NATIONAL GEOGRAPHIC

INDEX

—

January-June, 1966

VOLUME 129

PUBLISHED BY THE
NATIONAL GEOGRAPHIC SOCIETY
WASHINGTON, D. C.

Contents

Index

VOLUME 129

JANUARY-JUNE, 1966

January	pp.	1–152	April	pp. 447–594
February	pp.	153–296	May	pp. 595–742
March	pp.	297–446	June	pp. 743–888

Illustrations in bold face

A

Abaroa, Eduardo 158
'Abd al-'Aziz 10, 19, 20, 36
'Abd al-'Aziz Al Sa'ud, Faisal ibn, King (Saudi Arabia) 10, **11,** 13
'Abd al Rahman Al Faisal Al Sa'ud, 'Abd al-'Aziz ibn 10, 19, 20, 36
Abercrombie, Thomas J. 5; "Saudi Arabia: Beyond the Sands of Mecca." Jan., pp. 1–53
Abercrombie, Mrs. Thomas J. (Lynn) 28, 29, 30, 31, 33, **35**
Abhā, Saudi Arabia 5, 35, 36, 38, 41, **42–43**
Aborigines: Australia: " 'The Alice' in Australia's Wonderland." By Alan Villiers. Feb., pp. 230–257
Adjustment to modern life 250; Rehabilitation attempts 255–256
Art and artists 232, 247–249, **248–249**
Culture 250
Legends and myths 235, 240, 250
Occupation, Principal (working stock) 249, 250, 251, 252, 253
Aborigines: New Britain: "Blowgun Hunters of the South Pacific." By Jane C. Goodale. June, pp. 793–817
Abraham (prophet) 5, 40, 43, 44, 47, 48, 51
Abu Simbel temples, Egypt 412, **413;** "Saving the Ancient Temples at Abu Simbel." By Georg Gerster. May, pp. 694–742
Advisory groups 709
Coordination problems 710, 735, 736
Financing 709, 741
Methods 694, **694,** 696, **719, 722–723,** 733, **733,** 738, 741
Phase No. 1 (cofferdams) 696, 709, **724–725,** 733, 741, 742
Phase No. 2 (cliff and bulk excavation) **716, 720–721, 732,** 733–734
Phase No. 3 (block-cutting) 698–699, **717, 730, 737,** 738, 741–742, diagram **730;** Ramesses' face-lifting **694, 730–731**
Proposed plans 699, 706, 709; One-piece plans 706, 716

Protection with sand 709, **714–715, 718, 724–725,** 730
Rebuilding 696, **736,** 742, site **739**
Storage area 696, **738–739,** 741
Weather 698, 741
Academy of Medical Sciences, Moscow: President **337**
Acadia House Museum, near St. Martinville, La. **352**
Acadiana: "Cajunland, Louisiana's French-speaking Coast." By Bern Keating. Mar., pp. 353–391
Adams, Robert W. 585
Adam's Peak (mountain), Ceylon **464,** 466–467; Summit **465**
Ad Darb, Saudi Arabia **38–39**
Adelaide, Australia 230, 232, 234, 257
Adenauer, Konrad **104**
Aetna Life and Casualty Insurance Companies 265A, 529A
Africa: New nations 821, flags **821;** see also Egypt
Agena spacecraft 542, 552
Air Medal, U.S. **296**
Airport Road, Riyadh, Saudi Arabia 5, **12–13**
Aitkens, W. R. **387**
Alaska: Statehood 94, 96
Alba, Armando 184
Albert the First (Monaco): Statue **534**
Albrecht, F.W. 250, 255, 256
Albright, Horace M. 557
Al Ḥadīdah, Saudi Arabia 26; Meteorite near **35**
Al Hasa, Saudi Arabia 37
Al Ḥijāz, Saudi Arabia 5, 10
" 'The Alice' in Australia's Wonderland." By Alan Villiers. Feb., pp. 230–257
Alice Springs, Australia **232, 234–235;** " 'The Alice' in Australia's Wonderland." By Alan Villiers. Feb., pp. 230–257
Alinat, Jean 500, 504, 522, 529, 532
All American Canal, Calif. 615, 616
All American Indian Days: Sheridan, Wyo. **566–567**
Alliance for Progress 105, 153
Allied Land and Livestock Company 874, 880, 884; Shearing camp **874–875,** 883
Alligators: Louisiana 363, 364–365, 367
Al Madīnah al-Munawwarah see Medina

Alsaleh, Soliman 5, 10
Altiplano, Bolivian **154–155, 162, 172–173,** 176, 178
Alto Beni area, Bolivia 167
Altube, Pedro 881
Al 'Ulá, Saudi Arabia: Children **21;** Hills near **18–19**
Alzugaray, Fermin **870–871,** 888
Amazon River, South America 132, 135
Amboise, France **850–851,** 857, 860
Amboise chateau, **850–851,** 857, 860
Amerasinghe, Basil 452, 453
American Committee to Preserve Abu Simbel 741
"An American in Москва, Russia's Capital." By Thomas T. Hammond. Mar., pp. 297–351
Amieux Frères canning plant, Nantes **853**
Amoonguna settlement, Australia: Sewing class **250**
Amphibolite, Pyroxene, crystals **122**
Amun (Egyptian god) 698, 700, 717, 721, 723; Statue **708**
Anaheim, Calif. 601, 610
Anastasia Island, St. Augustine 202, 215, 221, 227, 229
Andes (mountains), South America see Bolivia; Colombia
Andrews, Julie: Quoted 601
Anemone fields, Oceanside, Calif. **614**
Angel of Christian Charity (statue), London **748**
Angelenos 595, 596, 599, 601, 602, 603, 604
Angels Camp, Calif. 649, 652
Angers, France 868; Gladiolus field **865**
Angers castle **864–865,** 868, 869
Angkor Wat, Cambodia **266**
Animals: "Capturing Strange Creatures in Colombia." By Marte Latham. May, pp. 682–693; see also Cattle; Killer Whales; Sheep; Weddell seals
Anjou, Counts of 868
Anjou, France 866
Anne of Brittany 857, 863
Annunciation, Cathedral of the, Kremlin **308**
Antarctica: "Stalking Seals Under Antarctic Ice." By Carleton Ray. Jan., pp. 54–65
Anthropology see Aborigines
Anuradhapura, Ceylon 486, **487,** 489

v

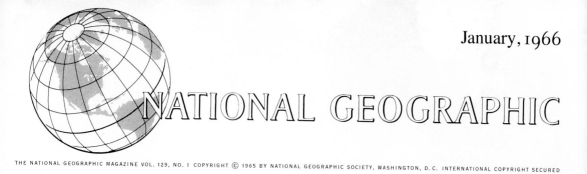

THE NATIONAL GEOGRAPHIC MAGAZINE VOL. 129, NO. 1 COPYRIGHT © 1965 BY NATIONAL GEOGRAPHIC SOCIETY, WASHINGTON, D. C. INTERNATIONAL COPYRIGHT SECURED

المملكة العربية السعودية

SAUDI ARABIA
Beyond the Sands of Mecca

ARTICLE AND PHOTOGRAPHS BY THOMAS J. ABERCROMBIE

National Geographic Foreign Staff

MULTITUDES packed the sacred hills and plains surrounding Mount 'Arafāt, praying and waiting through the blazing afternoon. Around me the rocky desert landscape shone with the white costumes of the pious pilgrim throngs. They stood in silent devotion, as had the prophet Mohammed thirteen centuries before. The white-hot sun slowly quenched itself in the caldron of haze above Mecca.

Sunset was the signal—the spiritual climax of the annual Moslem pilgrimage. The murmuring prayers of a million souls reached a crescendo. *"Laa ilaaha illa llaah!* There is no God but Allah!" shouted the immense congregation. "He has no partner. His is authority and praise."

A cannon boomed in the distance. The mountains came to life as a human landslide poured into the valley en route to the next holy place (pages 44-5).

From Khartoum, Cairo, and İstanbul they had come; from Pakistan, Nigeria, Iran, China, Indonesia—Moslems from all over the world. Businessman, Bedouin, blacksmith, bureaucrat; pasha and pauper—all equal in the eyes of Allah, all individuality obliterated by the simple *ihraam,* or pilgrim's garb.

The newly built four-lane pilgrim's highway overflowed with taxis, red Ford pickups, enormous diesel trucks, buses (their roofs piled high with baggage and passengers), bicycles, Cadillacs, and donkey-drawn water carts. I inched my Land-Rover through the slow tangle that stretched out of sight into the dusk. The hundreds of thousands on foot moved faster than those on wheels. Motor traffic was awash in a human tide.

Saudis Cautiously Welcome Progress

Never had I witnessed a greater display of unity and faith, or greater problems of logistics. Amazingly, the world's biggest traffic jam takes place every year in desert Arabia!

But Saudi Arabia, I found, is full of surprises. Recently, as a Moslem and a guest of the Saudi Government, I made the journey to Mecca and the little-known Arabia beyond.

1

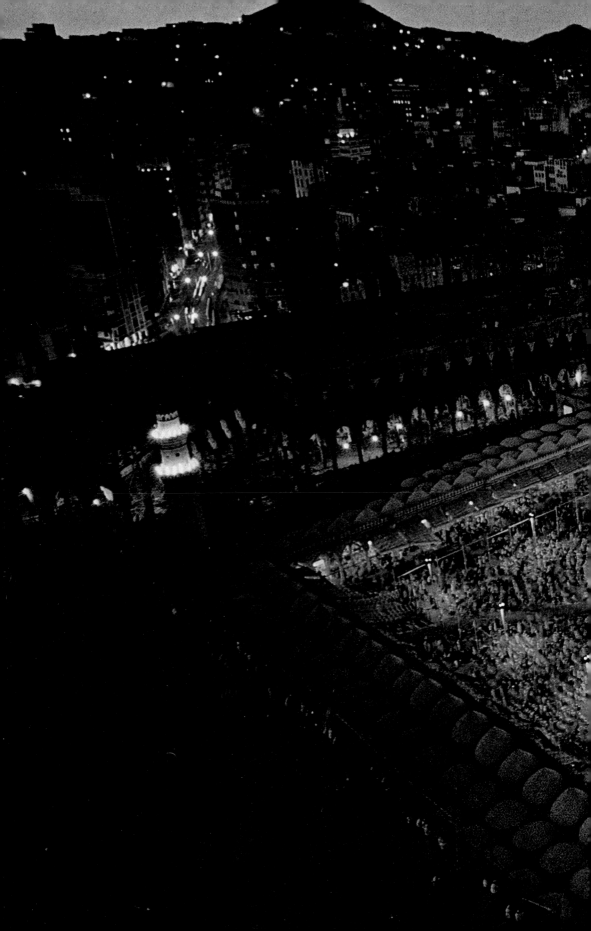

By Land-Rover, camel, and jet plane I traveled 20,000 miles through the sparsely settled peninsula, an area roughly the size of the United States east of the Mississippi.

Half of Saudi Arabia's 6,630,000 people cluster in booming cities and small oases that dot the desert kingdom. The rest, the hardy Bedouin, still graze their flocks across the endless sands (pages 18-19).

Like a Bedouin, I too roamed—from the green hills of Abhā to the sand-blown wastes of Ar Rab' al Khālī (the Empty Quarter), from ancient holy cities to modern oil towns along the Persian Gulf. Wherever I went, I found the Arabians welcoming the 20th century, but never with open arms. "Modernization we want, we need, and we will have," a Saudi friend told me, "but on our own terms."

From Jidda, an international port of entry, I flew to the government capital, Riyadh, to begin my journey (map, pages 8-9). The jet flight from Jidda was a typical Saudi blend of past and present. A Saudi prince wearing white robe and headcloth and black 'aba, or cloak, sat with his three wives; only their high heels showed beneath their all-covering black garments. A British geologist fanned his red mustache with a copy of *The Times,* while across the aisle a weathered desert sheik sat next to a bodyguard armed with a silver-mounted dagger and a Czech submachine gun.

We climbed above the steaming Red Sea coast, over the volcanic mountains of Al Ḥijāz, and across the Ḥarrat Rahaṭ, a lifeless plain of black basalt boulders that even the Bedouin fear.

Egyptian popular music poured from the cabin speakers while the steward served us cardamom-flavored Arab coffee from a long-beaked brass pot. We flew 500 miles across the desert plains of the Najd. Not a village or a palm grove did I see until we crossed the Jabal Ṭuwayq escarpment and let down into Riyadh.

It was here that I met young Soliman Alsaleh, my friend from the Saudi Ministry of Information.

"Modernization has changed the face of Riyadh since I was a boy," said Soliman as we climbed into his Volkswagen. "It's becoming a city of two different worlds."

Born in Riyadh and schooled in California, Soliman felt perfectly at home in both.

Glass and Steel Supplant Mud Brick

Huge glass-and-concrete buildings of the new Saudi Government ministries lined six-lane Airport Road (pages 12-13). Soliman pointed them out as we drove in from the terminal: Petroleum, Defense, Interior, Communications, Agriculture, Education, Health, Commerce and Industry, Finance—impressive symbols. I thought of the new responsibilities Arabia was taking on. Yet the old ways persist: In the shade of the Ministry of Finance a family of Bedouin had pitched their black tents.

In the busy suq, or market, around the Masjid al-Joma—the Friday Mosque—we wove through the colorful throng. A black-veiled woman clutched a bolt of gingham under her arm; a gray-bearded hawker waved bright red headcloths; a ragged boy peddled water from a pottery jug for two cents a glass.

(Continued on page 10)

Emotions at fever pitch, a quarter of a million Moslems jam Haram Mosque in the holy city of Mecca to pay homage to Allah. In a milling mass, those in the center—blurred in this time exposure—circle the black-draped Ka'ba, most sacred of Islamic shrines. Shouting, weeping with joy, pilgrims seek to touch its granite walls and thus achieve the goal of a lifetime. Moslems believe the prophet Abraham—like Mohammed a messenger of God—and his son Ishmael built the first structure here. And five times each day, from across the globe, the world's 456,000,000 Moslems turn toward Mecca to pray.

KODACHROME BY THOMAS J. ABERCROMBIE © N.G.S.

THIS PAGE FOLDS OUT

"Sand. Always sand. In my eyes, in my shoes, in my cameras." Author-photographer Thomas Abercrombie will never forget the cruel, gritty, all-pervading sand encountered during his four months of travel in the remote, long-mysterious kingdom of Saudi Arabia. As a Moslem, he obtained rare permission to photograph the annual pilgrimage to Mecca. As a guest, he found a welcome in homes of desert tribesmen and city dwellers alike. The result: an extraordinary portrait of a land isolated for centuries by its religion and its geography.

In the cool light of dawn, Bedouin break camp. By day they roam the deserts where only brittle shrubs scar the wastes. In bold contrast, the glittering airport terminal at Dhahran links the nation's far-flung cities by Saudi Arabian Airlines jets.

LEBANON
SYRIA
Damascus
Sayda (Sidon)
Haifa
ISRAEL
Tel Aviv-Yafo
Gaza
Nabulus
Amman
Jerusalem
Negev
Dead Sea
+5905
Petra
El Quseima
Ma'an
Elat Al 'Aqabah
Haql
SINAI
Gulf of Aqaba
8465
Nabq
Al Mudawwarah
Aynunah
Al Muwaylih
Jabal Shār
+6529
Tabūk
HEJAZ RAILWAY UNDER RECONSTRUCTION
3280
3212
Al Jawf
Sakākah
Jabal Rāf
Līnah
An Nafūd
Jubbah
Baq'ā
Ad Dār al Hamrā'
Taymā'
3888
+2559
Ha'il
Ash Shu'aybah
Al Kahfah
Jabal Shammar
Mada'in Sālih
Al 'Ula
Safājah
Al Ghazālah
Khaybar
Harrat Khaybar
Hulayfā'
Al 'Uyūn
Buraydah
Al Qasīm
Ar Rass
Unayzah
Ash Shaqrā'
Ma'aqalā
Rumāh
Az Zulfī
Al Hinākiyah
Ad Dawādimī
Durma
Ar Riyād (Riyadh)
Al Madīnah (Medina)
Al Hamrā'
Badr Hunayn
Yanbu'
'Afīf
Al Qay'iyah
Ar Ruwaydah
Qafarah
Harad
W. as Sahbā'
TROPIC OF CANCER
Bīr Shalatein
Masturah
Rābigh
Al Qadīmah
Sufaynah
Harrat al Kishb
Zalim
Al Muwayh
(Hauta) Al Hillah
Al Huwwah
Qalamat Nadqān
Al Kharfah
Al Badi'
Al 'Ubaylah
Al Hadidah (meteor craters)
Juddah (Jidda)
Makkah (Mecca)
Minā
At Tā'if
8415
Harrat Nawāsif
+5200
Ar Rawdah
Harrat al Buqūm
Wādi ad Dawāsir
As Sulayyil
Rayda
Urūq ar Rumaylah
Qalamat Khawr Al Juhaysh
Qalamat Fāris
Qalama
Al Mahāwiyah
Az Zāfir
Qal'at Bīshah
+1355
Ar Rab' al Khālī (Empty)
+1703
+1076
Al Lith
Ad Dūqah
Banī Shanfā
Tathlīth
Hamdah
SAUDI ARABIA
Port Sudan
Suakin
Suakin Archipelago
Al Qunfudhah
Abhā
Jabal Sawdā'
10279
Khamīs Mushayt
+3488
+2598
Ar Rab'
SUDAN
Haiya
Karora
Ash Shuqayq
Ad Darb
Zahrān
Qīzān
Abā Sa'ūd
Jazā'ir Farasān
Sa'dah
Eriba
Nakfa
Khamir
+4780
+3960
Tarim
Say'ūn
Hanīn
Qishn
Sayhūt
Kassala
Agordat
Massawa
Dahlak Arch.
Al Muwassam
Maydī
Khamir
Shabwah
Ma'rib
Asmara
Al Luhayyah
Kamarān
San'ā
Bayhān al Qisāb
Ash Shihr
Al Mukallā
Burūm
Harrah
Aksum
Adigrat
Danakil Depression
Al Hudaydah (Hodeida)
As Salīf
Yarīm
Zabīd
Dhamār
Ansāb
+5709
Balhāf
Al Hawrah
Makale
15158
Zuqar
Ibb
10003
Ad Dāli'
Lawdar
Shuqrā
Ahwar
ETHIOPIA
6986
Ta'izz
Al Mukhā (Mocha)
10587
Shaykh 'Uthmān
Gondar
Assab
Turbah
Perim (Barim)
ADEN U.K.
Crater
FRENCH SOMALILAND
Djibouti
Alula
Ras Asir
STATUTE MILES
PRODUCED BY NATIONAL GEOGRAPHIC SOCIETY CARTOGRAPHIC DIVISION
Abbai (Blue Nile)
Lake Tana
Bahir Dar
Tesissat Falls
Quoram
Tandaho
Aiscia
Berbera
Ras Khanzira
Ras Sura
Bosaso
Barg
Erigavo
SOMALI REPUBLIC
GULF OF ADEN

IRAQ
Ba'qūbah
Arak
Kāshān
Ar Rutbah
Ar Ramadi
Baghdād
Khorramābād
IRAN
Karbalā'
Babylon
Al Kūt
Esfahān
Al Hillah
Al 'Amārah
Dezfūl
Lālī
Naft-e Safīd
+1231
An Nāsiriyah
Hawr al Hammār
Ahvāz
Zagros Mountains
TRANS-ARABIAN PIPELINE
'Ar'ar
+2329
Al Ma'anīyah
1212
Rumaila
Raudhatain
Al Basrah
Khorramshahr
Bandar-e Ma'shūr
14030
Sahrā' al Hijārah
NEUTRAL ZONE
Saudi Arabia & Iraq
Abādān
Kāzerūn
FRONTIER UNDEFINED
Ad Duwayd
Wafra
KUWAIT
NEUTRAL ZONE
Saudi Arabia & Kuwait
Bushehr
Al Kuwayt
Qaryat al 'Ulyā
Safaniya
Manifah
PERSIAN GULF
Khārk
30
(Dhahran) Az Zahrān
Ra's at Tannūrah
40
39
Al Jubayl
Al Qatīf
Dammam
Abqaiq
Al Manāmah
BAHRAIN
Al Mubarraz
QATAR
Al Hufūf (Hofuf)
Ad Dawhah (Doha)
As Salwa
Coastal sovereignty undefined
HADRAMAWT
ARABIA
FRONTIERS

NORTHERN DESERT
AL HIJAZ
ASIR
YEMEN

Map labels (left map):

A F G H A N I S T A N

55° 60° 65° 70°

Ferdows
Tabas
Qāyen
Nā'in
Bīrjand
Yazd
Farah
Peshawarun
Dasht-e Lūt +9816
R S I A N A)
Zābol
30°

PAKISTAN

Railroads ——— **Roads** ——— **Tracks** ———
Places with Scheduled Air Service + **Oil Pipe Lines** ———
Oil Fields ⌷ **Ruins** ∴ **Water Holes** • **Sand** **Lava**
Dry Salt Lake **Below Sea Level** **Elevations in Feet** 15158
Soundings in Fathoms 2705

Persepolis
Shirāz
Sa'īdābād (Sirjan) +14500
Zāhedān
Fasā
Neyriz
Bam
Mīnjāveh
Jahrom
Sabzvārān
Khāsh +9242
Hālīl
11447+
Lār
+10760
Hāmūn-e Jaz Mūriān
Īrānshahr
Bandar 'Abbās
Mināb
Bampur
40°
Qeshm
+7390
13
Bandar-e Lengeh
Al Khaşab
Ra's Musandam
Nīkshahr
Oman
15
Ra's al Khaymah
Umm al Qaywayn
Dibbah
Dadnah
Jāsk
Ash Shāriqah
Ujmān
70
Dubayy
Al Fujayrah
Chāh Bahār
950
Umm Shaif
Al Maḩḑah
Gavāter 25°
Abū Zaby
Şuḩār
1005
Gwatar Bay
Tarif
Al Buraymī
1810
7
TRUCIAL STATES
Barkā'
Matraḩ
1848
Murban
Masqaţ (Muscat)
Ad Dafrah
TROPIC OF CANCER
al Jabal al Akhḑar
Ibri
Al Qurayyāt
Jabal ash Shām
10400
1814
+381
AL JIWĀ'
Umm az Zumūl
Izki
Ibrā 7060
Ra's al Hadd
Adam
Tiwi
Şūr
Al Qurayni
Muntarib
Al Hadd
As Suwayḩ
Al Ashkharah
Ra's Jibsh
66
+108
Dawwāh 1856
Khalūf
906 Al Maşirah
2355
Manāḑif
8
20°
Jiddat al Ḩarāsis
Khalīj al Maşirah
2200
404+
Al 'Ayn
26
Juwara
Ra's al Madrakah
1243
Mazraq
Dawḩat Sawqarah 1960
Mādir
Marmul +600 21
Ra's ash Sharbatāt
2020
47
Jabal Samḩān
Khūryān Mūryān (Kuria Muria Is.) U.K.
1375
4800
awf
Salālah
Mirbāţ
1448
Ra's Darbat 'Alī
Damqūt 1330
2270
A R A B I A N
880
2230
2340
15°
698
1574
1680
S E A
1560
1880
2080
Qaysā
Tamrida (Hudaybū)
766 4931
Socotra (Suquţrá) South Arabia
17
The Brothers
45
2705

Geographical Equivalents

Dasht	desert	Kūhhā	mountains
Hāmūn	lake	Nafūd	desert
Harrat	lava field	Qalamat	drilled well
Hawr	lake	Ra's	cape
Jabal	mountain, range	Wādī	valley, watercourse

55° 60°

SAUDI ARABIA

LAND OF MOHAMMED and fountainhead of an empire that once stretched from Spain to India, the Kingdom of Saudi Arabia (whose name in Arabic script appears on page one) today works to catch up with the 20th century. Income from petroleum eases the way; the barren desert country happily sits atop an estimated 10 percent of the world's oil supply. The government receives half the profits from this subsurface wealth and puts most of it into new roads, airfields, schools, water projects, and hospitals.

Three decades have brought spectacular gains, notably in the towns, where air-conditioned offices and apartments rise. In Mecca and Medina, electricity and running ice water await the devout hadjis, or Moslem pilgrims, who come from all parts of the world. Despite such progress, half the people

remain nomads. Another million are farmers; their thick-walled mud houses border groves of date palms and fields of grain that cluster around the scattered oases in this country lacking both lakes and rivers.

GOVERNMENT: Monarchy. **AREA:** 870,000 square miles. **POPULATION:** 6,630,000; 90 percent Arabs, 10 percent with Negroid ancestry. **LANGUAGE:** Arabic. **RELIGION:** Exclusively Moslem. **INSCRIPTION ON FLAG** (above): "There is no God but God, and Mohammed is the prophet of God." **ECONOMY:** Oil provides 83 percent of the nation's revenues. Pilgrims to Mecca bring in several million dollars a year. Dates, millet, wheat, and vegetables grown. **MAJOR CITIES:** Riyadh (population more than 170,000), royal capital; Jidda, port; Mecca, Medina, holy cities. **CLIMATE:** Dry and hot. Temperatures may soar beyond 120° F., and villages may go without rain for years. Humid coastal areas, temperate mountain localities. Riyadh average daily high 107° F. June-August; January maximum 70°, minimum 40°.

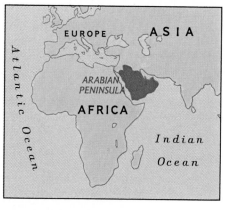

EUROPE ASIA
Atlantic Ocean
ARABIAN PENINSULA
AFRICA
Indian Ocean

9

Piles of gaudy merchandise spilled from tiny stalls into the narrow, crowded lanes. At one shop Bedouin haggled over giant brass coffeepots, leather sandals, and decorated incense burners. Next door a swarthy merchant sold expensive bits of aromatic wood and frankincense from an iron strongbox.

Later that afternoon we pulled up crude wooden chairs at one of the outdoor teashops in the midst of the market place. Metal shutters clanged down around us as we sipped the last of our hot, heavily sugared tea. Radio Riyadh, sounding through a transistor set at the next table, switched from music to readings from the Koran.

"*Salaat! Salaat!* Prayer time!" shouted a green-turbaned *mutawwa‘,* or religious policeman. He rapped loudly on shutters to speed closing for the evening devotions. When, moments later, the muezzin called from the minaret, the streets were deserted.

Daring Raid Launches a Nation

At the turn of the century, Riyadh was a small town administered by the powerful Rashid family. The traditional rulers, the Sa‘ud family, smoldered in exile in Kuwait. On a cold moonless night in January, 1902, a small, bold expedition, led by 21-year-old ‘Abd al-‘Aziz ibn ‘Abd al-Rahman Al Faisal Al Sa‘ud, set out to regain the disputed capital.

‘Abd al-‘Aziz and 40 followers slipped into a palm grove just outside the town. With six of his men, he scrambled over Riyadh's high mud-brick walls. He quietly opened the gates to the rest of his band. They hid throughout the night, drinking coffee and eating dates. They slept a little, and prayed.

Next morning, they attacked Emir ‘Ajlan as he emerged from his fortress with his bodyguards. Though outnumbered two to one by the emir's guards, they won the short, fierce battle and the town of Riyadh. The seed of the Saudi nation was sown.

A decade after re-establishing the house of Sa‘ud in Riyadh, young ‘Abd al-‘Aziz had consolidated most of central Arabia. In 1912 he founded the first of many cooperative farming communities of *Ikhwaan,* or Brethren. These colonies offered the Bedouin a more stable life and provided ‘Abd al-‘Aziz with a ready supply of loyal, zealous soldiers.

The following year the rising desert leader drove the Turks from the Eastern Province. By 1921 he had annexed the southern highlands of the ‘Asīr. Mecca and Al Ḥijāz had fallen to him by 1925. ‘Abd al-‘Aziz now controlled most of the peninsula and was proclaimed king. In 1932 his new nation assumed its present name, Saudi Arabia.

Wives Still Live in Old King's Palace

As the empire of ‘Abd al-‘Aziz grew, so did his capital. After World War II, on the tide of oil prosperity, Riyadh overflowed its walls and burgeoned into a desert metropolis of more than 170,000 people.

One day in Riyadh, Soliman and I drove along the high pink walls of the famous Naseryah Palace built by former King Sa‘ud. As the oldest surviving son of ‘Abd al-‘Aziz, he became king when his father died in 1953. (Both were known in their times simply as Ibn Sa‘ud.) Until he was deposed in 1964, the son reigned here in splendor and extravagance.

"Scores of his wives and ex-wives live in the palace with their children and servants," said Soliman. "Would you like to go inside?"

The mile-square palace complex was a city within a city, complete with mosques, schools, shops, and playgrounds. Rows of sumptuous villas lined the four-lane avenue leading to the giant pink reception hall. A few black Cadillacs passed us, their passengers hidden behind windows of one-way glass.

Otherwise it was quiet. The paint of some of the buildings was beginning to blister; here and there oleander and bougainvillea were drying up, untended. Electric traffic lights at once-busy corners blinked no more.

By contrast, Saudi Arabia's present ruler, Sa‘ud's half-brother King Faisal, lives a simple life in the same modest palace he occupied for years as foreign minister. His only wife, Emira Iffat, though never seen in public, works behind the scenes to better the place of women in the kingdom.

I waited for my audience with King Faisal at his new ultramodern office building, the Qasr ar-Riyaasa (literally, the "Palace of the Premiership"). Promptly at 4 p.m. sirens announced the arrival of His Majesty.

Enlightened monarch of 6,630,000 subjects, King Faisal ibn ‘Abd al-‘Aziz Al Sa‘ud seeks to shepherd his desert domain into the 20th century. While still in his teens, Faisal fought beside his father to unify Arabia. Later he traveled widely in the West and led Saudi delegations to the United Nations before succeeding his half-brother on the throne in 1964. Here in his garden in Riyadh, Saudi Arabia's royal capital, His Majesty wears traditional robes topped by a gold-wrapped agal, or headband.

Two-faced Riyadh keeps one visage turned to the past (left) and the other toward the present. Only a desert town twenty years ago, the capital prospered with the postwar oil boom. Palaces, apartments, schools, hospitals, and a university sprouted along wide avenues as Riyadh's population grew to 170,000, making it the kingdom's largest city.

Here gleaming new buildings housing government ministries flank tree-lined Airport Road (above). With assistance from the United Nations and other groups, the government plans similar urban-renewal projects in 40 other towns.

In the heart of Old Riyadh, castellated walls of mud brick shade rooftops where Saudi families often sleep to escape summer heat. Daytime temperatures rise as high as 113° F. and may fall no lower than 90° at night.

Date groves in the distance separate city from desert.

Beheaded traffic symbol identifies a pedestrian crosswalk in Riyadh. The sign placates Moslem puritans, who resent any form of human image.

Two red jeeps manned by soldiers followed the blue Chrysler up to the portico. King Faisal climbed the steps behind a phalanx of personal bodyguards wearing gold-mounted swords and daggers.

As I crossed the deep Oriental carpet of his office, the King came from behind an enormous walnut desk and led me to a divan set along the wall. A servant, in white and wearing a black leather pistol belt, poured coffee, then tea. His Majesty's manner was gracious, his expression calm and reflective. But his dark eyes glinted as he talked.

"Oil is our bounty from Allah," he said. "Our coffers are full, and we are thankful. But it will take more than money to develop our country. It will take time and experience.

"Most of our people do not even have a dependable supply of water to drink. Think of it—such a basic thing!

"Our country is large and the population is scattered. In the next ten years we must build 10,000 miles of new roads. We must encourage industry, foreign trade, improve our agriculture, expand our communications facilities, build and staff more hospitals.

"Education is the key that will open the way for all these things," His Majesty assured me. "We are making strides. Hardly a town is without its school. For the first time we are

13

Challenge of education absorbs boys at Riyadh's Model Capital School; they write in flowing Arabic script from right to left. A showcase institution, the school offers courses in art, mathematics, and chemistry, as well as traditional lessons from the Koran and Arabic literature. Within the past ten years the kingdom's Ministry of Education has tripled the number of schools. Today, as Saudi Arabia begins educating its women for the first time, nearly 60,000 girls attend public—but not coeducational—schools. Thus the nation seeks to recapture the glorious era when Arabic scholars helped keep learning alive during Europe's Dark Ages.

Bachelor's last fling: Clapping hands beat out the rhythm as a wedding dancer whirls on a street of Jidda. The groom invited these male guests; the bride's friends will gather at her home. Saudi parents arrange most marriages, usually between cousins.

enrolling girls in public schools—shattering traditions centuries old to do it.

"We continue to drill wells for water and oil; but most important is the well of knowledge."

Before leaving Riyadh, I visited the Institute of Light, one of the most impressive schools I have seen anywhere. I was greeted by the young, energetic director, Mr. Abdallah el-Ghanim. Abdallah was born 31 years ago in a small village near Riyadh. There, as a child, smallpox had blinded him.

"Being blind is perhaps less of a handicap in Saudi Arabia than in other countries," Abdallah explained. "Most Arab schools used to rely on oral education and memorization. But I knew if I was to amount to anything, I must learn to read. An Iraqi teacher in my village taught me Braille."

Soon Abdallah was not only reading with his fingertips, but teaching a small group of other sightless Saudis to do the same.

"We met at my house or in the mosque," he continued. "The shortage of material in Arabic Braille was our greatest problem. I began to study English in Braille to translate more material into our growing Braille library."

When Abdallah visited King Sa'ud in 1958 with plans for a small school for the blind, the King backed him generously.

"For the handicapped here, the world is changing rapidly," Abdallah said. "We must keep our eyes, so to speak, on the future!"

Cars Battle Donkeys in Jidda Streets

I decided to make my headquarters in Jidda, on the Red Sea. As the gateway to Mecca, Jidda had grown slowly over the centuries with the pilgrim trade. After World War II, spurred by oil money, it began to mushroom. Nowadays 35 ships at a time crowd its harbor, Saudi Arabia's largest.

Ten-story office and apartment buildings have risen above the automobile showrooms and department stores along bustling King 'Abd al-'Aziz Street. During the early-afternoon rush hour, squadrons of bright red American sedans jostle and honk. Strangely, the ear-splitting noise perturbs neither the bold breed of Jidda pedestrians nor the laden donkeys, which often add a bray of their own to the cacophony. I took refuge from the din in the covered suq nearby (following page).

I love the atmosphere of the Arab market place: The sound of the money-changers clinking coins; the shouts of the hawker selling holy water brought down from Mecca; the smell of saffron, cinnamon, and freshly roasted coffee; stray beams of sunlight flashing on bright-colored carpets and bolts of brocades.

But here, too, the noisy, persistent 20th century intrudes. A transistor radio blared the latest twangy tune from Cairo, the *"Hajji-Baba Cha-Cha-Cha,"* making bargaining for

15

Latticed balconies fronting tall stone houses of Jidda shelter ladies of the harems, or women's quarters, who peer discreetly at life pulsing in the streets of Arabia's major port. Early each evening, following sunset prayers, men gather to gossip at their favorite *gahwa,* or sidewalk coffee house. Gateway to the holy city of Mecca, Jidda owes its growth to pilgrim trade. Today steamships and dhows crowd its harbor, and cars jam both old and new sections of the city.

Camel saddles to carburetors, water pipes to water skis, Korans to comic books—Jidda's arcaded suqs offer goods that span the centuries. Customers may bargain for prayer rugs, tent poles, transistor radios, air conditioners, or holy water from Mecca. Here a veiled Bedouin wife carries home a roll of palm matting. Machine-woven carpets from Italy hang from rafters.

EKTACHROME (ABOVE) AND KODACHROME © N.G.S.

On endless trek, desert-roaming Bedouin shepherds lead their flock past tattered hills near Al 'Ulá. Watchdogs guard against strangers and an occasional wolf. Half of Arabia's

population wanders constantly in search
of pasture for goats, sheep, and camels.

a handful of pistachios almost impossible.
Labels on the "Persian" carpets showed they
were woven in Italy. Half a block away bulldozers were knocking down walls for a cross-
town expressway.

Later I followed a bevy of water-bearers
up a narrow street, past a precariously leaning minaret, to the heart of the old city. I had
a midmorning appointment with Sheik Mohammed Nassif, a scholar who bore the noble
title of sharif, at the House With The Tree.

Even in the labyrinth of tall stone houses in
Jidda's old city (pages 16-17), Sheik Mohammed's home was easy to find. The spreading
greenery of a giant Indian neem tree, a close
relative of the chinaberry, shaded his doorway and rose to the roof of his five-story mansion. Sheik Mohammed, heavy-set but still
spry at 90, met me on the front steps. He
wore a spotless white turban, and a white
suit coat over his robe.

Days in Arabia Begin at Sunset

Long retired from office, the old sage now
divides his time between his friends and his
books. In his cozy first-floor study, bookcases
lining the wall from floor to ceiling house Jidda's finest private library. Over small glasses
of mint-flavored tea, we talked about his tree
and his city.

"Fifty years ago, when I planted my tree,
the townspeople thought me mad," Sheik Mohammed told me. "Because of the water shortage, there was not another tree in all of Jidda.
In those days water cost a man as much as
his bread. Luckily, we have a small well under
the house. Our family sprinkled the tree each
day with water left over from ablutions. Now,
of course, water is piped in from the mountains, 20 miles away."

Sheik Mohammed led me up the stairs to
his penthouse, cool in the steady sea breeze.
Here former King 'Abd al-'Aziz often spent
his nights when visiting Jidda. Twenty windows offered a splendid panorama of the city.
In the distance I could see Jidda expanding
into the surrounding desert. Hundreds of
spacious villas were springing up, framed by
green gardens and shaded with billowing
tamarisks, pines, and eucalyptus. Sheik Mohammed's tree was no longer alone.

That evening I was to attend a Saudi wedding. Leaving the hotel, I checked my wristwatch. Specially made in Switzerland for the
Arabian market, it has two dials and four
hands. Reckoning Arabic time is simple
enough. The day begins officially at sunset,
which is always 12 o'clock. This puts noon

Relic of revolution, a rusting locomotive blasted by Lawrence of Arabia in 1917 still lies beside the abandoned Hejaz Railway north of Medina. The controversial British scholar and soldier T. E. Lawrence aided the Arabs in their successful revolt against the Turks in World War I. Then this train—which originally carried pilgrims from Damascus, Syria, to Arabia's holy cities—sped Turkish troops to ambush and death.

In festive frocks, children scamper through the doorway of their home in Al 'Ulá. For three days following Ramadan, the Moslem fasting month, Arabians put on new robes and stream through their villages visiting friends and relatives.

at about 6 a.m., depending on the time of year.

But Jidda's foreign colony complicates things. Most embassies, for instance, use "sun time," which is Arabic plus six. The military (and sometimes Saudi Arabian Airlines) take Greenwich time plus three. Out in the Eastern Province the Arabian American Oil Company uses daylight-saving time.

"I'm used to Friday being the weekly holiday," said the wife of one diplomat. "We all juggle our week accordingly. But then, if Friday is Sunday, I must remember not to serve meat to Catholic guests on Wednesday."

More than once I missed an important date, though my watch showed me both Arabic and sun time. Worse, the conflicting systems sometimes cost me a meal. In my hotel, the Kandara Palace, the reception desk was on different time from the dining room.

I arrived at the wedding promptly at four —or rather, ten—anyway, in plenty of time. The three-day festivities had just begun. The narrow street was aglow with strings of electric lights. In the midst of the noisy crowd of well-wishers, musicians tuned their drums over a blazing wood fire. Tonight's guests were men only. Tomorrow the bride would entertain the women at her home.

The bridegroom passed out tea and soft drinks. Men took turns in the circle, whirling and spinning to the quickening drumbeat, while the crowd chanted and clapped (pages 14-15). The groom seemed as nervous as any groom anywhere.

"It's his first wedding," teased an old man. "The second, third, and fourth marriages are always easier."

I could understand the young man's worry. Taking a bride one has never met before, and pledging a bride price of 5,000 riyals (about $1,100) for her, sight unseen, must certainly heighten any man's anxiety.

In Arabia the parents usually arrange the weddings, and most marriages are between cousins. A proverb I heard that night summed up the traditional Arab feelings on matrimony: "He who marries not his cousin deserves to have only girl children."

Arabian Lunch—Western Style

But many younger Saudis are beginning to break with tradition. Take my friend Hassan Yassin, for instance. The son of one of 'Abd al-'Aziz's most trusted advisers, Hassan spent much of his boyhood in Cairo schools, then four years at the University of California. He returned to Jidda with a master's degree in political science and a pretty American wife.

I stopped in at Hassan's small air-conditioned office at the Ministry of Petroleum and Mineral Resources. In typical Arab style he entertained many guests at the same time, plying us with cups of hot mint tea. In American

Sandstone sepulcher casts its shadow across a surrealistic setting at Madā'in Ṣāliḥ, 400 miles north of Mecca. A lone Bedouin trudges past one of more than 100 rock-hewn tombs, legacy of a once-prosperous people. For two centuries before and after the time

style he conducted his business with efficiency and dispatch. People came in with problems, and left with solutions.

Hassan and his bride Betty invited me to lunch at their home with some of their Saudi friends. I was the only one in Western dress. The meal was delightfully and thoroughly Arab—heaps of deliciously spiced rice and mutton. But I felt right at home in the lively discussions of the new jazz program on Radio Mecca, city planning, a cook-out at the beach on Friday, the newly formed women's club.

Arabian hospitality, though justly famous, is usually more apparent among men. At rare mixed functions the women of the visiting families eat with those of the household in the privacy of the harem, unseen by male guests.

Today was different. Around a large table set with silver and fine china, we all sat together, men and women alike. I enjoyed the

bold departure. It was one of the few chances I would have to meet the women of Arabia. The conversation turned to their role in a changing world.

"Polygamy is now rare among the educated classes," Hassan pointed out. "The Koran allows four wives—but all must be treated equally. Many of us believe it would be hard to do justice to more than one wife."

I wondered whether the Saudi women would ever be freed from the confinement of the veil. Though Betty does not wear one, many American and European wives of Saudi officials have resigned themselves to discreet anonymity in public. Women are still forbidden to drive in Arabia. If one is caught behind the wheel, her husband risks jail.

"You are lucky in your country," said Hassan. "You have no deep roots. Here, changes must fit into the patterns and traditions of

of Christ, the Nabateans grew rich on the peninsula's caravan trade in incense and spices; then Rome destroyed their power. Today many Arabians, awed by the sand-swept solitude and legendary past of the valley, believe it to be haunted.

orthodox Islam, for Islam is Arabia's law as well as its religion. This will take time."

The pressures of change in Saudi Arabia were first felt 750 miles east of Jidda, in the oil-rich sands along the Persian Gulf.

Oil is the lifeblood of modern Arabia. It gushes through shining pipes across the deserts where weary caravans once plodded. Each day the reeking black crude brings more wealth than all Arabia's frankincense and myrrh once brought in a lifetime.

Oilmen Tame Arabia's Eastern Deserts

Soon after the first oil agreements were signed between the Standard Oil Company of California and the Saudi Government in 1933, a trio of American geologists arrived at the small port of Al Jubayl on the Persian Gulf. By camel and truck they set out to explore the huge concession: 370,000 square miles of little-known desert, an area bigger than Texas and Oklahoma combined.

In 1938 drillers in Dhahran struck oil in commercial quantities nearly a mile beneath the sand. Soon after the end of World War II, increased oil demands spurred development. Drill crews worked night and day. By 1946, four American companies had joined in the ownership of Aramco, the Arabian American Oil Company.

In 1950 the trans-Arabian pipeline began carrying crude oil across 1,000 miles of desert to the Mediterranean port of Sidon. In the Persian Gulf, teams of seagoing oil workers floated giant platforms onto the shallow water at Safaniya to bring in the world's most productive offshore oilfield. On shore, welding crews laid pipelines creating a 300-mile-long complex of wells, pump stations, and a refinery and tanker port on the Persian Gulf.

HENNA GLOW OF SUNSET *tints grotesque sentinels brooding over Madā'in Şāliḥ. Wind-driven grit and sparse rains carved the sandstone giants. Red truck travels an ancient caravan route where camels once plodded toward Mecca.*

Today Aramco handles more than two million barrels a day, putting Saudi Arabia second only to Kuwait among Middle East oil producers. Beneath the Saudi sands lie an estimated 60 *billion* barrels of proven reserves.

Dhahran, the capital of the Aramco complex and home of 1,100 of its senior staff members, is a centrally air-conditioned town. Cooling stations pump chilled air through conduits to the homes of the company's employees. Green lawns and well-watered gardens nearly hide the bungalows lining the palm-shaded streets that curve from the modern supermarket up past the library, the swimming pool, and the Little League baseball field. Dhahran today looks more like a sedate suburb of Phoenix, Arizona, than an oil boomtown.

"Bonanza" Telecast in English and Arabic

Dhahran Television, HZ-22-TV, broadcasts daily in Arabic. Koran readings open the evening program. Most popular are wrestling matches and the Egyptian movies on the late show. Arabic dialogue is dubbed in on "Bonanza"; English-speaking viewers listen by radio to the original sound track, broadcast simultaneously by Aramco's radio station.

Much of Aramco's success in Saudi Arabia has been a result of its excellent relations with the Saudi people, Aramco president Thomas Barger told me. We talked in Aramco's gleaming glass-and-aluminum headquarters building in Dhahran.

"The geologists felt at home out on the sands," he said. "There was a sort of spiritual bond between us and our Bedouin guides. We both loved the simple life and the freedom of the desert. Of course as our operations grew and thousands of American workers arrived with their families, relations became more complex. We had to work at it."

"We've built training centers and roads and we guarantee home loans for our Saudi workers," interjected Homer Mueller, head of Aramco's Policy and Planning Staff. "Our Medical Center is as up to date as any in the Middle East."

"But our cultural exchange is even more important," Mr. Barger added. "Most business is conducted bilingually. Americans are given time off from work to study Arabic;

some 140 young Saudi employees are being trained in U. S. and Middle Eastern schools and colleges in Aramco programs."

Aramco's good-will campaign often touches subtle areas. During the Moslem fasting month of Ramadan, the firm shortens its working hours. Once, it turned over one of its cooks to the royal kitchen in Riyadh. Every day it wrestles into Arabic such technical oil terms as "fractionator reflux accumulator."

By truck, plane, and motor launch I toured Aramco's far-flung complex. Twenty miles out on the gulf, aboard Safaniya rig No. 1, two crews worked around the clock in 12-hour shifts (page 29). I sipped coffee with some of the Saudi drillers. Former farmers, Bedouin, fishermen, they were oilmen now.

"It's a completely different way of life for us," said Ali ibn Isa al-Majhad. "At first, working for the company was a shock: strange clothes, a thousand things to learn—and regular hours. *Wa-llaah!* To become a slave to the clock! But regular hours mean regular pay.

"I used to dive for pearls. It was dangerous work—seasonal too—and my split of the pearls was small. Now I earn as much in a month as I did in a year. Next year, Allah willing, I'll buy my own house."

Bedouin Bring Rumors of Giant Meteorite

Three hundred miles south of Dhahran, Aramco's seismographic crews were mapping the underground structures of promising future oil reservoirs in Ar Rabʻ al Khālī. I was determined to visit this windswept wilderness whose name, literally, means "the Empty Quarter"—especially after talking with young James Mandaville. Jim, a second-generation Aramcon, had grown up in Arabia and loved it. He spoke excellent Arabic and knew Bedouin dialects as well.

"The Bedouin have talked for years about a chunk of iron near a crater at Al Ḥadīdah, halfway into the Empty Quarter," said Jim. "They say it's the size of a camel's hump. Some of our exploration teams have visited the craters; they saw three of them, quite close together. They found only a few prune-size bits of meteoritic iron."

The Empty Quarter is one of the last of earth's great unknown areas. It remains a blank spot on the map, an undulating sea of

Geysers of sand explode from the desert of eastern Arabia as geologists probe for oil-bearing layers a mile beneath the surface. Delicate seismographs in the truck record reflected sound waves and provide clues to the region's mineral potential. American oilmen began in 1933 to explore an area the size of Texas and Oklahoma combined; their discoveries led to the formation of the Arabian American Oil Company.

sand as big as Texas (page 34)—its permanent population: zero.

"A trip into the Empty Quarter is no Sunday excursion," Jim warned me. "There's danger involved, and some fancy navigating. More than 400 miles with hardly a landmark. You'll have to carry every drop of water you'll need. God help you if your Land-Rover breaks down." I worried, too, about the lateness of the season. Any day a *shamaal*—a summer northerly—could plague us with stinging sandstorms.

My wife Lynn joined me in Dhahran just in time for the big adventure. For her it would mean a break from housekeeping routines.

The emir of the province assigned us a hefty Dodge Power Wagon, with a driver and cook, as a back-up vehicle. Aramco's exploration department briefed me and outfitted the Land-Rover with 900-x-15 sand tires. Lynn supervised the loading of canned food, charcoal, green coffee for baksheesh, or tips, 200

gallons of water, 400 of gasoline, and a small live lamb. At Al Hufūf oasis we picked up young Jabr, our guide. He was of the Murrah tribe, most famous trackers in Arabia.

Jabr was lean but tough as leather. He brought with him all his worldly goods: a turban, short white gown, cartridge belt, and rifle. He kept his hair in long ringlets and his black beard trimmed short, and he looked the world straight in the eye.

We crossed the Dammam-Riyadh railway at Ḥaraḍ and followed a faint trail for four hours to our first stop, Nadqān Well. A herd of noisy camels pressed around it; nearby a group of Murrah Bedouin had pitched their black tents (pages 32-3). One belonged to Jabr's father. We were among friends.

I left Lynn to set up camp and walked with Jabr to meet the camp's senior member, graybearded Emir Rashid ibn Nudaylah.

"*As-salaam 'alaikum!* Peace be upon you!" shouted Jabr. They rubbed noses in greeting.

Diamond-toothed drill bores a well at Safaniya, world's most productive offshore oilfield, which extends 50 miles out in the Persian Gulf. Aramco's 10,300 well-paid Saudi employees represent a new and dynamic element in Arabian society.

Gas flares fire the night at Aramco's Ras Tanurah refinery, north of Dhahran. Each day sparkling towers convert more than a quarter of a million barrels of crude oil into a variety of fuels, including aviation gasoline.

"Wa-'alaikum as-salaam," answered the old one. "And on you, peace."

We sat cross-legged on cushions in the welcome shade of the *bait ash-sha'r,* literally, "house of hair." Woven of black goat's hair, it was some 40 feet long. A colorful partition muffled the giggles and gossip of the harem. The emir had spotted us on the horizon. The coffeepot was already on the fire.

Fair-skinned Beauty Worth 45 Camels

The emir himself poured a swallow of coffee into a tiny china cup. Politeness demanded that I take three cups. I was tired and parched. I took them with relish. A gallon bowl of cool, sweet camel milk was passed around, followed by handfuls of dates.

The Arab loves his coffee break. It's the sum total of his social life (following pages). It often lasts all day, and it is strictly a man's affair. But this was a special case, and novelty won out over convention. At the emir's

insistence, Lynn joined us around the fire.

We talked about rising prices of rifles and wives. The emir had three of each.

"Wa-llaah, but this fair-skinned one is a jewel," said the old emir with a nod toward Lynn. "Worth thirty camels at least."

"Fifty," I countered, defending Lynn's market value.

"Possibly thirty-five."

"Forty-five (may you live long), forty-five!"

It was Lynn's first time on the auction block. She began to fidget—until all broke into laughter.

Inevitably the talk turned to the grazing. The Bedouin's harsh life is a constant search for grass for his camels, sheep, and goats. A few scattered showers had made this a good year, bringing up thin patches of grass and sedge between the dunes.

On our way down we had crossed the wide Wādī aṣ Ṣahbā', a shallow depression in the sandy landscape. Here water could be had for the drilling. The Saudi Government had sunk wells and started a small experimental farm. Eventually it plans to settle a thousand Bedouin families on five-acre plots. Had the emir and his people ever been tempted to settle down, I asked.

"Trade the whole world for a garden? Never!" he answered adamantly. "And what would happen to our camels? They give us the milk of life and hair for our rugs. They carry us and our burdens without complaint. They are our freedom."

Next morning we headed south over the sands. With Lynn and Jabr beside me, I led in the Land-Rover. The two vehicles bobbed over the dunes like small rafts on an ocean. By noon the Land-Rover was a crucible. Now not even a shadow broke the monotony of the blinding landscape.

Suddenly I hit the brakes. Just in time, I had stopped short of a sharp crest of sand. Another ten feet would have plunged us headlong down the steep 60-foot leeward side of the dune!

Five times a day we halted for prayer. Each time I checked my compass and odometer; Lynn put a check mark on the map. But when I drove, Jabr was my compass. With a faint wave of his hand he set the course.

Jabr broke the silence. "Two summers ago my family followed the rain clouds south. We took this same track."

Track! I saw nothing but dunes and, in the distance, a tiny black speck. As we drew nearer, I recognized it as the carcass of a long-dead camel. Jabr smiled. We were on course.

Just before sunset, 13 hours south of Nadqān, Jabr justified my faith in him.

"Al-hamdillaah! Praise be to God!" sighed Jabr. "Here is Wabar." I saw nothing. Then, over the dune, there was the crater.

We killed our lamb and feasted round the campfire. Jabr and Wahier, the cook, told us stories about the evil city of Wabar. Allah had destroyed it with fire from the sky.

I cross-examined Jabr, hoping for the secret of his remarkable navigating. Jabr couldn't explain his "sixth sense."

Hospitality at a Bedouin Well

THOUGH an arid, barren wilderness of boulders and sand, Arabia's Ar Rab' al Khālī —the Empty Quarter—provides a home to the hardy Murrah tribe. In summer, when temperatures soar to 120° F., these eternal wanderers camp close to wells along the northern fringes of a vast wasteland the size of Texas. After a day of grazing on the burning dunes, camels drink smelly, brackish water unfit for humans. Their masters live for months without drinking water; to quench their thirst, they milk the camels (upper left). Pitching his tent near Nadqān Well, Emir Rashid ibn Nudaylah offers guests large bowls of the fresh milk and heaps of delicious dates. His son (upper right) pours coffee—spiced with cardamom and ginger root—from a long-beaked pot into tiny china cups. Earlier, he boiled the water over a brushwood fire and ground the beans in a brass mortar. A guest customarily accepts three servings; shaking the cup with a rapid twist of the wrist signifies a sufficiency. Hospitality is a duty as well as a joy for the Bedouin. He will kill his last sheep to feed the stranger at his tent.

KODACHROMES © NATIONAL GEOGRAPHIC SOCIETY

"We are Bedouin," he said. "It is our life."

They were still chanting Bedouin songs when Lynn and I laid out blankets under the blazing stars.

Next morning we explored the 250-foot crater. Sand had nearly filled it. On the higher, western rim we picked up torn chunks of limestone bedrock and fragments of glassy slag—sand melted by the impact of a meteor.

"Here! Over here!"

It was Jabr's voice in the distance. We followed his footprints a quarter of a mile across the sand. Rumor had become reality; the biggest iron meteorite ever found in Arabia lay at our feet (page 35).

It was too big. Shaped roughly like a saucer, it measured about four feet in diameter and two feet thick at center. A little quick geometry put its weight at almost two and a half tons. We couldn't possibly bring it back.

Breakdowns Force a Desert Detour

The great nugget rang like a bell as I chipped a sample off the edge. Meanwhile, Lynn made a sketch map of its location. We surveyed the crater; then, our work finished, we retreated northward. The last item packed up was my thermometer. It read 127° F.

Troubles plagued our return trip; the heat and rough terrain of the Empty Quarter are hard on the best of vehicles. The Power Wagon threw a fan blade. I used up most of my first-aid kit on a torn radiator hose. Ali, the driver, patched the radiator with a mixture of barley flour and camel dung.

Then a short circuit in the Land-Rover burned out the generator, which began to screech. We decided to detour and stop for repairs at "Seismo-4," an Aramco exploration camp. I had the address in my notebook: Lat. 23° 40' 00" N., Long. 49° 32' 24" E.

The camp manager, Bob Anderson, greeted us with dishes of chocolate ice cream, promises of spares, and bunks for the night in one of the camp's air-conditioned trailers.

Like a black ghost at Halloween, a Bedouin woman peers through a slit-eyed veil. Henna stains her work-worn hands. Patterned drapery on the tent, hand-woven from dyed wool and goat's hair, partitions off the harem. Moslem law allows a man four wives —but only if he can treat them equally.

Bawling for water, thirsty camels await their turn to drink at Nadqān Well. Men sip coffee in the shade of goat-hair tents, while women tend to early-morning chores.

A long day's drive brought us safely into Dhahran. There I left Lynn back in the 20th century and flew across the country for a camel ride along one of Saudi Arabia's last regular caravan routes. Despite the hazards of sand, dust, and chassis-shattering roads, most of the kingdom's colorful caravans have given way to jeeps, buses, and giant trucks.

Two Days' Journey to Abhā Market

In the village of Ad Darb, on the sultry Red Sea coast, I caught up with tall, raw-boned Fahd ibn Muhassan, the boss of the camel drivers.

"Ah-lan wa-sahlan! Welcome!" he said, with a smile as wide as his beard. "You are just in time; we leave before sunset. We will be in Abhā for the Tuesday market, Allah willing, but it is two days' journey and two nights. And the road is steep."

We filed out of the village on foot, leading a string of 48 camels bawling under heavy loads. How different was this coastal desert from the rest of Arabia! The village of Ad Darb was typical—a cluster of tall, pointed huts, framed with poles and thatched with palm rope (pages 38-9). The dark-skinned people dressed for the sweltering climate. Men wore only striped loincloths and broad-brimmed hats; women walked about in bright calico, seldom veiled. The scene struck me as more African than Arabian.

Not until the first stars appeared did we mount. Fahd coached me in the art of climbing aboard a moving camel.

"We can't stop the whole caravan to get on and off," Fahd explained. "It would take an hour with the stick to get them moving again."

I tied my rifle and cameras opposite the clay water jug and coffeepots and pulled down slightly on my camel's head as I walked.

"Gurrrrah! Gurrrrrrah!" I trilled, quickly putting my knee in the crook of her powerful neck. Instantly I was airborne, swinging safely into the saddle.

Her good balance had earned my camel the name of Midwam, which means "spinning top." Now, loaded with 400 pounds of coffee and sorghum stalks, she moved with an especially smooth gait. I sprawled among the mixed baggage and tried to sleep. Far ahead in the dark, Fahd moaned a love ballad:

"The quickening wind unveiled a glimpse;
A slender neck, dark lovely eyes...."

Never had I seen such a show of stars. The night wore on. I dozed fitfully. The Big Dipper turned slowly round Polaris and finally poured out the red dawn. We stopped to rest.

Before noon we were loaded again and moving painfully across the hot, breathless desert, impatient for the cool mountains rising in the haze ahead.

We flushed larks and coveys of sand grouse and, once, a red-headed Arabian woodpecker.

KODACHROMES BY THOMAS J. ABERCROMBIE © N.G.S.

Silent shadows on the sand, Murrah Bedouin and their camels plod the Empty Quarter in search of grass. Wind-created "dunes" only a few inches high show as light streaks in the lee of scattered bushes.

Smashing in from space, this 4,800-pound meteorite dug a sandy grave near Al Ḥadīdah in the Empty Quarter. The author found the iron-nickel nugget, largest ever discovered in Arabia, after Murrah Bedouin guided him across 400 miles of desert.

I spied a pair of gray hornbills hooting from the yellow blossoms of a thorny *talh* tree. We passed a splendid iridescent blue lizard. He was doing push-ups on his forelegs on his rock perch. The camel drivers called him *dhubb as-salaat,* the praying lizard.

Suddenly I heard the terrifying sound of screams and rolling rocks on the hillside above us. I grabbed my rifle.

"Don't shoot!" laughed Fahd. "They are only baboons." I looked closer. A whole colony was on the move. The husky males formed a cordon around the females and young ones.

"They are harmless unless you scare them; then they shower you with stones," he said.

Some of the camels lagged. "Haaaa! Haaaa! A curse on your first milk!" shouted Fahd, driving them up to pace. As we trudged the last stretch of stony switchbacks, the air freshened and we passed cool springs. Goatherds, high above us, waved salutes. By afternoon we reached the windy pass.

Vista of Green Rewards Climbers

I looked back. Seven thousand feet below, the desert and the sea were veiled by sultry mist. Ahead, the trail led down through green terraces to Abhā.

Paying a courtesy call on the governor of Abhā, Emir Turki bin Madhi al-Sudairi, I found him holding *majlis,* a sort of "open court." At the far end of a richly carpeted room he sat in great dignity, hearing complaints and settling disputes, flanked by a dozen stern bodyguards wearing thick leather cartridge belts and armed with English rifles. I left my shoes at the door and advanced humbly. He met me halfway to trade the usual Arab greetings:

"Peace be with you!" I opened.

"And with you, peace!"

"Morning of goodness, O Emir."

"Morning of light."

"God grant you life."

"Our family, our gardens, be yours."

With dispatch, he settled the day's business. Two brothers disputed ownership of a small family field. The emir awarded it to the younger, who had planted it each year since his father's death. A woman was divorced because she was barren; her husband was ordered to return the dowry.

Outside, in the shadow of the emir's towering palace, the Tuesday market was reaching a climax. Here I met Husain Zaphir, a native of the region who spoke excellent English and offered his services as a guide. He led me through the bustle. Farmers crowded the temporary stalls to buy sheep and coffee, charcoal, tools, and trinkets. Others filled the noisy teashops that lined the town square.

Fodder for a Nonexistent Donkey

Young women from the nearby villages sold bundles of herbs and alfalfa. Few were veiled; many were striking in bright red or green dresses, beautifully embroidered at the neck and cuffs. Heavy silver anklets and bracelets rattled as they sorted their wares.

A smiling girl in a sheepskin coat and wide straw hat bargained with us over her wares.

"Ah, there are no more beautiful women in all Arabia," Husain assured me. "Here on Tuesday a man could find a bride."

Enchanted, he bought a bale of fodder. I remarked that it was too bad we had no donkey. Husain blushed and tossed the bundle of alfalfa in the back of a jeep we had hired.

We drove up the winding motor road above Abhā to the village of Sūqah. Near a crumbling stone watchtower, set among green terraces, we found an old farmer damming a small brook to water his field of barley. Here, I thought, was a man at peace with his land.

"It was not always peaceful here," the old man remembered. "Villages often fought each other, and the Bedouin raided us all. Twice, when I was a young boy, I huddled in this tower with my family, while raiders looted our homes and livestock.

"But 'Abd al-'Aziz (Allah's peace be upon him) put an end to the raiding. Now, you see, we use the watchtower for a granary, our rifles for hunting. Allah be praised."

Later I followed a shepherd's trail to the summit of nearby Jabal Sawdā', highest point in the kingdom. My pocket altimeter read

Waves of sand from a desert ocean lap the date groves of Al Ḥasā, the kingdom's largest oasis. Driven by the prevailing *shamaal,* or northerly wind, the crescent-shaped dunes choked hundreds of acres of fertile farmland and buried whole villages. Now fences and rows of tamarisk trees, pines, and castor plants help to halt the relentless invader. Scores of bubbling warm springs water this island of fertility.

Onion domes of thatch shelter the villagers of Ad Darb, who farm Arabia's coastal plain by the Red Sea. Donkeys bearing pottery water jugs plod in never-ending procession to and from the community well. Women of this seldom-visited region rarely wear veils.

Shaped like a knight's helmet, cap of woven palm leaves protects a farmer of Ad Darb from the sun. He raises sesame and presses oil from the seeds with camel-powered mills.

10,279 feet. Here, where the mountain milked precious raindrops from the clouds, I found a small "rain forest," perhaps 20 feet wide, along the edge of the escarpment. Tangles of gnarled junipers, bearded with gray-green lichen, sheltered tall red-blooming aloes. Tiny alpine flowers glowed among the rocks. A lazy hawk watched from a sapphire sky.

Lamb Slain for Emir's Guests

On my return to Abhā, Emir Turki bade me to lunch. The Arab is a determined host. For him hospitality is an obligation, a part of his code of honor, a bond between friends, and a truce between enemies. A poor Bedouin will boil his last rice for the stranger who appears in his camp; an important emir favors his guests with a feast.

I squatted on one knee at the emir's right, and the bodyguards took their place around the huge tray of rice piled high with steaming meat. A lamb had been killed for the occasion. Around the centerpiece lay dishes of salad, eggplant, and custard, and folded sheets of flat bread.

"Bismi llaahi r-rahmaani r-rahiim," the emir whispered, signaling the beginning of the meal. "In the name of Allah, the compassionate, the merciful."

We ate, as is customary, with the right hand only. The guards, I noticed, never took their left hands off their rifles. The emir tore out pieces of the lungs (good for the digestion) and the tongue and laid them before me.

"Who eats the tongue will speak the better for it," the emir promised with a smile. Often

in Arabia I was so honored, but it did little to improve my Arabic.

During the meal we spoke little and ate quickly. We rolled handfuls of rice into compact lumps and popped them into our mouths. A bowl of drinking water was passed around, then dishes of custard sprinkled with almonds.

Incense Smoke Marks Feast's End

Suddenly the emir stood up; the meal was over. We washed under a graceful brass pitcher held by a household servant. Another brought rose water for our hands and faces. A third passed around the incense burner. Each in turn, we held it under our headcloths to soak fragrant smoke into our beards. This signaled the party's end. The Arabs have a saying: *"Bakhkhir wa-ruuh.* Take the incense and go."

By the time I returned to Jidda, thousands of hadjis (pilgrims) were already arriving for Islam's greatest pageant, the climax of the long journey to Mecca.* The harbor was crowded with ships strung with festive lights. Brightly painted buses jammed the square. Regular airline service was suspended as special pilgrim flights droned into Jidda International Airport. In a few days the population of Jidda would double.

Jidda enjoyed the bustle. Many small merchants would count more profit during *Dhu l-Hijja,* the month of pilgrimage, than in all the rest of the year. The streets and market place overflowed with newcomers changing money and buying food, pilgrim clothes, and

*See "From America to Mecca on Airborne Pilgrimage," by Abdul Ghafur Sheikh, GEOGRAPHIC, July, 1953.

39

souvenirs. Some pilgrims were selling carpets (two are allowed duty free) for expenses.

Hotels and pensions were full to the rooftops. Special new barracks built by the Ministry of Pilgrimage along the waterfront and at the airport helped absorb the overflow. Thousands slept under buses in the park, or on the streets.

I had encountered the religion of Islam before, in the deserts of Iran, in the mountains of Yemen, along the coast of Turkey, and was impressed by its message.* It includes much that is familiar to us in the Old Testament and the New, and adds much. True, its rites are colored by the harsh desert life that nourished it. So, too, is its majestic simplicity. But in its essence Islam never veers from the oneness of God.

To the Moslem mind, Mohammed was God's messenger—no more than that—as were Jesus and Abraham before him.

A trip to the *qaadi,* or religious magistrate, in Jidda to file my petition of intention, a note scribbled under the Saudi visa in my passport

*The author described his travels "Behind the Veil of Troubled Yemen," in the March, 1964, GEOGRAPHIC.

—and I was admitted to the brotherhood of Islam.

"*Mubaarak!* Blessings!" said my friend Husain as we left the qaadi. He had driven back with me from Abhā on his way to the pilgrimage. Now we would go together.

Husain and I donned the *ihraam,* the pilgrim dress, consisting of two pieces of seamless white cloth, one wound around the waist, the other draped over the left shoulder (page 47). All pilgrims wear the same garb, from the lowliest servant to the King himself.

Money belt, sandals, and a green umbrella

Castles of mud rise above the village of Khamīs Mushayṭ in the cool ‘Asīr mountains. Fagot of firewood on her back, a young shepherdess heads homeward. She crosses a dry wadi, where ditches trap rain water to nourish scant grass and terraces of wheat and sorghum. The author reached this mountainous region after an arduous three-day camel trip from the Red Sea coast. Invited to dine with the local emir, he sat down to a banquet of whole roast lamb served atop a tray of steaming rice.

completed my costume—except for a small handbag filled with cameras and film. The Saudi Ministry of Information had arranged special permission for me to photograph the pilgrimage.

Pilgrims Ring Ka'ba 250,000 Strong

That afternoon we sped in my Land-Rover along the four-lane expressway that connects Jidda with Mecca, 45 miles away. Not so long ago the pious crowds crossed these sands on swaying camels. Now fleets of taxis, trucks, and buses hurried the pilgrims on their way. Soldiers examined our passes at the checkpoint just outside the sacred precincts, which extend roughly 15 miles from the city. Signs in English and Arabic warned: RESTRICTED AREA, MOSLEMS ONLY PERMITTED.

We passed huge new mansions and army barracks in the sandy outskirts of Mecca. Then, as we rounded the foot of a hill, the holy city itself burst into view.

"Labbayka Allahumma Labbayka!" At the sight, we shouted the traditional pilgrim's cry. "Here I am, at your service, O God!"

A wide avenue cut through the labyrinth of tall pastel-colored houses that crowded a protected valley and climbed up the steep black hillsides. Modern shops and hotels lined the square around the Haram Mosque, Islam's holiest shrine.

We washed; then, carrying our sandals,

entered the enormous outer galleries beneath two towering minarets. Just inside, young Mohammed Noor offered his services. He was a *mutawwif,* a professional pilgrim guide.

He led us across the carpets through the mosque's newer section. This $100,000,000 addition, now nearing completion, covers 15 acres and completely surrounds the original mosque, begun in the eighth century. We passed through the Gate of Salvation into the turbulent inner court.

Before me, rising above the white-robed crowds, stood the Ka'ba, the cube-shaped House of God, made of Meccan granite and draped with black brocade. Moslems believe the original, long destroyed, was built by Abraham and his son Ishmael. Wherever a Moslem may be, he turns toward it five times each day for prayer.

Barefoot, I followed my guide seven times round the Ka'ba, repeating after him in Arabic the proper phrases of devotion.

"O mighty Allah. This mosque is your mosque. This peace is your peace. This slave is your slave."

Each time we passed the sacred black stone set in silver on the eastern corner, we raised our hands and shouted *"Allaahu Akbar!* God is greatest!"

Bearers carrying the sick and the lame jostled us with their heavy wooden litters.

(Continued on page 48)

Layer cakes of slate, jutting from whitewashed walls, protect the mud-brick houses of Abhā from seasonal downpours. In autumn, the southwest monsoon dumps torrents of precious rain on this city beside Saudi Arabia's loftiest mountain, 10,279-foot Jabal Sawdā'. In Abhā's market place (below), hand-embroidered wedding dresses for sale emblazon a spice shop.

EKTACHROMES BY THOMAS J. ABERCROMBIE © N.G.S.

GHOSTLY HOST AT TWILIGHT, *drawn as moths to a sacred flame, streams across the plain of 'Arafāt, hallowed by its ties to Abraham. Each year a million pilgrims journey to Mecca and the surrounding countryside in answer to an edict in the holy Koran: "And proclaim unto mankind the Pilgrimage. They will come unto thee on foot and on every lean camel . . . from every deep ravine." Here cars, trucks, and buses join the slow-moving throng, creating the world's greatest traffic jam.*

44   KODACHROME BY SAFOUH NAAMANI © N.G.S.

Beating the devil, stone-throwing pilgrims jam the streets of Miná, a village six miles from Mecca. In this Fisheye-lens view, visitors hurl the traditional seven stones, a yearly event in the hamlet. Some toss shoes. The pillar marks one of three spots, Moslems believe, where the devil tempted Abraham as he prepared to sacrifice his son to God. Finding Abraham's faith steadfast, God substituted a ram.

Faces alight with glee, Moslems from Morocco to Indonesia pelt the pillar. Later, outside the village, they will slay thousands of sheep, cows, and camels to commemorate Abraham's offering. Men wear prescribed pilgrim garb, the white two-piece *ihraam.*

EKTACHROMES BY THOMAS J. ABERCROMBIE © N.G.S.

My legs and heels were torn by a thousand toenails. Old women, lean Bedouin, bearded savants, husky soldiers, whirled together, pressing and parrying. Tears of joy streaked the faces of many, for they were reaching at last the sacred goal of a lifetime.

After circling the Ka'ba, Husain and I ran back and forth seven times, as custom commands, between Safa and Marwa. These two hills, though nearly half a mile apart, have now been enclosed within the giant mosque. Moslem legend tells how Abraham left Hagar here in the desert with their son Ishmael. Frantically she ran between Safa and Marwa, searching for water for the child. Finally the angel Gabriel led her to a spring.

The same miraculous spring still feeds the Well of Zamzam. We stopped to wash our faces in its holy waters. The more pious doused themselves from head to foot.

Pilgrims Pause for Sunset Prayer

I climbed to the roof of the mosque and entered one of the minarets over the Gate of Abraham. I had taken a moment out from the pilgrimage rites, seeking a vantage point for my cameras. In darkness I groped my way up the precarious stairway that led around and upward inside the tower. Just at the call of sunset prayer I reached the cupola, 300 feet above the courtyard. I watched breathlessly while the most sacred and beautiful pageant of Islam unfolded (pages 2-4).

A quarter of a million people stopped where they were and turned toward the Ka'ba. They seemed to form an immense and beautiful Oriental carpet—each tuft a white-clad pilgrim—woven in ever-widening circles around the black square. Lamp posts added symmetrical patterns of luminous rosettes. Arcades and galleries of the giant outer mosque formed a border around the design.

The hushed whispers of the crowd rose in a muffled chorus under the Meccan sky. "Allaahu Akbar!" In unison, all foreheads reverently touched the gravel of the courtyard.

After prayer, the carpet came to life as crowds once more began their churning around the holy Ka'ba. Beyond the spectacle the first lights of evening began to twinkle throughout the winding Mecca valley. The blood-red sunset retreated before a charging full moon and its army of stars.

Next day on the plain of 'Arafāt, 14 miles east of Mecca, the pilgrimage came to a climax. In hundreds of thousands of tents packing the valley, the pilgrims, often whole families, spent the day resting and praying (pages

Shave of grace: White-bearded pilgrim in Miná bares his head to a sidewalk barber, completing the pilgrimage ceremonies. Now the man will shed the ihraam and put on his regular clothes for the trip home.

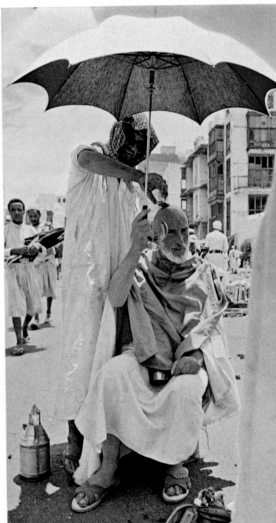

KODACHROMES © NATIONAL GEOGRAPHIC SOCIETY

Parched pilgrim pleads for water at the doorway of a hotel during the three-day rites in Miná. Wealthy Moslems book rooms in the village's large new hotels as long as a year in advance; others crowd the houses lining Miná's main street or pitch tents in the nearby hills. Thousands spread prayer rugs on the ground and sleep in the open. To cope with the annual invasion, the Saudi Government has built housing centers, drilled wells, and set up field hospitals.

44-5). Then, precisely at sunset, as a cannon sounded the signal, everyone left at once for the next stop, the village of Miná.

Soldiers and policemen, carrying camel sticks and wearing pistol belts over their pilgrim clothes, kept stern order during the exodus. They wrote no tickets, but dragged an occasional offender from his truck and thrashed him soundly with their sticks.

In our Land-Rover we ground through the deep sand around the stalled road traffic and the surging crowds, making the six-mile drive to Miná in two hours. Many trucks and buses didn't arrive till next day.

Blue Eyes Puzzle a Texas Arab

Husain and I checked in at the Taysir, one of several ten-story hotels that have sprung up recently in the small village.

"Min fain inta?" asked the young desk clerk. "Where are you from?" He stared suspiciously at my blue eyes. I showed my passport.

"America? Y'all from Washin'ton?" he gasped in fluent, southern-fried English. "Ah jist lef' Texas less'n two weeks back! Ah'm back heah helpin' in Dad's hotel fuh the rush season."

The rush season in Miná lasts only three days. During the rest of the year, I learned, the village is practically empty. That explained the high room rate: $100 a bed in a four-bed room. I was lucky at that. Most of the pilgrims were camped in tents in the bleak basalt hills around the town. Hundreds of thousands more slept on small prayer rugs in the hot dust of the streets.

Nonetheless, the days at Miná were happy ones. The rigors of the journey were forgotten in celebration of a successful pilgrimage. Swept along with exuberant crowds, I threw the allotted seven stones at each of three devil pillars in Miná's main street (pages 46-7). These stone columns mark the places where Moslems believe the devil tried to tempt Abraham to refuse to sacrifice his son as God had commanded. In the end, God provided a ram which Abraham sacrificed instead.

That sacrifice survives in tradition. Throughout the day, in the official slaughterhouse just outside town, pilgrims slit the throats of thousands of sheep, cows, and camels, and distribute the meat to the poor.

On the second day at Miná everyday clothes take the place of pilgrim's

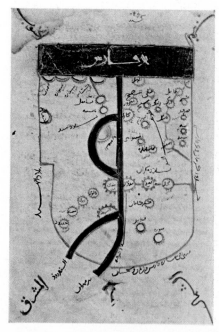

Glittering minarets spike the skyline of Medina the Radiant, second only to Mecca among the holy cities of Islam. Mohammed spent the last ten years of his life here, after fleeing from Mecca in A.D. 622.

Squatting at mahogany benches, scholars consult Arabic texts on science, law, and religion at the Sheik Hagmud Library in Medina. Priceless books and hand-lettered manuscripts crowd the shelves.

Time-stained map illustrates a centuries-old Arabic geography. The chart shows fortified cities as red circles and the Indus River flowing through present-day Pakistan on its way to the Arabian Sea. The Sheik Hagmud Library treasures the volume.

garb. Once a uniform white, crowds now are brightened by colorful costumes from many lands: brilliant red calicos from Nigeria, green turbans from Iran, blue Yemeni caftans, striped Egyptian galabias, and sarongs from Indonesia.

Medina Exerts a Special Pull

Few pilgrims return home without making the 300-mile trip north to Medina, Arabia's second holy city. Mohammed spent the last ten years of his life there after idol worshipers, alarmed at his rising popularity, drove him and a handful of followers from his native Mecca. The Moslem calendar dates from the year of his Hegira, or flight, in A.D. 622.

Before I left Arabia, I paid my respects to Mohammed's memory at his tomb in Medina, under the green dome in the Masjid ar-Rasul, the Mosque of the Prophet (opposite). Praying to Mohammed is forbidden by the Koran, but most visitors offer a prayer here to Allah for the Prophet. With his own hands, the Prophet helped build the first mosque on this spot. Over the centuries it has been rebuilt and enlarged, most recently by the Saudi Government in 1955.

Although the pilgrimage season was over, crowds still filled the mosque at prayer time and afterward bargained with cloth merchants on the front steps over bright-colored bolts of cotton and silk (below). Others, in the market place, purchased prayer beads and Korans. I bought a small morocco-bound edition for myself, taking care to argue only about the price of the binding. The holy pages inside are always included free.

That evening from the roof of my airconditioned hotel I stared out across the city. In the rose twilight the first lights began to twinkle, then quickly outshone the starry desert night.

Al Madīnah al-Munawwarah, the City of Light; it seemed a fitting name tonight. The sacred precincts were illuminated by roaring generators outside the town, manned by two lonely Englishmen. Welcome, 20th century, says Arabia, but don't rush me.

Medina was the seed from which sprouted the great Arab empires that stretched from Gibraltar to India. Dipping into the wisdom of Greece, Persia, and Byzantium, they relighted the lamps of Europe's Dark Ages. Now the West returns in kind. Slowly the impact is felt, modified, and finally accepted.

Arabia shone with the light of Islam long before Edison's electric illumination. It prospered without oil wells, occupied the deserts without trucks and fertilizers, conquered great distances without jet planes.

Now with all these modern boons, it will rise from its slumber, Allah willing, to shine anew, and put Aladdin's lamp to shame.

THE END

EKTACHROMES BY THOMAS J. ABERCROMBIE © N.G.S.

Bolts of bright cotton in a Medina market contrast with the somber garb of four Saudi women.

Banded arches of limestone and basalt with geometric designs—orthodox Moslem art bans human images—support the ceiling of Medina's Mosque of the Prophet. On rich red carpets men pray and read their Korans. They believe Mohammed helped build the original mosque of clay and palm trunks.

Religion remains the guiding force of Saudi Arabia, dictating its civil laws, monitoring its manners, and refreshing its spirit with the ecstasy of worship at holy sites.

Stalking Seals

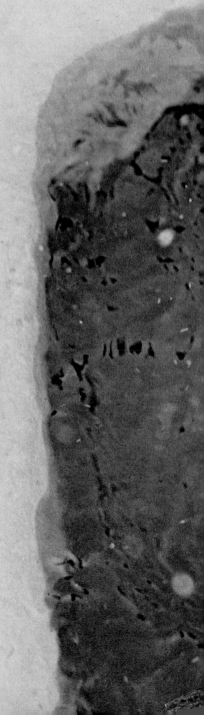

WITH SIX FEET of ice over my head and 300 feet of frigid water below, I swam through the half-light for our access hole to the surface. Ahead, bubbles streamed intermittently from the Aqua-Lung of Lt. David Lavallee. And toward us, aiming for the same objective, swam a nine-foot, 800-pound Weddell seal.

We eyed each other curiously, the seal and I. The thought occurred to me that this big fellow might not like the idea of our using his breathing hole.

Dave gave a final kick of his flippers and entered the hole. Now the seal was just inches from my swim fins. As I swam up behind Dave, the animal grasped my right fin gently in his powerful jaws, holding on for perhaps ten seconds. Then, as Dave hauled himself out of the water, the seal let go of my flipper.

Almost together the seal and I popped our heads through the access hole. On an impulse, I gave him a gentle pat on the snout, and then heaved myself out of the water.

Dave and I watched the animal breathe deeply and repeatedly for three minutes, his nostrils dilating and contracting like giant mechanical valves. Before he clamped his nostrils shut and dived again, he gave us one brief glance and that was all.

I couldn't have been more delighted by his casual acceptance of us—apparitions wearing rubber suits, face masks, and metal tanks. To him we were fellow marine creatures, and he was proving our motto: "If you want to study a seal, *be* a seal."

The Weddell seal, *Leptonychotes weddelli,* is the world's most southerly mammal—a behemoth that reaches 10½ feet in length and well over 1,000 pounds in weight. Our first expedition in 1963—supported by the National Science Foundation's United States Antarctic Research Program under a

Puppy-faced Weddell seal gulps air through its window on the world, a hole in six-foot-thick Antarctic ice. Daring scientists, diving through such openings into the unknown, for the first time swam with the huge mammals to learn the secrets of their life in polar waters.

Under Antarctic Ice

Article and photographs by
CARLETON RAY, Ph.D.
Curator, New York Aquarium
New York Zoological Society

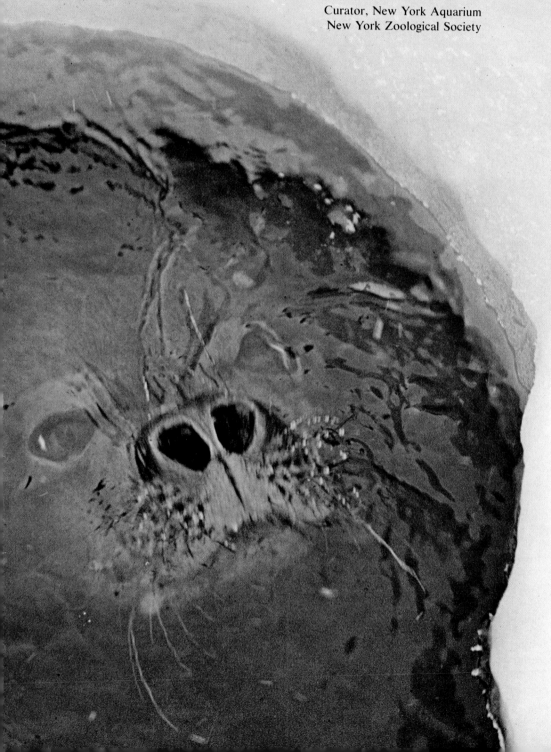

KODACHROME BY WILLIAM E. SCHEVILL © NATIONAL GEOGRAPHIC SOCIETY

Antarctic aquanauts brace for a plunge into the eerie, mysterious realm beneath the ice: Author Carleton Ray (left), chief diver Lt. David O. Lavallee, USN (center), and photographer Peter R. Gimbel. "The touch of sea on bare skin felt like the stab of an ice pick," Ray said after water seepage in his specially made suit of foam neoprene added pain to danger.

grant to the New York Zoological Society— had shown us the possibility of a unique research mission. Now, on a five-week expedition the following year, we were planning to study these marine mammals in their natural habitat—under the ice!

We wanted to learn, first of all, how seals navigate far beneath the ice-covered surface, where less than one percent of the overhead sunlight penetrates. How, after dives of perhaps 1,500 feet and half an hour's duration, do they find their way back to the holes they use for breathing? And how do they find the fish and shrimplike creatures they feed upon in the darkness of the depths? (We suspected that they use echo-location, or sonar.*)

Secondly, we wanted to know whether they communicate with each other by voice. What is the nature of seal "talk"?

Thirdly, how, in the coldest realm on earth, can seals bear the extreme temperatures on the surface and in the icy waters below?

In our search for answers, we joined forces with the Woods Hole Oceanographic Institution in the persons of bio-acousticians William E. Schevill and William A. Watkins—whose work was also supported by the National Science Foundation. The New York Zoological Society contingent included two extraordinarily capable biological divers and underwater

*NATIONAL GEOGRAPHIC published "Birds That 'See' in the Dark With Their Ears," by Edward S. Ross, in February, 1965; also "How Bats Hunt With Sound," by J. J. G. McCue, in April, 1961

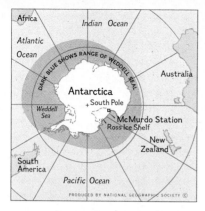

Earth's coldest domain harbors the seal named after British navigator James Weddell, who discovered the Weddell Sea in 1823. Expedition's camp lies on sea ice three miles from McMurdo Station, permanent United States research base.

Above and below the ice, scientists study how seals navigate, communicate, breathe, and forage. Submerged hydrophones capture seals' "talk" for a tape recorder in the hut; their vocabulary ranges from high trills to low moans. Divers drop through holes on photographic missions. Down below they face the risk of losing their way and running out of air. Though seals accepted the men as seagoing mammals, the equipment aroused their curiosity (below). One Weddell bit a hydrophone; another, hearing a playback of seal sounds, surfaced through the lab hole to see who was talking.

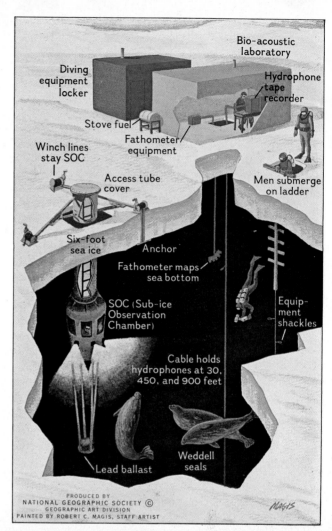

Bio-acoustic laboratory

Diving equipment locker

Hydrophone tape recorder

Stove fuel

Winch lines stay SOC

Fathometer equipment

Access tube cover

Men submerge on ladder

Six-foot sea ice

Anchor

Fathometer maps sea bottom

SOC (Sub-ice Observation Chamber)

Equipment shackles

Cable holds hydrophones at 30, 450, and 900 feet

Lead ballast

Weddell seals

Isolated porthole, the only one in half a mile, means life or death to the seal, who must find it to breathe. Dr. Ray (left) believes the animals use sonar, bouncing voice signals off the ice to locate such passageways. Constant use keeps the holes open even in the coldest weather; the seals enlarge them by sawing with their teeth. Blubbery bodies smooth the edges.

Sleek as a bullet, an 800-pound Weddell plunges through its hole in the ice. It survives long dives by constricting surface blood vessels to ensure a steady supply of blood to heart and brain. The Weddell also tolerates large amounts of carbon dioxide in the blood. Thus it can remain submerged for half an hour or longer, seeking food at depths as great as 1,500 feet—the deepest dive known for seals.

Flood-lamp eyes peer from the bucket-shaped capsule into the undersea gloom as divers—like astronauts afloat in space—circle amid a swarm of air bubbles. Light-reflecting paint flakes off the suit of the diver at right. Barring leaks in their suits, the men can withstand the 28.6° F. water for almost an hour. Submerged 16 feet below the icy surface, the observation chamber gave team members longer, more protected sessions in the deep. Scientists spent up to two hours in the cylinder despite temperatures in the chilly 30's. Like a submarine's periscope, the 12-foot access tube thrusts up through the ice. Long struts hold ballast for the six-foot-high compartment.

Around the hole "sunlight filtered through the ice as a bluish haze that resembled a cloudy sky," recalls Dr. Ray. "But dim surface illumination rapidly faded into blackness below."

EKTACHROME (ABOVE) AND DUOTONE (OPPOSITE) BY CARLETON RAY;
KODACHROME (TOP) BY DAVID O. LAVALLEE © N.G.S.

photographers, Peter R. Gimbel* and Lt. David O. Lavallee, USN, and myself. We made our base near the United States' McMurdo Station, 840 miles from the South Pole (map, page 57).

For our work we air-freighted close to two tons of equipment to Antarctica—everything from the most complex sound systems to thermal long johns and sun glasses. All our acoustical gear for listening to and tape-recording seal sounds would be installed in a 12-by-20-foot prefabricated, insulated hut equipped with an oil stove and a picture window. We would lower our underwater microphones through a hole in the floor of the hut.

"SOC" Designed to Keep Watch on Seals

To *watch* the seals while we listened, Bill Schevill had suggested, and David Lavallee had designed—and the National Science Foundation had had built—one of the strangest contrivances ever seen in Antarctica, the Sub-ice Observation Chamber, or "SOC." This tapered orange-yellow cylinder, with a 12-foot access tube and six windows, could hold two men. It would be secured by cables anchored to the underside of the ice.

We hoped to hear underwater seal sounds within a radius of five miles. We estimated there were 400 to 500 seals in the area of McMurdo; one day we counted almost 300 whiskered snouts on the ice at one time.

Here on the coast in the Antarctic spring, the coldest day we experienced was only 22° below zero F. in the shade. The temperature sometimes would climb to about freezing. Even in the much colder interior, it is the sudden and wild storms, especially winds, that make Antarctica so forbidding. That, and the continent's complete isolation by the Antarctic oceans—the most violent known.

Weddells are remarkable animals to be able to live on and under the ice of these cruel seas. They feed underwater, yet must breathe and whelp on the surface. Holes, kept open the year round through constant use and sawing with their teeth, comprise their only link between the two worlds.

During October and November—springtime down here—most of these seals gather in rookeries, where females give birth to 60- to 70-pound, 5-foot pups. On warmer days adult seals sunbathe like groups of lizards, while pups wander a bit. But on colder days the

Popping up for air, a Weddell surveys its domain, dominated by Mount Erebus, Antarctica's only active volcano, at left. White-splotched chest and benign expression distinguish this gentlest of seals. Two other animals stretch out to soak up the sun.

"They can sleep through gale-force winds in temperatures far below zero," says Dr. Ray. "But when a seal gets too cold in the wind, it slips under the ice to snooze while holding its breath. To my knowledge, our expedition was the first to observe seals sleeping beneath the ice."

Galaxy of starfish gleams 30 feet beneath the surface of McMurdo Sound. These creatures, smaller than a man's hand, detect food and light with upturned armlike rays. Like little mops, the starfish scour the sea floor's volcanic ash for shellfish and marine plants.

*Mr. Gimbel illustrated "By Parachute Into Peru's Lost World," by G. Brooks Baekeland, NATIONAL GEOGRAPHIC, August, 1964. Dr. Ray himself contributed "Three Whales That Flew," in the March, 1962, issue.

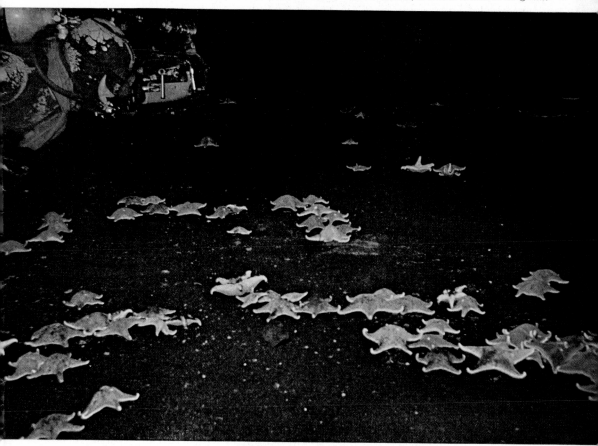

Food for seals, big Antarctic "cod" rarely reach the surface except when brought up from the depths by Weddells. Cruising in darkness, the seals find *Dissostichus mawsoni* by echo-location, scientists believe. Philip M. Smith, representing the United States Antarctic Program, scrutinizes two 60-pound specimens—no relation to the true cod—mauled by seals shortly before.

Flippers kicking, a diver swims toward a crystalline stalactite dangling from the sea ice. Water-filled pockets within the icy stalactite hold living creatures, including a smaller species of Antarctic cod and tiny shrimp-shaped amphipods.

Like a jeweled pin an inch in diameter, a brittle star adorns the sea floor.

KODACHROME BY CARLETON RAY © NATIONAL GEOGRAPHIC SOCIETY

snow-encrusted young huddle in the lee of mothers (pages 64-5). Within six weeks, pups approach 200 pounds, lose their fluffy tan hair, called lanugo, and take to the water.

Other adult seals gather in nonbreeding colonies along cracks in the sea ice or near the shore. Communal living is not, however, an invariable rule; individualists occasionally are found near isolated holes in the ice.

Our explorations beneath the ice by scuba diving, hydrophones, and observation from the SOC would help us understand the other side of the life of these amphibious beasts.

Cacophony of Sound Deluges Listeners

Shortly after we arrived at McMurdo, a C-130 Hercules landed with the observation chamber. We wanted a location well away from the base and the path of icebreakers, in about 1,000 feet of water. After several soundings, we found such a site and started to make a place for the SOC in the ice.

In four days a chain saw, ice drill, tongs, and dynamite removed about 22 tons of six-foot-thick ice to make three holes: one for hydrophones in the floor of our bio-acoustics hut; another for divers and seals just outside the hut's picture window; and a third, seven feet square, for the SOC (diagram, page 57).

We started moving our hut toward its hole three miles away, but were beaten back by a gale after the first half a mile. Next day we hauled the hut the rest of the way. By nightfall Bill Watkins had one hydrophone in place, and we settled in to listen.

What we heard held us transfixed for hours. The water was alive with the sounds of seals. There was not a moment's silence in the "silent world," but instead a never-ending chorus of seal trills, chirps, and whistles.

"No wonder the seals haul out onto the ice," said Dave Lavallee. "They have to get away from all that racket below!"

Two days later Navy Seabees, with their usual ingenuity, lowered the SOC into place. Two seals were already "in residence," using as a breathing hole the same opening the SOC was in. We were soon seeing and hearing the Weddell seal simultaneously, in the first prolonged acoustical-behavioral study of any large marine mammal in its own environment.

Lavallee, Gimbel, and I first dove near the SOC to install lights and clean its windows. Then it was time to "become seals" ourselves. Along a crack in the ice near shore, where the water was shallower, we found four holes made by seals, two of them large enough for divers. We would be going down with

EKTACHROME (BELOW) BY PETER R. GIMBEL; KODACHROMES BY CARLETON RAY © N.G.S.

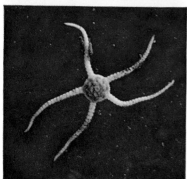

standard breathing equipment, but our suits had been specially fabricated for us of 5/16-inch-thick foam neoprene. The only exposed skin was a little area around the mouth, which we knew from experience would not get uncomfortably cold in the 28.6° F. sea water. We adjusted our outfits against leakage, and entered the water one by one.

As we descended, penetrating this forbidding frontier, we had a feeling of otherworldliness. I was apprehensive. This was truly the unknown, as hostile an environment as is found on earth. But, as we got accustomed to this blue crystalline world, the apprehension became mixed with a pleasant weightless feeling. We were one with the sea.

Antarctic Waters Teem With Life

Visibility proved excellent. We could see some 75 yards horizontally along the silver band of the crack. Overhead, from clusters of ice crystals—sometimes three to four feet long—emanated a blue-white light. The underside of the ice was stained brown with diatoms. Among the crystals dwelt a species of Antarctic "cod," one to three inches long, and little shrimplike amphipods (above).

In the water itself we found a multitude of delicate creatures: small ctenophores, or comb jellyfish; little pteropods, or winged snails, up to three-fourths of an inch long, flapping their "wings" like men trying to warm themselves on a cold day; huge jellyfish, as much as two and a half feet across the bell, with tentacles up to 35 feet long.

We followed the rays of light downward and on the bottom observed a plenitude of life: starfish, ranging from two to eighteen inches across, of two different species—a big orange type and a smaller blue one always found with the tips of its arms upturned, probably tasting for food (page 61); brittle stars; nemertine, or proboscid, worms up to three feet long and an inch in diameter.

Here and there patches of ice crystals had formed on the mud. The same fishes and amphipods found among the crystals above were also present among those on the bottom.

Many of these bottom animals fed on seal feces. The seals were contributing to an incredibly rich food chain by feeding far afield, bringing back nutrients, and fertilizing the area. All in all, I would judge there was as great a collection of bottom life as occurs anywhere in the world. In fact, during the summer, the Antarctic oceans are considered to be the richest on earth. Twenty-four hours of sunlight and the nutrients that accumulate

when the sea is ice-covered stimulate an amazing growth of plants and animals.

Seal-watching proved relatively easy. The animals seemed indifferent to us, and let us approach them in their various moods. We never saw them feed or mate, but we did spot them sleeping directly under the ice.

The Weddell will do this at times, the air in its lungs giving it the buoyancy needed to remain securely up against the ice.

One marvels at the magnificent metabolism allowing rest in the coldest environment known on earth, for the thermal conductivity of water at this temperature is 23 times greater than that of air at the same temperature. This means that the human body, for instance, would cool 23 times faster in 28.6° F. water than in air at the same temperature. The unprotected body could not produce heat fast enough to survive more than a few minutes.

Occasionally we saw seals fighting, at times rather vigorously. I witnessed one such fight from the SOC, while Lavallee and Gimbel were swimming outside. The two seals squared off just five feet under the ice, almost ignoring the divers a dozen feet away. When the seals approached each other, I heard one emit a long descending trill. Then they made loud chugging sounds, their throats pulsating with the power of the "music." They opened their mouths and wagged their heads, circling about counterclockwise. Then they lunged and once or twice made harmless contact. They squirmed and contorted, feinting. This continued for about 30 seconds; then the seals separated and swam away.

The struggle seemed to be for dominance, with each seal trying to assert authority over the other. In another fight, the seals were a bit more serious. They circled, each trying to get at the other's throat. They closed and whirled furiously, drawing no blood. This seemed to be a fight to protect a breathing territory and drive away an intruder.

Weddell seals kept us amused, amazed, and quite busy for the weeks we watched them.

On guard over her three-week-old pup, a mother Weddell cries "wa-a-a-ah" in protest over human intrusion. Whelped singly, seals weigh 60 to 70 pounds at birth; they feed on milk that contains up to 50 percent butterfat, gaining three to four pounds daily. Some adults grow to more than 1,000 pounds.

The data—including more than 75 miles of tape recordings—have not been completely digested and analyzed, but we've come to several tentative conclusions. Broadly speaking we are, of course, convinced that these seals echo-locate in much the same way some porpoises are known to do to find food. As yet we have no concrete proof, just sounds that indicate the capability.

We are pretty sure the seals use echo-location to find breathing holes and to hunt for food, particularly during the long Antarctic night. We recorded several distinct types of sounds while observing our subjects closely. We think a short chirp may be used by the seals to echo-locate. The Weddells may use this or other sounds to orient themselves to the sea floor or to the surface.

We are also convinced that Weddell seals can communicate with each other after a fashion. When one is severely agitated, it will clap its teeth and jaws together. This sound is a warning or threat. He's saying, "Watch it!"

Another noise, a chugging grunt, sounds like someone getting hit in the belly. This, too, is a warning or a threat.

A fourth noise we heard, a melodious bird-like trill, would start high on the scale and end in a low "chug!" We heard this only when a seal was near a hole. He seemed to be saying, "See that hole. It's mine. That's where I breathe." We plan to gather more evidence of seal "talk" on future expeditions.

Blubber Protects Against Extreme Cold

We also reached several conclusions as to how the seals are able to live in the frigid Antarctic. Their unusual metabolism offers part of the answer. Metabolism is sometimes likened to a furnace, and the Weddell seal's heating system burns more than twice as fast as that of land animals. Furthermore, the seal has an inordinately thick layer of blubber, one of nature's best insulators. This, together with an extraordinary ability to constrict its blood vessels, keeps the heat of the furnace from escaping.

Weddell pups are able to live through infancy on the ice because of the fluffy tan hair which coats them for the first six weeks or so. If this layer of wool-like fur gets wet, the moisture almost immediately freezes, and the ice crystals fall off, keeping the pups dry. Paradoxically, warmer temperatures are more hazardous; if the moisture does not freeze, the young seal's skin remains wet and chilled. By the time the pups shed the lanugo, they have built up sufficient blubber to protect themselves in the sea. Weddell seals' milk is 40 to 50 percent butterfat. On this rich diet infant seals gain three or four pounds a day—much of it blubber.

All this, and the other information we gathered, is just a small beginning. Much remains to be discovered about the relationship of the seal to its Antarctic environment.

Man has just begun to probe one of the greatest realms of mystery left on earth—the undersea. We are at the beginning of a new era of Antarctic exploration. The heroic age is over, but the scientific age of underwater exploration has barely begun in the globe's least hospitable domain. **THE END**

THE ATOMIC AGE: Its

Fearsome fireball of a 1952 hydrogen test explosion, spawning an ominous mushroom cloud, symbolizes the perils of the Atomic Age. The atom's annihilating force, unleashed during Franklin D. Roosevelt's Administration, has challenged the powers of every subsequent President in a tireless search for peace. Yet the "fearful engines of atomic might,"

By FRANK FREIDEL

Professor of History, Harvard University

Problems and Promises

T HE PRESIDENTS of the middle decades of the 20th century bore perhaps the heaviest responsibility in the history of the office: to guard the peace in a turbulent world while assuring the well-being of all the Nation's citizens. Much was demanded of these Chief Executives, from Franklin D. Roosevelt through Lyndon B. Johnson, and each labored long and hard to meet his obligations.

Their primary task was to maintain stability and prosperity, acting with Congress to throw the weight of the Federal Government into the economic balance as needed. Franklin D. Roosevelt's first goal was to pull the Nation out of a disastrous depression and to halt plummeting deflation. Each of his successors worked to prevent recessions from turning into depressions, and, during two decades of unprecedented prosperity, to restrain inflation.

With the outbreak of World War II, President Roosevelt assumed another major responsibility—to

*Earlier installments appeared in the November, 1964, GEO-GRAPHIC (Washington through John Quincy Adams); January, 1965 (Jackson through Buchanan); May, 1965 (Lincoln through McKinley); and October, 1965 (Theodore Roosevelt through Hoover).

KODACHROME BY THOMAS J. ABERCROMBIE © N.G.S.

UNITED STATES AIR FORCE

as President Dwight D. Eisenhower described the nuclear devices, can serve mankind. In 1953, he proposed the Atoms for Peace program to the United Nations.

Taming the atom revolutionized scientific endeavor in fields as varied as medicine and ship propulsion. Metal fingers in a shielded chamber hold a uranium sample for analysis.

foster collective security. Succeeding Presidents have been largely occupied with marshaling the economic resources and armed strength of the United States in behalf of poor or threatened nations.

Maintenance of economic stability at home and peace abroad have been frustrating and often thankless tasks, demanding the full energies and resourcefulness of each of these Presidents. Each has contributed his own approach to these persistent problems.

Roosevelt, within a humanitarian framework, was frankly experimental. Harry S Truman demonstrated an ability to make perilous decisions quickly and calmly. Dwight D. Eisenhower, the consolidator of the achievements of a score of years, stressed moderation. John F. Kennedy, bringing youth and style, focused on the demands of an urban age. Johnson, contributing a consummate skill in obtaining legislative action, has led the Nation toward a "Great Society."

The complex problems that these modern Presidents have faced contrast sharply with the basic problems that confronted George Washington: to establish a firm executive department for the fledgling Government and to obtain respect and security in a world dominated by unfriendly monarchies.

President's Task Remains Unchanged

The present generation knows both promise and peril beyond the farthest vision of the Founding Fathers, Kennedy pointed out in his Inaugural Address:

"The world is very different now. For man holds in his mortal hands the power to abolish all forms of human poverty and all forms of human life."

Nevertheless, he noted, the same beliefs for which Washington's generation had fought were still at issue throughout the world.

Thus President Johnson in proposing a national health program prefaced his message to Congress with a thought from Thomas Jefferson, as appropriate in the 1960's as in 1787:

OHN E. FLETCHER © N.G.S.; UNITED STATES AIR FORCE (BELOW); EKTACHROME (RIGHT) BY WILLIAM TAUB FOR NASA

"Without health there is no happiness. An attention to health, then, should take the place of every other object."

In a basic way, the role of the President has remained unaltered through almost 18 decades and the tenure of 35 Chief Executives. President Johnson expressed it eloquently in his State of the Union Message to Congress in January, 1965:

"A President does not shape a new and personal vision of America. He collects it from the scattered hopes of the American past.

"It existed when the first settlers saw the coast of a new world, and when the first pioneers moved Westward.

"It has guided us every step of the way.

"It sustains every President. But it is also your inheritance and it belongs equally to all the people that we all serve.

"It must be interpreted anew by each generation for its own needs. . . .

"It shall lead us as we enter this third century of the search for 'a more perfect Union.'"

From the High Tide of War Rise Hopes for Peace and a New Frontier in Space

D-Day, June 6, 1944, saw the Allies storm Hitler's western wall at Omaha Beach (center) and four other Normandy beachheads. Lessons of history's costliest war convinced world statesmen of the need for a permanent peace-keeping organization. Helping to establish the United Nations (left) and to strengthen it amidst the uncertainties of the cold war occupied the minds of America's mid-20th-century Presidents.

In the face of a shaky peace, successive administrations moved forward in the cause of freedom: rebuilding ravaged countries, aiding new nations emerging from the remnants of empire, and transforming the American economy from war production to a postwar prosperity dedicated to eradicating poverty. The United States entered the era of manned space flight in 1961 with the suborbital ride of Astronaut Alan B. Shepard, Jr. (right). By 1965, the Nation was making giant strides in its announced goal of putting a man on the moon by 1970.

FRANKLIN D. ROOSEVELT sought a more abundant way of life for the American people, and for all humanity. He demonstrated his warm concern for mankind with a flair for brilliant improvisations; like a 19th-century Yankee inventor, he sought his great ends through trial-and-error experimentation. His love of innovation, his wit and jaunty optimism made him an exciting leader.

He became President at a time of national despair, at the depth of the Great Depression. First he helped the American people regain faith in themselves; then he led in the enactment of the most sweeping program of social legislation in the Nation's history.

In World War II, he assumed leadership for the United States in the struggle against totalitarianism and helped plan the United Nations to maintain the peace. He died in office shortly before final victory in 1945, having served longer than any other President.

Roosevelt, like his fifth cousin Theodore Roosevelt, came from a patrician New York family. He was born in 1882 on a pleasant estate overlooking the Hudson River at Hyde Park, New York (page 76). Both his parents and his headmaster, Endicott Peabody of Groton School, impressed on the young Roosevelt his responsibilities toward those less fortunate. Throughout his career this attitude shaped his thought and action.

At Harvard he became editor-in-chief of the *Crimson,* the student newspaper, then attended Columbia University Law School. On St. Patrick's Day, 1905, he wed his distant cousin, Anna Eleanor Roosevelt, a willowy, shy young woman, who was given in marriage by her uncle, the President.

Franklin Idolized Cousin Theodore

Following the example of the first President Roosevelt, whom he enormously admired, Franklin D. Roosevelt decided to enter public service through politics. He had joined the Harvard Republican Club and in 1900 marched in a torchlight procession hailing the ticket of William McKinley and Theodore Roosevelt. But in 1910, in line with the tradition of his own branch of the Roosevelt family, he chose the Democratic Party. Campaigning flamboyantly in a red Maxwell automobile, he won election to the New York Senate.

Crisis President: The Nation's gravest depression and greatest war burdened Franklin Delano Roosevelt during his 12 years and 40 days in office—the longest span served by any American Chief Executive. Roosevelt fought for social justice —a "new deal for the American people"—and for a lasting peace based on international cooperation.

"I have seen war. . . . I hate war." Roosevelt performed brilliantly as Assistant Secretary of the Navy during World War I, but he itched to get close to the fighting. Several times his inspections of U. S. bases took him within range of German artillery. Here he disembarks from a Navy seaplane at Pauillac, France, on August 14, 1918.

FRANKLIN D. ROOSEVELT LIBRARY

Painting by Frank O. Salisbury, White House Collection

Gay and jaunty, cigarette holder cocked upward, the smiling F.D.R. won the confidence of millions of Americans who elected him an unprecedented four times. Here, at Warm Springs, Georgia, Roosevelt drives a Ford for which he himself designed hand controls for clutch, brake, and throttle.

Undaunted by his handicap, Roosevelt refused to become an invalid. He sailed and swam, developing the powerful torso of an athlete. Here, in 1933, he steers *Amberjack II* on a cruise from Marion, Massachusetts, to Campobello Island, New Brunswick, his beloved Canadian summer home.

There he immediately began to capture headlines as a progressive reformer.

President Wilson appointed him Assistant Secretary of the Navy, a post once held by Theodore Roosevelt, and during World War I Franklin D. Roosevelt became known in Washington as a man who got things done. He was Democratic nominee for Vice President in 1920 and campaigned vigorously for the League of Nations. This won him a national reputation, and the Harding landslide did him no harm.

But in the summer of 1921, when he was 39, disaster struck. While vacationing at Campobello, after swimming in the icy Bay of Fundy, he was stricken with poliomyelitis. With indomitable courage, he fought to regain use of his legs, particularly through swimming.

"The water put me where I am," he remarked, "and the water has to bring me back." He found the water so beneficial at a resort in Georgia that he risked his none-too-ample inheritance to buy the property and set up the Georgia Warm Springs Foundation to treat polio sufferers (page 77). His Little White House there is a state memorial.

Despite the wishes of his mother, Sara Delano Roosevelt, that he give up politics, he continued to be active behind the scenes, and dramatically appeared on crutches before the 1924 Democratic Convention to nominate Al Smith as "the Happy Warrior." In 1928, when Smith received the Democratic nomination, he persuaded Roosevelt to strengthen the ticket in New York by running for governor. Asked whether Roosevelt was physically qualified to serve, Smith retorted, "A Governor does not have to be an acrobat."

While Smith lost the Presidency, Roosevelt won in New York by 25,000 votes. In Albany he proved a strong governor, remarkably the master of a Republican legislature.

F. D. R.'s "Hundred Days" Stir the Nation

He was elected President in November, 1932, defeating President Hoover. The depression grew steadily worse, and by the time he was inaugurated, on March 4, 1933, industrial production had sunk to almost half that of 1929; one worker in four was jobless.

To the disheartened Nation Roosevelt brought hope. He promised prompt, vigorous action and asserted in his Inaugural Address, "The only thing we have to fear is fear itself." His first moves were reassuring to businessmen—the proclamation of a national bank holiday; then a cautious reopening of banks that could prove their solvency, along

Replanting a charred hillside, Civilian Conservation Corps men help change the face of America. Three million jobless, including thousands of Indians and veterans, served in Roosevelt's peaceful army. They put out fires, protected wildlife, fought insect pests, and restored historic landmarks. Many former CCC youths served the Nation gallantly in World War II.

SOCIAL SECURITY ACT
ACCOUNT NUMBER
008-07-3292
HAS BEEN   ESTABLISHED FOR
Ida May Fuller
12/10/36 *Ida M. Fuller*
DATE OF ISSUE   EMPLOYEE'S SIGNATURE

Social Security pioneer Miss Ida Fuller of Ludlow, Vermont, a retired legal secretary, received the first benefits under the Roosevelt-instituted program. Her initial check, for $22.54, was dated January 31, 1940. When payments increased in 1965, she again received the first check and a congratulatory telephone call from President Johnson—both on her 91st birthday. She now receives $59 a month.

with deep cuts in Government expenditures.

Next came the remarkable legislation of his first hundred days. He proposed, and Congress enacted, a sweeping program to bring recovery to business and agriculture and immediate relief to the unemployed and those in danger of losing farms and homes. Further, with the establishment of the Tennessee Valley Authority, he led the Federal Government into a precedent-setting venture in regional planning and development.

Like Teddy Roosevelt and Wilson, Franklin D. Roosevelt vigorously used all the powers of the Presidency. Like them, he wished the Government to function as an impartial arbiter among businessmen, farmers, workers, and consumers. But he went beyond them because of the drastic needs of the depression

years, and used the Government to provide strong aid to each group.

By 1935 the Nation was achieving some measure of recovery, but businessmen and bankers were turning against the "New Deal." They feared Roosevelt's experiments and concessions to labor, and were appalled that he had taken the Nation off the gold standard and allowed budget deficits.

Roosevelt's response to the attacks from the right was to push through Congress a new legislative program: Social Security, heavier income taxes, new controls over banks and public utilities, and an enormous work-relief program for the unemployed.

In 1936 he defeated Governor Alf Landon of Kansas, a Republican liberal, by a top-heavy margin, winning in every state but two.

Rebirth of a region: Tennessee Valley Authority, with its vast system of public and private dams, brought new life to a river basin encompassing seven states. Here Fontana Dam spans the Little Tennessee River. A Government-owned corporation, TVA generates power and provides flood control, produces fertilizer, facilitates navigation, and conserves natural resources. TVA power helped develop nuclear energy at Oak Ridge, Tennessee, during World War II. One of the most successful of Roosevelt's "New Deal" agencies, TVA has inspired similar projects throughout the world.

Fireside chats brought Roosevelt's warm and vibrant voice into living rooms across the land. In calm, reassuring tones, F.D.R. explained his policies to the people. "His face would smile and light up as though he were actually sitting on the front porch or in the parlor with them," recalled his Secretary of Labor, Frances Perkins, first woman to serve in a Cabinet post.

Latter-day St. George: Cartoonist Jerry Doyle of the Philadelphia *Record* pictured Roosevelt fighting the dragons of fear and deflation during early New Deal days. F.D.R. wields the sword of confidence and the shield of the National Recovery Administration, an agency that managed Roosevelt's emergency program for revitalizing industry. But a Supreme Court decision in 1935 brought NRA to an end.

He was inaugurated on January 20, 1937—the first President sworn in on the new date provided by the Twentieth Amendment. In his Inaugural, he declared:

"I see a United States which can demonstrate that, under democratic methods of government, national wealth can be translated into a spreading volume of human comforts hitherto unknown, and the lowest standard of living can be raised far above the level of mere subsistence. But here is the challenge to our democracy. . . . I see one-third of a nation ill-housed, ill-clad, ill-nourished."

The Supreme Court had been invalidating key New Deal measures as unconstitutional, sometimes by a narrow 5-to-4 decision. Early in his second term, Roosevelt sought legislation to increase the size of the Court. Vehement protests were raised against "packing the Court," and in their midst the Court began to hand down decisions favorable to the New Deal, often by a one-vote margin. Roosevelt

lost his Supreme Court battle, but a revolution in constitutional law took place. Thereafter the Government could legally engage in extensive regulation of the economy.

In his first Inaugural, Roosevelt had pledged the United States to the policy of the "good neighbor," and in our relations with American republics to the South he transformed the Monroe Doctrine. From a unilateral American manifesto it became a mutual arrangement for concerted action against aggressors.

In Asia and Europe aggressor nations threatened a second world war, which was precipitated in 1939 by Hitler's invasion of Poland. Roosevelt tried through neutrality legislation to keep the United States out of war, yet strengthen nations under attack.

After France fell and Britain came under siege in the summer of 1940, Roosevelt began to send Great Britain all possible aid short of war. In September the United States gave the British 50 over-age destroyers, freshly

'He who plants must cultivate," the Roosevelts read the motto on their coat of arms. Roses in a field represent the family name. F.D.R. could claim relationship by blood or marriage to 11 former Presidents—Washington, both Adamses, Madison, Van Buren, both Harrisons, Taylor, Grant, Theodore Roosevelt, and Taft.

Portrait of a zestful lady: Wife, mother, writer, humanitarian, Anna Eleanor Roosevelt filled a multitude of roles. "She would rather light a candle than curse the darkness, and her glow has warmed the world," the late Adlai E. Stevenson said of her upon her death in 1962. This magnificent and unusual portrait by Douglas Chandor—the only one for which she formally posed —hangs in the White House.

Stately Roosevelt home, a national historic site since 1946, overlooks the Hudson River at Hyde Park, New York. The original Victorian frame house in which the President was born evolved into this stucco and fieldstone mansion through additions, many by F.D.R. himself. He and Mrs. Roosevelt lie buried in the rose garden. Presidential papers and mementos crowd the nearby Franklin D. Roosevelt Library. More than 300,000 people a year visit Hyde Park.

Soothing waters of Warm Springs buoyed Roosevelt's spirits. The President inspired and led the March of Dimes that financed polio's eventual defeat through the Salk and Sabin vaccines.

Christening a gallant ship: Mrs. Roosevelt helps launch the carrier *Yorktown* in 1943. With her stands Rear Adm. Elliott Buckmaster, captain of the vessel's namesake and predecessor when the Japanese sank her in the Battle of Midway the previous year.

The storied "Big E," the carrier *Enterprise* (below), goes down the ways at Newport News, Virginia, in 1936. A Navy booster since his days as Assistant Secretary of the Department, Roosevelt pushed a naval expansion program that built up America's defenses and provided work for thousands of unemployed.

WIDE WORLD

repaired and equipped, and received 99-year leases on eight bases in the Western Hemisphere. It was, Winston Churchill later wrote, "a decidedly unneutral act."

In the winter of 1940-41, when British ability to buy arms was nearly exhausted, Roosevelt devised "lend-lease." If a neighbor's house were afire, he explained, certainly one would lend him a fire hose to extinguish the blaze. Roosevelt also brought economic pressure on the Japanese to try to prevent their taking over Southeast Asia.

Aid to Allies precipitated a bitter debate between U. S. isolationists and interventionists. In the campaign of 1940, however, Roosevelt's opponent, Wendell Willkie, also favored aiding the Allies. F. D. R. won, becoming the first President to serve a third term.

In January, 1941, though the Nation was not yet directly involved, Roosevelt proclaimed as war aims the Four Freedoms: of speech and worship and from want and fear. He met Churchill off Argentia, Newfoundland, in August, 1941, and they drew up the Atlantic Charter, which incorporated these aims.

Sunday Attack Brings War to U. S.

Before the year was out, the Nation was precipitated into the war. Japanese airplanes broke the Sunday calm of December 7, 1941, striking Pearl Harbor with devastating effect (opposite). Congress declared war the next day. Three days later, Germany and Italy declared war on the United States.

As wartime Commander in Chief, Roosevelt delegated much of his responsibility for home-front war production and concentrated on world-wide strategy and diplomacy. The ultimate decisions were his: the invasion of North Africa in 1942, the appointment of Dwight D. Eisenhower rather than George C. Marshall to lead the Normandy D-Day assault. He told Marshall, "I could not sleep at night with you out of the country." But even as he fought the war, he planned for peace, giving much thought to a United Nations.

In 1944, defeating New York's Governor Thomas E. Dewey, Roosevelt won a fourth term. But, as the Allies poised on the brink of victory over the Nazis, his health deteriorated. On April 12, 1945, while posing for a portrait in the Little White House at Warm Springs, Georgia, he collapsed and died of a cerebral hemorrhage. The Nation was plunged into mourning. As a sailor in Times Square lamented, "You know it's tough when one of your buddies has to go, and President Roosevelt was our buddy."

President and future President share a jeep in Sicily in December, 1943. F. D. R. had just named Eisenhower to command the Allied invasion of France. Roosevelt was the first President to travel outside the U. S. in wartime.

"Unprovoked and dastardly," Roosevelt termed Japan's attack on Pearl Harbor, December 7, 1941—"a date which will live in infamy." Here *West Virginia* (foreground) and *Tennessee* blaze in the chaos of "Battleship Row."

79

THIRTY-THIRD PRESIDENT 1945-1953

HARRY S TRUMAN, becoming President as World War II drew to a close, made some of the most crucial decisions in the Nation's history. He ordered the dropping of atomic bombs to hasten Japan's surrender. He broke the Soviet Union's postwar blockade of West Berlin with a titanic airlift. And he stemmed the Communist invasion of South Korea.

During his administration, the Nation grappled with problems of inflation and civil rights at home. Abroad, it initiated rehabilitation of war-torn areas, aid to underdeveloped countries, and new systems of collective security.

Truman was born in Lamar, Missouri, in 1884, and his birthplace there, at Truman Avenue and 11th Street, is now a state historic site. The son of a livestock dealer, he grew up in Independence, Missouri, and became a bank clerk. Then, needed on the family farm at Grandview, he spent 12 years, until he was 33, as a prosperous Missouri farmer, proud of his skill in planting a straight row of corn. He was the first President since Grant to have engaged in farming as an adult.

He went to France during World War I, and fought on the western front in the field artillery. Returning home as a captain, he married his childhood sweetheart Elizabeth Virginia ("Bess") Wallace, and with an Army friend opened a haberdashery shop in Kansas City, Missouri. The shop failed, but Truman refused to go into bankruptcy and paid off the debts.

County Administrator Becomes a Senator

With the support of fellow veterans and the political machine of Tom Pendergast, boss of Kansas City, Truman was elected a "judge" (actually, an administrator) of Jackson County in 1922. Except for one defeat at the polls, when the Ku Klux Klan opposed him, he remained in office until 1934, building a notable reputation for honesty and efficiency.

He was elected Senator from Missouri in 1934, as a Democrat pledged to support Roosevelt, and was re-elected in 1940. During World War II he became famous as head

"He met the war, the peace and old insistent friends with the same magnified modesty but also with clear self-possession," biographer Jonathan Daniels wrote of Harry Truman. Suddenly thrust into the Presidency, the man from Missouri held unshakable faith in his country and his countrymen.

Rocky road traveled in his first year might have destroyed a less valiant and resolute Chief Executive than Truman. In a volume of his memoirs, aptly entitled *Year of Decisions,* he recounts his meeting with Eleanor Roosevelt after her husband's death. "Is there anything I can do for you?" Truman asked. "Is there anything *we* can do for *you?*" she responded. "For you are the one in trouble now."

1946 HERBLOCK © CARTOON, THE WASHINGTON POST

"SURE YOU HAVEN'T MISSED ANYTHING?"

Painting by Greta Kempton, White House Collection

"**We fired our first barrage** on the night of September 6 [1918]," Capt. Harry Truman remembers. He led Battery D of the 129th Field Artillery during the Meuse-Argonne offensive of World War I. "We were occupying an old French position which probably was fairly well known to the Germans, and as soon as we had finished the barrage they returned the compliment. My battery became panic-stricken, and all except five or six scattered like partridges. Finally I got them back together without losing any men, although we had six horses killed."

Twenty-seven years later the veteran "redleg," as an artilleryman is called, became Commander in Chief of a Nation at war, and his firsthand knowledge of warfare proved valuable. His Chief of Staff, Adm. William D. Leahy, said: "...he was amazingly well informed on military history from the campaigns of the ancients, such as Hannibal and Caesar, down to the great global conflict...."

of the Senate war investigating committee, checking into waste and corruption in defense spending. Its work, he has estimated, saved the Nation as much as 15 billion dollars.

In 1944, when the backers of Henry A. Wallace, James F. Byrnes, William O. Douglas, and Truman waged a vigorous contest for the Vice Presidential nomination, President Roosevelt settled it by choosing Truman. During his few weeks as Vice President, after Roosevelt's fourth-term victory, Truman scarcely saw the President and received no briefing from him on the development of the atomic bomb or the increasing difficulties with the Soviet Union.

Stunned New President Takes Command

Suddenly these and a host of other wartime problems became Truman's to solve when, on April 12, 1945, Mrs. Roosevelt told him that her husband was dead. Truman was President of the United States. "I felt like the moon, the stars, and all the planets had fallen on me," he told reporters the next day.

Quickly he was briefed on the acute problems of both war strategy and peacemaking. V-E Day, end of the war in Europe, came less than a month later, but at the Potsdam Conference in the summer of 1945, he discovered firsthand how hard it was to make agreements with Stalin.

At Potsdam the Allies issued an ultimatum to the Japanese to surrender. Urged by his advisers in Washington, Truman decided that if the Japanese did not surrender, the United States would drop the newly developed atomic weapons on Japan. Two bombs were dropped. Japanese surrender quickly followed, and World War II ended. The new machinery hopefully fabricated to preserve the peace, the United Nations, already existed. President Truman had witnessed the signing of the charter at San Francisco in June (page 89).

Thus far, the new Chief Executive had followed almost directly the lines laid down by his predecessor. But by the fall of 1945 he was developing his own policies, and presented to Congress a 21-point program, later named the "Fair Deal." It covered expansion of Social Security, full-employment measures, a permanent Fair Employment Practices Act to protect minority rights, public housing and slum clearance, and Government aid to scientific research. In additional messages he recommended Federal aid to education and health insurance.

The Fair Deal, Truman himself has written, "symbolizes for me my assumption of

"**It is a mighty leap** from the vice presidency to the presidency when one is forced to make it without warning," Truman declared. In the White House on April 12, 1945, Chief Justice Harlan Fiske Stone swears him in as the 33d President. Witnesses are (from left): Secretary of Labor Frances Perkins, Secretary of War Henry L. Stimson, Secretary of Commerce Henry A. Wallace, War Production Board Chairman J. A. Krug, Secretary of the Navy James Forrestal, Secretary of Agriculture Claude R. Wickard, Deputy Chairman of War Manpower Commission Frank McNamee (behind Wickard), Attorney General Francis Biddle, Secretary of the Treasury Henry Morgenthau, Jr., Secretary of State Edward R. Stettinius (almost hidden by Truman), Mrs. Truman, Secretary of the Interior Harold L. Ickes, Margaret Truman, Speaker of the House Sam Rayburn, War Mobilization Director Frederick M. Vinson, and House Minority Leader Joseph W. Martin.

the office of President in my own right."

Congress enacted only a few of the measures the President recommended. A limited full-employment program provided for a Council of Economic Advisers; the Atomic Energy Commission was established; and a considerable reorganization of Government agencies included unification of Army, Navy, and Air Force under a Secretary of Defense.

The Truman Administration's efforts to check inflation had hard sledding, since business opposed price controls and labor chafed under wage ceilings. By the fall of 1946 few controls remained, and Truman removed most of those after Republicans won decisive victories in the Congressional elections.

The new 80th Congress also made its weight felt in labor policy, overriding a Presi-dential veto of the Taft-Hartley Labor-Management Relations Act, which placed restrictions on union activities. This law prohibited the "closed shop," in which a worker cannot be hired unless he belongs to a union, and allowed states to go still further by enacting "right-to-work" laws.

President Truman Criticizes a Critic

Truman delighted and sometimes dismayed the public with his peppery forthrightness. It helped him reach his great decisions and was invaluable in interpreting them to the Nation. But he created a national sensation, which he still relishes in retrospect, when he sent a blistering note to a Washington music critic who had written a harsh review of his daughter Margaret's singing.

His simple directness was a vital asset during the 1948 campaign. For 35 days he toured the country by train, traveling 31,700 miles, and making as many as 16 whistle-stop speeches a day. He had told Senator Alben Barkley, the nominee for Vice President, "I'm going to fight hard, and I'm going to give 'em hell!" In his plain, extemporaneous style, he did. And he won the crowds with his open affection for his wife and daughter. "How would you like to meet my family?" he would ask after his talk. Then he would introduce "the boss"—Mrs. Truman—and "my baby," who was also "the boss's boss," Margaret.

According to the polls, the President seemed to have little chance in the 1948 election. But directing his attack more against the Republican 80th Congress than against his opponent, New York Governor Thomas E. Dewey, Truman emerged the winner. He gathered the votes of many workingmen who resented the Taft-Hartley Act, of farmers disappointed by lawmakers' failure to provide crop storage

facilities, and of others who felt they had suffered from Congressional actions.

In foreign relations, President Truman provided his most effective leadership. When the Soviet Union pressured Turkey and, through guerrillas, threatened to take over Greece, the President, in March, 1947, asked Congress to aid the two countries.

Truman Offers Help to World's Poor

In his message he enunciated the doctrine that took his name: "... it must be the policy of the United States to support free peoples who are resisting attempted subjugation by armed minorities or by outside pressures."

Military aid was not enough; economic productivity had to be restored to counter the Communist threat. In June, 1947, Secretary of State George C. Marshall proposed a program of combined aid and self-help that came to be known as the Marshall Plan. Within three years, through the expenditure of 12 billion dollars, the United States helped lift

84

In a historic meeting, Allied leaders at Potsdam, Germany, draft an ultimatum to Japan in July, 1945, and debate postwar problems. President Truman sits at upper right, British Prime Minister Winston Churchill at lower center. Marshal Josef Stalin (leaning back) wanted to "act in concert about the surrender of Japan," although Russia had not yet declared war on the Asian nation.

Act of surrender: Aboard the U.S.S. *Missouri* in Tokyo Bay, Gen. Douglas MacArthur receives the Japanese surrender on September 2, 1945. Maj. Gen. Yohijiro Umezo signs for Japan. In a line beside Fleet Admiral Chester W. Nimitz (left) stand senior military and naval officers of the Allied powers. "My choice of the *Missouri* was an obvious one," Truman recalls. "She was one of the newest and most powerful battleships in our fleet; she had been named after my own state; my daughter Margaret had christened her...."

Western Europe's economy above prewar levels and diminish the strength of its Communist parties.

In his Inaugural Address, on January 20, 1949, President Truman proposed that the United States extend its aid to the "more than half the people of the world . . . living in conditions approaching misery." He listed a number of ways to help them, including the now renowned "Point Four" of his address: to provide them with technical assistance and investment capital so that they could expand their economies.

Out of his proposal came the Point Four program, which grew in time into the Nation's multibillion-dollar outlays for foreign aid. To Truman, elimination of poverty seemed one of the most promising as well as humane ways to check the growth of Communism.

Direct military moves by the Communists also had to be met. As the Western powers laid plans for self-government in West Germany, the Soviet Union imposed a blockade of Berlin in June, 1948.* Truman countered with his famous airlift (following pages) and a new military grand alliance for the protection of Western nations, the North Atlantic Treaty Organization, established in 1949.

Russia Balks at Inspection Plan

A new and more dangerous threat from the Soviet Union appeared in the atomic realm. Since 1946 Truman had been recommending to the United Nations the adoption of a thoroughgoing system of international supervision of atomic energy, including on-the-spot inspection. The United States offered to place its stockpile of atomic bombs under international control when the system was put into effect. The Soviet Union steadfastly blocked the American proposals. Then, in the fall of 1949, President Truman announced: "We have evidence that within recent weeks an atomic explosion occurred in the U.S.S.R."

*The GEOGRAPHIC published "Airlift to Berlin" in its May, 1949, issue.

KODACHROME BY NATIONAL GEOGRAPHIC PHOTOGRAPHER EMORY KRISTOF © N.G.S.

WALTER SANDERS, LIFE (ABOVE), AND WIDE WORLD

"**Operation Vittles,**" President Truman's dramatic answer to a Russian blockade of war-shattered Berlin in 1948, delivered as many as 7,000 tons of vital supplies a day. For eight months during the Berlin Airlift, supply planes made a landing on the average of once every three minutes, carrying everything from medicines to coal. Standing amid ruins, these Berliners watch a USAF C-47 roar in at Tempelhof Airport.

With the Truman Doctrine, the American people came face to face with the responsibility of aiding hungry, devastated nations. The Marshall Plan, named for Truman's Secretary of State, Gen. George C. Marshall (right), reached the humblest citizens, as evidenced by this painting on a Sicilian donkey cart (opposite) displayed in the Smithsonian Institution in Washington, D. C. Panels depict delivery of tractors, the restoration of farms, and rebuilding of cities.

First White House television tour: Truman escorts commentator Walter Cronkite through the Diplomatic Reception Room in 1952. Portrait shows Angelica Van Buren, daughter-in-law of the eighth President.

A committee appointed by Truman in 1948 inspected the White House and found it "standing up purely from habit." Renovation took three and a half years and cost $5,800,000.

British lion, Winston Churchill, and Truman motor through Jefferson City, Missouri, in March, 1946, en route to Westminster College at Fulton, where Churchill alerted the free world to Communist dangers: "... an iron curtain has descended across the [European] Continent."

"That's one for the books," a joyous Harry Truman said in St. Louis, Missouri, as he held aloft an early and erroneous headline in the Chicago *Tribune* of November 3, 1948. In a stunning upset, Democrat Truman defeated Republican Thomas E. Dewey by two million votes.

Active in retirement, former President and Mrs. Truman ride in a Venetian gondola during their 1956 European tour.

Harry Truman met Bess Wallace in Sunday school. "She had golden curls and...the most beautiful blue eyes," he wrote. They attended school together from fifth grade through high school, and married in 1919.

Mrs. Truman enjoyed being a Senator's wife, Truman later wrote, "and had fallen in love with Washington." But as First Lady she was "not especially interested...in the formalities and pomp or the artificiality which...surround the family of a President."

Truman's response to the Soviet test was to order rapid development of "super" atomic weapons, and on November 1, 1952, in Eniwetok Atoll, the first hydrogen explosion was set off, leaving a huge crater where a coral island had been (pages 66-7).

During these same years Communism was spreading rapidly in Asia, and by the end of 1949 had overrun the Chinese mainland. Suddenly, in June, 1950, the Communist government of North Korea launched a full-scale attack on South Korea. President Truman, conferring promptly with his diplomatic and military advisers, ordered American units into battle as the United Nations Security Council—with Russia boycotting its sessions—called all U.N. members to defend South Korea. The U.N. organized a force of other nations to fight beside the Americans and South Koreans.

U.N. Troops Hold Line in Korea

A long, discouraging struggle followed, as U.N. troops, predominantly American, were at first forced back, then drove almost to the Chinese border, only to be pushed back again, this time by hordes of Chinese. After counterattacks, the U.N. held a line above the old boundary of South Korea.

Truman insisted on a war of containment; he would not risk its enlargement into a major conflict with China, and perhaps Russia. When Gen. Douglas MacArthur, commander of U.N. forces in Korea, issued statements contrary to this policy, the President dismissed the "old soldier."

In 1953 Truman retired to Independence, Missouri, and continued to make lively comments on national and world affairs. He has published three volumes of memoirs and seen the creation of the Harry S Truman Library and Museum. But his real monuments are the Fair Deal program and the collective security systems which stemmed the tide of Communism in Europe and Korea.

Birth of the United Nations: Secretary of State Stettinius signs the charter in San Francisco on June 26, 1945. Truman, witnessing the event, said of the U.N., "If we fail to use it, we shall betray all those who have died in order that we might meet here in freedom and safety to create it." Five years later, Communist North Korea invaded South Korea. Truman announced U. S. intervention; the U.N. called for a defense force. And guns boomed in Korea for three long years (below).

KODACHROME BY ROBERT MOSIER © N.G.S.

Dwight D Eisenhower

THIRTY-FOURTH PRESIDENT 1953-1961

DWIGHT D. EISENHOWER brought to the Presidency not only his prestige as the victorious commanding general in Europe in World War II, but also a warmth of popular affection and respect.

He sought during his two terms to maintain peace and prosperity for the American people. He obtained an armistice in Korea and worked incessantly to ease the cold war between Communist countries and the United States and its allies. At home he pursued the moderate policies of "modern Republicanism," and as he left office he could say, "America is today the strongest, the most influential, and most productive nation in the world."

Born in Denison, Texas, in 1890, Eisenhower grew up in Abilene, Kansas, the third of seven sons of a creamery mechanic. Today the Eisenhower Presidential Library and Eisenhower Museum stand near his boyhood Abilene home.

In high school young "Ike" (a nickname he acquired as a child) excelled in football and baseball. At West Point he was a lithe, dynamic halfback until a knee injury ended his playing days. Stationed in Texas as a second lieutenant, he met Mamie Geneva Doud, whom he married in 1916 (page 99).

During World War I he failed to obtain assignment in France but rose to the temporary rank of lieutenant colonel. Through long years in the peacetime army he especially excelled in staff assignments, serving under Generals John J. Pershing, Douglas MacArthur, and Walter Krueger.

Gift for Organizing Marked Ike's Career

Soon after Pearl Harbor, Gen. George C. Marshall, in the light of Eisenhower's knowledge of the Philippines, brought him to Washington to plan moves in the Pacific. Eisenhower showed such great organizational ability and dealt so tactfully with other branches of the armed services that Marshall assigned him to command American forces in the European Theater of Operations.

Arriving in England in June, 1942, he was shortly named commander of the Allied forces for the November invasion of North Africa. On D-Day, June 6, 1944, he was Supreme

U. S. ARMY

After leading Allied armies to victory in World War II, national hero Dwight David Eisenhower was sought as Presidential standard-bearer by both Republicans and Democrats. But it was the Republicans who convinced him that he should seek public office in 1952. With shouts of "We like Ike" echoing across the land, Eisenhower swept his party to its first national victory in 24 years. Peace, progress, and prosperity were his keynote for eight years.

"Full victory—nothing else." The Supreme Commander of the Allied Expeditionary Force exhorts men of the 101st Airborne Division near Newbury, England, on the eve of the Normandy invasion.

Painting by Thomas E. Stephens, White House Collection

WIDE WORLD (ABOVE) AND CARL MYDANS, LIFE

Ike pledged to go to Korea if elected in 1952. Here the President-elect visits the front in December of that year; six months later an armistice was signed.

At the summit: The Big Four meet in Geneva in July of 1955. Eisenhower (upper center), with John Foster Dulles on his right, faces Britain's Prime Minister Sir Anthony Eden and Foreign Secretary Harold Macmillan. Nikita Khrushchev (far left) and Nikolai Bulganin of the Soviet Union sit opposite Premier Edgar Faure of France. The Russians rejected Ike's "Open Skies" proposal—aerial inspection and exchange of blueprints of military installations—but this first postwar summit raised hopes for relaxation of tensions.

Tireless diplomat John Foster Dulles, Eisenhower's first Secretary of State, traveled the world in a quest for peace. Here he consults his President at a villa near Geneva.

Commander of the troops invading France. He directed the operations of millions of Allied troops with a skillful mixture of firmness and diplomacy that won him loyalty and acclaim. His rapid promotion reached a climax in late 1944 with the fifth star of a General of the Army, a rank Congress made permanent in 1946.

At war's end, Eisenhower confided to friends that he had tasted enough of glory and would like to retire and become president of a small college, perhaps doing some farming on the side. Instead he became President of Columbia University in New York City. Then he took leave from that post to assume supreme command over the new NATO forces being assembled in 1951 for the common defense of the United States and its European allies.

Political Leaders Offer Dazzling Prospect

To his headquarters near Paris came emissaries from the Republican Party to urge him to run for President. In 1948 he had refused similar overtures from public figures of both parties, but in 1952 he consented to run to ensure continued American leadership in international affairs.

The electorate that year was troubled by inflation, by charges of a "mess in Washington," and especially by the drawn-out Korean war. The voters turned to General Eisenhower as a leader they thought could bring them security.

"I like Ike" was an irresistible slogan; he won a sweeping victory over Illinois Governor Adlai E. Stevenson.

"In the final choice," President Eisenhower declared in his first Inaugural Address, "a soldier's pack is not so heavy a burden as a prisoner's chains." Negotiating from military strength, he tried to reduce the tensions of the cold war. In the summer of 1953 the signing of a final armistice brought an armed peace along the border of South Korea.

The death of Stalin in the spring of 1953 also brought some shifts in relations with the Soviet Union. The new Russian leaders consented to a peace treaty neutralizing Austria. Meanwhile both the Soviet Union and the United States were developing hydrogen bombs—the Americans testing a device so powerful that it could have destroyed all New York City.

Nation Rallies to Stricken Chief

With the threat of such destructive force hanging over the world, President Eisenhower met the leaders of the British, French, and Soviet Governments at Geneva in July, 1955 (pages 92-3). At one of the sessions the President, putting down his glasses, unexpectedly proposed to the Soviets that they and the United States immediately exchange complete blueprints of their military establishments. He further suggested that each "provide within our countries facilities for aerial photography to the other country."

He explained, "I have been searching my heart and mind for something that I could say here that could convince everyone of the great sincerity of the United States in approaching this problem of disarmament." The Soviet conferees greeted the proposal with silence, but were so cordial throughout the meetings that a relaxation of tensions took place.

Suddenly, in September, 1955, President Eisenhower suffered a moderately severe heart attack while vacationing in Denver. As he lay in the hospital slowly recovering, tens of thousands of letters and telegrams came in. "It really does something for you," the President told Mrs. Eisenhower, "to know that people all over the world are praying for you."

As a birthday joke, White House correspondents gave him gaudy red pajamas with five gold stars embroidered on each collar tab;

when he began to improve, he good-humoredly wore them. He received Cabinet officers and more and more resumed his duties as President. After nearly seven weeks he left the hospital and flew back to Washington.

"Misfortune, and particularly the misfortune of illness," he said in a brief speech, "brings to all of us an understanding of how good people are." A panel of doctors in February, 1956, reported that the President's

EKTACHROME (BELOW) BY WAYNE MILLER, MAGNUM; KODACHROME BY GILBERT M. GROSVENOR © N.G.S.

Eisenhower's distinctive wave greets citizens of Anchorage, Alaska. "Ike is nifty, started out with 48; ended up with 50," rhymed a slogan in recognition of Alaska's becoming a state on January 3, 1959, followed by Hawaii eight months later.

Record Presidential traveler Eisenhower, his daughter-in-law Mrs. John Eisenhower, and the Prime Minister of India, the late Jawaharlal Nehru, pause beside the reflecting pool of the Taj Mahal. In the cause of world peace, Eisenhower visited 27 lands. His longest tour was reported in "When the President Goes Abroad," by Gilbert M. Grosvenor, GEOGRAPHIC, May, 1960.

injured heart muscle had healed. The way was clear for him to run for a second term, and in November, 1956, he again defeated Adlai Stevenson by a wide margin.

In domestic policy, modern Republicanism, as the President interpreted it, came to mean a middle-of-the-road course. He continued most New Deal and Fair Deal programs, but in a conservative way with emphasis on balancing the budget.

In 1954 Eisenhower obtained from Congress a tax-reform bill, almost a thousand pages long, aimed at stimulating business growth. In public-power development the President emphasized decentralization; he favored cooperation between the Federal

KODACHROME BY EMORY KRISTOF © N.G.S.

Government and local government or private enterprise over wholly Federal projects. For the Hell's Canyon project on the Snake River, he therefore preferred the construction of three power dams by a private utility rather than one large multipurpose dam by the Federal Government.

Similarly, he proposed limited programs of public health insurance and school construction, with the Federal Government helping underwrite local enterprise. He sometimes called this approach "dynamic conservatism."

Among Eisenhower's major achievements as President was his speeding of a large-scale highway program to build 41,000 miles of new interstate roads. About half this system —with the Federal Government paying 90 percent of the cost out of gasoline and other highway-user taxes—is now in operation, offering motorists multilane, limited-access roads with never a stop light.

History's Biggest Building Project

As Eisenhower has proudly described it, this is "not only the most gigantic federal undertaking in road-building" in U. S. history but also "the biggest peacetime construction project of any description ever undertaken by the United States or any other country."

During the Eisenhower Administration, Social Security and unemployment insurance were extended to millions more people. The 1959 labor-management act required union and business officials to file reports of transactions that affected the welfare of union members and the general public. The St. Lawrence Seaway was dedicated. And Alaska and Hawaii attained statehood.

As desegregation of schools began, in keeping with the 1954 Supreme Court decision, President Eisenhower sent troops into Little Rock, Arkansas, to assure compliance with the orders of a Federal court.

Eisenhower also ordered the complete desegregation of the Nation's Armed Forces. In 1957 he signed the first civil rights legislation to pass Congress in 82 years.

"There must be no second class citizens in this country," he wrote.

In his last State of the Union Message, while granting that problems of unemployment and recessions remained unsolved, Eisenhower noted the unprecedented economic progress during his two terms. With almost no new inflation, the productivity of the Nation had risen nearly 25 percent, the

CANADAWIDE FEATURE SERVICE

"Magnificent symbol" of Canadian-United States ties—thus Ike hailed the St. Lawrence Seaway as he and Queen Elizabeth II dedicated the joint project at Montreal in 1959. Biggest ditchdigging job since the Panama Canal, the system of locks, channels, and dams opened the Great Lakes to ocean shipping. Starting with Woodrow Wilson, every President had favored such a project.

Stairsteps to North America's middle, Snell Lock and six others lift vessels 224 feet in the 189 miles of seaway. Snell helps ships pass Moses-Saunders Powerdam, which harnesses Great Lakes drainage and generates electricity for the neighboring nations.

Concrete ribbons lace the states with high-speed expressways and fulfill a cherished dream. The Interstate Highway System, a joint state-Federal venture enacted in 1944, grew slowly at first. Eisenhower urged Congress to increase Federal participation to 90 percent, and it did so in 1956. Today motorists can travel half of the planned 41,000-mile network.

real wages of factory workers 20 percent, and average family income 15 percent.

Above all, President Eisenhower concentrated on keeping the peace in a world threatened with thermonuclear destruction. His Atoms for Peace program, announced in 1953, offered the United Nations loans of American uranium for peaceful use by "have-not" countries. Throughout his eight years in office, he tried to reach an accord with the Soviet Union to end atomic tests and limit nuclear armaments.

Rift Widens Despite Khrushchev Visit

In the fall of 1957 the hopes raised at the Geneva summit conference vanished. The Soviet Union, on October 4, launched the first earth satellite, giving rise to fears that it might now deliver thermonuclear warheads anywhere in the world.

The President responded to "sputnik diplomacy" by increasing American armaments and foreign aid, speeding an American satellite program, and then renewing his efforts to negotiate with the Soviet Union.

He even invited Premier Khrushchev to visit the United States, but, though the Premier came, new crises drove the two nations further apart: the shooting down of an American U-2 reconnaissance plane over the Soviet Union, and the breaking of diplomatic relations with Communist Cuba. The Soviets still refused to agree to a secure atomic test-ban treaty, and the best that could be achieved was a temporary abstinence from testing.

To maintain security as well as to assist suffering peoples, Eisenhower year after year requested large appropriations for the foreign-aid program. He himself in his final months of office visited many nations around the globe (page 95). To cheering multitudes wherever he went, he repeatedly proclaimed the American desire for peace.

Before he left office in January, 1961, for his Gettysburg farm, he urged the necessity of maintaining military strength, but cautioned that vast, long-continued military expenditures could breed potential dangers to our way of life.

The retiring President pointed out that the "conjunction of an immense military establishment and a large arms industry is new in the American experience.... We must never let the weight of this combination endanger our liberties or democratic processes. We should take nothing for granted."

He concluded with a prayer that "in the goodness of time, all peoples will come to live together in a peace guaranteed by the binding force of mutual respect and love."

Distinguished world traveler, Britain's Prince Philip receives the National Geographic Society's Special Gold Medal from President Eisenhower in 1958. Earlier, Society President Melville Bell Grosvenor, standing behind the Chief Executive, read the inscription: "To His Royal Highness, the Prince Philip, Duke of Edinburgh, whose questing spirit has taken him to the far corners of the globe and brought to millions a better understanding of our planet and its peoples." Dr. Gilbert H. Grosvenor, Dr. Hugh L. Dryden, and the late Dr. John Oliver La Gorce of the Society's Board of Trustees watch the presentation at the White House.

Four years before, Eisenhower had become the eighth President to present medals on behalf of the Society when he awarded the Hubbard Medal to Sir Edmund Hillary, Sir John Hunt, and Tenzing Norkey of the British Mount Everest Expedition for the first conquest of earth's highest mountain.

"**I've found my career** — and its name is Ike," said Mamie Doud Eisenhower early in her married life. Her experience as the wife of an Army officer and university president made easy the transition to First Lady. Mrs. Eisenhower's great interest in the historical traditions of the White House inspired donors to complete the Presidential china collection. Other contributions include Adam mirrors, a settee and three chairs for the Lincoln Room, and Federal-style furnishings for the Diplomatic Reception Room.

Her love for children prompted the First Lady to reinstate the custom of Easter-egg rolling on the White House lawn, a ceremony discontinued for 12 years during and after World War II.

Proud grandfather and his son Maj. John Eisenhower watch young David take two of his sisters on a pony ride at the President's Gettysburg farm. The elder Eisenhowers purchased the rolling Pennsylvania acreage in 1950, and the remodeled farmhouse became the first home of their own since their marriage in 1916.

PAINTING BY THOMAS E. STEPHENS, WHITE HOUSE COLLECTION

Fast friends, the President and Winston Churchill tour Ike's farm in a golf cart. Sir Winston visited the Eisenhowers in both Washington and Gettysburg during his trip to the United States in 1959. The two leaders first met in wartime Washington in 1942. Mutual trials and responsibilities strengthened their ties.

John F. Kennedy [signature]

THIRTY-FIFTH PRESIDENT 1961/1963

JOHN F. KENNEDY, the first President born in the 20th century, called on the American people in his Inaugural Address to enlist in "a struggle against the common enemies of man: tyranny, poverty, disease and war itself." The struggle would not be finished in a hundred days or a thousand, he predicted: "But let us begin."

Kennedy did begin, urging the "New Frontier" program upon Congress and resisting the Communist threats even into the shadow of nuclear war. To the leadership of the Nation he brought realism, efficiency, verve—and the promise of increasing greatness.

Abruptly, in November, 1963, when he was scarcely past his first thousand days in office, he died by an assassin's bullet. Kennedy was the youngest man elected President; he was the youngest to die. Yet in his brief tenure he had firmly embarked the Nation on a forward course; his successor could pay no higher tribute than to proclaim, "Let us continue."

The second of nine children, Kennedy was born in Brookline, Massachusetts, a suburb of Boston, on May 29, 1917. He was proud that his forebears came from Ireland, rising swiftly in America to wealth and political prominence. His maternal grandfather was Mayor of Boston; his father, Ambassador to Great Britain.

Young PT Skipper Saves His Crew

After graduation from Harvard, Kennedy entered the Navy in World War II. As a lieutenant (j.g.), he commanded a PT boat in the Solomon Islands (page 102). Shortly after midnight on August 2, 1943, a Japanese destroyer sliced through it. Kennedy's back, already weak from a football injury, was badly hurt, but after 15 hours in the water he led the survivors to a small island. He spent the rest of his naval service in hospitals and as an instructor.

Early in 1946 Kennedy fought his first political campaign, in a Democratic primary for a Congressional district in the Boston area.

Dashing vigor and handsome features of John F. Kennedy, youngest elected President, stirred the Nation and the world. With his strong sense of purpose, his tough yet supple mind, he projected an image of confidence that promised progress. But an assassin's bullet ended his life on November 22, 1963. This photograph was among Mrs. Kennedy's favorites; an official portrait had not been painted before his death.

Elegant and eloquent, Jacqueline Kennedy enriched the White House with art treasures and conducted a tour of the Executive Mansion on nationwide television. Traveling abroad with her husband, whom she called an "idealist without illusions," she charmed dignitaries with her command of languages. Here, in 1961, she holds Caroline, age 4, and John, Jr., 1.

PHOTOGRAPH BY ELLIOTT ERWITT, MAGNUM, COURTESY SATURDAY EVENING POST (OPPOSITE); MARK SHAW

Awaiting action in the Pacific during World War II, Lieutenant Kennedy relaxes in his torpedo boat, PT 109. When a Japanese destroyer cut the craft in half, Kennedy saved his crew and won the Navy and Marine Corps Medal. Asked how he became a hero, he replied: "It was easy—they sank my boat."

The 28-year-old candidate stumped energetically among the working people and received nearly twice as many votes as his nearest opponent. He won easily in November.

During his six years in the House, Congressman Kennedy labored for the betterment of his constituents, voting for slum clearance and low-cost housing bills, and opposing the Taft-Hartley bill to restrict labor unions. At a Washington dinner party, he met beautiful Jacqueline Lee Bouvier, whom he married on September 12, 1953.

By this time, Kennedy had advanced from House to Senate, defeating Republican Senator Henry Cabot Lodge in the 1952 elections. As Senator, Kennedy made good his campaign slogan to "do *more* for Massachusetts." But increasingly he took a national view; he voted for reciprocal trade legislation and the St. Lawrence Seaway, even though they were not popular in Massachusetts.

From Pulitzer Prize to Presidency

Kennedy's old back injuries had become increasingly painful, and in October, 1954, he underwent a critical operation. While convalescing, he wrote *Profiles in Courage,* sketches of eight Senators who had risked their careers for their convictions. The book won a Pulitzer Prize for biography.

In 1956 Senator Kennedy came close to receiving the Democratic nomination for Vice President; in 1960 he went forthrightly in quest of the Presidential nomination. He fought intensely in several primaries and won, and at the Democratic Convention was nominated for President on the first ballot. He offered to share the ticket with his most powerful rival, Senate Majority Leader Lyndon B. Johnson.

"We stand today on the edge of a New Frontier," Kennedy proclaimed in his acceptance speech. Millions watched his vigorous television debates with the Republican nominee, Vice President Richard M. Nixon (opposite). Kennedy won the election by 303 to 219 electoral votes, but his margin in the almost 69,000,000 popular votes was a hairline 118,574. He was the first Roman Catholic to be elected President. The only other Catholic nominated by a major party had been Democrat Alfred E. Smith, badly defeated in 1928.

On a tide of youth, Kennedy sweeps the nomination for President at the 1960 Democratic Convention in Los Angeles. "The torch has been passed to a new generation of Americans," he said at his Inaugural.

102

In his Inaugural Address, Kennedy, aged 43, said "a new generation of Americans" had taken leadership. To all Americans he said: "Ask not what your country can do for you—ask what you can do for your country."

His vision of America extended beyond the Nation's material needs to the quality of American life and culture. Perhaps no President has ever so recognized the central place of the arts in a vital society (page 108).

Kennedy sent message after message to Congress to outline the New Frontier program. He called for legislation to speed economic growth, cut unemployment, rehabilitate depressed areas, reform the tax structure, modernize cities, husband natural resources, improve the lot of farmers, aid education, and provide medical care for old people.

For the next two years, he faced a conservative Congress. Nevertheless, he obtained much new legislation, including a reciprocal trade act, aid to higher education, and measures to pull the Nation out of the economic setback of 1960-61. In 1963, he fought hard for new civil rights legislation and for a cut in taxes to stimulate the economy. Both bills became law after his death.

Under Kennedy, the United States made strides in space. In May, 1961, shortly after Astronaut Alan B. Shepard, Jr., had completed the first American suborbital flight, the President asked Congress to undertake Project Apollo, to land a man on the moon by 1970 and return him safely.

First Presidential candidates to debate on television, Kennedy and Republican nominee Richard M. Nixon argue issues in a New York studio in October, 1960. This and three other verbal clashes, which reached four out of five voters, recalled the Lincoln-Douglas debates of 1858 in impact and had a decisive effect at the polls.

"Ich bin ein Berliner—I am a Berliner." Kennedy practiced the phrase so he could speak it to West Berliners during his European tour in 1963. He termed it "the proudest boast" in the world of freedom. With Mayor Willy Brandt (center) and Chancellor Konrad Adenauer, he sets out to inspect the wall that tragically divides East and West Berlin. Crowds cheer (below) as Kennedy rides past the war-scarred spire of the Kaiser Wilhelm Memorial Church.

First Roman Catholic President calls on Pope Paul VI in Rome (opposite). Last October, Kennedy's successor, Lyndon B. Johnson, met with the Pontiff in New York—first visit of a Pope to the Western Hemisphere.

In foreign affairs, Kennedy asserted energetic, imaginative, and effective leadership—though his administration began with a fiasco. He permitted a force of anti-Castro Cubans, armed and trained by the United States before his Inauguration, to land on the coast of Cuba in April, 1961, in a disastrous attempt to overthrow the dictator.

In the aftermath of this setback, Kennedy pressed his Alliance for Progress program to eliminate the poverty that might lead to further Castro-style revolutions. This was "a vast new ten-year plan for the Americas, a plan to transform the 1960's into an historic decade of democratic progress." The United States offered loans and grants to assist our hemispheric neighbors in their development.

Another Kennedy program was establishment of the Peace Corps, which has trained thousands of idealistic Americans—mostly young people—and sent them to work in underdeveloped countries all over the world (page 106).*

In June, 1961, Kennedy went to Vienna to talk with Soviet Premier Khrushchev, particularly in regard to Soviet pressure on Berlin. But Khrushchev seemed to be set on driving the Western allies out of that city; he fixed an end-of-the-year deadline for settlement of the Berlin issue, and in July announced a one-third increase in the Soviet military budget. Kennedy reacted firmly, requesting Congress to authorize strengthening of American forces.

In August, Communist East Germany erected a wall of barbed wire and concrete blocks between East and West Berlin, and the Soviet Union announced a series of nuclear

*Peace Corps Director Sargent Shriver and several of his Volunteers reported on "Ambassadors of Good Will," in the September, 1964, GEOGRAPHIC.

tests that doubled the fallout from all previous tests. Reluctantly Kennedy resumed small-scale American tests. The tension over Berlin eased, only to be succeeded by the Cuban crisis.

In October, 1962, Kennedy received photographic proof of Soviet missile bases in Cuba. With intermediate-range missiles installed, Khrushchev could have commanded an arc covering the contiguous forty-eight states and parts of Canada.

Acting deliberately and coolly, President Kennedy, in a memorable telecast, announced a naval quarantine on all offensive weapons bound for Cuba. "I call upon Chairman Khrushchev to halt and eliminate this clandestine, reckless, and provocative threat to world peace," the President declared. "He has an opportunity now to move the world back from the abyss of destruction."

A week of tension followed. Kennedy personally directed the quarantine fleet, forbidding interceptions far at sea in order to give Soviet ships laden with missiles more time to stop and turn around. Finally Khrushchev removed the missiles.

After this confrontation, Kennedy repeatedly emphasized the necessity of great powers working together to preserve the human race. He obtained an agreement with Russia banning nuclear tests in the atmosphere, in space, and under water—the first arms-control treaty since the cold war began.

War on human misery: Rita Helmkamp and Edward Dennison, Peace Corps Volunteers in Bolivia, vaccinate a youngster against smallpox.

President Kennedy launched the Corps in March, 1961. Today its members number more than 12,000 and serve in 46 countries. Forsaking many luxuries, this good-will army performs a host of jobs to aid self-help efforts of other nations. On Caribbean islands, Volunteers teach in schools and toil on farms; in Tanzania they work in busy hospital wards; in India they have fostered a chicken industry.

Showdown on the high seas: In October, 1962, Americans learned that Russia was building missile bases in Cuba. "This . . . clandestine decision to station strategic weapons for the first time outside of Soviet soil . . . cannot be accepted by this country," Kennedy declared on television (right).

In Florida the largest invasion force since World War II massed to meet the Red threat 90 miles away. Simultaneously, the U. S. Navy established a quarantine around Cuba to block Soviet shipments. But the crisis ended when Russia met Kennedy's terms and ordered withdrawal of the missiles. The destroyer *Barry* (foreground) checks a Soviet freighter removing rockets from the island. Navy observer plane flies overhead.

For Dr. Melville Bell Grosvenor — with our deepest appreciation and good wishes always.
Jacqueline Kennedy
John F. Kennedy

6-28-62

"**And here's one for you too, Mr. President.**" The Chief Executive smiled approvingly as Dr. Grosvenor reversed protocol by presenting the first leather-bound souvenir copy of the White House guidebook to Mrs. Kennedy as its guiding spirit. The First Lady had invited the National Geographic Society, as a public service, to produce the guide (right) for the nonprofit White House Historical Association, headed by David E. Finley (center); the book sells for $1.25, providing funds for refurnishing the mansion. The Society's President later received this autographed picture.

Patrons of the arts, the Kennedys entertain novelist Pearl Buck and poet Robert Frost at the White House. For the Inauguration, Frost recited his poem, "The Gift Outright"—a J.F.K. favorite.

108

Before Kennedy could build further on these auspicious beginnings, he was murdered. On November 22, 1963, while riding with his wife through the streets of Dallas, Texas, hailed by happy crowds, the President was shot from behind by an assassin. The Nation mourned his death with an outpouring of grief comparable to that which marked the death of Abraham Lincoln.*

He is buried at Arlington, Virginia, in a simple grave marked by an eternal flame. Hundreds of sites and memorials around the world have been dedicated to his memory. The most famous are Cape Kennedy, the

*In "The Last Full Measure," in the March, 1964, GEOGRAPHIC, President-Editor Melville Bell Grosvenor and the Society's staff told how the world paid tribute.

United States space center in Florida formerly known as Cape Canaveral; Mount Kennedy, a peak in the Canadian Yukon; and three acres of ground and a memorial at historic Runnymede, England. Future memorials will include the John F. Kennedy Center for the Performing Arts in Washington, D. C., and a library at Harvard University.

Kennedy exemplified intelligence, vitality, charm, and what he had referred to as "that most admirable of human virtues—courage." President Johnson, two days after the funeral voiced the feeling of the Nation: "No words are sad enough to express our sense of loss. No words are strong enough to express our determination to continue the forward thrust of America that he began."

Signing the nuclear-test-ban treaty in October, 1963, the President seals a pact outlawing atomic explosions in the atmosphere, space, and under water by the U. S., United Kingdom, and Soviet Union. Vice President Lyndon B. Johnson (right) and other dignitaries cluster in the Treaty Room of the White House. Restored to its Victorian elegance, the chamber had not beheld such a ceremony since the signing in 1898 of the protocol that ended hostilities in the Spanish-American War.   109

EKTACHROME BY CECIL B. STOUGHTON © N.G.S.

[signature: Lyndon B. Johnson]

THIRTY-SIXTH PRESIDENT 1963-

LYNDON B. JOHNSON rallied the American Nation toward a "Great Society." In his first years in office, backed by a broad consensus of the electorate and heavy majorities in Congress, he gave the country a legislative program of extraordinary scope.

Congress acted on the President's recommendations with unusual speed. It passed historic measures to protect the civil rights of minorities, to wipe out urban and rural pockets of poverty, to provide medical care for the aged, to assist education, to improve transportation, to beautify the countryside, and, through tax cuts, to stimulate the economy. By means of such legislation, Johnson sought to bring the Nation closer to its goal of a more abundant and meaningful life for every level of American society.

Johnson was born on August 27, 1908, in the grasslands of southwest Texas, not far from Johnson City, which his family had helped settle. His grandfather had fought in the Confederate Army and served as a member of the Texas Legislature; his father, who also served in the legislature, was a firm opponent of the Ku Klux Klan.

Johnson felt the pinch of rural poverty in the 1920's; while attending high school he worked as a shoeshine boy.

"I know that as a farm boy I did not feel secure," he has reminisced, "and when I was 14 years I decided I was not going to be the victim of a system which would allow the price of a commodity like cotton to drop from 40 cents to 6 cents and destroy the homes of people like my own family."

While working his way through Southwest Texas State Teachers College, he took a year off to teach Mexican-American children at Cotulla, Texas. A classmate remembers him as "a beanpole who was 6 foot 3, as tall as he is now, but who then weighed only 135 pounds. Lyndon was full of nervous energy ...always doing two or three things at a time."

With a "Great Society" as his goal, Lyndon Baines Johnson signed into law more major bills in his first two years than any President since his mentor, Franklin D. Roosevelt.

The dynamic Texan entered the Presidency with greater legislative experience than any predecessor. He had come to Washington as secretary to a Texas Representative in 1931. Election to the House of Representatives followed, then to the Senate, and finally to the Vice Presidency. Upon Kennedy's tragic death, Mr. Johnson became Chief Executive, and in the 1964 election won by an unprecedented popular majority.

Under sunny Texas skies, the President strolls with Mrs. Johnson and daughters Luci Baines (left) and Lynda Bird at the LBJ Ranch. Roots here run deep: Mr. Johnson was born in a modest homestead only 800 yards down the road. In Austin, 65 miles east, he courted and won Claudia Taylor, known from childhood as Lady Bird.

111

"I do solemnly swear. . . ." Only two hours earlier a sniper struck down President John F. Kennedy as he rode through cheering throngs in downtown Dallas, Texas. Now Vice President Johnson takes the oath of office, his right hand raised in pledge, his left hand on a small leather-bound Bible. Thus, in the midst of chaos, the orderly transfer of power takes place. The Nation was shocked by the fourth Presidential assassination in its history, but it was not paralyzed.

At 12:30 p.m. on November 22, 1963, Mr. and Mrs. Johnson rode two cars behind President and Mrs. Kennedy in a motorcade through the Texas metropolis. At the first crack of the rifle, a Secret Service agent threw himself across the Vice President in a protective move. The Johnsons' car sped to the hospital where the mortally wounded Kennedy had been taken. Alert to the possibility of a widespread plot against the Government, Mr. Johnson hurried under guard to the Presidential plane at the Dallas airport for the flight to Washington. After Mrs. Kennedy boarded, Federal District Judge Sarah T. Hughes swore in the 36th President of the United States, becoming the first woman to administer the oath of office. Beside the new President at the sorrowful oath taking stand Mrs. Johnson and Mrs. Kennedy, who still wears the pink suit chosen for what had promised to be a gay occasion.

Arriving in Washington that evening, President Johnson made a brief statement, concluding: "I will do my best. That is all I can do. I ask for your help—and God's."

Across the land, the people mourned. Addressing Congress five days later, President Johnson paid tribute to his predecessor and recalled Kennedy's dreams for the Nation. He urged, "All my fellow Americans, let us continue."

After graduation, while he was teaching speech at a Houston high school, his inner drive for public service steered him into politics. In 1931 he went to Washington as secretary to a Texas Congressman, Richard M. Kleberg. On a visit to Austin in September, 1934, he met Claudia "Lady Bird" Taylor, who has said she was taken aback at first, "then I realized he was handsome and charming and terribly bright." They were married in November.

Johnson became the Texas director of the National Youth Administration in 1935, and within two years developed what was regarded in Washington as a model among state youth programs. In 1937 he campaigned for the House of Representatives on a New Deal platform and defeated his nearest opponent two to one. In the House he became an effective lieutenant of Majority Leader Sam Rayburn and a protégé of President Roosevelt.

Immediately after Pearl Harbor he volunteered for active military service, and as a Navy lieutenant commander, won a Silver Star in the Pacific before he and other Congressmen were recalled to Washington.

Heart Attack Fails to Halt Career

In 1948, after five and a half terms in the House, Johnson won the Democratic primary contest for Senator by a margin of 87 votes. Once nominated, however, he easily defeated his Republican opponent.

The young Senator was elected Democratic Minority Whip after only three years' service and, in 1953, Minority Leader at the age of 44—the youngest in Senate history. When the Democrats gained control of the Senate in 1954, Johnson became Majority Leader and a commanding figure in Congress.

He suffered a severe heart attack in July, 1955, but made a complete recovery. As a Democratic Majority Leader in a Republican administration, he won a reputation for the statesmanlike way in which he supported or opposed White House measures on their basic merits. He refused to engage in partisanship as he guided through the Senate vital measures of national security and civil rights.

When Johnson failed to obtain the Democratic nomination for the Presidency in 1960, he accepted Kennedy's offer of the Vice Presidential nomination. On November 22, 1963, when President Kennedy was assassinated in Dallas, Texas, Vice President Lyndon Johnson was sworn in as the 36th President of the United States (above).

As President he tried to exemplify the view

Making friends for the United States, the genial Texan visited 27 countries as Vice President. The National Geographic Society recognized his extensive travels on June 8, 1962, by presenting him with its Jane M. Smith Award, a citation praising his "efforts to bring the peoples of the world closer together." He made a trip to Scandinavia in 1963, the first time such a high-ranking U. S. official had toured that area. Here, with Lady Bird and Lynda, he inspects a Lapp's reindeer in Finland. Vice President Johnson described his journey in the February, 1964, NATIONAL GEOGRAPHIC.

One of the most active Vice Presidents in history, Johnson was chairman of the National Aeronautics and Space Council, the National Advisory Council of the Peace Corps, and the President's Committee on Equal Employment Opportunity.

"**Come now,** and let us reason together." In the spirit of his favorite Biblical verse—Isaiah 1:18—Senate Majority Leader Johnson confers with colleagues in 1960: Senators Mike Mansfield (center) of Montana, Joseph S. Clark (left) of Pennsylvania, and William Proxmire of Wisconsin. Working 12 to 16 hours a day, Johnson piloted through the Senate the first civil rights act in 82 years. He impressed even opponents as "one of the ablest political craftsmen of our time."

EKTACHROME (ABOVE) BY VOLKMAR WENTZEL © N.G.S.; GEORGE THAMES, NEW YORK TIMES

"A triumph for freedom as huge as any victory won on any battlefield," the President calls the 1965 Voting Rights Act, which struck down practices denying minorities the vote. His words echo around statues of Lincoln in the Capitol Rotunda. He signed the bill in the President's Room, where, in 1861, Lincoln freed slaves impressed into the Confederate Army.

Strike against Viet Cong: In South Viet Nam, copters land paratroopers seeking out Communist guerrillas. Mr. Johnson ordered bombing of Red supply bases in North Viet Nam and by late 1965 had increased the U. S. troop total in South Viet Nam to more than 160,000.

Waging war on poverty, Mr. Johnson inspected the economically distressed Appalachian region in April, 1964. "I know what poverty means to people," he has said. "I have been unemployed. I have stood in an employment office, waiting for an assignment. . . ." Here he visits a jobless sawmill worker.

"**Immense excitement**" marks the lively discussions at L. B. J.'s Cabinet meetings, according to former Postmaster General John A. Gronouski (left, foreground). Reviewing administration policy in July, 1965, from left: U.N. Ambassador Arthur J. Goldberg; Robert S. McNamara, Defense; Orville L. Freeman, Agriculture; W. Willard Wirtz, Labor; John W. Gardner, incoming Health, Education and Welfare; Anthony J. Celebrezze, retiring HEW; John T. Connor, Commerce; Nicholas deB. Katzenbach, Attorney General; Dean Rusk, State; the President; Henry H. Fowler, Treasury; and Stewart L. Udall, Interior.

he had expressed in 1958 that it was unacceptable in the American Nation for a question to be settled by a partisan majority overriding a minority. "I do not believe," he said, "we have arrived at an answer until we have found the national answer, the answer all reasonable men can agree upon." To Congress in January, 1964, in his State of the Union Message, he recommended what he believed to be some of the national answers:

"Let this session of Congress be known as the session which did more for civil rights than the last hundred sessions combined; as the session which enacted the most far-reaching tax cut of our time; as the session which declared all-out war on human poverty and unemployment in these United States.... All this and more can and must be done."

Congress did accept these answers. The Civil Rights Act of 1964 strengthened earlier legislation, opened large categories of public accommodations to Negroes, and enlarged their opportunities. Congress also enacted tax-reduction and antipoverty measures.

Great Society Becomes New Goal

Johnson envisaged going still further, toward the goal of what he called a Great Society. In accepting the Democratic nomination for the Presidency in August, 1964, he declared: "This nation, this generation, in this hour has man's first chance to build a great society, a place where the meaning of man's life matches the marvels of man's labor."

In the 1964 election, Johnson won against Republican Senator Barry Goldwater by the biggest popular margin in American history —more than 15,000,000 votes.

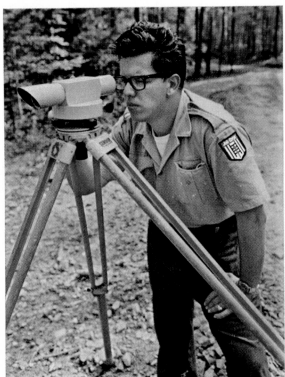

KODACHROMES BY JIM ATHERTON © N.G.S.

Embarked on new careers, Job Corpsmen train at the Blue Jay Conservation Center in Pennsylvania. Bruce Templeman drives an end loader, Neil D'Camera sights through a level, as they build a new sewer line for the camp. Eventually, they will acquire skills in such fields as reforestation, fire control, and wildlife management.

Modeled after the Civilian Conservation Corps of the 1930's (page 73), the Job Corps gives out-of-school, out-of-work youths, aged 16 to 21, the basic education and skills needed to hold jobs. By late fall of 1965, 64 rural and urban Job Corps centers in 30 states housed 13,500 young people.

To the 89th Congress, meeting in January, 1965, he outlined his objectives: Aid to education, an attack on disease, urban renewal, beautification of America and elimination of air and river pollution, development of depressed regions, control and prevention of crime and delinquency, removal of every obstacle to the right to vote, honor and support to art and thought, and a vigorous campaign against waste and inefficiency. Congress, at times augmenting or amending, rapidly enacted the legislation he recommended to make a beginning on each of these programs.

Congress gave the President bipartisan support when, in response to the frustrations of Negroes seeking to register to vote in some areas of the South, he proposed a bill to strike down restrictions to voting.

"To deny a man his hopes because of his color or race, his religion or the place of his birth," Johnson declared, "is not only to do injustice, it is to deny America and to dishonor the dead who gave their lives for freedom."

For the signing of the Voting Rights Act of 1965, Johnson went to the President's Room in the Capitol, where Lincoln had affixed his name to a bill freeing slaves forced to serve in the Confederate Army.

Truman Proposal Finally Becomes Law

Similarly, he flew to Independence, Missouri, and signed the Medicare-Social Security measure in the presence of former President Truman, first Chief Executive to propose health insurance as part of the Social Security program. In the presence of Mayor Robert F. Wagner of New York, son of the leading New Deal proponent of public housing, the President signed a housing bill going far beyond any of its predecessors.

"We must make sure," he said, "that every family in America lives in a home of dignity, in a neighborhood of pride, a community of opportunity and a city of promise and hope."

Johnson enlisted the support of many Republicans as well as most Democrats. He was unusually successful in convincing businessmen that the Government wished to aid rather than hinder them. He made frequent and effective use of television.

Under Johnson the country scored spectacular advances in space. It so effectively cut the Russian lead that only 11 weeks after a Soviet cosmonaut floated outside his space vehicle, Astronaut Edward H. White II took a "walk" in space. Little more than two months later Astronauts L. Gordon Cooper, Jr., and Charles Conrad, Jr., kept Gemini V in orbit a

Spadework for beauty: The First Lady plants an azalea to dramatize her drive to make the Nation's Capital a showcase. Campaigning to beautify all America, she pushed legislation to restrict billboards and junkyards beside major highways; L.B.J. called it "Lady Bird's bill" and gave her the first pen he used in signing it.

record-breaking eight days. An unmanned vehicle, Mariner IV, after a flight of 325.1 million miles, transmitted the first close-up photographs of Mars.

In relations with other nations, President Johnson inherited a serious and perplexing problem in South Viet Nam, where the United States had long sought to stem the tide of Communism threatening Southeast Asia. Under the Geneva Agreement of 1954, all the Indochina states had won their independence and all—including North Viet Nam—had accepted neutralization. This agreement was flouted almost immediately. Communist guerrillas, the Viet Cong, encouraged and supported from the North, increasingly threatened to take over South Viet Nam.

The Eisenhower Administration sent aid and advisers, and Kennedy, stepping up the commitment, dispatched 3,200 military advisers and technicians in 1961. During the Johnson Administration the growth of Viet Cong forces led to still sterner countermeasures. American troops entered more directly into the fighting by the summer of 1965. President Johnson asserted that he was planning careful additional steps toward the paramount goal—"to bring an end to aggression and a peaceful settlement."

Dominican Revolt Brings a New Crisis

When reports of a revolution in the Dominican Republic reached the White House in the spring of 1965, President Johnson acted quickly. He landed troops to protect American lives in a situation that appeared to be developing sinister dimensions.

"The American nations," he later declared, "cannot, must not, and will not permit the establishment of another Communist government in the Western Hemisphere."

He turned to the Organization of American States, and within a few days that body negotiated a cease-fire, began to work toward a peaceable settlement, and dispatched an Inter-American Peace Force. By September, through these efforts, the rival factions had agreed on a new government.

Beyond and above these crises, President Johnson strove for the goals he enunciated to the United Nations a few weeks after he became President:

"We know what we want: The United States wants to see the cold war end; we want to see it end once and for all; the United States wants to prevent the dissemination of nuclear weapons to nations not now possessing them; the United States wants to press on with arms control and reduction; the United States wants to cooperate with all the members of this organization to conquer everywhere the ancient enemies of mankind—hunger and disease and ignorance; the United States wants sanity, and security, and peace for all, and above all."   THE END

"The best instrument yet devised to promote the peace of the world." Thus President Johnson described the United Nations when he renewed his country's support of the international body in an address to the General Assembly on December 17, 1963. He once defined a peaceful world as a place "where differences are solved without destruction, and common effort is directed at common problems."

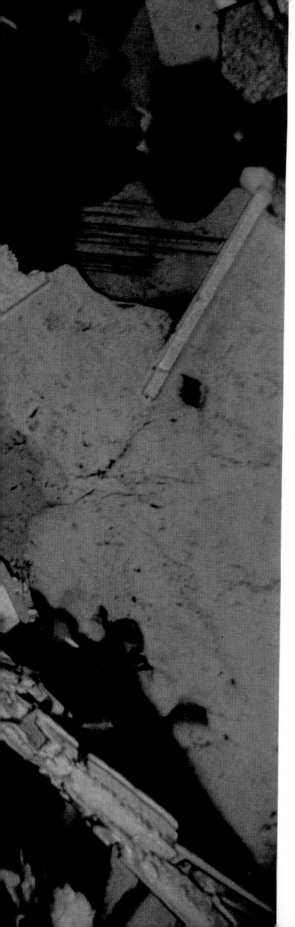

Finding Rare Beauty in Common Rocks

Article and photographs by
LORENCE G. COLLINS, Ph.D.

PEOPLE cock an eyebrow when I tell them abstract art is about as modern as a dinosaur. In the first place, they can't imagine that a geologist knows much about art. Yet I work with a dazzling array of colors and free forms every day.

To prove my point, I project a few slides from my collection. The doubters usually admit that no museum can match my display of abstract shapes and colors.

Churning forces within the globe have been creating "modern art" since the beginning of geologic time. Volcanoes, earthquakes, and seeping water stir earth's crust into infinite patterns of beauty.

Unfortunately, few people see them. So I enjoy showing my photographs of rock thin sections—wafers of stone three times thinner than this page—taken through the petrographic microscope. Such a microscope differs from others in that it polarizes light. Like picket fences, crystals in the microscope's optics block out all rays except those that filter between the crystals' parallel rows, or planes,

Nature's genius and polarized light create a masterpiece that a painter might entitle "Autumn Leaves." The geologist, peering through a petrographic microscope, sees muscovite, biotite, quartz, and feldspar crystals—here magnified 100 times—and calls the mixture common gray granite.

of atoms. As did Alice with her looking glass, I use this instrument to enter another world—a microscopic realm of dancing colors and shapes.

Nature builds rocks with tiny particles of minerals. Most minerals crystallize into characteristic shapes and boast a distinctive set of optical properties. Like lenses and prisms, the crystals bend light and break it into separate rays.

The color of a mineral seen through the petrographic microscope depends on the mineral's alignment with the plane of polarization. As I rotate a thin section in polarized light, the mineral alignment continually changes, and I can see a constantly shifting assortment of colors. It reminds me of a child's kaleidoscope.

Gleaming diamonds, rubies, sapphires, emeralds, and opals in thin sections appear almost colorless, to the amazement of my new students in petrography at San Fernando Valley State College. But shimmering beauty may lurk in a drab, lichen-covered stone that nicks your lawn-mower blade.

By systematically studying samples ground to uniform thickness, geologists have determined the characteristics of every mineral. Now we can quickly learn a rock's mineral components by observing the colors and shapes of thin-section grains.

The relationship of different crystals to one another and changes in them caused by chemical reactions, heat, or pressure also tell important stories. Sometimes they lead us to the hiding places of petroleum or metal ores.

While geologists employ petrographic analysis to study earth's crust, other professions as well find it helpful. In the police crime laboratory, it can turn up valuable clues, such as the source of dirt particles on a suspected slayer's shoes. It helps military researchers assess the sea ice of potential Arctic airstrips. When scientists of Project Mohole recover the first sample of earth's mantle from three miles beneath the ocean floor, they will prepare thin sections for petrographic inspection.* Undoubtedly, the first men on the moon will gather rocks for study under the petrographic microscope.

For me, the colors and patterns that unfold the mysteries of matter turn a tedious task into gripping adventure. And when I hear artists declare they have broken the bonds of objective art, I know nature really did it first.

*Samuel W. Matthews described the first steps of Project Mohole in the November, 1961, NATIONAL GEOGRAPHIC.

The author films nature's abstracts with a camera atop his petrographic microscope. Dr. Collins uses his slides in classes at San Fernando Valley State College, Northridge, California, where he teaches petrography—rock description and classification.

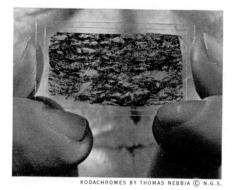

Rock thin section appears drab in ordinary light. Polarized beams kindle sparkling hues in its tiny crystals. Technicians prepare thin sections by slicing wafers from rock samples with diamond saws. They cement the wafers to glass slides, then grind each to a thickness of 1/1000 of an inch.

Close-up of a stained-glass window? Farmland from 30,000 feet up? Neither. Rose, orange, and mottled pink identify augite. Geologists recognize the other colors as hornblende, usually green or brown in thin section. Combined, the two minerals produce pyroxene amphibolite—a black rock to the naked eye.

Crushing force, perhaps millions of years ago, shattered portions of tremolite-actinolite. The small granules, rotated during crushing, have alignments different from the solid center; thus light from them is affected differently, many appearing brown instead of yellow, red, and blue.

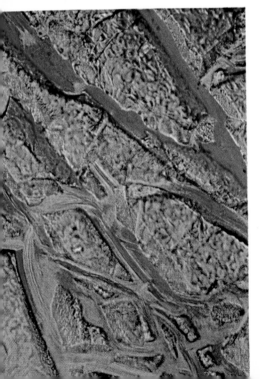

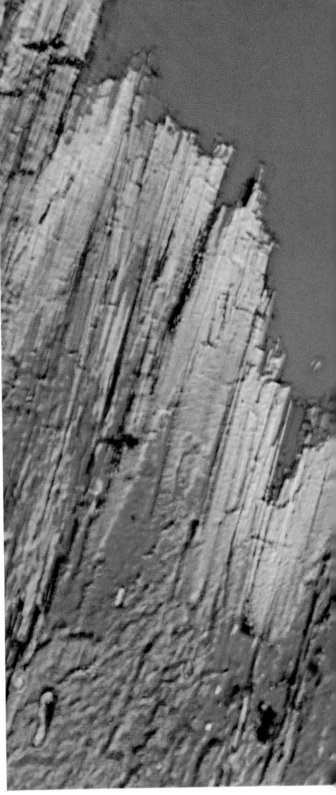

Snakes writhe in a lava bath. Formed in molten rock, olivine fractures when it cools and hardens. Water seeps into the cracks and sets off chemical reactions that alter the reddish-appearing olivine to serpentine (green). The author inserted a quartz wedge into the microscope to enhance the colors of this rock, which otherwise appears dull.

Sunrise glows on a skyscraper skyline traced by the jagged edge of a tremolite-actinolite thin section—another view of the same mineral seen at upper left. Dr. Collins's years of training as a geologist had little to do with his selection of pictures for this article. "I tried to look down my microscope with the eye of an artist," he explains. "You might find any of these rocks in a vacant lot. Certainly, none of the pictures reveals anything startling to a geologist. But I think they do demonstrate that nature puts brilliant beauty into even its humblest creations."

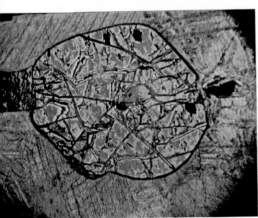

"**Fossilized flounder**" of olivine swims in a marble sea. The tiny crystal tells geologists that very high temperatures baked the marble from limestone.

Bold bars of rainbow color march in a "modern" abstract design created eons ago (below). Cleavage planes of a single calcite crystal cast these rhombohedral patterns.

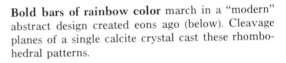

Dazzling free forms created by heat, pressure, upheavals, and chemical reaction daub a miniature "canvas" (below). Hornblende provides the green pigment, feldspar the yellow, biotite the red.

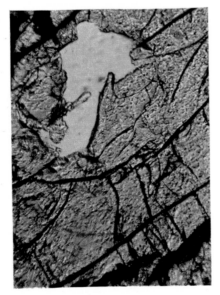

Ghostly yellow grain of quartz floats in dead tree limbs; actually, fracture lines brand the augite background.

Mottled mosaic records the transformation of grayish feldspar into golden grains of epidote. Hot-water seepage, deep in the earth, works the seeming magic.

Meteor shower of muscovite, an ordinary mica, rains through a midnight sky of microcline feldspar. Like frightened birds, fractures flit through the downpour.

127

Fiery river of muscovite roars down a quartz canyon. Extreme heat and pressure created this brilliant display in what probably was once sandy shale. A single mineral presents many faces and hues to the petrographic microscope. This semicircular arrange-

"Butterfly wings" flutter as the microscope stares down a fracture. Muscovite fans out into microcline feldspar when moisture enters the fracture and starts the metamorphosis. The muscovite glistens with gemlike luster in a microscopic world of polarized light. Ironically, diamonds, rubies, emeralds, and sapphires—minerals man prizes because they sparkle on his finger—offer drab, colorless thin sections.

Students study a granite thin section in a geology class. Since only one student at a time can see a slide under the microscope, Dr. Collins photographs and projects thin sections for an entire class to view at once.

KODACHROMES BY LORENCE G. COLLINS AND (BELOW) NATIONAL GEOGRAPHIC PHOTOGRAPHER THOMAS NEBBIA © N.G.S.

ment of muscovite blushes through every intensity of color as the fingerlike grains are rotated a full 360 degrees on the stage of the microscope. Startlingly different portraits of muscovite appear at bottom left and on page 127.   THE END   129

THE WAURÁ
BRAZILIAN INDIANS
OF THE HIDDEN XINGU

Article and photographs by HARALD SCHULTZ

Taut young warrior measures his scarecrow enemy before hurling a spear.

IN THE BEGINNING, there was no man. Flying through the darkness, the son of the bat fell in love with the daughter of the jatobá tree. Out of their love, two boys were born: the sun and the moon.

The brothers made many bows and arrows and set them up next to each other in a long row. Then they made large cigars and blew the smoke against the bows and arrows, changing them into human beings—the ancestors of all the Indians who dwelt among the headwaters of the Xingu River....

We are flying toward the remote heart of Brazil. The shadow of our Brazilian Air Force DC-3 skitters batlike over the green roof of the endless Amazon forest, reminding me of the creation myth of the upper Xingu region—our destination, and one of the last fortresses of primitive man.

Far to the south, the Mato Grosso Plateau gives rise to five major rivers. Trickling across savanna, coursing through stands of towering forest, gushing in foaming rapids, they finally merge in the jungle to form the Xingu River

The game sharpens his skill for a joyous mock war with a neighboring tribe. 131

(pronounced sheengoo), some 1,000 winding miles from its confluence with the Amazon (map, page 135).

The immense wilderness separating these rivers is a hidden world ringed by once-dreaded tribes: Chavante, Tshikão, Tshukahamae, Cayapó....

Here too dwell many peaceful tribes who cling to an ancient way of life. One of them, the Waurá, is particularly fascinating to me as a scientist and student of Brazilian Indian culture.* The Waurá know the secret of making pottery. They still practice age-old ceremonials. I now had the rare opportunity to live among them.

Park Created to Save Ancient Tribes

The jungle rises to meet us. We glide down through roiling heat currents to a patch of red earth in a forest clearing. Our plane bumps and rolls past mud-walled huts to a stop before a large wooden sign:

PÔSTO LEONARDO VILLAS BOAS
PARQUE NACIONAL DO XINGU

The bearded men who meet us are Orlando and Claudio Villas Boas. With their late brother, for whom this jungle post is named, they have spent many years befriending, pacifying, and protecting Indians of the Xingu from the fatal onrush of civilization. They now control admission to the area.

When the German explorer Karl von den Steinen first entered this region in 1884, he found a populous paradise of 3,000 Indians; they spoke a medley of tongues and lived in 35 villages. In 1962 the World Health Organization reported a population of only 500.

In an effort to halt this devastation, the Brazilian Government created Xingu National Park in 1961 and set rigid admission rules. Experienced jungle pilots of the Brazilian Air Force, navigating to landing strips—no more than scratches in the wilderness—keep open the lifelines. Without them, study of these tribes would be almost impossible.

The plane must return to civilization. Soon after, clearance for my visit is granted, and I set out with three Waurá guides in a bark canoe for the journey to their village.

The village lies by a lake at the end of a long path from the Tamitatoala River. Five houses

stand like giant haystacks around a large square of beaten earth (pages 134-5). Here live 85 Waurá Indians, the last in the world.

Ikiana, a chap about 22, steps forward. He has worked for a year at Campo de Diauarum, an outpost of civilization 65 miles to the north. He can serve as my interpreter among the Arawakan-speaking Waurá.

"Where shall I go with all my belongings?"

"We will build a house for you," says Malakiyauá, the courteous and kindly chief of the village. "You must give everyone who helps build it a bush knife and an ax."

As the days pass, about eight men work continually. The sides of the house are made of thin tree trunks. The roof is covered carefully with sedge.

"Your house is finished!" says Malakiyauá. "Now you must pay." He calls the youths and men together. They line up in long rows.

"Here are eight knives and axes," I say.

"No!" replies the chief seriously and firmly. "Everyone gets an ax and a knife."

There are 18 men and youths. Not all of them worked at the same time, but nearly all the village seems to have worked a little. But I gladly pay, for Malakiyauá knows how to look after the welfare of his village.

Too Many Cooks Crowd the Hearth

"Now I have a house, I need a cook."

"I will be your assistant. I can cook, too," Ikiana says to me.

The following morning not one but two cooks are stirring the fire.

"This is Akaintobi, the son of Chief Malakiyauá. He is *my* assistant."

In the afternoon still a third works around our hearth. "And who is he?"

"It is Apá, the son of the storyteller Praguai. He is Akaintobi's assistant."

At breakfast two of Ikiana's nieces and nephews appear at the table—a large flat tree root set upon four posts.

"These little ones get only a half cup of chocolate. This is the end," he says.

---

*Memorable accounts by Harald Schultz of other remote Brazilian tribes have appeared in NATIONAL GEOGRAPHIC: "Children of the Sun and Moon," March, 1959; "Tukuna Maidens Come of Age," November, 1959; "Blue-eyed Indian," July, 1961; "Brazil's Big-lipped Indians," January, 1962; and "Indians of the Amazon Darkness," May, 1964.

Tinkle of a bronze bell, given by the author to his friend Kari-Kariis, sounds a whimsical counterpoint to the rhythm of a war dance performed now only for games. Living in Brazil's jungle with other pacified Xingu tribes but surrounded by still-savage and marauding Indians, the last 85 Waurá left in the world preserve an ancient, primitive culture. Vivid festivals highlight the dry season, a time of plenty.

If the plane were not bringing more supplies, we would indeed be nearing the end.

Nights during the dry winter—July to September—are bitterly cold. Inside the large communal houses, each Waurá family keeps a fire crackling. They hang their hammocks close to the blaze.

In the house the Indians built for me, I huddle in wool blankets, but still the chill creeps in. This house has no door that can be locked, and in the middle of the night I sense someone standing next to my rubber mattress. It is pitch black. I fumble for my flashlight and ask, "Who is there?"

"Corimágua!" says a soft unfamiliar voice.

At last I find the light. In its beam stands a strange person in rags, holding his hands over his eyes against the glare.

"Who are you?"

"Corimágua!" he answers. He appears to be cold and points at my blanket.

"Go away and let me sleep. We will talk about it tomorrow."

"Corimágua!" he says reproachfully.

I am a little frightened and cannot get back to sleep for a long time.

In the welcome light of morning, I ask Ikiana, "Who is Corimágua?"

"It means 'I am your friend.' "

"And who goes about nights into the houses and disturbs the sleeping?"

"It is the widower, Kaulukumã. Come, I will show you 'your friend.' He lives with me."

In Ikiana's large dark house, where several families dwell, is a cage made of arrow shafts. Inside on an old hammock lies "Corimágua."

"Whenever someone loses his wife," Ikiana explains, "his head is shorn and he is locked up in a cage inside the house, like the young fellows who will soon be men and the girls when they reach womanhood. Only at night can the widower leave his hiding place to roam around and visit his friends. When his hair has grown long again, he is free."

Many of the Indians of the Xingu fear the spirits of the dead. The widower must remain in his cage until it is certain his wife's spirit has departed.

Pot of poison beneath her sieve, a Waurá woman grates juicy manioc root. Boiling disposes of the volatile prussic acid and leaves a potable soup. Coarse paste, rolled into balls (background), as well as starchy residue in the tub, will be dried to make *beiju* cakes, tribal staff of life.

Gleaming arteries of water cross the heart of the South American Continent and join to form the Xingu River, which flows north 1,000 miles to its confluence with the Amazon. In 1961 Brazil set aside 8,500 square miles of dense tropical forest to form the Xingu National Park for the protection of primitive tribes and flora and fauna.

Haystack houses in a forest clearing comprise the remote village of the Waurá Indians. Path at right leads to a large lake. In the white patches around the dwellings, women make manioc flour during the dry season. The author lived in the house under construction near the landing strip, used by the Brazilian Air Force to fly in medical aid.

KODACHROMES BY HARALD SCHULTZ © N.G.S.

Pacific Ocean

Amazon

Atlantic Ocean

B R A Z I L

Xingu

SOUTH AMERICA

AREA ENLARGED BELOW

★ Brasília

0   1000
STATUTE MILES

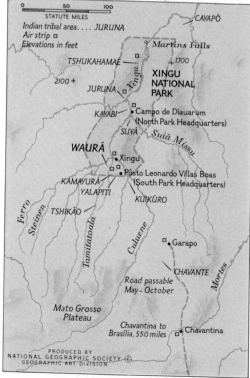

0   50   100
STATUTE MILES

Indian tribal area.... JURUNA
Air strip ◻
Elevations in feet

CAYAPÓ

Martins Falls

TSHUKAHAMAE

4 1700

XINGU NATIONAL PARK

2100 +

JURUNA

KAYABI

Campo de Diauarum
(North Park Headquarters)

SUYÁ   Suiá Missu

WAURÁ

Xingu

Pôsto Leonardo Villas Boas
(South Park Headquarters)

KAMAYURÁ
YALAPITI

KUIKÚRO

Ferro

Steinen

TSHIKÃO

Tamitatoala

Culuene

Garapo

CHAVANTE

Mortes

Road passable
May - October

Mato Grosso
Plateau

Chavantina to
Brasília, 550 miles

Chavantina

PRODUCED BY
NATIONAL GEOGRAPHIC SOCIETY ©
GEOGRAPHIC ART DIVISION

Blood-red helmets of hair decorate men for daily wrestling bouts. Sticky dye, made from the oil of pressed *urucú* seeds boiled into paste, wards off both supernatural beings and real insects. Men believe that tight bands on arms and ankles increase strength. The mask house, an exclusive male "club," provides storage for painted faces and straw suits that represent spirits (pages 148-9). Men meet here after work and paint themselves for tests of strength. Sacred flutes (page 140), which women may see only on their deathbeds, lie hidden in the thatch walls.

"I have no wife who can make me a new hammock," the widower says. "Look how old and worn it is. Give me your hammock."

Such a pitiful widower! I give him a hammock and a blanket. A few weeks later, during the visit of a Yalapiti Indian, he trades them for something else he wants.

"Corimágua," he says brightly.

Dancing Amazons Relive a Legend

It is still early morning. Mist hangs in the air. The men are gathered in the village square. Chief Malakiyauá is seated on a stool cut from a solid block of wood.

A chorus of women is singing in the chief's house. In the gloom of the vast interior, two groups are decorating each other blood-red with *urucú* dye. They are putting on new *uluri*—tiny triangles of fiber—their only body covering. Two of the women are adorned

with magnificent diadems of yellow feathers, from which protrude long arara, or macaw, tail feathers.

One of the leaders appears in the dark entrance of the hut. She dances across the square toward Malakiyauá, singing and swinging two arrows up and down (pages 142-43).

The chief rises, carefully takes the woman by the hand, and leads her for a few steps. She continues alone until she disappears again into the chieftain's house.

Shortly after, the second leader of the dancing Amazons appears. She repeats the dance across the square.

Then the chorus appears in two long lines, one moving forward with swaying hips and the other taking small steps sideways. While singing, they dance into and out of the houses.

Praguai, the wise village storyteller, begins his tale: "Once there lived the Jamarikumá

Nature's dazzling patterns inspire makeup for war games. Markings indicate tribal rank, from lowly sea gull to kingly jaguar. Takara tops off a wild-fowl motif with a plaited straw hat (left). Lapokitee wears a precious necklace of jaguar claws (center). Under a diadem of treasured toucan feathers, Kapalukate models the dashing raiment of a hawk (bottom). Waurá boys (below) wear customary gull design, but the chief's grandson enjoys the right to a privileged pattern—polka dots.

LIVING GALLERY OF GEOMETRIC ART: *Abstract designs symbolic of
jungle creatures—hawks, pumas, armadillos—whirl, dip, and
bob during a rousing dance following daily practice for war games.
Warriors shoulder blunt-tipped spears for mock combat
and carry wooden spear throwers.*

tribe. For many days the men stayed away and sent no fish to the women. An old man named Kamatápirá, who had been left behind, told the women that their men were bad and would return to kill them. Going to the jungle, he found three giant armadillos. He commanded the animals to dig a long tunnel. Then he and the women followed the armadillos far into the earth, until they came out again at the Tamitatoala River.

"The women danced, painted with urucú and adorned with yellow feather diadems. They made bows and arrows and learned to use them. They learned to live without their men. Nothing more has ever been heard from them. We know only the place by the river where they came from the ground."

In two long lines the chorus of women dances across the square, stamping behind the leaders, retelling with song and step the old story of the lost Amazons of the Xingu.

These Jamarikumá dances are a welcome change for the Waurá women, who work from dawn to dusk during the long dry season. Each morning they dig out the heavy roots of the bitter manioc plants growing in the nearby fields. Using the starchy pulp from these roots, the Indians make *beiju* cakes—their staff of life (page 135). Manioc is "bitter" because it contains deadly prussic acid, a small portion of which would kill a man.

Trouble Stems From Secret Skill

Mats are spread under open palm shelters behind the houses. Here the women peel the manioc roots with clam shells and grate them on boards set with pointed teeth of palmwood. The pulp is then squeezed on a palm-rib sieve to press out the poisonous fluid which, along with fine particles of starch, is collected

in a pot. Coarse pulp left on the sieve is formed into balls and dried as beiju. The liquid, boiled to rid it of prussic acid, becomes nutritious soup. Starchy residue in the pot is dried to make fine flat cakes.

The large pots used for preparing manioc, and the smaller gray ones adorned with images of forest animals, confer upon the Waurá great prestige: Of all the tribes living in the upper Xingu, only the Waurá have the secret of ceramics, learned in an unremembered past (page 150).

This skill is also the cause of personal grief. While nearby tribes acquire their pottery by trading with the Waurá, the wild hunters of the distant forests, like the Tshikão, prefer to "steal the factory"—attacking before dawn to carry off Waurá women. The raids are an ever-present danger, even though the steady approach of civilization and the diplomacy of the Villas Boas brothers make their occurrence less and less frequent.

Dusk gathers. The village square is now quiet. Children and women sit in the doorways of the huts.

Vatuku, the best fisherman of the village, carries a glowing ember, a wooden stool, and some large cigars to a place near the mask house, where the masks and sacred flutes are kept. He is joined by Praguai, the storyteller, and Ayumá with the kind eyes, then by Kraptá, the brother of Chief Malakiyauá. Other men gather. Finally comes the chief.

In the evening they sit on stools in a circle and smoke long cigars.

"Come sit with us, Kukoi." The Waurá have difficulty with Vuvu, the name given to me by the Kraho Indians. The closest they can come to pronouncing it is "Kukoi."

Now there is deep concern.

Her "shadow" gone, a woman dies

EKTACHROME (ABOVE) AND KODACHROME BY HARALD SCHULTZ © N.G.S.

EVIL SPIRITS lurk in lakes and streams to steal human "shadows," or souls, the Waurá believe. When spirits hold a shadow in captivity, a person grows ill and will perish unless his soul is rescued. In these rare photographs the author captures a poignant struggle to ward off death. Shaman (above) blows magic smoke over a woman whose shadow has been stolen. Chief shaman (right), with assistant, inhales cigar smoke to induce a trance during which he sees spirits and asks for the soul's return. In a last attempt to save her, men play the sacred *jakui* (left), flutes of awesome power; women hide indoors. When even these spirits fail, the tribe ascribes death to witchcraft invoked by another tribe.

Striding out of a legend, Waurá women tell by step and song the tale of the Jamarikumá Amazons—legendary Xingu women who fled from their selfish husbands and learned to make weapons and live without men. Dance leader (opposite) offers a gift of ceremonial arrows to the chief, representing an old man who helped the Jamarikumá wives escape. Early explorers named the Amazon region after seeing armed women like those the Xingu myth describes. Living isolated in tropical jungle, the primitive Waurá wear little or no costume the year round, recalling Christopher Columbus's account of Indians on San Salvador Island in the Bahamas, "quite naked as their mothers bore them."

In the chief's house, where several families live, Kregmá's wife has been lying for a long time in her hammock. She is wasting away. The shamans think that an evil water spirit, a *sapukiyauá,* has stolen her "shadow," or soul, away. A shaman must go to see the water spirit and ask for the return of the woman's shadow. He can do so only in a state of trance, for only then are the spirits visible to him.

Five large cigars are lying in front of Malakiyauá. On an empty stomach, he smokes one cigar after another. He inhales deeply, then with a hissing sound, he quickly exhales the smoke through half-closed teeth.

Trance Turns Shaman Into "Mad Dog"

His solid round face grows stiff; sweat covers forehead and neck; his eyes are tightly closed. With a jerking motion he rises. Shrieking, he runs into the darkness. He disappears down the path to the lake, and soon can be heard crying, talking, and moaning.

He approaches again. Bowed, almost crouching, Malakiyauá runs across the village square. He is not the kind, serene chief I know so well but a strange animal that, driveling and crying, runs into the house where the sick woman lies.

Now crawling, now stumbling to his feet, the dazed shaman passes his hands over the woman's body. He groans and gasps as though contending with the invisible power of the water spirit. He turns in a frenzy, drops to his knees, and with flashing teeth bounds toward me like a mad dog. Horrified, I dash from the house. The men laugh loudly.

"Everywhere, in the rivers and lakes, the spirits wait to snatch the shadows of men," Ikiana tells me. "If Malakiyauá cannot get the shadow of Kregmá's wife back, she will soon die."

The shaman, groaning and moaning as though ill, returns to the circle of men and places his head in Kregmá's lap. Slowly he awakens. I speak to him.

"Did you want to bite me, Malakiyauá?"

He looks at me with surprise. He is again the serene, sensible, and always kind chief.

"I know nothing about it, Kukoi."

As time goes on, more attempts are made, while in a state of trance, to persuade the water spirit to return the shadow.

Whenever an ailing person recovers, he may after a time ask his friends to make a portrait of the spirit that held his shadow. These portraits are the masks that hang in

Clay Fish and Wooden Souls Work Magic

During the dry season, Chief Malakiyauá (left) hides a fish charm (above) in a wicker basket. Then it is sunk in the lake to lure a good catch. The Waurá found the image in a place five days' journey from their village where, they believe, the sun lived when he was a human. As the water level falls lower and fish seek deeper pools, the Indians perform the *patápu* ceremony with bull-roarers, wooden blades carved and painted to represent the souls of fish (lower left). Whirled from the end of a long pole by a skirted man (below), the blade creates a deep humming—a song to call fish back to fill empty Waurá nets.

the men's house. High-spirited Waurá men and boys use them not only in ceremonials but in lighter-hearted moments.

Hardly a day goes by without the lively maskers bounding out to harry the women for food or playfully deprive the fisherman of his morning's catch. Dressed as water spirits, wearing suits of straw, they stare from sightless shell eyes and talk in high falsetto voices to the busy women (pages 148-9):

"Give us beiju cakes! We are hungry!"

Finally, to be rid of the nuisance, the women oblige. Happy now, the maskers skip away, the small ones following spiritedly like little billy goats.

As afternoon shadows lengthen, more of the men return from fishing. They gather in the mask house to paint themselves with red urucú (page 136).

"Urucú is beautiful!" Ikiana says. "It also protects us against the supernatural beings."

Laughter and joyous singing ring out, and then I hear another sound quite like the call of jaguars: *"Huka! Huka! Huka!"*

In the center of the village square, Ayumá and Kregmá are sparring with one another. With quick movements they roughen their hands with earth and crouch—fists held forward like the paws of beasts. They grasp one another's hands, seeking to get an armlock around the neck. Each tries to throw his opponent flat on his back.

One of them is thrown. He gets up again. The winner helps him. Another pair takes their place. The Waurá men wrestle nearly every afternoon the whole dry season long.

As dusk gathers the men form a long line. The women stand opposite them. Singing and rhythmic stamping fill the air. Tomorrow will be another day of work and joy!

EKTACHROMES (BELOW AND OPPOSITE LOWER); KODACHROMES © N.G.S.

It is the cold hour before dawn. Suddenly shrill cries ring from the square. A happy crowd of young boys bursts into my hut.

"Come and bathe with us, Kukoi!"

Each morning the boys of the tribe forsake their warm hammocks by the fires to race through the cold air to the lakeside. We go down the path, whistling and singing. Some of the boys carry burning logs, and others gather dry branches along the way. Overhead, a full moon washes the sky of stars.

Not far from the lake a fire is kindled. Smooth brown bodies huddle close to it. Then with a singing roar the boys dash into the icy water. Rhythmically thrashing hands and arms, they practice the warriors' chant, the stirring song sung at their war games. They keep this up for half an hour without breaking the tempo.

In the east, the sun, once a human warrior and father of all the Indians of the Xingu, casts a gleaming spear against the night. The boys leap from the water and race for the village, whooping in high spirits. They learn early that nature gives nothing away and that life is a daily struggle, but one in which there can be beauty and fun.

Monkey Stew Precedes War Games

I am surprised one day to find the tribesmen stewing a big howler monkey.

"I thought you Waurá ate no animals."

"Has no one told you, Kukoi? It is coming time for *javari*—the war games!"

The javari are the climax of the dry season, a time of joy and festivity. This year there is a special excitement, for Malakiyauá has invited the tribe's recently dreaded enemies, the Suyá, to the games.

Only the older men will eat the rare meal of stewed monkey, but each man and boy in the village has a part to play in the games. They practice every day for weeks.

The boys have made a large straw man in the square. The tribe is divided into three battle groups. Youths under 15 are covered with white clay, then painted with black patterns. Screaming in high voices, running and

hopping with deeply bent knees, flapping crooked arms, these are the sea gulls.

Older men paint themselves in the mottled patterns of wild fowl, hawks, otters, monkeys, and armadillos. But the kings of the javari games are the adult warriors who have proven themselves brave and skillful in combat. They wear the markings of the harpy eagle, the king vulture, the tawny puma, and the spotted jaguar. Most distinguished of all are the black jaguars, strong bodies painted with charcoal and white clay.

First the sea gulls, from the end of the line of battle, sweep to the attack, their long javari spears with blunt stone tips striking the straw figure. They are followed by the otters and hens and others of the middle group. Finally, the eagles and jaguars drive the shafts into the enemy, howling triumphantly at each hit (pages 130-31).

After weeks of practice, the Waurá begin a realistic rehearsal for the games. Praguai has stretched a flat layer of cotton over a ring of bark and painted it red. Wedged in his lower

Reaping a slippery harvest, Waurá fishermen flail the surface of a stream with long poles (left). Frightened fish, hidden under the dense cover of water hyacinth, dart into waiting nets held by men in the sterns of the canoes. For many years the Xingu tribes made boats by laboriously peeling large sections of flexible bark from *jatobá* trees and curling them by fire. Now the Waurá own dugout canoes, acquired by trading pottery with dugout-making tribes downriver.

Wealthy Waurá tribesman brings in a net of tasty *matrinchá* fish, a harmless relative of the savage piranha and a favorite food on the Xingu. Takara wears a necklace and three-strand belt of fresh-water clam shells, signs of affluence. Spreading from the end of a long pole, his net pulls shut when fleeing fish hit the palm-fiber mesh. Indians kill fish by biting the backbone and, after grilling, sprinkle them with salt extracted from water-hyacinth ashes.

147

lip, it is an excellent imitation of a Suyá lip disk. He is now chief Pentotí of the Suyá, the "big-lipped Indians." He struts into the square in an exact and amusing impersonation.

Malakiyauá, dressed in his finest fur headband and necklace of jaguar claws, receives his guest with great solemnity. The two chiefs sit on stools in the center of the square. The maneuvers begin.

Two lines of chanting, roaring warriors, stamping the ground with excitement, square off about 100 feet apart. Suddenly the air is filled with whistling, glinting spears unleashed from wooden throwers. The warriors on both sides dodge the missiles and the files close until only a narrow corridor is left between them.

Out steps a single warrior holding only a thick bundle of staves. His opponent, armed with a blunt-tipped spear, advances between the noisy columns. They feint and twist. The man behind the loose shield turns to make himself a difficult target. The enemy throws. With amazing agility the defender leaps aside as the spear whizzes past.

Shields Scorned by Bravest Waurá

Now the roles are reversed, as the attacker becomes the attacked. The enemy seizes a bundle shield and retreats. Again the whir of the long javari spear splits the air, and again it misses the target.

Two new warriors step into position. The attacks and counterattacks continue. So skilled are the combatants that few are hit. When one is, however, a peal of triumph resounds. The "wounded" man is expected to nurse his burning bruise with stoic calm.

Last of all, the birds of prey and great jungle cats step forth without shields of any kind. Standing proud in the sunlight, their skins vivid with color, the bravest of the Waurá offer their nude bodies to the spears of the enemy. They are seldom hit.

Malakiyauá is pleased with his men. In the

morning, swift *pariatus*—messengers painted all in black—are sent to invite the Suyá. But others follow quickly to bring them back. A messenger swifter than any man has entered the village and soon will claim the soul of Kregmá's wife.

Carefully, the women have closed the doors of their houses. The village seems deserted.

Strange flute music resounds from the lake: The jakui, mightiest of spirits, are coming.

A procession of young men and boys, wearing crowns of yellow feathers, crosses the square. They play long flutes (page 140).

Slapstick spirits in straw suits and woven masks demand beiju cakes. With falsetto voices, they threaten cooks with a slashing fish-toothed weapon. The happy horseplay, intended to cadge extra food from hardworking women, occurs daily. In fashioning the masks, representing dangerous water spirits, artisans follow descriptions by sick persons whose shadows were rescued by shamans. After the author bartered for a mask, Waurá friends told him the spirits so resented it they charmed a live fish into the chief's stomach, giving him cramps.

In the dark corner of the chief's house, the dying woman, wasted away to skin and bones, lies in a hammock (page 141). The young men step up close. The flutes fade away. The first one removes his yellow feather crown and places it upon her head, saying, "I offer you this feather crown, mother."

Each of the men repeats this simple ceremony. Then they blow cigar smoke over the sick woman. Sounds of mourning are heard. From everywhere Indians gather. The wailing grows louder as death comes at last.

In front of the mask house, men have dug a round hole. Wrapped in her hammock, the woman is buried with her face toward the east: "So that every day she can see the rising sun." The widower's wailing is heard throughout the village. He repeats the same heartbreaking sounds for many days, until finally they fade away.

Fish Called by Singing Shadows

For weeks now, the water in the lakes and rivers has been steadily falling under a bright sun and cloudless skies. The boats must often be dragged over the sticky clay of exposed

Secret skill of ceramics, known only by the Waurá among Xingu peoples, confers prestige and trading power, but makes them the target of raids by unpacified tribes seeking pottery-making wives. To create a permanent finish, the chief rubs a dye of root juice and charcoal into the huge clay vessel and fires it upside down over burning logs.

Joy of invention absorbs a boy as he constructs an aircraft copied from those he has seen land on the little village airstrip.

Sculptured birds adorn the lake shore. A young Waurá smooths mud "feathers" of an egret built on a skeleton of branches. Clay heron watches as a gull glides on the water.

150

riverbanks. The men no longer fish with mesh nets. Instead, they use woven baskets to capture individual fish in the shallow water. The day comes when not even the superb skill of Vatuku can fill his vine basket. The fish have gone downstream to the last deep pools.

During their evening smoke, the shamans agree that the time has come for the *patápu* ceremony to call the fish back.

In the mask house, the men are chanting as they carve and paint with bright colors the patápus—flat, elliptical wooden shapes representing the souls, or shadows, of fish. Each man makes two, male and female, tying them with long vine cords to slender poles.

Two of the men take their places in the square, while the women retreat inside. Slowly at first, the men swing the poles, whirling the heavy patápus around and around, higher and higher overhead. A deep humming sound grows in intensity until the whole earth seems to vibrate with its rhythm. The deep-throated roaring of the patápus goes on for several days as the men take turns swinging the fish souls through the sky (pages 144-5).

"Now," says Praguai, "the fish will be moving upstream from where the rivers join to form the Xingu. We made the fish shadows and they are singing to the fish to return. Now there will be plenty of fish. There will be plenty of *piquiá* too!"

For a long time no one has talked of any-thing else but piquiá. The succulent yellow fruit and its juice provide a special treat for the Xingu Indians. All year they wait for it to ripen, then move to the groves and spend days on end gorging themselves.

"Piquiá," Malakiyauá says, patting his stomach, "is good!"

Dolls of Death Lure the Unwary

We have gone up the Tamitatoala to gather turtle eggs and hunt ducks.

Smoke rises from somewhere far away in the forest or out in the savanna. Someone is burning a new clearing before the rains come.

"Tshikão!" the Waurá whisper excitedly as they point to the smoke column. Their interest is aroused, but they have no fear.

A few years ago the wild Tshikão Indians from the southwest raided the Waurá village and carried off two children. In retaliation several Waurá men, joined by a group of Kamayurá Indians, paddled upstream and, after a march of a day and a half across the savanna, killed two Tshikão men.

The Suyá, until the Villas Boas brothers pacified them, also preyed on the Waurá.

Along the banks of the Tamitatoala we find nine fire sites and a small carelessly plaited basket containing bits of manioc. A straight path leads far into the savanna.

"Tshikão!" the Waurá whisper again as they eagerly inspect the sleeping places and

Innocence of Eden lights the painted faces of a young Waurá family. Despite the dry season's nighttime cold, the Indians wear no clothing. The Brazilian Government seeks to protect the peoples of the Xingu region and preserve their ancient way of life. Even limited contact with civilization has had a harmful effect upon all the Xingu tribes; an epidemic of measles a few years ago killed many Waurá.

ashes of a campfire left by the wild Indians. Then my friends freeze in their tracks. Seated upon three poles, blocking the path, are crude human figurines made of dried leaves tied together with thin vines.

Each of the dolls holds a tiny bow. In each bow is a tiny arrow aimed at our hearts. The effect of this sign of warning is grotesque, almost frightening.

I walk closer for a better look. But I stop immediately when a loud warning cry sounds out: "Kukoi! No farther!"

The earth opens at my feet. It is a trap! I stand on the brink of a pit. Ten feet below me, the tips of eight large spears are visible in the dark hole. Each one is capped by a point of needle-sharp jaguar bone.

A hideous death awaits the unwary who falls into such a trap. We pull the spears out and place in the pit an arrow pointing straight up. As a present, some feathers used in making arrows are hung over the shaft; I tie a

little steel knife to it—signs of wishing peace.

"If the Tshikão discover us here, they will crush our skulls. They attack before dawn. We must set up a watch."

The night's sleep is broken not by the feared attack but by a torrential downpour. The long dry season has ended. We huddle over a hissing fire until dawn.

Chief Offers a Farewell Gift

As we return, the streams are swelling. In the parched forest, fires ignited by lightning or Indians are going out. Nature is renewing itself. My visit has come to an end.

Malakiyauá says a sad farewell.

"Here, Kukoi, this is for you."

He hands me a simple wooden spatula that he himself has carved. Coming from this good man and his generous people, it is a gift I shall always treasure—a reminder of the dignity, simplicity, and tradition of their ancient way of life.

OUR FIRST NIGHT together in Bolivia, my wife Sue and I slept in a graveyard overlooking the legendary birthplace of the Incas, Lake Titicaca.

We huddled in our car on a hillside, watching the wind blow blossoms from withered wreaths and scatter them among the adobe tombs. Moonlight glittered on the Strait of Tiquina, near the southeastern end of the big lake Bolivia shares with Peru. We had left Peru's capital, Lima, five nights before.

After ten years in Peru, I was on my way to join the U. S. Operations Mission to Bolivia, one of the aid programs now under the Alliance for Progress. Having left our two sons with missionary friends in the Amazon headwater country, my wife and I were now only two hours' drive from La Paz, the Bolivian capital that was to be our new home.

Ferrymen Halt Traffic at Nightfall

But first we had to cross the Strait of Tiquina on a wind-driven ferry. Earlier that evening we had arrived at the lake shore, to find the Aymará Indian ferryboat crew busy hoisting sail. When I asked the helmsman to ferry us, he refused flatly:

"Not after dark, for any price."

Any price? I offered double fare. No. Triple? No. The boat slid away into the night.

Parked on the stone jetty in the bitter cold, we wondered glumly if we should have driven south around the lake instead (map, page 160). But there, too, we might have been caught, for iron gates at both ends of the border bridge slam shut before nightfall.

We were not alone. Hundreds of human shapes lay rolled up in ponchos on the rocky beach. Some of them got up, and soon dozens of staring faces pressed against our windows.

Locking the car, we pushed our way through crowds of muffled figures to a little red hotel on a hill. Its dim halls were packed with travelers. Clearly, there was no room for us.

"Pilgrims," explained the innkeeper. "It is Holy Week, and this is a stopping-off place between La Paz and Copacabana.

"Usually they have prayed for a great favor, like the recovery of a loved one from illness. They promise the Virgin of Copacabana that

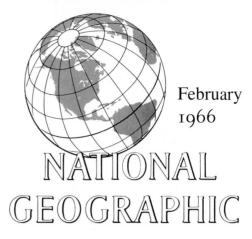

February
1966

NATIONAL GEOGRAPHIC

THE NATIONAL GEOGRAPHIC MAGAZINE VOL. 129, NO. 2
COPYRIGHT © 1966 BY NATIONAL GEOGRAPHIC SOCIETY, WASHINGTON, D. C.
INTERNATIONAL COPYRIGHT SECURED

Flamboyant
is the word for
BOLIVIA

Article and photographs by
LOREN McINTYRE

Derby on her head and doll on her back, an Aymará Indian girl copies her mother. But old customs fade as change sweeps Bolivia. This youngster, who goes to school near La Paz, will be able to vote when she grows up, a right granted women after 1952's revolution.

TELCHROME © N.G.S.

WORLD'S LOFTIEST CAPITAL, La Paz sprawls across
the slopes of a river-gouged canyon 11,900 feet
above sea level. The city's Spanish name—Paz
means "peace"—belies a history of more than 150
uprisings since Bolivian independence in 1825.
Jet runway of El Alto Airport scars the vast

they will walk the hundred miles to her shrine. Here they rest after crossing by the ferry."

Finally we found a pilgrim-free resting place: a hillside graveyard. Sue shuddered. "You didn't warn me it would be this rugged."

"No seas kkaima," I said. "Don't be wishy-washy."

Bolivians use "kkaima," an Indian adjective for tasteless food, to describe weak opinions,

---

The Author: Seattle-born Loren Alexander McIntyre, a 48-year-old officer of the U. S. Agency for International Development, has spent 17 years in South America—as a naval adviser in Peru, as a private film producer, and as an audiovisual expert for the U. S. foreign aid program. For 5½ years he worked and lived in Bolivia, taking his cameras and a scholar's knowledge of Latin American culture to all parts of that sky-high land.

Sail-driven ferries shuttle cars and people across the three-quarter-mile-wide Strait of Tiquina in Lake Titicaca. Deckhands pole the stern-loading craft to and from the landings. Bolivia and Peru share this highest of the world's navigable lakes, at 12,506 feet. The Incas revered Titicaca as sacred, claiming it as their birthplace.

Shopwindow wonders and the velvet lights of La Paz delight a Bolivian of mixed Indian and Spanish blood, who cradles her infant against evening chill.

flaccid politics, and lackluster personality.

In Bolivia, I reminded my wife, very little is kkaima. Flamboyant is the word for Bolivia. Mountains leap sharper and higher, colors are brighter, people tougher, revolutions bloodier. "And visitors sleep in graveyards," Sue added grimly.

At daybreak I shaved in Titicaca's chill water, and then drove our car aboard a ferry. Our crossing was a brisk one, under a wide sail. Soon we were driving into La Paz, highest capital city in the world.

All Ways in La Paz Lead Down

I had seen La Paz many times before. But Sue's first view of the city, sprawling across a canyon 11,900 feet above sea level, took her breath away. Beyond the far side of the canyon towered the triple peaks of Illimani, more than 21,000 feet high.

"It's impossible to get lost in La Paz," I told Sue. "You simply walk downhill. All the city is a funnel, with a single main thoroughfare running out the bottom toward the residential districts in the lower valleys."

I pointed out two boys riding a homemade coaster wagon. "They can coast 12 miles without a stop. They whiz down 2,300 vertical feet so fast it makes their ears pop, to the end of the road in Calacoto, down in the valley to the right. There's where we'll live."

We drove over the canyon rim and snaked down a concrete boulevard in wide, sweeping curves. We inched through a religious procession that wrapped the roadway like a bright scarf. A herd of llamas watched us haughtily. Halfway down, in the middle of the city, the funnel was clogged. The Sunday morning promenade filled the Prado, the main thoroughfare of La Paz.

The institution of the promenade—an occasion for boys to eye girls, and vice versa, while circling a plaza—has become mechanized in La Paz. The young men promenaded

in sedans, jeeps, and pickup trucks, creeping around the Prado.

We lived down in Calacoto five and a half years. With red cliffs and desert-dry air surrounding us, it was like living at the bottom of the Grand Canyon. Our sons used to ride horseback into a primeval wasteland riddled with secret caves—only five minutes from the house.

A block uphill from us, in a rented house, lived the President of the Republic, Hernán Siles Zuazo. When President Víctor Paz Estenssoro succeeded Siles, he lived about four blocks downhill.

Calacoto had neither stores nor offices. They were in La Paz, back up that roller-coaster road.

Trouble Stalks the City of Peace

The city of Nuestra Señora de la Paz, Our Lady of Peace, has seldom lived up to its name since its founding in 1548 by order of Pedro de la Gasca, an envoy to whom the King of Spain had entrusted the rule of the empire seized from the Incas.

Conquistador Francisco Pizarro, his companions-at-arms, and their sons and brothers and heirs had slain one another in senseless civil wars during the 16 years following the conquest. Then they were all gone, the last eliminated by de la Gasca.

Presiding from Lima, de la Gasca marked this moment of peace by founding the new city. He delegated Alonso de Mendoza, a Spanish captain, to find a site. Mendoza became the first "mayor" of the town, a position henceforth granted only by the Spanish monarch and apparently much in demand.

In 1590, a council, acting for the crown, denied the job to Miguel de Cervantes Saavedra, who had yet to write *Don Quixote*. I once heard a Bolivian schoolteacher tell his class that, but for this dastardly denial by the king, the literary classic would have been published in La Paz instead of in Madrid.

Revolts troubled the nearly three centuries of Spanish rule. Hordes of Aymará Indians under Tupac Catari besieged La Paz for six months in 1781, a year when uprisings of latter-day Incas extended from Cusco, Peru, to Tucumán, Argentina.

Pride of heritage draws a capacity crowd to a folk-dancing festival at the national stadium in La Paz. Sponsored by the education ministry, the show featured performers from every part of the nation, rewarding city-dwellers with reminiscences of rural childhood days.

"We want our sea—*Queremos nuestro mar,*" chant parading women of the Seamstresses Union as they carry a 100-foot Bolivian flag past La Paz's Plaza Abaroa. Held each March 23, the procession honors national hero Eduardo Abaroa, who died in 1879 in the War of the Pacific, when Bolivia lost its seacoast to Chile.

Esperanza

Rio Branco

Bom Comércio · Abuná
Rio Negro · Manoa
64°

PRODUCED BY
NATIONAL GEOGRAPHIC SOCIETY ©
CARTOGRAPHIC DIVISION

Chandless

Iaco

Canamari

Villa Bella
Yata
Vila
Murtinho
Yata (Yata)

Railroads   Roads
Places with Scheduled Air Service
Oil Pipe Lines   Dry Salt Lake
Glaciers   Elevations in Feet 21391
Soundings in Fathoms 4360

Mercier · Nacebe
Cachuela Esperanza
Guajará Mirim
Guayaramerín
(Puerto Sucre)

Xapuri
Brasiléia
Bella Flor
Humaitá

Bolpebra
Cobija
Las Piedras
Riberalta
Moreno
Iberia
Iñapari
Porvenir
Puerto Rico
Ivón
Concepción

P A N D O

B R A Z I

0   100   200
STATUTE MILES

Piedras

Filadelfia
San Miguelito

Sena

Serra dos Parecis

Pimenta
Bueno

Puerto Maldonado

Puerto Pardo
Chive
Puerto Heath

San Lorenzo

Bolívar · Fortaleza

984+

Lago de
los Arroyos

Príncipe da Beira

Pedras Negras

Madre de Dios

Manupari

Lago
Rogoaguado
Puerto Siles
Baures

Mateguá

Quince Mil
Marcapata
Ollachea

Astillero

Ixiamas

Lago Pató

Lago
Rogoaguado

San Joaquín

Exaltación
San Ramón

Magdalena

Puerto Villazón
Piso Firme

Puerto Alegre
San Cristóbal
Porvenir

Macusani

San Buenaventura

5984+

Lago
Rogagua

Santa Ana
Lago de San Luis
Huacaraje

Baures

Puerto Saucedo
Huachi

B E N I

Laguna
Concepción
Puerto Frey

Sandia

Asillo
Ayaviri
Putina
Huancané
Cojata

Apolo
Pelechuco

19682+

Reyes
Rurrenabaque

San Borja

Yacuma
Rápulo

San Pedro

Pensamiento
Perseverancia

San Pablo
Ascensión

Cururu

Lampa
Juliaca

Mocomoco
Chuma
Tipuani
Guanay

Mapiri

Santa Ana

San Francisco
San Lorenzo

San Ignacio

Trinidad

San Andrés
Loreto
Limoquije

San Pablo

San Martín

Puno
Ilave
Copacabana

Lago Titicaca
Isla del Sol

Puerto Acosta
Sorata
Illampu

Zongo
Valley
Caranavi

Sécure

Grande

El Puente
Concepción

Ubinas
18480 HWY.

Yunguyo
Guegui
Milluni

Coroico
YUNGAS
Chulumani

BOUNDARY
UNDEFINED

Ichoa

San Javier
San Ignacio

PAN AMERICAN HWY.
17008+

Desaguadero
Tiahuanacu
Viacha

La Paz
21201

Illimani
Inquisivi

Todos
Santos

Chapare

Pto. Villarroel

Grande
Piray

Gral. Saavedra

San Miguel

Mazo Cruz

Moquegua

Calacoto
Comanche

Corocoro
Luribay
Yaco

Independencia
Villa Tunari

B O L I V I A

Buena Vista

Montero

S A N T A

Tarata

Visviri

Umala

Cochabamba
COCHABAMBA

Portachuelo
Warnes

L. Concepción
El Cerro

Volcán Tacora
18646

Charaña

Sicasica
Tomás
Colquiri

Quillacollo
Tarata

Punata
Arani

1291+

Totora
Pojo

Santa Cruz
Cotoca
Paurito

Ser. de
San José

Pachia
Nevado
Sajama
19882

Curahuara
de Carangas
Challacollo
Barrón
Paria

Arque
Capinota

Mizque

Pampa
Grande
Samaipata

Tacna
Puquios

Corque

Oruro

Sacaca
Torotoro

Aiquile

Trigal

Quirusillas
Vallegrande

Arica
Azapa

Turco

El Choro

Challapata
Lallagua
Uncía
Pazña

Poroma

Mojocoya

Pucará

Cabezas

Codpa

Huachacalla

Lago Poopó
Orinoca

Ravelo

Sucre

Villa Serrano

Bañados del Izozog

Cuya
Camiña

Sabaya

Poopó

O R U R O

Huari
Ocurí

Zudañez
Yotala

Padilla
Sopachuy

Gutiérrez

Charagua

Pisagua

L. de Coipasa

Sevaruyo
Tinguipaya
Yocalla

Betanzos

Villa Vaca
Guzmán

Lagunillas

Negreiros
Huara

PAN AMERICAN
HWY. 19669

Salar de
Coipasa

Salinas de
G. Mendoza

Potosí

Puna

San Francisco

Humberstone
Iquique

Llica
Río Mulatos
Porco

Camiri

Pozo Almonte
Anita
Pintados
Victoria

Salar de
Empexa

Salar de
Uyuni

Huanchaca
Uyuni

San Lucas
Vitichi
Toropalca

Cuevo
Boyuibe

Fortín
G. Mendoz

Fortín Coronel
E. Garay

Punta Lobos
Lagunas

P O T O S Í

Villa Martín

Río Grande
Atocha

Camargo
Cotagaita

Villa Abecia

Huacaya
Carandaiti

Puesto Estrella

Salar de Llamara

Quillagua

Oro Ingenio

Villa Montes

Tocopilla
Maria Elena
Vergara

Rica Aventura

Toco

Chiguana

Chuquicamata

Oyahue

Ascotán

Collaguasi

San Lucas
Tupiza

Moraya
Mojo

Villazón

Entre Ríos

Uriondo
Padcaya
Tarija

T A R I J A

Itaú

Cañada Oruro
Santa Victoria
La Esmeralda

Yacuiba
Pocitos

Campo Durán
Ballivián

Pedro de Valdivia
Deseada

Calama

Quetena

Laguna
Colorada

San Pablo
Pan de Azúcar
Santa Catalina

La Quiaca
PAN AMERICAN
HWY.

Puesto del
Marqués
Abra Pampa

Aguaray

D'Orbigny

Ciro Echesortu
Tranquitas

Mejillones
Salinas

Unión

San Pedro
de Atacama

Coranzuli

Cochinoca

Tartagal

Capitán J. Page

Antofagasta

La Chimba

Salar
de Atacama

Toconao

Tilcara

A R G E N T I N A

Humahuaca
Susques

San Ramón
de la Nueva Orán

Pichanal
Hickmann
Morillo

Puerto
Irigoyen

TROPIC OF CAPRICORN

Cobres

Salinas
Grandes

Calilegua
La Estrella

Los Blancos

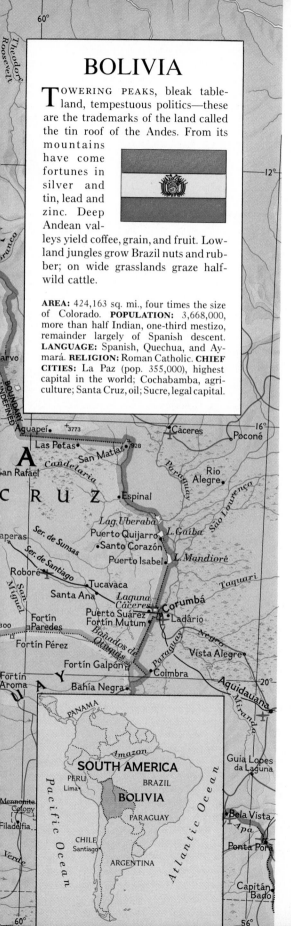

BOLIVIA

Towering peaks, bleak table-land, tempestuous politics—these are the trademarks of the land called the tin roof of the Andes. From its mountains have come fortunes in silver and tin, lead and zinc. Deep Andean valleys yield coffee, grain, and fruit. Lowland jungles grow Brazil nuts and rubber; on wide grasslands graze half-wild cattle.

AREA: 424,163 sq. mi., four times the size of Colorado. **POPULATION:** 3,668,000, more than half Indian, one-third mestizo, remainder largely of Spanish descent. **LANGUAGE:** Spanish, Quechua, and Aymará. **RELIGION:** Roman Catholic. **CHIEF CITIES:** La Paz (pop. 355,000), highest capital in the world; Cochabamba, agriculture; Santa Cruz, oil; Sucre, legal capital.

In 1809, the colonists of Alto (High) Peru, as Bolivia was then called, became the first South Americans to proclaim independence from Spain. They were the last to achieve it, on August 6, 1825.

Simón Bolívar, liberator of northern South America, became the first leader of the country named for him. He resigned a year later, in 1826, and was succeeded by six presidents in the next three years. During the following 126 years, 50-odd men held the top spot. Fifteen of them lasted only days or weeks, tumbled by one or another of more than 150 uprisings in this period. Ten were assassinated.

Browsing through musty records, listening to old scholars, or questioning young students, I reached the conclusion that political conspiracy is part of the fabric of Bolivian life. One phrase I read in an old manuscript said: "Presidents do not know how to step down in time; they have to be shot out of office."

Opposite Palacio Quemado (Burned Palace), often ravaged during its 120-year history, two soldiers stand guard by a lamppost where the mutilated body of President Gualberto Villarroel was strung up by a mob in 1946. Every day, as he enters the palace, the current president sees this reminder.

Revolution Breaks Political Pattern

In 1952 the usual pattern of politics and recurrent palace revolt was shattered in Bolivia by a major social upheaval. Its leader was Víctor Paz Estenssoro.

Before his own sudden ouster in 1964, I called upon President Paz in his office. Land titles lay heaped on his desk. As we talked, he signed them. Beginning a third four-year term, President Paz looked as peaceful as his name, although his personal history has been as turbulent as that of the city of La Paz.

"For ten years we fought the tyranny of tin barons, underground and above ground, in the mines and at the ballot box," he said. "The MNR [National Revolutionary Movement] party did not conspire to make a mere *motín*. Your word is mutiny, a good word to describe what happens in most Latin American countries where they do not make real revolutions. Our goal was to overthrow the entire social order. To win, we had to destroy the army. And we did. Then our MNR government nationalized the three big tin combines and diversified the economy. We decreed universal suffrage and forced agrarian reform."

"Your enemies make many charges, Your Excellency," I pointed out.

"That may be." He picked up a land title. "But no one denies that we gained the dignity

161

of citizenship for more than half the Bolivian people, the Indian farmers who had been serfs for centuries."

In November, 1964, only some seven months after this interview, President Paz was overthrown, victim of a classic motín and of the army, which he had permitted to be rebuilt as a deterrent to Castro-communist insurgency. He fled the country.

The inheritor of the Palacio Quemado was Paz's newly elected vice president, Gen. René Barrientos Ortuño, who three years earlier told a U. S. military observer: "My followers will thrust me into the presidency some day." His non-followers cherished other hopes. The bold young air force general's body bears scars from repeated attempts on his life.

President Barrientos quickly granted voice and action to elements of Bolivian society that had been suppressed by the one-party MNR regime. His supporters looked to him to rescue the nation from revolutionary excesses before complete collapse of the economy. He has concentrated on streamlining the tin-mining industry—heart of Bolivia's economy—and controlling repeated uprisings among the country's tough, discontented miners. In May, 1965, Gen. Alfredo Ovando Candia, commander in chief of the armed forces, joined Barrientos as co-president in an effort to bring order out of the years of chaos.

Gunfire Adds Zing to Political Parade

The sound of gunfire became a familiar experience during our residence in La Paz. I remember its effect on a visiting minister of a new nation who shared the palace balcony with the president one ninth of April, anniversary of the 1952 revolution.

From a palace window above the presidential box, I was photographing the parade of MNR adherents, including miners in yellow raincoats packing loads of dynamite on their backs or strung like leis around their necks.

KODACHROMES © NATIONAL GEOGRAPHIC SOCIETY

Crisply modern, the new Faculty of Medicine building adds to the stature of San Andrés University in La Paz. Indian and mestizo homes cling to the slide-prone slope below the Altiplano and peaks of the Cordillera Real.

Highland tunes set costumed dancers whirling in a La Paz park on Bolivia's Independence Day, August 6. Lampshade hats, embroidered ponchos, and multilayered skirts—*polleras*—bedeck the spirited performers.

Soldiers in Germanic helmets goose-stepped past in review. Behind them limped veterans of the Chaco War, a bloody territorial dispute with Paraguay in the early 1930's which resulted in the loss of more than 50,000 Bolivian lives and most of the Gran Chaco—a sparsely settled scrubland in the southeast.

Then a contingent of MNR youth loosed a few bursts of automatic-weapons fire into the air. Bullets brought down masonry from the cornice above my head. Others felled a 6,600-volt power line, which lashed about in the street like a Chinese dragon, scattering sparks with reports as loud as the gunfire.

Spectators reeled back, the marchers detoured, and somehow everyone escaped electrocution. The president remained imperturbable. But one figure on the balcony had crumpled—the visiting minister.

Moments later I was asked to vacate my window in the palace because a certain foreign dignitary had to be carried into the room.

"Has he been shot?" I asked in alarm.

Heiress of the conquistadors: Ana Taborga de la Quintana, of Spanish descent, attends La Paz's Convent of the Sacred Heart. Although Spaniards in 1624 founded one of the Western Hemisphere's first universities in Sucre, only one Bolivian in three can read.

Morning to evening, La Paz's main boulevard teems with activity fostered by shops, hotels, and crowded sidewalk cafes, such as this at Hotel Copacabana. The broad Avenida 16 de Julio, commonly called "El Prado," honors the date of Bolivia's armed revolt against Spanish rule in 1809.

On Sunday mornings a modernized version of the old-fashioned Spanish promenade circles the tree-lined mall: Girls parade on foot, while ogling young men ride countercurrent in a slow procession of jeeps, trucks, and automobiles.

"Happily not, *caballero*. He has been struck by *sorojche* [altitude sickness]."

Well, it might have been sorojche. I remember when the National Symphony Orchestra of Washington, D. C., performed at the La Paz Municipal Theater in 1959. Howard Mitchell, the director, told me: "Many members felt ghastly that first night. Some of the string instrumentalists would never have lasted the performance without whiffing from portable oxygen tanks. The wind section seemed better adjusted."

Planes Play Tag Below Andean Peaks

I once discussed the hazards of high-altitude take-offs, landings, and parachute jumps with Gen. Javier Cerruto of the Bolivian Air Force. The general suggested, with a twinkle in his eye, that I join a flight of Military Air Transport (TAM) planes to Tipuani.

"Why Tipuani, *mi general?*" Tipuani, 70 air miles north of La Paz, is a jungle village on the other side of the Cordillera Real (map, page 160), where an American mining company dredges for gold. I had no particular desire to go there.

"Well, on the Tipuani flight you will learn very quickly about the agricultural diversification made possible by varieties of climate," said General Cerruto. "You will see all the world's latitudes, from the North Pole to the Equator, in less than four vertical miles."

I planned to forget the offer. But the general declared, "You shall go as soon as the weather clears." Two days later he announced that the moment had come. Three Douglas DC-3's took off, with me in the copilot seat of the lead plane, TAM 06.

We leveled off at 17,000 feet. I knew that snow peak after snow peak towered above our flight path. On better days they thrust above the clouds like a slalom course for Andean deities, but now they lurked in torn vapors through which we raced.

During the next five minutes of blind flying, I wanted to go to Tipuani less than ever. 165

Abruptly we burst into clear afternoon sunshine, followed by the other two DC-3's.

The commander pushed his wheel forward and pointed the plane at the rain forest far below. He shouted in my ear, "Have you ever seen TAM 05?" I shook my head. "Then let me show you." He flew parallel to a high jungle-clad ridge. "There is TAM 05." Strewn all over the crest of the ridge glittered bits of aluminum that had been a DC-3.

"Perhaps now you would like to see TAM 07?" shouted the commander.

"Not this time," I replied. I remembered we were flying TAM 06.

The two other planes now led us toward Tipuani, veering through the steep green valleys like great silver condors. Suddenly the lead plane flipped into a vertical bank to the left and disappeared. Moments later, the second plane followed.

Our turn came. We sank into a canyon between cliffs so close together it seemed the wings could not pass. Then we snapped into a left turn. I caught a fleeting glimpse of a rope suspension bridge over a gorge. We flipped back to horizontal, and there ahead stretched a grassy meadow. But less than a thousand feet of meadow . . . not enough!

We dropped fast, bumped over a hump, and more runway appeared. We braked and could have stopped with plenty of grass to spare, but the commander rolled to the end of the runway. I peered over a precipice to a coffee-and-cream river far below.

"You are perspiring," observed the commander. "It is very hot here in the jungle, no?"

Silver heirlooms arranged in a ceremonial arch welcome worshipers at the door of the centuries-old Church of San Francisco in La Paz. Parishioners beautify the temple with treasured possessions on Corpus Christi and other religious feast days. Beneath the gleaming array, vendors—whose Indian ancestors carved the church's baroque reliefs —unwrap trinkets for sale to churchgoers.

Cliff of death: Five alleged political conspirators, including Chaco War hero Lt. Gen. Demetrio Ramos, were shot and tossed over this awesome precipice in 1944. A cross marks the spot at El Balcón (The Balcony), where the road turns right.

A truck filled with migrants twists toward the valleys of Alto Beni—the upper Beni River area. Since 1954, that fertile region has undergone development through a government-sponsored land-settlement program.

Lacquered in gold by the rising sun, a fleet of new reed boats awaits fishermen on Lake Titicaca.

Tipuani itself was little more than a cluster of grass shacks. Crewmen unloaded the supplies we had brought and put our return cargo aboard: sacks of empty beer bottles destined for refilling at the brewery in La Paz. Within 15 minutes the daily air circus flew off the Tipuani strip the same way it had come in.

The commander piloted me on a short flight to the Yungas, the steep, humid valleys descending eastward from La Paz. Tiny towns brightened the summits of hills like white spume on the crests of gigantic green billows. A tenuous net of roads linked the towns.

Along such roads, bordered by wild orchids, trudge Indian girls so shy they turn their backs on passing vehicles. Narrow terraces on the steep Yungas slopes grow coca plants (page 178), whose dried leaves are chewed by many Andean peoples for narcotic effect.

The pilot put me down at the village of Caranavi, where the government spearheads a massive attempt to resettle highlanders in the fertile tropical lowlands. A road built with U. S. assistance carries migrant farm workers downhill and ripe fruit back up to La Paz. I joined a truckload of farmers to ride up this road, from the Amazon jungle to the roof of the country, in eight hours by night.

Mountain Driving Safer After Dark

It was safer in the dark. The cliff-hanging road is too narrow for vehicles to pass, except on occasional shoulders. By day it can be fatal to meet a truck suddenly coming around a hairpin turn. By night the lights of approaching vehicles at least flash a warning on the canyon walls.

On our right, a river rushed toward the Amazon, wasting its untold energy like a thousand other rivers along the eastern slopes of the Andes. On our left the piercing notes of crickets and other night creatures sounded

From a dark summer squall, a rainbow drops a luminous foot on the western horizon.

from dripping ferns and mosses. Sometimes we passed a candle-lit hut. Our headlights picked up a hitchhiker's beckoning thumb. A flashing smile brought us to a brief halt.

Our new passenger was 14-year-old Teófilo. "Sí, caballero," he told me. "I go to look for work in La Paz. No, caballero, I have never left home before. Sí, caballero, my mother gives permission."

A voice came from among the passengers. "That boy's ancestors were African slaves."

"True," said another. "They came to this valley three centuries ago. My grandfather used to tell of their small kingdom over yonder, and of their last king, Bonifacio."

We climbed until the vegetation thinned, the engine faltered, and jungle-born Teófilo gasped for oxygen. Dense clouds muffled the road, and we could not see the brink. No human lived nearby to note our passing, were we to fall into the forest a mile below.

At the summit, new snow mantled the road. A sign advised that the elevation was nearly 16,000 feet. Minutes later we broke free into a clear, moonless Andean night. We paused in the sterile silence while I helped the driver finish a thermos of coffee. So much of the earth's atmosphere lay below us that the stars shone almost as crisply as if seen from a spaceship.

We rolled swiftly downhill, while Teófilo huddled in a blanket, awaiting but not believing in the spectacle that I told him lay just ahead. Then, suddenly, we rounded a bend and looked down upon La Paz, glittering like a chest of jewels in a pirate's cave. Towering Illimani stood guard in the starlight.

"*Mamitay*—Mother of God," whispered Teófilo. He made the sign of the Cross.

On our journey we had passed hundreds of roadside crosses marking the deaths of earlier travelers. One huge concrete cross stood atop the most awesome cliff of all, The Balcony, near Chuspipata (page 167). The cross bore the date 1944 and five names, not of luckless motorists but of victims of politics.

I learned more about this tragedy on New Year's Day, 1960, when I was returning to La Paz from a seaside holiday at Arica, Chile, where Bolivians have free-port privileges.

Tale Unfolds Aboard "The Smuggler"

On a train nicknamed *"El Contrabandista"* I shared a seat with a small, proud, elderly lady with threadbare clothing, a pasteboard suitcase bound with twine, and a paper bag of lunch.

As the train labored up into the Andean foothills, it lurched and the paper bag spilled its contents. I retrieved an orange for the señora. Soon we were friends.

Most Latin Americans are extremely nationalistic, and I was surprised when she said: "I am sorry to say that I am Bolivian. I live in Santiago, Chile. Like 30,000 of my countrymen, I am an expatriate. I go now to La Paz only because I need money. I have to sell my little house there. That's the only thing in life that matters. Money!" She snapped her fingers derisively.

Hours later, while attendants were offering oxygen, my companion pointed from her window to a distant snow-capped peak. "That looks like a Bolivian mountain."

"No, señora, that is the Volcán Tacora, in Chile. Bolivia lies a little farther on."

A while later she spied grazing llamas and clutched my arm. "There are no llamas in Chile. Now we are in Bolivia!"

"No, señora. But soon. . . ."

At sunset the train slowed at the border village of Charaña. The señora peered at huge scrawls on an adobe wall: "Up with Paz" and "Down with Arce."

"Ah," she said, "now we come to my country."

The train wheezed to a stop. A bugle call sounded. A red-yellow-and-green Bolivian banner sank down a flagstaff for the night. The

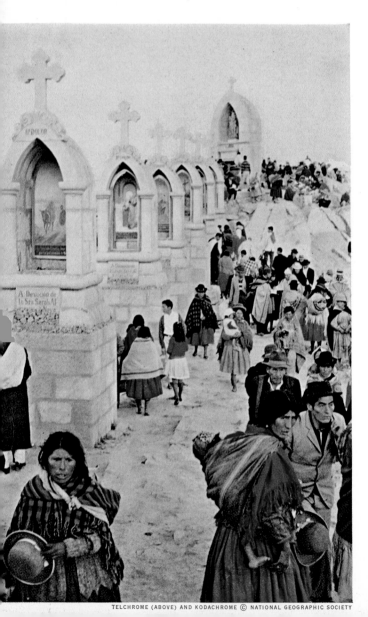

Jam-packed pilgrims, many from foreign lands, crowd Copacabana each year to honor her famous Virgin. A copy of the Virgin's statue rides in procession amidst the noise of firecrackers and the prayers of the pious. The original, carved by the Indian Francisco Yupanqui in 1576, never leaves Copacabana's basilica; tradition forbids its movement lest the waters of Lake Titicaca rise in flood.

A trudge up a hill called Calvario highlights the three-day August fiesta, Bolivia's foremost religious event. Some pilgrims make the climb on their knees, carrying small stones from the bottom as proof of their devotion. They deposit the stones around hilltop shrines that depict the Virgin Mary's seven sorrows.

Illimani's frosted splendor towers over Indian farms on the soil-poor Altiplano, the Andean high plateau. Green plots of beans patch the tawny landscape. Living proves

EKTACHROME BY LOREN McINTYRE © N.G.S.

harsh in this cold, unyielding country, but Altiplano Indians resist leaving their rocky acres for the tropical lowlands, despite the government's promise of an easier life.

señora, suddenly sobbing, pressed her face against my sleeve.

Darkness obscured the arid plains of Charaña. A customs official opened the pasteboard suitcase, shrugged, and went on through the train.

Softly I chided the señora: "Why were you not truthful with me? Why did you say that nothing matters but money?"

She lifted her face. Her eyes flashed.

"You have traveled to the North Yungas, no? And you have seen a great cross at the most fearsome cliff, no? Marking that spot where the circling vultures betrayed an evil secret 15 years ago? And have you read the names on that cross?"

"I have read them, señora, but I do not remember them."

"Then remember one the rest of your life. The name of a hero of the Chaco War. A gentle man, laughing when they took him away, because he knew he was innocent of any conspiracy. They said they were taking him to exile in the jungle. But they stopped by that cliff and shot him with the others. He was my husband, Lieutenant General Demetrio Ramos!"

A few days later, in La Paz, I dialed the number of the Señora de Ramos. An unfamiliar voice answered.

"Ay, but the señora left this life only yesterday. Her heart was tired."

It could have been the altitude.

Two-mile-high Lake Holds Monster Trout

During our years in La Paz, we roamed our flamboyant world from the ski lift at Nevado Chacaltaya (90 minutes from home and 17,536 feet high) to the jungles of the Zongo Valley (two hours' drive beyond the snows and two vertical miles lower). To me, the best place of all was Lake Titicaca.

As a schoolboy in Seattle, Washington, I used to write about imaginary adventures sailing reed boats on Titicaca, the sacred lake of the Incas (pages 168-9). Thirty years later I set sail there in my own 18-foot reed boat, new and golden green. It cost $15.

Within a year my boat turned black with rot. My next craft was a homemade twin-outboard cruiser, which generated only half its 120-horsepower rating at the 12,500-foot elevation, but was nevertheless the fastest craft on the lake.

I explored almost every cove and inlet of this 3,200-square-mile lake, partly for the

Flowery exclamation point, a *Puya raimondii* punctuates an isolated granite height. Only after 150 years of growth does this world's tallest herb, an Andean cousin of the pineapple, shoot skyward from a spiny base.* It dwarfs in age even the largest of Mexico's agaves, popularly called century plants. Atop a ladder, a man plucks one of the 8,000 blossoms on the 30-foot-high spire, which dies even as it blooms.

Rare lifelike head, a pre-Inca Tiahuanacan jar, shows the long nose typical of today's Andean Indians; some anthropologists consider it the mark of a people adapted to breathing the thin, cold air of their lofty land. The five-inch ceramic effigy wears an ornamental plug through its lower lip.

His face a look-alike of his ancestor's portrait in clay, an Aymará Indian squats by remains of a wall at Tiahuanacu. The monoliths were hewn by his forebears, who flourished here from 600 B.C. to A.D. 1200.

joy of adventure and discovery, and partly in search of the big rainbow trout.

In 1959 I found them. During the next three years my boat and its crew won all nine Bolivian sport-fishing trophies. My biggest rainbow weighed 26 pounds. The largest caught by rod and reel in Titicaca, to my knowledge, weighed 34 pounds, and was taken in 1956 by Iowa's Senator Bourke B. Hickenlooper.

Before 1939, only small fish inhabited Titicaca. Then U. S. specialists introduced trout into many Andean lakes and rivers to improve the protein content of highlanders' diets. Titicaca's rainbows throve and grew to sizes equaled only in Pend Oreille Lake, Idaho.

The Isla del Sol—Island of the Sun—rises out of Lake Titicaca like the spine and limbs of a sea monster held motionless by some forgotten enchantment. Legendary birthplace of the Incas and shrine of the earlier Colla peoples, the Island of the Sun bewitched me with its abandoned stone temples, crystal lagoons, white beaches, and lofty cliffs from which one can see across the lake to Peru.

Lake Titicaca has a living monster—or so some highland folk believe. The monster has

*See "Puya, the Pineapple's Andean Ancestor," by Mulford B. Foster, GEOGRAPHIC, October, 1950.

been reported swimming with its nose above water, creating great waves and a frightful noise, leaving lacerated gill nets in its wake.

But it did not come home the night I spent at its supposed lair. The creature has been sighted only on Sunday evenings at twilight. That is when the alcoholic weekend fiestas of the lake-shore people draw to a close.

"Easy" Sightseeing Trip Almost Fatal

South of the lake stretch vast wastelands, remote and risky to traverse by car. I had long wanted to see them the easy way, by air. The day I succeeded, I nearly died.

At El Alto Airport, I engaged a light plane with eight hours' fuel capacity. I asked the pilot to remove the door so that I could take pictures. He complied, with some misgivings, and I strapped myself into the rear seat.

As soon as we were airborne, I knew I was in serious trouble. A 100-mile-an-hour gale tore through the doorway, whipping mercilessly under my parka, stealing my body heat, whirling it out the door and into the Andean sky. By the time we leveled off at 18,000 feet,

with no oxygen bottle and the temperature below zero, I was almost insensible from the cold. Yet I had seven hours of flying ahead, unless I chose to abandon the long-awaited flight. Up front, the pilot was more protected from the frigid blast.

We followed the railroad tracks across the Altiplano from La Paz to the mining and railroad center of Oruro. Thousands of flamingos rose from the marshes, scattering coral reflections like Oriental fireworks.

I envied the pilot in his many layers of clothing, although he too was shivering. We flew over Challacollo, an adobe Venice, whose children fish from their doorsteps with conical nets. Their elders pole reed boats along flooded streets leading to fields of *quinoa*. This nourishing grain, with potatoes (native to the Andes), forms a staple of the highland diet.

We crossed the Desaguadero (Drainage) River, which carries the overflow from Lake Titicaca 200 miles southeast across the flatlands to Lake Poopó, where much of it evaporates. Over Lake Coipasa we looked down upon 200 square miles of saturated brine in a

Plumed headdresses of flamingo and rhea feathers nod above a band at an Altiplano festival. A trumpeter signals dancers with a blast on the *pututu*, a bull's horn at the end of a hollow cane. In bygone days, Indians blew pottery pututus from summits to rally warriors. Other musicians play reed panpipes called *sicuris*, Indian instruments since pre-Columbian times. Unlike lowlanders, whose festive songs shimmer with fiery Spanish rhythms, these highlanders keep cadence with an austere beat.

Black-braided grape peddler weighs her wares at Tarija, a town near the Argentine border. Her wide-brimmed derby, like other regional hats, takes shape from soaked wool, pounded to a cardboard texture and starched.

Vegetable vendor binds her child in a woven *cinturón*, a decorative belt. She tends her curbside grocery in the colonial city of Sucre, still Bolivia's legal capital.

Shy sloe-eyed bride wears wedding-gift money pinned to her shawl by guests, an Altiplano custom. Of sturdy Aymará stock, she walked 20 miles with her husband to her new mountain home.

EKTACHROME (BELOW) AND KODACHROMES © N.G.S.

salt flat seven times larger. Nearly 9,000 square miles of salt deposits occupy this end of the Altiplano. The largest, the Salar de Uyuni, glistened ahead. I was glad to be flying above Uyuni and not adding my brine-bleached skeleton to those of lost travelers.

We might have been flying over Antarctica, it was that cold. By the time we turned for home, I could feel consciousness slipping away. Although I didn't quite pass out, they had to carry me from the plane after six hours aloft. A doctor took my temperature.

"Only four degrees Centigrade below normal," he said—92° Fahrenheit. An hour in a hot tub fixed that.

My icy ride was a minor ordeal compared to the adventures of Portuguese explorer Aleixo Garcia, believed to have reached Bolivia in the early 1520's. Marooned on the coast of Brazil, he recruited hundreds of In-

dian followers as he pushed west across an unknown continent a decade before the Spaniards rode up the Inca road from Peru.

Garcia's expedition was comparable to a trek across North America from Cape Cod to the Rockies, and occurred a century before the Pilgrims landed at Plymouth Rock.

The barrier of the Andes and the Inca warriors turned the Portuguese adventurer back just short of fabulous riches and a place in history. It was the Spaniards who won the golden goblets and silver mountains.

Llamas Grace Bolivia's Highlands

In 1964 I made a long swing around the country with a young Bolivian named Napoleón Vilela. Near Oruro and the big tin mines, despite the huge increase in truck traffic over roads improved through U. S. assistance, we saw pack llamas everywhere—

Indigo-shadowed valleys, the Yungas enfold terraces of coca. Mother and daughter fill their aprons with the pain-killing leaves, revered for centuries by highlanders who recognized their narcotic properties. Used in manufacture of cocaine, the dried herb when chewed can dull the pangs of cold and hunger or quiet a crying baby. A dampened wad stuck to the forehead cures a headache, Indians believe. Attributing sacred powers to the plant, superstitious Aymarás offer it in a ritual to mountain deities.

Spinning yarn as she walks, a bare-foot Aymará twirls magenta-dyed wool around a spindle. Years before the Spanish conquistadors overran Bolivia in the 16th century, Indians wove colorful textiles from the wool of alpacas and llamas. Today's highlanders, like their ancestors, wear garments made from yarn produced while sitting in the market, tending flocks, or even dancing. Many multicolored Andean creations now reach stores in the United States.

Across the valley cling white-roofed houses near Sorata, where in 1780 leaders of 100,000 Aymarás vowed to exterminate the Spaniards. After damming mountain rivers, they released backed-up waters that swept away the town and thousands of its inhabitants.

KODACHROME © NATIONAL GEOGRAPHIC SOCIETY

stately in stance, regal in coats of grays or tans or crazy-quilt hues (pages 184-5).

In a meadow by the highway, we watched a pure white llama being born. He got up and teetered proudly on soft hoofs. A shepherd came to kill him for his pelt. Quickly I asked, "What price will the pelt bring?"

"White pelts make choice quilts. Sixty thousand bolivianos." Five dollars. We lifted him into the jeep, and I sewed a strand of colored yarn into his ear to mark him mine, as the peasants do. At the next village, I bought a nursing bottle and a can of evaporated milk. But my llama would drink only while standing up. We stopped driving. When we started again, he got carsick.

We saw a little boy crying by the roadside. His kite had caught in a telegraph wire. He stopped crying when I gave him my llama.

I've often read that llamas spit at people. I have never seen one do so. But I have seen herdsmen spit at llamas. As we neared Colquiri, a mining town north of Oruro, 20 runaway llamas came galloping into a village. An Indian stopped them in their tracks by standing in their way and spitting furiously at them.

The llamas were loaded with *ttola,* an aromatic shrub used as domestic fuel. The springy ttola has another use. When a tire went flat, a truck driver showed us how to stuff it with ttola. It carried us comfortably into Colquiri.

Tin-mine Tío Bedevils Picture-takers

Minerals, principally tin, account for 94 percent in value of Bolivia's exports. To see how men wrest the ore from deep inside mountains, I followed an engineer more than a mile into the main tunnel at Colquiri.

Several miners said Tío would spoil any pictures I made inside the mine. Tío is an

LIFEBLOOD OF BOLIVIA, *tin ore flows by narrow-gauge railroad from deep galleries within snow-shrouded Huayna Potosí to the refinery at Milluni (foreground). The metal, which brings in three-quarters of the nation's foreign exchange, stains the valley orange where tailings have been dumped and imparts a metallic taste to lake water that helps supply La Paz, ten miles away.*

idol, the painted image of a mischievous devil, seated in a niche in one of the mine galleries. As we walked, the temperature soared.

"The miners spend a great deal of their lives, besides working time, in the mine," the engineer told me. "They cook here, eat, conduct meetings, and set aside one day of each work week for recreation." "Recreation" in the mine, I learned, amounted to drinking astonishing quantities of fiery *aguardiente*—raw cane alcohol.

In a cloudy cavern hotter than a steam bath, shaken with unnerving noise, we found Pedro Salas and Juan Condori, clad in breechclouts, attacking the tin lode with a compressed-air drill.

With sweat streaming into my eyes and down my back, I set up my camera. Then I realized that Tío was up to his tricks. Humid air was condensing on the cold lenses. Water ran off in trickles. Wiping was useless until the camera warmed up. Previous photographers must have tried to take pictures with lenses clouded or film streaked with moisture. I thwarted Tío's "ghosts" by cooking my camera and lenses under floodlamps until they were warm and dry.

Miner's Redoubt: His "Skyscraper" Home

Pedro Salas invited me to share dinner with his family in Rascacielos (Skyscraper) No. 547, his house high on the mountain above the mine. Pedro's wife rose from her treadle sewing machine to greet me. His Quechua mother was busy in the kitchen, a small sooty alcove. His daughter put away her primer and stood at attention with her baby brother.

Pedro removed his home-study books on automotive engineering from the table to make room for supper. He offered me his only chair.

Adobe walls were papered with pages from a magazine story about a sick boy in the slums of Rio de Janeiro. "My wife and I are very sorry for this boy," said Pedro. "We tried to send him some money."

Supper was mostly rice. Afterward, Pedro played the guitar, talked about politics and child rearing, and questioned me about opportunities for work, both in his country and in mine.

I slept at Colquiri in a sleeping bag at Pedro Salas's home. More than a home, the single room at No. 547 was Pedro's redoubt. His troops were his wife and the boy and girl. His secret weapon was faith in the individual's ability to make his own future. His flag was hope.

Few miners have a redoubt like Pedro's. Some seek substitutes in alcohol and coca. Most have learned they now have a voice in national affairs. Sometimes they try to magnify their voice with Mausers and dynamite. The men who mine tin are the most combustible element of Bolivian society.

Stair-step eyries climb a mountainside at Colquiri, where families of tin miners cook, eat, and sleep in one-room homes, roofed with corrugated-iron sheets. Adobe bricks wall off front-yard garden plots and play areas for children.

Bundled against cold and damp, miners at Milluni pierce a vein of tin ore beneath a glacier. Raincoats shed water used to control dust as the pneumatic drill hammers and bores into solid rock. In hotter and deeper mines, drillers wear only breechclouts.

Nationalization of major mines in 1952 provided benefits for the miners: low-cost commissaries, medical aid, and a shorter work week. But production declined because of politically inspired work stoppages, inexperienced management, and rundown equipment—problems the present government strives to solve.

After Colquiri, Napoleón and I headed for Potosí, where mining in the New World began in April, 1545. Along the shore of Lake Poopó, we passed mine after deserted mine.

Each dilapidated processing plant was marked by steel towers that carried high cables from abandoned borings in the distant mountains. When the industry was nationalized after the 1952 revolution, many mines shut down abruptly and remain closed today.

Rusty buckets still swung from aerial cables. I climbed a tower to try to photograph some of the buckets with the ramshackle buildings in the background. All the buckets were full of ore, left there when the last crew walked away years before!

Long hours from Poopó, beyond the crumbling arches of Romanesque aqueducts built by 16th-century Basque engineers who settled in Potosí, we sighted the cone-shaped mountain that has yielded nearly two billion dollars' worth of silver (page 189). After the precious artifacts of the Incas and Aztecs had been melted down to finance the rise of Spanish power, this was where the subsoil of the New World was first and most massively exploited, to catapult the kings of Castile into pre-eminence among Europe's monarchs.

Art Survives in Remote Mining City

We drove into a city little changed from the age when it was the largest and richest in the New World. Potosí, highest and one of the most remote cities ever populated by Western man, has few equals as a repository of Spanish colonial art and architecture.

Little or nothing remains of the old city's eight fencing schools and 36 gaming houses. But we stood on balconies and walked across ballrooms where, in 1616, the year Shakespeare and Cervantes died, the ladies of Potosí danced at 13,600 feet altitude. They wore silks from Cathay and pearls from Isla de Margarita, off Venezuela. Meanwhile, inside the mountain chambers, unnumbered Indians worked, died, and were buried.

When adjacent populations became depleted, miners were conscripted by a Spanish adaptation of the *mita,* a system the Incas had used to resettle huge numbers of their conquered peoples. Records show that caravans of as many as 2,500 conscripts, with 5,000 members of their families and 30,000 animals, were sent yearly to Potosí from Peruvian towns as far away as 400 miles. How many completed their period of service and returned? The records do not say.

Even with conscript labor, it took 20 years to construct the Casa de Moneda, which was the mint, the prison, the Bastille of Potosí. A massive building occupying a city block, the Casa de Moneda now houses the finest museum in Bolivia. Director Don Armando Alba opened its doors with a huge ring of keys.

"The four great wooden machines which rolled silver bars into long strips are still in working condition," he declared. "Only we no longer keep convicts in our dungeons to turn the shafts of the presses and to strike coins from the silver strips."

Since the exciting days of three centuries ago, the population of Potosí has fallen from 150,000 to one-third that number. The rustle

Nuzzling her newborn calf, a mother llama welcomes it into a world of toil. Llamas provide highlanders with wool, milk, meat, and transport. Ancient Andean peoples domesticated this cousin of the camel.

Pack train of llamas, loaded with dung for fuel, picks its way across the crumpled, treeless highlands. Bearing an equal burden, the herder hisses commands to his sole companions on the trek. Such caravans also freight grain, tin ore, and blocks of rock salt.

KODACHROME (ABOVE) AND TELCHROME © N.G.S.

of silk is gone, but the glottal chatter of the woolen-shawled women in the marketplace goes on as before. The silver lodes are exhausted, and now the smell of sulphur from processed tin ore pervades the streets.

The mountain is almost all hollowed out. Its entrails clog the valleys. Indian women sift through them ceaselessly, seeking chunks of tin ore. There is no money today to keep up the buildings and repair the furniture left behind when the conquerors went home to Spain. Rain splashes through the rotting roofs of churches and dribbles over huge sooty paintings hanging awry on the adobe walls.

Asian Immigrants Find a Good Life

Following a side trip to the red-roofed city of Sucre, we drove south to Tarija, a miniature of old Spain near the Argentine border. Then we turned north to follow the trans-Andean pipeline through oilfields marking the easternmost spurs of the Andes.

After two weeks of travel on dirt and gravel, we finally reached the only paved highway in Bolivia, which runs 300 miles between Cochabamba and Santa Cruz and then 40 miles north to Montero (map, page 160). But only minutes later we rolled off the pavement into an incredible quagmire of city streets.

This was Santa Cruz, a booming center of oil-field development, sugar mills, cotton farms worked by migrants from the highlands, and rice plantations cultivated by Japanese and Okinawans. Gradually these agricultural enterprises are swinging the national economy from importation to exportation of such staples as sugar and rice.

Massive castlelike buttresses anchor a suspension bridge across the Pilcomayo River between Sucre and Potosí. Nearly empty truck rolls over the one-lane wooden roadway; a light pickup will shuttle the truck's cargo across to avoid overloading the old bridge. In astonishing feats of engineering, the Incas likewise once conquered major river barriers with suspension spans.

For an instant at sunset, Potosí—a city that silver built—seems to regain its long-vanished grandeur. In 1545 the Spanish began mining Cerro Potosí, beyond the end of the street; it came to be known as Cerro Rico, the Hill of Riches. Before its lode ran out, it yielded an estimated two billion dollars in bullion and transformed a treeless mountainside into the largest and wealthiest city in the New World.

Most of Santa Cruz's people are descendants of Spaniards who arrived half a century before the first Englishmen settled in North America. Among more recent immigrants we found Ng Pak See, from Communist China. He had been spirited out through Hong Kong in 1963 by the World Council of Churches, which has settled many refugees in Bolivia.

Mr. Ng, patriarch of a four-family colony composed of his sons and their wives and children, served us a lunch of chicken, eggs, and rice while telling us of his new life.

"What good fortune touched us, out of millions of people!" exclaimed Mr. Ng. "Here we have all the land we can manage, with grapefruit and corn and oranges and rice and pigs and chickens. And we have freedom!"

I met only one settler who wanted to go back home, a Spaniard who tried unsuccessfully to sell me his 21-acre farm, complete with tomatoes ready to harvest, for $1,500.

Aid Program Transforms an Economy

Santa Cruz's prosperity illustrates the high rate of return that comes of a well-invested Yankee dollar. Under the United States Point Four aid program, the impact of more than 300 projects in one area over a ten-year period has completely transformed the economy.

A tale of one project, livestock improvement, was given world-wide publicity by critics of the U. S. foreign aid program. It seems a prize Texas bull was flown to Santa Cruz at a cost of several thousand dollars to better the breed of local cattle. But shortly after its arrival, the bull was barbecued by the Bolivians, who held a fiesta to thank the United States for this fine gift.

The fact is that the Point Four livestock specialists authorized slaughtering the bull because it had tried to hurdle a barbed-wire fence and was permanently incapacitated.

To get from Santa Cruz to Puerto Suárez, where the easternmost bulge of Bolivia meets Brazil, Napoleón and I considered a quick, $20 flight on Bolivia's national airline, Lloyd Aéreo Boliviano. But a four-day, $4 train trip suggested greater possibilities for adventure.

Our third-class accommodation was a few square feet of an open flatcar, where we rigged an awning against sun and rain. It was preferable to second class, the gloomy interior of a stifling boxcar. For two dollars more, we might have traveled first class—a wooden seat in the one wooden coach.

The train started like the fall of a stick of bombs, the bursts beginning in the distance, bracketing each car in turn, right up to the inevitable detonation under our seats. It braked with a shudder, hesitated, started again with a neck-snapping jerk, gathered steam to crack the whip around the next turn, lurched along the straightaways, wrenched to a stop once more, then simmered on sidings for hours while the engine crew hunted for firewood. We became grateful for these delays, the only time sleep was possible.

Most of our fellow passengers were *comerciantes,* small merchants on their way across the continent by rail with suitcases of Bolivian curios for sale in São Paulo, Brazil.

"We should have come fourth class," said Napoleón. "I met some nice people up there."

"You're joking. Where?"

"On *top* of the boxcars."

I tried it. The footing was tricky but the scenery was better, and the roof was uncluttered by women, children, domestic animals, baggage, and the inevitable types bound for Brazil to escape arrest.

Cowboys Populate South America's Heart

Finally we reached Puerto Suárez—in five days, not four. Here we were close to the geographical center of South America and, at 440 feet, nearly at Bolivia's lowest elevation.

A port? I saw only a dusty frontier town, bleached under the sun, not dead but apparently moribund. I had the feeling that any moment a stagecoach might come careering up to the hotel; an eastern lady, gathering her skirts fastidiously in a gloved hand, would be helped down by a dude; and a gunman would come busting out of a bar.

Cowboys we found, tough hombres, but they were up to their necks in flowers. They were swimming their horses deep into a profusion of water hyacinths, rounding up their herds of zebu cattle.

My map said Puerto Suárez was a port on sizable Lake Cáceres, with access to the sea via the Paraguay and Paraná Rivers. But

Onetime El Dorado of silver, Potosí's Hill of Riches looms over the city it spawned and the cemetery it filled with those who extracted its wealth. Today miners work tin veins that still thread the mountain; women sift the tailings in search of ore.

Grinning Bacchus, god of wine, watches over a courtyard of Potosí's Casa de Moneda. In this "House of Money," now a museum, colonials minted gold and silver coins for the Spanish Empire. Coinmakers in Madrid sent "samplers" to the New World to illustrate the coin markings of Spain. The model above, with a 1770 Madrid mint mark, shows alphabet, numbers, and symbols around a Spanish crown. Potosí minters transferred letters and designs to their own coin dies. After nearly 400 years the mint stopped work in 1951, when paper money replaced the last of the hard currency.

EKTACHROME (OPPOSITE, LOWER) BY ROBERT F. SISSON; KODACHRO

the decayed dock now led only to a vast meadow where cattle grazed belly-deep in the mud. The lake had all but dried up; its channel was choked with water hyacinths.

We soon learned that the streets were quiet because all the activity was indoors. And when we found out what was going on inside, we began to understand why illiteracy, so commonplace in the highlands, is rare in many Bolivian lowland communities.

All the children and many adults were in school. Their drive for learning derives from generations of missionary schooling.

Bomber Becomes Flying "Meat Wagon"

We flew back along the edge of the great rain forest stretching 2,000 miles from the Andes to the Brazilian coastline. Our plane touched down at some of the oases in that green desert, towns with names like Concepción or Ascensión, bestowed centuries ago by the Jesuit founders. In them dwell white descendants of the early Spaniards, many with daughters so pretty that it has long been the custom for gentlemen from the highlands of Bolivia to look for wives there.

We saw cargo planes bring in cabinet ministers and missionaries, barbed wire and beer, nylons and cement. In San Ignacio they had unloaded a bullet-riddled command car that once served Rommel's Afrika Korps and is now an ambulance driven by an Austrian nun.

Napoleón and I traveled to Bolivia's north-central savanna, in the Beni region, in an empty "meat wagon," a converted B-17 bomber used to fly beef to Altiplano markets.

For 100 miles the pilot hedgehopped at 200 feet. We flushed rheas—South American ostriches—deer, and a jaguar roused from its siesta. Occasionally we stampeded cattle.

"There's a lot of cattle rustling in the Beni," said Napoleón. That was understandable. We saw no fences, nor any human beings.

"The only way to find a ranch is to follow the wagon tracks," explained our pilot. Changing course, we followed two parallel ruts nearly 30 miles before we flashed over a grove of trees and a ranch house.

Go east, young man! And Bolivians do, east of the Andes, where lies 70 percent of the nation's land. Here, as in the American West, pioneers find a future in cattle raising, in planting cotton, sugar, rice, and citrus fruits. These vaqueros (left) herd zebu and *criollo* cattle near the eastern border town of Puerto Suárez. In the north-central Beni region, boundless grasslands could feed 25 million head.

Cotton-picking migrant, a mestizo from Cochabamba, labors on a wide-spreading plantation near Santa Cruz.

Ball of latex from the far-northern jungle cures over a smoky fire. Bolivia profited from rubber in the early 1900's, but no longer ranks as an important producer.

Fangs bared, glass eyes glaring, a devil dancer personifying evil flails his arms in a threat to good during the Diablada, Oruro's annual pageant. Silver coins on his girdle jingle to the blare of a brass band. Catholic priests nearly 200 years ago introduced the morality play to converts, whose descendants continue to make costumes and choreography more elaborate. Lucifer emerges from a mineshaft at midnight. He meets the archangel Michael, who battles seven devils, the deadly sins, into submission. Master craftsman Trifón Quiroga (below) paints a dragon face on a devil mask.

KODACHROMES BY LOREN McINTYRE © N.G.S.

North of the grasslands lies more jungle, merging into Brazil, threaded with broad rivers like the Beni. Life along the rivers is much like that along the Mississippi a hundred years ago—perhaps easier, because the waters and the woods provide abundant natural foods, as well as cash crops such as rubber (preceding page), quinine bark, and Brazil nuts.

Rivers Patrolled by "Fluvial Fleet"

In the port of Riberalta, on the northern reaches of the Beni River, I learned that the United States Army has recently helped give birth to a Bolivian river-and-lake force. Gutemberg Barroso, a Bolivian army major, told me, "I will soon command our 'fluvial fleet,' the boats your army has supplied to patrol the jungle against Cuban-inspired guerrillas. My commission is being changed, and soon I'll be on my way to study at the Peruvian naval academy on the Pacific coast near Lima."

When I replied that I had once taught gunnery there, he fired eager questions about blue water and tall ships. For the commander of Bolivia's navy had yet to behold the sea.

As in the eastern lowlands, most of the children of the northern Bolivian jungle communities were in school. Except for isolated and extremely primitive Indian tribes, there seemed to be little illiteracy. But up in the highlands, three-fourths of the adults remain illiterate. Like Ignacio.

When Sue and I rented our home in Bolivia, an Aymará Indian boy came with the house. Ignacio had no schooling and could not write his own name. In atrocious Spanish he said he was 19, and waved a tattered pink card. "My army discharge," he explained.

My elder son offered to teach him to read and write. Ignacio showed no interest. He would sit for hours in the kitchen, when his work was finished,

with a kitten or a puppy in his arms. Sue and I became, in a sense, his foster parents.

One day in 1962, several years later, my son asked Ignacio when he expected to marry. "Not yet. I'm only 19—too young for girls." What's more, observed Ignacio, getting married required "papers."

Still 19? I asked again to see his documents. He produced only the pink card. "Does it not say I am 19?" It did, but it was dated 1954.

No Identity Card, No Identity

Without an identification card, Ignacio could not seek formal employment. He could not stay at hotels. He could not vote or marry. His freedom of movement and choice was completely circumscribed by society's demand that he have paper proof of his existence as a human being.

I ventured the first step of a bureaucratic minuet. First, Ignacio would need a birth certificate. At a tiny municipal court, a judge helped me—as he had legally helped thousands before me—to invent the birth of a child in a certain Altiplano town, to such-and-such parents. We dated it August 6, 1935.

To obtain the ID card which all Bolivian males should carry, Ignacio would also need a military service record. With his tattered pink card, I applied to army headquarters.

"I'm sorry," said the clerk. "This is a week-end pass."

Ignacio had been given the card one day in 1954 and told he could "go home." He had never returned; unknowingly, he had deserted.

So I paid a fine, and Ignacio re-enlisted under his new surname. A week later, I paid a mustering-out fee to buy him out of the service. However, when Ignacio went to pick up his discharge papers, he stood in the wrong line and unwittingly re-enlisted for a two-year hitch. I paid again.

On August 6, 1962, Bolivia's Independence Day, we gave Ignacio his first birthday party, with 27 candles on the cake.

The next day he strutted a bit as he chatted with the door-to-door fruit vendor.

"Do not doubt my age," said Ignacio. "I have papers to prove it."

"Ay... and how old are you?"

"Nineteen!"   THE END

Smiling with love, a Quechua mother in Potosí finds pleasure in the nearness of her baby, strapped to her back in a shawl. For such little ones Bolivia struggles to improve its economy, establish schools, and raise standards of health.

St. Augustine, Nation's

THUNDER FROM THE PAST:
*Spanish cannon "La Sibila"—
the fortuneteller—fires atop
Castillo de San Marcos, a 17th-
century citadel administered
by the National Park Service.
Surviving the plagues of war
and famine, this Florida city,
oldest European settlement
in the United States, welcomes
the world to its year-long
fourth centennial.*

KODACHROME BY NATIONAL GEOGRAPHIC
PHOTOGRAPHER ALBERT MOLDVAY © N.G.S.

Oldest City, Turns 400

By ROBERT L. CONLY

Assistant Editor

ALL YOU NEED is an ounce of imagination and half an ounce of luck. Armed with these, stroll at dusk or dawn to St. Augustine's waterfront. Choose one of the quiet streets, arched by ancient live oaks and Spanish moss. Then sit down where you can look out over the gentle blue harbor and watch the birth of the oldest city in the United States.

Off to the right the massive gray bulk of the Castillo de San Marcos broods over the town and the waters it has guarded since the 1670's. But for the moment we must pretend it does not exist, for the event we are about to see took place much earlier, and in those days the oaks and the cedars grew right down to the waterfront.

Galleons Anchor Outside the Bar

As you look out across the bay, you will see dimly, through the half-light, the white breakers where the Atlantic Ocean pours through a narrow inlet into the bay. And, if you are lucky, you

"With many banners spread, to the sound of trumpets and salutes of artillery," the Spaniards dedicate St. Augustine on September 8, 1565, as their chaplain recorded. One of Spain's foremost admirals, Pedro Menéndez de Avilés, kneels to kiss the Cross and possess the land in the name of King Philip II. "A large number of Indians watched these proceedings and imitated all they saw done," wrote the priest. "All the captains took the oath of allegiance to him [Menéndez] as their general and governor." A French fortification on Florida's St. Johns River spurred Spain to plant a colony in the land claimed 52 years earlier by Juan Ponce de León. St. Augustine became capital and chief stronghold of Spanish Florida.

Specially commissioned by NATIONAL GEOGRAPHIC, the paintings accompanying this article bring to life St. Augustine's early history. The city's 400th-anniversary celebration extends to September, 1966.

will glimpse, as I did one evening, the lights of a boat coming through this inlet, bobbing, disappearing, reappearing as it rides the rollers that carry it over the shallow bar.

Now imagine that these are not the electric lights of a modern boat. They are ship's lanterns shining 400 years in the past, on September 6, 1565. The ships—there are three of them, and two more out of sight beyond the inlet, galleons too big to cross the bar— are loaded with Spanish soldiers. They have been two months at sea, dispatched by King Philip II of Spain to occupy La Florida and drive out an impudent band of French Huguenots who have settled there. For Florida is, by Papal decree, Spanish territory.

The men wear steel helmets, breastplates, and chain mail, and they are armed with arquebuses, steel-tipped pikes, and swords. The shore they approach is crowded with Indians who have also seen the lights come through the inlet. The Spaniards are not worried about the Indians. Their real peril is approaching from behind them—and not far behind, either.

The Spaniards beach their boats and disembark, led by two captains. The chief who approaches them, a tall Indian named Seloy, is friendly and turns over to the visitors a large house near the waterfront.

Now the Spanish soldiers, on orders of their captains, spring into a frenzy of activity. They have perhaps a day or two—they hope! —to fortify the house against a French attack they know is coming. For they have found the Huguenots, and learned to their dismay that the French colony, only a few miles away, has a strong fort already built, more soldiers than they do, more and better ships, more arms.

This Spanish landing was the beginning of St. Augustine, and in a very real sense the start of the first chapter of the Nation's history. The city, now celebrating its 400th anniversary, was founded in haste and fear in three days—September 6 to 8, 1565. This was 42 years before Jamestown and 55 years before the Pilgrims reached Plymouth. Thus St. Augustine is easily the oldest surviving European settlement in the United States.

When I visited the city, I found that it was, in a commercial sort of way, very much aware of its antiquity. As I drove in, a maze of advertisements urged me not to miss the Old Jail ("authentic, educational"), the Old Sugar Mill, the Museum of Yesterday's Toys, and the Oldest Wooden Schoolhouse, to mention just a few. During my stay my shirts were washed with modern efficiency by the Ancient City Laundry & Dry Cleaners, and on the radio a singing commercial advertised "the Oldest Bank in the Oldest City."

In the middle of all this decrepitude it is amusing to find, of all things, the Fountain of

proach to St. Augustine ugly, and, I suspect, encourage many travelers to speed on rather than to stop.

And that is a sad thing, for St. Augustine, if you stay awhile, will tell you its own story, one of the most important and dramatic in the history of the New World. I have seen no other place in the United States where history is so visible and touchable.

There are several ways to get a quick survey of the city and a capsule of its history. One is to visit the Oldest House, a handsome restored Spanish dwelling maintained as a museum by the local historical society. Anoth-

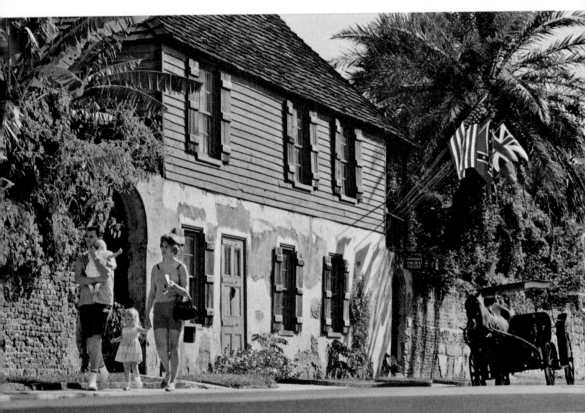

KODACHROME BY ALBERT MOLDVAY © N.G.S.

Youth, where—who can prove otherwise?—Juan Ponce de León may have paused on his exploration of Florida in 1513, more than half a century before the founding of St. Augustine. Here any visitor can get a lecture tour and a paper cup of spring water (from a well, not a fountain) for a mere $1.00. Long ago there was a rival Fountain of Youth on the other side of town, but it closed down for lack of business.

All this is a surface phenomenon, mainly aimed at prying a dollar or two out of the one-day tourist. And who can criticize that? Well, I can. Garish billboards make the ap-

er is to take a short tour—by boat, by small rubber-tired train, or by horse and carriage—each with a guide who gives you his own story of St. Augustine.

Traditionally, the most lurid accounts are given by the carriage drivers, mostly elderly Negroes in derby or top hat. Their red-and-yellow buggies sparkle in the sun; their horses are tasseled. I took one of these. The driver said his name was Major; he had been driving a carriage since 1910. No, he had never been in any army—Major was his Christian name. His mare was named Jezebel. He flicked her reins, and off we went.

KODACHROMES BY NATIONAL GEOGRAPHIC PHOTOGRAPHERS ALBERT MOLDVAY (ABOVE) AND WINFIELD PARKS © N.G.S.

Four flags that have flown over St. Augustine—Spanish, British, Confederate, and United States—flutter from the city's Oldest House, which dates from the 1720's. Hand-hewn beams support low ceilings of the venerable structure.

Page from the past, a worm-eaten document lists one of the earliest recorded weddings in the United States: Vincent Solana to Maria Viscente, July 4, 1594. Some 20 Solana families still live in the city. Father Michael V. Gannon, director of the Mission of Nombre de Dios, examines the entry in the parish register, oldest surviving U. S. record of baptisms, marriages, and burials.

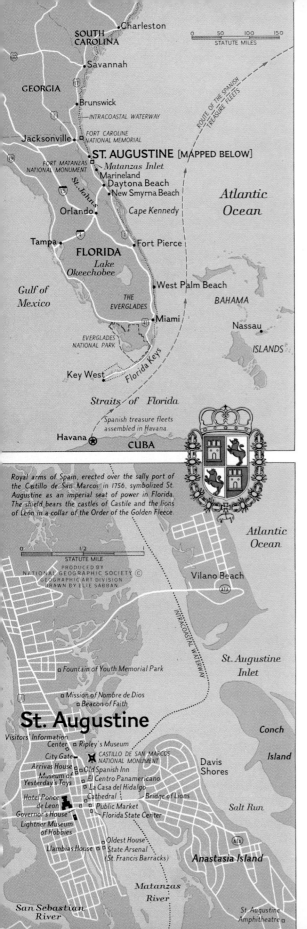

Royal arms of Spain, erected over the sally port of the Castillo de San Marcos in 1756, symbolized St. Augustine as an imperial seat of power in Florida. The shield bears the castles of Castile and the lions of Leon in a collar of the Order of the Golden Fleece.

PRODUCED BY
NATIONAL GEOGRAPHIC SOCIETY ©
GEOGRAPHIC ART DIVISION
DRAWN BY ELIE SABBAN

When he saw me taking notes, he asked, "You going to write this up?" I said yes.

"To be printed?" I said yes.

He said: "Well, now, don't you believe everything I say. You just believe about *half* what I say, then you safe."

He thought this over, and added reflectively, "I talk long enough, there bound to be *some* truth in it."

Cars Thread Streets of Spanish Days

Actually, Major's discourse on St. Augustine was reasonably accurate. I learned that the city was founded by the Spaniards, who held it for two centuries, then taken over by the British, then by Spain again, and finally, in 1821, by the United States.

We clip-clopped along the pleasant waterfront, past the massive old Spanish *castillo*, through the stone City Gate and along streets with Spanish names—Cordova, Sevilla, Granada, Cadiz. Some of them seemed too narrow for cars (though cars nosed through most of them anyway), and balconies leaned out overhead from the two-story Spanish houses. Other streets were wider, and these were walled and roofed by giant shade trees; here the houses were big, square, opulent—reminders of the end of the last century when wealthy Americans "discovered" St. Augustine and made it a fashionable spa.

St. Augustine today is a city of 15,000. The old town faces the Matanzas River, part of the Intracoastal Waterway that links Florida and New England. The Bridge of Lions spans the river and lets the city expand on Anastasia Island, where modern houses line the waterfront. A few miles down the island there are ocean beaches, but the city itself is not, strictly speaking, a seaside resort.

It is customary for visitors to call St. Augustine a sleepy Spanish town, and parts of it are. On the edge of the business district, in fact, the townspeople and the State of Florida

On the sea road from the Spanish Main, the Florida peninsula saw riches flow past in Spain's treasure fleets. With gold to be plundered—and protected—Spain established St. Augustine to guard her galleons against corsairs. Today history embellishes the old town; suburbs spill across the river.

Swathed in satin, her mantilla-draped head bowed behind a fan, Nancy Russell adds Spanish elegance to St. Augustine's Easter Week Festival. She traces her ancestry to Minorcans who came to the town in the 1770's.

are spending millions of dollars to bring back this Old World atmosphere by reconstruction, restoration, and preservation of several blocks of old Spanish houses.

Downtown St. Augustine, however, is quite wide awake. It crawls with traffic; there are modern shops, restaurants, office buildings, parking meters, and motels, motels, motels. The city has a small fishing industry; it was once a major center for shrimping, but that has dwindled as new and more productive grounds have been found in the Gulf of Mexico and farther south.

As we drove around the central plaza, laid out in Spanish style, I saw another modern phenomenon: pickets—young people, some Negro, some white, carrying signs protesting segregation. St. Augustine was undergoing a period of racial strife which brought it unhappy nationwide publicity.

French and Spanish Vie for Treasure

But the city's main products are antiquity and history. They bring in visitors by the hundreds of thousands and provide St. Augustine with three-fourths of its income.

Furthermore, the history has a hero, a strong, audacious, contradictory figure whose life is only vaguely known to most historians. Before saying goodbye to Major and Jezebel, I drove with them along the wide avenue that bears his name—Avenida Menendez.

Don Pedro Menéndez de Avilés founded St. Augustine as the capital of La Florida— which at the time meant capital of much of North America. For to the Spaniards, Florida extended all the way north into Canada and west beyond the Mississippi.

Menéndez, before our story opens, had been captain general of the Spanish treasure fleet, whose ships were carrying millions of dollars' worth of gold, silver, and other riches from the New World to Spain.* Now the

*See "Drowned Galleons Yield Spanish Gold," by Kip Wagner, NATIONAL GEOGRAPHIC, January, 1965.

"Little city of the deep," as Ralph Waldo Emerson called St. Augustine, lies in the lazy embrace of meandering tidal rivers, guarded by the massive walls of Castillo de San Marcos. Travelers who enter through the City Gate at lower right ride into the restoration area on St. George Street (pages 208-9). Spanish Renaissance towers spring from the red tile roof of the Hotel Ponce de Leon, opened by Henry M. Flagler in 1888 to help develop Florida's east coast into an "American Riviera."

French Huguenots, led by a bold captain named Jean Ribault, were threatening this fleet. The French had built their new colony, Fort Caroline, on the St. Johns River—a perfect spot from which to pounce on Spanish ships sailing north along the Florida coast.

King Philip of Spain had protested angrily to the French court; then he summoned Menéndez, appointed him *adelantado* (commander) of Florida, and told him to drive the

heretics out and occupy the land for Spain.

His were the ships that sailed through St. Augustine's inlet that September day 400 years ago. They had left Cádiz two months earlier and had run into a storm so fierce that less than half of Menéndez's original fleet was still with him. A special disaster was the disappearance of his supply ship. He had started with 1,000 soldiers and settlers; now he had 600.

He had found the French the day before, 35 miles up the coast—well entrenched, better equipped and manned than his own tattered remnant. After a skirmish at sea (below), he retreated to St. Augustine, the nearest suitable harbor. But he knew Ribault would not be far behind. The enemy he had come so far to demolish now threatened to demolish him.

A few days after the Spaniards had dug in as well as they could, Ribault's ships, as expected, did appear outside the inlet. They did not attack, however, for just then Menéndez had a stroke of luck. According to his chronicler, Gonzalo Solís de Merás, "... God Our Lord performed a miracle; for the weather being fair and clear, suddenly the sea rose very high, and a strong and contrary north wind came up...."

Miracle for the Spaniards, perhaps, but ruin for Ribault. The "contrary north wind" drove his ships irresistibly southward and wrecked them on the sands near what is now Daytona Beach.

Menéndez, having seen the French fleet running south, reasoned that Fort Caroline must now be weakly garrisoned. With 500 men he set out on foot through the wind and rain, across swamps and swollen rivers, to attack it (pages 212-13).

It took four days to make the march. At dawn on the fifth day the Spaniards fell on the fort. They found it defended by only 150 French soldiers, a few artisans, some women and children. It was all over in an hour: more than 130 Huguenots killed, not a Spaniard lost. Menéndez renamed the fort San Mateo, garrisoned it, and marched back to St. Augustine in triumph.

How to Bring History to Life

In introducing Don Pedro Menéndez, I said that historians know little about him. But I found in St. Augustine a studious yet genial man named Albert Manucy, a historian with the National Park Service, who has studied Menéndez's life, off and on, for 20 years. When I met him, he was typing away at a biography, but did not yet have much down on paper.

"The way to bring this history to life," he said, "is to see it for yourself." So we got into a car the next day and set out to follow Menéndez to Fort Caroline. It isn't much of a trip in a modern car over a fast road, and this seemed to worry Mr. Manucy, who felt the need to explain why it took Menéndez four days.

As we approached the St. Johns River, he pulled the car off the road, and we climbed out. Off to the right lay an evil-looking swamp, waist-deep muck and water, a place for snakes, leeches, mosquitoes, and spiders. Behind it lay a thick pine grove, and all around us an impenetrable thicket of brush. It was typical of the countryside we had been driving through.

Storm-crippled flagship of Governor Menéndez, the *San Pelayo,* fires futilely at the fleeing French; another Spanish ship stands by, foreground. Near the mouth of the St. Johns River, Menéndez spied enemy galleons anchored off Fort Caroline. Despite loss of spars and rigging in an Atlantic storm, he attacked. But the French, after shouting "many shameless and insulting words against the King," cut anchor cables and escaped into the night.

"Look at that," said Mr. Manucy. "Saw palmetto. Feel the edges of the stems." They felt like sharp saws. Other bushes had thorns like needles. "Try walking a few feet through that stuff." I was wearing a new pair of slacks, so I declined. But it was easy to see why Menéndez and his men, carrying heavy battle equipment, took so long to make the march—especially through a storm.

We got back in the car and drove on to see Fort Caroline (upper map, page 202). We couldn't really see the original settlement, for the land on which it stood has been washed away by the St. Johns River. But the National Park Service has established a memorial a thousand feet or so from the original site, and when I got there they were finishing a reconstruction of the old French fort (pages 214-15).

"It's as accurate as we can make it," said Superintendent John DeWeese. "A few Frenchmen escaped Menéndez, and one of them was an artist, Jacques le Moyne. Later a book of his pictures was published. One shows the fort quite clearly."

Invasion Threatens Grassy Earthworks

We strolled down a shady trail through the woods to the reconstructed fort itself, a pretty spot overlooking the quiet river. As we inspected the newly built earthworks,

208

Fort Caroline was suddenly reinvaded—by two busloads of schoolboys. They swarmed over the grassy earthworks in a way that would have put the Spaniards to shame.

"With invasions like this," said Mr. De-Weese, "it's hard to keep grass growing."

Well, maybe so. But what's the use of rebuilding a fort if small boys can't recapture it now and then? I asked one of them what he thought of it. "It's neat," he shouted, and clambered up the wall.

Another day, again with Mr. Manucy, I set out for Matanzas Inlet, 14 miles south of St. Augustine, to see the horrifying end of this particular portion of Huguenot history.

Aged stone walls bask in the golden glow of lamplight on St. George Street, a thoroughfare of colonial days. Here cars pass under balconies where mantilla-draped señoritas once gossiped; the Old Spanish Inn transports visitors into the past. During a festival last September celebrating the city's 400th anniversary (below), celebrants sing and dance down St. George Street. Crumbling in decay only a decade ago, this section of the city provided a pilot project for the St. Augustine Historical Restoration and Preservation Commission, headquartered in the balconied Arrivas House at left center. 209

Moss-hung tunnel of live oaks, Magnolia Avenue makes a dappled way for Major, a carriage driver (right), and Jezebel, his horse. The good-natured driver regales visitors with his own blood-and-thunder version of St. Augustine's stormy history.

A few days after Menéndez returned to St. Augustine, he got word from friendly Indians of many white men farther south. Some of Ribault's men had survived the wrecking of the French ships and marched up the beach, hoping to return to Fort Caroline. They were blocked by an inlet too deep for them to ford. Menéndez took 60 soldiers and a boat and pushed south.

So did Mr. Manucy and I. There is a bridge across Matanzas Inlet now, and the sand has shifted over the years, but the scene must be approximately the same. We stopped the car short of the bridge and climbed a dune—as Menéndez also did when he got there.

Across the water he saw the pathetic group of 200 French soldiers. They had salvaged some weapons, but they were starving—some, in fact, were searching for shellfish when he spotted them.

"You have to remember," said Mr. Manucy, "that Menéndez had only 60 men with him. Also that he was under orders to kill all heretics. It was a tricky situation."

It was, and criticism of what Menéndez did next still goes on after four centuries.

Menéndez Delivers an Ultimatum: Surrender or Starve

Don Pedro had some of the French leaders brought over in his boat. He fed them, but he offered no compromise. They could either surrender or stay where they were and starve.

Finally the Frenchmen gave up. They handed over their few weapons and their banners. The Spaniards ferried them over the inlet ten at a time and tied their hands, telling them they were to be marched to St. Augustine. Instead, as each group passed behind a dune, they were slaughtered.

A few days later the rest of the French force—some 350 men led by Ribault himself—reached the inlet. The same bloody scene was re-enacted, except that this time perhaps 200 of the Frenchmen decided to walk south, taking their chances with the Indians. (Menéndez captured them later near Cape Canaveral, today's Cape Kennedy.)

The others gave up, were ferried across the inlet and killed (pages 216-17). Menéndez spared only the trumpeters, fifers, and drummers, plus a few soldiers who professed to be Catholics. That was on October 12, 1565.

Today small red flowers grow near the water's edge at Matanzas Inlet, and in the dunes there are thousands of tiny shells of a mollusk, *Donax variabilis,* which give the sands a reddish hue, as if even four centuries of sun and rain have failed to bleach them clean. And the name the Spaniards gave to the inlet and to the fort they later built there perpetuates the deed, for the Spanish word *matanza* means "slaughter."

So the French threat was destroyed; Spain secured control of Florida and held it for the next two centuries. But it was a precarious control, and St. Augustine, the capital, could hardly be called a successful colony. It produced no silver or gold, and the Spaniards had little luck in their attempts to farm its sandy soil.

Menéndez himself sailed back to Spain and died there in 1574. His colony remained an outpost, and because it had no adequate fortification for the first 100 years, it was vulnerable to raids by every passing pirate and privateer.

Lookout Tower Lures an English Sea Dog

One of the passing privateers was Sir Francis Drake. By this time (1586) England's sea power was growing fast; Queen Elizabeth I sat on the throne, and with her blessing Drake was joyfully looting Spanish settlements in the Caribbean. St. Augustine was scarcely worth looting and might have escaped entirely, except for an ironic twist.

According to Drake's own chronicler, here is what happened: "... wee descried on the shore a place built like a Beacon, which was in deede a scaffold upon foure long mastes...." Drake looked at the tower and decided "to see what place the enemie held there: for none amongst us had any knowledge thereof at all." The "scaffold" was a lookout tower—built to warn the citizens of approaching pirates.

Poor St. Augustine! It had 150 soldiers; Drake had some 20 vessels and 2,000 men. The Spaniards fired a few shots and fled. After Drake had burned the town to the ground and sailed away, they crept out of the bushes and rebuilt on the ashes. They hung on, but just barely.

Parish records dating back to 1594, the oldest written records in the United States, are still kept by the Mission of Nombre de Dios in St. Augustine. One day I went to see them—wormeaten, tattered, almost indecipherable: *Bautismos, Matrimonios, Entierros*—baptisms, marriages, burials (page 201). Judging by the baptisms, a score or more babies a year were born in the early days. Population was probably less than 600.

One of the earliest marriages shown is that of a Vincent Solana, on July 4, 1594, to Maria Viscente. St. Augustine's telephone directory today lists more than 20 Solanas, and their genealogy has been traced back to this wedding. They are the oldest surviving United States family on record.

I talked to some of the Solanas. One is a priest, another a postmaster; another, Carl Solana, was maître d'hôtel at a restaurant where I ate frequently.

I asked him, "How does it feel to be a member of the oldest family in the United States?"

He shrugged: "When you've known it all your life, you get used to it."

His reticence was typical of the town's old Spanish families, but once a year, at Eastertime, they show their pride of ancestry. Out of trunks and cedar chests come costumes and heirlooms—mantillas, tall combs, jewelry—and there is an Easter parade which makes St. Augustine's plaza look again the way it looked centuries ago (page 203).

In a Hurricane's Fury, the Spanish March on France's Fort Caroline

"God Our Lord performed a miracle," wrote Gonzalo Solís de Merás of a violent storm that drove French commander Jean Ribault's ships southward, away from a planned attack on St. Augustine and far from their harbor at Fort Caroline. Realizing the enemy fortress would be undermanned, Governor Menéndez and 500 soldiers struggled for four days through "great darkness and the great tempest of wind and rain." Surprising the French, drenched pikemen and arquebusiers captured the stronghold without losing a man.

213

The rest of St. Augustine's early history reflected what was taking place in Europe. As a sea power and a colonial empire, Spain was going down, England coming up. By the middle of the 17th century, Boston was a thriving port of 15,000 people; St. Augustine had fewer than 1,500.

In the early 1600's the King of Spain, now Philip III, seriously considered abandoning St. Augustine entirely. One strong factor in saving it was that at last it began to produce a successful crop: not gold, not silver, but souls—Indian converts.

The Franciscan missions in St. Augustine's early years are perhaps its chief success story. The humble friars had a peculiar ability for making friends with the Indians and winning them over to Christianity.

Perhaps it was because they were willing to endure hardship, poverty, and even martyrdom, to move out into the woods and live among the savages. As one historian relates, "A lone Franciscan, with no weapons other than his Cross and Bible, could do more with the Indians than 100 men-at-arms."

The first handful of Franciscans reached Florida in 1573. By 1606 a visiting bishop from Cuba was able to confirm 2,000 Indians as Catholics, and that was only a beginning. By 1655 the Franciscans had established more than 30 mission centers, stretching north to what is now Georgia and South Carolina, and west beyond Tallahassee. They had some 26,000 converts.

Sea-shell Fortress Survives the Centuries

Yet despite its success as a missionary headquarters, St. Augustine as a military outpost continued to teeter on the brink of oblivion. There were more raids, and the early wooden forts continued to be overrun; they were burned down, or they rotted away and had to be rebuilt. The early records indicate a succession of nine forts built and destroyed. Meanwhile the danger grew worse. The English, like a dagger pointed at St. Augustine's throat, were moving south. In the 1670's they settled in Carolina, only 225 miles north.

Then a great event took place in St. Augustine. By order of the crown, work was begun in 1672 on a massive and impregnable fortress that would defy the most powerful cannon, big enough to shelter the entire population of the town in an emergency. It was called the Castillo de San Marcos; it took 24 years to build; it still stands today, and it has never yet been taken by assault. The most remarkable fact about it, however, is that it is made of sea shells.

Beneath the sands of Anastasia Island the

Green walls of Fort Caroline, near Jacksonville, memorialize France's brief hold on the peninsula. Two and a half years after the Spanish massacre of the colony in 1565, vengeful Frenchmen returned to the St. Johns River and wiped out the Spanish garrison. This National Park Service reconstruction of the stockaded earthwork stands near the original site, which washed away in the 19th century.

Cross and Sword, a symphonic drama by Pulitzer Prize-winner Paul Green, portrays St. Augustine's early years. In the finale, colonists bid farewell to their governor as he sails for Spain. "Yea, our city lives!" exults Menéndez. "For here we did our best." 215

Dune of doom crests above the sea as steel-willed Menéndez orders the execution of the red-bearded Frenchman Ribault and his soldiers, shipwrecked south of St. Augustine during the hurricane (pages 212-13). Finding a large force of Frenchmen marooned on a peninsula, Menéndez divided the enemy into groups of ten and ferried each small party across an inlet. Then they were bound and marched behind a dune, to be put to the sword. The massacre ended the French threat to Florida but gave the inlet its grim name—Matanzas, meaning "slaughters."

Halo of vines crowns a quiet chapel at the site of St. Augustine's Mission of Nombre de Dios, founded by secular priests in 1565. A century later, Franciscan friars had built chains of Indian missions westward and northward, and could count 26,000 converts to Christianity.

KODACHROME BY ALICE BIXLER; PAINTING BY STANLEY MELTZOFF © N.G.S.

Spaniards discovered a substance they called *coquina*. Made of countless tiny shells of *Donax variabilis* (the same mollusk that tints the sands at Matanzas Inlet), stuck together by time, lime, and their own weight, coquina is softer than most stone, easy to quarry and shape, but resilient. As the English learned, firing cannon balls at a thick coquina wall is like throwing pebbles at a rubbery round of cheese. They either bounce off or are absorbed, and the wall remains intact.

The castillo, now administered by the National Park Service, is St. Augustine's greatest historic attraction. Close to half a million visitors a year come to marvel at it, for even by modern standards it is a fantastic piece of engineering (pages 222-3). I spent hours roaming its ramparts and the dark chambers that lie between its inner and outer walls.

My best visit, though, was with a man named Luis Arana, like Mr. Manucy a historian for the National Park Service. The fort is his specialty.

On a sunny spring afternoon I walked with Mr. Arana across the greensward that now surrounds San Marcos. A

With solid blows, planker Michael Hall sinks a nail into a wooden hull at the DESCO boatyard in St. Augustine. World's largest manufacturer of commercial shrimp boats, the company turns out 100 vessels a year. Shrimpers from Kuwait to Borneo, British Guiana to Italy, work from the Florida-built trawlers.

Powdered with dust from sanding a trawler's hull, yard worker Lee Green wears a mask to protect his lungs.

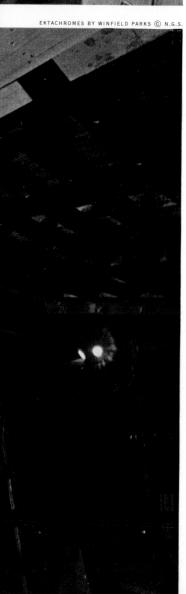

flotilla of ducks swam in the Matanzas River, which laps a stone seawall a few yards from the fort, and at the water's edge a few fishermen dozed in the sun.

Along the walkway through the park some old iron cannon have been set up—just for atmosphere—and there were a few dozen tourists strolling about. I noted that each male tourist between the ages of five and eleven, as he passed a cannon, stared hopefully into the barrel, as if half expecting to see a cannonball coming out.

"Doesn't it scare you to have a big gun pointed at your head?" I asked one of them.

"It didn't," he said. "I pointed my head at it."

Castillo's Court Offered Haven to 1,500

The pastoral surroundings make the castillo itself look, by contrast, incredibly menacing. Its massive gray walls, studded on top with heavy guns, loom 30 feet high; a moat makes them look even higher. During siege its inner court has sheltered as many as 1,500 people.

Luis Arana and I crossed the moat over a wooden bridge and entered an office. Mr. Arana picked up a pencil and a pad of paper. I quickly learned that as a bird cannot fly without wings, neither can Mr. Arana expound and explain without drawing and writing.

"The outer walls are 14 feet thick at the base," he said, "tapering to 9 feet at the top." He drew a cross section of the wall, wrote "14" at the bottom, "9" at the top.

"The fort was remodeled, starting in 1738. At that time they moved the inner wall back and added the arched coquina ceilings to the chambers between the walls." He wrote down "1738" and sketched a coquina arch.

Several hours later Mr. Arana's scratch pad was full, and so was my head. We had walked over every square foot of the place, and I wished I had coquina arches in my feet. Mr. Arana explained how the first big attack was made on the fort.

That was in 1702. England and Spain were at war, and Governor James Moore of Carolina swept south with ships, cannon, and perhaps 1,000 men. Occupying the town, he bombarded and besieged the fort for nearly two months, then gave up and went home.

Although the battle ended in victory for the castillo and its defenders (pages 224-5), it was a sad two months for the town itself. Moore, as he retired, destroyed most of the buildings left standing. Later he also systematically burned the Franciscan missions in western Florida.

There is no structure in present-day St. Augustine—except the castillo—that dates from earlier than 1702. The city's Oldest House is a sturdy coquina building that can be traced to 1727 (pages 200-201). But of the original settlement, only archeological fragments and documents remain.

I talked to the manager of the St. Augustine Historical Society, Mr. J. Carver Harris, about this. He said, rather wistfully: "You'd think that the oldest house in the oldest city would have to be the oldest house in the United States. We used to think so, too, but when the historians went to work, they found it just wasn't so. There are quite a few older houses in New England, for example. The *towns* aren't as old—they just weren't burned down so often."

Eventually the British flag did fly over the Castillo de San Marcos. In 1762 a British force captured Havana; the following year Britain and Spain signed a treaty which, in effect, traded Florida for Cuba.

When word of this treaty reached St. Augustine, the citizens—numbering more than 3,000—were horrified. They had worked for 200 years to keep the English out. Almost to a man they moved away, taking their belongings with them but abandoning their homes (some of them by this time handsome coquina houses), their churches, and their castillo. The real irony was that in a mere 20 years, Britain gave Florida back to Spain.

Minorcans Came Under British Flag

I had not been in St. Augustine many days when I began hearing a phrase that puzzled me. When someone's name (Mr. Manucy's, for instance) was mentioned to me in conversation, it was very likely to be followed by the

Built from the bounty of the sea, Castillo de San Marcos rises in the 1670's. Spanish masons shape blocks of coquina, sea shells cemented by their own lime, and set them with mortar made from oyster shells. Indians (far left) raft blocks from quarries on Anastasia Island. The resilient walls frustrated attackers; the rock "will not splinter," complained an Englishman, "but will give way to cannon ball as though you would stick a knife into cheese...."

comment, "He's a Minorcan." I met a man named Mr. X. L. Pellicer, a bank official, who told me that he was a Minorcan. Why so many Minorcans?

"While the British occupied Florida," Mr. Pellicer explained, "they brought one of my ancestors, Francisco Pellicer, and more than 1,400 others from the Mediterranean, mostly from Minorca, to start a colony at New Smyrna. That's about 60 miles south of here. The colony failed, and its people gave up. About 600 survivors walked to St. Augustine and settled here."

When Britain failed to quell the American Revolution and gave Florida back to Spain, most of the British moved out, but the Minorcans stayed on. Their descendants are still in St. Augustine, many of them leading citizens. One local Minorcan family produced a couple of America's best writers and poets—Stephen Vincent and William Rose Benét.

The Second Spanish Period (as the historians call it) in Florida did not last very long. St. Augustine itself, with its garrison, fort, and walls, did relatively well. But the rest of Florida under Spain became a lawless place, a hideout for escaped slaves and fugitive Indians who eventually banded together under the name Seminole, which means "wild."

Trouble led to trouble, until in 1818 Gen. Andrew Jackson led American troops into the territory in a punitive campaign, destroying several Seminole villages. Finally Spain ceded all of Florida to the United States. In 1821 the Stars and Stripes at last flew over the Castillo de San Marcos.

Wildcat Breaches Fort From Within

During the Seminole War of 1835-42, San Marcos served as both a headquarters and a prison. To it in 1837 were taken a group of Seminoles, including two famous leaders, Osceola and Coacoochee, who had been captured by treachery under a flag of truce. Osceola fell sick, but Coacoochee (also called Wildcat), locked up in a dark, high-ceilinged chamber, plotted an escape.

According to Coacoochee's own account, he and a companion, Talmus Hadjo, made ropes out of their bedding and waited for a moonless night. Then Wildcat somehow scaled his dungeon wall and squeezed through a tiny window. From the window he dropped one end of the rope inside for Hadjo to climb; on the other end he slid down the outer wall into the moat. Hadjo followed. All told, 20 Seminoles escaped that night (page 226).

Coacoochee rejoined his tribesmen to lead

IMPREGNABLE THROUGH THE CENTURIES, *Castillo de San Marcos and its bristling bastions held Florida for Spain. Protected by jagged outer wall and tidal moat, the fortress spreads a four-pronged fighting deck over barracks, chapel, jail, and armory. Visitors crowd the courtyard.*

Agony of a town aflame: Spanish Governor Joseph de Zúñiga y Zerda, right, watches cannoneers fire from the Castillo de San Marcos, trying to stop St. Augustine's spreading blaze by concussion. The night: December 29-30, 1702. But the town burns on, as the forces of England's Carolina colony give up a futile seven-week siege of the fort.

further resistance. Though most of the Seminoles were eventually resettled in the West, they have never signed a peace. More than a thousand still live in southern Florida.*

St. Augustine remained remote and relatively quiet until a hurricane struck it in the 1880's. Unlike 1965's Hurricane Betsy, this was a human hurricane named Henry M. Flagler. He was a multimillionaire, a partner of John D. Rockefeller, and he had decided to turn Florida's east coast into an "American Riviera." Before he left St. Augustine, it had acquired two enormous new hotels and a railroad—the Florida East Coast line.

The grandest of the hotels, the Ponce de Leon, is still open in the winter, and no visitor should leave town without at least seeing it. It's built in the style of a Spanish Renaissance castle. When it opened in 1888, the Ponce was described as the world's finest hotel, and I can believe it. The ceiling in the main dining room arches 68 feet high; balconied guest rooms overlook a walled Spanish patio full of flowers and palm trees, with a fountain splashing in the middle.

New Viewpoint for a New England Family

St. Augustine now gets half a million visitors in a good year. I talked to a lot of them, asking them why they had come and what they thought of the place.

"The golf course is great," some of them said. Or, "We're on our way home from Miami, and we got tired of driving."

But many knew exactly why they had come, and what the city symbolized. My favorite tourists were a family from Connecticut—Mr. and Mrs. Max L. Kopko and their daughters, Gail, 11, and Cynthia, 9. Gail told me, quite seriously, that she had come to write a history of Florida. I thought she seemed a bit young for such an enterprise, but her father explained.

"We're from New England," he said. "When I went to school, I was taught that the Pilgrims settled this country in 1620. It wasn't until I came to St. Augustine a few years ago

*See "Florida's 'Wild' Indians, the Seminole," by Louis Capron, NATIONAL GEOGRAPHIC, December, 1956.

on business that I learned the Spaniards got here first. This time I brought my family along to see it for themselves. Gail has to write a report about it for her history class."

The Kopkos had visited the historic sites, including the Oldest House and the castillo. When I last saw them, they were preparing to relax by seeing Ripley's Believe It or Not Museum, which has nothing much to do with St. Augustine except that it's there, but contains a charming collection of shrunken heads, an Egyptian mummy case, and, quite naturally, a model railroad bridge made of more than 31,000 toothpicks.

Gail promised to send me her history of Florida after the teacher got through with it, and she did. It's an *illustrated* history, with flags and flowers on the covers, and pictures of oranges, lemons, scenic views, and even a clump of Spanish moss. At the end of it Gail's teacher had penciled in "V.G.," which I presume means Very Good, and is an understatement, but that's the way teachers are.

The text ends: "The place that I liked best was the first church. I liked the church because it was so peaceful."

I was glad Gail felt this way, because I did, too. What she saw was not really the first church, but a small chapel standing on the site of the first mission, the Mission of Nombre de Dios, founded by Menéndez and his priests to convert the Indians. The original buildings have long since been destroyed, but the grounds are kept much as they must have looked 400 years ago, with great shade trees, quiet paths, and votive candles flickering. There is an outdoor altar, and in the chapel (page 216) rests the wooden coffin of Menéndez, a gift from Spain in 1924, when his body was reinterred in Avilés.

To mark St. Augustine's 400th birthday, the Catholic Church is building near the old

mission a new research library, a church, and at the water's edge, a Beacon of Faith—a 200-foot-high illuminated stainless-steel cross. For all this the church was raising $3,000,000, part of which will also be used to sponsor research into Florida's early history.

This is only one of many ways in which the city is celebrating its 400th anniversary year, calling attention to its Spanish heritage and entertaining visitors who come to join its year-long birthday party.

Wooden Guns for *Cross and Sword*

In a basement workshop I met a man named Tom Rahner, who was making guns by the dozen. He was also making a cannon about eight feet long, with a metal lining so it could actually be fired. With him was another man named W. I. Drysdale, who had just bought 2,000 chairs. The chairs and the guns and the cannon were part of a plot to lure visitors to town and make them stay longer. The guns were authentic-looking 16th-century arquebuses made of wood.

With Mr. Drysdale and Mr. Rahner, I drove across the Bridge of Lions to Anastasia Island. There, in a quiet wooded setting near the sea, stood a splendid 2,000-seat amphitheater, still under construction but nearly complete.

"Isn't it a beauty?" said Mr. Drysdale. "It ought to be. It's costing us $325,000 to build." To fill it, the St. Augustine town fathers commissioned Pulitzer Prize-winning playwright Paul Green to write a symphonic drama telling the story of the founding of the

In dark of the moon, Seminoles led by chief Coacoochee, known as Wildcat, escape from the castillo. Twenty Indians—captured by the U. S. Army in 1837—scaled the interior wall, squeezed through a small window, and let themselves down on a rope made from bedding. They fled across the marshy moat, now filled with water (right). Later Coacoochee related, "We had been growing sickly . . . and we resolved to make our escape or die in the attempt."

Rejoining his tribesmen, Coacoochee became a scourge and thorn to the Army. His leadership revived the waning spirits of other chiefs, prolonging the Seminole War for five years.

oldest city. It's called *Cross and Sword.*

Mr. Drysdale, a leading local businessman, was in charge of construction; his 2,000 chairs were just being installed. Mr. Rahner, an actor with several years' experience in another outdoor drama (North Carolina's *Unto These Hills),* is general manager of the production. The arquebuses? The cannon? "Props," he said. "I enjoy woodworking, so I'm making them myself."

Later, when the 400th year was getting under way last September, I went back to St. Augustine and saw the finished product: a fine, exciting, two-hour show with never a dull minute (page 215). Its cast of 100 includes beautiful Indian maidens, stalwart conquistadors, and saintly priests; and in the final battle scene Mr. Rahner's cannon is fired with a tooth-rattling boom, and clouds of white smoke fill the stage. *Cross and Sword,* in its outdoor theater, is on only in the summer months; children under 12 get in free and will love it as much as grownups.

EKTACHROME (BELOW) BY WINFIELD PARKS; KODACHROME BY ALICE BIXLER © N.G.S.

"**Farewell;** and fair befall thee, gentle town!" wrote Ralph Waldo Emerson, when he left St. Augustine in 1827 after regaining his health. Today, retired citizens come to stay; some spend the afternoon in the Public Market, enjoying a game of cards. At dusk, the streets grow quiet and traffic no longer crowds the Bridge of Lions, connecting Anastasia Island to the mainland. Now the span's light poles seem to change into Spanish pikemen, standing guard over the Nation's oldest city.

St. Augustine's biggest effort, not strictly part of the 400th anniversary but important to it, is a $20,000,000 restoration program. Financed by state and local funds, it aims for something like Williamsburg, Virginia, but with Spanish architecture instead of Georgian. This is under the direction of Earle W. Newton, the same historian who guided the reconstruction of Old Sturbridge village in Massachusetts.

The restoration is a 20-year project, slow-moving because, as Mr. Newton points out, "You can't just tear down a living city of 15,000 people and rebuild it. Williamsburg didn't have quite the same problem."

Even so, the city has completed a section equivalent to several city blocks. Here, along narrow St. George Street, just inside the old City Gate, St. Augustine looks much the way it did during its Spanish heyday. (Earlier, I complained about billboards. In the restoration area, not only are billboards banned and signs strictly regulated, but even the parking meters are being removed.)

"Contrary Wind" Helps Mark an Anniversary

When I returned to St. Augustine to see the 401st year in, I watched the dedication of the beautiful Casa del Hidalgo (house of the nobleman), built in 16th-century Spanish style by the Government of Spain as a permanent showplace in Florida. Another dedication, across the street, opened El Centro Panamericano, to which Latin American countries will send exhibits of their art, crafts, and culture.

Climax of the anniversary celebration was to be a High Mass, offered by Archbishop Joseph P. Hurley of St. Augustine and eight other priests simultaneously. Since one of the first things Don Pedro Menéndez did when he landed was to hear Mass at an outdoor altar on September 8, 1565, the priests in St. Augustine decided to have theirs outdoors, too, at an altar on the old mission grounds.

But on September 8, 1965, by a 400-year coincidence, the sky turned to lead and once again "suddenly the sea rose very high, and a strong and contrary north wind came up. . . ." It was the gale fringe of Hurricane Betsy, and it blew the outdoor Mass indoors. The congregation, incidentally, included distinguished delegates from Spain who flew across the Atlantic to visit their former colony on her birthday.

"All this," said Mr. Newton, "the visitors, the restoration, and the rest, are to emphasize America's Spanish heritage, which is so often neglected in our history books. St. Augustine was, and in a sense still is, the northeastern corner of Latin America."

If we do not read much about our Spanish heritage in history books, perhaps it is because, as someone has pointed out, "the winner writes the history." But the heritage is here, in our art, our music, our literature, and our architecture, and it spreads far beyond the little settlement Don Pedro Menéndez founded 400 years ago.
                                                    THE END

"The Alice" in Australia's Wonderland

By ALAN VILLIERS

Photographs by
JEFF CARTER and DAVID MOORE

"YOU'LL LIKE ALICE," they all said, with a special note in the voice. Everyone I met throughout Australia told me the same thing, whether or not they had ever visited Alice Springs. Ah, the Alice, or just Alice—never its full name—*that's* the place!

As I flew north from Adelaide over the arid zone of South Australia, I wondered what any town in such a hinterland could possibly have. Below, the country looked like a red-brown nowhere. Large lakes, marked in blue on the map, turned out to be dry salt pans. Waterless rivers scribbled twisting gray lines across the red landscape. In the dim past this had been a seabed. Now everything appeared barren, burned, useless.

The airplane began to descend. A brown

scar marked the railroad that snaked in from the south. We skimmed above blue-gray scrub—saltbush, mulga, and spinifex. In the distance the corrugated, sun-burned earth heaved itself into the fantastic shapes and colors of the Macdonnell Ranges (page 244).

"I love this land!" said a young woman, her lively eyes glued to a window. I looked out at the red, parched terrain, wondering what she found to admire.

Here, centered in the lower third of Australia's Northern Territory, lay the geographic heart of the continent (map, page 233). I am Australian-born but, like many others, I knew little about this vast red-rock highland, girt by fearsome deserts, that sprawls out and away from Alice Springs in every direction.

CROWNING A REALM *of vast distances, waterless rivers, and pioneer living, a diadem of stone glows in the first rays of dawn. A fantasyland five miles across, the domes of the Olgas rise 3,507 feet above sea level, keeping lonely vigil over a sandy plain in the remotest outback.*

EKTACHROME BY DAVID MOORE © NATIONAL GEOGRAPHIC SOCIETY

231

Could I, in a few weeks of roaming this region, come to know it, respect it—even love it, as my plane companion did?

My first sight of the town of Alice Springs gave no clue. It was a sunny winter's day, the sky a Mediterranean blue, the sun warm but not hot. The airport bus rolled to a stop between a large gum tree and the airlines terminal. Nearby I noted a "stockmen's shop," which could at a quick glance have been a cowhands' store in Cheyenne, Wyoming. It carried much the same shirts, boots, headgear, even the chaps. But the cowhands lounging outside were Australian aborigines—a characteristic feature of the Alice scene (above).

Bombs and Bitumen Help Alice Grow

The growth of Alice Springs in recent years has astonished inhabitants of the Northern Territory and some officials in Canberra as well. In the 1920's the population numbered fewer than 100; by World War II, it had risen to only 1,000. But after the Japanese bombed Darwin, territorial offices moved temporarily to Alice. Stuart Highway—still called simply "the bitumen"—was completed from Darwin to Alice, a distance of 954 miles.

Now a prosperous town of 6,000, Alice attracts hordes of tourists; they come especially for the fine winter weather (June-September), to see the spectacular scenery and the famed aboriginal artists centered in Alice,

and to visit surrounding cattle stations— ranches—some bigger than Rhode Island.

Alice was born in the mid-19th century after discovery of a sheltered, watered plain amid the Macdonnell Ranges. By 1872 a telegraph station had been built at a water hole beneath a rocky hill. It was called Alice Springs, for the wife of Charles Todd, superintendent of telegraphs back in Adelaide.

Next came the prospectors looking for any metal—preferably gold—and finding little. They left a ghost town at Arltunga, not far from Alice. Once, back in the 1880's, they thought they had found rubies by the carload. Jubilant prospectors loaded camels with sacks of them. Soon 24 companies were at work. But the "rubies" proved to be cheap garnets, not worth transporting.

Cattlemen soon followed, for much of "the Centre," as Australians call the area, is not desert but marginal land that provides good feed when it rains. They knew the rains would be far between, but when rains came, cattle fattened quickly and kept their condition on the long stock drives. If a route had growing feed, it didn't matter how long the cattle took to walk it. The pioneers felt that one good season could carry five bad ones. But it has often had to carry six—even eight.

I first visited the Centre in 1962 and returned in 1964. Although a few spasmodic showers fell here and there, on both occasions

Stone Age blends with 20th century in Alice Springs, as aborigines gather to swap yarns before a bank. The 6,000 people of this urban outpost, only town in a raw interior region one and a half times the size of Texas, think of it as "the Alice."

Windmills whirring beside them, homesteads merit spots on a map of the untamed Centre, as Australians call the arid heart of their continent. So-called lakes and rivers stand dry most of the time. Aborigines wandering the sparsely settled land recognize "soaks," where water lurks just below ground, but cattlemen must depend on water pumped by the wind from bores hundreds of feet deep. Just a few inches of rain a year can keep sandy wastes abloom with wildflowers, grasses, and shrubs. But eight years of drought has reduced the area to a dust bowl of starving cattle. For the future, residents look to promising mineral resources and growing numbers of tourists lured by the open spaces and rugged beauty of the Macdonnell Ranges.

AUSTRALIA

0   500   1000

STATUTE MILES

233

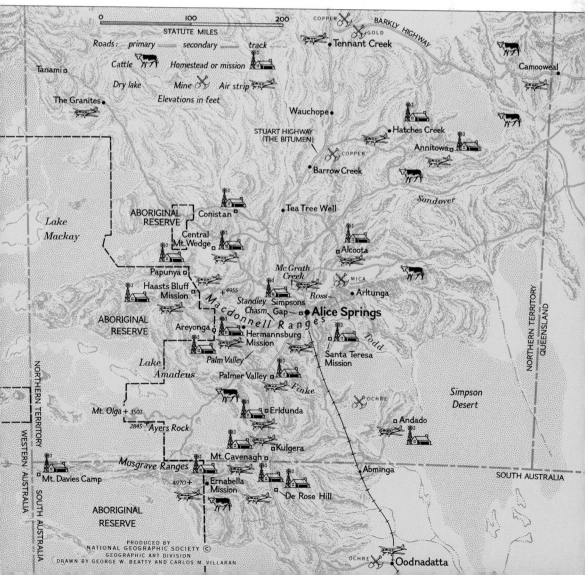

PRODUCED BY
NATIONAL GEOGRAPHIC SOCIETY ©
GEOGRAPHIC ART DIVISION
DRAWN BY GEORGE W. BEATTY AND CARLOS M. VILLARAN

Oasis of civilization in the harsh red heart of Australia, Alice Springs sprawls near Heavitree Gap, gateway to the south in the Macdonnell Ranges. Anzac Hill (center) raises a white monument to Australian and New Zealand dead of two World Wars.

A telegraph station in 1872, Alice grew slowly until a railroad linked it to Adelaide in 1929. The dusty, tin-roofed town often exploded with the revelry of cattlemen and miners. World War II put it on the map as a military base.

To Centre dwellers, Alice is THE city. It offers hotels, night spots, and smart shops like those in Gorey's Arcade (right). Nevil Shute captured its flavor in his book *A Town Like Alice,* published in the United States as *The Legacy.*

234

I found general conditions very poor. By mid-1965, over a great deal of the area the situation had deteriorated into the "worst drought in living memory"—which in central Australia is saying something.

Rain is spotty and at no time abundant. Records at the Alice—where ten inches a year is average—show that just under seven inches fell during 1958, when the surrounding district nourished 353,000 head of cattle. After several poor years, almost eight inches fell at Alice in 1962, but stock by then had dwindled to 176,000. In 1963 rainfall was four inches; in 1964 just under five; through October, 1965, just over one inch. This was disastrous. Barely 136,000 head of livestock remained.

Conservationists, agricultural economists, botanists, and Alice old-timers fear that the whole area may turn into a huge dust bowl, an Australian Sahara.

"Dust is mentioned now in almost every weather forecast," wrote a friend in July, 1965. "I had to drive 40 miles southeast from Alice the other day, toward Simpson Desert. The whole way I could barely see my own radiator because of a dust storm. This place isn't going to be much use again until it really gets a soaking rain and then is left to recover, ungrazed, for many years."

Biggest "Pebble" Towers 1,143 Feet

One answer to the region's economic woes may lie deep underground. Engineers report discovery of the continent's largest known gas field in the Lake Amadeus area, and have concluded that a major oil deposit lies close by.

District Officer Dan Conway sees a bright future in the tourist business: "Thousands of visitors a year, and they all find plenty to interest them."

From my earlier trip, I already knew several of the attractions. Like Standley Chasm, a cleft in the Chewings Range, 24 miles west of town, where the dirt track suddenly becomes the stony bed of a waterless creek, and the noon sun, striking almost straight down, changes the red canyon face to a burnished gold (page 238). Or Simpsons Gap, 10 miles out, with the smallest cattle station in the Alice Springs District: only 120 square miles!

Then, a 90-minute flight from Alice—or nine hours by bus—looms the tremendous monolith of Ayers Rock, called Uluru in aboriginal myth and legend (pages 239-41). Terra-cotta red, fiery crimson, and delicate mauve by turns in the shifting sun, Uluru towers 1,143 feet above the plain and is six miles around—the biggest "pebble" in the world, dropped in a desert as flat as the sea.

Out Ross River way is a dude ranch in colorful red hills. Up at Alcoota lies a mound littered with fossils of giant marsupials and emu-like birds as tall as 10 feet.

Yes, there was plenty to see.

On the main street of Alice itself stands a memorial church to the man who pioneered the famous Royal Flying Doctor Service—a missionary named John Flynn, born in my home state of Victoria in 1880, died 1951, buried by the roadside outside Alice. A stone cairn calls him simply "Flynn of the Inland."

At a time when radio and flying alike were primitive

ADELAIDE – 1062

WARNING

TRAVELLERS •

CHECK YOUR FOOD, PETROL AND WATER • THE NEXT PUBLIC STORE IS KULGERA, 168 MILES SOUTH

When wind sweeps the Centre, dust churns into clouds that obliterate the sun. Even with headlights burning, drivers can see only a few yards ahead. Grit sifts through windows and doors. Dirt roads disappear overnight beneath drifting dunes.

No sensible motorist ventures into the wastes without maps, compass, water, and four-wheel drive. A breakdown can bring death, as a grim prankster reminds with a makeshift monument of the bones of a horse, behind the wheel, and a cow. Even on good days, tires bog in talcum-fine red dust. Iron oxide gives the soil its striking rust color. Dust storms increase as years-long drought lingers. Denuded of plant cover by grazing and lack of rain, topsoil blows away. Conservationists fear that even the return of average rainfall—ten inches a year—will not rejuvenate much of the lost grazing land.

and far from accepted, tough John Flynn used both and urged his reluctant country-men to spread them over the whole of the outback. There is no telling how many lives have been saved since the R.F.D.S. was begun in neighboring Queensland in 1928.*

Every day physicians at 13 centers such as Alice Springs hold radio "clinics," giving instructions for treatment to isolated stations and camps—each equipped with standardized medicine chests containing more than 80 items. In emergencies a nurse or doctor flies to the patient (page 243).

I walked from the Elkira Court motel in the sunshine of Bath Street toward R.F.D.S. headquarters. Aboriginal children played with hoses that revived lawns with water from the town's deep wells. A four-wheel-drive vehicle, red with the sand of the desert, drove by, its canvas water bag slung on the front bumper. Big diesel trucks were loading from freight cars in the railroad yard—building materials, drums of oil, live sheep.

Help Never More Than Hours Away

At R.F.D.S. headquarters—a pleasant bungalow in the shade of Billygoat Hill—I met Base Director George Brown, ex-radio officer in the British Merchant Navy.

"People come to Alice on a visit, like it, and stay. That's what I did," he told me.

"Before this service operated, the patient had either to be brought to the doctor, or else the doctor, alerted by a messenger, traveled overland to the patient. At times distances of hundreds of miles were involved, and local pioneer residents can recall journeys of 14 days over rough bush tracks, by horse-drawn buggy, to reach the nearest busy hospital. Nowadays we can bring skilled medical help to any outpost on the network within three hours."

We thumbed through a file of flight

*For more on the flying doctors see "Australia," by Alan Villiers, GEOGRAPHIC, September, 1963.

Fingers of gold fleetingly probe Standley Chasm, a day-long round trip from Alice Springs. Only at noon does the sun dip into the shadowy cleft whose walls, 20 to 30 feet apart, tower 23 stories.

Answering the challenge of Ayers Rock, sightseers attack the west ridge, a safety line their sole aid on the steep ascent. "I climbed Ayers Rock" badges reward the hardy ones who reach the top.

EKTACHROME (OPPOSITE) BY DAVID MOORE; KODACHROME BY JEFF CARTER © N.G.S.

EKTACHROMES BY DAVID MOORE © N.G.S.

MONUMENT TO CREATION *in aboriginal minds, Ayers Rock springs 1,143 feet above a scrub plain. Tribesmen cloak the 2¼-mile-long monolith in legends of the "Dreamtime," their version of man's beginnings. And how did this mammoth boulder come to lie in the middle of a plain? It fell from the sky, one legend says. Religious symbols smeared in ocher and splashes of human blood drawn from arm veins decorate caves riddling the rock's base.*

Visitors line Sunset Strip, a sand ridge, to see Ayers Rock turn deep gray in cloud shadow (top, left), then burn red in the setting sun.

240

records, open on a side table, while the pretty girl radio operator monitored a call about a stockman on a station hundreds of miles away who had been found unconscious in a gully an hour or so earlier. Pursuing stampeding cattle in the night, he had apparently ridden into the low bough of a tree.

There was also a problem with a dehydrated baby having a convulsion near Ayers Rock.

In cool, reassuring tones the voice of a nurse could be heard dealing with these more or less routine matters, while a messenger was bringing the doctor—an Englishman—and mechanics warmed up a plane at the airport to fly him to a patient.

Drama leaped from the flight report pages:

> Alice Springs to Mount Davies. Aboriginal infant. Complaint not ascertained. Sister [nurse] Keady traveled to attend infant. Sister and Pilot Donnard had considerable trouble to get wild bush mother, a desert woman, into the aircraft. Cost, £90.
>
> Male aborigine age about 30. Severe wound in arm and fractured elbow in boomerang fight over a lubra [woman]. Cost, £35.5.0.

Government funds and public contributions defray the costs of the R.F.D.S. For the fiscal year 1964-65, the service's Cessnas, twin-engine Beechcrafts, and four-engine Herons logged 91,000 miles on 255 emergency flights out of Alice Springs. They brought in 320 patients for hospitalization.

"You should hear the 'galah sessions,'" said Mrs. Nan Brown, the director's wife. The galah is a bush cockatoo much given to noisy chatter (page 245). Mrs. Brown explained that now and again the R.F.D.S. throws its network open to the outback women for a sort of free-for-all chat. And how they chat! As if they were all in the same room instead of scattered over an area one and a half times the size of Texas. The greatly enjoyed galah session shatters isolation. But it ceases the second an emergency call comes in.

Light Planes Link Cattle Stations

The flying from Alice is done by an extraordinary group of bush pilots supplied by Connellan Airways. In addition to its R.F.D.S. flights, Eddie Connellan's airline covers by scheduled bush-mail flights more than 120 stations in a 600,000-square-mile area. Its little planes take off day after day for places as far away as Wyndham in Western Australia or Maningrida on the north coast.

The pilots usually put down at station strips, but they will obligingly land any place that provides a wind sock, a once-whitewashed stone or two to locate the landing spot, and—most important—radioed confirmation that the strip is serviceable.

"Our primary purpose is service to the territory people—at the remote cattle stations, the mining fields, and the native welfare settlements and missions," Damian Miller, the airline's director of training, told me. "But if we have a spare seat, we'll always try to fit in

KODACHROME BY JEFF CARTER © N.G.S.

Conga line of fuzzy caterpillars migrates from tree to tree to feed on leaves. Girls keep their distance, since stinging hairs inflame the skin. Playing follow-the-leader, these larvae of the bag-shelter moth earn the name "processionary caterpillars."

KODACHROMES BY ROBERT B. GOODMAN (ABOVE) AND JEFF CARTER © N.G.S.

Crisis in the bush: Ambulance plane rushes an ailing aborigine to a hospital. Family physician to the outback, the Royal Flying Doctor Service ministers to isolated homesteads, camps, and missions for aborigines. Doctors diagnose ills by radio and prescribe for minor ones from standardized medicine chests stocked by every station.

Vital to the Centre way of life, the R.F.D.S. radio network also relays messages (right), instructs pupils of the School of the Air, and permits gossip sessions by housewives.

243

Parrots of the outback, rose-breasted cockatoos called galahs flock to their daily feeding at Pitchi Ritchi, a bird and flower sanctuary near Heavitree Gap. The spirited chatter of the noisy birds has led homesteaders to call housewives' radio gossip fests "galah sessions."

Worn and polished by time, the Macdonnell Ranges furrow the Tropic of Capricorn. Their vivid stripes—ancient sediments tilted vertically in a fold—ripple 250 miles across Australia's abdomen.

Wielding cruel claws, the perentie stalks other reptiles and even small kangaroos. The huge Australian lizard grows as long as eight feet.

EKTACHROMES BY DAVID MOORE © N.G.S.

an interested visitor. It's a good way to see Australia's Centre."

I joined Damian on one of Connellan's regular mail runs from the Alice airport. On the return flight we were to bring back a sick aboriginal child from the Ernabella Mission, 210 miles to the southwest, across the border in South Australia.

KODACHROME BY JEFF CARTER © N.G.S.

Aboriginal elder faces the future with stoic calm, characteristically ignoring the bush fly in his eye. Many aborigines earn their way as stockmen, but efforts to turn nomads into landholding pastoralists have met with little success (page 255).

The control tower gave us our weather forecast: dust squalls and—surprisingly—rain, light and localized.

Our take-off resembled a grasshopper's jump. A burst of power, the briefest of full-throttle runs, and our twin-engine craft was in the air. Moments later the runway of Alice airport was still below us, for it is long enough

to handle the biggest jets. After that, the red-brown nowhere stretched for miles.

Twenty minutes of flight and Damian began coming down. At first, I couldn't see why. After much searching, I noticed an old wind sock, a few white rocks, a waiting truck. A gray-bearded aborigine with a couple of big cattle dogs in a truck accepted mail and parcels without a word. We roared off again, climbing above a roughly fenced corral and the tin roofs of the homestead.

"Palmer Valley," said Damian.

At Erldunda, the next station, there was no one in sight at all. We waited for ten minutes, then put out the mail, and took to the air again.

I asked Damian where all the livestock was.

"The stock's run down because of the drought," he said. "A lot of it is dead. Even the kangaroos have died on some stations."

Next stop was a place called Kulgera, 145 miles from Alice toward the South Australian border. In a small garden, its wooden fence thatched against sand, a few optimistic tomatoes showed red badges of courage in their unequal fight against the drought.

Ominous clouds of approaching dust squalls darkened the skyline to the north and east. The big corral was empty, and diesel road trains—trucks that have several livestock trailers—stood idle in the yard.

"It hasn't really rained here for almost five years," station owner Len McConville told me over coffee and cakes. "We're down to 300 head of stock. I don't know that I care to hang on here much longer."

Soon the plane was refueled and we were airborne once more, headed toward the next station, called Mount Cavenagh.

"Do you see what I see?" asked Damian. "It's been *raining*. This place is actually wet!"

In we came, flaps down. Up rushed the brown earth, marked with dark boggy streaks. Damian skillfully sought and found firm ground—except for one deceptive soft patch.

Down plopped the nose wheel, right in it. Over nosed the plane, starboard propeller biting the earth. But our seat belts held us.

We climbed down, dug out the nose wheel, and examined the hopelessly bent prop.

"There's still that sick child at Ernabella," said Damian. "I'll have to get another airplane to fly him out."

The radio at the station homestead was occupied with the School of the Air, conducted by Mrs. Nance Barrett in her studio classroom at the high school in Alice. Childish voices piped up from remote homesteads and camps all over the 125,000 square miles of Mrs. Barrett's "classroom." They answered questions on Australian history with assurance. They fired back answers to awkward arithmetical problems in pounds, shillings, and pence—a difficulty that should end in February, 1966, when Australia is scheduled to convert its currency to a decimal system. The session ended with a song to the notes of Mrs. Barrett's piano, hundreds of miles away.

Sun Shrouded by Swirling Dust

Damian soon has another Connellan airplane winging out from Alice toward nearby Kulgera strip, where the rain hasn't struck yet. We go there and watch as the plane makes several passes before landing. A turbulent crosswind catches it in gust after gust, and it is hard to see how the craft can escape being dashed to the ground. The pilot nurses it with bursts of power just off the runway, to touch down perfectly at last and stay down.

The young pilot jumps out smiling. This is all in the day's work. I climb aboard, strapping myself good and tight in the seat.

We get up all right, but the weather deteriorates. We can see dust squalls, some so dense they look solid, and the sun glints like a pale red moon through the lighter dust high up. When the strong winds want to pick up dust anywhere around this area, they have plenty to work on (pages 236-7 and 254-5).

For a while we dodge the squalls, the aircraft pitching and tossing like a yacht fighting a strong gale. The air hits us like pieces of invisible mountainside. Sometimes, with no warning, the plane leaps vertically, then shakes its wings and drops again. At other times the pilot, flying on instruments, throttles back and glides over the humpback of five thousand feet of what looks like solid dust.

We toss and pitch over the foothills of the Musgrave Ranges. Below, with the air clear of dust at last, the red granite mountains and valleys make a terrain ferocious and challenging. Who, I wonder, would want to live in this wild place?

"It is the land of the Pitjantjara tribe," says my pilot friend.

We fly over the Ernabella Mission—some well-kept buildings with shining tin roofs, a cement-brick church, a garden decking the red earth with pale green. Beyond is the strip. The wind sock is distended straight across it, denoting a stiff crosswind.

Coming in, we rush above a knot of aboriginal wurlies—rough huts of bark, branches, twigs, and leaves—at the end of the red runway. We touch, bounce, touch, bounce. The strip is long, and I am glad of that. We touch again, and the wheels stay. We are down.

No time is wasted. With his dark, bearded kinsmen gathered compassionately around, a little boy with a chest infection is lifted aboard and strapped in the rear seat with another patient—a thin young woman—beside him. We roar once more into the sky, to buck the turbulent air 210 miles to Alice.

We skid through hail, lurch along the edges of rain squalls. Some have left pools of water on the ground—but not for long. The sun's evaporation and the rain-hungry earth will soon see to that. The little boy and the young woman sit wide-eyed, silent, accepting the gyrations of the airplane, I suppose, as another oddity in the white man's way of life.

At last the runways of the Alice airport show up ahead. The little airplane lands on a tenth of one strip; we taxi, it seems, for miles. An ambulance waits, with Sister Joyce Ellis— a stately brunette from Queensland dressed in white—ready to receive the little boy.

"Nice flight?" she asks.

Outback Colors Inspire Aboriginal Artists

I had tasted the violence the Centre can brew. But it can also be astonishingly colorful, with brilliant reds and purples. No wonder it is the home of Australia's amazing aboriginal art movement. Long ago, observers noted that the aborigines possessed an extraordinary flair for producing abstract designs in color. But only anthropologists and primitive-art enthusiasts paid much attention.

Then came Albert Namatjira.

Everybody in Australia knows something of the Namatjira story—how Albert, an aborigine reared at Hermannsburg Mission, 70 miles from Alice, became an artist of world stature. His is not an isolated case. Albert Namatjira went on to inspire a school of Aranda tribesmen artists (following pages). Now some of his sons are becoming equally famous, and Gabriel, his grandson, is following in their footsteps.

The great artist's grave lies just outside Alice. The headstone bears a text from the First Book of Corinthians 15:10—"by the grace of God I am what I am"—in Albert's own language, and the simple inscription:

ALBERT NAMATJIRA
BORN AT HERMANNSBURG, JULY 28, 1902
DIED AT ALICE SPRINGS, AUGUST 8, 1959

I found Rex Battarbee, the artist who fostered the Namatjira art movement, in a pleasant house in a wide street by the side of the Todd River. His house overlooks the gum trees that crowd the dry riverbed. Inside, the rooms shine with his own glowing water colors alongside those of native artists.

Rex Battarbee, born at Warrnambool in Victoria, severely wounded fighting as a

member of the Australian Imperial Forces in France in World War I, told me that he started coming to the Centre to paint during the 1930's. He took Albert Namatjira as his camel boy. Albert developed a great interest in the white man's paintings of the color-splashed Centre.

"Then one day," Rex told me, "Albert said very quietly, 'I could do that. Just teach me how to prepare the paints.' I showed him. He learned fast. We used water colors—no oils; the dust and the bush flies stick to oils here. Within a fortnight he was painting tolerably well, and he went on from there."

Gradually Albert's gift found appreciation beyond Hermannsburg Mission. At a 1938 exhibition in Melbourne, his paintings sold for as much as six guineas (then $25).

lost persons and criminals over deserts and through the bush with the baffling skill they began to acquire in earliest childhood.

Some trackers still work at Alice Springs, though Police Inspector G. L. Ryall told me that the automobile and the bitumen had largely done away with the need for them. I met the inspector's two trackers—quiet, taciturn men in khaki uniforms.

"Yes, I can tell all the tracks," tall Walbiri tribesman Larry Jabaljari admitted, as if the skill were so commonplace as not to be worth mentioning. "They're different."

His mate, Willie Martin, nodded approval.

One Track May Tell a Whole Story

I gathered that to them a track—whether of lizard, snake, wallaby, emu, aborigine, white man, or child—was not just a blur left uselessly in the bush. It was a picture story.

The local tribe is the Aranda, or Arunta. To the southwest and over the South Australian border live the Pitjantjara. Northwest of these, on two government settlements and a few cattle stations, are the Walbiri. They

With a bold brush Gabriel Namatjira portrays the ghost gums and dramatic terrain of his native land (left). Landscapes by Albert Namatjira, his grandfather, won world acclaim and inspired fellow tribesmen to paint.

Second-generation Namatjiras, Oscar and Keith (below), turn out quick sketches that tourists buy at Alice Springs for $15 apiece. But the brothers amass little wealth; tribal law demands they share earnings with their many relatives. They work in water colors because dust and flies stick to oils.

KODACHROMES BY JEFF CARTER © N.G.S.

Now many are worth thousands of pounds.

"The Australian aborigine can be a talented and an able man," said Rex Battarbee. "For years we thought him capable only of scrawling rough totemic designs—circles, spirals, bird tracks, animal footprints—on bits of bark or the dark walls of caves. Look at this work by Ewald, Albert's son."

We looked at a striking painting of a mountainous landscape after a rain squall, with an astonishing quality and amazing light.

"No artist could have done better in this manner," Battarbee concluded.

This awareness of the natives' artistic ability is relatively new. For decades they have been regarded mainly as convenient stockmen on cattle stations, or useful trackers for the police. Their practiced eyes can trail

and other area tribes all speak similar dialects, and all have complex social organizations, and a rich heritage of myth, ritual, and beliefs in magic. Strict tribal laws control every essential activity and relationship. Transgressors are severely dealt with, even to the death. Some are punished by "pointing the bone"— execution by psychic magic: Executioners point a bone at an offender and sing the prescribed chant; if he believes, he may give up his will to live, wither away, and die.

"Simple" Nomads Command 40,000 Words

Australians—both officials and plain citizens—are trying to understand the Stone Age viewpoint. But no one regards it as easy.

"The aborigine is still a wanderer in body and in mind," said Father Summerhayes at Santa Teresa Mission when I visited there. "Perhaps it is his greatest failing."

The Commonwealth Government's Welfare Department declared: "Assimilation is our

policy. But it will take a long, long time." The government's goal was to grant Australian aborigines full citizenship—a step since taken. Eventually, officials expect, aborigines will enjoy the same manner of living and accept the same responsibilities as white Australians. But everyone agrees it will take a long time.

Pastor F. W. Albrecht, former superintendent of the Finke River Mission at Hermannsburg, has spent most of his life among the aborigines.

"You can't turn a food gatherer into a food producer overnight," he told me. "The aborigine is not a simple nomad searching for a way of life. He is an efficient collector of his needs, with a social system that suits him, disciplines him, and is workable.

"To survive in a country like this and bring up a family in it, to have a language of at least 40,000 words, a culture, a social system, a religion and philosophy suited to him —these are hardly the achievements of a dull and stupid nomad. The more we get to know about their system of life and themselves, the more we admire them. But we have to train them in a new sort of responsibility.

"The aborigine is a good stockman," Pastor Albrecht pointed out. "In that work he feels, and is, responsible. He knows he has a place in the community. He feels he belongs."

Thereafter I looked at the dark stockmen of the Alice with new eyes. I went out along the bitumen 30 miles or so north to meet a gang droving their livestock down the old cattle route, not far from the road. Although the diesel road trains carried a lot of cattle, a good deal of bush droving was still going on. I was fortunate to see this spectacle, for the drought has left most of the surviving cattle

EKTACHROME BY DAVID MOORE © N.G.S.

Learning to sew, aboriginal women at Amoonguna settlement make hospital caps. Such way stations between nomadic and settled living, run by government or church, help aborigines adjust to modern ways.

Primitive Pintubi tribespeople find food, clothing, and nursing care at Papunya settlement. Crude windbreaks shelter family groups on the reserve's fringes.

Aborigines who demonstrate a willingness to learn win permanent housing in Papunya. Those who find the new life lacking may return to the old whenever they wish. Until recent years, few of the desert-dwelling Pintubi had seen a white man.

too weak to walk to the railhead at Alice.

Just north of McGrath Creek in the low scrub country, with lots of flowers about, we met the mob of cattle—big, nervous beasts plodding along behind a tough-looking boss steer. Mick Wagoo, the chief drover, told me that a mob always has a sort of born leader that takes over the job by natural right.

Mick was just about to bring the mob to a halt for the night. It was around four in the afternoon. I stayed, fascinated, for I had never seen anything like this before.

Mick was a fine-looking aborigine, on a sturdy horse. He wore high-heeled boots and dusty old clothes, with a colored kerchief bound around his head beneath his bashed-up, wide-brimmed hat—a more or less standard outfit. His crew numbered eight other aborigines. They had 40 horses, no wagon.

The mob settled down, two or three of the horsemen still watching them, always ready for a "rush"—Australian for stampede.

"We lost 30 beasts in a rush three nights ago," said Mick. "We'll pick most of them up again when we bring in another mob."

There were, I gathered, four more such mobs to be brought to Alice during that season. This was the third. They'd come about 150 miles and had already been three weeks on the road, he thought. (Mick wasn't very good on time.)

Trail Dinner: Damper and Kangaroo Stew

The cattle stood watching us, looking now and again at their leader. Big and wild, they seemed to me ready to rush at any moment.

"How do you cope with a rush?" I asked.

"We try to head them off and get around them," he said. "We try to get them into a ring. Then they rush around and around. They get tired and stop."

I stayed while the drovers made camp, hobbling the pack horses, putting bells on them, and letting them go.

Unbowed victim of drought, Central Mount Wedge station-owner Bill Waudby corrals horses used to work 300 cattle he hopefully keeps as breeding stock. Once his Rhode Island-size spread supported 2,000 head. From Alice Springs, 150 miles away, he hauls beef for his family and feed for the remnant of his herd.

Striking contrast drawn by a barbed-wire fence: land on the left retains cover and will spring to life with rain. Starving cattle stripped the other side bare; it may never recover.

Cowboy ballads, down-under style, waylay tourists. Aranda tribesmen will offer curios for sale following their concert, performed beside the road to Palm Valley, where a freak of geography permits palm trees to grow. Aborigines in cattle country so admire American movie cowboys that they wear wrangler's clothing whether they work stock or not.

Astride a wild cow, a daredevil of the Hermannsburg Mission shows his skill at an annual rodeo that attracts spectators from hundreds of miles around. Founded in 1877, the Lutheran settlement, 70 miles west of Alice Springs, offers a permanent home for Aranda tribesmen who work the mission's 1,500-square-mile cattle station.

"Things will get better," insists cattleman Bill Waudby. Accustomed to periodic drought, cattle-station managers normally anticipate only one good year in five. But the current drought began in 1958. Some cattlemen, located near scenic attractions, now cater to tourists by providing guesthouses. A few operate dude ranches.

Specter haunting the Centre, a dust squall rips into Undoolya station. It gobbles up topsoil, containing grass seeds waiting to germinate, then redeposits the load in arid wastes elsewhere. Dust storms may occur every few days during droughts.

"We have to work a shift system," Mick explained to me. "We can't just leave the mob. At least two or three of us must always be on our horses, keeping watch. We have special horses trained for night work. These cattle have never seen anybody but us, and they're easily scared."

The stockmen listened silently and settled among their packs, almost blending into the bush—at home here and quietly competent, ready for anything. Bush flies flocked in from nowhere, as they always do, and settled on men's and horses' faces, and in their eyes. Accustomed to this from birth, neither man nor beast paid much attention.

The shadows lengthened and the fire crackled for the simple evening meal of kangaroo stew and unleavened bread called "damper," baked roughly in the wood ashes. The stew smelled good. The damper tasted wonderful. It wasn't hard to brush the bits of ash from it.

The stars began to come out, lovely in the dark velvety blue of the tropic night. We yarned along, about dingoes and kangaroos, about the aborigines' life. Mick didn't volunteer anything, but he answered questions well. The others said nothing whatever.

In the lull I thought I heard voices singing. Singing? I was fooling myself. Singing out there, in the wilderness?

But someone *was*—chanting, sometimes in a way I'd never heard before; sometimes humming, quietly and continuously. Who and why?

I asked Boss Mick. He seemed surprised at my ignorance.

"The boys sing for the cattle," he explained. "It quiets them. We always sing—all night, where the cattle can hear. We ride slowly round and round, stop often. And always we must make a little noise. So they know that we are there."

Children of the Past Ignore the Future

The stockmen rolled into their blankets, still in their clothes minus only their big felt hats. Soon they would be sleeping soundly, ready for their turn, before the morning came, to sing and chant softly from the saddle to their beasts. Before sunup the mob would be on the way again. They'd be another week or

so to Alice, rest there a while, and be freighted away to the stockyards in Adelaide. Then the dressed beef would be shipped—perhaps halfway around the world.

I wondered why men so good as stockmen could not progress a little further and become station managers and owners themselves? After all, no one could have more right to some of this land.

I asked Pastor Albrecht about it when I returned to Alice Springs.

"We've tried that," he told me. "In 1944 we settled some of our good stockmen as pastoralists in their own right. We started a concern that we called the Hermannsburg Aboriginal Pastoralists Association. We financed experienced family men, with repayment to

255

be made within a certain time. The idea was to give them a feeling of social responsibility, pride of ownership, a sense of ambition. All this would help assimilation.

"We found they just weren't interested in what we thought of as their economic rehabilitation—just couldn't see the sense in any such thing. To people who never had accumulated anything, property ownership meant less than nothing. They ran the stock all right. They paid off their debts. But they could not get hold of our idea of providing for the future, of working now to profit later.

"'You white people always worry, worry, worry—about clothing, about money, rain, cattle,' one of them said to me. 'We never worry. In this country it is no use.'

"Back for thousands of years," Pastor Albrecht continued, "they had seen this harsh land defy them with prolonged drought, time and time again. Why develop what certain drought must certainly destroy?

"We stuck to the experiment for years. It didn't work. Their past was too strong in them. They gave up, and drifted back to the mission.

"It will take time and patience to change these attitudes. But we must press on."

I thought of Mick and his fellow tribesmen coming down the droving track from

256

the north, his stockmen singing lullabies to the cattle through the tropic nights. These men live in the open, free and simple, their wants taken care of, their families sharing the communal life of the tribe. They would deliver the mob at Alice and go back with their horses for more.

A strange town, Alice. It gets hold of you. Late that night I walked along the streets thinking about it all. It was a soft night with the southern constellations glowing. I nodded a greeting to a group of barefoot aborigines on the sidewalk, one of them with a handful of spears. The night was heavy with the scent of flowers.

Next morning I caught an airplane for Adelaide. As Alice faded behind and below, I stared at the fantastic red landscape slipping by—the dry, harsh heart of the continent. But somehow it no longer seemed a dead, forbidding place.

There *was* life down there: people. They were tough, tenacious people; scattered all over the outback, many of them, and perhaps a bit lonely. Some were black, older than history, wise in the ways of survival. Others were white, with courage and patience and faith in a stern, raw land.

I knew now how they could grow to love it.

THE END

Kangaroos diminish during the drought, adding to the problems of aborigine food hunters, but the Centre, despite its empty appearance, supports many forms of life. Lizards scurry about, and dingoes—wild dogs—howl dismally at night. Eagles and ostrichlike emus range the area. Moisture-craving bush flies plague eyes and mouths of men and animals, but they do not bite.

KODACHROMES BY JEFF CARTER © N.G.S.

Clinging to bush life and the company of his dogs, an aborigine carves boomerangs, spears, and woomeras (spear throwers) for sale. He offers camel rides to sightseers who stumble onto his camp. Imported a century ago from India, dromedaries packed supplies before motor vehicles outmoded them. Today the beasts rove in wild herds, and many have perished in the drought. Aborigines use them to haul gear on walkabouts.

Giant Comet Grazes the Sun

By KENNETH F. WEAVER
National Geographic Senior Staff

I AM A SEA-BRED THING. When I feel happy, or lonely, I come down to the sea, for it fills my heart with deep emotion. That night I was dreaming of the sea. I was walking along the shore....

I do not know why, but on that night my wife woke me, very faithfully. Usually she discourages me from observing the stars. Exposing myself to the night dew, she thinks, cannot be any good for my health. Still, she woke me.

At four o'clock I climbed up to the observing stage on the roof of a storehouse in my courtyard. The starry sky was beautiful, transparent, as though swept clean by the typhoon two days before. Fine weather! I put my eye to the telescope.

At a quarter past four something refracted through my lenses—a queer, pale celestial body. My heart shook. I broke the stillness before the dawn:

"A new comet!"

Thus does Tsutomu Seki, writing to NATIONAL GEOGRAPHIC, recall his discovery.

Yet, even as Seki, in the Japanese city of Kōchi, was exclaiming with delight over his find, another young comet hunter, Kaoru Ikeya, was poring over star charts in Benten Jima, 250 miles away. Ikeya, too, had seen the fuzzy object, "shining like a street lamp on a misty night." Nowhere could he find it on the charts.

"From my experience observing," he said later, "I judged the image to be real, and not merely the reflection of some city light, some ghost image in my eyepiece, or a fleck of cloud." His experience was not negligible: Since the age of 13 he had been making telescopes and watching the heavens. At 22, he already had two comet discoveries to his credit.

Hastily, Ikeya climbed down from his corrugated

Ghostly searchlight against a dawning sky, Ikeya-Seki flaunts a 75-million-mile tail flowing away from the sun. Luminous gas and dust torn from the glowing head form the transparent streamer. GEOGRAPHIC photographer Victor R. Boswell, Jr., made this remarkable Ektachrome near Beltsville, Maryland, on October 30, 1965.

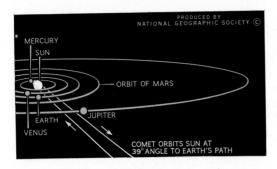

Diving in from space, Ikeya-Seki sweeps past earth, wheels around the sun, and streaks away. At its closest approach to the sun, the comet misses by a mere 300,000 miles. Solar wind—a steady blast of electrified particles—blows the tail ahead of Ikeya-Seki as it recedes. Dates in blue show when the comet passes below the planets' orbits.

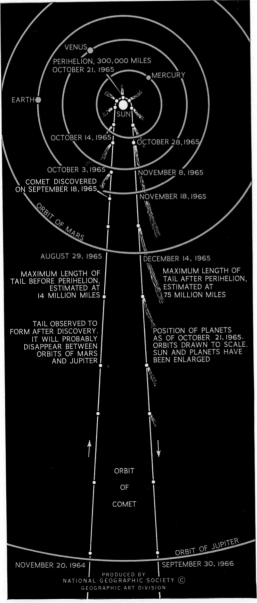

roof, jumped on his bicycle, and rode three miles through the still-sleeping streets. At the post office he sent an urgent telegram to the Tokyo Astronomical Observatory, reading simply: "4 A.M. 19TH. COMET? MAGNITUDE SEVEN. 0845 SOUTH 0837. IKEYA."

Translated, the cryptic message meant: "I think I discovered a comet at 4 o'clock this morning, September 19 [it was still September 18 in the Western Hemisphere]. Its brightness is 7th magnitude [just one step below visibility to the naked eye]. Its location in astronomical coordinates is right ascension 8 hours 45 minutes and declination minus 8 degrees 37 minutes. Ikeya."

Unmistakably it was a comet, quickly confirmed by the international clearinghouse for such matters at the Smithsonian Astrophysical Observatory in Cambridge, Massachusetts. These scientists enrolled it as Comet 1965f, signifying the sixth comet spotted that year, and named it for Ikeya and Seki. For each man, it was the third comet to bear his name.

Tail Grows as Comet Nears Sun

As September gave way to October, Ikeya-Seki, suddenly world-famous, hurtled on toward the sun. The glowing ball expanded hugely. Visible to the naked eye now, it trailed an ever-lengthening tail so transparent the stars shone through it undimmed (page 258).

In its flight, faster and faster as it neared the gravitational heart of the solar system, Ikeya-Seki at first seemed destined to plunge into the sun. But its path through space saved it; on October 21, barely 300,000 miles out, it skidded around the sun in a hard crack-the-whip turn, changing its direction by 130 degrees within six hours.

At perihelion, point of closest approach to the sun, the comet reached a speed of a million miles an hour. Under the intense gravitational force of the sun, its nucleus split into three parts. Then the broken comet swung away, traveling now against the sun's pull. It embarked on the outward leg of an enormous cigar-shaped orbit that will take it far beyond the outermost planet.

By February, 1966, still visible to a telescope, this comet will have lost 95 percent of its speed. In several hundred years it will have slowed down so much that it can no longer resist the sun's pull. Once more its parts will plunge sunward, to be rediscovered perhaps a millennium from now.

Comets are so common that the orbits of some 870 have been computed, yet so rare that only about eight a year are spotted, half

KODACHROME (LEFT) BY THOMAS M. BEERS, NATIONAL GEOGRAPHIC STAFF,
AND EKTACHROME BY EIJI MIYAZAWA © N.G.S.

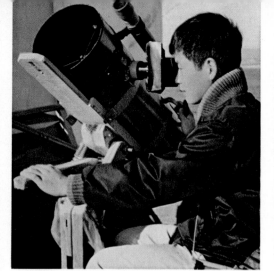

"I wanted to see the sky, so I built a telescope to look," says 22-year-old Kaoru Ikeya of Benten Jima, Japan, who began observing the stars at 13. Ikeya, a piano-factory worker, discovered Ikeya-Seki last September 19 (Japan time).

"Sky hunter," as Tsutomu Seki, 34, calls himself, teaches guitar at his home in Kōchi, Japan. Like Ikeya an amateur astronomer since youth, he spied the comet the same night. Each found two earlier comets, credited to them by name.

of them newly known. On infrequent occasions—fewer than ten times a century—a truly brilliant one blazes in the daytime sky to fill the superstitious with awe and terror.

Halley's comet, most celebrated of all, has returned to frighten the world approximately every three-quarters of a century for at least 2,200 years. The Chinese recorded it in 240 B.C., and history has noted every return since then. Its next coming is expected by astronomers in 1986.

Halley's visits coincided with the Jewish revolt of A.D. 66 and the last great battle of Attila the Hun against the Romans in 451. Halley's glared in English skies in 1066, just before William the Conqueror defeated King Harold and his Saxons at Hastings.

In 1910, Haitians freely bought "comet pills" to protect themselves from Halley's poisonous gases. They need not have feared. Scientists say the earth has passed through hundreds of comet tails without mishap.

Actually, Ikeya-Seki's tail and coma (the luminous head) are about as near to nothing as they can get and still be something. They probably contain less than an ounce of matter to the cubic mile.

The only part of a comet with any real substance is the nucleus, measuring from one to perhaps fifty miles in diameter. According to the widely accepted theory developed by Dr. Fred L. Whipple, Director of the Smithsonian Astrophysical Observatory, this nucleus is a "dirty snowball" of frozen water

*See "The Sun," by Herbert Friedman, NATIONAL GEOGRAPHIC, November, 1965.

and gases, such as methane and ammonia. It is mixed, like a raisin pudding, with bits of porous, fragile, earthy material.

When Ikeya-Seki swept near enough to the sun to become heated, the outer layers of the nucleus vaporized. The intensely luminous gas and dust thus released formed the comet's glowing head, which expanded till it was larger than a planet, and the tail, which reached the enormous length of 75 million miles. It is the tail that gives comets their name: *komētēs,* in Greek, means "long-haired."

Where did Ikeya-Seki come from? Dr. Whipple suggests that billions of comets may have condensed out of gas and dust at the same time and in much the same way as the sun and planets.* Those that survived collision with the planets were thrown far out to the fringes of the solar system, where they circle as outriders of the sun.

Occasionally a passing star disturbs their motions and throws some of the comets toward the sun. These eccentric wanderers, like Ikeya-Seki, come unheralded and mysterious, to remain visible for a few weeks or months, then vanish again into darkness.

Every two years or so, a comet can be seen with the unaided eye. But even before the dim patch of light becomes visible, some lonely stargazer such as Kaoru Ikeya or Tsutomu Seki will find it with a telescope. And he will feel the surge of joy that Keats described when he wrote:

Then felt I like some watcher of the skies
When a new planet swims into his ken....

THE END

Saga of a Ship, the *Yankee*

By LUIS MARDEN
National Geographic Senior Staff

ON FEBRUARY 11 a lovely lady—the world-wandering brigantine *Yankee*—stars in the National Geographic Society's third nationwide television program in color on the Columbia Broadcasting System network. Here a veteran member of the GEOGRAPHIC's far-ranging staff tells of *Yankee*'s 54 years of life—from pre-World War I duty in the North Sea to a coral reef off Rarotonga. — THE EDITOR

I WELL REMEMBER the first time I saw her. Like a vision from the heroic days of sail, she rose up from the dark-blue shield of the Pacific. Topgallant, topsail, stunsails, bellying forecourse, and the gleaming triangles of headsails, staysails, and the main grew slowly upward from the horizon until the whole vessel lay on the hard edge of the sea. From the top of solitary Pitcairn Island, almost in the exact center of the South Pacific, I looked down on an immense circle of white-flecked cobalt and watched the brigantine *Yankee* sail over the rim of the earth.

At dawn that morning the long-drawn-out cry of "Sail ho-o-o!" had sounded from the lookout high above Bounty Bay, and five strokes of the island bell, the signal for a ship sighting, had clanged out again and again.

Pitcairners were about to welcome an old friend: Capt. Irving Johnson, the crack New England shipmaster who once every three years took an amateur crew round the world under sail. For nearly 25 years Captain Johnson had been a good friend to the people of Pitcairn, bringing them mail-order parcels, carrying them more than a hundred miles to another island to cut wood, and even on one occasion dynamiting the rocky bottom of Bounty Bay to make a safer entrance for the longboats that traded with passing ships.

Captain Johnson had promised me passage to Tahiti, and I was in the first longboat that pulled out through the white breakers to the brigantine. As we climbed out of the trough, I saw suddenly revealed the 96-foot-long vessel straining at her anchor chain as she rose and fell with the scend of the sea.

My eye ran down the graceful curve of her clipper bow, then aloft to the crossed yards glistening in the sun, and I felt as if I had gone back in time to the day in 1790 when the forebears of the Pitcairners, the mutineers in the *Bounty,* had brought their little ship here to her last resting place.

Free as the wind, the brigantine *Yankee* slices through a long Pacific swell as brisk trades fill her outstretched wings. *Yankee* cruised four times around the world under Capt. and Mrs. Irving Johnson; youthful crews shared labor and expenses. Topgallant carries the Johnson family emblem.

KODACHROME BY WILLIAM L. NEWTON III © NATIONAL GEOGRAPHIC SOCIETY

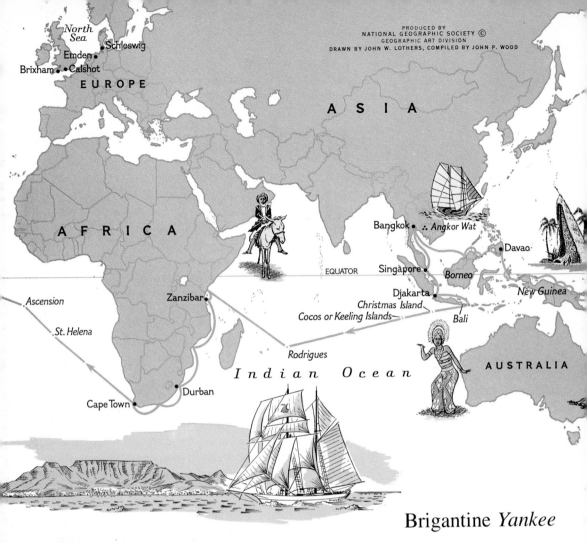

PRODUCED BY
NATIONAL GEOGRAPHIC SOCIETY ©
GEOGRAPHIC ART DIVISION
DRAWN BY JOHN W. LOTHERS, COMPILED BY JOHN P. WOOD

North Sea

Schleswig

Emden

Brixham • Calshot

EUROPE

A S I A

A F R I C A

Bangkok • ∴ Angkor Wat

Davao

EQUATOR

Singapore

Borneo

Zanzibar

Djakarta

Christmas Island

New Guinea

Ascension

Cocos or Keeling Islands

Bali

St. Helena

Rodrigues

AUSTRALIA

Indian Ocean

Durban

Cape Town

Brigantine *Yankee*

With the islanders I went aft to shake the hand of Irving Johnson, a broad-shouldered, powerfully built man with piercing blue eyes and an aquiline nose shaped like a well-cut jib, and of his wife Electa, "Exy" to *Yankee* crews and friends in many ports of the world.*

Before the second World War, Irving Johnson had sailed his first *Yankee,* a schooner, three times around the world, each time with an expense-sharing amateur crew.

All during the war Johnson, then a lieutenant commander in the U. S. Navy, took the survey vessel *Sumner* through the waters he knew so well, charting and sounding. His intimate knowledge of the reefs, currents, and coasts of the Pacific was invaluable.

After the war the Johnsons received proof of this from a friend in the Tonga Islands to whom they had sent a copy of their book

*See, in NATIONAL GEOGRAPHIC: "New Guinea to Bali in *Yankee,*" December, 1959; "Lost World of the Galapagos," May, 1959; "South Seas' Incredible Land Divers," January, 1955; "*Yankee* Roams the Orient," March, 1951; "The *Yankee*'s Wander-world," January, 1949; and "Westward Bound in the *Yankee,*" January, 1942—all by Irving and Electa Johnson.

SUPER ANSCOCHROME BY THOMAS J. ABERCROMBIE © N.G.S.

Shooting the sun, Capt. Irving Johnson navigates the brigantine *Yankee*. He gave the same proud name to her predecessor, a schooner, and to her successor, a ketch.

WATCH "THE VOYAGE OF THE BRIGANTINE YANKEE"
ON MOST OF THESE CBS TELEVISION STATIONS

(A few stations may schedule the program at a later date. Check your newspaper for day and time.)

ALABAMA
Birmingham WAPI-TV (13)
Dothan WTVY (4)
Huntsville WHNT-TV (19)
Mobile WKRG-TV (5)
Montgomery WCOV-TV (20)

ARIZONA
Phoenix KOOL-TV (10)
Tucson KOLD-TV (13)
Yuma KBLU-TV (13)

ARKANSAS
Fort Smith KFSA-TV (5)
Little Rock KTHV (11)

CALIFORNIA
Bakersfield KBAK-TV (29)
Chico KHSL-TV (12)
Eureka KIEM-TV (3)
Fresno KFRE-TV (30)
Los Angeles KNXT (2)
Sacramento KXTV (10)
Salinas-
Monterey KSBW-TV (8)
San Diego KFMB-TV (8)
San Francisco KPIX (5)

COLORADO
Colorado Springs-
Pueblo KKTV (11)
Denver KLZ-TV (7)
Grand Junction KREX-TV (5)

CONNECTICUT
Hartford WTIC-TV (3)

DELAWARE*

DIST. OF COLUMBIA
Washington WTOP-TV (9)

FLORIDA
Fort Myers WINK-TV (11)
Jacksonville WJXT (4)
Miami WTVJ (4)
Orlando WDBO-TV (6)
Tallahassee WCTV (6)
Tampa-St. Peters-
burg WTVT (13)

GEORGIA
Atlanta WAGA-TV (5)
Augusta WRDW-TV (12)
Columbus WRBL-TV (3)
Macon WMAZ-TV (13)
Savannah WTOC-TV (11)
Thomasville WCTV (6)

IDAHO
Boise KBOI-TV (2)
Idaho Falls KID-TV (3)
Lewiston KLEW-TV (3)
Twin Falls KMVT (11)

ILLINOIS
Champaign WCIA (3)
Chicago WBBM-TV (2)
Peoria WMBD-TV (31)
Quincy KHQA-TV (7)
Rockford WCEE-TV (23)
Rock Island WHBF-TV (4)

INDIANA
Evansville WEHT (50)
Fort Wayne WANE-TV (15)
Indianapolis WISH-TV (8)
Lafayette WFAM-TV (18)
South Bend WSBT-TV (22)

IOWA
Cedar Rapids-
Waterloo WMT-TV (2)
Des Moines KRNT-TV (8)
Mason City KGLO-TV (3)
Ottumwa KTVO (3)
Sioux City KVTV (9)

KANSAS
Ensign KTVC (6)
Goodland KLOE-TV (10)
Hays KAYS-TV (7)
Hutchinson-
Wichita KTVH (12)
Topeka WIBW-TV (13)

KENTUCKY
Lexington WLEX-TV (18)
Louisville WHAS-TV (11)

LOUISIANA
Baton Rouge WAFB-TV (9)
Lafayette KLFY-TV (10)
Monroe KNOE-TV (8)
New Orleans WWL-TV (4)
Shreveport KSLA-TV (12)

MAINE
Bangor WABI-TV (5)
Portland WGAN-TV (13)
Presque Isle WAGM-TV (8)

MARYLAND
Baltimore WMAR-TV (2)
Salisbury WBOC-TV (16)

MASSACHUSETTS
Boston WNDH-TV (5)

MICHIGAN
Cadillac-
Traverse City WWTV (9)
Detroit WJBK-TV (2)
Kalamazoo WKZO-TV (3)
Lansing WJIM-TV (6)
Marquette WLUC-TV (6)
Saginaw-Bay
City WKNX-TV (57)

MINNESOTA
Duluth KDAL-TV (3)
Mankato KEYC-TV (12)
Minneapolis-
St. Paul WCCO-TV (4)

MISSISSIPPI
Columbus WCBI-TV (4)
Greenwood WABG-TV (6)
Jackson WJTV (12)
Meridian WTOK-TV (11)

MISSOURI
Cape Girardeau KFVS-TV (12)
Hannibal KHQA-TV (7)
Jefferson City KRCG (13)
Joplin KODE-TV (12)
Kansas City KCMO-TV (5)
Kirksville KTVO (3)
St. Joseph KFEQ-TV (2)
St. Louis KMOX-TV (4)
Springfield KTTS-TV (10)

MONTANA
Billings KOOK-TV (2)
Butte KXLF-TV (4)
Glendive KXGN-TV (5)

Terre Haute WTHI-TV (10)

NEBRASKA
Lincoln KOLN-TV (10)
Omaha WOW-TV (6)

NEVADA
Las Vegas KLAS-TV (8)
Reno KOLO-TV (8)

NEW HAMPSHIRE*

NEW JERSEY*

NEW MEXICO
Albuquerque KGGM-TV (13)
Carlsbad KAVE-TV (6)
Roswell KSWS-TV (8)

NEW YORK
Albany WTEN (10)
Binghamton WNBF-TV (12)
Buffalo WBEN-TV (4)
Carthage-
Watertown WWNY-TV (7)
New York WCBS-TV (2)
Rochester WHEC-TV (10)
Syracuse WHEN-TV (5)

NORTH CAROLINA
Charlotte WBTV (3)
Durham-Raleigh WTVD (11)
Greensboro WFMY-TV (2)
Greenville WNCT-TV (9)

NORTH DAKOTA
Bismarck KXMB-TV (12)
Dickinson KDIX-TV (2)
Fargo-
Valley City KXJB-TV (4)
Minot KXMC-TV (13)

OHIO
Cincinnati WCPO-TV (9)
Cleveland WJW-TV (8)
Columbus WBNS-TV (10)
Dayton WHIO-TV (7)
Steubenville WSTV-TV (9)
Toledo WTOL-TV (11)
Youngstown WKBN-TV (27)

OKLAHOMA
Oklahoma City KWTV (9)
Tulsa KOTV (6)

OREGON
Klamath Falls KOTI (2)
Medford KTVM (5)
Portland KOIN-TV (6)

PENNSYLVANIA
Altoona WFBG-TV (10)
Erie WSEE (35)
Harrisburg WHP-TV (21)
Johnstown WJAC-TV (6)
Lancaster-
Lebanon WLYH-TV (15)
Philadelphia WCAU-TV (10)
Pittsburgh KDKA-TV (2)
Scranton-
Wilkes-Barre WDAU-TV (22)
York WSBA-TV (43)

RHODE ISLAND
Providence WPRO-TV (12)

SOUTH CAROLINA
Anderson WAIM-TV (40)
Charleston WCSC-TV (5)

Great Falls KFBB-TV (5)
Helena KBLL-TV (12)
Missoula KGVO-TV (13)

Columbia WNOK-TV (19)
Florence WBTW (13)
Spartanburg WSPA-TV (7)

SOUTH DAKOTA
Rapid City KOTA-TV (3)
Sioux Falls KELO-TV (11)

TENNESSEE
Chattanooga WDEF-TV (12)
Jackson WDXI-TV (7)
Johnson City-Bristol-
Kingsport WJHL-TV (11)
Knoxville WBIR-TV (10)
Memphis WREC-TV (3)
Nashville WLAC-TV (5)

TEXAS
Amarillo KFDA-TV (10)
Austin KTBC-TV (7)
Beaumont KFDM-TV (6)
Bryan KBTX-TV (3)
Corpus Christi KZTV (10)
Dallas-Ft. Worth KRLD-TV (4)
El Paso KROD-TV (4)
Harlingen KGBT-TV (4)
Houston KHOU-TV (11)
Laredo KGNS-TV (8)
Lubbock KLBK-TV (13)
Lufkin KTRE-TV (9)
Odessa KOSA-TV (7)
San Angelo KCTV (8)
San Antonio KENS-TV (5)
Sweetwater-
Abilene KPAR-TV (12)
Waco KWTX-TV (10)
Wichita Falls KAUZ-TV (6)

UTAH
Salt Lake City KSL-TV (5)

VERMONT
Burlington WCAX-TV (3)

VIRGINIA
Bristol WHIL-TV (11)
Harrisonburg WSVA-TV (3)
Norfolk WTAR-TV (3)
Richmond WRVA-TV (12)
Roanoke WDBJ-TV (7)

WASHINGTON
Bellingham KVOS-TV (12)
Pasco KEPR-TV (19)
Seattle KIRO-TV (7)
Spokane KXLY-TV (4)
Yakima KIMA-TV (29)

WEST VIRGINIA
Charleston WCHS-TV (8)
Clarksburg WBOY-TV (12)
Oak Hill WOAY-TV (4)
Wheeling WSTV-TV (9)

WISCONSIN
Green Bay WBAY-TV (2)
La Crosse WKBT (8)
Madison WISC-TV (3)
Milwaukee WISN-TV (12)
Superior KDAL-TV (3)
Wausau WSAU-TV (7)

WYOMING
Casper KTWO-TV (2)
Cheyenne KFBC-TV (5)
Riverton KWRB-TV (10)

**See neighboring states*

NATIONAL GEOGRAPHIC
Voyage
of the
Yankee

SEE IT ON TV
Friday,
February 11

Friday, February 11, 1966, *Yankee* sails the Seven Seas — to exotic adventure

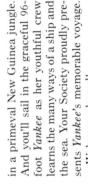

CIRCLE FEBRUARY 11 on your calendar and stand by to board a blue-water sailing ship. Destination: the Seven Seas. On that Friday evening, switch on your television set and ease into your armchair. High adventure awaits in visits to faraway ports.

You'll enjoy "The Voyage of the Brigantine *Yankee*," third in a series of hour-long TV true-life adventures produced by the National Geographic Society in association with David L. Wolper. The Columbia Broadcasting System televises this unique color film (see station listings on back page) under sponsorship of Encyclopaedia Britannica, Inc., and the Aetna Life and Casualty Insurance Companies.

Orson Welles narrates the thrilling around-the-world voyage of Capt. Irving Johnson (at wheel, above), his wife Electa, and 22 young men and women. You'll watch them put in to Pitcairn Island (above, left) and meet descendants of the *Bounty* mutineers. You'll witness New Hebrides islanders proving their manhood by hurtling headlong 73 feet from a tower. You'll mingle with Stone Age aborigines in a primeval New Guinea jungle. And you'll sail in the graceful 96-foot *Yankee* as her youthful crew learns the many ways of a ship and the sea. Your Society proudly presents *Yankee's* memorable voyage. Welcome aboard!

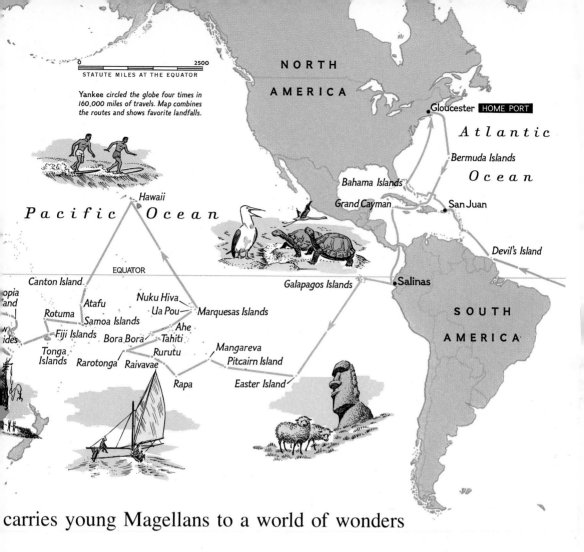

STATUTE MILES AT THE EQUATOR

Yankee circled the globe four times in 160,000 miles of travels. Map combines the routes and shows favorite landfalls.

NORTH AMERICA

SOUTH AMERICA

Atlantic Ocean

Pacific Ocean

Gloucester HOME PORT

Bermuda Islands

Bahama Islands

Grand Cayman
San Juan

Devil's Island

EQUATOR

Galapagos Islands
Salinas

Hawaii

Canton Island

Nuku Hiva
Ua Pou

Atafu
Marquesas Islands

opia and

Rotuma
Samoa Islands
Ahe

w ides
Fiji Islands
Bora Bora
Tahiti

Tonga Islands
Rarotonga
Rurutu
Raivavae

Mangareva
Pitcairn Island

Rapa

Easter Island

carries young Magellans to a world of wonders

describing a voyage aboard the first *Yankee.*

"American ships touched at our island frequently during the war," said the man. "One day one of your admirals called on us, and seeing your book, asked if he might borrow it. I couldn't refuse him, but I said to my wife, 'That's the last we'll see of that book.'

"However, about five weeks later the admiral—his name was Halsey—unexpectedly strode into the house and tossed down the book, saying, 'Thanks very much for the book. It won me a battle.' I asked how, and he said, 'When Irving Johnson said he could take a big ship through a certain channel, I believed him. Evidently the Japanese didn't, and I got round behind them. Thanks very much.'"

At war's end, Johnson's first thought was to obtain another sailing vessel, so he could return to the life he loved. Sterling Hayden, later a well-known actor, had sailed with Johnson on his second world cruise, and at Schleswig, Germany, Hayden found the right ship for his former skipper. She was claimed as a war prize by the British and taken to Calshot in southern England.

Master mariner Alan Villiers saw her there, with her stumpy steel masts and decks littered with loose gear, and later he told Irving:

"She looked like a treasure the dog brought in, not knowing its value."

Like the previous *Yankee,* this one began life as a German North Sea pilot-training ship, the schooner-rigged *Duhnen.* Built at Emden in 1912, she was the last of the German pilot-training boats to operate under sail. She served as a school ship for the Hitler Youth, and in World War II she became a radar target vessel for the Luftwaffe.

Built of steel with high bulwarks and no portholes, *Duhnen* was designed to stay dry in boisterous North Sea waters. Her only deck openings ran down the 'midships line, so that she would not fill in case of a knockdown. She was a safe ship.

TELEVISION ANNOUNCEMENT ▶
on the attached pages may be torn out, folded, and kept as a reminder for members and friends to watch "The Voyage of the Brigantine Yankee.*"*

Like floating jackstraws, slender Tikopian outriggers cluster about *Yankee's* awninged afterdeck. A Solomon Islands chief and his aide climb aboard seeking gifts. Others bring pandanus mats to trade for tobacco.

Robed in radiant saffron, Buddhist priests stroll through the massive ruins of Angkor Wat. Khmers, ancestors of today's Cambodians, built the temple in the 12th century; its lower gallery extends for half a mile.

Volcanic spears pierce the sky above Ua Pou in the Marquesas. Only these giant lava plugs remain of an ancient volcano that eroded away. Crew members keep watch as *Yankee* noses toward shore.

Skipper's wife, Mrs. Electa Johnson, embroiders in the captain's cabin; her needlework map depicts the vessel's adventures.

Memento of a mutiny: *Bounty's* anchor, found by *Yankee* crewmen, emerges from 50 feet of water off Pitcairn Island. Earlier, author Luis Marden had discovered *Bounty's* lime-encrusted remains close inshore.

It took three months of negotiation to purchase the ship, and when finally she was his, Captain Johnson sent her round for refitting to the yard of J. W. and A. Upham at Brixham.

There Devon shipwrights, whose ancestors had sailed with Drake against the Spanish Armada, went lovingly to work on *Yankee.* Topmasts and yards were dubbed out of North American pitch pine by old-timers with adzes, a tool, says Exy Johnson, which "no one under 60 seems qualified to handle."

Mrs. Johnson loved listening to the yardmen talk among themselves of "t' *Yank.*" She heard one old boy say to another, "Her'll take a heap o' drivin'." "Aye," replied his mate, "her'll go. Ain't nothin' to stop she."

Years of sailing had taught Irving Johnson what was needed in a ship to circumnavigate the world with an amateur crew in comfort and safety. *Duhnen's* schooner rig had been best for coastwise navigation, variable winds, and handling with a small crew. But as *Yankee* she would sail for long periods in the steady, unvarying trades. For running before a stiff breeze, square sails are more efficient as well as safer, as there is no danger of an accidental jibe. On the other hand, for beating to windward, fore-and-aft sails are superior, as they permit the ship to sail closer to the wind. To have the best of both worlds, Johnson rerigged her as a brigantine.

Here again Johnson's original thinking baffled some observers, though not the experts. When I showed a photograph of *Yankee* under full sail to Howard Chapelle, the Smithsonian Institution's authority on sailing ships, he said, "She's a brigantine, all right, but...." It is this "but" that gives pause to others who know only conventional rig. For example, her foremast should have one more yard, which

Irving Johnson omitted to simplify sail handling. Her topsail is smaller than her topgallant, the next sail above, the reverse of the usual practice, and so on. Nevertheless, "She's a brigantine, all right."

In all, *Yankee* could set 11 sails, totaling 7,775 square feet of canvas. Often we sailed at 10 knots. When the brigantine was heeled down in a breeze, I sometimes braced my arms against the lee bulwarks and looked down at the sea rushing and hissing by. It seemed we were going fast enough, I can tell you.

During the passage from Pitcairn to Mangareva, on a damp night of distant electrical storms, I saw a phenomenon I had only read about. As the ship drove through the moonless and starless night, there blossomed at the tip of each stunsail boom a plume of pale-blue lambent light. This discharge of atmospheric electricity is called St. Elmo's fire, after the patron saint of sailors.

I was aboard *Yankee* some five weeks in all. At the island of Nuku Hiva, in the Marquesas, we found an old Scot standing on the foreshore with tears streaming down his cheeks.

"It's the first time since I jumped ship forty years ago that a vessel with square sails has entered this harbor on wind alone," he said.

In *Yankee* I approached Tahiti as God intended that fair island to be approached—by sea.* I went ashore, but *Yankee* continued around the world, returning home to Gloucester, Massachusetts, after 40,000 miles.

To me, the achievement of the Johnsons in picking congenial and able crews was no less impressive than the consummate seamanship with which they sailed seven times around the world without a single serious mishap. Picking a crew of high-spirited boys and girls was almost as delicate a matter as selecting a crew for a submarine. Yet not only did Captain Johnson's crew invariably end the voyages as friends; shipboard romances blossomed into as many marriages as cruises.

At the end of her fourth voyage—the Johnsons' seventh world cruise—the *Yankee* was sold. Irving and Exy Johnson had always wanted to sail across Europe through its rivers and canals. Obviously *Yankee* was too big for this; so, reluctantly, the Johnsons parted with her, to build a new *Yankee,* a 50-foot ketch, in Holland.†

The brigantine *Yankee* then changed hands three times. Under the third owners, she sailed once around the world, then set out on another world voyage—an ill-starred one.

*Luis Marden's many GEOGRAPHIC articles include "Huzza for Otaheite!" April, 1962; "Tahiti, 'Finest Island in the World,' " July, 1962; and "I Found the Bones of the *Bounty*" (Pitcairn Island), December, 1957.
†In NATIONAL GEOGRAPHIC the Johnsons wrote "Inside Europe Aboard *Yankee,*" August, 1964; and "*Yankee* Cruises the Storied Nile," May, 1965.

MAJESTIC EVEN IN DISTRESS, Yankee *lies at the mercy of pounding surf at Rarotonga. Braving the sea, one member of a boarding party works his way to the ship while companions pull taut a lifeline. On a world cruise under new owners,* Yankee *broke adrift from her anchors off this South Sea isle and drove helplessly on to the reef.*

Yankee was anchored off the reef at Rarotonga when a gale struck. Unfortunately her batteries were dead, and her auxiliary engines would not start. First the chain of one anchor parted, then a fluke sheared off the other, and *Yankee* drove stern first on to the reef. Seas smashing broadside forced her higher until she lay 60 feet from deep water, tightly locked in a coral embrace.

That was in July of 1964. At this writing she lies at Rarotonga still, although a California syndicate hopes to refloat her by dynamiting a passage through the reef and pulling her off to deep water. *Yankee*'s many friends hope she will furrow the seas of the world again, for, as Exy Johnson has written:

"She was a ship worth all our efforts. She belonged at sea, making long passages, carrying a cloud of canvas, meeting any kind of weather. She was not built for weekend sailing. If she was not to lie neglected at the dock, her best use was in sailing around the world. At sea she was a thing of beauty. And she was as good as she was beautiful."

I well remember the last time I saw her. From the pierhead in Papeete I watched her sail toward the blue peaks of Moorea. From his post beside the wheel, Capt. Irving Johnson lifted his arm in farewell.

He is a sailor, and she was a ship.

THE END

What was a woman doing there?

A RAINBOW decorated the western sky that early morning of November 4—the second day of Operation Black Ferret. Action began at 0745 when American Marines moved toward a cane field surrounding a village held by the Viet Cong near Chu Lai, South Viet Nam.

A foot brushed a concealed nylon fishing line, a booby trap roared, and shrapnel shredded the damp foliage, felling six Marines and a lady from Milwaukee, Georgette Louise ("Dickey") Chapelle. She died moments later, half a world from home.

What, you might ask, was she doing there? Dickey, a veteran war correspondent, had asked that same question in her autobiography, *What's a Woman Doing Here?* Her mother had taught her that "violence in any form is unthinkable." But she came to believe we could have peace only by being strong.

She became a correspondent in World War II to be near her husband, Navy photographer Anthony Chapelle. Perhaps it was the shock of photographing the death and horror of Iwo Jima and Okinawa that led her to dedicate her life to "telling the folks back home" how cruel war can be. Almost a quarter of a century later, her byline now famous, this remarkable woman is mourned in a dozen languages.

Because I knew and loved Dickey from working beside her in Cuba, Viet Nam, northeast India, and Ladakh, word of her death shocked and sorrowed me—but it did not surprise. Dickey and danger were never far apart.

The evening before her death, she dug her own foxhole and huddled under a poncho as a light rain fell through the glare of aerial flares. Though I wasn't there, I'm sure she opened her breakfast of cold C-rations with the Swiss Army knife she always carried.

Staff Sergeant Albert P. Miville told me later what had happened next.

"She asked if she could go with us. I said, 'Sure, Dickey, fall in behind me.' Five seconds later she was hit. I was only a step away. Some brush saved me. I yelled for a corpsman. He looked at her and told me, 'Sergeant, there is nothing I can do.'"

The sounds of the violence she had been raised to abhor became the siren song that lured Dickey to every scene of political mayhem since World War II: Korea, Cuba, Quemoy, India, Algeria, Lebanon, Laos, Viet Nam, and the Dominican Republic. While helping smuggle penicillin to Hungarian Freedom Fighters, Dickey was captured and spent six weeks in solitary confinement, with terrifying interrogations, before the United States consul was able to free her. "Thank God I'm an American," she said.

One recent winter Dickey lived in Florida near Cuban exiles. She stored their nitroglycerin in her icebox. Her brother, Professor Robert Meyer, didn't approve.

"But I sent her two Du Pont handbooks on high explosives," he told me. "I thought if she was going to be fooling with the stuff, she should know what she was doing."

Personal integrity forced Dickey to write only stories she had "eyeballed"—to use her phrase. Official government handouts, complained Dickey, "have all the authenticity of patent-medicine ads."

From 1935 when, at age 16, she entered Massachusetts Institute of Technology on a scholarship, Dickey became part of a man's world. She married at 22 and then became a pilot, a parachutist, and a combat photographer. Between wars, Dickey and her husband covered the work of a dozen relief agencies over the world. They reported in NATIONAL GEOGRAPHIC on locust plagues in Iraq (April, 1953) and village life in India (April, 1956).

To her death, Dickey and Tony remained friends, though their marriage was dissolved in 1956. A lone red rose at her gravesite in Milwaukee carried the one word "Tony." Nearby was a bouquet, also of roses, from the Hungarian Freedom Fighters.

Never did Dickey tolerate favors in the field because of her sex. She hid her figure in loose khakis and bandoliers of cameras and film cans. Her long blonde hair, rolled into a bun, nestled in a floppy Australian bush hat. Makeup was not part of her field kit.

In 1962, after five weeks with the Indian

Army on the Chinese front, Dickey and I were flown directly to Calcutta, still in field gear. She excused herself at the airport, but returned almost immediately, laughing as she told me, in her gravelly, drill-sergeant voice, how successful her disguise had been: "I just got thrown out of the ladies' room."

In the field her only jewelry was the military insignia presented to her by fighting units. She fell wearing the globe and anchor of the Marine Corps Commandant, Gen. Wallace M. Greene, Jr., who took the insignia from his own uniform and gave it to Dickey

Of her many honors, I suppose Dickey most treasured the Overseas Press Club's award for "reporting requiring exceptional courage and enterprise." When she wasn't with her adopted military families, she worked for the club, serving on its Board of Governors.

Some who knew Dickey were ill at ease in the presence of her nervously loud voice and exuberant manner. But these characteristics stemmed from an enviable enthusiasm for life, and a dynamic mind and heart. Dickey found an identity and purpose in life we all envied. It freed her of inhibitions and fears.

KODACHROME © NATIONAL GEOGRAPHIC SOCIETY

War reporter Dickey Chapelle, born Georgette Louise Meyer in Milwaukee, Wisconsin, March 14, 1918, became the first American woman correspondent to die in action when she fell in South Viet Nam on November 4, 1965. Dickey was not on assignment for the GEOGRAPHIC when killed, but had been a contributor since 1953, and the article that follows was awaiting publication. Here, in the field in Viet Nam, she wears insignia earned by jumping into battle with U. S. and Vietnamese paratroopers.

before her departure for Viet Nam last fall.

To keep in condition and not be a burden on the men she photographed and wrote about, Dickey ran two miles a day when in New York between assignments.

In a lecture to Midwestern high-school students, she accused them of being "baby-soft teen-agers whose idea of exercise is to switch channels on the idiot box. . . ." Two boys challenged her to a 25-mile hike the next day.

"You know," she reported, "those kids were delighted when we finished. I knew I could do it, but they weren't sure they could."

She knew the odds against a moth that flies too close to the flame, but for years she beat those odds. She lived the hundreds of lives of the men she wrote about and photographed. Life was precious to her; her own was taken too soon. But she had used it well.

As a free lance writer-photographer, she had gone often to Viet Nam. Now, in the pages that follow, we present the last article for the GEOGRAPHIC by the courageous lady who always went where the action was.

W. E. GARRETT

WATER WAR IN
VIET NAM

Article and photographs by DICKEY CHAPELLE

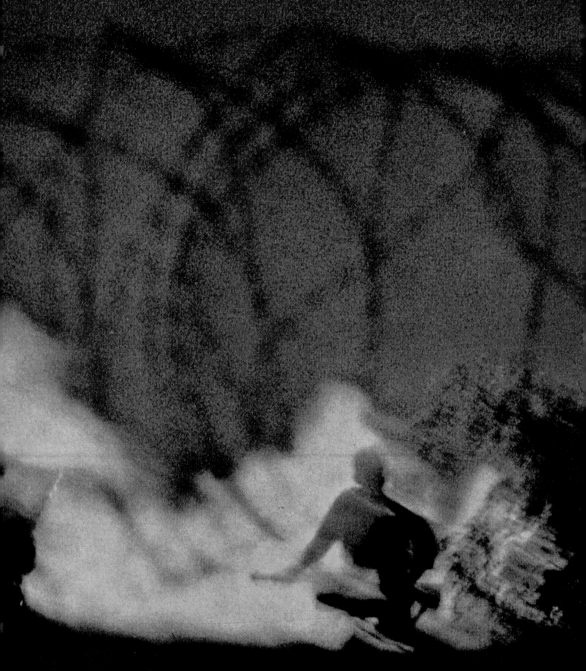

"**AS SOON AS THE LIGHT GOES,** so will our patrols." In the tropical twilight, the words sounded softly at my ear.

Lt. Harold Dale Meyerkord, United States Navy, was too professional a fighting man to dramatize his statement. But it was enough to disquiet me, to remind me that today we had already buried a comrade, exchanged fire with Viet Cong, and twice set out fruitless ambushes.

"We" meant River Assault Group 23, one of the Vietnamese Navy's daring gunboat forces. Each group, known for its initials as a RAG, operates a miniature fleet of shallow-draft patrol craft

FLAMING INFERNO, *ignited by a South Vietnamese patrol, flushes Viet Cong from a hut. "Night fighting is sudden, vicious, deadly," wrote combat correspondent Chapelle. During this action she crouched behind barbed wire on the bank of a canal, one in a maze of Mekong Delta waterways patrolled by River Assault Groups.*

EKTACHROME © N. G. S.

Each is commanded by a Vietnamese lieutenant and advised by an American naval officer—in this case, Lieutenant Meyerkord.

The RAG forces constitute the military presence of South Viet Nam on thousands of miles of waterway spanning the vast delta region of Indochina's Mekong River (map, page 281). Together with militia on fixed posts and infantry flown into the area, the little boats are trying to keep for the free world the coveted rice bowl of Southeast Asia.

One RAG Patrols Three Provinces

The delta is as rich in people as in rice: Five million of the 15,700,000 South Vietnamese live here. I had waded its fields three years before, photographing Vietnamese paratroopers and marines in action.* Water-borne forces were also fighting here, and now I'd come back to witness their operations. One of these, the Vietnamese Navy's so-called junk fleet, patrolled the coasts of the South China Sea and the Gulf of Siam. The river gunboat groups, the RAG's, operated across the broad flood region between the two coasts.

RAG 23 was responsible for safeguarding three of the 13 delta provinces—Vinh Long, Vinh Binh, and Kien Hoa. These are crisscrossed everywhere by majestic rivers, meandering streams, straight canals. The way of travel and even the way of life here is water-borne, aboard sampans and junks. Most people rarely see or use the few highways.

On this tense twilight we were in the heart of the delta, some 20 miles south of our RAG's home base at the provincial capital of Vinh Long, and more than 75 miles southwest of Saigon. We had swept

*Dickey Chapelle's first-person account of the grim and gallant "Helicopter War in South Viet Nam" appeared in NATIONAL GEOGRAPHIC in November, 1962. Continuing to risk her life in combat, she took part in December, 1964, in the river and coast patrols she describes here. Since then American commitment to the Viet Nam struggle has increased markedly, and many more U. S. Navy and Coast Guard men are fighting side by side with Vietnamese water-borne forces against the Communists.

Packaged death—a Viet Cong mine—may lurk under any water weed. Here a canal's surface erupts, but harmlessly, as South Vietnamese crewmen of River Assault Group (RAG) 23 set off a charge to detonate hidden mines. A few hours earlier, a mine destroyed a gunboat and killed two men. Seven assault groups, each with 19 boats of various types, combat the Viet Cong in thousands of miles of river and canal lacing the vast rice bowl known as the Mekong Delta.

"In this deadly game of hide-and-seek ... [you] feel joy at simple survival," wrote one who did not survive—Dickey Chapelle. Another who gave his life, United States Navy Lt. Harold Dale Meyerkord, here returns VC fire with an automatic rifle from the deck of his command boat.

Ramming the canal bank, gunboats land South Vietnamese infantrymen to battle a Viet Cong detachment. Redscarfed fighters of the Popular Force (below) embark for a foray. This barefoot, lightly armed group functions much like a volunteer fire company in the United States. Farmers and merchants by profession, its members go into action only when the enemy threatens their villages.

down the Mang Thu River the previous night to aid an embattled district headquarters, Cai Nhum. The Viet Cong had broken off their assault as we arrived.

But neither we nor the other Vietnamese forces here then were winning. For months Viet Cong strength had been outgrowing ours. And turmoil in Saigon was sapping the confidence of the fighting men.*

I could not think of the canal banks beside us as details on the map of the free world. Instead, like the lieutenant and the RAG sailors, I considered them suspect places from which at any time, without warning, we might be shot at. My misgivings applied particularly to the American beside me.

The Viet Cong were shifting their priority target from Vietnamese to Americans. A few days earlier I had learned just how grimly successful the drive to kill Americans had been in this province. Of 40-odd American military men in Vinh Long—naval and infantry advisers, helicopter pilots, supply and maintenance experts—the enemy had killed or wounded 18 in the field and hit one, with a grenade, in his shower. The casualty rate for this single group of Americans was running at more than 40 percent.

Viet Cong Rule by Kidnaping or Killing Anti-Communist Leaders

True, this was not the kind of big action in which countries crumble overnight. But the Viet Cong tactic of kidnaping or killing local anti-Red leaders, now openly aimed at Americans, was as deadly as any tactic in any war we had ever fought.

Perhaps that was why the surviving Americans were so determinedly cheerful, why they so often joked about themselves. For example, Lieutenant Meyerkord's radio code name always drew a chuckle. It was "Hornblower," after the spirited hero of C. S. Forester's novels.

Now, telling me about the patrols, he held his chin pugnaciously high. I tried to imitate his discipline, to mask what I, too, felt. I fixed my eyes on the low silhouette of huts and bushes marking the canal bank beyond the rail of our 60-foot command gunboat.

Despite myself, I tried to slow the setting sun, to hold back the dusk now purpling the muddy fields and so delay the patrols. But I knew better than that. Their purpose was to safeguard our gunboats from mines. Unless our little landing teams did go, there was a

*See "Saigon: Eye of the Storm," by Peter T. White, NATIONAL GEOGRAPHIC, June, 1965.

good chance that more of RAG 23 might be destroyed. Its survivors might once again fish from the turbid water more bodies like the one retrieved earlier in the day—a RAG gunner killed by a Viet Cong mine at the canal junction where we were now anchored.

The mine had been no crude gadget, but an electrically fired device big enough to shear off the heavy bow of the 56-foot launch and kill two of the crew.

A furtive villager had crept aboard our boat to report seven more mines in position in the 300 yards of canal behind us, rigged to wreck us as we returned after arranging the burial. If true, that meant there were at least seven Viet Cong hidden on the canal bank at this moment, one to detonate each mine, together with an ambushing force.

Our RAG commander, Vietnamese Navy Lt. Nguyen Van Hoa, briefed the little landing force, sending his instructions in shrill whispers over an American field radio.

Half the men, under a veteran Vietnamese officer, were to scour the east canal bank for the mines' detonating wires. The other half, under a Vietnamese ensign, were to patrol the west bank with Lieutenant Meyerkord. If either patrol force found a target too big to handle, the boats would come up to help. One comfort was the firepower of the RAG—20-mm. and 40-mm. cannon, .30- and .50-caliber machine guns, even an old 81-mm. mortar.

Isolation Favors the Viet Cong

Still, it would be a nervous business, with the odds favoring the enemy. Vinh Long Province, like the rest of the delta, had never been truly a part of any Indochinese state.

Here Khmer control ebbed centuries ago. The French, a generation back, sometimes taxed, but never ruled. Before River Assault Group 23 appeared, many villagers had not seen a representative of Saigon since the 1950's. Local warlords, river pirates, and now the Viet Cong had installed themselves without hindrance from any central government.

For two small bands of government troops to try to make their way in darkness, for hundreds of yards past houses and fields and jungle familiar to the enemy, was an act of daring. And an act of necessity.

Lieutenant Hoa, slight and erect, summed it up in his precise English: "Now that we have lost one boat, I could not tell my conscience or my admiral that I had sailed others into the same trap. The patrols will go first, the boats will follow."

I watched Lieutenant Meyerkord count ammunition clips into his pockets. Yet somehow it seemed unreal that I was going with him, and was slipping extra clips into my own pocket.

The war in Viet Nam marked the first time in more than twenty years as a war correspondent that I had carried a weapon in the course of my work. I'd begun it at the urging of the men I photographed, who reminded me that civilians were treated as spies when captured by the Viet Cong. Now, like most reporters covering combat operations in Viet Nam, I went armed.

Tense Patrol Begins With a Jest

"Where do you want to walk on this hike?" Lieutenant Meyerkord asked.

"Right behind you—you have the broadest shoulders, so you make the best bullet stop." I tried to make it sound light, but the words rang shrill.

The lieutenant abruptly dropped his stern-faced pose. With his normal gaiety he said, "Never thought I'd see the day when I'd have a *woman* behind me with a loaded carbine. Fire it one shot at a time, will you?"

I started to say I wasn't planning to fire it at all, but I started to chuckle instead. The lieutenant laughed frankly at his own joke. The Vietnamese sailors around us, caressing their own guns, laughed with him as if they'd understood.

"Nothing like something funny to settle them down, is there?" murmured the lieutenant fondly.

The first man climbed up to the bow where it pressed into the bank, jumped down, and disappeared. A second followed. The slight figure of the ensign disappeared next. Then it was Lieutenant Meyerkord's turn. When I reached the bow, the last sunset glow glinted on the mud surface as I jumped.

As I fell into the hypnotic rhythm of the patrol—we were moving between trees and

In a moment of serenity, while tides of terror rise and fall around them, Vietnamese youngsters play in a sampan. Strife seems far away; yet the deadly war inflicted upon the country by the Communists may destroy their village and snuff out their lives at any time. For the future of innocents like these, Americans fight and die in Southeast Asia.

cane fields, stepping high so we would not trip and clatter on the uneven ground—I was obsessed by a question that had plagued me on other walks in other wars: Why?

Why was it that humans still got along so badly that conflicts were settled like this, by young men betting their lives at hide-and-seek? Did I truly think I could, with the camera around my neck, help end the need for the carbine on my shoulder? Did I think I could make plain how warring really was, how quickly the cutting edge of fear excised every human virtue, leaving only the need to live? Here, now, the supreme virtue was the ability to shoot fast. Or first.

And why were Americans like Meyerkord here? They had brought all their expertise and dedication and raw nerve from the security of their home towns to the ultimate insecurity of guerrilla warfare as far from

home as it was possible to go.* Was that the American idea of global leadership? I knew it was at least one American's idea—mine.

Lieutenant Meyerkord halted and gestured toward a dark mass on our left. It was a building too big for a house. I remembered something Lieutenant Hoa had told us: The earlier mine had been assembled in a little factory of some kind on the canal bank.

What we were passing was such a place, perhaps a sugar-cane mill. Half our file already had passed. No one had fallen out to search the building for Viet Cong. Was the little factory really deserted?

I heard the snick of the safety catch on Meyerkord's rifle; my carbine's safety clicked in turn. He led a squad from the rear of the line around the dark reed-wall structure.

*See "American Special Forces in Action in Viet Nam," by Howard Sochurek, GEOGRAPHIC, January, 1965.

RAG rescues a village. For three days Cai Nhum, a district headquarters, lived in fear. Encircling Viet Cong lobbed in mortar shells. The market closed. Cai Nhum radioed for help, and RAG *23* responded with enough force to scatter the enemy. Now, with the protective fleet standing by, farmers in sampans come to reopen the market.

Ragged coast and river-laced tip of Viet Nam offer hideouts and highways for the Viet Cong. Junks and river boats patrol thousands of miles of shore and waterway, from 1954's demarcation line to the Mekong Delta and the Gulf of Siam. (An indexed map of Viet Nam in color, 11½ by 20½ inches, is available for 50¢ from the Society, Washington, D. C.)

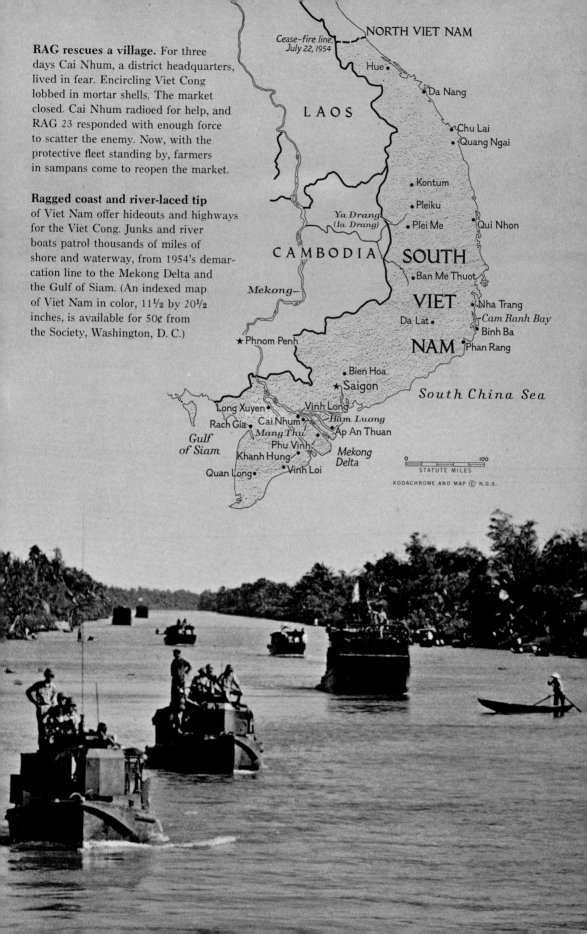

NORTH VIET NAM

Cease-fire line, July 22, 1954

Hue

Da Nang

LAOS

Chu Lai
Quang Ngai

Kontum

Pleiku

Ya Drang (Ia Drang)   Plei Me   Qui Nhon

CAMBODIA   SOUTH

Ban Me Thuot

Mekong—   VIET   Nha Trang
Cam Ranh Bay
Da Lat   Binh Ba

★ Phnom Penh   NAM   Phan Rang

Bien Hoa

★ Saigon   *South China Sea*

Long Xuyen   Vinh Long

Rach Gia   Cai Nhum   *Ham Luong*
Mang Thu   Ap An Thuan
Gulf   Phu Vinh
of Siam   Khanh Hung   *Mekong*
Delta
Quan Long   Vinh Loi

0   100
STATUTE MILES

KODACHROME AND MAP © N.G.S.

Starlight glinted on several huge metal pots. Then we could make out what might have been a press. The building seemed to have only three walls. The lieutenant decided it was empty and took up the patrol again.

He murmured, "They don't know they must search *every* building—we've just begun to train them for shore parties."

"Will they do whatever they see you do?"

"This is where we find out." He pointed to a row of huts ahead.

At each he led the men through the palm-sweating, knee-weakening, heart-stopping routine of stepping into the total blackness inside, finger on the trigger. The huts had been deserted—hastily, judging from the warm embers. By the time he approached the ninth hut, I knew the answer to my question.

Lieutenant Meyerkord had a team of Vietnamese searchers behind him. Two riflemen had figured out how it was done. They first kept the lieutenant covered; then they themselves began to search, passing the word to the men behind to cover them in turn.

"Now they *are* going through each hut," said the lieutenant, beaming.

Village Woman Warns of Viet Cong Hiding Place

The last hut was not deserted. We found the Vietnamese ensign in whispered conversation with a group in the entrance. He explained in fragments of English what a woman there had told him: No mine wires had been rigged from this side of the canal today. But the woman thought that some probably led from a house on the other side.

The lieutenant offered the woman a wad of currency. Vehemently she refused. He chuckled as he came back to the path. "Even in the Viet Cong's territory, not everyone hates the American adviser."

As we walked on, it grew terribly still. Or maybe it only seemed quiet in retrospect because of what came afterward—the sudden crash and chop of machine-gun fire.

But we were not the targets.

Crouched, we could see through a screen of grass that our patrol across the canal was firing at a hut from which streaks of tracer came at them. The sound echoed in short professional bursts, stuttering against a counterpoint of single shots. Then there were too many shots to count. Finally a finger of flame ran up one wall and turned to follow the roof line. The hut burst into flame. The firing stopped.

By the light of the burning hut, we took stock of our position. There was a barrier of looped barbed wire a little way up the canal bank; soon we were crowded behind it (pages 272-3). The Vietnamese ensign squatted to the lieutenant's left; I sat on my heels to his right. A soldier from the rear guard ran up, bringing word that the lady in the last house said there

Gagging smoke from a white phosphorus shell envelops an island of trees suspected of harboring the enemy. RAG troops advance through a field; moments later their gunboat will fire high-explosive shells into the woods.

Fallen comrade, a South Vietnamese rifleman killed by Viet Cong machine-gun fire, goes to his grave. Buddhist flags flutter above the mourners, who bear a model of a Vietnamese house and offerings of food, money, and candles for use by the departed in the hereafter. Even at a funeral service, armed guards (left) must protect the people.

283

were 30 Viet Cong in a cane field at our back.

"If they charge through the cane, we'll hear them in time," the lieutenant said. "But if they set up a machine gun and sweep their fire...." He looked up and down the line of crouched figures.

I knew what he meant; we ought not to be huddled where one long burst could hit most of us. Reluctantly I moved back a few yards. Immediately three Vietnamese riflemen filled the space between us. They, too, wanted to be warmed by Dale Meyerkord's assurance.

Patrol Cannot Radio Its Danger

Now I could hear the ensign whispering frantically to his radioman. He seemed to be asking whether anyone remembered the radio frequency of the boats. No one replied.

This was not a simple matter, like remembering one's telephone number. The Viet Cong used captured American radios and usually listened in. So new channels were chosen by the Vietnamese just before each operation and confided only to its commanders. Somehow, nobody tonight had noted the frequency on which the boats would be listening for us.

A new fear gripped me. The RAG commander would know from the firing that there were Viet Cong about, and he might decide to move in, guns blazing at the area from which the enemy had fired on the other patrol. The canal curved gently here; this meant we were now halted close to what could become the boat's line of fire. Lacking radio contact, we could not tell the commander that. Would he guess in time?

With all the resignation I could summon, I rolled half to my knees and tried to recheck camera settings by feel. The next sound I heard was what I wanted most to hear: approaching boat engines. Just engines, not guns. The Vietnamese skipper had concluded correctly, from the end of the firing and the dying hut blaze, that no Viet Cong remained to detonate mines here. In ten minutes he had located and picked up the patrol on the far bank and our own.

We found the skipper studying maps under a flashlight aboard the command boat. The

Metallic eagle lifts a wounded brother high above the fertile rice fields of the Mekong Delta. Pilots of the twin-engine helicopters refer to themselves as a "road-service company," but their job of rescuing smaller choppers downed by the enemy brings them under fire on nine out of ten missions.

Death rides their shoulders; dawn calls them to duty. South Vietnamese marines march past

light reflected on his composed, ivory-skinned face; he did not look his age, which I knew to be 30.

"Our landing party must have driven the enemy away, carrying their mines," he told Meyerkord. "Since they did not keep firing, it must have been only a rear-guard action. *If,* of course, our information was correct in the first place...." His voice trailed off.

Lieutenant Meyerkord had regained his usual ebullience. He grinned. "Well, as the newspapers tell us, it's a frustrating war."

Junk Navy Creates Its Own Legends

How to deploy small forces over large areas is the eternal problem of the Viet Nam war. It is true of the RAG's and equally of the Hai Thuyen, the armed junks guarding 1,200 miles of seacoast against the infiltration of men and guns from North Viet Nam. Some 500 little boats, operating out of a score of bases, must police tens of thousands of boat movements and check the identity of a million people afloat every year.

Since 1960, the junk force has spawned almost as many legends as it has missions. I

had heard that every junk-force sailor could sail and fight expertly, that each was tattooed with his oath to kill Communists (page 288) —and hence would be shot if captured—and that each wore only the civilian garb of black pajamas on both land and sea.

The last tale, I quickly learned, was no longer so. But after several weeks with the "junkies," I came to accept all the other stories. Later I retold them myself, proudly wearing the force's unique silver twin-sail insignia. But the junkies had not let me wear it till I had been shot at with them several times.

When I first joined them, such an experience did not seem very probable.

"We just don't come under fire every day, as we used to," was the first thing told me by Lt. James Monroe Vincent, USN. I was unpacking cameras in a reed building at the junk-force base near Ap An Thuan village, at the mouth of the Ham Luong River some 60 miles south of Saigon.

The sturdy lieutenant sat cross-legged on the bare wooden boards he used for a bed. He was one of four Americans serving on roving duty to all the junk divisions of the Third

shell-tattered trees in an eternal silhouette of war, here reflected in the water of a rice field.

Coastal District, Vietnamese Navy. (The South Viet Nam coastline is divided into four such districts, roughly matching the corps areas of the army.)

My briefing by Lieutenant Vincent ended with a characteristic understatement: "The junk divisions' function simply is to check every coastal boat that comes or goes, to be sure it's not serving the Viet Cong. We try not to do any more fighting on land. All those stories about land raids we've made—sure, a lot of them are true, but we made them only to secure our own bases."

He pulled out a well-creased map. The junk bases nearby all lay at the eastern edge of the delta, an area traditionally under Viet Cong control. Within a day's walk of where we sat, it was believed, enemy units were so deeply entrenched as to operate a rest camp, a hospital, and an officer training center.

"I know they're there," Lieutenant Vincent said. "Every time we sail past those beaches, somebody shoots at us."

He explained that neither type of operating junk—a motorized 50-footer and a motor-sailer 45 feet long—carried any armor plate.

He finished generously, "To take pictures, you can sit anywhere you like. There's no safe spot aboard, anyhow."

On my first few patrols, there were no bullets. Our most hazardous mission, it seemed, was our daily showing of the flag in Ap An Thuan village, whose huts came up almost to the earth wall of the base. The base had been situated here because of the proximity of the village market and its food supply.

Viet Cong Set a Trap for Americans

One morning an informant brought word that two Viet Cong agents had been planted in the village to kill the American advisers at the junk base, Lieutenant Vincent and Chief Gunner's Mate Edmund Canby. The VC were not bluffing with such threats. A few months earlier, a mine detonated at the village gate had missed other Americans for whom it was intended, but it had blown legs off four junk sailors who had come in their place.

Also while I was there, Ap An Thuan faced another threat: mortar fire at night. No artillery is more dreaded, for a mortar shell— which can kill up to 40 yards from point of

287

SAILOR OF THE JUNK FORCE *wears the Vietnamese words for "Kill Communists!" tattooed over his heart. With his comrades, he cruises the coast in these light, fast-sailing vessels. The armada's goal: to deny the Viet Cong use of the sea as a supply route. Needing no fuel, the craft circle offshore near Binh Ba. If they spy suspicious traffic, they radio to better-armed motorized junks. Navy destroyer escorts and Coast Guard cutters from the United States recently reinforced the fleet.*

288

KODACHROMES © NATIONAL GEOGRAPHIC SOCIETY

impact and wound much farther away—gives no warning. It can easily be lobbed over earth walls like those around the junk base.

"Now, if we're mortared, it may mean they'll try to overrun us," Lieutenant Vincent said. "We'll have to start shooting. The enemy uses the village as a shield. They know we try not to shoot toward the huts, no matter where their fire comes from. We'll have to go into the village again, and we don't want to spend the rest of our lives wondering who hit the women and children."

Three days later, I found out what he meant. The lesson came at high noon when, just back from a sea patrol aboard a motor junk, I had felt so secure that I'd taken off my boots and was wearing rubber shower shoes while sorting film. At first, I didn't believe my ears. I knew there were a dozen local militiamen in position nearby; could the stuttering shots I heard be the test-firing of their weapons? I went outside to hear better.

I had heard well enough. Those shots were fired from at least one American-made submachine gun and two automatic rifles, and the *zing-zing* of the bullets was coming in over our heads from the marketplace. The weapons obviously had been captured and were now being turned on us by the Viet Cong.

The incoming fire grew to a roar. I threw myself into a position on the base wall nearest the village, holding camera and carbine tightly because my hands suddenly were slippery. I saw that Lieutenant Vincent was in the next position along the earthwork. Here we were shielded—bullets don't go through earthworks. But I wondered: Since we had to turn back the Viet Cong somehow and they were shooting from inside the village, would our sailor-riflemen fire into the huts after all?

Junk Fleet Counterattacks—on Foot

Not for 12 minutes did the fire slacken. But I never saw one of our men aim toward a hut.

During a break in the firing, a sergeant ran in through the gate in our barbed wire. He said his dozen men had returned the fire from beyond the village until their ammunition ran out. He was telling Lieutenant Vincent and the officer commanding the junk division that we were still in deep trouble.

The enemy force—40 in all? More? He did not know. Still breathless, he told us three of his men were wounded.

Silently slipping from dark-sailed junks, Vietnamese sailors train near Cam Ranh Bay. Later the author joined a real assault in Phuoc Tuy Province, where a Viet Cong contingent had wiped out half of another battalion.

Baleful eye on the bow wards off demons, but the .30-caliber machine gun proves more effective against the VC. American naval architects helped design this command craft, one of 250 boats built in Viet Nam for the junk force.

Hope in a box: Hungry for learning, Vietnamese youngsters solemnly accept CARE kits containing notebooks, pencils, and rulers from the hands of a U. S. Strike Force officer in Kien Phong Province. American infantryman at Cai Nhum (right) shows a mother with a sick—and scared—child how to use a medicine dropper. Both scenes illustrate a conviction of Dickey Chapelle's. "Perhaps some-

day," she wrote, "compassion as an infantry tactic will be taught to every American soldier. He will still need to know his rifle number, his general's name, and how to kill.... And, when he kills, he will ask... if it is necessary. It will be that last reflex—the wondering why, the compassion for others... that may someday be America's unique contribution to the history of force."

I don't remember that anybody used the word counterattack. But a few minutes later I was moving through the empty market square, running to keep up with the figures around me. Ahead was the junk division's junior officer, Thanh Phu, carrying a grenade launcher; Lieutenant Vincent with an automatic carbine; and a dozen others. I looked back and saw perhaps 40 more. Our base was emptying itself of every able-bodied man.

The two lieutenants, one American and the other Vietnamese, led us through a paddy field, across a patch of jungle, and up a steep sand hill. I could see now that we were heading toward the next village, from which our patrol junks often were fired on. Past another high ridge, I heard firing on the left—the inland side. At first I was not sure it was incoming, but Lieutenant Vincent was wiser; when I squinted into my camera's view finder, he grunted, "Don't stop for any reason on this high ground. You'll be silhouetted against the sky. An easy target."

"I won't," I assured him fervently, and ran on.

Fleeing Enemy Drops List of Weapons

The firing sputtered out, and I found myself in a little glade just behind the Vietnamese lieutenant. He was bending over to pick up some things the Viet Cong obviously had dropped in haste. They proved our run in the sun had not been in vain.

The lieutenant was holding a fistful of enemy papers and insignia. One neat, ink-written notebook page listed the weapons of our attackers, including captured American-made ones. Also in the glade were many empty cartridges and a few unfired ones which I pocketed. They proved to be Chinese.

Then I was running again over the uneven ground, toward 293

the first huts of the village. Firing burst out to our right. I could see several of our men, small in the distance, shooting deliberately. I fixed my eyes on the huts and prayed our momentum would not carry us—barely a reinforced platoon—straight into a whole Viet Cong village.

Lieutenant Vincent threw back over his shoulder at me, "How many clips you got? I only have ten." I wondered what kind of battle he expected; his clips held 180 rounds.

"I've got four," I replied. "But can't they support us from the base with the big mortar?"

"Not much help if this thing goes hand to hand," he answered. "You know, *we* can be cut off from our base, too, just as we've been trying to cut off the VC. Though I think they've gotten clean away."

Just then the Vietnamese officer seemed to realize how far we had charged. He waved

"He was a *man*," said Dickey Chapelle of Lieutenant Meyerkord (above). It was her highest accolade. Automatic rifle in hand, Meyerkord directs fire from his gunboat. "Doughty but aging," the author described this craft, called FOM after the initials of the former French colonial administration in Viet Nam. Lightly armored, it carries one turret-mounted .50-caliber machine gun and three of .30 caliber.

in all his men except two flanking parties.

One junk sailor said he had been fired on from an adjoining hut. A petty officer and four riflemen searched the building and came out carrying a shiny brass Viet Cong grenade, its casing obviously cast from a mold of an old U. S. grenade. The sailors at first proposed to set fire to the house. But a militiaman objected that he had a friend who lived in the neighboring reed house, and if one burned, the second would, too.

Lieutenant Phu ordered us to start back on a cart trail circling toward the beach. Every 20 yards or so along its drainage ditches we saw a deep-dug rifleman's hole.

Lieutenant Vincent came alongside. "If they try to ambush us, you know enough not to jump into one of those holes, don't you?"

"Booby-trapped, maybe?"

"Good girl," he grunted, and again took his place in our rear guard, nearest the enemy.

His warning made me so sure we'd be ambushed that a sensation of relief flooded me when we reached Ap An Thuan. The deserted marketplace, bullet-crossed two hours be-fore, now seemed as secure as the Pentagon.

A few minutes later, back inside the base, Lieutenant Vincent stared at my feet in their thonged rubber shower shoes.

"We must have covered five miles. Did you wear those foolish things all the way?" he asked incredulously.

"That's right," I answered. "You said there wouldn't be any more land operations—remember?"

We laughed too much at the joke, because it felt so good to laugh at all.

Laughter—and Death—on the Delta

But laughter seldom lasts long on the delta, where sailors fight a strange kind of war—as much on land as on the water.

Shortly after I returned home, there appeared on the casualty lists another name: Harold Dale Meyerkord. Audacious, ebullient Lieutenant Meyerkord of River Assault Group 23, once of St. Louis. Dale Meyerkord, husband, father, leader and teacher of men, dead of a bullet in the brain on a muddy canal 9,000 miles from Missouri.

"Great personal risk ... was routine" for Lieutenant Meyerkord, Secretary of the Navy Paul H. Nitze declares as he presents the Navy Cross—its highest decoration—to the officer's widow, the former Jane Schmidt. His parents, Mr. and Mrs. Harold E. Meyerkord of St. Louis, hold the Air Medal, also awarded the officer posthumously on November 9, 1965. Wounded from ambush, Lieutenant Meyerkord continued firing until a second shot killed him.

NATIONAL GEOGRAPHIC

THE NATIONAL GEOGRAPHIC MAGAZINE VOL. 129, NO. 3 COPYRIGHT © 1966 BY NATIONAL GEOGRAPHIC SOCIETY, WASHINGTON, D. C. INTERNATIONAL COPYRIGHT SECURED

An American in
MOCKBA
Russia's Capital

By THOMAS T. HAMMOND, Ph.D.

Illustrations by National Geographic photographer DEAN CONGER

A LOUD KNOCK shook the door of my sleeping compartment. "Wake up!" shouted the train conductress. "We'll be in Moscow in half an hour."

"*Spasibo*—thank you," I shouted back. "How cold is it?"

"Twenty-two degrees below zero!"

I shuddered. This centigrade figure meant nearly eight below zero on the Fahrenheit scale—a real introduction to Russian winter. I pulled on my long underwear, woolen shirt, heavy tweed jacket, and galoshes. The conductress brought me hot tea served in a glass, the usual Russian way.

Munching on a breakfast of *pirozhki,* meat pies, I looked out the window at a world all white, gray, and black. Snow lay everywhere, hanging gracefully on the pines that lined the railroad tracks and burdening the rows of log cabins in the villages. Even the sky seemed covered with snow, since the orange ball of the sun was barely visible behind a curtain of white clouds.

Peasants rode by in heavy horse-drawn sleds or plodded through the snow in huge felt boots. The men wore fur caps with thick flaps covering their ears, while the women were wrapped in so many woolen scarves that they seemed to have no necks. Both men and women were bundled in dark-blue jackets of quilted cotton; they looked so rotund I thought they might roll more easily than they walked. Clouds of steam rose from their mouths as they puffed along.

Moscow Revisited—Student Style

Our train from Warsaw now passed through forests of lovely white birches, past suburban railroad depots and rows of new apartment buildings, each topped with dozens of TV antennas. Finally, the train squeaked to a halt in the Belorussian Station.

Though I had been to Moscow three times before, I was as excited as a country boy on his first trip to New York. On my previous visits I had been a tourist, staying no more than a few weeks, and the Intourist travel agency had catered to all my needs.* This time I would be in Moscow five months, and I would live like an ordinary Soviet citizen.

*See "Firsthand Look at the Soviet Union," by Thomas T. Hammond, GEOGRAPHIC, September, 1959.

Hearthstone of Mother Russia, Moscow's Red Square glows on a frosty winter night. Above its snow-buried cobbles loom the crenelated walls of the Kremlin, citadel of tsarist and Communist masters; the boxlike Lenin Mausoleum; floodlighted Spasskaya

(Saviour's) Tower, topped by a glowing star; and onion-domed St. Basil's Cathedral.
Living among Muscovites for five months, the author came to know the Soviet people
and their pride in a metropolis intimately linked with their nation's turbulent history.

I had come to do research on a book dealing with Russian history. Selected by a committee of American scholars under the official cultural exchange program of the U. S. and Soviet Governments, I would be quartered in a Moscow University dormitory.

Living like a student again after 15 years as a professor would be strange enough, and like a Soviet student still more so, but I would get closer to the reality of Soviet life than is ever possible for a tourist.

I hailed a taxi, and the driver—a friendly, chubby type with a day's growth of stubble on his face—helped load my suitcases.

"To M.G.U. [Moscow State University]," I said. "And please go through the center of town, so I can see what the Kremlin looks like in winter."

Sparkling Snow Beautifies the City

As we rode along, I stared out the window, wide-eyed lest I miss something. A light snow was falling, and red-faced women were busily shoveling the drifts into the streets— presumably the same women one can always see sweeping the sidewalks at other times of the year. Moscow, with its fresh blanket of white, seemed much more beautiful in February than in summer. Snow hid the cracks in the plaster, covered piles of trash in courtyards, and gave even log cabins an air of mysterious loveliness.

We headed down Gorky Street, the main shopping thoroughfare, which Russian students call "Broadvey" (map, page 305). We passed through Mayakovskiy Square, dedicated to the colorful "poet of the Russian Revolution"; then, a few blocks farther on, through Pushkin Square, honoring the 19th-century writer whom Russians consider their greatest literary genius. Behind Pushkin's statue I saw a strikingly modern building with a massive glass façade.

"That's the new Rossiya cinema," said the driver, "the most beautiful movie house in the world."

On either side of Gorky Street stood shops of various kinds; some had large modern display windows, with goods arranged in a more attractive manner than any I remembered seeing before. None of the shops bore the

names of private firms; these, of course, were abolished long ago. Instead, signs said "Book Store No. 100," "Grocery Store No. 14," "Pharmacy No. 36," or simply the name of the chief commodity—"Shoes," "Milk," "Wine."

There were only a few of the big neon signs one would find on our Broadway, and these were mostly political: "Glory to the Communist Party of the Soviet Union," "Long Live Leninism," "Forward to the Victory of Communism," or "Atoms for Peace." Some offered advice: "Insure Your Property With the

Jubilant students greet dawn with a song as they celebrate high-school graduation night in Red Square, a local tradition. The luckiest will continue educations or work in Moscow; military service or factory jobs elsewhere in the Soviet Union await others.

State Insurance Trust," "Keep Your Money in State Savings Banks," or simply "Drive Carefully."

The sidewalks teemed with people hurrying along, as if driven by the cold. They seemed better dressed than I remembered them in summer; almost everyone wore a fur hat—many of black or gray karakul from the steppes of central Asia—and some had matching fur collars on heavy wool coats.

On the street corners we passed brightly painted little wooden kiosks selling cigarettes, theater tickets, artificial flowers, cakes and cookies, meat pies, or fruit-flavored drinks. To my surprise, I saw a heavily bundled woman selling ice-cream sticks.

"Oh, sure," said the driver. "We eat as much ice cream in winter as in summer. We Russians are tough—we don't mind the cold."

Continuing to the end of Gorky Street, we came to Manezh Square. Straight ahead rose the old-fashioned red-brick turrets of the Historical Museum; to the right loomed the Kremlin wall, while in between I could see 301

EKTACHROME BY DEAN CONGER © NATIONAL GEOGRAPHIC SOCIETY

part of Red Square, the Lenin Mausoleum, Spasskaya Tower, and fantastic St. Basil's Cathedral.

We turned right, passing some older buildings of Moscow University, with their white classical columns and plastered walls of bright yellow. Then came the Lenin Library, a clean modern sculpture in gray marble. A few blocks on I saw a beautiful little Orthodox church, gaily painted in white, red, and green.

"What church is that?" I asked the driver.

"I don't know," he replied. "I'm an atheist."

Soon we had left the old part of town and were speeding along a broad new boulevard, Komsomol Prospect, bordered by rows of new apartments—most of them built since my last visit, six years before.

"See that tallest building over there?" asked the driver. "The architect who designed it forgot to include elevators, so the judge sentenced him to ten years—ten years of living on the top floor!" He grinned at his own joke.

Double-decker Bridge Carries Moscow Subway

We ascended a long bridge over the Moscow River, leading up to the steep bluff called Lenin Hills. The bridge was also a new addition since my last trip.

"It's a two-story bridge," said the driver, with a touch of pride in his voice. "The subway goes underneath!"

Now I could see the huge wedding-cake tower of Moscow University (pages 322-3), sitting grandly on a bluff by the river. As we reached the top of the hill, I asked the driver to stop so I could look back at the magnificent panorama of Moscow—the same vista that Napoleon had when he arrived with his army in 1812.

Since most of Moscow is flat and I stood on its highest point, almost the entire city was visible. I could see, immediately across the river, the huge bowl of Lenin Stadium, which seats more than 100,000 people for holiday celebrations and sports events (pages 324-5). Beyond was 440-year-old Novodevichiy Convent, surrounded by an ancient fortresslike wall as if to protect it from the modern city that has grown up around it. Its great bell tower and many churches are much the same as they were in 1598, when Boris Godunov received a delegation that came to ask him to become tsar.

In the far center of the horizon I glimpsed the Kremlin itself (painting, pages 308-9), with its golden domes, highest of them the Bell Tower of Ivan the Great. For centuries it was the tallest structure in Moscow, but Stalin surpassed it after World War II with no less than seven skyscrapers —tall, pointed towers adorned with elaborate curlicues in a style sometimes called "Stalinist Gothic."

Behind me soared the tallest and most imposing of these

To share the moment with folks at home, a soldier armed with camera as well as automatic rifle records the excitement of May Day, when the Soviets display their might in Red Square. In the hours-long spectacle, workers, farmers, athletes, and the men and machines of war pass in review before Soviet leaders. Only officials and selected guests, diplomats, journalists, and foreign visitors gain admission to Red Square; ordinary citizens who do not take part view it on television.

303

MOSCOW
Forest and park belt shown in green, subways in red

PRODUCED BY
NATIONAL GEOGRAPHIC SOCIETY ©

Cultural capital of the Soviet Union as well as its industrial and political center, fast-growing Moscow ranks as the world's fifth largest city, with a population of nearly 6,400,000. Owning few cars, people take advantage of the city's elaborate and well-run subway system (pages 316-17).

Spider web of boulevards and subways weaves out from the Kremlin, heart of Moscow. Palaces, museums, theaters, and libraries cluster in the downtown section, cut by the looping Moscow River. The name for both city and river—Москва in Cyrillic, pronounced "mos-kvah"—may have derived from a Finnish word meaning "waterway."

grandiloquent skyscrapers, the main building of Moscow University, 32 stories high, my home for the coming months.

My room, on the fifth floor, measured about 12 feet by 9—small by U. S. standards. But at least I had it all to myself; some Soviet students live two or three to a room. The furnishings included a table covered with oilcloth on which sat a cut-glass water carafe—one bit of elegance that is found in even the plainest Soviet offices and waiting rooms.

I had also been provided another typically Russian item: a large aluminum teapot. The English may insist upon having tea in mid-afternoon, but Russians keep the pot boiling all day long. On trains your sleeping car may not have hot water for shaving, but the porter will surely have a water heater for tea.

The room also had a loudspeaker that broadcast Radio Moscow. I couldn't dial another station, nor could I get foreign countries; I could only turn the speaker on or off.

Next to my room was another just like it

occupied by my suitemate, Aleksandr Yosefovich Primenko, or Sasha as we called him. Between us we shared a toilet, a wash basin, and a shower with plenty of hot water.

By Soviet standards, these quarters were luxurious. Even in Moscow, where thousands of new apartment buildings have gone up in the past ten years, it is still common for three or four people to live in one room and for several families to share the same toilet, bath, and kitchen. Homes in some parts of the city still lack running water, and housewives have to fetch it from outdoor pumps.

Indeed, the dormitory rooms are so superior to much of Moscow's housing that many unauthorized persons try to live at the university. Guards at all entrances require everyone to show his *propusk* (pass) for admittance. Even so, by using a borrowed pass or by some other ruse, many individuals manage to live in the dormitories without permission.

One night around 12:30 I was trying to go to sleep, when suddenly there was an insistent knock on the door. Three young men walked in and demanded, "Show us your passport!" I was completely bewildered. Were they secret police? What had I done wrong? I hastily handed them my passport. To my relief they said, "Everything's in order."

"What's it all about?" I asked.

"We belong to the Voluntary People's Guard for the Preservation of Social Order. We're looking for people living here illegally."

Student Committee Polices Dormitory

The People's Guard was not the only group checking on me to see that I followed the rules. The Sanitary Committee examined my room once a week, graded me on its cleanliness, and posted the grade on the bulletin board. Other inspectors looked for vermin, spraying poisons where necessary. I never saw a mouse, a roach, or an ant in the dormitory

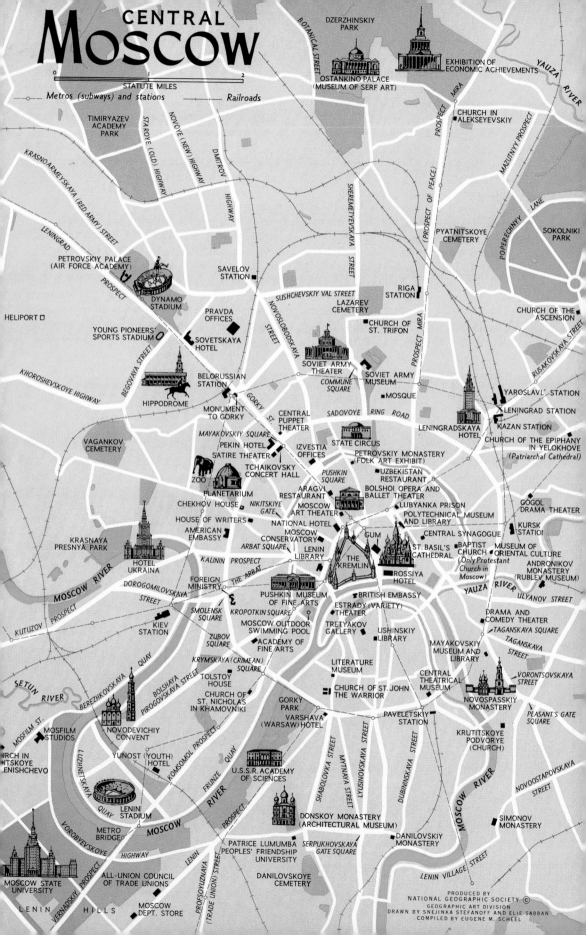

CENTRAL
Moscow

STATUTE MILES

Metros (subways) and stations   Railroads

DZERZHINSKIY PARK

BOTANICAL STREET

OSTANKINO PALACE (MUSEUM OF SERF ART)

EXHIBITION OF ECONOMIC ACHIEVEMENTS

YAUZA RIVER

TIMIRYAZEV ACADEMY PARK

STAROYE (OLD) HIGHWAY

NOVOYE (NEW) HIGHWAY

DMITROV HIGHWAY

SHEREMETYEVSKAYA STREET

PROSPECT MIRA

CHURCH IN ALEKSEYEVSKIY

MAZUTNYY PROSPECT

POPERECHNYY LANE

SOKOLNIKI PARK

KRASNOARMEYSKAYA (RED ARMY) STREET

PYATNITSKOYE CEMETERY

RUSAKOVSKAYA STREET

LENINGRAD PROSPECT

PETROVSKIY PALACE (AIR FORCE ACADEMY)

DYNAMO STADIUM

SAVELOV STATION

SUSHCHEVSKIY VAL STREET

LAZAREV CEMETERY

RIGA STATION

CHURCH OF THE ASCENSION

HELIPORT

YOUNG PIONEERS' SPORTS STADIUM

PRAVDA OFFICES

NOVOSLOBODSKAYA STREET

CHURCH OF ST. TRIFON

SOVETSKAYA HOTEL

BELORUSSIAN STATION

BEGOVAYA STREET

GORKY ST.

SOVIET ARMY THEATER

COMMUNE SQUARE

SOVIET ARMY MUSEUM

MOSQUE

YAROSLAVL' STATION

LENINGRAD STATION

KHOROSHEVSKOYE HIGHWAY

HIPPODROME

MONUMENT TO GORKY

SADOVOYE RING ROAD

LENINGRADSKAYA HOTEL

KAZAN STATION

CHURCH OF THE EPIPHANY IN YELOKHOVE (Patriarchal Cathedral)

VAGANKOV CEMETERY

MAYAKOVSKIY SQUARE

CENTRAL PUPPET THEATER

STATE CIRCUS

PETROVSKIY MONASTERY (FOLK ART EXHIBIT)

PEKIN HOTEL

SATIRE THEATER

IZVESTIA OFFICES

UZBEKISTAN RESTAURANT

GOGOL DRAMA THEATER

ZOO

TCHAIKOVSKY CONCERT HALL

PUSHKIN SQUARE

BOLSHOI OPERA AND BALLET THEATER

KURSK STATION

PLANETARIUM

ARAGVI RESTAURANT

LUBYANKA PRISON

KRASNAYA PRESNYA PARK

CHEKHOV HOUSE

NIKITSKIYE GATE

MOSCOW ART THEATER

POLYTECHNICAL MUSEUM AND LIBRARY

CENTRAL SYNAGOGUE

HOUSE OF WRITERS

AMERICAN EMBASSY

NATIONAL HOTEL

MOSCOW CONSERVATORY

GUM

ST. BASIL'S CATHEDRAL

BAPTIST CHURCH (Only Protestant Church in Moscow)

MUSEUM OF ORIENTAL CULTURE

HOTEL UKRAINA

ARBAT SQUARE

LENIN LIBRARY

THE KREMLIN

ANDRONIKOV MONASTERY (RUBLEV MUSEUM)

MOSCOW RIVER

FOREIGN MINISTRY

THE ARBAT

KALININ PROSPECT

ROSSIYA HOTEL

YAUZA RIVER

ULYANOV STREET

DOROGOMILOVSKAYA STREET

SMOLENSK SQUARE

PUSHKIN MUSEUM OF FINE ARTS

KROPOTKIN SQUARE

BRITISH EMBASSY

ESTRADY (VARIETY) THEATER

DRAMA AND COMEDY THEATER

KUTUZOV PROSPECT

KIEV STATION

ZUBOV SQUARE

MOSCOW OUTDOOR SWIMMING POOL

TRETYAKOV GALLERY

USHINSKIY LIBRARY

TAGANSKAYA SQUARE

MAYAKOVSKY MUSEUM AND LIBRARY

TAGANSKAYA STREET

ACADEMY OF FINE ARTS

KRYMSKAYA (CRIMEAN) SQUARE

LITERATURE MUSEUM

CENTRAL THEATRICAL MUSEUM

NOVOSPASSKIY MONASTERY

VORONTSOVSKAYA STREET

TOLSTOY HOUSE

CHURCH OF ST. NICHOLAS IN KHAMOVNIKI

CHURCH OF ST. JOHN THE WARRIOR

PEASANT'S GATE SQUARE

BEREZHKOVSKAYA QUAY

BOLSHAYA PIROGOVSKAYA STREET

GORKY PARK

VARSHAVA (WARSAW) HOTEL

PAVELETSKIY STATION

KRUTITSKOYE PODVORYE (CHURCH)

SETUN RIVER

MOSFILM ST.

MOSFILM STUDIOS

NOVODEVICHIY CONVENT

LUZHNETSKAYA QUAY

YUNOST (YOUTH) HOTEL

KOMSOMOL PROSPECT

FRUNZE QUAY

U.S.S.R. ACADEMY OF SCIENCES

SHABOLOVKA STREET

MYTNAYA STREET

NOVOLUZHNAYA STREET

DUBININSKAYA STREET

MOSCOW RIVER

NOVOOSTAPOVSKAYA STREET

CHURCH IN TKITSKOYE ENISHCHEVO

METRO BRIDGE

LENIN STADIUM

MOSCOW RIVER

DONSKOY MONASTERY (ARCHITECTURAL MUSEUM)

DANILOVSKIY MONASTERY

SIMONOV MONASTERY

VOROBYEVSKOYE HIGHWAY

MOSCOW STATE UNIVERSITY

VERNADSKIY PROSPECT

ALL-UNION COUNCIL OF TRADE UNIONS

MOSCOW DEPT. STORE

PROFSOYUZNAYA (TRADE UNION) STREET

PATRICE LUMUMBA PEOPLES' FRIENDSHIP UNIVERSITY

DANILOVSKOYE CEMETERY

SERPUKHOVSKOYE GATE SQUARE

LENIN PROSPECT

LENIN VILLAGE STREET

LENIN HILLS

PRODUCED BY
NATIONAL GEOGRAPHIC SOCIETY ©
GEOGRAPHIC ART DIVISION
DRAWN BY SNEJINKA STEFANOFF AND ELIE SABBAN
COMPILED BY EUGENE M. SCHEEL

—surprising, since most students kept food in their rooms. Nor was I ever bothered by bedbugs, though a friend was less fortunate.

As a resident of the dorm, I took my turn at floor duty. This involved sweeping the corridors and the two kitchens on our floor, as well as answering the telephone in the parlor for half a day.

The Student Committee, made up of activists from the Komsomol, the Communist Youth League, supervised all these matters. If a student was extremely lax in his academic and social responsibilities, the committee could recommend expulsion.

More than a score of American exchange scholars were quartered at the university during my stay, and all of us were objects of special supervision. Our suitemates, usually members of the Communist Party or the Komsomol, probably were required to report on us. We assumed microphones were hidden in our rooms. One of the Russians on my floor, a member of the People's Guard, inquired among the other students as to who came to my room and why.

Under these circumstances, many students were reluctant to drop into my room for a chat. They thought it would not look good on their records. Some of my dormitory mates were friendly nonetheless.

"*Nichevo,*" one said, "what the heck. If anybody asks me what I'm doing here, I'll say I'm practicing my English. I don't care; I never expect to be a Party member or have an important job anyhow."

One student from another Communist country was afraid even to speak to me, lest his compatriots find out about it. He asked a Soviet student to ask me if I would be willing to sell him some American cigarettes.

I refused, lest I be accused of *spekulatsiya*—black marketeering—but offered him some as a gift. He was afraid to take them from me directly, but suggested that I give them to a Soviet friend, who in turn would give them to him. Only after I assured him repeatedly that I would tell no one did he reluctantly hide the cigarettes in his pockets.

"If anyone knew, it would be this for me," he said, drawing a finger across his throat.

University "City" Fills Most Needs

My suitemate, Sasha, 37, was an attractive Ukrainian with bushy brown hair, a sharp nose, and usually a broad smile on his lips. He served in the army during World War II, was wounded three times, and lost one leg.

Sasha, a graduate student, aimed at becoming a history professor. Although he worked hard writing his dissertation, frequently typing till 3 a.m., he was always ready to answer my questions or simply to bat the breeze, and he helped greatly to ease my adjustment to Soviet life.

The towering home of Moscow University (or, to use its full name, "Moscow Order of Lenin and Order of the Red Banner of Labor State University Named for M. V. Lomonosov") is a self-sufficient community. It has a grocery store, shoe-repair shop, laundry, drugstore, a small clothing shop, a watch-repair kiosk, theater-ticket bureau, photo studio, post office, several book and newspaper stands, a movie hall, a barbershop (where I got excellent haircuts for 40 cents), and a beauty parlor where coeds get fancy hairdos for their weekend dates.

On my first visit to the student cafeteria, I was introduced to one of the most common

(Continued on page 311)

EKTACHROMES © NATIONAL GEOGRAPHIC SOCIETY

With heel-clicking precision, the guard changes at Lenin Mausoleum exactly on the stroke of the hour. During visiting hours, long lines wait patiently to view the glass-encased embalmed body of the father of the Union of Soviet Socialist Republics. Cyrillic letters over the door spell "Lenin."

Flowers alone grace the grave of a downgraded Stalin, dictator of the Soviet Union until his death in 1953, though busts mark the plots of less-famous Bolsheviks behind the Lenin shrine. A de-Stalinization program after his death rewrote the nation's history books and stripped the mantle of greatness from the long-time leader. In 1961 officials moved his remains here from a place of honor beside Lenin in the mausoleum.

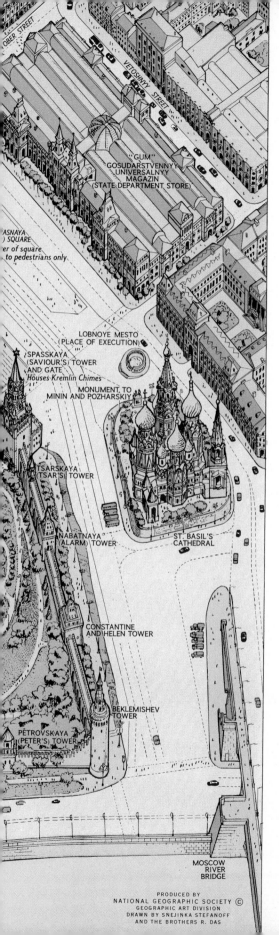

PRODUCED BY
NATIONAL GEOGRAPHIC SOCIETY ©
GEOGRAPHIC ART DIVISION
DRAWN BY SNEJINKA STEFANOFF
AND THE BROTHERS R. DAS

КРЕМЛЬ

K REMLIN—its very name conjures a fore-boding image in Western minds. Thus the magnificent buildings, capped by bulbous cupolas of gold and silver, often surprise foreign visitors with their beauty.

The Kremlin—literally "the citadel," the fortified center of the medieval city—stands where Prince Yuri Dolgorukiy, founder of Moscow, built a rude wooden fort in the 12th century. Later rulers rebuilt and improved it many times, erecting palaces, churches, and government offices befitting the seat of Russian empire. At the time Columbus was planning his voyages of discovery, Europe's foremost military engineers raised the protecting brick battlements around the Kremlin's 65 acres.

Succeeding the tsars in this traditional home of authority, the Bolsheviks imposed their new order. Paradoxically, the stronghold of an atheistic ideology preserves its former churches as historic treasures—the Cathedral of the Assumption, where the tsars were crowned; the Cathedral of the Annunciation, where they were wed; and the Cathedral of the Archangel Michael, where many lie entombed.

In the Hall of Arms, descendants of serfs see priceless riches of tsarist days. Diplomats sip vodka and eat caviar at gala receptions in St. George's Hall of the Grand Kremlin Palace.

Some visitors complain that the modern glass-and-marble Palace of Congresses, completed in 1961, looks out of place. The Soviets reply: "Other periods of Russian architecture are represented here—why not ours?"

Beyond Spasskaya Tower, the main Kremlin entrance, spreads Red Square, bounded by the Historical Museum, GUM (State Department Store), and St. Basil's Cathedral (pages 298-9). The square's Russian name, Krasnaya, once meaning "beautiful" as well as "red," predates the 1917 Revolution by centuries.

This precisely scaled painting shows the Kremlin in unprecedented detail. Since Soviet security regulations bar aerial photographs, artists gathered all available diagrams and ground-level photographs. They drafted a sketch that was carried to Moscow and corrected on the spot by a GEOGRAPHIC assistant editor.

features of Russian life—the queue. In this case there were two queues, operating on a pay-before-you-see-the-food basis.

After 10 or 15 minutes of waiting, I got close enough to read the menu posted on the cashier's cage. The menus were almost illegible and difficult to translate, even though I knew Russian. Several words meant stew; chopped meat had countless names.

Upon arriving at the head of the line, I faced the impossible task of deciphering the menu, translating it, and making a choice—all in a few seconds. If I dallied, the cashier would start shouting at me.

As I sounded off each item, the cashier would punch the cash register, which simply recorded the sale. She added up the total on an abacus (the standard device for adding in Russia). She then handed me the cash register tape in return for my kopecks (cents).

I now had the privilege of moving to the second queue and waiting another ten minutes or so before getting to the serving counters. At the first counter I presented one of my receipts to the girl, who reached into a trough, threw some mashed potatoes on a plate, and then plopped a bit of stew on top.

At the next counter I got my borsch, served in a shallow bowl filled to the brim; I carried it delicately lest it spill on my clothes. (This would have been a catastrophe, because of the poor dry-cleaning facilities in Moscow.)

The serving of bread occupied the full-time attention of still another girl, since it was not sold by the slice, but by the gram. The bread girl carefully weighed each piece, adding a bit here or cutting off a bit there, so no one would get slightly more or less than his two kopecks' worth.

There was one other feature of the student cafeteria that I will never forget—the complete lack of knives. Either I had to pick up my meat with a fork and bite off a chunk at a time, as most of the Russians did, or painfully pry the meat into pieces with the edge of a spoon.

Students Live on $40 a Month

The only virtue of the student cafeteria was its cheapness. I usually spent from 50 cents to 80 cents for dinner, never as much as a dollar. Cheapness, of course, is important for students who have to live on scholarships of $40 a month. Fortunately for me, there were two other eating places at the university. The professors' dining room (open to all) and the dietetic dining room both had better food, with table service, at somewhat higher prices—about $1.00 for an average dinner.

Of course, there were several good restaurants downtown. Among my favorites were

EKTACHROME (BELOW) AND KODACHROME BY DEAN CONGER © N.G.S.

Early tsars ruled and reveled in the throne room of the Kremlin's Hall of Facets. Beneath the arched ceiling at Christmas, 1553, Ivan the Terrible feted the first Englishmen to visit Russia. Allegorical frescoes glorify the power and the wisdom of the tsars.

Hoard of riches amassed by Russian rulers —gilded presentation pieces, crown jewels, golden carriages and sleighs, and diamond-studded robes—awe visitors to the Hall of Arms in the Kremlin. Stalin barred citizens from admission during his rule; not until 1955 could they tour the citadel.

Government by "*Da*—Yes"

RUBBER STAMP OF THE COMMUNIST PARTY, the Supreme Soviet meets in the Grand
Kremlin Palace. Unlike the Congress of the United States, this body wields little
power, approving decisions already reached by the Party's Presidium. Every four years
citizens dutifully elect nearly 1,500 deputies to the two Supreme Soviet chambers, casting their ballots for unopposed candidates selected by the Communist Party.

At a joint session last fall, Party Presidium members (from right) Leonid Brezhnev,
Alexei Kosygin, Anastas Mikoyan, Nikolay Podgorny, and Mikhail Suslov take front-
row seats by rank. Mikoyan later resigned as President of the Supreme Soviet, and Podgorny succeeded him. Brezhnev, First Secretary of the Party, and Kosygin, Chairman of
the Council of Ministers, hold positions once occupied by Nikita Khrushchev alone.

313

the Aragvi (specializing in Georgian foods and wines), the Uzbekistan (serving central Asian dishes), and the National Hotel (with a varied, predominantly Russian cuisine). Even these de luxe restaurants were inexpensive by American standards: A Soviet couple could have dinner, listen to a jazz orchestra, dance, and sip *shampanskoye*—Russian champagne—for about $5.00 a person. And, best of all, tipping was more or less voluntary.

Metropolis Retains Village Flavor

Though I spent most of my time in libraries doing research on Russian history, I set aside weekends for sightseeing. I walked the streets of Moscow for five months, yet every time I turned a new corner I found surprises —a little jewel of a church hidden beside a factory wall, a ramshackle log cabin on the edge of a new housing development, or a neoclassic palace built by some noble in the time of Catherine the Great.

Moscow is fascinating and confusing. It's a modern industrial metropolis with a population of 6,388,000, and yet it's only an overgrown peasant village. It's the capital of the biggest country in the world, but it is provincial and ingrown. It is at the same time clean and shabby; magnificent and dowdy; exhilarating and depressing; dynamic and stagnant; planned and chaotic; revolutionary and conservative. And it's always changing.

Moscow is the center of one of the world's most highly centralized countries. All major decisions—political, economic, scientific, or cultural—are made here. Soviet trains and planes operate on Moscow time. Outlying newspapers copy the contents and format of *Pravda* and *Izvestia,* published in Moscow. Moscow has the most industry, the most governmental offices, museums, monuments, scientists, and the most famous theaters.

Of all Russian cities, only Leningrad (formerly St. Petersburg), with 3,607,000 people, makes any claim to challenging Moscow's predominance. Peter the Great moved the capital to St. Petersburg in 1714; there it remained during most of the 200 years to 1918, when the Bolsheviks returned it to Moscow.

Leningraders still insist that their city is the most civilized metropolis in Russia, and regard Moscow as crude, backward, and drab. If Moscow is Washington and New York combined, Leningrad is Russia's Boston.

I tried to cover as much of Moscow as I could. Sometimes I boarded a bus or streetcar and rode to the end of the line, just to see what would turn up next. At other times I took the subway to look at the people, perhaps stopping along the way to admire the ornately decorated stations (pages 316-17).

Often I knocked around town with my closest Soviet friend, a graduate student in linguistics, whom I shall call Boris. A tall young man with finely chiseled features, high forehead, and curly black hair, Boris was one of the most cultured Russians I met, with a great knowledge of literature, history, art, architecture, and Soviet life in general.

He spoke German and English fluently and asked me to teach him American slang, which he found fascinating. Whenever we met, he would look at me with a grin and say, "What's cooking, Doc?" And when we parted, "See you later, alligator."

"Student From the Moon" Intrigues Boris

Boris obviously got a thrill out of having a friend from the United States, and he used to come by my room often to look at my magazines and newspapers. I once asked him why he was so interested in America.

"If a student from the moon came to your university, wouldn't you want to meet him?" he replied. "Our press has a lot of articles about the United States, but they don't tell the whole truth. I want to know for myself."

Like most Russians, Boris was generous. Frequently he brought gifts—a rare book on Russian history, a toy wooden bear for my son, or a cigarette box decorated with a miniature painting of a Russian fairy story.

Not long after my arrival, I made a return visit to the biggest tourist attraction in all Russia—Red Square and the Kremlin. Though Boris had seen them a hundred times, he was glad to go along.

In Red Square we joined the crowd in front

Fairy-tale fantasy mirrored in a rain pool, St. Basil's Cathedral embodies the splendor and mystique of old Russia. Built by Ivan the Terrible to commemorate his victory over the Tatars in 1552, the flamboyant masterpiece lifts domes of many shapes and colors above chapels linked by a labyrinth of passages. Napoleon, who called St. Basil's a "mosque" and stabled horses here, wanted the cathedral torn down. But it survived to become a historic monument. Around the platformlike Lobnoye Mesto, or Place of Execution (left), citizens once gathered for tsarist proclamations and public beheadings.

of Lenin's tomb to watch the changing of the guard. As three trim soldiers goose-stepped from the Kremlin, we watched to see if they would succeed in taking their places at the precise moment when the clock on Spasskaya Tower struck the hour (page 307).

"Perfect!" said Boris, beaming, as the click of their heels coincided exactly with the first "bong."

Swimmers Splash Amid Swirling Snow

On another day we visited GUM, the huge State Department Store (Gosudarstvennyy Universalnyy Magazin) across from the Kremlin (page 345). I had come to Moscow without a fur hat, and my Russian friends seemed worried that I would die of pneumonia. The smart karakul caps were too expensive—$75 —but I found a muskrat one with ear flaps for $20.

One of the strangest sights to me was the Moscow swimming pool—an enormous outdoor pool that operates even in below-zero weather. The water, of course, was heated, so a huge cloud of steam billowed up,

"World's most beautiful subway," say Muscovites of their Metro. But hurrying commuters rarely glance at the Stalin-era mosaics and chandeliers like these in Kiev Station.

Nearly three million people a day pay 5 kopecks (about 5½ cents) to travel in cars that run smoothly and on time. Four-lane escalators whisk them to and from stations as much as 200 feet below city streets.

Camped beneath an ornamental window, a subway hawker sells state lottery tickets for 30 kopecks. First prize: a small Moscow-made sedan worth about 3,500 rubles ($3,885).

giving the impression of a vast Turkish bath. It was odd to stand in a whirling snowstorm and watch hundreds of men and women splashing a few feet away in scanty bathing suits.

Another day we went to the Exhibition of Economic Achievements, a sort of permanent world's fair, except that only the U.S.S.R. is represented (pages 326-7). Spread across 534 acres, many of the pavilions reflect architectural styles of the Union's different republics and nationalities. They hold thousands of displays of the most up-to-date developments of Soviet industry, construction, transportation, and agriculture. Special halls proclaim achievements in "Space," "Atomic Energy for Peaceful Purposes," "Electronics," "Livestock Breeding," and so on.

Additives Turn White Bread Tan

An exhibition boasting of Russia's agricultural achievements seemed a bit ironic, because the food situation that year was the worst the country had seen in a long time. Indeed, the crop failure was so serious that Russia was forced to buy wheat from the United States.

Inhabitants of Moscow felt the shortage most keenly in bread, always a large part of the Russian diet. The delicious white bread I had eaten as a tourist was available now only in the most expensive restaurants. Elsewhere people had a choice of either the traditional black bread or a bread that, though described as "white," was actually tan in color and rather unpleasant in flavor.

The queer taste was the result of adding one or another substitute to the flour—corn meal, peas, beans, and so on. The students had a sarcastic comment: "Did you hear what they're adding to the bread this week?"

"What?"

"Flour!"

The crop failure also affected other foods; macaroni, rice, buckwheat, and similar grain products disappeared from the stores completely. Friends told me that outside Moscow the food situation was, as usual, much worse. In provincial villages and towns there were periods when only black bread was available, and customers had to wait in long lines for that.

"There are always shortages of one thing or another," a Moscow housewife told me. "They

Face as round and red as the beets she sells, a vendor hunches against the cold in a Moscow free market. Her stolid strength reflects the Russian spirit that wore down Napoleon's invading legions and checked Hitler's panzers in the rubble of Stalingrad. Like hundreds of farm folk who stream into the city each morning, she offers produce raised on a private plot tilled on a collective farm. For stall and scale she pays a nominal rent and pockets the rest of her earnings.   EKTACHROME BY DEAN CONGER © N.G.S.

boast that our economy is a planned one, but it doesn't show many signs of being planned in the sale of the goods I need. But if you think Moscow is bad, you should see the other cities. I mail my sister in Archangel a package of foods every month—things she can't buy at all."

On my trips as a tourist I hadn't felt the food shortages, since the hotel restaurants where I ate offered a wide variety of dishes. This time, however, I shopped for food regularly, mostly in the university's *gastronom* (grocery store), and found it quite a chore.

I would have liked to buy milk every day, but I never knew when the gastronom would get its supply—one day it would be in the morning, the next day in the afternoon, and the third day in the evening. Sometimes they would have only milk, sometimes only yogurt, and sometimes neither. And even when they had exactly what I wanted, I might stand in line for 15 minutes, only to find the supply exhausted before my turn came.

"If It's for Sale, Buy It"

During winter the arrival of eggs was a rare event. Word would spread through the dormitory—"Eggs!"—and students would come hurrying from all directions. The eggs came packed in large wooden crates. This meant that the purchasers had to perform a balancing trick—carrying home their limit of 30 eggs on a piece of the indented cardboard from the crate.

Living in a country where shortages are common, one develops new attitudes. I soon adopted a basic rule of Communist society: "If you see something for sale that you want, buy it, because tomorrow there probably won't be any."

I seldom eat oranges, but when I unexpectedly found them on sale in Moscow, I very much wanted some—until I discovered the price: 20 to 30 cents apiece. Soon, however, the lure of the scarce luxury became irresistible, and I queued up for oranges whenever they were available—usually shipped in from Spain, Morocco, or Israel. As a result, I ate more oranges in those five months than I ordinarily eat in five years.

Pensive poet Robert Rozhdestvenskiy often aims his blank verse at Stalinist repressions. Though a confirmed Communist, he aroused Khrushchev's ire with his protests; later he publicly confessed his "errors." He and other liberal young poets enjoy the popularity of matinee idols. Public readings on Poetry Day pack Moscow's many Houses of Culture and even fill Lenin Stadium with a capacity crowd of 100,000 poetry lovers.

Interviewing Rozhdestvenskiy in his Moscow flat, photographer Conger found him "always moving—gesturing, pacing, changing chairs." Twice a visitor to the United States, the 33-year-old poet at times waxes anti-American in his verses.

Guitars are in, balalaikas out, with Russia's jazz-loving young people. Reclining on rented slat chairs, this group whiles away leisure hours at Silver Pine Forest Beach on the Moscow River.

AGLOW FOR MAY DAY, *Moscow University rises above a fountain-studded pool. The city's tallest building bristles with "Stalinist Gothic" towers and ornamentation; its hundreds of well-equipped laboratories reflect Russia's stress on science. More than 30,000 undergraduates, a third of them coeds (inset), compete for admission and attend tuition-free. Living in student quarters, the author found the university a self-contained community complete with stores, barbershop, and bank. Guards at each entrance intercept would-be squatters lured by the relative luxury of the dormitories.*

The Soviet regime encourages its subjects to accept the shortages and hardships of today by holding out the promise of the glorious future awaiting them "in a few more years." According to the official line, what they have today is called "socialism," while the future system, in which everybody will have plenty of everything, will be called "communism."

The government has made many promises in the past, and Soviet citizens have become somewhat cynical. One day Boris asked me: "Did you hear what it's going to be like at the end of the next five-year plan? Every family will have a TV set and a private jet plane."

"I can see why everybody would want a TV set," I replied, "but why will they need a jet airplane?"

"Well," he said, "when we see on TV that eggs are on sale in Vladivostok, we can jump in our planes and fly there to buy some."

A similar skepticism about the utopian future was revealed in the remark made to me on a bus one day. When I first arrived in Moscow, I noticed that the buses bore signs saying "No Conductor." Instead of someone to collect fares, there was a box near the entrance, where each passenger was supposed to drop his 5 kopecks and take a ticket. I asked the young man seated beside me about the new system.

"Not long ago," he said, "all the conductors were removed, and we changed to the honor system. This shows that we have achieved socialism, since all citizens have rid themselves of capitalist greed and think only of the collective good.

"And when we achieve communism," he added with a grin, "there will be no drivers."

Western Fashions Invade Moscow

Though the food situation in Moscow had deteriorated since my last trip, clothing seemed much improved. The heavy utilitarian shoes for ladies had been replaced by slim pumps with spike heels, most of them imported. Dresses were of better fit and fashion. Parisian coiffures had replaced the dowdy hairdos of the past, and use of lipstick and mascara (which the Bolsheviks had once denounced as "bourgeois") was common.

The typical Soviet man of the past wore jackets with sleeves (by Western tastes) too long, trousers with cuffs too wide, and shoes that were broad and ungainly. Now many Soviet men have gone Italian—with form-fitting jackets, narrow trousers, and pointed shoes.

My first impression in 1956 had been that almost everybody looked like either a worker or a peasant; now, eight years later, most

Poised for a slalom, skiers await their turn on a steep slope in the Lenin Hills near the university. The run ends at the ice-paved Moscow River.

From these bluffs in 1812, Napoleon first spied the turreted Oriental city he held so briefly. "She lies at my feet," he gloats in Tolstoy's *War and Peace,* "her golden domes and crosses flashing and twinkling in the sun." Now viewers see the honeycomb tiers of Lenin Stadium and phalanxes of new apartments.

Muskrat *shapka* warms the author's ears in a city so cold that passersby search each others' faces for frostbite. Professor of Russian History at the University of Virginia, Dr. Hammond speaks Russian and has made four visits to the U.S.S.R.

Market-bound *babushka*—"grandmother" in Russian—tows a snow-time perambulator with bundled cargo.

Muscovites looked middle class. One evening at the Bolshoi Theater I sat next to a gray-haired gentleman who was so distinguished-looking in his neat white shirt and well-tailored navy-blue suit that I assumed he was from some Western country, perhaps the United States. His wife wore a big beehive hairdo, an ermine cape, and diamonds on her fingers. Yet during intermission, when they began to talk, I discovered that they were both Russians, evidently members of the new upper class. Perhaps he was a Party or government official, a scientist, a successful author, or a university professor.

One could not say, however, that today the stores are filled with attractive, well-made clothing. Foreign visitors still meet black marketeers who are ready to buy the clothes off their backs for high prices. One student I knew paid $22 for a nylon shirt from Yugo-

slavia because, he said, the quality was superior to similar Soviet products.

Foreign clothes are a status symbol, especially among the youth. Once in downtown Moscow I saw a boy about 19 or 20 whom I immediately identified as an American from his clothes—a seersucker jacket, madras shirt, khaki trousers, and loafers. "What part of the States are you from?" I asked.

He looked puzzled. *"Chto vy skazali?—* What did you say?" he replied in Russian.

He *was* Russian. He had bought his American outfit, he explained, from American tourists and Soviet black marketeers.

Shoe Speculator Draws Jail Term

The chronic shortage of quality goods also has led to what the government calls "speculation"—buying scarce items and reselling them at a profit. I ran into a case of this one

325

day when I attended a trial at a People's Court, lowest in the Soviet judicial system. The defendant, a man about 45, was accused of buying a pair of ladies' shoes for $23, then trying to sell them for $28 to a girl at the end of the line.

He denied it. "I bought them for my niece, but that girl begged me to sell them to her, so I was going to let her have them for the same price I paid."

The judge interrupted impatiently: "Are you trying to tell us that after waiting in line several hours you were going to sell the shoes for the same price? That's not believable! You're a professional speculator; you've been in court before for the same offense, and your pockets were full of earrings when the police arrested you."

The man finally admitted his guilt, but pleaded for mercy on the basis of his service in World War II. His sentence: two years in prison.

Consumer goods may be scarce in Moscow, but cultural activities abound. The city's numerous theaters operate on the repertory system, and the variety of performances that one can see (if he has the time and money) is overwhelming.

During one typical ten-day period, Muscovites could attend no fewer than 221 different plays, 12 ballets, 19 operas, 12 operettas, 16 puppet shows, a circus, and 23 plays written

Showcase of a nation, the Exhibition of Economic Achievements attracts huge crowds. Housed in templelike pavilions, the 100,000 displays in this permanent fair range from sputniks to laying hens, computers to milking machines. Streaming past the Friendship of Peoples Fountain, more than 8,000,000 visitors a year crisscross the parklike grounds in north-central Moscow.

Hoops of pretzel-like *bubliki* appeal to all ages at the exhibit. Boiled, then baked, the crusty rings ride like bracelets on the arms of matrons in scarves and chic younger women with bouffant hairdos.

especially for children. This is not counting the concerts, which are numerous and of high quality. Tickets, moreover, are quite cheap. Even at the Bolshoi Ballet the top price is only $3.85.

Many people have seen the Bolshoi dancers on world tours in recent years, but nothing compares with seeing them in their own home theater, with its huge stage, gilded balconies, red-plush upholstery, and crystal chandeliers —an appropriate setting for the classical ballets they do so well.

And it is particularly fun to watch the spectacle with an enthusiastic Soviet audience (pages 334-5). Russians are fanatics about ballet; the leading stars are national heroes. One night at the Bolshoi I shared a box with two schoolteachers who could tell me in detail the professional histories of each of the principal dancers, where they had studied, how long they had been dancing, their best roles, and what their particular virtues were.

The performance that night starred Maya Plisetskaya, one of the most honored ballerinas in Russia, in a ballet concert. Whenever Plisetskaya was about to appear, the audience began to applaud, and before she had finished each dance, they began to applaud again. At the end she had to repeat "The Dying Swan." Then huge bouquets of flowers were brought onto the stage, while she bowed for nearly 20 minutes. Never before had I seen such love between audience and artist.

"Dangerous" Books Withheld From Public

The main purpose of my coming to Russia, as stated in my application, was to collect information for a book on the Russian Revolution of 1905, an event which paved the way for the Bolshevik Revolution of 1917.

The staff of Lenin Library, the Russian equivalent of our Library of Congress, served

EKTACHROMES © NATIONAL GEOGRAPHIC SOCIETY

Riding the giant Ferris wheel, rowing on the lake, or giggling at images in funhouse mirrors—Gorky Park on a soft summer evening offers something for everyone. Less-active visitors relax in formal gardens, dine in restaurants, or attend plays in the amphitheater. Most popular of the city's 11 "parks of culture and rest," Gorky stretches along the Moscow River. The capital lacks true night clubs, but in a number of restaurants revelers such as these May Day celebrants may dance to popular music.

Flame of faith lighting her face, a supplicant offers a candle in a Russian Orthodox church. Schools teach militant atheism and church membership closes the door to good jobs, but religion persists despite decades of persecution.

Hallowed Virgin of Vladimir, a 12th-century Byzantine masterpiece, hangs in Moscow's Tretyakov Gallery. It inspired many icons by Russian artists during an age of religious fervor.

me politely and efficiently, though the library had some rather strange regulations. Many books, newspapers, and magazines were not included in the card catalogue because they were considered too heretical for the general public. Publications considered especially dangerous were kept in a secret part of the library called the "Special Fund," inaccessible to all but the most stalwart supporters of the Communist regime.

Though Lenin Library proved useful, the most important place for my research was the Central State Historical Archive. It contains invaluable original source materials—letters, diaries, government records, and other unpublished materials that exist nowhere else in the world.

When my application to study in Moscow was sent to the Soviet authorities in the spring of 1963, I stated clearly that I wished to do research in archives, and I listed the archives by name. I stated further that I would do preliminary reading on my topic in the United States, using a 15-volume series of documents published by the Soviet Academy of Sciences.

Red Tape Drags On for Months

On my arrival in Moscow in February, 1964, the university said that before using the archives I must first submit a "Research Plan" —my work, like everything else in the Soviet Union, having to be planned. I prepared the plan, emphasizing again that my main interest was in archival materials.

EKTACHROMES © NATIONAL GEOGRAPHIC SOCIETY

Next I had to submit a detailed three-page list of the collections I wished to use in the archives. After a few weeks of waiting, I was assured that I had permission to use the archives "in principle," but that I would have to give the archivists time to get the materials together for me.

Throughout March and April I was repeatedly told that the collections would be ready "in a few days." Finally, on May 22, I was handed a letter from the Main Archival Administration. It stated that it was not necessary for me to use the archives, since I could find all the necessary documents in the 15-volume series of the Academy of Sciences.

The net result of my three-and-a-half-month wait was a suggestion that I read the books I had already read in the United States!

The final chapter occurred only after I returned home, where a letter awaited me from the U. S. Embassy in Moscow. An official of the Ministry of Education had telephoned the embassy on July 7—five days after my departure—to say that permission for me to work in the archives had been granted, and they were terribly sorry to have "just discovered" that I had left.

While the archives story is evidence that Stalinist bureaucracy and suspicion of foreigners is far from dead in the Soviet Union, I found indications of liberalizing trends and greater respect for the truth.

I was particularly impressed by public meetings which the Institute of History held

to discuss the draft of a book on the history of the Soviet Union during the time of Stalin's dictatorship. Although the draft apparently was much more truthful than earlier Soviet histories, it still was not sufficiently honest to satisfy some of the speakers.

"During the time of Stalin," said one critic caustically, "we described everything as either great or awful, black or white, with nothing in between. We still do the same thing; we are still under Stalin's influence. Have we ever given a balanced evaluation of a person, showing both his good and bad sides? No, always a person is a god or a devil. We must not continue this. We can't write just for today; we must write so that in ten years we won't blush."

Problem of Truth Plagues Soviet Historians

Other members of the audience attacked the book for not telling enough about the great purges of 1935-38, the Stalin-Hitler pact of 1939, or the ruthless way in which Stalin collectivized agriculture. Still, there seemed to be tacit acknowledgment by those present that Soviet authorities would not permit historians to tell the *whole* truth.

As one speaker commented, "There are many fabrications in this volume, and *some* of them can certainly be eliminated."

In other areas also I found greater freedom and less fear of the police than on previous trips. Voice of America broadcasts to Russia are no longer jammed (with the unfortunate result that people seem less eager to listen), and jazz is no longer condemned (with the unfortunate result that I was kept awake nights by recordings of the loudest kind of rock 'n' roll). American music is played fairly often on the Soviet radio; one night I was startled to hear "Wagon Wheels," "Indiana," and "Beautiful Ohio"

KODACHROMES © NATIONAL GEOGRAPHIC SOCIETY

High-rise apartments lift above rustic cabins near Moscow University as the capital expands. The prefabricated structures provide more than 100,000 new units annually, and families accustomed to communal baths and kitchens clamor for the apartments' comparative luxury—even while criticizing the mass-produced buildings for shoddy workmanship. Women masons, carpenters, and painters labor side by side with men on the projects.

Bolshoi Ballet: big and beautiful

TRADITIONALLY, the ballet enjoys tremendous esteem in Russia, which has produced some of the world's foremost dancers—Pavlova, Nijinsky, Ulanova, Nureyev. The celebrated Bolshoi company features extravagant productions and extraordinary physical feats. Bolshoi means "grand," and the troupe justifies its name in classics like "Swan Lake," performed here in the Kremlin's Palace of Congresses before a capacity audience of 6,000.

The Bolshoi's 250 dancers, supported by their own orchestra and an army of technicians, live in a world apart. Wards of the Ministry of Culture, solo ballerinas like Yekaterina Maximova (below) begin their careers at age 9 or 10. Each year 30 youngsters, chosen from 1,500 applicants, enter the Bolshoi's school for nine years of rigorous training. To make the picture below and others of Russian artists and professional people (pages 320, 336-7, and 339), photographer Conger had the assistance of the Institute of Soviet-American Relations, a government agency dealing with American visitors.

KODACHROME (ABOVE) BY THOMAS T. HAMMOND; EKTACHROMES (BELOW AND RIGHT) AND
KODACHROME BY NATIONAL GEOGRAPHIC PHOTOGRAPHER DEAN CONGER © N.G.S.

—American voices singing along with Mitch Miller.

A few Broadway hits are now performed on the Moscow stage, though they are usually chosen to show the degeneration of American life (Tennessee Williams's *Orpheus Descending*), or the class divisions of American society (*Two for the Seesaw* by William Gibson).

Another landmark in the removal of Stalinist restrictions was the first presentation since the Revolution of ballets by the Russian émigré composer Igor Stravinsky, such as "Petrushka" and "Fire Bird."

336

Workaday world of Moscow women

SPURRED BY STAGGERING WAR CASUALTIES, the necessity for more family income, and governmental encouragement, Soviet women invade fields regarded in many lands as male domain—from unskilled labor to top-notch professions. Today 55 percent of employed Muscovites are women, including three of every four doctors. They earn equal pay for equal work with men, but predominate in lower-wage occupations.

Dr. Nadezhda Blokhin teams with husband Nikolay, President of the Academy of Medical Sciences, in cancer surgery. Yelena Prosvetova spends long hours at her desk as deputy mayor of Moscow. Dark-haired Elina Bystritskaya, a screen and stage star, turns heads in a Moscow park. When women grow too old for jobs like tending textile looms, they care for children (opposite, above) and thus free young mothers for work.

I also heard much talk about two Soviet movies which dealt with hitherto forbidden subjects. One, called *Silence,* showed the secret police of Stalin's era arriving in the middle of the night to arrest a man who was probably innocent, and then pictured a meeting of a Party cell where his son was unjustly expelled. In another film a leading character was Grigoriy Zinoviev, an early Bolshevik who was purged by Stalin and became for many years an "unperson."

State Still Controls Soviet Arts

In general, however, intellectual and cultural life in 1964 was less free than it had been at other times since the death of Stalin. Yev-geny Yevtushenko and a number of other somewhat rebellious writers and artists were condemned by the Party in 1963, and political controls were tightened. Today Soviet Russia, the land of revolution, remains extremely conservative in art, literature, ballet, and drama.

One thing that surprised me was how often I heard Russians criticize Nikita Khrushchev, then the premier. While they were afraid to say anything disrespectful when fellow Soviet citizens were around, some of them spoke to me quite freely and spontaneously, as though they were in the habit of talking like this with their friends. Intellectuals were particularly contemptuous of him. *"Kakoy durak!* What a fool!" they used to say.

In Russia there is an infinite series of jokes about things supposedly said by the radio station in the capital of Armenia, Radio Yerevan. Usually they are in the form of requests by listeners for information, which the announcer tries to answer. One of the most popular of these stories involved Khrushchev:

Question: "Can you tell the best way to get rid of baldness?"

Announcer: "I'm sorry, but we do not discuss political questions."

Criticism of Khrushchev Mounts

A Russian professor I met was especially critical. "Stalin may have been cruel and despotic," he said, "but at least he had dignity. But this *kukuruznik* [cornball] we have now is always boasting about some new harebrained scheme of his.

"One year he sent the students out to Siberia and Kazakhstan to help plow up the virgin lands, but that was a flop. Then he said that all the farms had to grow corn, and that

was a fiasco, too. And of course we were shocked by the Cuban missile crisis—one day he denied that there were any Soviet missiles in Cuba, and the next day he promised to remove them! That scared us. We've had enough of war, and we don't like this playing around with brinkmanship."

"I have no great love for Khrushchev," I said, "but still he seems to me an enormous improvement over Stalin. Don't forget all the reforms he's put through."

"You Americans are all alike!" said the professor. "All your newspapers talk about are the good things Khrushchev has done. But in 1962, when he raised prices on meat and butter, you didn't publish anything about the food riots in Novocherkassk. And what about the food shortages now? If we had an intelligent man at the top, this wouldn't happen."

How typical these views were is hard to say. But when Khrushchev was removed from power after my return to the United States, it was interesting to read official criticisms of

"Baa, baa, black sheep," sing Young Pioneers, practicing English with a nursery rhyme in Sokolniki Park. Most youngsters from 9 to 14 belong to Pioneer clubs, learning woodcraft as well as Marxist doctrine.

Colossus of Lenin dwarfs the noted sculptor Matvey Manizer. On the balcony a full-bearded Karl Marx broods beside smaller works. Copies of Manizer's works adorn schools and plazas throughout the U.S.S.R.

him in the Soviet press similar to those I had heard from private citizens.

There are still many reminders, however, that Russia is a police state. One night I was chatting with friends in a Moscow apartment when the hostess got up and closed the windows. "No need to arouse the curiosity of the neighbors," she commented.

Another day I was enjoying a gay dinner with several Soviet students in a dormitory room. We were having such a good time that I decided to photograph the occasion.

"Be sure you don't publish any of those pictures," said one of my friends.

"Why not?" I asked. "What trouble could you get into because of such pictures?"

"In Russia," he laughed, "anything is possible. The authorities might think that the room looks too shabby and that our food isn't fancy enough. They might ask why we let you take our pictures unless we had champagne and caviar on the table."

Russians Keep "Tongue Behind Teeth"

Once I asked Boris which restrictions he felt most keenly.

"Well, for one thing," he said, "I'd like to be able to travel abroad as freely as you do. I've never been outside the U.S.S.R., and I may never get out. Even if I should get a passport some day, I'd have to leave my family behind as a guarantee that I'd come back.

"And, of course," he added, "every Soviet citizen has to learn to keep his tongue behind his teeth. You never know who might report on you and get you into trouble. This makes it difficult to have close friendships, or to speak frankly with anybody."

I learned what he meant the hard way, for unintentionally I got someone into trouble myself. In one of the downtown restaurants there was a young waitress, a peasant girl fresh from the country. Since she gave good service, I usually sat at one of her tables, and we used to chat. When she learned I was from America, her eyes bulged with wonder.

"Are you . . . are you a . . . a capitalist?" she asked hesitantly, as though she were seeing the devil himself.

Another time she asked: "Tell me, why do you drink water? Don't you know that only peasants drink water?"

I found her naivete both charming and amusing, and in a conversation with my friend the head waiter, I repeated her questions. Later that day I chanced to pass her

Romance blooms in a shady nook of Pushkin Square. Lack of privacy, due to overcrowding, throws a major obstacle in the path of young love. Couples often must court in parks and cafes to escape prying eyes of parents and little brothers.

on the sidewalk in front of the restaurant. Tears were streaming down her face.

"What's the matter?" I asked.

"Why did you talk to the head waiter?" she said. "Now I've lost my job."

I was astounded. How incredible that they had fired this innocent girl just because she was friendly with an American and had asked some foolish questions! "I'm going to choke that head waiter," I said.

"Oh, don't say anything to him about it," she pleaded, "because I'll be in worse trouble for telling you."

"But what can I do?" I asked.

"Nothing," she said. "It's too late now."

"Can you get another job?"

"Yes, but it may take a while to find one. And besides, I have my mother to support."

The only thing I could do was to give her some money and wish her luck. I had never felt so helpless and frustrated.

The Soviet citizen I felt most sorry for, however, was Arash, an Armenian—or, as he would say, an American of Armenian descent—whom I met one day in the American Embassy. Born in Boston of immigrant parents, he had moved with his family and 300 other Armenian-Americans to the Soviet Socialist Republic of Armenia after World War II. The Soviet regime, playing on Armenian nationalist pride, had urged Armenians all over the world to "return" to a fatherland which most of them had never seen.

"The Soviet agent in Boston told us that if we didn't like it in the Soviet Union, we could simply pack our things and come back to the States," said Arash. "Well, that's what I've been wanting to do since the day I got here, and they haven't let me out yet."

"Why in the world did you come in the first place?" I asked.

"Well, we wanted to help worship in the Armenian church, and where we wouldn't feel like outsiders.

"The day we arrived," he continued, "we knew we had made a mistake, but then it was too late. Those who complained were packed off to Siberia, and that silenced the rest."

"Why did the Soviet regime play such a cruel trick on your people?" I asked.

"When we came," said Arash, "the Armenian Republic was nothing—just slums—and they wanted us to help build it up. We brought

EKTACHROME © NATIONAL GEOGRAPHIC SOCIETY

Tsarina for a day, a bride legalizes her vows in a Marriage Palace. Elegantly decorated, such chambers lend glamor to drab

bulldozers and tractors and all sorts of machinery—why, one guy even brought a complete shoe factory, which the Soviet Government took away from him. Compared with Soviet citizens, we were rich, and we brought everything with us."

"What are you doing here in the American Embassy?" I asked.

"I was hoping they could help me, but there's nothing they can do unless the Soviets give me permission to leave. You see, when we came, we gave up our American citizenship and became Soviet citizens."

"Do you still hope to go back to America some day?" I asked.

"I *am* going back," he shouted. "They've let a few of us Americans out, and I'm gonna make it some day, even if I have to send my application in a thousand times. I read the *Daily Worker* regularly—it's the only foreign newspaper in English that I can get—and I listen every night to the American Armed

"Citizens," flashes a giant neon warning, "before stepping from the sidewalk into the street, be sure that the crossing is absolutely safe." Lighted signs, rare in dim downtown Moscow, promote safety, sobriety, and Communism.

Crossroads of the U.S.S.R., Komsomol Square at dusk channels luminous veins of traffic between major railroad stations. Trains of the Trans-Siberian line rumble out of spired Kazan Station. Leningrad and Yaroslavl Stations at left send passengers northward.

Forces radio network. I'm an American, and I'm gonna be an American till the day I die!"

My encounter with Arash depressed me—and Moscow weather didn't help. April was a dreary month. There were no more snowfalls, but the gutters were still filled with dirty snow and ice, mixed with all the trash that had accumulated during the long winter. The wind was cold, the trees were bare, and the parks were brown and drab. It was as if Moscow had lost its beautiful white ermine robe and had been left with only some dirty rags.

Muscovites Emerge From Winter

Early in May I had a chance to go south on a trip to Transcaucasia and central Asia, and I was delighted to get away. But on my return at the end of the month, I found that Moscow had been miraculously transformed.

Driving into the city from the airport, we passed through fields that had suddenly become a brilliant green. Shrubs thrust forth their blossoms as if in celebration that the long freeze had ended. In the little park in front of the Bolshoi Theater pansies had been planted, and delicate pink blooms covered the apple trees. The whole city gave the impression of having been newly washed and painted.

The people of Moscow had emerged from their furry cocoons and joined in worshiping the newborn sun. They lay in the grass in the parks—some in bathing suits, some simply in their underwear—soaking up the warmth as though their bodies were starved for it. Every afternoon the courtyard in front of my dormitory was filled with students playing soccer, volleyball, and badminton. On Sundays some of us would walk down to the river to sunbathe, mingle with the crowd, and watch the excursion boats—some of them speedy hydrofoils—go whizzing by (page 346).

One beautiful afternoon some friends and I

Like women the world over, shoppers delight in trying on hats at the new Moscow Department Store in the southwest section. Quality and variety of clothing improve as Russians demand more consumer goods.

Macy's of Moscow, GUM offers everything from sausages to perfumes—when available. Recent economic reforms permit stores to order goods directly from factories, specifying styles and colors most desirable to buyers.

Skimming at 40 knots, a hydrofoil whisks sightseers along the winding Moscow River as the hull lifts free of the surface on underwater wings. Swift hydrofoils like *Meteor 3* have captured the imagination of Soviet planners, who send them sprinting by the scores over Russian waterways. Already they ease Moscow's chronic fresh-food shortage, bringing in vegetables and fruits from gardens far to the south.

Though locked in the heart of Eurasia, Moscow docks an increasing tonnage of water-borne commerce and wears the title Port of Five Seas. Canals linking the Moscow, Volga, and Don Rivers reach south to the Caspian, Azov, and Black Seas; others carry trade northward to the Baltic and icy White Sea. But the boats bow to trains when ice paralyzes shipping—at least four months a year.

Savoring every sunlit hour of the all-too-brief summer, bathers stroll the banks of the Moscow River. Once a narrow waterway that shrank in summer droughts, the river today winds broad and steady through the city, its level controlled by locks. Swimmers flock to this spot beside Metro Bridge, where autos roll above the glass-enclosed subway. Partial to bikinis, some Russian girls make their own suits and wear them impartially on beach or badminton court. This teen-ager plays in the Lenin Hills.

took the subway out to the northern section of Moscow to Ostankino, formerly one of the estates of the fabulously wealthy Sheremetev family, and now a public museum and park. Before entering the palace, we were required to put cloth slippers over our shoes, lest we scratch the elaborate inlaid floors.

Inside, posters and pictures explained to visitors the horrors of pre-Revolutionary Russia, when this one aristocratic family was able to own hundreds of thousands of serfs. The building was furnished as if its former owners had intended it to be a museum—paintings crowded the walls, and the rooms were filled with ornate furniture. A huge ballroom had doubled as a theater; Count Sheremetev had built it for his wife, a former serf, who was a famous actress.

Outside, classical statuary studded the gardens. It was Sunday, and the grounds were crowded with ordinary working people—families eating lunch, children chasing one another, women with their shoes off playing cards, and men drinking beer or lying in the grass with their chests bared to the sun. The whole scene seemed to symbolize the Revolution, the overthrow of the old aristocracy, the confiscation of their property, and the enthronement of the working masses.

Argument With an Ice-cream Seller

An old woman with a wrinkled face, twinkling eyes, and a scarf round her head was selling ice cream from a pushcart. We stopped to buy some. Seeing by my clothes that I was a foreigner, she asked where I came from.

"A-mer-i-ka!" she exclaimed in surprise. Then the smile on her face faded. "I don't like America," she said. "There the capitalists are the bosses. Here I'm my own boss."

"You mean the state is your boss," I replied. "In the old days you could work for yourself, but now you sell ice cream for the state, which takes away most of your profit."

"No," she insisted, "here we have no bosses any more. My mother and father were serfs, but now everybody is free."

We argued in a friendly fashion, but I

seemed unable to convince her. Then she changed the subject.

"I'm so sorry that your President Kennedy was killed," she said. "He was a good man; he was for peace. I hope your new President will fight for peace also."

Such expressions of sympathy I heard over and over, from simple working people like this woman, as well as from sophisticated intellectuals who praised the late President's firmness and restraint in the Cuban crisis.

In the summer my friends and I also got together for picnics. From the university we

Three hundred pounds of limp lion drape a trainer in the grand finale at the Moscow State Circus. Bengal tigers crouch motionless on stools at ring's edge as Walter Zapashny, once a professional strongman, daringly mixes high-strung cats of different species. European circuses, unlike America's three-ring spectacles, stage one act at a time to ensure that the audience misses nothing.

could catch a bus to the outskirts of the city, where the forests had not yet surrendered to the onward march of apartment houses and factories. One afternoon four of my closest Russian friends took me with them to a little pond hidden in the heart of a quiet grove of white birches. It was a farewell party, since I would soon be heading home and they would be leaving the university to begin work at their newly assigned jobs.

The youngest of the group was Grigoriy, a broad-faced Cossack from Rostov on Don, who was going home to marry Nina, his child-hood sweetheart. He had been assigned to teach history in a high school in Bratsk, far off in Siberia, where Russia has built the world's largest hydroelectric power station. We kid-ded him about being "exiled" to Siberia.

"Oh, it won't be so bad," he said. "At least I won't be separated from my wife. Nina has a job there as an electrical technician. The pay is high, and we can save some money. Besides, I can go hunting and fishing. Who knows, maybe we'll like it and stay there."

My friend Boris was less optimistic about his job in Tallinn, the capital of Estonia.   349

Soldiers of the playing field, athletes parade their colors past the Kremlin on May Day. White flag flutters above the standard bearer of the Dynamo Sports Society; a streamlined diesel rides the red banner of the Locomotive Sports Society.

At every school, farm, factory, office, and military unit, calisthenics and games promote physical fitness. The Soviet Union constantly strives to win world recognition in international competitions.

Pondering the pageantry of sport, a young Muscovite perches on top of her father's shoulder.

"I've heard that the Estonians hate the Russians," he said. "When a Russian goes into a restaurant in Tallinn, the waiters serve all the Estonians first. I don't think I'll stay there any longer than I have to."

Hot Dogs, Caviar, and Conversation

Luckiest of the three was Dmitri, a fun-loving graduate student in his 30's with many friends—a man who knew how to get ahead in the world. His red-headed wife Olga was from Moscow, and through family connections she had managed to get her husband a job there.

"I wish I had *blat* [pull] like you," said Boris. "I could get a nice soft job in Moscow."

"Why should we have to move?" retorted Olga. "I want to be here with my family and friends. And besides, Dmitri has already taught for four years in the provinces. Now it's his turn to live and work in the big city."

We built a fire and roasted hot dogs; they laughed when I translated the name into Russian. Olga had brought some dried fish, salami, smoked cheese, caviar, and fresh black bread. I opened a bottle of Khvanchkara, the best of Georgian red wines. A friend at the U. S. Embassy had given me some marshmallows—the first my Russian friends had ever seen—and we toasted them, American style.

Since we knew that this might be the last time we would see each other, we felt a bit sad, and the talk took a serious turn.

"Do you think that Russia and America will go to war?" asked Olga.

"I don't think so," I replied. "Both sides realize that you can't win an atomic war."

"But," said Grigoriy, "some fanatic might start a war. I read there are many fascists in

America. Or some Pentagon general might push a button and blow up the world."

"I don't think you have to worry," I said. "We have safeguards that make it impossible for one madman to trigger a war."

"Wouldn't Have Dared" Ten Years Ago

I changed the subject. "What about your future here in Russia—do you think things will be better, or will they stay the same?"

"Better," said Dmitri. "The repudiation of Stalin was a tremendous step forward. Now there's no turning back. The regime has got to give the people more freedom and a better life. And we'll never let another man become as powerful as Stalin was."

"We have a lot more freedom now," said Boris. "Ten years ago we wouldn't have dared to be so friendly with an American like you.

Ten years ago there weren't any American exchange scholars at the university. In Stalin's day this picnic would have been impossible."

"He's right," said Dmitri. "You probably don't realize how much it means for us to have an American friend—it's like having a window to the outside world, through which we can see things that have been hidden from us. Besides, it's hard to hate Americans or be afraid of them when you know one personally and find he's just a human being like us."

"It's the same with me," I said. "It's good to find that Russians are basically the same as the people back home. And it's nice to have friends who tell me what they really believe, instead of feeding me propaganda."

"Let's drink a toast to more American-Russian friendships!" said Boris.

I poured the last of the wine.   THE END

351

CAJUNLAND
Louisiana's French-speaking Coast

By BERN KEATING

Photographs by CHARLES HARBUTT, Magnum, and FRANKE KEATING

T HE SHRIMP BOATS were late, and by mid-morning we all nodded, drowsy from squinting into the wintry sun that glinted on the shimmering bayou at Lafitte. The roustabouts sprawled on the dock, softly chatting in the French dialect of coastal Louisiana.

I was waiting with my wife Franke—my photographer on this trip—for a launch to carry us to Barataria Bay. The shrimpers ignored us; our city clothes marked us as beneath their notice. They talked indiscreetly (certain social sets along this coast regard poaching as a year-round sport) in what they fondly believed was a private language. But with my French-Canadian rearing, I could eavesdrop shamelessly.

A big-eyed Cajun girl, a toddler of no more than three or four, tussled with a fisherman, punching him playfully on the biceps. When the playing became rough, the child picked up a stick to augment her puny strength. I couldn't keep quiet any longer.

"Lâches le bâton, méchante," I scolded.

I could not have stopped the conversation quicker

Like phantoms out of the past, Cajun dancers whirl beneath a moss-hung live oak at Longfellow-Evangeline Memorial State Park near St. Martinville. The old plantation grounds and home, now the Acadia House Museum, commemorate poet Henry Wadsworth Longfellow and his heroine Evangeline. Her people, exiled from Canada, settled in southern Louisiana and gave the region a distinctive name, Nouvelle Acadie—New Acadia. Rich marsh and woodland watered by twisting bayous offered peace and plenty then as now.

Sundown's blaze silhouettes a trawler chugging the quiet waters of Barataria Bay, a marsh-ringed lagoon south of New Orleans. Slipping through Barataria Pass, Cajun shrimpers sweep coastal waters of the Gulf of Mexico. They stay out for days at a time, dropping trial nets in likely spots. When they find shrimp, a large trawl goes overboard to scoop up the harvest. Then the trawlers dash for packing houses and a few days of leisure on Grand Isle (below). One of the Nation's top shrimp producers, Louisiana landed 60,000,000 pounds last year.

by firing a ten-gauge shotgun into the crowd. All heads snapped around. All eyes bore down on me with astonishment.

One of the fishermen said in English, "You speak French, mister?"

"Since I am a baby."

"But you not from Lafitte!"

"Oh, man, people speak French lots of places besides Lafitte."

"Yeah, I guess you right. Lafayette, Houma, Thibodaux, all them Loo-zeean places the folks speak French, so they tell me."

Thus reminded of the widespread use of

the Gallic idiom, the dockers resumed their drowsy hum, but now they amiably included me. I spoke French; ergo, I was a Cajun.

That is how the *habitants* have always treated me in Cajunland—or Acadiana, as sophisticated Cajun journalists have started calling it. During 15 years of travel in southern Louisiana, I have used French as my passport into the Cajun world. The estimated quarter of a million French-speaking dwellers of the Louisiana coastal marsh do not accept strangers easily. Louisiana Frenchmen show an un-Gallic reserve, possibly because their English-speaking neighbors have often misunderstood them.

For instance, before I began my latest tour of Acadiana, I chatted with an Anglo-Saxon state official who expressed alarm at my free use of the word "Cajun."

"Don't let them hear you call them Cajuns," he said. "It's a dirty word to them."

Like most of his Anglo-Saxon neighbors, the nervous official has managed to spend his life among the French-speakers of southern Louisiana without once noticing that Cajun is precisely what they call themselves.

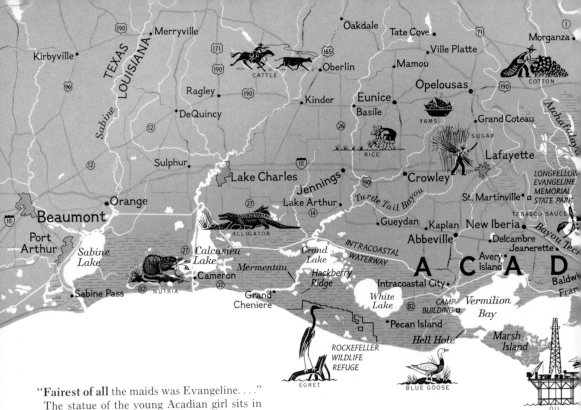

Map labels (top to bottom, left to right):

190 Merryville · Oakdale · Tate Cove · Ville Platte · Morganza · 71 · 1

Kirbyville · TEXAS LOUISIANA · 171 · 165 · Mamou · COTTON

190 · CATTLE · Oberlin · Opelousas · 190

Ragley · DeQuincy · 190 · Kinder · Eunice · Basile · YAMS · Grand Coteau · SUGAR · Atchafalaya

96 · 12 · 26 · Lafayette

Sulphur · 12 · 10 · Lake Charles · RICE · Crowley · St. Martinville · LONGFELLOW EVANGELINE MEMORIAL STATE PARK

Jennings · 90 · TABASCO SAUCE

Orange · Lake Arthur · 14 · Turtle Tail Bayou · Kaplan · New Iberia · Bayou Teche

Beaumont · 27 · ALLIGATOR · Gueydan · Abbeville · Avery Island · Delcambre · Jeanerette · A C A D

Port Arthur · Sabine Lake · Calcasieu Lake · Mermentau · Grand Lake · INTRACOASTAL WATERWAY · Intracoastal City · Baldwin · Fran

Cameron · 27 · Hackberry Ridge · CAMP BUILDING · Vermilion Bay

Sabine Pass · 82 · NUTRIA · Grand Cheniere · White Lake · 82 · Pecan Island · Hell Hole · Marsh Island

ROCKEFELLER WILDLIFE REFUGE · OIL

EGRET · BLUE GOOSE

"Fairest of all the maids was Evangeline. . . ."
The statue of the young Acadian girl sits in
St. Martinville atop the grave of Emmeline
Labiche, whose story may have inspired
Longfellow's poem. In 1755 the British de-
ported 6,000 French settlers from Acadia, today's Nova Scotia, after they refused to swear
unqualified allegiance to the Crown. Emmeline and her betrothed, Louis Arceneaux, became separated. Several years later she found
him in St. Martinville, wed to another—and
died heartbroken. The poem's tragic tale differs: Silver-haired Evangeline discovers her
Gabriel dying in a Philadelphia almshouse.

Gulf of Mexico

KODACHROME BY CHARLES HARBUTT, MAGNUM © N.G.S.

A shrewd Cajun farmer from near Baldwin, Johnny Derouen, laid this question of
terminology to rest for me.

"Tell me, Johnny," I asked, "does it insult
you Louisiana French to be called Cajuns?"

"Only when an outsider call us *damn* Cajun, whether he say damn out loud or not."

Storms Sweep Low-lying Coast

Acadiana is a strip along the Louisiana
Gulf Coast stretching roughly from the Texas
border to the mouths of the Mississippi (map,
above). It comprises a brackish marshland,
plus a narrow band of drained farmland and
low-lying ridge just in from the coastal marsh.

The lowland produces a wealth of game,
rice, sugar, fur, and oil, but the marsh inhabitants have suffered in recent years from
devastating hurricanes. This past September
Hurricane Betsy roared up the Mississippi.
With her deadly eye paralleling the river, but
30 miles to the west, Betsy laid waste the

eastern end of the marsh. The storm rapidly lost strength as it bulled upstream, but not before its 150-mile-an-hour winds had hurled a nine-foot wall of Gulf water across the delta and Grand Isle, 45 miles westward.

After the storm, I flew over the devastated area with Dick Yancey, Assistant Director of the Louisiana Wild Life and Fisheries Commission, who wanted to survey damage to marsh wildlife.

Banking his plane, Dick pointed to an ocean-going oil-rig tender perched on the Mississippi River levee where the tidal surge had lifted it (page 359). The streets of the towns that line the riverbank had become canals, and returning refugees poled pirogues between car tops peeping above floodwaters. Boxcars lay scattered like jackstraws in a yard where rescue crews found 15 bodies. In the occasional grove, the wind had blown the very bark from the weather side of what few trees still stood.

Grande Isle was marked by a column of smoke from burning debris. Betsy had mauled it as severely as she had the delta. I recognized most of the surviving structures, but the storm had pushed them a block, two blocks, half a mile from where they belonged. Miles away in the marsh, buildings, trailers, and automobiles wallowed in the backwash. But a few miles farther west damage dropped off sharply. By the time we reached Cameron, at the extreme western end of the Cajun country, we didn't see a misplaced shingle.

"Betsy hit Grand Isle hard," Dick said after we landed. "One man drowned there. Cameron Parish lost 544 people in Hurricane Audrey in 1957, and hardly a building stood on its own lot. Today you'd never know the area had suffered such a tragedy.

"Eventually the delta and Grand Isle will be as good as new. These are hardy folk, or they would never have lasted two hundred years on this coast."

Beached ships, broken homes, and miles of debris attest the fury of Hurricane Betsy. Raging across the Gulf last September, Betsy slammed into southeastern Louisiana with 150-mile-an-hour winds followed by a nine-foot wave. Grand Isle caught the full blast. A restaurant, swept from its foundations by wind and rushing waters, blocks the island's main highway (above). Mrs. Amy Rhine takes shelter in a ruined building (left). Wall of water moving up the Mississippi River lifted the oil tender and its tugboat onto shore (right). The Red Cross erected tents for the homeless; the Coast Guard provided dry clothes and coffee.

Dr. Thomas Arceneaux, of the University of Southwestern Louisiana in Lafayette, researches the saga of his Acadian ancestors as a scholarly hobby, so I consulted him about the origins of this Gallic enclave.

"According to historians," he said, "Cajun is a corruption of Acadian. The original Cajuns were peaceable French farmers whose ancestors had lived since 1604 in the French colony of Acadia, in what is now the Canadian Province of Nova Scotia. Nobody knows for sure what Acadia means. One guess is that it's a corruption of Arcadia. Another is that it comes from a Micmac Indian word. In either case, the connotation seems to have been 'place of plenty.'

"In 1713 Acadia fell to the British as a prize of war. At first the new rulers urged the French farmers to remain. But in 1755, as war with France raged anew, the British demanded that the Acadians take an unqualified oath of loyalty. When the farmers refused, their homes were burned, and they were scattered among English colonies of the Atlantic seaboard.

Derrick-spiked islands of steel probe for undersea oil and gas in the Gulf of Mexico. The tender, anchored at the rig, serves as floating hotel and supply depot; helicopters land supplies and new crews at a pocket-size heliport on the ship's stern. Gleaming hard hat protects a driller guiding a bit (left). Development of offshore oil fields has boosted the state's petroleum production; it ranks second in the United States after Texas.

Gradually many of the exiles trickled into the French-Catholic country around New Orleans."

The tragedies of separation and loss which followed the dispersal of the Acadians are known to virtually every schoolboy through Longfellow's "Evangeline." She was an Acadian maiden who lost her lover during *Le Grand Dérangement*—The Big Upheaval.

Around St. Martinville, every other enterprise bears the name Evangeline, the whole area is called the Evangeline Country, and a statue to Evangeline marks the graveyard (page 356). Surely, all this reverence for a fictitious heroine is a tribute to the poet's art.

Nostalgia Survives Time and Distance

The flesh-and-blood Cajuns arrived in Louisiana with a terrible nostalgia for their lost Acadian meadows. They shunned the city life of New Orleans and settled the empty lands west of the Mississippi. Their descendants have remained a rural people. They hunt, trap, raise sugar and rice, and tend 380,000 head of cattle—some of which seem almost aquatic.

"Acadians have remained true to their ancestors," Dr. Arceneaux said, "those devout people who suffered the intruder to burn their homes and drive them into penniless exile

rather than swear allegiance to Britain. So powerfully does Acadian nostalgia for the old ways work that even outsiders who have married Cajun girls have blended completely into the community. The once-Anglo-Saxon Bradberries and the Germanic Hoffpauirs and Shexnayders speak French as merrily as the Boudreaux and LeBlancs."

Toward the edges of Acadiana the Cajun culture blends into the Anglo-Saxon culture that surrounds it. In westernmost Cameron Parish, cattle ranches dot the squashy coastal strip. Hereford steers happily splash about in knee-deep water; prickly-pear cactus grows on the occasional low ridge; French-speaking cowboys fasten hidalgo spurs to rubber boots and swing whips behind their herds, giving a Wild West look to the landscape (pages 366-7). Nobody has to tell the visitor that Texas lies just across the Sabine River.

But Cameron is not Texas; it is French Louisiana, and the people's accents show it.

Recovered from the 1957 hurricane and virtually untouched by Betsy, the western marshes of Louisiana grow the biggest and glossiest muskrat and nutria on the fur-rich coast. Cameron's annual winter fur festival was under way when I arrived. The waterfront main street teemed with merrymakers.

On the flat bed of a truck parked in the

Harsh honk of a blue goose, blown in imitation of the wild bird, may win a prize for Kenneth Duhon in the goose-calling contest at the Fur and Wildlife Festival in Cameron, Louisiana. Judges rate him on the quality and variety of his calls.

Explosion of wings erupts from the waters of Hell Hole, an inlet of Vermilion Bay. During winter months, some 400,000 blue and snow geese from Canada find haven in 450,000 acres of coastline set aside for the preservation of wildlife.

Fur-clad fishermen, marsh raccoon (left) and otter roam the bayous in search of food. With muskrat, mink, and nutria, they keep Louisiana among the Nation's leaders in fur production.

KODACHROMES BY BERN KEATING (ABOVE) AND FRANKE KEATING © NATIONAL GEOGRAPHIC SOCIETY

center of town, Robert Mhire, a powerfully built trapper wielding an oversize jackknife with blade honed down to razor-weight, skinned a nutria in a race against time. Hurling a flayed cadaver aside, he attacked the next of his allotted two animals.

"What's in it for the winner?" I asked a rubber-booted spectator.

"Championship of Loo-zeean," he said, without taking his eyes off the blade. The tone of his voice indicated that in Acadiana a fur-skinning title outranks a Nobel Prize.

"I'm a pretty fast knife, me, and I was going to skin some nutria myself, but when I hear that Robert Mhire is coming in, I back out. No use to let him skin the nutria and me too in front of all these people."

Mhire skinned both animals in a total of two minutes and 21 seconds, then threw his hands overhead to the applause of the throng.

"That Mhire," said the booted man, "he can skin a running camel and peel a bucketful of gnats for lagniappe while I'm only reaching for my knife."

Later, I struck up a conversation with the new champion and discovered that, paradoxically, as a wildlife commission employee he is more concerned with caring for fur bearers than with skinning them. Then, at the oyster-shucking contest, or maybe it was the wild goose calling, or even at the gumbo tasting, Mhire introduced me to his fellow conservationist, Raymond Mayard.

"I got to go in the marsh tonight to put a tag on some little bitty alligator so we know how fast he grows," Raymond told me. "Want to come along?"

The sun had set by the time we started for

the Mayard home at nearby Grand Cheniere. As dark fell, the wild inhabitants of the marsh came to life and swarmed across the road.

"Them coons and rabbits, otters and minks and muskrats, and especially nutria, they crowding the marsh so thick they shouldering each other onto the road," Raymond said. "Sometimes the road-striping crew don't even have time to stop the machine to throw the dead ones out of the road. They just drag the white line smack across them."

Housewives the world over have a built-in hostility toward the unannounced dinner guest, so I approached the Mayard house with some nervousness. "Come in, *cher*," Mrs. Mayard called cheerily, and her good humor survived even the discovery that Raymond had brought home a surprise visitor.

A glance at the table showed why Mrs. Mayard was undisturbed. She had prepared a suitcase-size roasting pan four inches deep with *chevrettes étouffées,* jumbo shrimp smothered in a sauce that filled the room with perfume of herbs and spices lightly spiked with Tabasco and chili peppers. Hungry as Raymond and I were, we could make only an insignificant dent in the massive dish.

"Ghost Fire" Makes Bayous Glow

We needed all the calories we could absorb, too, for after supper we bundled into hunting clothes and sortied into the chilly night to go after the 'gators. I held an electric spotlight in the bow, and Raymond guided our boat down seemingly endless canals and bayous.

"Blow out your light," Raymond whispered as we entered a shallow lake. He cut the engine and we glided through water that leaped to life in the sudden darkness. Everywhere it glittered with the silent fire of phosphorescent plankton. Minnows dashing for cover trailed wiggling darts of light before the blazing track left by a marauding redfish. A flock of ducks, alarmed by the sudden stop of our motor, exploded from their feeding grounds and sprayed the night with a shower of falling stars. Raymond plunged his hand into the water and brought it up glowing with phosphorescence.

"You bring good luck," he said. "I never seen the ghost fire so bright before."

I snapped on my lamp. Its beam caught a pair of flashing eyes that looked as big as oranges. Transfixed by the light, a six-foot alligator let us ease up to him and, with a minimum of thrashing, allowed us to slip a noose over his head and pull him into the boat.

"Cold weather makes bad traveling in the

Nutria gives all to the fur industry: Its pelt goes into coats (above), and its meat feeds mink. A South American native, the nutria (below) rejuvenated Louisiana's fur trade 30 years ago when a dozen of the rodents escaped from private pens on Avery Island. Eating their way with beaverlike teeth across the swamplands, the prolific creatures usurped the domain of M'sieu Mus'rat, former king of the marsh. Louisiana trappers sent more than a million and a half nutria pelts to furriers last year.

Smiles announce good hunting for Robert Chiasson and Victor Tabor, but they rarely talk about the abundance of nutria—to do so might bring bad luck; it also might bring other hunters. To control the rodents, trappers may bag them in daylight hours without limit.

marsh," Raymond said, "but it also makes the alligator sleepy, and that's the best kind of alligator I like if I got to tag him."

We found two more alligators, both already tagged; so Raymond loaded them into the boat to be taken to the laboratory for a growth study. Their jaws and legs were tied, but I shied from the thrashing tails. "That business about a 'gator's tail breaking your leg," Raymond said, "don't you believe it. A 'gator's tail ain't no stronger than my arm."

Tame 'Gator Begs for Lunchtime Handout

I had already marveled at the slender Raymond's wiry strength in hauling the heavy boat and motor over portages; his figure of speech was not reassuring. I gave the alligators all the room available in a 14-foot boat.

"The 'gator is the most lied-about animal I know," Raymond said. "You can hold a big 'gator's mouth shut with your hands and he doesn't want to bite. I been living with 'gators all my life, and I ain't never heard of one biting folks. We don't taste good, I expect.

"And the story that 'gators take forever to grow and live forever in the same den. These tagged 'gators are big boys and girls six feet long and roaring for romance when they only 6 or maybe even 5 year old. And don't they ramble! Everybody see the 'gator sleeping in the zoo think they drag along, but when we catch one on dry land, he can run along on them stumpy legs faster than we can walk. We got to trot to lasso him. We find 'gators 8 or 12 or even 20 miles from where we put them out of the boat. But of course they was males; the ladies stay closer to home.

"They ugly fellows, but you be surprised how fast you can like them. One fellow hung around the boat dock at the refuge for years, begging for handouts at lunchtime. It got so some of us was packing an extra sandwich for that scaly bum. He got run over by a boat, and we like to held a funeral for him."

Cowboy spurs and rubber boots mark a wrangler in the soggy grassland and river-bottom of Cajun country. Muzzles high, cattle from the Carter Ranch swim the Mermentau River (below) to winter pasture on marsh-locked Hackberry Ridge. Cowhands crack whips (right), sending a reluctant calf scampering. On the ridge, cattle graze Louisiana-straw and sprig-tail grasses that shoot tall and green during winter on land that was burned off in September. The Carter herd of 1,000 reflects a slow build-up after the devastation of Hurricane Audrey in 1957, when 2,000 head were lost.

Next afternoon a wildlife commission plane carried me 50 miles east to Vermilion Bay, in the heart of the marsh, where 125,000 geese from Canada spend the winter. I wanted to photograph the flocks at dawn.

Dick Yancey piloted the plane and followed a more tortuous course than a small boy's errand to the grocery store, for he had to make a side trip to investigate every deer, every flock of pintail and teal, every alligator basking in the first feeble rays of the sun, to be sure the central coastal wildlife had escaped the worst of Betsy.

He set me down on a primitive landing strip behind a camp building.

"The rangers stationed here will put you up and take you back to civilization when you have your pictures," he said, and took off immediately.

Unexpectedly, the camp was deserted. I sat on the front steps and shrank from the brooding silence of the vast landscape. Slowly, however, the marsh came to life for me,

KODACHROME BY CHARLES HARBUTT, MAGNUM, © N.G.S.

as my ears grew attuned to a humming, buzzing, droning, splashing cacophony. The sun declined, and one special thin whine mounted steadily. A million salt marsh mosquitoes, ravenous after a day of fasting in their grassy bed, drove me behind the refuge of the camp's screen door.

A pirogue ghosted up to the dock, and a stocky fisherman climbed out carrying a long string of fish and a bucket of live crabs. He jumped and almost scattered the crabs into the bayou when I walked up and spoke to him from out of the twilight.

"Man, I thought the devil had finally come for me," he said. "Why you walk up so quiet? You should make a big noise when you come up on somebody out here, else you make him jump out of his shoe."

Gamble on Gumbo Pays Off

After apologies for my tenderfoot behavior, I exchanged introductions with Malon White, who has dwelt in the marsh, as he put it, "since before alligators was invented."

"Unless you like a bologna sandwich, you going to eat my cooking," Malon said. "If your insurance ain't paid up, I say take the bologna."

"What are you planning to cook?"

"A pot of gumbo with some nice young crab in him. Maybe a little fresh mullet to fill

out the corners. You skin the fish, I brown the roux, and we both say some prayers the supper don't kill us."

Malon's professionally able movements around the kitchen quieted my fears. The outdoorsmen of Acadiana for generations have had to feed themselves during lonely months at fishing and trapping camps, and they have had to learn how to substitute the pleasures of the table for the pleasures of society.

Scattering a handful of flour into a pan of hot oil, Malon stirred furiously at the mixture to keep it from burning.

"Any time you see some smoke coming from your roux, throw it away, or you be sorry," he said. "A burned roux look fine, and the bad cook he'll try to sneak it by you, but he just spoil his fish and his crab if he too lazy to make a new one."

When the roux was right, Malon turned it out into a soup kettle and pitched in onions, a bay leaf, three dashes of Tabasco, crab meat, fish fillets, a bit of water. He brought the gumbo to a simmer and sat down to talk.

"You came to the right place for goose pictures. We get up an hour before the sun tomorrow, and I take you to Hell Hole. There's a strip of sand there maybe 20 feet wide, the only sand around, and the goose comes at sunrise to fill his craw. He needs that sand for chewing, for he don't have no teeth.

Room without walls distinguishes the old Cajun home of Mr. and Mrs. Aldes Vidrine of Tate Cove. As important to the family as its kitchen, the *galerie,* or porch, provides an outdoor parlor that fills to overflowing when the family gets together—*grandmère, grand-père, maman, papa, les enfants,* and a seemingly endless supply of *cousins.* Outside staircase leading to the *garçonnière,* or bachelor's quarters, affords young men privacy and protects maman's rugs from their muddy feet.

Bounty from a *boucherie,* a cooperative butchery, fills the table at the Terry Vidrine home in Mamou. When the north wind blows, relatives and neighbors round up hogs for slaughter; in warm weather the meat would spoil quickly. The women cook all day—stuffing sausages, layering smoked pork in crocks, frying *gratons,* or cracklings, and preparing *boudin,* a delectable pork dish with rice and spices.

KODACHROMES BY CHARLES HARBUTT, MAGNUM © N.G.S.

Homemade sunbonnet frames the face of Mrs. Frank Pitre, who lives near Opelousas. She and her husband celebrated their fiftieth wedding anniversary last year; they have four children, 17 grandchildren, and seven great-grandchildren.

Pirogue-borne fisherman drops his net in the shadow of a cypress stump on Bayou Teche. Fish swarm around pilings of the oil-pumping rig. Cajuns paddle the narrow, flat-bottomed pirogues through root-laced swamps and along rivulets that ribbon the marshes. The craft, they say, "can ride on a heavy dew."

For jambalaya or gumbo—and for tables beyond Cajunland—rice grows in abundance near Crowley. Huge tires keep combines from miring. Louisianians, who use rice in Creole and Cajun dishes, each consume 30 pounds a year, five times the national average.

"Hide yourself in the wire grass there and you'll get some pictures, man, a thousand pictures. That goose'll walk all over you with his bare feet, to get a mouthful of that sand."

Malon soon set the table with a gumbo that would have been a credit to the great Escoffier. I am referring, of course, to Cyprien Escoffier of Turtle Tail Bayou, for a true gumbo is not a French invention but a combination of African or Indian recipes, Spanish seasonings, and Cajun culinary genius.

Before sunrise the next morning, Malon shook me awake and guided my uncertain steps to the boat landing. Vermilion Bay was covered with fog that cut visibility to zero, but Malon pushed forward as if he knew precisely where he was going.

The boat bumped against a bank, and Malon said, "Hell Hole . . . you get out here. Me, I've seen a goose before. I'm going around the bend to do a little fishing."

As the first watery rays from the sun lit the   371

banks of pearly fog, the birds found their way to the sand spit. They wheeled and floated down, necks outstretched, feet paddling, wings spread to brake their swift descent. Within minutes of the first arrivals, I was listening to the gabble of masses of geese, the closest just barely beyond arm's reach. Only a goose hunter can know what a triumph it was to be so close to thousands of blues and snows, which are among the world's wariest game birds.

When I had my fill of pictures, I leaped to my feet for a try at capturing on film an explosion of feathers and thrashing wings (pages 362-3). Malon heard the great flocks passing over and, guessing what had happened, coiled his lines and came to carry me to the dock at Intracoastal City, south of Abbeville.

Fugitives Thrive in New Home

From the time the first Canadian exile moved into the bogs west of New Orleans until this century, pelts of fur-bearing swamp animals provided a steady but small portion of the Cajuns' income. During the 20th century, however, the proliferation of two animals new to the marsh boosted trapping to a major industry.

The muskrat probably did not arrive till just before the turn of the century. He sneaked in while everybody was busy elsewhere, but these immigrants from northern stream banks found a cushy home in the coastal marsh. For long, Louisiana produced more muskrat pelts than all other states combined, but saltwater invasion of the marsh has seriously altered the habitat, and the take of pelts dropped from a record ten million in the 1922-23 season to less than a quarter of a million in 1964-65.

Nevertheless, Louisiana still traps a lot of muskrat. Betsy killed thousands of fur bearers in the delta, but Dick Yancey told me replacements will pour into the ecological vacuum from the surrounding overcrowded marshes. The total fur harvest may not suffer at all.

Just before World War II, the nutria from Argentina invaded the (Continued on page 377)

Bunched like a bouquet, crawfish await the chefs at Don's Seafood and Steak House in Lafayette. From their bayou-threaded crawfish "ranch," the owners annually harvest 200,000 pounds of this freshwater cousin of the lobster. Using recipes handed down from cook to cook, Don's creates an all-crawfish platter including bisque, pie, patties, and fried tails.

KODACHROME BY CHARLES HARBUTT, MAGNUM © N.G.S.

Fiery pepper pods fill boxes on Avery Island, an inland hump surrounded by cypress swamps and the waters of Bayou Petit Anse. Walter S. McIlhenny (center) weighs the crop, chief ingredient in the famous Tabasco sauce produced on the island by the McIlhenny Company, of which he is president. His uncle, Edward Avery McIlhenny, won distinction as a conservationist and helped save the snowy egret from extinction.

373

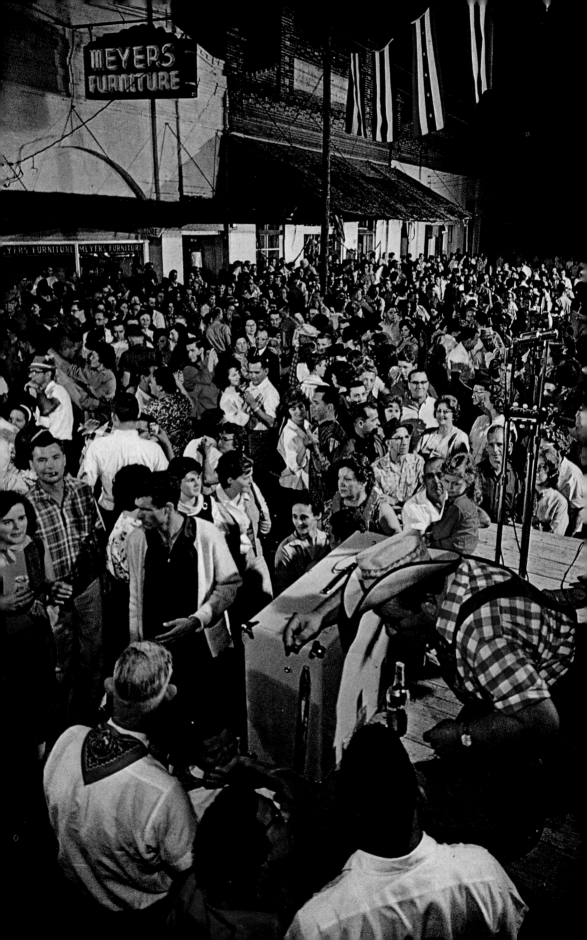

Dancers jam Main Street at the Sugar Cane Festival in New Iberia. Couples do the Cajun two-step to the cadence of Happy Fats and his country band. Bass viol and guitars augment accordion and fiddle, traditional Acadian instruments. As in the old Saturday-night community dance, called a fais-do-do, children join their parents for the evening.

Harvest in, farmers and townspeople burst out in a three-day celebration with dancing, parades, and exhibits. The crowning of a beauty queen highlights the occasion. Always ready for a get-together and a good time, Acadians also honor rice, yams, cotton, dairy products, furs, shrimp, and crawfish with festivals.

In the quiet weeks after harvest, men of Mamou (below) relax over *bourré,* a Cajun combination of bridge and poker.

Dollar for good luck adorns the bridal veil of newly married Mrs. Wayne Ridout of Basile. She and her groom welcome guests at their *Bal de Noce,* or wedding dance, in Eunice.

KODACHROME (OPPOSITE) AND EKTACHROMES BY CHARLES HARBUTT, MAGNUM © N.G.S.

Canopy of net hangs from the mast of a shrimp trawler at Delcambre; the name rhymes with "welcome," say residents.

Haunt of pirates more than a century ago, Grand Isle now harbors fisherfolk and oilmen. In the early 1800's dashing Jean Lafitte organized the privateers of Barataria Bay. From Grand Isle and Grand Terre, the distant smudge of land at right, they preyed on Spanish merchantmen in the Gulf. During the War of 1812, the British offered Lafitte money, land, and rank to join their side. Instead, he volunteered services to U. S. Gen. Andrew Jackson. For help in winning the Battle of New Orleans, Lafitte and men won praise and pardon.

Oysters go to bed in Barataria Bay. Transplanted from seed grounds where they have been growing for a year or more, the shellfish will now mature in a 1,000-acre underwater field leased from the state.

marsh. The heavy-bodied rodent multiplied so wildly that Cajun trappers have fabricated an elaborate and ribald mythology about the fecund creatures. Among other tall tales, the Cajuns say that the female nutria has her teats beside her backbone so that her young can suckle as she swims—which preposterous folk tale happens to be exactly true.

Trapping Helps Balance Nature

To get the straight story on the nutria, I called on Ted O'Neil in Abbeville. Ted is head of the wildlife commission's fur division and the top expert on Louisiana trapping.

I sat down with him in his kitchen to split a pot of tar-black Cajun coffee, and for two hours Ted talked about nutria without seeming to come to an end of his knowledge. During a storm about 30 years ago, he said, a dozen of the 18-pound beaverlike crea-

tures escaped private pens on Avery Island. "With no important disease and no enemies," Ted said, "the nutria have increased till you can hardly put your foot down in the marsh without stepping on a nutria footprint —or sometimes even on a nutria himself.

"Lucky for us, the nutria is the great American Shmoo, fearless and sublimely stupid, so that you don't even have to bait traps; just put them where he'll obligingly step into them.

"He grows a durable fur, one of the most easily dyed, and so prized that a nutria coat of finest pelts and craftsmanship sells for around $1,500. Besides, each carcass yields about eight pounds of red meat to feed ranch mink in the north. So, as a pelt or as mink food, the nutria ends up as a fur coat."

To let me see the nutria in its unbelievable numbers, Ted O'Neil passed me along to the Louisiana Land and Exploration Company in   377

EKTACHROME (OPPOSITE, UPPER) BY CHARLES HARBUTT, MAGNUM; KODACHROMES BY FRANKE KEATING © N.G.S.

Houma, owner of 650,000 acres of marshland. The marsh lay at the western edge of Betsy's devastation, but the game had survived.

Chester Voisin, a French-speaking guide, rounded up a party of native bogtrotters, and we set out in an immense and powerfully engined amphibious tractor with aluminum cleats on its gigantic tracks. We headed for a shell mound called Congo Island (named for the venomous cottonmouth moccasin, *congo* in Cajun French).

The marsh literally crawled with nutria. It was a cold day and the tractor had to stop every 50 to 100 feet to keep from running over colonies of nutria huddled together for warmth. Sometimes even a cottontail rabbit burst out of this fur ball when we stirred the nutria up with a stick.

The dullest eye (mine) could count 20 nutria waddling away from our racket at any given second during the two-mile trip. Mink and coon, muskrat, otter, and rabbit kept the landscape jumping. It seemed impossible that the marsh could support such a teeming population (pages 362-5).

"Sometimes it can't," Chester told me. "If we don't trap them nutria hard enough to keep them thinned out, they'll eat up all the grass in the marsh, turn it to naked mud, and then they'll sure enough die, every last one of them."

We had a picnic lunch on Congo Island, actually a ridge in the marsh built by generations of Indians who scooped the meat from millions of clams and tossed the shells over their shoulders. The shell pile finally rose high enough to support live oaks and Spanish moss.

Cajun Trappers Careful Not to Brag

From the bayou north of the island, we heard the snapping of .22 rifle fire. Two trappers poled a pirogue into view. The pirogue's waist was piled high with nutria.

Chester called, "How is the luck? Plenty of nutria, *hein?*"

"No, man, scarcer than snake shoes," one of the trappers complained. "You can't make a dollar no more off this nutria. Pretty soon us trappers got to skin cockroaches if nutria get more scarce."

Gloomy-faced, the trapper pair poled on down the bayou, their pirogue overloaded so grossly that occasional trickles of water ran over the gunwale. I wondered aloud what the trappers would possibly consider an abundance. Chester explained that they were only catering to a fear that bragging would stir the wrath of the gods and bring bad luck.

EKTACHROME (ABOVE) BY CHARLES HARBUTT, MAGNUM
KODACHROME BY FRANKE KEATING © N.G.S.

The Cross leads as altar boys and parishioners circle the square of St. Martin Catholic Church in St. Martinville at the beginning of the Corpus Christi Procession.

Cascading moss graces the driveway of the Sacred Heart Church in Grand Coteau, where Marius Thibodeaux parks his buggy each morning on the way to Mass. Braids of an Indian princess gave Louisiana its Spanish moss, a legend relates. When she died, a grieving brave hung her raven locks on a limb above the grave. Turning gray with time, the strands blew from tree to tree, and finally all the land wept for the maiden.

East of these swamplands, State Route 1 runs beside Bayou Lafourche for 100 miles. The road is lined by a continuous strip city which is in most places only one house deep. Beyond lies the marsh, aswarm with game but void of human life, except for the weeks following Betsy, when power and telephone company linemen cut away the tangle of storm-toppled poles and wires.

On my way to Grand Isle only days after Betsy struck, I could trace the increasing fury of the storm by the angle of the power poles leaning over the highway. For the last 20 miles of the drive south, if a single pole stood upright, I missed it.

Sea Hawk Rides Out Betsy's Fury

At the Grand Isle town limits, civil authorities and rifle-bearing National Guardsmen stopped all cars to turn back idle sightseers or potential looters. The guards searched every car leaving Grand Isle to be sure it carried no goods stolen from the wreckage.

Bulldozers chuffed through the desolate lanes, stacking the splintered debris of houses. Where Grand Isle's liveliest juke joint had once stood, the bulldozers piled a mound of concrete blocks and broken boards, the remains of a dozen vanished dwellings.

With some nervousness, I looked for the house of my old friend Capt. Charles Sebastian, "for 20 years the South's most famous fisherman," as his charter-boat shingle proclaims. Fortunately, his house, built on eight-foot pilings, was intact, except for a door split open and half a ton of sand spread on furniture and floor.

"The *Sea Hawk* rode out the storm without a scratch in the bayou at Lafitte, 30 miles inland," Charles reported. "When I brought

Feathers fly as Mardi Gras celebrants raid a chicken yard—with the owner's permission. Preserving a custom of the 1780's, men of Mamou rise before dawn on Shrove Tuesday. Hiding behind masks (left) and bizarre costumes, they ride on horseback across the countryside, calling at each farm to collect food for a feast. After a steaming cup of *café noir* (right), the thick black coffee Cajuns drink a dozen times a day, they gallop to the next stop. From the collection of ducks, chickens, sausage, onions, and spices, wives concoct huge pots of gumbo. Following the meal, tired riders still find the energy to dance to fais-dodo music until midnight, when Lent begins.

KODACHROME (BELOW) AND EKTACHROMES BY CHARLES HARBUTT, MAGNUM © N.G.S.

381

House that sugar built, Shadows-on-the-Teche in New Iberia opens its gardens to belles in tulle and taffeta as in years past, when visiting Creoles from nearby plantations danced the magnolia-scented nights away. David Weeks built the mansion in 1830 as a town house for his vast domain of sugar land. The home drifted to ruin after the Civil War. Then in 1922, descendant Weeks Hall began restoring it to its original grandeur, a task completed by the National Trust for Historic Preservation. Today the Shadows provides a romantic isle of yesteryear for beauties such as Gail Romero (right).

her to Grand Isle the next day, my boat's radio was one of the few links with the outside world till the Coast Guard's regular transmitter went back in commission."

We walked to the boat, moored at Fisherman's Wharf, where in happier times I had whiled away evenings listening to pungent conversation in the local French patois, larded with words from Spanish, Portuguese, Italian, and Choctaw. Lafitte's corsairs, drawn from many maritime nations, left behind this exotic mishmash of a language when they sailed from these islands for New Orleans to help Andrew Jackson rout the British in 1815.

The groceries, chandleries, bars, and seafood packing plants that once had lined the wharf lay in ruins, but already the air rang with banging hammers, and power saws snarled through tangled heaps of wreckage.

Fish Swarm Near Oil-rig Pilings

We boarded *Sea Hawk* to inspect the fishing sites. Charles steered for the mile-long platform of the Freeport Sulphur Company's underwater mining rig, standing on immense steel stilts seven miles out in the Gulf of Mexico (following pages).

"The storm damaged many offshore oil platforms and the sulphur rig, but Betsy won't stop production for long," Charles said. "Good thing too; the wells in the marsh and offshore pump 500 million barrels of crude a year. More than 42,000 Louisianians make a living out of the industry nowadays, and a pretty good living, too [pages 360-61].

"What concerns me, though, is the fishing grounds. These offshore rigs along the Louisiana and Texas coasts have made some of the fattest fishing waters in the world out of what used to be ordinary pickings.

"When you build a new rig, first the barnacles and the water plants fix themselves on the pilings. Then the little swimming stuff that feeds on the barnacles and plants comes along, and right behind them come the big swimming things that eat the little swimming things. Pretty soon you have a whole swarming underwater world hugging the shade and shelter of the rig.

"I wouldn't care if they never found oil or sulphur with these rigs, so long as they put down plenty of piling. Now let's find out if Betsy messed up my underwater world."

We tied up to one of the towering, stiltlike piers of the sulphur rig and threw lines over the side. Within minutes we were pulling in firm-fleshed red snappers—each as big across as a serving platter—sand trout, sheepshead, channel bass, and spadefish. From the bottom we pulled up croaker, grouper, and grunt. The waters clearly still teemed with fish.

Grinning for joy, Charles broke out the spinning gear and went after the surface feeders, which that day were bluefish and Spanish mackerel. Farther offshore he caught six amberjack weighing 40 to 60 pounds each.

"This boom in the fish population often happens after a storm," Charles said. "Sometimes the fishing is enormously better for a few days after a big wind riles up the water. The turbulence must bring up nutrients from the deep or something. And, of course, the rigs provide perfect shelter."

Back ashore, Tony Cheramie, shrimper and dock worker, helped us tie up. He took in the report about fishing conditions without surprise. During the thirty or so years he has lived on this seven miles of sandy ridge, he has survived many storms.

"The shrimping is always much more better after a blow," he said. "And with the marsh to hide in, even the little water things do all right."

Tony told of cruising the marsh to see what Betsy had done to the fish world. As a proper Baratarian with a big stake in the fisheries, he had searched the marsh waters and could report happily that the little sea creatures still hid there in unimaginable billions.

"Them little water babies sneak around in the thick grass, hide from the wind and the big fellow. All day they drink the soup of the marsh and grow big. Some of them little fellow, they only good for fish food, but some of them is shrimp and oyster. When they grow big enough, we catch them for the pot. Man, that marsh is just one big seafood gumbo."

Monday morning at the wildlife commission's marine laboratory on Grand Terre just

Offshore sulphur mine yields a golden hoard

across Barataria Pass, I got a sadder report. Dr. Lyle St. Amant, the state's seafood conservation expert, said the storm had smothered hundreds of oyster reefs with silt.

"The tides will eventually flush out the silt," he said, "but much of this year's crop of Barataria Bay oysters has been killed."

"Will the beds reseed themselves?"

"Reseed themselves? Yes, but only on natural-producing reefs, controlled and operated by the state. On privately leased beds, an oysterman works like a sugarmill mule to make his crop. He must plant seed oysters annually and move them about as they grow, to take advantage of changes in salinity. We harvest a million barrels of oysters in a normal year only because we farm them like sweet potatoes."

He focused a telescope on an oyster lugger steaming in circles on Barataria Bay, then passed the glass to me. Through the lens I could see muscular young oystermen, half-naked and sweaty, shoveling tons of seed oysters over the side (page 376).

"Those oystermen are reseeding their silted reefs," he said. "They are planting seed oysters

KODACHROMES BY FRANKE KEATING (BELOW) AND CHARLES HARBUTT, MAGNUM © N.G.S.

Blades whirring, a helicopter chugs aloft from Freeport Sulphur's mile-long Y-shaped mining platform off the Louisiana coast. Here superheated water, forced 2,000 feet beneath the Gulf to a subterranean deposit, melts the sulphur. Conveyed by pipeline to shore, 80 percent of the mineral goes into storage for sale in liquid form; the remainder solidifies in vats at Port Sulphur (opposite).

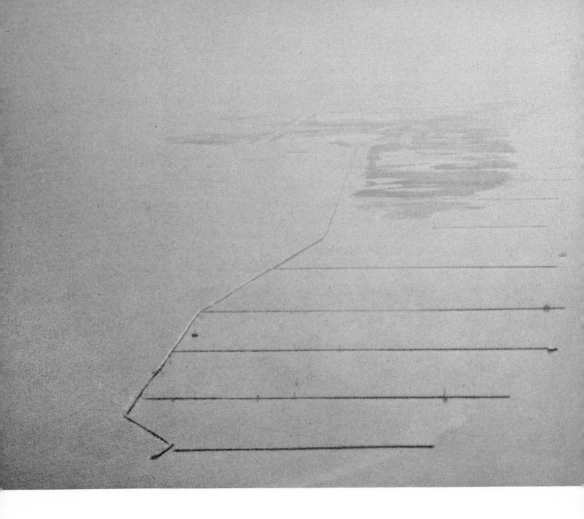

that have set on old shell which they get from seed beds on the other side of the Mississippi.

"The normal method in Louisiana involves the removal of seed oysters from natural reefs owned and managed by the state. The seed oysters are planted on privately leased bottoms, where they grow to market size and fatten. Though predators occur in these areas, the annual plantings, rapid growth, and a rotational system of planting result in good production—frequently as much as three to one over the natural-reef output.

"And oystering pays pretty well. The shrimp and oyster harvest brings us about 60 million dollars in a normal year. Of course, the oyster crop probably will be 20 to 50 percent less this year, but they grow fast. Production should return to normal by next season.

"At least 15,000 people work in the shrimp and oyster fisheries," Dr. St. Amant continued. "They're a rugged bunch, and the fisheries have survived worse than the storm.

"A few years ago shrimp production declined from an unknown cause, but it has come back to almost what it used to be. We expect 60 million pounds a year from now on."[*]

Next day, I went out with Junior Duet on his oyster lugger, and for a test of my aging arteries I took over a shovel myself. The young oystermen eyed me dubiously as I attacked the seed-oyster heap with an old-fashioned coal stoker's scoop big enough to hold half a bushel at a bite. Within ten minutes I collapsed over a capstan with eyes bulging and sides heaving like a sunfish out of water.

The oystermen swung their shovels steadily on, till five tons of seed were over the side. From that moment, I have eaten my fat Gulf oysters with more respect for the men who keep them coming.

Lafitte's Ghost Lingers in the Marsh

After my essay at oyster farming, Théard Rigaud, a local skipper, invited me to go on a more relaxed kind of oyster harvest—a search of the Grand Terre marsh for "wild" oysters that had seeded and fattened themselves as

*Dr. Clarence P. Idyll wrote of the industry in two GEOGRAPHIC articles: "Shrimp Nursery," in May, 1965, and "Shrimpers Strike Gold in the Gulf," May, 1957.

Southwest Pass, one of two chief mouths of the Mississippi River, provides a gateway for vessels heading up the delta to New Orleans. By confining the channel with a system of jetties and dikes, engineers accelerate the river current. The increased flow helps keep the passage clear and minimizes dredging. Spur dikes collect sediment that would otherwise drop in the ship channel.

Treacherous fogs add to the dangers faced by a Mississippi River bar pilot. At Pilottown, near Head of Passes, W. R. Aitkens awaits a ship guided by a river pilot from New Orleans. Here the bar pilot takes over to direct the vessel through the lower channel to the Gulf.

Haven for study and relaxation, the Memorial Student Union of the University of Southwestern Louisiana at Lafayette overlooks a cypress lake where native iris bloom in the spring. Another kind of Cajun beauty, a coed (above), wears silver crawfish earrings and brooch. A fellow student (top) leads a bonfire rally for her football team, the Bulldogs, nicknamed the "Ragin' Cajuns."

Established in 1898 as the Southwestern Louisiana Industrial Institute, the school achieved university status in 1960. Its six colleges and graduate school enrolled 8,500 students this year. The College of Agriculture maintains some 600 acres of farmland for experiments in horticulture and animal and poultry science.

best they could in the old-fashioned, easygoing way.

Grand Terre is bare of buildings except for the marine laboratory and the ruins of Fort Livingston, built before the Civil War and smashed in the hurricanes that have harried this coast. But the name Grand Terre stirred memories of great doings.

"What's the history of this place?"

"Why, this was Lafitte's town," Théard told me. "Hundreds of pirates once lived here, when they weren't at sea robbing the Spanish. Come, I'll show you the brick pillars of old Fort Lafitte."

COME, MON CHERIE, TO ZEE U.S.L. HOMECOMING TO SEE ZEE BULLDOG SKONK ZEE SPARTANS ZEE BAND CLUB'S PEPÉ LE PEW

We picked up the bushel of wild oysters we had gathered in the shallow bayou and loaded them into the pirogue. But before leaving we searched the spot where stumps of massive pillars had stood the last time Rigaud passed that way, ten years before. We found only brickbats, scattered probably by Hurricane Audrey in 1957 and again by Betsy in 1965.

Louisiana Grows 100 Feet a Year

About 15,000 square miles of land, almost a third of Louisiana's area, was built by the Mississippi River. With a million tons of sand and silt coming down the river every day, the delta—or at least that part of it around the mouths of the Mississippi—grows southward at the rate of 100 feet a year, a mile every half-century or so.

The road below New Orleans runs along the top of a natural levee formed by periodic river overflow. The land falls away on either side. Citizens of the delta grow their oranges, tend their oil wells, skin their nutria in a strip of land 75 miles long and just wide enough in places for a baseball diamond.

On the delta's eastern side, a new 2,000-acre lake of brackish water glitters where Betsy's winds and tides rolled up the life-supporting

layer of marsh plants and threw this cyclopean mud pie against the coast 17 miles northward. More than 200 deer that once flourished here have disappeared forever, or at least for the decades it will take for river silt to rebuild the marshy habitat.

The dwellers of the delta are not exactly the breed you find elsewhere on the coast. A glance at the faces and names along the delta road shows that the Cajun character of the marshland culture is diluted below New Orleans by Spanish and Slavic blood.

The river road ends just beyond Venice, a fishing and trapping village 20-odd miles up from the river mouths. I wanted to go all the way to the Gulf; so, despite a heavy fog that made travel dangerous, parish authorities detailed a boat to take me to Pilottown, a station near the end of the line.

Conversation there rarely drifted far from the recent storm. The station escaped with only minor damage, but on down the river, where six bar pilots rode out the storm, the tidal surge heavily damaged pilot shelters. Nevertheless, bar and river pilots moved ships up and down the river 24 hours after the hurricane passed.

After two days of cribbage forced on me by the persistent fog, I persuaded my boat captain to sneak us through the fog back to the road head so I could drive to the unofficial capital of Acadiana, at Lafayette, more than 200 miles to the northwest.

Lafayette Flaunts Gallic Flavor

"*Bienvenu à Lafayette*" says a highway marker at the edge of town. On the main street the eavesdropping passerby hears as much French as English. The gas-station attendant sings out your bill in piastres. He is not so quaint, however, as to turn down a proffered American dollar, for that is exactly what a piastre is in Lafayette.

The television broadcast day opens at sunrise with "*Passe Partout*," a live news and farm show in French. Commercials proclaim that a certain store offers its goods at "*les prix* wholesale *à tous.*" Wholesale prices to everybody, more or less.

For luncheon, I went to Don's Seafood and Steak House, where I met the host, Ashby Landry. He calls himself "*le roi d'écrevisse du monde*"—the crawfish king of the world—and maybe he is at that.

Ashby briefed me on the care, feeding, and cooking of the crawfish, a decapod crustacean that is not only the No. 1 delicacy of the Cajun cuisine but also the totem of the Cajun clan, just as the bulldog is the British totem, the eagle is American, the rooster French.

Plate after plate of crawfish dishes whisked by me for a sampling. Bisques followed gumbos, *étouffées* followed patties, jambalayas followed pies (page 372).

"Don't eat too much of the *écrevisses étouffées*," Ashby warned. "You not good started yet, so save plenty of room in you insides."

Ashby's dining room resounded with a happy babble of French and English, as Cajuns and Texas-Oklahoma oil immigrants pitched into aromatic Louisiana dishes. Those oil men, I am told, come grudgingly to the Cajun country, but kick like bee-stung mules when the companies try to transfer them away.

Cajuns Persist in a Changing World

How long can this exotic pocket of Gallic individuality last, I wondered.

On my way home, I snapped on the car radio and tuned in a program of Cajun waltzes and two-steps. The music faded fast as I went north, as did the French names on the roadside mailboxes. Almost inaudible now, the radio swung into a bilingual song by Cajun singer Rod Bernard and his friend Jack Clement. It was about a modern Cajun girl at the fais-dodo, a Cajun-style Saturday night hoedown. The English version went:

She don't like to ride in my pirogue,
Don't even know how to cook gumbo.
She upsets her Cajun papa
When she does the twist at the fais-dodo.

So even the Cajuns are nervous about remaining themselves. But I think they will survive. Their resilient recovery after the storm showed of what tough stuff they are made. Surely, the American gumbo still needs the Cajun world—the Tabasco pepper that gives a piquant flavor to the whole.   THE END

Softly the evening came. The sun
  from the western horizon
Like a magician extended his golden
  wand o'er the landscape....

Longfellow's lines capture the beauty of waning day in Acadiana. Although industrialization spreads across the land, the Cajun people—fun-loving, steadfast, devout—keep the spirit of "Evangeline."

THE STARTING PISTOL CRACKS, the checkered flag whips down. My ground crew and I sprint the hundred yards to my balloon, a 79-foot-long, plastic-coated nylon bag spread out on the hot sand like a discarded awning.

I throw a lighted match into the propane-fueled ground inflation unit, and the hot-air blower roars into action with a whoosh of flame. You can always tell a racing balloon pilot by his singed eyebrows.

Two of my six-man crew hold open the skirt around the mouth of the bag. A bubble of hot air creeps inside to the crown, like a cat under a blanket.

The big bag slowly swells to life, straining to right itself. Now I light the two in-flight gas burners on the gondola's aluminum frame and pour in more hot air. "Let go of the crown," I shout. The balloon

Hot-Air Balloons Race on Silent Winds

NYLON BAGS UNFOLD *like giant blossoms as a balloon race gets under way near Reno, Nevada.*

By WILLIAM R. BERRY

Photographs by
DON W. JONES

EKTACHROME (BELOW) AND KODACHF

swings upright with a powerful pull, filling to its 60,000-cubic-foot capacity—a thing of beauty.

We fight to keep the gondola on the ground. I scramble aboard, and my weight—180 pounds plus parachute—momentarily halts the upthrusting globe. Then my crew heaves upward on the bottom of the wicker basket. It is just eight minutes after the gun, I note with satisfaction. I am airborne.

Ten other balloons blossom around me—contestants in a special cross-country event of the four-day National Championship Air Races at Reno, Nevada, in September, 1965. Ours is a time-distance race; whoever flies farthest and lands within one hour will win.

Balloons Gain New Favor in an Era of Rockets

Our vehicles, lofting us skyward, are something special themselves. In an age of rocketry, they hark back to one of the oldest principles of flight: Heated air, imprisoned in a bag, struggles to rise through the colder, denser air around it—and can carry a man with it.

The "rediscovery" of hot-air ballooning in 1960—when Ed Yost of Sioux Falls, South Dakota, flew a 40-foot fabric envelope for an hour and 35 minutes—opened a new era in a fascinating sport. Balloonists no longer need depend on expensive gas and cumbersome ballast. Adjustable propane burners heat nature's own air within the bag; now we can rise or descend at the turn of a valve.

My burners roar their frenzied song. The altimeter needle winds swiftly around its dial. I recheck the ground handling lines dangling below and shudder, recalling a harrowing ascent two years ago: I had fancied I heard a muffled shout over the roar of the burners as I climbed swiftly past 300 feet. I shrugged it off, intent on watching the rate-of-climb indicator.

Later, as I cut back the burners at 3,000 feet, I heard someone call again—this time unmistakably.

"Please, mister, won't you get me down?" a child's voice whimpered desperately.

I looked overboard. The memory of what I saw still gives me nightmares. Somehow a boy had gotten a line wrapped tightly around his hand, and I had unwittingly lifted him with me!

I couldn't reach him, for the ground lines dangle straight down from the sides of the balloon, far from the gondola. As quickly as I could, I brought the balloon down, talking to the boy quietly, telling him to look at me, not at the ground.

(Continued on page 402)

Off at a dead run in a Le Mans Start—named after the famous French auto race—author Berry, in red flying suit, and his crew dash to the lifeless balloon. Moments later, hot-air blower roaring, the bag billows. While one crewman holds the skirt open, a second braves the 120° F. air inside to free fouled lines. Others, visible through the crown, restrain the balloon.

Flames spurt from dual propane burners in a preflight test designed to guard against flameout. If burners should fail in high-altitude flight, the balloon would descend out of control and eventually crash.

395

STRAINING SKYWARD *as burners
pour hot air into the envelopes,
balloons fight their crews'
efforts to hold them in place until
they swell to full size. Then,
with a final push upward, the
bags will soar. Capacities range
from 27,000 to 87,000 cubic
feet. Commercial firms sponsor
most racers; Mr. Berry's entry
bears the banner of Holiday
Magic, Inc., a cosmetics firm.*

Gemlike sun peers from behind the author's glowing balloon (above) as it climbs skyward. Exhaust ports at top of skirt allow cooling air to leave the bag. To descend, the balloonist vents hot air through the "hoohoo," a valve that shows as a vertical slit on the gold gore left of the registration number.

Eyeing his instruments as well as his competitors, Berry soars at 5,000 feet above Nevada. Red strap attaches to a rip panel that deflates the balloon for landing. Fire-breaks stripe the sage below. Using a camera suspended from the balloon by photographer Don W. Jones, the author snapped this unusual picture by remote control.

FOLLOWING PAGES ▶

Dangling on a spiderweb of steel, the wicker basket rides heavenward below the rising balloon. Berry's gondola provides only enough room for the pilot and an infrequent passenger, plus two eight-gallon propane tanks—sufficient for two hours' flying. The ground swims dizzily below the balloon's mouth and ports. Burn hole at upper right— no hazard to flight—occurred during a previous inflation.

Camera hanging inside the bag, installed by Jones, captured this action photograph.

399

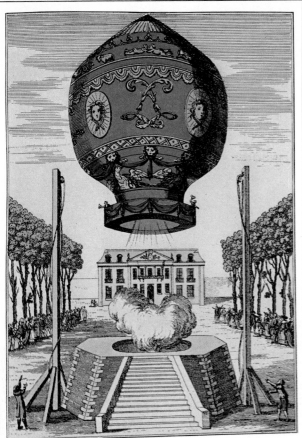

COURTESY C. H. GIBBS-SMITH
AND ARIEL PRESS, LONDON

Old idea wins new fans

PARIS CROWDS CHEERED on October 15, 1783, when the "aerostat" devised by the Montgolfier brothers lifted Pilâtre de Rozier more than 80 feet into the air. The long-sought secret of flight: A huge, fragile, linen-and-paper balloon filled with smoke and hot air from blazing straw and wool. But De Rozier was not the first balloonist. A month earlier, as Louis XVI and the glamorous Marie Antoinette watched, a duck, a rooster, and a sheep rode aloft for eight minutes, landing safely.

In November, De Rozier and the Marquis d'Arlandes became the first men to travel by free-flying balloon when they made a 25-minute flight across Paris. The aeronauts, above, proudly bow to the acclaiming throng.

Light gases soon supplanted hot air. Today, however, nylon bags and propane burners carry airmen in a new application of the Montgolfier principle. Of 64 balloons certified by the Federal Aviation Agency, more than half are hot-air bags. The sport centers principally in the western United States. The National Aeronautic Association sanctions meets such as the one last September near Reno, Nevada (described in the accompanying article), and another in November at Palm Springs, California.

Author Berry, a business executive in Oakland, California, nurtures a long-range ambition: to soar beneath a hot-air bag across the United States—and eventually the Atlantic Ocean.

(Continued from page 395)
Finally, two miles from our take-off point, 11-year-old Danny Nowell of Mill Valley, California, hit the earth —a little hard, and terribly frightened, but miraculously unscathed. Ever since, I have checked my ground lines with extra care.

I now look for the other ten racers to see where the winds take them. Some soar above me; others still struggle to leave the ground.

Elevation at Reno Sky Ranch, our take-off point, nine miles northeast of Reno, is about 4,500 feet. My altimeter shows 8,500 feet, and I am

Biggest hot-air balloon, an 87,000-cubic-foot Semco competes in a spot-landing event in the Nevada air races. Four piles of burning tires like the one

climbing at just under 1,000 feet per minute
—fast enough. If I rise too rapidly, the terrific
resistance of air flattening the crown of my
balloon could cause it to split.

I head for 17,000 feet. Up there, in the cold,
brilliant sky, I hope to find the strongest
winds. In this race, direction does not matter.

Below I see several antlike jeeps, following
balloons as far as possible to measure their
flight. The judges will plot distances on a
map to determine the winner. I also look for
the red truck that will try to follow my drift.
I spot it far away, kicking up a cloud of dust
along a penciled road.

Again I check my altimeter, now showing
15,000 feet, and I shut down the burners,
leaving only the pilot lights on. The balloon
will coast to altitude on its own momentum.

The ground below me spreads out in an
endless pattern of firebreaks crisscrossing the
desert sage (pages 398-9). To the north glistens
Pyramid Lake—a cold, wet bath for anyone
who lands there. Luckily, a 15- to 20-knot
wind blows me away from the water, toward
the Virginia Mountains, a rugged range just
to the east.

With burners off at this high altitude, the
sudden silence startles me, as it always does.
Only up here have I heard such absolute quiet.

People sometimes ask me why I like ballooning. I find it hard to answer. I love the air
—everything about it. For years I have flown

at left, marking the points of the compass, raise smoke beacons about two miles from the
center take-off point. Pilots have an hour to land as close as possible to one of the mark-
ers. During the four-day meet, balloonists also played hare and hounds—a balloon chase
—and vied in an altitude-control match, following preset up-and-down patterns.

Touching down, pilot Mal J. Fink releases his gondola and, with less weight, the balloon rises again. But two lines attached to the gondola pull taut and rip open side panels on the bag. A retaining line at the crown tips the balloon, and hot air spills out with a rush. The landing method differs from the author's, whose Raven balloon has a rip panel in the crown.

light planes and gliders, and I'm a sports parachutist. Since I discovered ballooning three years ago, I go up in balloons whenever I can.*

For all my love of the air, however, I think it's the quiet that appeals to me most in ballooning—the quiet, and the sense of freedom, and the challenge. I am alone, and I must match myself against the deceptively peaceful sky and the waiting ground.

Return to Earth Requires Skill

I have now reached "17 grand"—17,000 feet—in my frail basket, dangling on steel cables from the nylon bag. I can still see three balloons; the rest have sailed out of sight, soaring on other winds, at other altitudes.

Every few minutes I turn up my burners. The air inside the envelope must be kept 100 or more degrees hotter than the air outside, or the balloon will begin a rapid descent. I watch my pyrometer carefully; if the air inside the bag gets much hotter than 250° F., the skin may become brittle and crack.

The mountain range passes far below me. Time, in this race, is running out, and I must find a place to land.

Now begins the tricky descent. I pull the cord that opens the maneuvering vent—popularly called the "hoo-hoo" (page 399). This slit high on the side of the envelope normally remains closed but, when open, allows hot air to escape and thus reduces the buoyancy of the balloon.

The rate-of-climb needle points down and the altimeter unwinds. If my balloon comes down too fast it will fill with cold air and smash into these boulder-strewn mountains. So I slacken the cord and the pressure of hot air in the bag automatically closes the valve. I turn up the burners and the balloon gently levels off. I have come down 1,000 feet on an invisible aerial staircase. Repeating the process, over and over, I take giant 1,000-foot steps toward the earth.

As I approach ground, an unexpected updraft holds me eerily just above a cliff—no place for landing. I fire up the burners and leap-frog past the hazard.

At least there are no wires strung across this open country. I think of my young friend

*For other NATIONAL GEOGRAPHIC accounts of the fascination of ballooning, see "Across the Alps in a Wicker Basket," by Phil Walker, January, 1963; and "Braving the Atlantic by Balloon," by Arnold Eiloart, July, 1959.

Like a limp dishrag, Mr. Fink's balloon drops toward desert sage. Below, Berry (white short-sleeved shirt) helps his crew portage gondola and balloon from a ravine where he landed.

Dick Pollard, of Denver, Colorado, killed two years ago when his balloon drifted across high-tension lines.

Now I detect a worrisome ground wind driving me into a deep, rocky ravine. Ground wind can drag a balloonist, shredding bag and gondola.

No Lions This Time

A few feet above ground.... Now! I yank a line that pulls off the big rip panel in the crown. The balloon collapses, and I land with a jarring thud, dragging 30 yards.

On other flights I have landed in water, among trees, and once right next to a lion pit in a zoo, but never in worse terrain than this. It takes my ground crew, who have been trying to follow the balloon by truck, four hours to catch up with me; we have to portage the balloon and gondola a quarter of a mile (right). Later I learn I have drifted 12 miles and tied for sixth place. Jim Craig of China Lake, California, went 15 miles and won the race.

Despite the rough landing, I can hardly wait to get back in the air, again to ride on silent winds beneath a nylon bag.

SPORT OF HOT-AIR BALLOONING
brings a bright new constellation
to Nevada's daytime skies.

Adventure, science, history, exploration spring to life in your Society's new program of

Special Publications

By MELVILLE BELL GROSVENOR
LL.D., Sc.D.
President and Editor, National Geographic Society

AGRATEFUL MOTHER in Louisville, Kentucky, not long ago wrote to the GEOGRAPHIC to tell us "how much your articles on the Presidents have helped our son in his 8th-grade work. . . . He has received an A-plus. . . ."

Her letter was typical of hundreds. So was one from "an ardent history reader" in Westminster, California, urging that "this series about the Presidents . . . be published in book form." An English member stated flatly, "I am going to get them made into a book." A Georgian requested a Presidents book "at a price I can afford."

The book they suggested is now available —*Our Country's Presidents.* With it the National Geographic Society inaugurates a new service—a series of Special Publications as rich in interest and varied in scope as the Society's magazine itself.

What President Sat His Horse Sideways?

Our Country's Presidents, in its 248 pages, combines the widely hailed series of five articles written for NATIONAL GEOGRAPHIC by Frank Freidel, professor of history at Harvard University. The book brings vividly before us each of the leaders of our Nation, from George Washington to Lyndon B. Johnson, as only dramatic illustrations and concise,

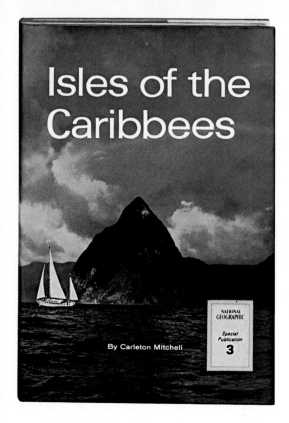

Isles of the Caribbees

By Carleton Mitchell

NATIONAL GEOGRAPHIC
Special Publication
3

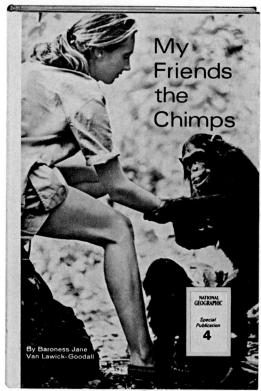

My Friends the Chimps

By Baroness Jane Van Lawick-Goodall

NATIONAL GEOGRAPHIC
Special Publication
4

informative text can do. Zachary Taylor, for example, becomes far more than a name when we see the gruff, determined face of this warrior President—and read how the Mexican War hero directed battles while wearing a straw hat and sitting his horse sideways.

Every chapter presents a wealth of little-known fact. Which President was elected to the Confederate Congress? John Tyler—though he died before taking his seat as a Representative from Virginia. Which three became bridegrooms while living in the White House? Tyler, Cleveland, and Wilson. Who was the first "dark horse?" Polk in 1844. Who originated the "front-porch" campaign? McKinley in 1896.

During the Civil War, President Lincoln found late-night strolls relaxing. A young trumpeter of the 9th Massachusetts Battery has preserved such a moment for us on his sketch pad: the gaunt President pulling a wrap around his burdened shoulders. For years this rare drawing lay unappreciated in the archives of the Library of Congress—until its interest and importance were recognized by National Geographic picture editors.

Similarly, the Society's researchers studied a photograph of Harry Truman taking the oath of office—and completed the identification of witnesses both for the book and for the records of the Truman Library in Independence, Missouri.

Thus even the best-informed adult will find photographs and facts to enrich his knowledge of America, while the pictures lure his children into reading history brought to life.

Though these Special Publications represent a new effort by the Society, a further

---

HOW TO RESERVE YOUR BOOKS

A PROMPT REQUEST will bring you first editions of the four books as they appear:
Our Country's Presidents, by Frank Freidel, 248 pages. Available now.
The River Nile, by Bruce Brander, 200 pages. Available in July.
Isles of the Caribbees, by Carleton Mitchell, 200 pages. Available in October.
My Friends the Chimps, by Baroness Jane van Lawick-Goodall, 200 pages. Available in February, 1967.

The books are bound in hard covers of gold-stamped linen vellum and contain a profusion of color illustrations.

Send no money with your order. You will receive a bill for $4.25 with each book.

Address reservations to National Geographic Society, Dept. 300, Washington, D. C. 20036.

means of "increasing and diffusing geographic knowledge," their editors are veteran members of the Society's staff. Headed by Robert L. Breeden, they have been responsible for production of such public-service projects as the official White House guidebook for the White House Historical Association; the guide to the United States Capitol, *We, the People;* and the new Supreme Court book, *Equal Justice Under Law.* Each has been received with superlatives.

"Stunning," said the *Christian Science Monitor* as it praised "the superb craftsmanship of the National Geographic Society."

"An exacting quest for perfection," said the Washington *Star.*

But the compliment I personally value most highly came from Mrs. John F. Kennedy. In a letter of thanks for the White House guide, she lauded "the excellence of the book." And she added, "Only the NATIONAL GEOGRAPHIC could have done that."

The same pursuit of excellence marks the second volume in the new series—*The River Nile,* to be ready in July. Our editors are now racing both time and the river, for rising waters backed up by the Aswan High Dam are even at this moment drowning much of Egypt's past.

A few years ago my mother traveled 30,000 miles through Africa. "In all that trip," she said, "the most magnificent sight was the sunrise

From fledgling Nation to world leader, the United States has grown under the direction of 35 men, and their ambitions and achievements crowd the pages of *Our Country's Presidents.*

New Yorkers witnessed the oath-taking of George Washington, first Chief Executive. Thomas Jefferson, drafter of the Declaration of Independence, almost doubled the size of the country during his administration. Andrew Jackson leaped to prominence as hero of the War of 1812. A rail splitter in his youth, Abraham Lincoln gained a national reputation in debates with Stephen A. Douglas and, as President, preserved the Union during turbulent Civil War days. A century later President John F. Kennedy and his wife Jacqueline brought vitality, youth, and charm to the White House.

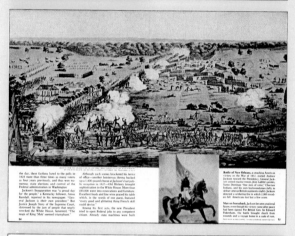

view of the rock-hewn temples at Abu Simbel."

In recent months those temples have presented an even more extraordinary sight. Engineers have been carving the great statues into pieces and lifting them 225 feet for reassembly above high water. Our Society photographers have filmed each step in this project. At the same time, they have photographed archeologists at work in the doomed valley and recorded their recent discoveries.

New Chapters in the Nile's Old Story

Capturing this intensive activity in pictures and words, *The River Nile* is a book both timely and timeless. It tells two giant stories: A part of the past never again to be seen, and a technological revolution about to change the face of this ancient valley.

Author of *The River Nile* is a widely traveled GEOGRAPHIC staff member, Bruce Brander, who did much of his research on the river itself. To visit archeological sites and to see the great stream from its mouth to its headwaters, he flew along it by jetliner, sailed it at the pleasure of the wind in a graceful felucca, and roamed its bordering deserts by camel and Land-Rover.

The book retells one of the world's oldest geographic stories—the quest for the source of the Nile. The ancients were tantalized by tales of the river's birthplace in great lakes and mountains to the south. Nero sent an expedition, to no avail. All through medieval times, the Nile's origin remained unknown. Not until 1862 did the English explorer John Hanning Speke finally trace the White Nile to Lake Victoria, on the Equator.

The River Nile takes us even farther south, to the true headwaters in the tiny republic of Rwanda. Moving downsteam, we course past the Mountains of the Moon—the Ruwenzori —and through the country of pagan cattle worshipers in the Sudan.

We watch the upper Nile ooze through the swampy Sudd, where dry land is so scarce and bird life so plentiful that birds must sometimes take turns landing. In the wet season these swamps grow to the size of England; their changing channels and floating islands have baffled experienced river pilots. In 1881 the Italian explorer Romolo Gessi was trapped for three months in the watery maze. Most of his 400 men starved in the swamp, and he died shortly after reaching Egypt.

Today the longest river on earth serves as a mighty source of electrical energy, while still linking monuments of civilizations that flourished millenniums ago. *The River Nile* encompasses it all—4,145 miles and 5,000 years.

Carleton Mitchell's *Isles of the Caribbees*, third of the books, takes you on an armchair voyage of discovery. You will cruise under sail

Silent flows the lifeblood of Egypt, past remnants of vanished grandeur. A new NATIONAL GEOGRAPHIC book, *The River Nile,* captures the sweep and pageantry of the world's longest river.

Like ships of Pharaohs, a *gaiassa* slips by the crumbling Kôm Ombo Temple. The new Aswan High Dam, 35 miles upstream, poses no threat to it, but the rock temples of Abu Simbel in Nubia (right) would have been lost forever under Lake Nasser except for an international project to carve them into blocks for reassembly above the rising waters.

Skilled workmen slice the crown from one of four colossi of Ramesses II that guard the entrance to the main temple of Abu Simbel. Children thrill to a ride down the gigantic sand pile that protects the façade during dismantling.

Golden funerary mask of King Tutankhamun preserves the features of the young Pharaoh. His tomb, discovered in 1922, revealed a treasure trove of precious artifacts buried with him 3,300 years ago. Today the Egyptian Museum in Cairo exhibits the unique collection.

To isles of winter sun

W ARM WHISPERING WINDS, the fragrance of
flamboyants, the lilting rhythms of a steel band
—few can resist the spell of the Caribbean.

In *Isles of the Caribbees,* readers cruise in the
yawl *Finisterre* with veteran yachtsman Carleton
Mitchell (below), his face stung by spray. Sailing a
turquoise sea, he drops anchor at the Virgin Islands,
St. Kitts, Antigua, and Guadeloupe, glamorous
names in the Leeward Islands. In the Windwards,
he calls at the equally romantic Grenadines, St.
Vincent, St. Lucia, and Martinique (above), where
fishermen dry their nets on a palm-fringed beach.

On Grenada, southernmost of the Windward Islands, steep verdant hills enfold the harbor of St.
George's, and fiery blossoms of royal poinciana cas-
cade above a banana boat taking on cargo. Sails
furled, an island yacht drowses at anchor.

along the sun-washed crescent of Leeward and Windward Islands, the Lesser Antilles, which stretch in a 700-mile arc from Puerto Rico to the coast of South America.

It was my own good fortune to sail with Carleton Mitchell on his cup-winning ocean-racer *Finisterre* from St. Christopher—nick-named St. Kitts—to St. Thomas in the Virgin Islands, as he gathered much of the material for this book. I shall always remember our first view of the Dutch island of Saba, rising from the sea like Napoleon's cocked hat. Strangely, you must climb 900 feet to reach Bottom, its largest town. "It really is a bottom," said skipper Mitchell, "the crater of a dead volcano."

With our yachtsman-author we meet the living history of half a dozen melded cultures from Europe, Africa, and Asia, brought to the shores of the New World by galleons, pirate ships, men-of-war, and slavers. On the French island of Guadeloupe, where a guillotine in 1794 beheaded 27 Royalist officers in one day during France's Reign of Terror, cane knives decapitate roosters and goats in a traditional East Indian ritual. Ghosts of British naval officers of Nelson's day seem to stalk a restored dockyard at English Harbour, Antigua, still under the Union Jack. The Dutch island of St. Eustatius dips its colors to *Finisterre,* a reminder that its salute in 1776 to a United States brig-of-war was the first official recognition of this infant nation.

With *Finisterre* you visit planter isles that time passed by, and tourist isles building new fortune on "fun in the sun." Anyone hoping to visit the West Indies should own *Isles of the Caribbees;* those who may never sail there   415

EKTACHROMES BY WINFIELD PARKS © NATIONAL GEOGRAPHIC SOCIETY

Friends from different worlds, Baroness Jane van Lawick-Goodall and burly Figan play together. *My Friends the Chimps* recounts the fascinating discoveries and experiences of the attractive British scientist studying these apes in the wilds of Tanzania.

Fishing for dinner, Fifi pokes a grass stem into a termite mound; she will pull it out laden with clinging insects. Her mother Flo (above) nibbles at choice large termites; small ones go free, rejected by the discriminating diners. Baroness van Lawick reported the animals modifying stems to fashion fishing poles for termites, proving that chimpanzees in the wild make crude tools. She found they also create sponges from chewed leaves and sop up drinking water with them.

416

will find this book the stuff of dreams.

In the fourth volume of the series, *My Friends the Chimps,* the Baroness Jane van Lawick-Goodall tells the full story of her life among wild chimpanzees in the Gombe Stream Game Reserve of Tanzania.

As Jane Goodall, she began her field study in 1960 at the suggestion of the noted anthropologist Dr. Louis S. B. Leakey of Nairobi, Kenya. "Chimps demonstrate the rudiments of reasoned thinking," she has written. "We hope that study of their social habits in the wild will throw new light on the growth of early human cultures."

For five years the Society has supported the research of this remarkable English girl; through her two GEO-GRAPHIC articles and our Society's television documentary, millions have followed her as she moved into the bush alone, as she gradually won the confidence of wild chimpanzees and made scientific history with her observations.

Of first importance, she discovered that these chimpanzees make primitive tools—for extracting termites from nests (opposite) and for sopping up water for drinking. She found that chimpanzees, like humans, gain reassurance from a friendly touch and greet each other by embracing, even kissing.

A turning point—and a romance—came when the Society assigned an outstanding young photographer of African wildlife, Dutch Baron Hugo van Lawick, to record Miss Goodall's work on color film. They married and now conduct the study as a husband-wife team. Through the young scientist's eyes and her husband's extraordinary photographs we see the powerful Mike bolster his ego with wild bouts of kicking empty kerosene cans. We watch "charging" displays, in which excited apes rush about dragging branches, swaying on limbs, and stamping the ground.

With illustrations that also stand as major contributions to science, *My Friends the Chimps* will interest anyone who enjoys personal adventure, anthropology, or a trip to the zoo.

These, then, are the first four of our Society's Special Publications. By making a prompt reservation, your family can share these varied worlds (for details see page 409). THE END

EKTACHROMES BY BARON HUGO VAN LAWICK
© NATIONAL GEOGRAPHIC SOCIETY

Human expressions—whimsy, complacency, humility, pride—flit across the faces of chimpanzees. Physical characteristics and mannerisms distinguish each animal, enabling the Baroness van Lawick to recognize and name many. David Greybeard's grizzled chin, for example, makes him easy to spot. White irises around his pupils identify Mr. Worzle. The scientist knows others by their long faces, short faces, bald shoulders, and body builds.

Making Friends With

PREPOSTEROUS PLAYMATES, *man and killer whale swim together for the first time, exploding the popular belief that the marine behemoth will attack any creature in the sea. Chin to chin with the author, 24-foot Namu accepts a slab of salmon. Underwater photographer's Fisheye lens records the antics in Rich Cove, on Puget Sound. Spectators peer from a floating dock above.*

M Y HEART POUNDED with excitement, although I felt no genuine fear. The killer whale, all 24 feet and five tons of him, exhaled a cloud of vapor from his blowhole and swam toward me in a lazy arc.

Clad in a black neoprene wet suit, I squatted on a floating dock at Rich Cove, near Seattle, Washington, and dangled a 12-pound salmon enticingly over the water.

"Come on, whale!" I called, then switched to a nasal imitation of the beeps and squeals of whale talk.

I clung, as always, to my confidence that this dangerous animal somehow sensed and returned my friendly feeling. Yet with *Orcinus orca* there is no escaping—what shall I say?—apprehension. The

a Killer Whale

By EDWARD I. GRIFFIN

killer whale, also called orca from his Latin name, is like man in being one of the few mammals that kill for sport.

The tall dorsal fin cut the water like an ax blade as the whale glided across the fenced and net-enclosed pool. Up through the surface came the blunt head. The cool steel-gray eye blinked, the jaws gaped, the jagged array of conical teeth closed on the salmon.

Now for the new trick! I kept a firm grip on my end of the fish. The whale slid past, pulling me with him into the frigid water.

Deliberately, I hung onto the salmon until the killer had dragged me thirty feet or so. Then I released the fish, and the orca gulped it down.

The trick completed, I started to swim toward shore. But the animal had other ideas.

He came up from below and, carrying me on his back like the boy on the dolphin in Greek myth, delivered me to the end of the dock. The greedy fellow wanted more salmon!

Learning to Trust a Killer

Killer whales, found in all the oceans of the world, are reputed to be the most bloodthirsty predators in salt water, yet this individual, through a strange set of circumstances, had become my playmate and won my trust. But it was always up to the whale, in the last analysis, to decide if I would emerge from the pool alive and unmarked.

"Either you're crazy, or you have courage running out your ears," a spectator said when I waded ashore.

I disclaim both lunacy and excessive cour-

Fame for Namu begins by a rocky headland of British Columbia. Caged behind nets close to shore, he receives visits from relatives at large, possibly his mother and younger brothers or sisters.

On a stormy June night in 1965, commercial fishermen William Lechkobit (top right) and Robert McGarvey (below) snared Namu in a salmon net. They promptly contacted marine scientists and exhibitors, hoping to sell their rare catch, one of the most intelligent of sea creatures.

Edward I. (Ted) Griffin, owner and director of the Seattle Public Aquarium, flew to the little cannery town of Namu that gave the whale his name (map, next page). For $8,000 he acquired what was then the world's only captive specimen of *Orcinus orca;* another killer, harpooned near Saturna Island a year earlier, had died after 87 days in captivity at Vancouver, British Columbia.

Now Griffin faced an almost impossible task: transporting his five-ton purchase to Seattle, Washington, 450 miles to the south.

KODACHROMES BY PAUL V. THOMAS © N.G.S.

age. I have simply wanted very much to get to know and understand this whale, and to have him accept me. For that, I have been willing to take certain chances.

I am owner and director of the Seattle Public Aquarium, and last summer I gambled $60,000—a sum I had to beg, borrow, and bargain for—to purchase, transport, and exhibit a bull killer whale called Namu.

Captain Ahab lost a leg, and later his life, trying to vanquish the white whale Moby Dick; getting my saw-toothed orca home safe to Seattle, I risked losing my shirt.

Just one item—400 pounds of salmon, my whale's daily ration—at 25 cents a pound multiplies out to $100 a day. That's $700 a week just to feed the animal, and my wife and children have to eat, too.

Namu got his name from the British Columbia cannery town near which he trapped himself by blundering into a salmon net (map, next page). For several months Namu was the only killer whale in captivity. Then last November we captured a 14-foot female. Though apparently too young to be a mate for Namu, the new calf romped happily with her more ponderous playmate, and the pair became great pals.

My biggest surprise has been Namu's friendly behavior—so far, at least. One reference work describes the killer whale as having "the appetite of a hog, the cruelty of a wolf, the courage of a bulldog, and the most terrible jaws afloat."

Orcas at sea feed exclusively on live or fresh-killed prey. They will eat fish, squid, and birds, but for the main course they prefer red meat. From huge blue and gray whales as much as twenty times their size, killer packs strip the lips, tongues, and pectoral fins, then wait until their victims die from loss of blood before devouring the carcasses.

Or they swallow seals, dolphins, and penguins whole: One killer whale stomach, when opened, contained 13 dolphins and 14 seals. Another held 32 full-grown seals. Only the tusked adult walrus holds the orca at bay. Stories about human remains in killers' stomachs lack verification, but a photographer on Robert Falcon Scott's last Antarctic expedition in 1911 was threatened when killers, trying to get at dogs staked on an ice floe, bumped the ice from beneath, breaking it around man and dogs.

Like others of his species, Namu is a power-

EKTACHROMES BY TED SPIEGEL (BELOW), K

ful, efficient killer. In this respect I find him fascinating. Yet some strange affinity has drawn me closer and closer to him over these past months. It is something I find impossible to explain.

"Aren't you risking death," friends ask, "every time you swim with that whale?"

In a way—yes. But from the very start I was convinced that neither Namu nor any orca associates man with his feeding pattern. I also knew that killer whales in the wild have few if any enemies and should feel no fear. Hence, I reasoned, orcas don't have to use their teeth defensively. So I counted on my whale's regarding me with curiosity, but not with hunger or with fear.

From our first meeting, in the swirling tidal waters of British Columbia, I began to prepare myself for swimming with Namu. I

Eager to spy Namu, thousands line the bridge at Deception Pass, Washington, backing up traffic for miles on each side. Tugboat *Iver Foss* pulls Namu's floating pen of steel mesh. A wait for suitable tides forced a day's layover here.

"Namu's Navy," as reporters dubbed the bizarre convoy that towed the whale to Seattle, crossed some of the most treacherous waters on the Pacific coast: wind-whipped swells of Queen Charlotte Sound, whirlpools of Seymour Narrows, and open stretches of the Strait of Georgia.

Pod of killers overtakes the flotilla on the fourth day out. Dorsal fins poke menacingly from the sea. Trying to help the captive, they repeatedly charged the cage but, warned by their own built-in sonar, stopped just short of it. After several hours, they vanished as suddenly as they had appeared. Only a cow and two calves, possibly Namu's family, stayed with the tow for 150 miles.

Not all Seattle welcomed Namu's arrival on July 28, 1965. Two placard-bearing pickets paraded the docks demanding his release.

423

wanted to know this animal as intimately as a human could. Really close contact was possible only in the whale's medium—the sea.

In the water I would be relatively helpless. To be safe, I would have to be completely accepted by the animal. I must get him used to my presence, even to count on it.

After we finally got Namu to the aquarium at Pier 56 in Seattle, I spent long hours on the catwalk of his floating cage watching him, studying his behavior, noting his moods.

I began by rowing a small boat about the whale's pen. At first this made Namu nervous and he would sulk on the bottom. When the whale accepted the boat, I then approached him in a small rubber raft. Soon the animal allowed me to touch and pet him.

Within a few days, instead of my pursuing the orca, he was chasing me. Yet never did he make the slightest aggressive gesture with mouth, teeth, or mighty tail flukes. It was like

Bow and arrow shoots a massive dose of vitamin-B complex into Namu to perk up a lagging appetite. Research technician Darrell Bills fires the syringe. Below, Mr. Griffin mans oars as an assistant removes the dart.

Prowling the jade-green waters of Puget Sound, Namu inspects photographer Schulke as he takes this rare underwater photograph at close quarters. Eyes far back on the head (under the white patch) enable the killer whale to see sideways as well as straight ahead.

being followed around by a big friendly dog.

On a memorable day—Friday, August 27, 1965—I ventured for the first time into the water with my whale. Clad in my wet suit, I slipped into one corner of the pen.

Was I frightened? Yes—plenty! But optimistic as well, and too busy to get panicky.

Whale Enjoys Scrub-brush Grooming

I put my masked head under water, so that I could see my quarry and cope with him somehow if he became an adversary. All O.K. I could see the burly black-and-white form holding position with a lazy rocking motion, fore and aft. His eye held mine. Gradually I felt secure.

With a short-handled brush I approached Namu under water. With a light touch, I scrubbed his head, nose, and chin. The whale made no move to withdraw or to attack me.

Later the same day I swam right around Namu. He stayed stock-still, seeming almost to disregard me.

I slid onto his back and tugged gently at his huge dorsal fin. He swam two or three times around the pen with his unfamiliar burden, then casually bucked me off, almost as if with a shrug and the thought, "That's enough of this nonsense for now."

From that point on it was like a honeymoon. We got along beautifully.

I found that my whale loved to have his hide scrubbed with a long-handled brush. Killers often rub against each other, perhaps to slough off dead skin and maintain their sleek smoothness. We began regular back- and stomach-scratching sessions that scraped and groomed Namu's skin.

Namu seemed ecstatic, and soon permitted me to row the boat right over his back. He could then scratch himself on its bottom. One day I happened to block Namu's blowhole   425

EKTACHROME (BELOW) BY FLIP SCHULKE; KODACHROMES BY MERRILL P. SPENCER © N.G.S.

with the boat. He had to swim away to suck in a breath of air. Soon he learned to roll away upside down if this happened.

Within a few days he was actually chasing the boat while swimming upside down. He would go under the boat, clamp his disk-shaped pectoral fins on each side, and carry the cockleshell craft around the pool. Sometimes the only way to end this fantastic game was to throw a fish in front of him, then row like mad for the catwalk.

People on the pier clapped and cheered as Namu cavorted about, his curiosity guiding him to new experiences almost daily. I believe my constant presence reassured the whale during this trying period of adjustment.

To understand how I feel about Namu, you must realize that from earliest boyhood I have collected, cherished, and observed wild creatures, particularly fishes and other

426 (Continued on page 433)

Mate or mother—Namu's guardians could not tell which—circles the pen. Once when Namu squealed loudly, she charged the cage. Apparently satisfied as to his safety, she backed off.

Massive jaws agape, Namu dines on salmon. He rejects the roe of the female fish, a delicacy to humans, by squeezing it out the side of his mouth.

Royal welcome to Seattle finds spectators jamming the waterfront as the *Robert E. Lee,* which shared the tow with the *Iver Foss,* pulls the pen between the reception barge and the author's aquarium on Pier 56. While press and pleasure boats provide escort, Namu rolls on his back and flashes his white underbelly.

427

EKTACHROME (ABOVE) BY K. GILBEY HEWLETT; EKTACHROME (BELOW) AND KODACHROME BY PAUL V. THOMAS © N.G.S.

TUXEDOED ACROBAT *catapults from the water with scarcely a ripple and lands with a mighty five-ton splash. Radiantly healthy, Namu puts on this awesome show almost daily, often after devouring his $100 ration of salmon. Enclosed in Rich Cove, 12 miles west of Seattle, the whale began his first winter in captivity with plenty of room for exercise.*

428 KODACHROME BY PAUL V. THOMAS © NATIONAL GEOGRAPHIC SOCIETY

OPPOSITE PAGE FOLDS OUT

inhabitants of the sea. Over the years it became my prime ambition—almost a ruling passion—to capture a killer whale alive.

In July, 1964, Dr. Murray A. Newman, Curator of the Vancouver Public Aquarium, sent a party to harpoon a killer whale for use in preparing an exhibition model. But the harpoon, while holding the 15-foot orca, inflicted no serious injury. This killer, called Moby Doll—although discovered later to be a male—unfortunately died after three months in captivity.

Once previously a killer had been taken alive: Marineland of the Pacific netted a sick orca in 1961 off southern California. It died two days later.

Months before Namu swam into my life, I had taken up the search for these magnificent mammals, hunting them with small boats, helicopters, and tranquilizer guns in the salmon-rich waters of Puget Sound.

But success eluded me until about midnight last June 23 when my phone rang.

"Mr. Griffin? This is Walter Piatocka. I'm a fisherman and I'm calling from Namu, British Columbia. Two men here have caught a pair of killer whales, and the animals are for sale. These fellows thought you might be interested."

I gulped. Live killers at last!
"How much?" I asked.

Mounting his sea steed for a thrilling 15-minute ride around Rich Cove, Ted Griffin kneels on Namu's back and holds tight to the high dorsal fin. "So sensitive is the fin," says Griffin, "that at first the touch of a finger alarmed Namu, and he would quickly shake me off. But later I could stay on as long as I desired. Sometimes he even goes to sleep with me on his back, and I have to swat him to make him go." The author wears a neoprene wet suit in the 47-degree water.

Bubbles rise from Namu's blowhole. Like dolphins, killers communicate with sonarlike high-frequency sounds, most of them originating in the larynx and many inaudible to human ears. Hydrophones have captured Namu's underwater signals from three miles away; whales probably detect them much farther.

Tuning in on Namu, an acoustic engineer from the Boeing Company records the whale's voice and imitates it. Research vessel *Maribo II* houses the instruments.

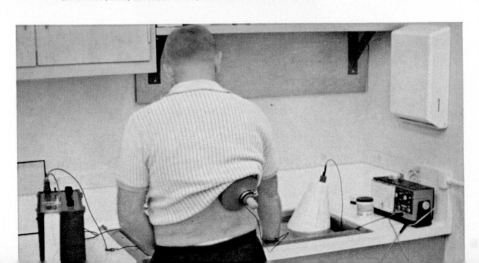

434

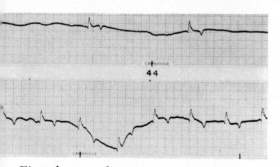

First electrocardiogram ever made of an uninjured, unrestrained killer whale reveals a surface heartbeat of 60 pulsations a minute (lower graph) but only 30 beats under water (upper). A medical team from Seattle's Virginia Mason Hospital Research Center, directed by Dr. Merrill P. Spencer, obtained Namu's cardiogram, using a suction cup to attach electric sensors directly over the whale's heart as he rolled on his back to take food. The instrument recorded Namu's heartbeat as squiggles on a roll of graph paper.

Technician (opposite) tests the suction power of the plungerlike cup before fastening it onto Namu's skin.

"Don't know exactly. The whales are up for grabs, but the fishermen think they're worth a lot of money."

"I'll be up there tomorrow," I replied.

Next day in a float plane of Lake Union Air Service, I flew to Namu, where I met red-bearded Robert McGarvey and husky William Lechkobit (page 421). They told me how they had come into possession of two orcas—"blackfish," they called them.

On the evening of June 22, 1965, Bob and Willie set their drift nets for spring salmon in Fitz Hugh Sound, in the mid-part of British Columbia's fiord-slashed coast. As they drifted with the tide, each in his own boat, they chatted by radiotelephone and prepared to turn in for the night.

Sunday Collection Saves the Day

Off Warrior Cove it began blowing up. Willie's net wrapped around a reef and he found himself drifting dangerously close to the breakers. Willie had no choice: To save his boat he cut the net loose. Then he headed for one of the cannery wharves at nearby Namu and tied up for the night.

Bob McGarvey's net drifted clear and he stayed out. In the morning he swung over to see how Willie's net was doing. He blinked when he saw what was inside: two killer whales—a big one and a baby.

"The big blackfish was kinda pushin' the little feller to get him out of there," Bob said. "But the baby wouldn't go, so the big one slipped out through a space between the net and the rocks, showing the young one the way to get free. The little one stayed put, so the big whale went back in behind the net.

"I called Willie by radiophone," Bob went on. "He came right out and saw those killers. His eyes bugged and he said, 'Give me a hand, and we'll get those things out of there.'

"'No you don't!' I said. 'We're going to sell those blackfish, Willie. They're worth more than any netful of salmon!'"

Word of the capture spread like prairie fire. "Whale Caught by a Fluke," headlined one newspaper. Other bidders were interested, and the best offer I could make was turned down. Heavyhearted, I flew back to Seattle.

Two days later the whale calf escaped. No one saw it go.

"With the little whale gone, we lost our best bargaining card," Bob McGarvey said later. "Everybody wanted that baby."

Fearful that the big whale also might escape, the fishermen phoned me. "The first fellow up here to Namu with $8,000 in cash

435

will get the whale," Bob said. Then he added, "The deadline is Sunday night—that's tomorrow. Otherwise, we let him go. We can't afford to keep feeding salmon to this brute, and besides, we've got fishing to do."

I was stunned. It was Saturday night, with the banks already closed, and they wouldn't reopen until Monday! I had only a few hundred dollars at the aquarium.

Friendly merchants saved the day. On Sunday I took a couple of shopping bags and ranged the Seattle waterfront. Everywhere I went cash drawers were emptied for me. I scraped together the required sum, mostly in small bills—ones, fives, tens, and twenties.

When I reached Namu, no other purchaser had arrived, and next morning, June 28, we closed the deal. My mood was ecstatic. I felt tremendous joy and relief. A live killer whale finally was mine!

Now all I had to do was to keep him alive for the 450-mile journey south. Seattle suddenly seemed very, very far away.

To guard and feed the whale, I posted Don Goldsberry, collector and keeper from Tacoma's Point Defiance Aquarium, who later entered my employ. My veteran seal trainer, Homer Snow, also was on hand to help.

British Columbia Packers, Ltd., generously offered the facilities of their cannery and a wharf at Namu as construction site for a floating pen in which to tow my prize home.

Brute Manpower Moves Three-ton Pen

From Seattle I flew up 4,000 pounds of precut structural steel. Our Tinkertoy pen took shape—a metal basket with angle-iron stiffeners, crisscrossed by quarter-inch rod welded on two-foot centers. The cage would be 60 by 40 feet, 16 feet deep, floated by 41 fuel drums, rimmed with a catwalk (page 427).

With forklifts and seine-boat booms we tried to lift the completed pen into the water. One side of it crumpled like spaghetti.

After repairs were made, I beckoned to the crowd of two or three hundred spectators. "We aren't getting anywhere," I called out. "If any of you would like to volunteer, we'd surely appreciate your help."

The crowd moved in, mostly men, but a few women. They surrounded my Rube Goldberg contraption—it weighed three tons— and in minutes eased it into the water.

Robert Hardwick, Seattle disc jockey, brought up his yacht *Robert E. Lee* as escort vessel. For crew he had reporter Stan Patty and photographer Bruce McKim of the Seattle *Times*. The *Lee* towed the pen out to the reef, where Namu waited behind a triple wall of nets. Bob and Willie from the first day had thrown salmon to the whale, and he ate them with relish.

"He's even eating salmon that've gotten caught in the nets," Don Goldsberry told me. It was a relief that our captive was feeding.

Sonar Warning Stops Whale Charge

But trouble struck with an "attack" by a pod of 30 or 40 killer whales. The herd came, we can only suppose, in response to a cry for help from Namu. They would charge the nets, singly or in small groups, but they always pulled up just short of the flimsy barricade. Any of these huge animals could easily have burst right through the nets. Why did they always stop short?

I have come to the conclusion that we might have imprisoned Namu in a sack of tissue paper. It is evident that when an obstruction looms before this killer or his kin, something tells them, "You mustn't try it."

That "something" is the killer whale's marvelous sonar. Like dolphins, orcas use echo-location to zero in on prey and to avoid obstructions. Rapid-fire clicks, probably originating in the larynx, bounce off obstructions in the water and return to the whale. From the elapsed time and direction, the orca can compute the obstacle's position.

Always present, and often nose to nose with Namu on the other side of the nets, were an adult female and two calves (page 420).

"I'm sure those three are Namu's relatives," Don said. "One of the calves, I'll bet, is the little guy that escaped from the net."

The press, of course, made it a love story— captured father and solicitous mother and young. Perhaps so—science lacks enough data to say for sure. My view is that Namu is only 8 or 10 years old and not yet a father.

Contemptuous of the small perch darting about him, Namu heads topside for a more substantial meal of salmon, the only food he eats in captivity. To sustain their distinguished visitor, Washington State fisheries authorities waived a law prohibiting the use of salmon to feed animals. Namu gobbles 400 pounds a day. "He'd eat a ton if we let him," claims one of his keepers.

PRANKSTER WHALE *takes his owner for a ride—
then abruptly dumps him! "In roomy Rich
Cove,"* says the author, *"Namu quickly learned
that by upsetting the skiff he could not only gain my
companionship but also dine sooner when all the
salmon spilled out." Diving below the boat (underwater view), Namu tips it with sure, swift motions,
and the boatman ends in the brine (sequence at left).
"Pray Namu remains captive all his life, or pity the
unsuspecting sailors he meets," muses Mr. Griffin.*

EKTACHROME (ABOVE) BY FLIP SCHULKE; KODACHROME BY MERRILL P. SPENCER © N.G.S.

More likely the others are his mother and two younger siblings.

At Warrior Cove, I entered the water close to Namu, but still with a net between us. The whale peered curiously at me, and here took place our first eyeball-to-eyeball talks.

All of us working above water with the animal had heard his strange noises—sometimes they resembled the wailings of a lovesick cat. Namu beeped and squealed both on and below the surface.

Now, swimming beside him there at the reef, I tried for the first time to match his sounds. This proved easier under water, for some reason, than in the air. By the time we had Namu in his pen, he was responding to me. Admittedly, these were strange conversations. I hadn't the faintest idea what I was saying to him with my own feeble vocalizing.

Whales "Home-in" on Namu From Afar

Finally the day came when the purse seiner we had hired, the *Chamiss Bay,* skippered by Capt. Vivian Wilson, arrived to tow Namu to Port Hardy, 100 miles away on Vancouver Island. There the *Chamiss Bay* left us to return to fishing. For the onward voyage, I chartered the *Iver Foss,* a harbor tug in the

"Just a little lower. That's the spot. Now scratch, please." As if giving directions, Namu lolls belly-up for a stomach rub from Ted Griffin.

Swimming on his back with pectoral fins in the air, Namu circles Rich Cove with Griffin astride his chest and holding his lower jaw. Minutes later the incongruous water sprites begin a favorite game: cat-and-mouse. "I slip off and swim at full speed toward shore," Griffin explains, "but I never reach it. Namu races toward me, surfaces, and with me prone on his back, streaks to deep water again. I jump off, and we start all over. He never tires of the sport."

capable command of Capt. George Losey.

The morning our flotilla left Port Hardy, I had to make one of my frequent shuttle flights to Seattle. As my float plane took off, Namu was acting up—dashing around the pen, slapping his tail, swimming upside down, beeping and squealing. I guessed that he must be in contact with other killer whales.

We were several miles out, still climbing, when I caught sight of a pod of orcas broaching about five miles to the north (pages 422-3). They were swimming directly toward the tow.

So this was the cause of Namu's restlessness! The whales heading for Namu seemed

to show the great range over which killers can communicate by underwater sounds.

Doubling back toward Port Hardy, we kept the moving pod in sight. When this group of whales neared the towing pen, they became much excited by Namu's presence. From our plane we could see them mill about madly. Namu, too, whipped the water in a frenzy.

I learned on my return that, although most of the pod soon moved on, a cow and two calves stayed behind.

"These were the same whales who kept us company at Warrior Cove," said Don. "I am positive, from scars and markings on them. Namu's family can't stay away from him."

For several days cow and calves stuck with the tow. The smaller calf slid over its mother's back, playful as an otter.

On July 15, near Kelsey Bay, Namu began thrashing, rolling, squealing, and lifting his head out of the water. We learned shortly what had stirred him up.

A powerful bull orca hove into sight and started cavorting with the cow and the calves. The interloper kept showing off. The *Robert E. Lee* finally drove off the troublemaker, and calm was restored. The cow and calves fell farther behind and soon were lost to sight. Probably they rejoined their herd.

Jazz Band Welcomes a Captive Killer

Our flotilla entered U. S. waters in Haro Strait on July 24, and on Wednesday, July 28, Namu's cage slowly edged into place beside Pier 56 on the Seattle waterfront (pages 426-7). A Dixieland band played, and in his floating pen Namu bobbed and splashed, showing off his handsome black tuxedo coat and white shirt front.

I leaned on the front of the cage and cried.

Men thrust microphones at me. "This is the most exciting moment of my life," I said.

Namu was an instant success. Record crowds pushed in to see the fearsome killer turned tame. The first Sunday nearly 5,000 spectators showed up! By the end of September, 120,000 visitors had come to see my whale.

Right away we placed a plastic liner in the pen, under and around the whale. This almost totally excluded the foul surface water of the harbor. Into the lined pen a hose poured clean water, pumped up from a depth of 60 feet.

During his first weeks in his new home, Namu ate hardly anything. To stimulate the whale's appetite, we gave him B-complex vitamin shots, using a bow and arrow firing a hypodermic dart to make the injection (page 424). Namu didn't even move.

Whether because of the shots, or for other

Lobtailing—thrashing the water with triangular flukes—Namu expresses displeasure. For an hour Griffin, in the skiff, has scrubbed the whale's hide with a long-handled brush. Now, like a child balking at bedtime, Namu refuses to accept the end of the grooming.

Surfacing to breathe, Namu sprays a rainbow. He can stay submerged for as long as 10 minutes, but normally comes up once a minute. Amazingly, he can blow to exhale and draw in fresh air in less than a second. A muscular flap locks the blowhole shut when he dives.

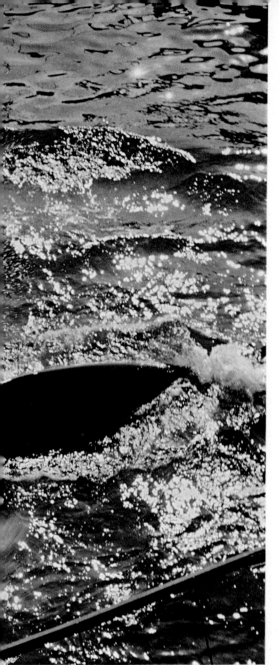

KODACHROMES BY ANDREW H. BROWN (ABOVE) AND MERRILL P. SPENCER © N.G.S.

reasons, the whale's hunger soon sharpened. By the first of September we were feeding him 200 to 400 pounds of salmon daily.

It was about this time that our ponderous pet displayed a craftiness I found amusing. One morning I noticed that he seemed greedier than usual: When I would throw him a salmon, he would sink down with the tidbit clamped in his bear-trap jaws and drop out of sight, which was unusual. Very quickly he was back, begging for another. I kept feeding him fish, and he kept wheeling back for more.

"I think that big devil's up to something," said Don.

Our suspicions aroused, I pulled on my wet suit and jumped into the water. It took only moments to discover a pile of fish, stacked like cordwood in a corner of the pen. Namu was hoarding rations, apparently for a quiet salmon break between regular feedings!

Many people have written begging me to set Namu free. Such an action, I believe, would be a disservice both to science and to the curious public.

Dr. Dixy Lee Ray, Director of the Pacific Science Center in Seattle, echoed my feeling when she spoke in an interview in defense of holding Namu for exhibit and research.

"Like timid animals in nature, we humans fear what we do not understand," she said. "By understanding Namu, learning more about him, there will be less wanton killing of his kind. He has much to teach us."

Namu Becomes a Science Project

To qualified people, I have, of course, made Namu available for study. Dr. Merrill P. Spencer, Director of the Virginia Mason Hospital Research Center in Seattle, had worked closely with me to develop techniques for capture and handling of killer whales. Namu gave Dr. Spencer a long-awaited opportunity to study the physiology of *Orcinus orca*.

"First thing I want to do," Merrill told me, "is to take an electrocardiogram of Namu."

Merrill and his assistant, Darrell Bills, brought to the pier an electrode set in a rubber suction cup. The pickup cup was mounted on the end of a long pole, with the wire leading to an electrocardiograph on the catwalk (pages 434-5).

During September and October two excellent heart readings were obtained, spanning several respiratory cycles, which last, usually, from 30 seconds to a minute and a half. The records showed that Namu's heartbeat speeds up sharply to 60 beats a minute for the few seconds when he comes up to blow. Between breaths, while the whale is diving, the heart slows to 30 beats a minute.*

Killers are strangely and wonderfully built. As warm-blooded mammals, their structure to some extent parallels that of land creatures. Orcas have vestigial hip bones. Flesh and muscle compose their tail flukes and dorsal fins, but five "hand" bones strengthen each round pectoral fin.

Mother orcas, like dolphins, have a remarkable way of nursing their young. When the

*For further background, see "Hunting the Heartbeat of a Whale," by Paul Dudley White, M.D., with Samuel W. Matthews, NATIONAL GEOGRAPHIC, July, 1956.

infant orca, about seven feet long at birth, wants to feed, it nuzzles its parent's abdomen near the tail, and with powerful muscles the mother whale, through an aperture, shoots a jet of milk directly into the youngster's mouth. Each squirt takes only a second or two.

Killer whales, of course, are close kin to dolphins: Both animals belong to the suborder Odontoceti, toothed whales. Orcas and dolphins share many characteristics of structure, behavior, and intelligence.

Killers, like dolphins, have unusually large brains in proportion to their bodies: Young Moby Doll, the ill-fated Vancouver aquarium captive, tipped the scale at slightly over a ton; his brain weighed 14 pounds. A 7-ton elephant has a brain of only about 12 pounds.

"The precise relationship between brain weight and intelligence is a rather slippery area of science," Merrill Spencer told me. "As yet we have no sure conclusions."

But that orcas, like dolphins, are astonishingly smart is beyond question.

Broad Vocabulary Marks "Whale Talk"

Dr. Thomas C. Poulter of the Stanford Research Institute came to make underwater recordings of Namu's remarkable vocabulary. Dr. Poulter has been interested in killers since his Antarctic days, when he was second in command and senior scientist of the Byrd expedition of 1933-35.* He told me that most of Namu's sounds originate in his larynx. When surfaced, he emits sounds through his blowhole. When submerged, however, the sounds travel through body tissue, which is a good conductor, directly into the water.

"We can now tell the sex of killer whales just from underwater tapes," Dr. Poulter said.

I sat spellbound for 45 minutes listening to the recordings. Rarely could I spot exact duplication of any sound or group of sounds, familiar as I was with Namu's chatter.

Whales can transmit sounds over a wide

*"The Society's Special Medal Is Awarded to Dr. Thomas C. Poulter," NATIONAL GEOGRAPHIC, July, 1937.

range, from 50 cycles per second to at least 40,000, and perhaps even 100,000. Humans can hear only within a range from 50 to 20,000 cycles per second. So we may be hearing only a fraction of the sounds Namu emits.

"The question is," says Merrill Spencer, "does a whale use the information from the sounds he generates in the higher frequency ranges? We just don't know—yet."

The sensitivity of the orca's sonar is extraordinary. Merrill stood beside me on the

With incredible familiarity, Griffin pries open Namu's mouth to reveal some 50 formidable teeth. As large as a man's thumb, they interlock like the jaws of a steel trap. "During his first months in captivity, I constantly worked and played with Namu, ever alert for some aggressive sign on his part," says the author. "I never saw one. He was always affable. Would all killers behave as well in captivity? I don't know. That's one reason I hope we get more—to find out."

pen one afternoon when I tried to get Namu to accept albacore tuna. Naturally, he favored the more expensive fish—salmon!

We managed to get the whale to swallow two or three albacores only by luring him with salmon and then dropping the cheaper fish into his open mouth.

I continued the experiment with him at night, when he could not see the fish. I held an albacore in the water in front of him, perhaps 25 feet away. I pulled the tuna out of the water and then dunked it again with a splash. Namu showed no interest.

But as soon as I dipped a salmon in the water, Namu swung his head back and forth, apparently scanning the new target. Then he slowly swam over and helped himself to the choicer offering.

He was making a lot of audible sounds and probably more that we couldn't hear. The two fish were about the same size and shape. To me it was a striking display of the killer 445

whale's ability to discriminate and select solely by use of sonar.

Came the end of September and autumn's onset, and every day fewer people visited Pier 56. Namu's cage was beginning to fall apart, and I wanted to get the whale away from the harborside debris that would slop into his pen in winter gales.

At Rich Cove in Puget Sound, 12 miles away, I found a splendid wintering-over spot for my whale. By building wing fences and by stringing nets and boom logs across the mouth of the cove, we made an ideal enclosure.

At last Namu had room enough—a roughly circular pool 500 feet across—to disport himself freely. Often after feeding, he vaulted clear out of the water in great leaps that ended with explosive splashes (pages 428-30).

I wanted to capture more killers, and Namu's Rich Cove pool could hold another whale or two. Pods of orcas often range up and down this part of Puget Sound.

In November, as I mentioned earlier, Merrill Spencer and I caught a young killer whale in a net. It was a 14-foot female, which we named Shamu. She shared Namu's enclosure until late December, when she was moved to an aquarium in San Diego, California.

Namu Declines Swimmer's Leg

Before Thanksgiving, Namu had a chance to sample a human drumstick—but passed it up. I was feeding him under water. Namu slid up alongside on my left. I laid one hand on Namu's nose, and with the other I held out a salmon, tantalizingly, in front of his partly open mouth. I shouldn't have done it.

He gave a quick nod with his head, and I lost my hold on the whale's snout. This threw me off balance. Trying to straighten up, I slapped Namu in the face with the fish held in my other hand.

At this instant, Namu was pushing at my hip. Instantly he opened his mouth, feeling for the salmon, and sucked in my leg instead. It was all over before I had time to feel scared. Namu, by simply turning away his head, at once rejected my leg from his maw. I never even felt his teeth.

Although I now take liberties with Namu inconceivable a few months ago, in a way there is a keener edge of suspense each time I enter the water with him. I know more now, much more, about the killer's capabilities—

*See Dr. Kellogg's article, "Whales, Giants of the Sea," in NATIONAL GEOGRAPHIC, January, 1940.

his speed, his strength, and what he can do with those teeth.

The whale knows more about me, too: for instance, that I am slow in the water and speak his language atrociously. Today my friend, tomorrow he could pick up habits of disdain, carelessness, or even aggressiveness that would imperil our relationship.

Though I try not to let the whale know it, I have discovered that he has a mean side. Beware, I have taught myself, when he swings his head sharply or jerks it upward. Especially take care when he bobs his head up and down swiftly. This marks his most severe displeasure and peevishness. "Leave me alone now," it says, and I take the hint.

A Friend—but a Dangerous One

I am no longer the only individual who has entered the water with my whale. A few others have ventured to swim with him: Don Goldsberry, my brother Jim (not enthusiastically!), Flip Schulke to get photographs for this article, divers filming a motion picture written around Namu, and one scientist. Also a high-ranking naval officer. Yes—the U. S. Navy, too, is interested in killer whales.

I am convinced that Namu, Shamu, and their kind can be trained to match the agility and adroitness of dolphins in tricks involving controlled leaps and swimming maneuvers.

But anyone working with a killer whale still must realize that this is a dangerous and unpredictable creature. Its intelligence can be both a reassurance and a threat.

I have recently been in touch with the noted biologist Dr. A. Remington Kellogg, a member of the National Geographic Society's Committee for Research and Exploration. Formerly Assistant Secretary of the Smithsonian Institution and U. S. Commissioner to the International Whaling Commission, he is one of the world's leading authorities on whales.* Reviewing the photographs accompanying this article, he was amazed to see the prince of marine predators in effect playing pat-a-cake with humans.

"I'm afraid we must toss away some of our earlier preconceptions about these animals," said Dr. Kellogg. "This behavior of Namu is entirely contrary to what anyone could have expected. I would be cautious, though, about generalizing from the actions of this one killer whale. I wouldn't use my trust in this animal as a passport to familiarity with another."

Amen.

A CANNON BOOMS, breaking the still of evening under the August full moon. Echoes, scampering across the hills, knock on every door, summoning all to the celebration. From the Chalet Guest House, my wife Donna and I watch as the beautiful city of Kandy, couched in the mountains of Ceylon, dresses in light for the annual procession climaxing Perahera, the city's age-old Buddhist festival.

Below us the Temple of the Tooth flares suddenly in the dusk as white lights blaze along its crenelated outlines. Fountains in the nearby lake play in pastel patterns, and the surrounding hillsides twinkle with twisting ribbons of gaily lit bungalows. Even the fireflies seem to bear brighter torches.

Kandy's storied temple enshrines a relic venerated for centuries as an eyetooth of the Buddha. Though the precious tooth itself never leaves the temple, tonight a symbolic golden casket will be borne through the streets. And tonight Ceylonese from all reaches of the island nation will relive the pomp and pageantry of their ancient royalty.

Within minutes of leaving the Chalet, our car is entrapped in a mesh of humanity. We

Bright as a butterfly, a woman in a flowing skirt flutters across a terraced rice field in Ceylon's highlands, balancing on a dike as if on a tightrope.

447

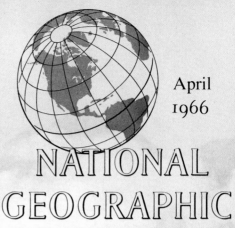

April
1966

NATIONAL
GEOGRAPHIC

THE NATIONAL GEOGRAPHIC MAGAZINE VOL. 129, NO. 4
COPYRIGHT © 1966 BY NATIONAL GEOGRAPHIC SOCIETY, WASHINGTON, D. C.
INTERNATIONAL COPYRIGHT SECURED

Ceylon

Article and photographs by

DONNA K. and
GILBERT M. GROSVENOR

Senior Assistant Editor

Festival lights

WHEN MIDSUMMER's full moon silvers Ceylon's skies, peaceful Kandy turns into a fantasy of light and sound for the celebration of Perahera. From the moated Temple of the Tooth (left) emerges a golden casket, copy of one that holds a relic vener-

flare in Kandy

ated as a tooth of the Buddha. While the relic stays behind in the temple, the casket goes on parade, riding atop Rajah, an elephant with gold-sheathed tusks. He leads scores of others, three abreast, down Kandy's streets. Clothed in shining satin, the pachyderms twinkle with portable electric lamps. Drummers, musicians, acrobats, and dancers join the exuberant procession. For ten days, Kandy becomes a fairy-tale town out of the far-distant past.

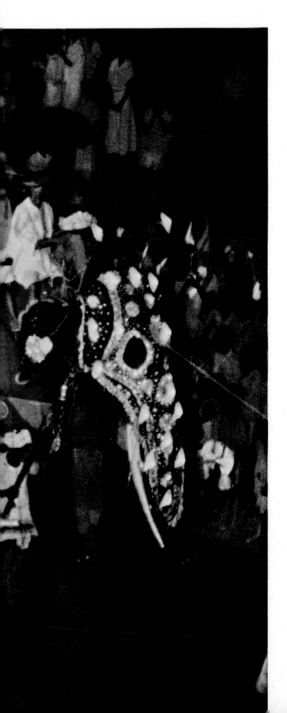

Man and nature combine to turn night into day during the Perahera. The moon, electricity, and torchbearers with braziers of flaming copra light the glittering observance. Major events in the life of the Buddha occurred at the time of the full moon, and believers schedule religious festivals like the Perahera to coincide with it.

abandon it and wriggle our way along on foot. As we reach the temple, a final cannon shot signals the beginning of the procession.

Rolling drums pound cadence, and crackling whips welt the air. Torchlit waves of dancers tinkling with silver ornaments leap and whirl to the stirring rhythms of martial music. Elephants—an incredible, orderly herd of close to a hundred—lumber three abreast, their gray hulks spangled with satin emblazoned with myriad lights.

"Madam, there's Rajah!" Dan Dias, our driver-guide, points to a huge elephant draped in shimmering brocade, its tusks bound with gold (preceding pages). "For many years Rajah has carried the eyetooth casket of our Lord Buddha. He knows that all eyes watch him. See how carefully he steps upon the carpet of white linen unrolled before him?"

Behind Rajah parades a stately figure: the Diyawadene Nilame, lay guardian of the temple, swathed in bulging layers of magnificently jeweled ceremonial robes and wearing brocaded slippers.

Ceylon Turns to the West

The last elephant passes, crowds flow into the streets, and Kandy reverts to the 20th century. But the explosion of light and color and sound, with its admixture of carnival atmosphere and reverent mysticism, has given Donna and me a glimpse into Ceylon's legendary past. Even today that kaleidoscopic past is everywhere evident.

We had arrived at a crucial time in the little nation's affairs. After drifting perilously close to bankruptcy and Communism, the island voted its leftist government out of office in March, 1965, and installed a democratic regime friendly to the West.

Now Ceylon, custodian of a culture 2,500 years old, struggled valiantly to establish a 20th-century identity. Its new government sought to broaden the economy, largely dependent on tea, rubber, and coconut products, and to instill a sense of unity and purpose among a diverse population of 11 million.

For seven weeks Donna and I crisscrossed the island, finding it surprisingly varied in

terrain and climate for such a relatively small area. Under a fiery sun we explored the northern plains, parched with drought from June to October but often inundated by northeast monsoon rains during the winter months. We climbed tortuous roads into Ceylon's south-central highlands, an area where nature rations rain and sunshine in delicate proportions to nurture tea bushes blanketing the contoured hills. And we followed the crescent of the southern plains, like the north a farming region subject to the capricious extremes of the monsoon cycle (map, page 454).

Between forays around the island, we savored Colombo—sprawling seaport capital, a city where bullock carts plod along in the shadow of modern skyscrapers. Not a section of Ceylon's largest city escaped our fascinated inspection. But, like most visitors, we always returned to the Pettah, or marketplace, whose narrow clogged streets resound in a raucous symphony of blaring horns from vintage cars and battered buses, of rumbling carts and chattering humanity (page 457).

A sweating porter, bent beneath bulging bags of rice, nudges me against a wall of tin kettles. Bounding out of his stall, a bearded Moor seizes upon my embarrassment at his tumbled wares to barter for a quick sale. I veto 10-gallon pails, but buy a Thermos jug.

In one cluttered shop, permeated with the pungence of fish and curries, I stop to finger the grocer's latest selection of large dried fish; they swing like stiff cardboard from a hook above baskets of Bombay onions, little red chilies, and black peppers.

Everywhere we hear betel vendors hawking a five-cent chew. Donna edges close to a vendor and watches. His customer selects a few choice chunks of areca nut, places them on a fresh betel leaf, then dips a dirty finger into a white paste of powdered limestone. He spreads the sticky lime on the nut and leaf—like mustard on a hot dog—then rolls up the concoction and pops it into his mouth. When the vendor offers Donna a sample, she flees.

The Pettah abruptly yields to Colombo's administrative and commercial center, the Fort, once the site of a Portuguese and later

Dark skin and golden nose "trills" identify this tea picker as an Indian Tamil. Her people have been brought from southern India since the 1830's to work on coffee, tea, and rubber plantations. Now more than a million strong, many still have close ties with India. Unlike them, a million Ceylon Tamils, whose forebears came centuries earlier, are citizens and may vote. Both groups are Hindu, set apart by religion and language from the Sinhalese, the island's Buddhist majority.

of a Dutch stronghold. Stark modern skyscrapers dwarf rows of government buildings
(above), boutiques and jewelry shops, and the
century-old Clock Tower. Money-changers
hustle rupees, street traders peddle National
Lottery tickets, and cycling salesmen push
Elephant House brand ice-cream wagons.

"Industrialize!"—Though Funds Are Scant

On the fringe of town Donna and I see another facet of Colombo's personality. Ducking
down a sleepy side street, we walk into the
roar of a new can factory. Huge hydraulic
presses slam in vibrating staccato, spitting
out thousands of tin cans. Above the din of
rending metal, away from the searing heat of
soldering machines, Mr. Basil Amerasinghe,
one of the owners, proudly tells us:

"Our factory marks one of Ceylon's first
efforts toward medium-scale manufacturing.
When we built it in 1963, we committed ourselves to mass production with expensive
machinery. Financing proved difficult, as few
European countries would risk new capital

here. Also, we had to train every technician—none could be found in Ceylon. But with enough capital and increased tin imports, I could employ more men, run at greater capacity, and meet all Ceylon's needs for cans."

Although Mr. Amerasinghe is succeeding, tremendous financial obstacles discourage many others from risking investments.

"The West strives to inspire the capitalist system, but won't support private industry," echoed another manufacturer. "Loans are negotiated only on a government-to-government

"A great island . . . resort of ships," wrote the sixth-century Greek trader Sopater of the land known today as Ceylon. The description holds. From the ends of earth ships still come, dropping anchor in the protected harbor of Colombo to take on tea, rubber, and coconut products. And a democratic government, now looking to the West, builds toward a return to onetime greatness. In the House of Representatives and the Secretariat, right foreground, government officials strive to keep faith with the island's original name—Lanka, the Resplendent.

453

Ceylon

Kankesanturai • • Point Pedro

Palk Strait

Jaffna •

PAKISTAN ★ **CHINA**
New Delhi ★ NEPAL
Karachi • PAKISTAN
• Calcutta
Bombay • **INDIA** BURMA
Rangoon ★
Arabian Sea
Bay of Bengal
0 — 500
STATUTE MILES
Indian Ocean Area enlarged
INDONESIA

Automobile and railroad
ferry service to
Dhanushkodi, India

Adam's Bridge
Mannar •

Gulf of Mannar

• Mullaittivu

Kanakarayan

Paranki

Ma

Vavuniya •

China Bay • Trincomalee
• Mutur

RUANWELI
DAGOBA

Anuradhapura •

Puttalam •

Kala

Mi

SIGIRIYA
FORTRESS

Sigiriya Fortress □ • Sigiriya
• Dambulla

• Polonnaruwa

Mahaweli

Maduru

• Eravur
• Batticaloa

Chilaw •

Maha

Kurunegala • • Matale

• Kalmunai

Katugastota
Kandy •
Negombo • Kegalla • Peradeniya

Gal Oya Dam

• Akkaraipat

Ekala •

*Pidurutalagala
8281 feet*

Kitulgala • Nuwara Eliya • Badulla
Colombo ★ Kolonnawa Norton • Dimbula Demodara
Kotte • Bridge Namunakuli
Adam's Peak 6671 feet
Moratuwa • *7360 feet* **U V A**
Panadura • • Haputale

• Pottuvil

Ratnapura •
Kalutara • • Balangoda
• Opanake
Beruwala •

TEA

RICE

Rakwana •

RUBBER

Ambalangoda •

Gin

Menik
RUHUNU
NATIONAL PARK

COCONUTS

Hikkaduwa •
Kaluwella •
Galle
Weligama •
Matara • *Dondra Head*

Walawe

• Hambantota

PRODUCED BY
NATIONAL GEOGRAPHIC SOCIETY ©
GEOGRAPHIC ART DIVISION
PAINTED BY LISA BIGANZOLI, COMPILED BY JOHN P. W

0 — 30
STATUTE MILES

CEYLON

PEARL pendant off the tip of India, the 270-mile-long land of the Lion People, the Sinhalese, is justly famed for gems and tea. This parliamentary state became an independent British Commonwealth member in 1948. Traditionally tolerant, Ceylon gives voice to four world faiths: Buddhism, Hinduism, Islam, and Christianity.

AREA: 25,332 sq. mi., slightly bigger than West Virginia. **POPULATION:** 11,000,000; 70 percent Sinhalese, 22 percent Tamil. **LANGUAGE:** Predominantly Sinhalese; Tamil and English also spoken. **ECONOMY:** Agricultural; second (to India) in world tea output, fourth in rubber. **MAJOR CITIES:** Colombo (510,947), capital and port; Trincomalee, port; Kandy, center of Buddhist culture and pageantry.

basis. Ceylon pleads to businessmen, 'Industrialize!' But when we respond, our national banks cry, 'Sorry, no credit available!' "

Near Colombo, at Ekala, the government has built an industrial complex to stimulate small manufacturing. It offers inexpensive factory facilities, electricity, water, and abundant labor. But limited foreign exchange has forced cutbacks of imported raw materials.

An owner who invested in the project lamented: "I have the finest German machinery for making carbon paper. My papers and ribbons equal any European imports into India or Southeast Asia. I know I can undersell those imports, if only Ceylon would lift its meager import quota for carbon black. Without carbon black, I'm finished. How can I pay for idle machines?"

Bare Treasury Confronted New Prime Minister

The destiny of Ceylon's fledgling industries—indeed of the entire nation—rests in the hands of Prime Minister Dudley Senanayake (below). Elected in March, 1965, he inherited a treasury so bare that funds had to be borrowed to meet payrolls for civil employees.

Earlier Ceylon writhed in economic chaos and political discontent. A leftist government, headed by the modern world's first woman prime minister, Mrs. S. W. R. D. Bandaranaike, threatened to suppress a critical free press. Rumors had it that she would

Prime Minister Dudley Senanayake heads a neutral coalition government struggling to stabilize and modernize Ceylon with help from the West. At the Royal Colombo Golf Club he plays with Dr. Bede Muller, a Burgher, as descendants of early European settlers are called. Declining to stoop, the caddy retrieves a golf ball with his toes.

EKTACHROMES (ABOVE AND BELOW) AND KODACHROME BY GILBERT M. GROSVENOR © N.G.S.

nationalize the large tea estates, which provide 65 percent of Ceylon's foreign exchange. As the government gravitated toward the Communist bloc, Western nations lost confidence in Ceylon.

"Our country was fighting for its life in perhaps its last free election," a brilliant Ceylonese lawyer told me. "All of us—professional men, intellectuals, and businessmen alike—laid aside our jobs, fanned out across the country, and vigorously campaigned against Mrs. Bandaranaike.

"For forty days I ran from speech to speech—sometimes ten a day. I'd leave home at dawn with three shirts and a flask of tea. The issues were fundamental, rising above caste, community, religion, or party.

"When Dudley Senanayake carried the vote, our country turned the corner. We chose not to be just cogs in the wheel of state, not to belong to the state, but rather to have it belong to us," the lawyer concluded.

Donna and I called upon the prime minister several times. A kind, modest, soft-spoken man, he discussed candidly the difficult problems confronting his country.

"First we must stabilize the economy," said Mr. Senanayake. "Our United National Party controls almost 100 of the 157 parliamentary seats, enough to ratify our programs.

"Like many small developing nations, we need foreign exchange to bolster our critical imports of food and raw materials, machinery and

Freshly cooked curries in covered platters await delivery by bicycle to businessmen in Colombo. Each morning boys collect the lunches from customers' homes and gather here in Cinnamon Gardens to sort them according to office buildings. After serving, they wait for the plates, sort them again by neighborhood, and return the empties—all for about five rupees ($1) a month.

Bullock carts rumble down the street. Autos honk through crowds. Sidewalk salesmen hawk eggs, fruits, brassware, and betel chews. Chickens squawk in portable cages (left). The time: any daylight hour at the Pettah, Colombo's market.

With trunk and toes, an elephant hoists a log at a lumbermill near Kitulgala. His mahout directs the work by shouted commands and pressure behind the ears. Bulldozer of Ceylon, the animal can haul 1,000-pound loads through trackless forests, yet it needs no spare parts, yearly tune-ups, or imported fuel.

Ceylon's elephants once roamed the island freely, property of kings. But shrinking jungle domain and elephant roundups cut numbers from 10,000 a century ago to fewer than 1,200 today. The government no longer grants licenses for capturing wild elephants for training.

Kneeling for a daily bath, the lumberjacks have hides scrubbed by their mahouts. At the command *"Dheri udheri"*—"Rinse, please"—they raise trunks like fire hoses and shoot water over spots freshly cleaned.

consumer goods. To earn additional foreign currency, we must increase our exports; tea, rubber, and coconut products are not enough."

The prime minister sighed. "But without raw materials, the task is difficult. For the next two or three years, aid is essential."

"Do you plan new industries?" I asked.

"We wish to encourage small industries to manufacture products that we now import or do without," he replied. "To support these industries, my government has recently lifted the ban on many essential imports, especially spare parts for lorries and machinery. Also, Western capital is again beginning to flow into Ceylon."

Economic Problems in a Land of Plenty

Later, strolling Colombo's crowded ocean front, I wondered if many Ceylonese shared Prime Minister Senanayake's deep concern over the nation's economic problems. I recalled the words of a Ceylonese friend: "In my land, where starvation is unknown, life touches our people lightly. Just thrust a stick into the ground, and it will bear fruit. Crack open a fallen coconut, and you will find nourishment."

We lingered with the throng of carefree Ceylonese families gathered on Colombo's mile-long ocean-front stretch of emerald turf known as the Galle Face Green. When the scorching sun lies spent on the horizon and cooling breezes blow across the green, a medley of faces, fair and dark, mingle here in a profusion of vivid saris and white sarongs, gay print dresses and European business suits.

Few small nations can claim a more plural society than Ceylon. The eight million Sinhalese Buddhists mix with two and a half million darker-skinned Hindu Tamils, plus a sprinkling of fairer Christian Burghers, who descend from early European settlers. Europeans and Ceylonese Moors add to the cultural montage.

More than 2,000 years ago, when much of Europe was still inhabited by barbarians, Ceylon boasted magnificent kingdoms built by Sinhalese upon the foundation of a great religion, Buddhism. The Sinhalese, a people from northern India, came by sail in the fifth or sixth century B.C. to settle on this island off the toe of India. They constructed huge artificial lakes and dug intricate irrigation canals. Appropriately, they called the land Lanka, meaning "resplendent." *

Buddhist Lanka prevailed for 1,800 years, despite repeated invasions by fierce Hindu warriors from southern India, the Tamils. For centuries the Sinhalese and Tamils fought, until finally all the dams and canals were destroyed and the land ravaged. What war had started, malaria finished, and by the early 16th century both the Buddhist and Hindu kingdoms had withered.

Ceylon, divided and exhausted, endured occupation by the Portuguese, and later by the Dutch and British. The island did not regain its independence until 1948.

Choice of Language Leads to Riots

Despite centuries of coexistence, Ceylon's diverse groups have maintained, in general, their own ethnic identities, even languages. Although the British endowed the island with an international tongue, in 1956 a fervid nationalistic government proclaimed Sinhalese the official language. This decision, rekindling ancient Tamil-Sinhalese feuds, led to bloodletting riots in 1958 and serious unrest as recently as early 1966.

Seeking a solution, the predominantly Sinhalese parliament has decreed that districts

*See "Ceylon, Island of the 'Lion People,'" by Helen Trybulowski Gilles, NATIONAL GEOGRAPHIC, July, 1948. 459

with Tamil majorities could use Tamil in their schools and local governments. However, since the central government and many businesses are conducted in Sinhalese, Tamils suffer a handicap when they compete with Sinhalese.

As one Ceylonese friend put it, "When we rejected English as our national language, we went from the solution to the problem."

But such concerns seem remote on Galle Face Green. The band plays "oom-pa-pa" melodies, children trot by on ponies, and 20-foot cobra kites dance overhead.

By late dusk the crowds melt away. Even the audacious crows, Ceylon's omnipresent pests, scavenge their last morsel and fly off, leaving the crashing breakers playing to an empty house. Piercing the solitude, a lighthouse beacon sweeps its watchful eye over the vital port, illuminating ships under all the flags of the globe waiting to exchange rice, flour, and dried fish for tea.

We, too, drift home to Cinnamon Gardens, where flaming sentries of flamboyant trees, flanked by walls of bougainvillea, guard the city's most fashionable residential suburb. Once it was a Dutch plantation, but its spice bushes have long since yielded to spacious, elegant houses, among them the home of our friends Cynthia and Vere de Mel.

"String-hoppers" Cool Fiery Curries

When we first arrived in Colombo, Cynthia had said: "You can't capture Ceylon from hotel rooms! You must come live with us."

The De Mels typify modern Ceylon. Although both are Sinhalese, Cynthia was reared as a Christian and English-educated. She married of her own choice, while girlhood friends still expected parentally arranged matches. Bright, beautiful, and effervescent, Cynthia skillfully manages her own travel agency. Vere, devoutly Buddhist and a former transportation official, owns Colombo's taxi service, Quickshaws.

Through Cynthia and Vere, we touched the pulsebeat of Ceylon, its gentle people. We ate torrid curries, always careful to take plenty of "string-hoppers"—spaghetti-like patties—as fire extinguishers for the more flammable dishes. Cynthia taught Donna to drape a sari, to bargain for fruits and vegetables in the market, and to prepare many Ceylonese delicacies.

We came to understand the old saying, "The Ceylonese are happiest with a stranger in their streets or a visitor on their doorstep."

Every day at the De Mels' was rewarding. But I vividly recall one evening in particular. Cynthia informed us: "The cook isn't well. He has been told an evil eye is cast upon him. Only a lime ceremony will drive away evil spirits, he feels."

"A lime ceremony?" I asked.

"A part of bali, devil worship," she said.

Bali, whose roots trace back to northern India, mysteriously blends astrology, demonism, and ancestor worship, forces that inexorably govern the lives of many Ceylonese. Vestiges of primitive popular religions, animism and witchcraft, are intricately and often subtly woven into contemporary religious behavior. Devotees calculate propitious moments for every act by the planets—the controlling spirits. Magic rites exorcise evil spirits and curry favor with benevolent ones.

"Go, Go You Devils"

At 9 p.m.—the auspicious time—the ceremony begins. Areca palm fronds and seven species of flowers adorn the altar—a porch chair. "There must be flesh from sea and land —see the dried fish and strip of leather?" Cynthia whispers. "The seven limes mean purification; the coins appease the gods."

The cook sits on a straw mat, hands folded in prayer on the altar. A bearded man in white sarong and open shirt begins chanting and throws incense into a smoldering pot.

"He's the *kapurala,* or doctor of magic lore," murmurs Cynthia. "First he invokes all the gods—Yama, Lakshmi, be present!—and names all the devils who must leave."

Squeezing a lime over the cook's head, the kapurala chants: "...all gods in heaven and earth stand witness.... Go, go you devils from the joints, and from the head let evil go away...." After touching each limb with split limes, he drops the limes into a bowl of water.

"He talks to the devils in a scolding manner, slipping from Sinhalese into Tamil," Cynthia explains. "Now he'll watch to see if an odd number of limes float face up to the surface— a very good sign."

Suddenly, a huge insect lights on Donna's arm. She swings viciously but misses. "Don't worry, he's a friendly spirit," Vere chuckles.

After 30 minutes of unbroken recitation, the kapurala ties a string around the patient's arm. A sprinkle with lime twigs, an anointment

Hanging onto a short tusk, a mahout brushes his elephant's teeth with a coconut husk. Light splotches are natural markings, not the result of wear and tear on hide.

"**Second Eden!**" Thus early Islamic traders called Ceylon, believing that Allah sent
Adam and Eve here to console them for the loss of Paradise. And beauty yet abides—

in exquisitely terraced and contoured hillsides, in watery mirrors being readied for
rice seedlings ... and in rolling, distant highland slopes, green with gardens of tea.

with hot oil, and the ceremony ends. If the doctor mispronounces even one word, the ceremony is unsuccessful.

"How long before the cure works?" I ask.

"When the aches and pains are gone, it has worked. The therapeutic effect isn't unlike a psychiatrist's couch," says Cynthia.

Next morning the cook looks happier, if not healthier. But several days later, when we leave the De Mels' for a journey into Ceylon's upcountry, I notice he still clings to the security of his string.

As always, we depart from Colombo at dawn, the city's most glorious hour. Not a soul stirs; only the screeching *koha* birds pierce the quiet of first light. Ocean breezes rustle the rain trees, and they unfold their leaves, splashing Colombo's pavements with cupfuls of moisture collected during the night. Nearby, smoke curls skyward from the waning embers of a funeral pyre.

Ceylonese Scarecrows Wear Sarongs

In scattered villages, as we pass, shadowy forms of children squat beside thatch-roofed houses and slosh themselves clean with jugs of water.

Foliage crowds the road with a wild luxuriance of palms and fruit-bearing trees: mango, breadfruit, jak, banana, pawpaw. Clusters of villages, tucked into the folds of hills, lie amid a woven pattern of paddy fields fringed with dark-green coconut palms. Croaking frogs and humming cicadas serenade sarong-draped scarecrows policing the fields of this pastoral paradise.

Rice knows no season here. Some fields near harvest as others are prepared for planting. Teams of buffalo heave powerful shoulders against wooden plows that sink deep into the rich ooze of watered fields. Lean sinewy men, naked to the waist and caked in mud, scold their protesting beasts. When the turf is turned, men paddle the mud into smooth sheets, now ready for flooding and planting.

Along the road slender barefoot women bear 60-pound bundles of wood atop their heads with a grace befitting royalty. When we stop to watch, inquisitive children swarm out of nowhere, surrounding us like bees around buttercups. Dark faces press so tightly about the car that windows fog.

Our driver Dan, perhaps embarrassed by their enthusiasm, explains, "Madam, they're as curious about you as you may be about them. Few Europeans stop to talk to the villagers."

We had not driven far when we saw him: an elephant, ponderous and gray, with his trunk twisted around a mass of palm fronds. We slowed our car as he swayed across the road. Perched on his back, like a flea on a moving mountain, a tiny mahout shouted commands and prodded with a spiked pole.

Just beyond, at a lumbermill near Kitulgala, these Ceylonese bulldozers neatly rolled huge logs

Sacred pinnacle hallowed throughout history, Adam's Peak (below) stands alone against the sky, 7,360 feet above the sea. Its crown cradles a three-foot-long depression shaped like a human footprint. Who stepped there? Followers of the Buddha believe he left the mark on one of his three

trips to Ceylon. Hindus see it as that of the god Siva. Certain early Christians gave St. Thomas credit for making the print. And Moslems hold that Adam himself stood on the peak.

Pilgrims join by night to climb the four-mile trail. At the holy summit (opposite), they pay homage to the footprint and greet dawn with prayer. Beyond these worshipers another wonder appears: The shadow cast at sunrise by the sacred mountain rises high against the clouds.

KODACHROMES BY GILBERT M. GROSVENOR (ABOVE)
AND BRIAN BRAKE © NATIONAL GEOGRAPHIC SOCIETY

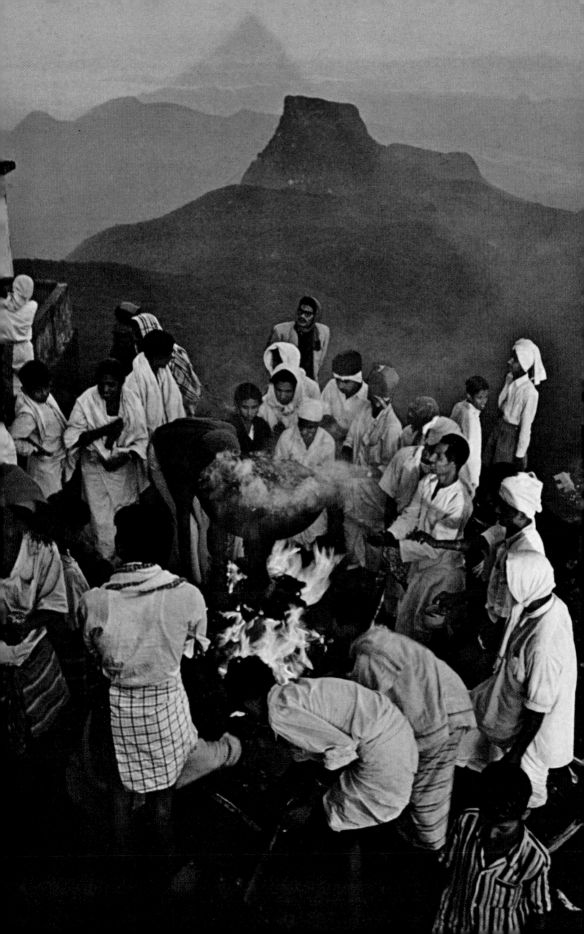

with their foreheads and feet. Then, hoisting the logs with their trunks, they flung them like twigs onto a pile.

In Ceylon's jungles, machines cannot compete with elephants. No mass of metal, bolts, and gears could daily tramp along rivers, weave through miles of tangled, swampy undergrowth, gather up a felled tree, and drag it back to the mill.

Elephants offer 50-year warranties—no parts, no overhauls, just a few hundred fronds and a daily wash (pages 458-9 and 461). Ceylon's elephant, an Indian breed, frequently tuskless, is considered more easily tamed than the larger African elephant.

"Owning an elephant brings great pres-

tige," Dan remarked. "Depending upon training, age, and ability to work, they cost from 10,000 to 20,000 rupees [$2,000 to $4,000]."

Adam's Peak Bears Hallowed Footprint

We continued ascending into the clouds as the road coiled around sheer mountain walls. Dizzily they spilled away into a panorama of misty waterfalls tumbling down a verdant backdrop of undulating hills. Among the hills the cone of Adam's Peak rose like a natural cathedral (pages 464-5). A shallow depression at its peak is hallowed by three great religions.

Predictably, Dan knew well the mountain's legends. "We Buddhists believe that Adam's Peak bears the holy footprint of Lord Buddha.

Plucking tea "flushes"—the tender buds and adjoining two leaves—workers at Norton Bridge toss them into baskets without a backward glance. After withering, rolling, fermenting, and drying, teas go to tasters. At the Brooke Bond tea plant in Colombo, Mr. Michael Tissera spits out a sample, one of perhaps 200 he will taste in a day. Judging taste, color, and aroma, he decides how much his company will offer the grower.

Hindus deem it their god Siva's mountain. Moslems say that Adam, hurled from Paradise, stood here a thousand years atoning for his sin. Finally he was reunited with Eve, and they lived in Lanka for many centuries, propagating humankind."

Generations of pilgrims have toiled by torchlight up the perilous cliffs to await sunrise and the mysterious shadow cast by the sacred mountain. Today sturdy stairs and protective rails ascend the cliff face, replacing notched stone steps and huge chains anchored into the solid rock by unknown hands centuries ago.

"Many times I've climbed to the summit with pilgrims when the weather was favor-

able," Dan told us. "But in times past, climbing Adam's Peak was very dangerous. I've heard that high winds used to sweep pilgrims from the cliff face and hurl them into the valley below. But still the aged, the ill, and the crippled hobbled painfully up the final precipice, driven by faith and hope."

We could not follow the time-worn trail trod by the ranks of pilgrims. It was the time of the southwest monsoon, when the climb was most treacherous. Paths lighted at other times were dark; resthouses along the way were shuttered tight; and leopards and other threatening animals prowled the slopes.

Reaching the mountains of mile-high Nuwara Eliya, Ceylon's picturesque resort area

EKTACHROMES (ABOVE AND BELOW) AND KODACHROME © N.G.S.

about 100 miles east of Colombo, we looked out on a patchwork quilt of cultivation. Serried ranks of tea bushes stretched across the horizon, contoured to peak and valley like a tailored knit dress. The delicately manicured plants had been "tipped," or trimmed, waist-high, bushy and flat-topped. Tea bushes (*Camellia sinensis*) would tower 40 feet high unless severely pruned every one to five years. Many produce for 50 years.

Tamils Tend Ceylon's Tea Crop

More than 400,000 Indian Tamils, workers and offspring of workers imported during the past century from southern India, tend the 590,000 acres under cultivation. Unlike Ceylon Tamils, whose ancestors came much earlier, many of these Indian Tamils still have close ties with India.

Throughout the upcountry, in tea-growing altitudes between 2,000 and 7,000 feet, large estates offer Tamil families free housing, schools, and hospital care. Although individuals are paid very little, households frequently include four or five wage earners. Women tend tea slopes, men operate heavy machinery, and children often work between classes, or full time after elementary schooling.

Since independence, successive Ceylonese governments, struggling with chronic unemployment, have debated deporting these unfranchised Indian Tamils back to the continent to create jobs for the Sinhalese. I asked an estate manager about this problem.

"Tea production would cease without Indian Tamil labor," he said. "Most Sinhalese refuse to till the soil for these wages. 'They'd rather eat jak fruit,' as the saying goes. Without tea exports, everyone, including the government, would be unemployed."

While we talked, a rainbow trail of brightly

Like green-carpeted stairs, rice fields climb a hill near Kandy; a fringe of palms breaks the symmetry. Though some farms harvest two crops a year, Ceylon must still import $60,000,000 worth of rice annually, half the amount eaten by her people.

Golden chaff rains from the basket of a worker winnowing rice near Demodara.

Love of water sends this Sinhalese beauty to the village stream for a daily bath. Love of company holds her there, chattering with friends as she pours potfuls of water over her head—so many for luck, so many for health, so many for coolness.

Skimming the waves at close to 15 knots, its single sail ballooning, a fishing outrigger off Negombo heads for home. In these slender, seaworthy craft, Ceylonese sailors venture 65 miles from home ports. Such primitive methods, however, make the industry

clad Tamil women (page 451) wound past us. The women bore loaded wicker baskets cinched high on their backs by straps over their foreheads. Earlier, I had watched these nimble-fingered women pluck the new, tender "flush"—two leaves and a bud. Now they headed for the processing factory.

We followed them to the top floor, where green leaves were thinly spread over nylon "tats," or shelves, for withering.

"Hold your skirt!" the teamaker warned Donna as we walked over grill-covered ducts. "Our huge blowers circulate hot air through the withering lofts, evaporating moisture from the leaf and leaving it soft and pliable."

He led us down steep wooden stairs to a floor crowded with monstrous machinery. Puzzled, I asked, "Do you really need such heavy equipment to crush a tiny tea leaf?"

"These rollers must daily twist and curl thousands of pounds of leaves," said the teamaker. "The machines crush cells to liberate aromatic juices—the essence of tea. They must work quickly, yet delicately.

"Then we put the leaves in a cool, moist room to accelerate oxidation, during which green tea turns bright copper. The tricky part is deciding when to choke off oxidation, at precisely the proper time, by 'firing,' or heating. The copper leaf turns black, as carefully

470

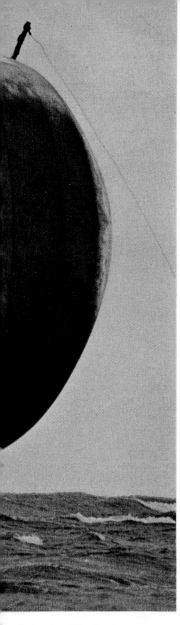

inefficient, and Ceylon must continue to import fish until modern vessels replace the outrigger fleets.

Toddy tapper inches across a taut ropeway between coconut palms to gather sap in the treetops. Liquid collected in the pot yields potent Ceylonese drinks.

controlled driers reduce water content to 3 percent. Finally, we sort the 'made tea' into commercial grades, ready for shipment."

Taste of Tea Reveals Weather in Uva

Competition in the sale of tea is keen. Samples are whisked daily by jets from Ceylon to world markets. We visited the Brooke Bond tea company, where Mr. T. Jayalingam, sales director of the Colombo office, predictably invited, "Join me for tea?"

"Hmm, not bad," he brightened, taking a sip. "Weather's still clear at Uva."

"Yes, we've just returned from there. But how did you know?" I asked naively.

"This new tea sample from an Uva estate is top quality, with good body. Only dry days and cool nights produce such quality," he explained. "Tea contains tannin, an astringent; caffeine, a stimulant; water; and an essential oil for flavor. The oil remains mysterious, but we know that flavor varies with an estate's altitude, rain, sun, soil, plucking, processing, blending, and other factors."

"Blending?" I questioned.

"Naturally. Americans prefer 'pointy,' light-flavored, high-grown teas from Dimbula or Nuwara Eliya; the English like 'thick' teas, with more body, from Uva," he explained.

"Pointy? Thick?" This was another tongue.

Ceylon's fabulous gems, to early Chinese, were the crystallized tears of the first man. Arab traders, too, marveled at the precious stones; in *The Arabian Nights,* Sindbad visited the King of Ceylon "on the battlements of whose palace are a thousand jewels."

A Colombo jewelry firm, Macan Markar, treasures this collection, including a 485-carat sapphire at upper right. Others are a chrysoberyl cat's-eye, lower right, star ruby, yellow sapphire, two star sapphires, square-cut aquamarine, and alexandrite at lower left. Rare stones also garb the ivory elephant.

Pit sunk in mud at Ratnapura yields gem-bearing gravel. Miners pan and sort their hauls in the clear water of a nearby stream.

Like cranes standing on one leg, fishermen perch on stilts to cast for spotted herring in shallow waters near Matara.

"Tasters classify teas with specific terms," said the patient Mr. Jayalingam. "Pungent, pointy, meaty, body, bakey, thick—those terms describe taste. Coppery, dull, bright—those define infusion, or the moist tea leaf. We're tasting now. Have a look."

White-robed technicians whispered in a room so quiet you could hear a tea leaf drop. Then I detected a curious "shush," like sand sifting into a tin pan, followed by a "slurp," and finally the sound of spittle finding a spittoon.

A crisp voice announced, "Alpha, little flaky, thick, bright, rupees 2.20."

"He's rated another lot of medium-grown tea," Mr. Jayalingam whispered.

Light Must Be Right for Tasting

Tiptoeing past a long table lined with bowls of tea, each beside a tin of tea, I unwittingly paused beside a window.

"Please move," the taster requested.

"He tastes only against north light," Mr. Jayalingam explained (page 467). "Color of the infusion and of the liquor are vital in judging tea, and change with light. We taste under precise conditions to match established standards."

I felt like a bull among tea cups.

"We prescribe 6.5 grams of tea per bowl, steeped exactly six minutes with freshly boiled filtered water, plus two teaspoons of fresh, TB-tested milk. No sugar. When the tea cools, we taste," said Mr. Jayalingam.

"You try it," he insisted. "First sift dried tea through your fingers into the tin tray to determine texture. Slurp up a sample of tea—it's polite in tea-tasting society—in fact a necessity, to fully savor the flavor; now, swish the tea around your palate; then, spit. Never swallow!"

Slurping was trained out of me at an early age, and I found it difficult to emulate the taster. But I must admit to getting the range of the spittoon after only one dribble on my tie and a squirt on the taster's shoes.

I soon distinguished subtleties between estate teas, but invariably judged the top quality to be inferior. Just when I thought I had learned the art, I spat out a thick tea, declaring it unfit to drink. Mr. Jayalingam winced. I had defamed his finest Uva sample.

He sighed. "Time for a break."

Back in his office, Mr. Jayalingam excitedly read an overseas cable. "Oh, no! They're fluorinating their water. I must alter the blend. Let's see, add pungence and...."

"Tea Party" Colors China Bay

We left our friend to his problems and headed toward Trincomalee, Ceylon's northeast port, whence much tea is shipped overseas. From his dockside office, Mr. Lionel Keess, manager of the Trincomalee Tea Administration, surveyed the fleet of freighters anchored in the China Bay harbor.

"We've just loaded one million pounds of tea. That gray freighter's bound for England, via Aden and Suez; the one moored close aboard heads to Australia; that black one getting up steam sails for Boston, New York, Philadelphia, Baltimore, Jacksonville, and Galveston. An average day," Mr. Keess mused.

Below us, laborers, their backs lumped black with calluses, muscled 125-pound tea chests aboard lighters that ferried the cargo to the ships. Booms angled out from the freighters like tentacles of an octopus, holding nets to haul aboard the precious cargo.

"Ceylon exported 455 million pounds of tea in 1963, and again in 1964," Mr. Keess said. "Trincomalee handled 315 million of those pounds in 1963, while Colombo and Galle shared the balance. With the cyclone, Trincomalee's 1964 volume shrank to 265 million."

"The cyclone?" Donna inquired.

"It hit December 22, 1964—I'll never forget it!" Mr. Keess said. "A howling northwest gale blew up and forgot to stop. Winds gusted to 150 miles per hour. All 36 lighters sank, and 8,000 chests of tea, almost a million pounds, floated in the harbor—our Trincomalee tea party," the Englishman joked.

Later, driving toward the beach in search of Trincomalee's fishing fleet, Donna groaned and commented, "It's sure a long way from plucking 'two leaves and a bud' to dunking a 'Flo-thru' tea bag."

Fishermen Race Home Under Sail

We found the long sandy beach bare of boats. The fleet had taken to sea the previous night, but it was expected back soon from fishing grounds five to ten miles offshore.

How curious, I thought, that Ceylon should be so dependent upon an agrarian economy when it floats in an ocean teeming with a limitless wealth of fish. Why does Ceylon yearly import 50 million rupees' worth of dried or tinned fish? I would soon find out.

At first only white specks dot the distant blue waters. As I watch, the specks blossom into canvas; then long slender hulls and outriggers pop above the horizon (page 470). They race at a fantastic pace, driven by a fresh quartering breeze and following sea, planing at top speed of perhaps 15 knots.

Smartly, each helmsman spills the wind and slides off the waves, killing momentum just as his outrigger grounds. I join eager lads on shore, lending a hand to beach the craft.

The skipper calls cadence in rhythm with the breaking surf. Together we push the vessel far up the shore, well above the tide line.

"Any luck?" I ask.

"Not much for a night's work—a few seerfish, some mackerel, and a couple of tuna," answers a tired, discouraged fisherman.

After dark, I squeeze aboard a small outrigger. I help my fishing mate, Paddy Singho, paddle. In his small boat, we dare not venture out of sight of Trincomalee's lights.

Breeze-whipped cloud of cotton cloth, destined for saris, dries at a fabric-printing factory at Ekala, 15 miles north of Colombo. Although part of an industrial complex built by the government, the factory wrestles with a problem common to other new Ceylonese enterprises. Capable of producing a thousand saris a day, the factory turns out only 480 because of the scarcity of cotton cloth, which must be imported from India. Thus the lack of materials and limited foreign exchange hamper Ceylon's industrial growth.

Bellying in the breeze, outrigger sails dry in the late-afternoon sun at Trincomalee. Ceylon's magnificent port on the Bay of Bengal. Slender coconut palms bend their

Three miles off the shore Paddy lowers a square-framed net about five feet down; then, to attract fish, he lights a bright kerosene lamp lashed amidships. Carefully, we rehearse the routine: When a fish surfaces below the light, Paddy will jerk the net upward, trapping the catch. With a smaller hooplike net, I will scoop the fish aboard.

A dark sky broods on the horizon. Thunderbolts clash and lightning sparks the night, but directly overhead the stars shine. Like a reflection of these stars, two hundred kerosene lights twinkle in the undulating seas.

For hours we thrash about in the growing swell. No fish. More hours pass.

The thunder growls. Lightning stabs closer, but we hold to the sea. No fish.

First a sprinkle, then the wet sound of the approaching downpour. Now I see the curtain of rain closing across the bay. Still no fish.

We blow out the light and paddle for the beach. On shore, we are not the only ones heading for home—away from the fish market. Until a modern deepwater fleet replaces outriggers, fishermen will reap scant harvests, and Ceylon must import dried fish.

Government Recognizes Fishermen's Needs

When Paddy Singho and I parted company, I was filled with pity for this frustrated, lonely man, whose family lived far away in Kaluwella village, along Ceylon's southwest coast. He could afford neither the bus fare nor the time to visit them. Not until the southwest

EKTACHROMES © NATIONAL GEOGRAPHIC SOCIETY

ıfted heads to the murmuring voice of the sea—
ıithout which, say the islanders, they cannot live.

monsoon passed would Paddy dare sail his outrigger home to Kaluwella.

As Donna and I drove south, my thoughts drifted back to Prime Minister Senanayake. He knew the plight of Ceylon's fishermen.

"When the Bandaranaike government subsidized the fishing industry, funds evaporated into fishermen's villages for housing, food, and other needs," said the prime minister. "But we're investing our rupees in a more efficient fleet: ocean-going ships, hydraulic winches, nylon nets, electronic gear. Our vessels will range far out into the Indian Ocean, where vast quantities of fish are caught."

Perhaps someday Paddy Singho will not return to port empty-handed.

Beyond Haputale, as we continued south,

the crisp, clear air and tropical lushness of the hill country abruptly wilted away to low scrub jungle. Here a sparse populace scratched parched soil for a meager subsistence. Salt flats stretched across the land's blanched face near the village of Hambantota. At Ruhunu National Park, elephants, deer, and bears wandered its vast expanse, desperately seeking some undiscovered pool (map, page 454).

But at Dondra Head, Ceylon's southernmost tip, the monsoon breezes were bracing. A lonely lighthouse guarded the headlands, as if to cover scars incised when the great temple of Dondra was desecrated by the Portuguese in the 16th century. Those were ruthless days.

When Portuguese caravels probed for rich   477

Oriental markets, they first touched Ceylon at Galle. As trade routes to the Far East developed, the Portuguese took cinnamon, gems, and elephants from Ceylon to Europe, spreading the island's fame afar.

The Portuguese brought the Cross to Ceylon. Dr. Richard Spittel, an elderly surgeon and anthropologist, bluntly expressed Ceylonese feelings when he commented to us, "The Portuguese forced their faith with fire and sword on 'heathens' whose traditions and religion predated Christianity."

Near Matara, as we followed the coast from Dondra Head, we spotted near-naked fishermen seated precariously atop slender vertical poles in the frothy surf (page 473).

Sunlight reflected a glint of wriggling silver as one man jerked rod and line upward and deftly unhooked a tiny fish, which he stowed in a straw basket belted about his waist.

"They are after *korrumburua,* a small fish we use in our hottest curries," Dan told us. "Because the fish frighten easily, the men must sit very quietly on their stilts. Only during the southwest monsoon, when seas are too high for boats to sail offshore, do they fish here. On a good day a man may catch 300 little herring, worth about 15 rupees."

On the beach a wiry, weathered old man, with long silver hair knotted behind in a tortoise-shell comb, broke open a young coconut, offering us a drink of its sweet, clear water.

"*Bohoma stuthi,*" Donna replied. His face-splitting grin beamed approval of her Sinhalese "thank you."

Late-afternoon shadows were creeping across Galle when we stopped for the night at the charming Hotel Closenberg, overlooking the town's churches and red-tiled Dutch rooftops. Quiet ramparts of the old Dutch fort still stand, facing the sea on three sides.

After the Dutch wrested control of the island from the Portuguese in 1658, they developed inland trade and ruled with a gentler hand. When Napoleon overran the Netherlands, Great Britain seized the opportunity to take control of Ceylon.

As dawn broke we continued our journey, hugging tiny silver bays and sanded expanses of beach carved into the southwest coast. At Hikkaduwa resort, a miniature Great Barrier Reef sparkled under sapphire seas

Leaves of plantain for their plates, the floor for their table, the Kandasamy family dines on rice and tortoise in a one-room home on China Bay. Mr. Kandasamy pilots a lighter shuttling tea crates from docks to ships in Trincomalee's harbor.

Whirling into a trance, dancers transform a courtyard into a festival ground at Kolonnawa, a Colombo suburb. To honor two Hindu gods, Vishnu and the God of Kataragama, they twirl ecstatically, lifting arched wooden frames called *kavadis*. Buddhists, also recognizing the Hindu deities, fly their bright flags. Suddenly, drummers pound faster. Villagers push closer. And those who will fulfill religious vows by self-mortification step forward.

EKTACHROME © N.G.S.

in a kingdom of coral gardens, a skin-diver's paradise.

A few miles farther, at Ambalangoda, Dan told us, "We are in the heart of bali country. We should visit one of the fine devil dancers and mask carvers who live here."

Chips were flying from a partially chiseled grotesque mask when we interrupted Mr. Ariyapala Wijesooriya, a sun-bronzed man with silver hair and piercing eyes. Laying down his mallet, he spoke proudly of his heritage.

"My family has danced and carved masks for a hundred years. My father taught me; his father taught him. To my eldest son I will pass on the secret bali charms and a knowledge of astrology, enabling him to read a sick person's horoscope and prescribe the healing charms."

We handled several of his beautifully carved enameled masks—Nagaraksha, the cobra god; Gurularaksha, the bird god with hawk eyes and parrot beak. In devil dancing, particular masks for specific illnesses must be worn to drive away the evil spirits.

The old man noticed Donna scrutinizing a gold chain and amulet adorning his neck.

"The rulership of the planet Saturn threatens ill omens for me. I wear this astrological sign, which I charmed 100,000 times, to ward off any evil effects. Saturn will rule 19 years, six of which have already passed."

"What form would this evil take?" I asked.

"Perhaps sickness, or loss of favor with friends or in my work," said Mr. Wijesooriya.

Astrology touches every stratum of society in Ceylon. A person's horoscope is predicted by reading mathematical charts pinpointing the planets' positions at the time of birth. Movement of these planets during a person's lifetime determines his fortune, chronicled on *ola* leaves (talipot palm) by an astrologer using a metal stylus and black powder.

Horoscopes oftentimes influence the selection of a profession, or even a marriage partner. Each day newspapers carry advertisements such as this: "Goigama Buddhist family seek suitable husband for attractive 25-year-old daughter with stenographer skills.

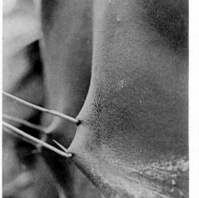

Dowry 10,000 rupees. Bring horoscope. Apply at. . . ."

We tested astrology for ourselves when Mr. P. A. Ediri-weera, Dan's employer at Ceylon Tours, surprised us by having our horoscopes cast by his astrologer. With astonishment we read accurate accounts of significant, and even minute, incidents from our pasts: A back injury of mine, almost to the day; an important decision by my wife was detailed (thank goodness she answered "Yes!"). However, there seemed to be one slight anomaly: While we both are to be proud parents of a daughter, I some-how am to be blessed with additional dividends—two sons. If the astrologer found this difficult to explain, I find it downright impossible!

Leaving Hikkaduwa and driving along the coast, we headed inland 40 miles to Ratnapura, City of Gems. I needed no astrologer to remind me that Donna auspi-ciously timed our arrival to coincide with her birthday.

Hooks pierce, lances stab, but no expression reveals pain in age-old rites shocking to Western eyes. Ful-filling vows, ten men stop frenzied dancing to endure the ceremony of flesh-piercing. Prime participant, Mohotty first rubs their skin with sa-cred ash. Then, grimacing, he forces lances into the flesh of a stoic wor-shiper, and drives a skewer through the cheeks of another, shown with a tongue depressor. Not a drop of blood flows. Mohotty promised one of his gods to endure an ordeal each year if a murder charge against his father was dropped. With hooks sunk into his back (above), he drags a heavy cart (right) while wearing spiked sandals.

Enthusiastically, she hinted that the Queen of Sheba's jewels were found near Ratnapura, and that Ceylon's famous gems sparkle in the world's finest collections.

Some enchantment faded as we watched men toiling in slimy pits and semidarkness 60 feet beneath a paddy field. Basketfuls of *illam,* or gem gravel, were hoisted to the surface, then swished round and round in a nearby river until all the mud washed away. Amid the residue of colored pebbles, perhaps a priceless treasure would appear.

But, as Mr. Bhadra Marapana, a friend and gem collector, told us: "More fortunes are squandered in the search than are made by hitting the jackpot. If you wish stones from Ceylon, purchase a sapphire or a cat's eye. Colombo has many fine gem stores."

Suddenly Donna was anxious to return to the capital, a two-hour drive from Ratnapura.

In Colombo, Dan steered us to Macan Markar's, a jewelry shop specializing in unique stones. Deep in its vault, Donna gingerly fingered in one hand a 485-carat blue sapphire valued at $250,000 (page 472); in the other she held a 105-carat cat's eye, worth $150,000.

"Ceylon has the finest cat's eyes in the world," a director told us. Noting Donna's covetous sparkle, he added, "But this one is not for sale. It's been the family mascot for a hundred years, bringing good luck to all three generations of sons in the firm."

I found it vastly flattering to be thought a prospective buyer of a $150,000 stone.

A Vow to Walk the Fiery Path

We had just reached the De Mel home when Dan telephoned. He told me, excitedly, "I have learned of a fire-walking ceremony in Kolonnawa village, near Colombo. Before the

481

ceremony, a man named Mohotty will pierce his body with needles and pull a cart roped to hooks in his back."

Now it was my turn to be excited, if a bit skeptical. Hurriedly I gathered up my camera gear, and we piled into Dan's car for the short drive. From the main road we heard lively flutes and drums resounding from the small courtyard of a village house. Fronds of margosa, the tree of purity, decorated doorways; coconut flowers, alms to the Hindu God of Kataragama, adorned the doorstep of the house; and Buddhist flags of brilliant blue, yellow, red, white, and orange flew from ropes strung around a small shrine laden with fruit and incense (page 479).

"Why do they fly Buddhist flags at a Hindu ceremony?" asked Donna.

"Madam, many Buddhists take part in Hindu ceremonies of piercing and fire walking," explained Dan. "The Hindu deities for these rites, Vishnu and the God of Kataragama, are recognized by Buddhists, and Hindus in turn pay homage to the Buddha."

A tall, fragile-looking man with soft, calm eyes appeared and introduced himself as Mohotty. Anticipating our questions, he explained: "I walked the coals in devotion many times as a young man, but when my father was falsely accused of murder, I vowed that if he was found innocent, I would reconfirm my faith each year by walking the fiery path and enduring the needles. This I have done ever since he was freed 16 years ago."

EKTACHROMES (ABOVE AND RIGHT) AND KODACHROME © N.G.S.

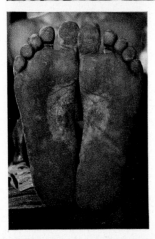

Fire-walker possessed by belief dances across coals measured at 1,328° F.—hot enough to melt aluminum—yet he shows no sign of pain. Other men, women, and children follow, not once but two and three times, believing that the longer they stay on the coals, the more merit they gain. Afterward, the feet of Mohotty (left) bear traces of ash on the instep and dirt from the ground around the fire, but not a blister. Skeptics offer explanations: Villagers harden their soles by years of walking barefoot; ash on the coals serves as insulation; perspiration protects the feet. But to the few who consider the fire the only way to fulfill religious pledges, the answer lies in steadfast conviction.

Stream of the faithful, their raised hands cupping lotus blossoms, flows humbly before the huge figure of the Buddha, reclining in the attitude of entering nirvana, the state of eternal happiness. The standing figure may be that of the living Buddha or his disciple Ananda, his grief forever etched in stone. The shrine survives amid the ruins of Polonnaruwa, majestic

Mohotty's words sent my eyes searching his face and body for puncture scars. Not a mark could I find.

Suddenly, drums pound a faster rhythm, and the villagers crowd closer as ten dancers, thrashing their heads violently from side to side, whirl around the courtyard.

The dancers kneel, and Mohotty rubs their cheeks, arms, and chests with sacred ash. They stare with glazed, half-closed eyes,

bodies motionless, as Mohotty forces skewers through each man's cheeks. Not a drop of blood seeps from the wounds, nor is there any expression of pain.

Mohotty Submits to Steel and Fire

Then steel pierces Mohotty's own cheeks; needles drive into his arms from shoulder to wrist; tiny arrowheads sink into his chest and stomach; spiked clogs are lashed to his feet.

capital of medieval Ceylon. In the 12th century King Parakrama Bahu the Great had the reclining Buddha carved and the city adorned with parks and palaces, baths and temples; he wanted to make all Lanka "a festive island . . . like unto a wishing tree." But Parakrama's wishing tree withered, and his capital fell to the jungle. Excavation began early this century.

Straining, three men drive fearsome hooks into Mohotty's lower back, but only once does he sway, as if faint. He seems coherent, but lost in utter supplication to his gods.

Ropes attached to the cart and tied to hooks in Mohotty's back pull taut against stretching flesh. Slowly, he draws the creaking cart around the courtyard. We gasp. Children, wide-eyed, reach for their mothers' hands. Only Mohotty remains expressionless.

"What is your secret?" I question him later.

"My secret?" he repeats. "Faith, total faith in my gods. Now, if you'll excuse me, I will enter my little shrine to pray."

A great fire smolders until long after midnight, when chanting dancers, gleaming with perspiration, circle the red-hot embers. One man collapses; others drag him away.

At 4 a.m. my friend Ed Lark, an American movie photographer and lecturer, measures the temperature of the coals with an optical pyrometer from the Ceylon Institute of Scientific and Industrial Research. The pyrometer registers 1,328° F. Since Ed is also a trained engineer familiar with this precise instrument, I trust his measurement.

Crowds perching on banks fall still as a young man dances across the 20-foot carpet of coals, twisting his body and feet as he moves (page 483). Then another man follows, scooping up handfuls of embers and throwing them over his shoulders. Nearly twenty men, women, boys, and girls firewalk, not once, but two and three times.

Mohotty crosses the fire four times, twice with his young son on his shoulders.

The crowds chant, *"Haro-hara."*

When it is over, we rush to thank Mohotty for letting us photograph the ceremony. Smiling, as if reading our minds, he sits and lifts his feet. They bear no trace of burns or blisters.

Well after dawn we fall into bed, but sleep evades us. Our minds cannot digest the incredible sights we have witnessed, nor can we explain them by hypnosis or drugs, tricks or gimmicks. What we saw was real, as real as the faith upon which these believers base their immunity from pain of steel or flame.

Religious faith has always shaped Ceylon. This was especially true in ancient days when faith, inspired by the Buddha, brought about the rise of the Sinhalese Kingdom.

Seeking the remnants of that splendid ancient civilization, we journeyed northward across the scorched, wasted plains, beyond the cities of today, to where the buried citadels of Ceylon's golden age sleep.

Saffron-robed youngsters, carrying begging bowls and parasols, study to be monks at a Buddhist school in Colombo. Mrs. Grosvenor asked one why he wished to be a monk. "To make my journey to nirvana shorter," he told her.

Ceylon's most famous dagoba (opposite), Ruanweli preserves relics of the Buddha at Anuradhapura, the island's capital even before Polonnaruwa. Built of brick, the shrine has at its top a crystal, the gift of Burma, that refracts sunlight into all colors of the rainbow.

At Anuradhapura, oldest, most glorious Sinhalese capital, we paused in quiet meditation beneath the sacred bo tree, planted 2,250 years ago, according to Buddhist belief, as a branch from the parent tree under which Buddha attained enlightenment.

Before us, huge domed dagobas (opposite), impenetrable structures of brick enshrining the holy relics of the Buddha, brooded over the crumbling bones of great palaces, pavilions, and shrines, outlined by weathered walls and ruined promenades. Wooded parks and sparkling man-made lakes suggested the ordered splendor of the past. We explored silent paths once trod by 10,000 saffron-robed Buddhist monks. At the grassy basement of the Brazen Palace, we imagined its fantastic nine stories, its rooms festooned with gold and silver, the ivory throne of its great hall.

Enriched by 90 kings, Anuradhapura stood from the fifth century B.C. until treasure-seeking Tamils finally destroyed it in the 11th century.

We, too, retreated from the heat of Anuradhapura, guided by bands of chattering black-faced langur monkeys in the trees lining the road that weaves 65 miles to Polonnaruwa, second great capital of the Sinhalese.

An oasis set in north-central Ceylon, Polonnaruwa is a monument to King Parakrama Bahu the Great, who in the 12th century carved vast statues and built shrines that still exist (pages 484-5). But the water system he left marks perhaps his greatest achievement.

"The tank [derived from the Portuguese word *tanque,* meaning "reservoir"] is still one of our largest," Dan told us. "The ancient

bund damming the valley stretches eight and a half miles. At capacity, the man-made lake covers 18,000 acres.

"A few years ago, engineers reconstructed the tank," Dan recalled. "It had lain in ruins ever since invading Tamils destroyed it 800 years ago. The engineers unearthed the king's original sluices and spillways—precisely where the new ones were to be placed."

Citadel of a Remorseful King

Forty miles from Polonnaruwa, we explored a huge russet-and-black mound of granite that looms like a great sulking beast 600 feet above the plains. There, at Sigiriya, the spirit of once-upon-a-time still broods (opposite).

In the fifth century A.D., in Anuradhapura, lived King Dhatu Sena with his two sons—one wicked, the other good. The wicked son, Kasyapa, murdered his father and seized the throne. The good son, Moggallana, fled, escaping assassins sent by his usurper brother.

Haunted by remorse for his deed, fearing his exiled brother and the quiet condemnation of his subjects, Kasyapa abandoned Anuradhapura for Sigiriya, the great rock rising sheer and lonely out of the wilderness.*

Around the base he cleared 50 acres for a city and encircled it with a mighty moated wall. On the very summit Kasyapa built an

*See "Sigiriya, a Fortress in the Sky," by Wilson K. Norton, NATIONAL GEOGRAPHIC, November, 1946.

EKTACHROME (ABOVE) AND KODACHROME BY GILBERT M. GROSVENOR © N.G.S.

Fortress built in fear: A terrified king who had murdered his father lived atop Sigiriya, or Lion Rock, a 600-foot-high granite monolith. Kasyapa moved his capital here from Anuradhapura to escape his brother's vengeance. A gallery, starting between gigantic lion's paws, leads up the sheer cliff to the three-acre top. Only ruins remain of Kasyapa's majestic palace. Donna Grosvenor, climbing the slippery face, braves whipping winds and the hordes of wasps that are the only inhabitants of Sigiriya.

Classic features of a Kandyan dancer echo the golden beauty of the Sigiriya frescoes. Of 500 figures that once graced the ascent to Kasyapa's lofty palace, only 21 remain, protected by a granite overhang. The ladies stand half-hidden by clouds, and though seemingly barebreasted, they actually wear gossamer blouses. Charmed visitors scratched verses of praise on a polished wall nearby—among the earliest examples of Sinhalese poetry.

Goddesses or court ladies? No one knows. But these voluptuous damsels glow with a life of their own—a tribute to unknown Sinhalese artists of 1,500 years ago.

Exquisite climbing lily, *Gloriosa superba* lives up to its name, but its yamlike root contains a deadly poison.

Vedda boy, descendant of Ceylon's nomadic aborigines, roams the jungle in search of food. He carries a bow and arrow and an ax. Veddas cling to traditional customs, but their numbers dwindle under pressure of advancing civilization and intermixture with other races.

Highland capital of the last Ceylonese kings, flower-scented Kandy borders a limpid lake. During the full moon of midsummer, the sleepy city throbs with animation as visitors come to witness Perahera (pages 448-9).

impregnable fortress in the sky, from which he ruled his kingdom for 18 years.

To reach the summit fortress, we hiked up endless terraced stairs, then walked halfway around the rock along a narrow corridor cut into the cliff and flanked by a 9-foot-high parapet. En route we stopped to admire Kasyapa's art gallery—the exquisite frescoes of the renowned and sensuous "Ladies of Sigiriya," who forever hide their identity behind taunting smiles (preceding pages).

Emerging on a broad, flat balcony between two huge brick paws of the Lion Rock, we began the hazardous zigzag ascent

to the final high plateau. We clung like acrobats to the near-perpendicular walls and clutched a metal railing to sustain us against the lashing winds. Leg and arm muscles ached from crouching and straining for a foothold as we inched up the cliff's slippery, notched face (page 489).

Fearful King Dies by His Own Sword

We dared not speak for fear of arousing the menacing hordes of wasps that now alone inhabit the three acres of the once-great palace, the pink throne room, baths, and galleries of the king's domain.

At the summit, still breathless, we gazed out upon a panorama of jungle, lakes, and mountains. From this same spot Kasyapa's sentries, watching day and night for any approaching enemy, finally reported Moggallana's army gathering on the plains below.

Perhaps because even the safety of his wondrous palace in the sky could not protect the sorrowing Kasyapa from his own bitter conscience, he descended to battle his brother.

In the midst of the fray, the king's elephant came to a marsh. When he turned the beast to find surer footing, his armies, thinking that he was fleeing, faltered and scattered.

493

"Rainy Day" and "White Horses" show the brilliant colors and rhythms of child artist Senaka Senanayake.

Gods dance, elephants parade, and lotus blossoms unfold on panels of batik cloth at the Colombo home of Mrs. Osmund de Silva. She supervises girls using hot wax and dye to decorate fabrics with Ceylonese designs.

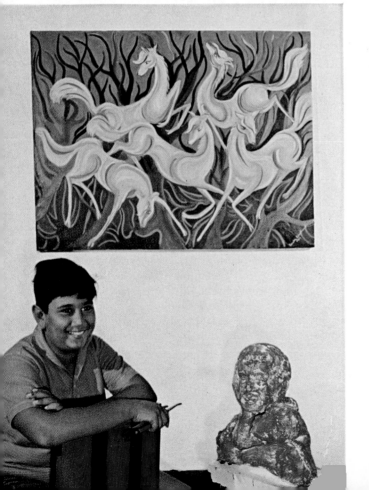

Famous at 15, Senaka Senanayake —nephew of Ceylon's prime minister—began his career at 6, painting on brown poster paper. Since then he has sent 42 one-man shows to cities around the world, exhibiting twice in Washington, D. C. A mural he painted hangs in United Nations headquarters in New York. Yet, happy and natural, he remains interested in sports and stamp collecting. "I really want to be a doctor," he told the authors. An accomplished sculptor, he sits beside "Father and Son," one of his recent works.

EKTACHROMES (ABOVE AND OPPOSITE LOWER) AND KODACHROME © NATIONAL GEOGRAPHIC SOCIETY

Without dismounting, Kasyapa unsheathed the royal dagger and slit his own throat.

Whatever infamy surrounds Kasyapa the king, it cannot tarnish the glorious creation of Kasyapa the architect, the artist, the engineer. Sigiriya stands as final testament to the monumental efforts of Kasyapa the man to claim salvation for Kasyapa the king.

From the searing plains of the buried cities, we retreated to the cool of Kandy's hills. The tinsel of Perahera had gone; quiet hung along the city's winding drives (pages 492-3).

Suddenly, without warning, rain descended upon us. First came the dull thump of heavy raindrops on an elephant-ear plant, then the clean smell of breezes driven before a torrent. Finally a steady sheet of water streamed from the skies with such determination that one might have wished for the security of a Noah's Ark and two reserved spaces aboard her.

Moments later, just as suddenly, the scowling clouds broke open, flooding the sky with color. Only rivulets running off rooftops, the squishing of bare feet on muddy paths, and the reflection of passing vehicles in the shiny streets proved the rains had come at all.

The deluge over, we probed the Peradeniya Royal Botanic Gardens near Kandy, 150 acres of flora from many tropical lands. Dan guided us through a scented spice reserve, where we sniffed nutmeg, cinnamon, clove, cardamom, and pepper. We found avenues lined with palms, a fairy glen of ferns, pools of lotus lilies, and greenhouses and laboratories where orchids are delicately nurtured.

River Jaunt Atop an Elephant

As we left the gardens, Dan had only to mention elephants bathing, and we headed for the river at Katugastota, near Kandy.

"Madam, you've wanted to ride an elephant. I know the mahouts; we'll find the best one for you," Dan promised.

Momentarily, Donna regretted ever having

mentioned the subject. Dan scurried off, returning with a mahout leading an elephant.

"Madam, meet Lechchimi. She's gentle."

"What should I do?" Donna asked.

"Madam, just stand there; Lechchimi will do the work," Dan instructed.

Blowing hot air in my direction, a great bewhiskered trunk reached out, hoisted my wife aloft, and gently set her down on the beast's broad forehead. The mahout shouted, "Head higher!" Lechchimi obeyed with an upward jerk of her head, and Donna slipped. Instantly the great trunk folded securely about her waist, holding her fast.

Now confident, Donna climbed astride Lechchimi's back for a stroll in the river. Only a few tasty slices of cocoa fruit from Donna, plus a sharp prod in the posterior from the mahout, persuaded Lechchimi to meander ashore.

"How was it?" I asked.

"Great, but she could do with a shave," Donna replied candidly.

At the Chalet Guest House in Kandy, Donna retreated to shower off essence of elephant, while I took time to relax and to scan the latest edition of the *Ceylon Observer*. Little had changed during the seven weeks Donna and I had traveled through this beautiful land. The world's spotlight was still cast on the troubled Asia around us. India and Pakistan battled for the Vale of Kashmir; blood flowed in the Red River Valley and Mekong Delta of Viet Nam; the Federation of Malaysia faltered; Indonesia seethed with discontent.

But here in the tranquil hills of Kandy the sounds of distant war and political turmoil echoed only faintly. One could still hear, clear and unchanging, the timeless voice of Lanka —the voice we had heard in the giggle of an upcountry girl, the trumpeting of a wild elephant crashing through primeval jungle, the roar of surf spending its fury against sandy shores, the rhythmic pounding of barefoot Kandyan dancers, and the shrill wind that sends dust eddying across the hallowed ruins of Buddhism's buried cities.   THE END

Cooling off under a golden shower, a worker ends his day at Anuradhapura, with the massive brick dome and spire of the Ruanweli Dagoba rising in the distance. The lake, part of an ancient system of irrigation reservoirs and canals, is named for King Tissa, Sinhalese monarch of the third century B.C. who first embraced Buddhism.

Walking with natural grace, women carry water jugs to a village near Anuradhapura.

Working for

Weeks on the Sea Floor

By CAPT. JACQUES-YVES COUSTEAU

Photographs by PHILIPPE COUSTEAU and BATES LITTLEHALES

THE OCTOBER SUN gleamed on the white stone lighthouse at Cap Ferrat and reflected from a jetliner beginning its climb from Nice-Côte d'Azur airport on France's south coast. Off the cape a statuesque water-skier crossed the sparkling sea. Oblivious to the vivid scene, a dozen of us sat closeted in the lighthouse watching closed-circuit telecasts of a historic event taking place 370 feet below the skier's foaming wake. We were witnessing one of the first steps in man's economic occupation of the ocean floor.

I had wagered a $700,000 project, involving 150 technicians and a dozen vessels, on the skill and dedication of a few young men shivering in the cold darkness of that lonely and forbidding realm. It was an expensive gamble on a tough and tricky task. But if they proved me right, millions

EERIE OUTPOST IN THE WILDERNESS OF SEA, *a spherical house-workshop known as Conshelf (Continental Shelf) Three crouches on the Mediterranean floor. The station's "street lamps" and the ghostly glimmer of day outline the author's famous diving saucer, above, probing the chill depths like a shark. Working out of the sea house for three weeks, six "oceanauts" boldly advanced man's exploitation of the ocean bed.*

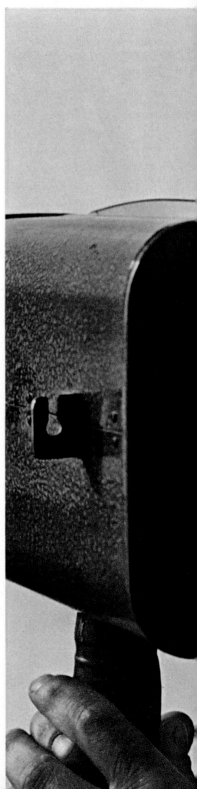

of square miles of offshore territory would be added to the regions exploitable by man.

On our screen a passing fish lent the only movement to a picture of a strange knobby totem pole picked out of the dark by haloed lights (painting, page 518). Slowly into the scene came an apparition, a big globular body with wide astonished eyes. In the pupil of each eye there was a man's face. This monster that swallowed men cast a glaring light on the scene.

"It's the diving saucer," said my wife Simone, as if to reassure our guest viewers. "You can see the crewmen at the portholes."

A Halloween skeleton drifted into the picture. "Raymond Coll," someone said. Only the light-colored tapes on the seams of Coll's black rubber trousers and sleeves showed in the darkness. Another skeleton appeared. A watcher identified him: "Christian Bonnici." The image shifted as an invisible diver, who could only have been my son Philippe, the cameraman, picked up the undersea TV camera and approached the totem pole.

"Christmas Tree" Simulates Submarine Oil Well

That singular structure was now recognizable as a production-type oil-well head, a vertical stack of pipes and valves known to oilmen as a "Christmas tree." Although it did not stand atop an actual oil well, the Christmas tree had been fitted with a tank of compressed air to create the internal pressure of a working wellhead.

Oil wells, whether on land or offshore, are controlled by Christmas trees, whose valves are adjusted to produce

Shaved pate bristling with electrodes, expedition chief André Laban turns human guinea pig. As red light flickers in the hand-held panel during a test ashore before the dive, sensors record his brain waves. Later, on the bottom, another electroencephalogram will show any effects of pressure and helium atmosphere. This, together with other mental and physiological records taken under water, revealed an amazing ability by the oceanauts to withstand the fatigue of their long ordeal. "The most modern machines often failed in the depths, but the men, never," says Captain Cousteau.

501

an even flow. Sometimes they choke up or run wild. On land, trucks with cranes lift tools and men for maintenance and repair.

On the bottom of the sea, in place of a crane, one of our practical underwater engineers, Albert Falco, had tethered over the wellhead an air-filled steel globe with a half-ton upward pull. From it hung a chain hoist, with which the oceanauts could raise and lower heavy tools. A diver seeking to mount the rig simply flipped his fins and soared.

Oceanauts Tackle "Impossible" Job

Our six divers, or "oceanauts" as we call the new breed of sea-floor technicians, had been working on the bottom for two weeks without surfacing. Each day they ventured from a spherical undersea house 150 feet away to carry out their assigned tasks. Now came the crucial test: The success of Continental Shelf Station (Conshelf) Three, the most advanced outpost yet established by man in the offshore wilderness, would be judged by the way these men managed the work they were about to begin.

With me were several skeptical oil engineers from the French Government's Bureau de Recherches de Pétrole, which helped to sponsor our third undersea settlement. They had their stop watches ready to time the oceanauts on the difficult operation. Several colleagues from the National Geographic Society, also a sponsor, had joined us.

We watched Bonnici attempt a key aspect of a wellhead repair job which oil technicians considered almost impossible under water. This consisted of threading a stiff wire through a thick pack of pressure-proof seals. Coll lent stability by sitting on his shoulders.

Bonnici trembled from head to foot with

"You first!" grins Cousteau as chief biologist Raymond Vaissière, project dietician, samples one of his own menus. Dr. Charles Aquadro, an American member of the staff, helped test Conshelf's breathing mixture.

Oceanauts ate frozen dinners like those served by airlines. Told that sauce for lobster thermidor would be banned because it might be difficult to digest, the gourmet divers said *"non"* to the lobster, too.

Trial dive in Monaco harbor seals six men in Conshelf Three. When the research vessel *Espadon* raised her gangplank, the unique sea station pumped water into ballast tanks for an 85-foot descent to the harbor bottom. Two Galeazzi decompression chambers, underwater "lifeboats," rode down with the sphere. Each of these cylinders could lift three men to the surface if pressure failed in the sea house or some other disaster occurred in the depths.

EKTACHROMES BY BATES LITTLEHALES © N.G.S.

cold and concentration. He retreated several times to the house for infrared warm-ups, but he persisted—and he prevailed. When the oilmen saw him ease the wire through the last seal, they stood up and cheered.

After seven hours in the water, Bonnici dragged himself into the house and learned that his coordination test that night would consist of threading needles!

Conshelf One: 33 Feet for 7 Days

Oceanauts had made much progress since our first manned undersea base was established in September, 1962. In Continental Shelf Station One—Conshelf One, as we called it—Albert Falco and Claude Wesly remained submerged for a week at a depth of 33 feet off Marseille. Using Aqua-Lungs, they labored outside as long as five hours a day at depths as great as 85 feet. They were supported—or rather oversupported—by a clutter of vessels and men; as other divers and just plain well-wishers dropped in, they sometimes felt as if they were living in a bus station.

Conshelf One proved that divers could live and work efficiently for a significant period while continuously submerged. The key word here is work: The reason for putting manned stations on the bottom is to multiply divers' work capability by hours and fathoms.

For Continental Shelf Station Two, we set a larger challenge, that of making a precursor of underwater society. We wanted to see what would happen to a group of average men during a month-long sojourn.

Conshelf Two, the first human colony on the sea floor, was set up in the Red Sea off 503

Port Sudan during the summer of 1963. The main settlement, 36 feet down, housed five men for a full month. There was also a deeper camp in which two men lived and out of which they worked for a week in a regimen of half helium, half air, pushing the work range of oceanauts to 165 feet.*

Our first continental-shelf structures were combinations of cylinders and domes. For Conshelf Three our engineering team, headed by Commandant Jean Alinat, went to the most logical form: the sphere. Our new undersea station, 18 feet in diameter, had two stories, the lower for diving, sleeping, and sanitation, the upper for dining, communications, and data gathering (painting, page 519).

The oceanauts swam out to work through a bottom hatch that was open to the sea during their whole time below. Pressure inside the house equaled pressure outside, so that water could not rise above the hatch. The steel globe rested on a 48-by-28-foot chassis that held 77 tons of ballast (half of it in iron pellets), water ballast tanks, and reservoirs of helium, oxygen, and compressed air.

On the open deck of the chassis were nine tons of wash water in a big neoprene bag, and a bin of canned table water and fruit juices. Here also were the "lifeboats"—two three-man Galeazzi decompression chambers, whose bottom hatches were kept open while the station was on the sea floor. In a life-or-death situation the men could enter the chambers, close the bottom hatches, and soar to the surface, there to undergo controlled decompression in big medical pressure chambers.

Fewer Ties Link Men With Surface

Before Conshelf Three reached the planning stage, I had come to the conclusion that it was wrong, expensive, and dangerous to bind the underwater people to a welter of ships, machinery, and specialists on the surface. I wanted to deliver them from total dependence on vulnerable cables, pipes, tackle, processions of support divers, and people who wanted to hit their knees with rubber mallets.

Our early oceanauts had lived in endless calm down below, but were at the mercy of surface storm damage to their communications and supplies. It was ridiculous. I set out to lessen Conshelf Three's reliance on the surface, even though the new station was to be nine times deeper than earlier ones.

The oceanauts would not be able to breathe air, because its nitrogen content would be lethal at 11 atmospheres; they would need an atmosphere of helium and oxygen, "heliox"

for short. They would be in darkness; at 100 meters, 328 feet, daylight is weak and dull. They would be alone; compressed-air divers from the sunlit world could not safely venture so deep. Only the diving saucer could visit them, and the only hand it could lend was its cold steel claw.

As oceanauts, we selected from our underwater research group skilled men in superior physical and mental states, who had performed well in difficult situations. If a man had personal reasons for declining, all he had

*See "At Home in the Sea," by Capt. Jacques-Yves Cousteau, NATIONAL GEOGRAPHIC, April, 1964.

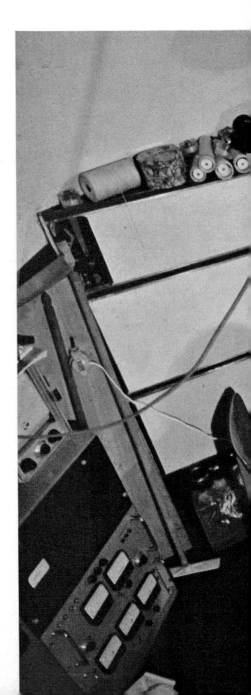

Farewell to sunshine: Raymond Coll and Christian Bonnici queue up in the water off Monaco to board their undersea home. André Laban, beside the sphere, breathes oxygen to purge his lungs of nitrogen before ducking through the bottom hatch.

At home in the sphere, though still afloat in the harbor, oceanauts undergoing pressurization top off a roast-beef lunch with fruit. Laban pinches his nose and blows to equalize the pressure on his eardrums.

EKTACHROMES BY PHILIPPE COUSTEAU (BELOW) AND BATES LITTLEHALES © N.G.S.

Human cargo inside, the sea house eases past Monaco's north harbor light on its way to the diving site seven miles away. Directing the move from the deck of *Espadon,* Cousteau sets a course that at no time crosses depths greater than 165 feet, so that if the sphere should accidentally sink, conventional divers could come to the rescue. Yellow fin and a pair of buoys steady the wobbly sea house. Lights of the Casino of Monte Carlo blaze from the hillside.

Trouble waited at the diving site. When Conshelf Three prepared to descend, mounting seas tore away power cables and forced a return to base. For two days divers made hurried repairs while the oceanauts, still under pressure, waited in the sphere. Then, once more, the flotilla said farewell to Monaco.

to do was tell me. We were not making an underwater home for heroes, but pitting capable working men against tough tasks.

Of fifty candidates, we initially took three men in whom we had firm confidence (page 520). We started them in five months' training as oil-well technicians. Christian Bonnici at 29 was an intense, driving worker, a good mechanic and self-reliant diver with no time for comedy. Raymond Coll, 27, had joined our group at 16. He was one of the coolest, most resourceful, and likable people in our outfit. Yves Omer, 24, was the youngest of the lot, a diligent worker with a flair for underwater rigging and learning new jobs.

We named a total of 12 oceanauts to undergo full training, dividing them into "A" and "B" teams, the latter as standbys for members of "A" team who might be disqualified for medical reasons. Heading "A" team and slated as *chef de mission* of Conshelf Three was André Laban, 37, an engineer with 14 years in our undersea group (pages 516-17). Laban is a slim, taciturn, easy-smiling individual with a shaven head and talent as a musician, painter, and cameraman.

As scientific chief of the undersea station we picked Jacques Rollet, a 28-year-old physicist from the laboratories of the Oceanographic Museum (pages 514-15). The demanding job of producing the film and photo record of the deep colony went to my younger son, Philippe, 24, recently schooled as a professional cinematographer (see nominations page at

EKTACHROMES BY BATES LITTLEHALES © NATIONAL GEOGRAPHIC SOCIETY

beginning of magazine). He has been diving for 20 years. I put a miniature Aqua-Lung on Philippe when he was four.

A year of training, testing, and construction went into Conshelf Three. The oceanauts helped build their house and furnish it.

Doctors Test High-pressure Heliox

In Marseille, our physicians put goats and sheep through prolonged heliox exposures in pressure chambers, simulating a depth of 660 feet. Only then did we make the first human trials. Dr. Charles F. Aquadro (page 503), an American member of my staff, and Dr. Jacques Chouteau spent three days in a tank of heliox at 13 atmospheres of pressure, the equivalent of 400 feet down in the sea.

We stinted nothing to make the underwater base efficient and safe. Time after time, I put off the launching date in order to improve the self-contained heliox breathing center. When you are pitting a new, unproven life-support system against the pressures of the deep, you cannot allow a schedule to interfere.

To place working men so deep for so long, we had to surround them with unfamiliar and exotic appliances. The heliox breathing center, our most radical departure, was a large installation called a cryogenerator, named after cryogenics, the study of extreme cold. The cryogenerator circulated the gases the oceanauts breathed, froze out carbon dioxide and other noxious gases, and dehumidified the house. It also served as a deep-freeze locker

507

and refrigerator for three weeks' food stocks.

To keep a close watch on their breathing mixtures, the oceanauts had gas analyzers whose findings could be read simultaneously in the house beneath the sea and by electrical transmission in the lighthouse above. This equipment was backed by a miniaturized mass spectrograph that continuously recorded the presence of every gaseous element in the oceanauts' environment. To rid the sphere of nitrogen, we created a vacuum inside it that wrung all gas out of its porous materials; then we filled it with heliox.

At last the top hatch was sealed and the lower hatch opened to welcome aboard the adventurers of Conshelf Three. The oceanauts entered it at noon on September 17, 1965 (page 505). They closed the bottom hatch, laid on heliox pressure, and reached 11 atmospheres in six hours. Still on the surface, they now lived under the equivalent pressure of 328 feet of water.

Heliox Changes Bass to Soprano

As soon as the men breathed heliox, their voices reverted to babyhood. Helium is so light that it does not slow the vibrations of the vocal cords, and a basso profundo turns to a mezzo-soprano. Days would pass before the oceanauts could understand each other.

They had to learn to speak slowly and succinctly, and to avoid high-pitched sounds. Omer described it: "Sooner or later, you were bound to get excited, and when you saw the genuine puzzlement on the other fellow's face, your hot emotion turned into a big laugh."

As we readied our 140-ton undersea house for its seaward journey, the panorama on the south jetty at Monaco was one of splendid chaos. Four vessels, several launches, and a hundred line-handlers crowded the quay. It was crammed with helium and oxygen tanks, a road crane, miles of spooled cable, camera crews, communications huts, hundreds of spectators, and the inevitable small child standing under the heaviest weight that was being transferred. Watching were naval observers from the United States, Britain, Italy, Sweden, West Germany, and France.

Half-hidden in the work party, giving no orders but keenly scanning the tumultuous scene, stood a pioneer among oceanauts, the safety chief of our complicated operation. Albert Falco's veteran eye and undersea wisdom perceived every aspect of the three-dimensional operation. He did not need symbols of authority. Our people knew he was there.

As our smaller research vessel, *Espadon,* slogged through the darkening sea with the sphere in tow (pages 506-7), a reporter on board said to Simone, "Madame Cousteau, you must be concerned about your son in there." She replied, "Monsieur, I have six sons in there, and I am thinking of all of them."

We reached the station site in the morning, and the weather turned hostile. One of the big marker buoys got out of control and tore up three of the power and communication cables that ran out from the Cap Ferrat lighthouse to the dive site. We could not submerge the house without its cables, nor leave it afloat in a rising storm, so we hauled it ignominiously back to Monaco. The oceanauts remained sealed up on the surface of the harbor for two days, while our electricians repaired the multiconductor cables in the water. All was ready again on the morning of September 21.

We anticipated that there would be two great critical periods for Conshelf Three: the descent and precise landing on the bottom, and the return to the surface under the control of the oceanauts themselves.

A considerable flotilla was engaged in preparing Conshelf Three to slide down a tight guide wire to its destined site on the floor. Five seagoing vessels, our diving saucer, and half a dozen launches and rubber boats were involved. Most of them had walkie-talkies, whose messages could be transmitted via headquarters on Cap Ferrat to the diving saucer and the deep-sea station itself. Under the surface, 15 divers made the sea house ready to descend.

Husky Bernard Delemotte's job was to plug in 14 multiconductor cables beneath the house. With compressed air he blew water out of the 3-by-5-foot entry tube and squeezed into it with cable ends, tools, and a three-tank Aqua-Lung. He dried himself and his gear, removed waterproof compound from the connections, and joined them with many turns of protective tape. Three hours of this unseen agonizing work gave the oceanauts warmth, telephone, and TV transmission.

The currents began changing. Ships and divers eased restraining lines or made them taut to keep the undersea house in position. The sea put kinks in the cables hanging on yellow drums between shore and sphere. Launches tugged at the writhing power lines to keep them in order (page 511).

The sun set. A lot of work remained. I

listened as privately as possible to French Navy weather reports. They predicted imminent gales. A storm would put us in a terrible mess.

I kept quiet and stood on the foredeck of *Espadon* as if I had no cares. My role was to concentrate on problems we had not foreseen.

It was nearly midnight before we could release the sea house from its support buoys. From its position under the surface, it started down unseen. The string of yellow floats diminished as they were hauled under, one by one.

The oceanauts had no sensation of sinking. They felt the legs of the house touch softly. From the saucer, Falco saw it land within one foot of the place he had picked (next page). It was 15 minutes after midnight, September 22, 1965.

Thus began a test of human ingenuity and adaptability, of dogged courage and kindling spirit that I am convinced will lead mankind to greater rewards than the space race.

Hatch Opens to Darkness

The oceanauts unbolted the bottom hatch to expose the liquid door through which they would pass to their labors on the ocean floor outside. The water was naked, clear, and black. The diving well looked like a barrel of tar. The oceanauts swallowed secretly. They were sunk in perpetual night.

The first chore was to bring in the ends of the 200-foot breathing hoses, strapped outside on the chassis, and expel water from them. Philippe put on a three-bottle Aqua-Lung filled with heliox and slipped into the cold, concealing water.

"As soon as I venture away from the *maison sous-marine*," said he, "I am struck by one overwhelming fact—we have lost the surface. It is far above us, out of sight, buried in treacherous night. The surface means death. Here on the bottom is safety—life itself. I reach down and touch the ground, our friend, our salvation."

Philippe passed the heavy hoses up to his companions. Taped together were each man's yellow inhalation pipe and a black hose to

EKTACHROME BY BATES LITTLEHALES © N.G.S.

Wake of bubbles traces a diver's path beside the sphere. Here in protected Villefranche Bay, a mile from the point of descent, Aqua-Lungers working off the ship *Winnaretta Singer* adjust Conshelf's metal legs and check external fittings. The station traveled the last mile to the diving site submerged beneath pounding surface waves.

Name of the support ship honors the daughter of sewing-machine manufacturer Isaac M. Singer. A foundation she established donated the vessel to Monaco's Oceanographic Museum, which Cousteau heads.

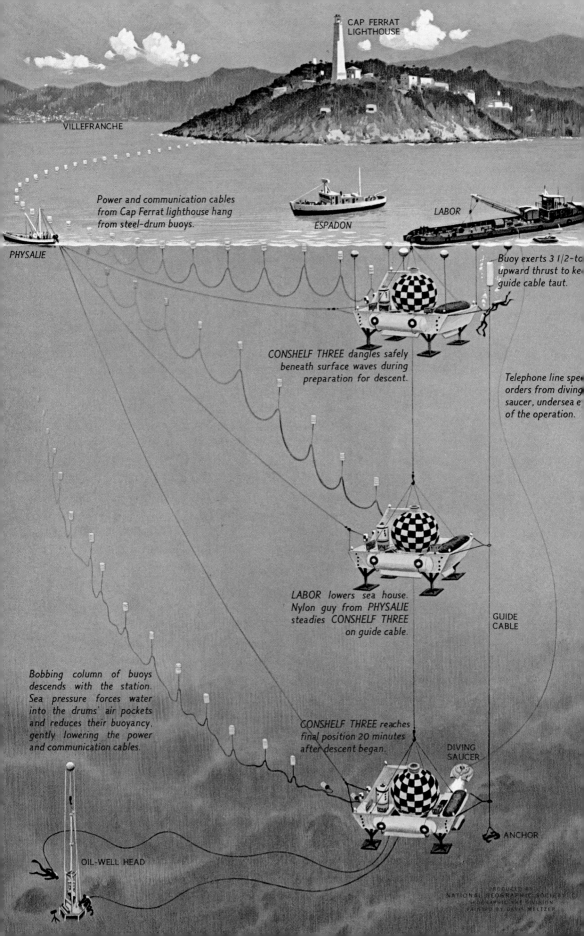

CAP FERRAT LIGHTHOUSE

VILLEFRANCHE

Power and communication cables from Cap Ferrat lighthouse hang from steel-drum buoys.

ESPADON

LABOR

PHYSALIE

Buoy exerts 3 1/2-to[n] upward thrust to kee[p] guide cable taut.

CONSHELF THREE dangles safely beneath surface waves during preparation for descent.

Telephone line spe[eds] orders from diving saucer, undersea e[ye] of the operation.

LABOR lowers sea house. Nylon guy from PHYSALIE steadies CONSHELF THREE on guide cable.

GUIDE CABLE

Bobbing column of buoys descends with the station. Sea pressure forces water into the drums' air pockets and reduces their buoyancy, gently lowering the power and communication cables.

CONSHELF THREE reaches final position 20 minutes after descent began.

DIVING SAUCER

ANCHOR

OIL-WELL HEAD

carry his exhalations back into the house. The oceanauts were forced to recover their helium, purify it, and replace expended oxygen. They could not, like compressed-air divers, blow bubbles into the sea. Three of them would have drained the house of gases and flooded it in a matter of hours.

A compressor forced heliox through the yellow pipe, and a "depressor," or reversed compressor, pulled the gas back through the black pipe. The oceanaut at the end of this giant respiratory system wore two heavy foam-rubber wet suits; on his chest was our new two-way regulator for high-pressure heliox; and on his back he carried a conventional Aqua-Lung filled with heliox. Like a provident parachutist, he had a reserve pack.

Between wet suits the oceanaut wore an in-compressible vest, the armor with which we hoped to overcome the ocean's main threat to deep fish men—sheer cold, exaggerated by pressure and the heat-stealing effect of helium.

Insulating Vests Resist Flattening

Near the surface, foam rubber will adequately insulate a man at 55° F., but 11 atmospheres of pressure will compress its air bubbles and destroy their insulating quality. To permit oceanauts to work in deep water, we had to have incompressible foam rubber.

The patent consists of enclosing microbubbles of gases in tiny ebonite spheres, no bigger than motes of dust, and filling a rubber blanket with millions of them. There wasn't time to make enough yardage for complete suits. We settled for vests to preserve the heat of

Half-mile arc of buoys, holding up power and communication lines, links the diving site with Cousteau's headquarters in the Cap Ferrat lighthouse. Line to left helps the research boat *Physalie* fight the current as her crew awaits Conshelf Three's descent.

Vertical voyage to a new world: Intricate maneuver of ships and men drops Conshelf Three 328 feet to a tiny patch of level bottom. As Cousteau watches from aboard *Espadon,* divers couple the sphere to a vertical guide wire. Then *Labor* slowly lowers away. Later, at a depth of 370 feet, Conshelf technicians erect an oil-well head, or "Christmas tree."

GROPING IN RELENTLESS GLOOM *that man-made lighting never quite dispels, André Laban inspects every inch of his command for rust, loosened cables, or any other defect. Emergency heliox tanks supplement standard breathing hoses trailing tail-like behind him. Glaring eyes of the diving saucer shine down to guide his rounds.*

the central organs of the body. Legs and arms can become numb and recover, but life is in danger if heart and lungs get too cold.

Conshelf Three itself soon got very cold, because of the heat conductivity of helium under great pressure. Here body warmth was lost 77 times faster than in normal atmosphere. The oceanauts turned on extra heaters to reach the ideal 90° F. temperature.

I did not forbid them to smoke. I did not need to. When you light a match in high-pressure heliox, the phosphorous tip fizzles out and the stem will not catch fire. If you put a glowing electric lighter to a cigarette, the tobacco and paper will not stay lit. Organic substances do not retain enough heat to burn.

Helium's heat diffusion also played tricks with food preparation. Although the deep-freeze meals needed only warming, the oceanauts had to heat water for tea and coffee. The water never boiled, although it reached temperatures half again as high as the sea-level boiling point.

Helium is a mischievous, merry element.

Old-fashioned apparatus of flasks and tubes stands by to analyze the breathing mixture should modern electronic testers fail. Chief scientist Jacques Rollet's laboratory doubles as Conshelf's dart-throwing range.

Reporting to the surface by means of a television camera on the ceiling, Rollet posts a measurement of the breathing mixture—oxygen: 2.5 percent. An increase to 5 percent could cause anemia in the divers; a drop below 1 percent, blackout. Written messages prove better than speech because the helium atmosphere distorts voices into high-pitched squeaks. In off-duty moments, oceanauts crack nuts and assemble model planes. Red wool *toques* have been worn proudly by generations of divers. Rollet and Yves Omer go shirtless in the sphere's 90° F. temperature, kept high to offset rapid loss of body heat in helium.

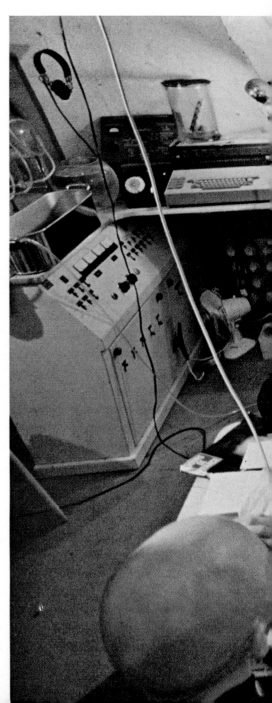

While it treats underwater man well, it gives his inventions and artifices a very bad time. The machines and electronic systems in Conshelf Three had passed short pressure tests in helium, but during days below, high-pressure helium infiltrated everything.

Artificial Atmosphere Disables Machines

The cryogenerator, the oceanauts' fountain of life, fell victim to helium's tricks. Air in the cells of the insulating material had been replaced by the insidious gas, robbing the unit of cold retention. The oceanauts had to help the sick machine with our emergency chemical atmosphere purifier.

Television tubes, too, suffered in the helium environment. There were two waterproof television cameras for outside work, plus two fixed units in the upper and lower stories of the station, on which we watched the men 24 hours a day. Continuous monitoring was vital to the security and documentation of the operation. We also used the interior cameras as videophones: If we could not understand

515

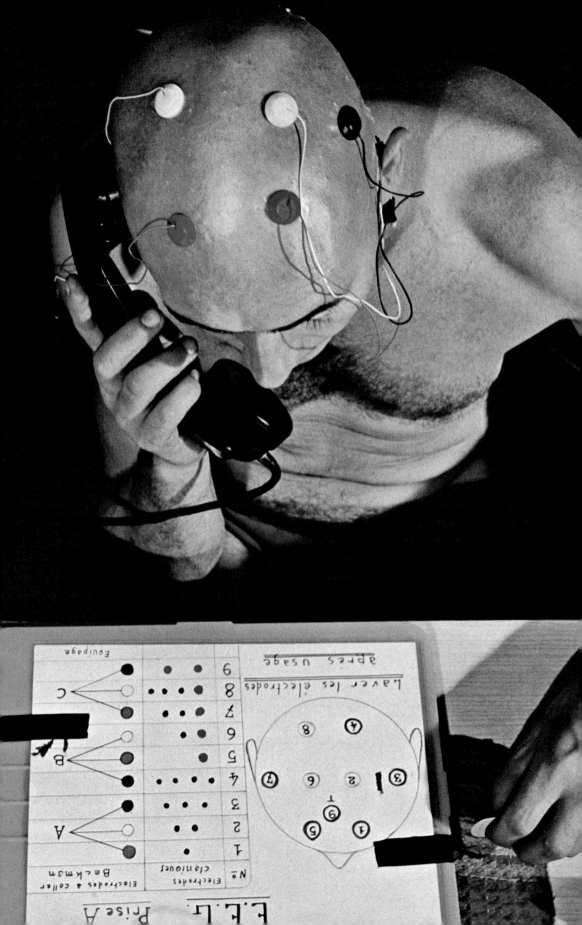

the oceanaut's falsetto, we could watch his lip movements, gestures, and scribbles held up to the lens (page 515).

But two or three days after Conshelf Three reached 11 atmospheres, its crewmen's images faded out on television. They replaced the "defective" vidicon tubes, and the replacements failed. A container sent from the surface brought fresh tubes and carried back the dead ones. The new tubes clouded over after three days. Tests showed the mischievous gas had infiltrated them. It cost $250 a day to keep Conshelf Three in TV tubes.

Sea-floor "Desert" Crawls With Life

The divers explored the sea-floor scenery. "The desert around us is no desert," Philippe found. "It crawls with life." Spiny lobsters with long antennae surrounded the house. There was a large octopus in residence atop a neighboring rock. Scorpionfish loitered on the bottom, confident of their camouflage. The oceanautic acres were littered with civilization's leavings, from pre-Christian amphorae to contemporary beer cans.

Myriad tiny creatures came to the lighted diving hatch; small frantic fish and prancing shrimp jammed into the glowing arena and made the water sizzle with their jerky celebrations of light. In his hand Laban dipped up the wriggling little things and downed them as the freshest of sea-food cocktails.

By the third night the chief's animated appetizers were gone. Big fish had discovered the little ones jigging against the station lights, and were robbing Laban from below.

We had confidence in Conshelf Three; so we invited the public to watch the experiment unfold. Scores of thousands of visitors to the

Impulses from electrodes stuck to Laban's scalp record brain waves during the exhausting weeks below. Readings flowing to a computer ashore, for comparison with an earlier surface test (page 501), showed no ill effects. The diagram tells Laban where to place the multicolored detectors. With all of them properly affixed, he telephones instructions to "tune me in."

Fatigue contorts Laban's face after a dive; weary hands unfasten the regulator. The station chief not only bore the burden of making all final decisions; as the team's top electrician he had to repair failure-prone machines. Eldest oceanaut at 37, he was sustained by strength of will, huge meals, and a steady stream of vitamin pills.

EKTACHROMES BY PHILIPPE COUSTEAU © N.G.S.   517

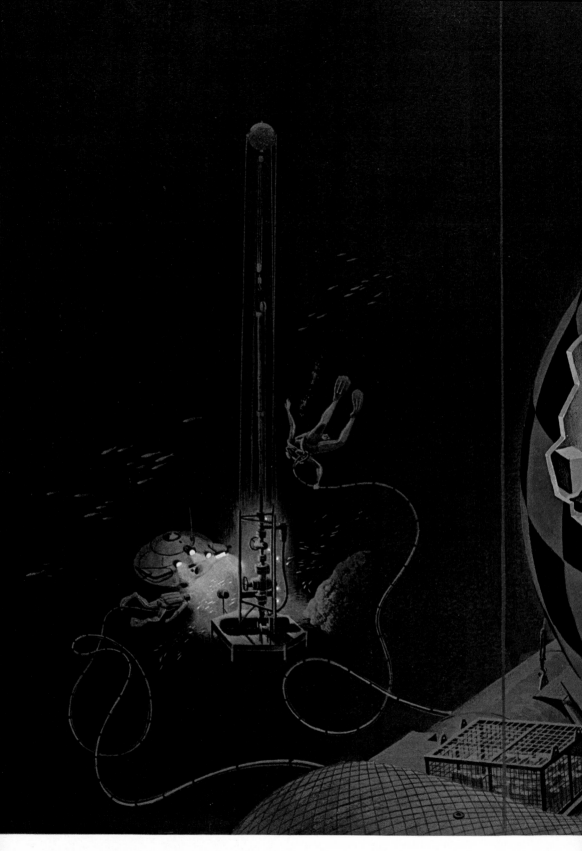

Every inch serves a purpose in the 18-foot-wide
Conshelf sphere, seen here in cutaway. While
station chief Laban telephones ashore, his mates

operate an IBM teleprinter, ready a motion-picture
camera at the diving hatch, and labor outside at
the oil-well head in the glow of the diving saucer's

headlights. Kitchen, dining room, and data-gathering equipment crowd the upper level. Spiral stairs beside the cylindrical deep-freeze lead down to hatch, shower, lavatory, and bunkroom. An outside chassis holds ballast tanks, a mesh pantry box, and net-covered bag with nine tons of wash water.

Oceanographic Museum saw the computer center, where data recorded in the sphere were analyzed and direct telecasts were received from the sea bottom (page 534). Indeed, people were looking into the diving room when an oceanaut stepped into a hot shower without realizing he had crossed in front of the camera.

While everyone could see the oceanauts, they could see none of us. They only heard voices from the surface, mostly that of the duty television monitor, whom they irreverently called "God."

After watching them for a while, Simone said: "Look at Dédé [Laban]. Up here you can't get him to say an extra word. Down there he is a chatterbox. *Regardez* Rollet! A serious face. He never laughs. Now look at him. All smiles and jokes." Then of her younger son: "And Philippe! The biggest playboy in town has become a man who is not satisfied with working less than twenty hours a day."

Living in high-pressure heliox affected the tactile senses. "I feel a kind of perspiration all over my body," reported Laban. "But when I wipe my forehead, it is dry. Another modification of our senses is the almost complete disappearance of smells. Most of us complain we can't taste the food."

Luckily for us, the bad weather predicted for the descent operation held off until Day Four. The oceanauts and their sea-stead were then safely beyond range of surface disturbance. Yet, when the storm broke overhead,

the turbulence echoed minutely even in their refuge. The water in the diving well rose and fell two inches.

We were scheduled to lower the oil-well head on Day Four, but the weather held us off. The storm mounted on Day Five. Torrential rains lashed the coast. Rockslides rumbled behind us on the coastal corniches.

I stood on the lighthouse terrace, watching the most vulnerable aspect of Conshelf Three, the point where the power and communication cables passed into the raging water. To minimize exposure of the cables to wave action, we had planted a stable A-frame out from the rocks and passed the heavily cushioned cables over rollers on top of it. The sea threatened to chafe away the cables on the

EKTACHROMES BY PHILIPPE COUSTEAU © N.G.S.

Lonely sentinel at the door of the sea house (right), Bonnici tends the hoses of two oceanauts. He cocks an ear to the throb of compressors behind the grid. They pump heliox through the yellow hose and retrieve exhalations through the black line.

"Crossroads of the world," divers called the cluttered hatch area. Laban (above) hands up canned food from the outside pantry. Water pushes up at 160 pounds per square inch through the open hatch, but equal pressure of heliox inside the sphere holds the black flood at bay.

Bonnici, Coll, and Omer discuss tools needed for work on the sea-floor oil rig.

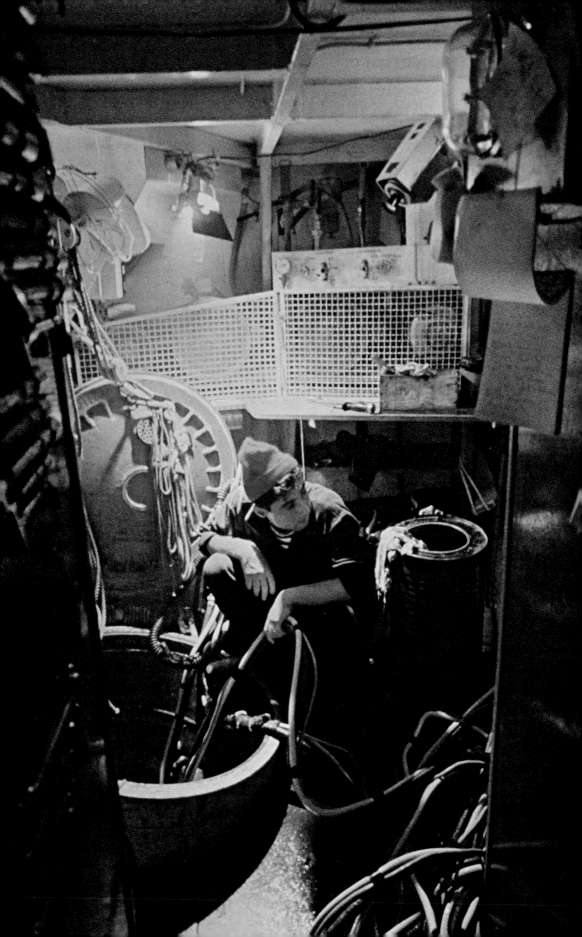

rocks. One of the lightkeepers told me helpfully, "We are getting the heaviest swells we've known here since 1947."

Nobody left our lighthouse headquarters for lunch. Simone appeared with a basket of bread, cheese, ham, and pizzas, which we ate gloomily on the terrace, sheltered from the rain in jeeps and TV vans, while looking down at the waves rising around the arteries and central nervous system of Conshelf Three.

Storm Tears at Conshelf's Lifelines

Foaming waves battered the A-frame, carried away its plank deck, and snapped one of its mainstays. I hurriedly conferred with my engineering chief, Alinat. We put the oceanauts on emergency standby to surface. If the A-frame were destroyed, the cables would part; we could not continue to transmit power to the station. In that case Laban was to button up the sphere, break out his two-week supply of atmosphere-regenerating chemicals, and jettison ballast to ascend.

Once free from the bottom, the oceanauts were to get into bed in down sleeping bags and cover themselves with blankets and outer clothing, for without their electric heaters they could well freeze to death in a few hours in helium. They had iron rations to chew while hibernating. The sphere could ride out any storm, provided we could maintain lines on it to hold it off the lighthouse rocks.

After noon another stay parted. Falco and Raymond Kientzy climbed the A-frame and strung new stays that saved Conshelf Three.

By morning it seemed that we had withstood the worst of the storm. For miles out, the Mediterranean looked like potato soup, and the oceanauts were at the bottom of the tureen. Apparently all unattached grains of sediment on the southern slope of the Maritime Alps had been flushed into the sea. It was bad news for our photo and TV coverage.

We lowered the five-ton oil-well head to its chosen place 150 feet downslope from the undersea house. This Christmas tree was going to an unprecedented depth. An oil well
(Continued on page 527)

Human phantoms, in a beam from the diving saucer, labor on the Christmas tree. Bubbles escape a diver as his lips shiver uncontrollably on the mouthpiece. Umbilical cords carrying heliox vanish in the darkness.

"We were buried in treacherous night," recalls the author's oceanaut son, Philippe, who as the crew's photographer brought back extraordinary still and motion pictures.

Toll of a day's work in numbing cold and forbidding darkness shows in the eyes of Coll and the "dishpan" hands of Laban. Outside chores lasting more than an hour caused mounting discomfort in the 50° to 55° water, but the sphere's infrared heating warmed the men in 15 minutes. Threading a repair assembly into the Christmas tree, Bonnici labored in the sea for seven aching hours—a working day unparalleled at such depths.

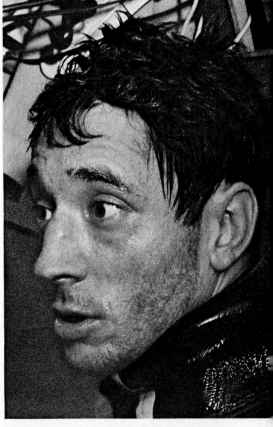

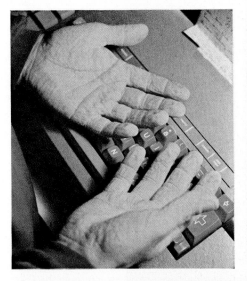

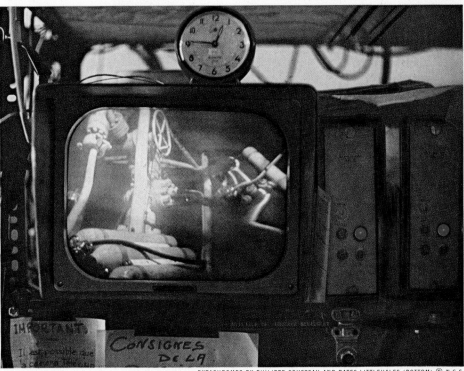

Toiling oceanauts attach the 400-pound repair assembly to the wellhead as television flashes the drama to oil engineers ashore. The divers performed the feat more quickly than land crews, proving that men can operate heavy equipment at twice the depth heretofore possible.

Like a fiddler with his bow, Rollet manipulates a pellet tube for a test of bottom turbulence. When he places it in a metal frame (opposite), it drops plastic balls that settle slowly, wafted by the subtlest currents. Grid on the sea floor measures their deflection.

Locked in battle with the cold, divers wore two wet suits with a special vest between. At these depths, pressure crushes air pockets of conventional foam rubber, making it useless as insulation. Bright yellow stripes of tape on the suits help the divers keep track of one another.

Flooding a "greenhouse" with light, Rollet tries to cause photosynthesis in the sunless deep. The experiment tests whether the depths harbor enough spores to build life under artificial illumination.

"Increasing the productivity of the great dark oceans," declares the author, "could help save half of humanity from malnutrition."

EKTACHROME (ABOVE) AND EASTMAN COLOR BY JACQUES-YVES COUSTEAU © N.G.S.

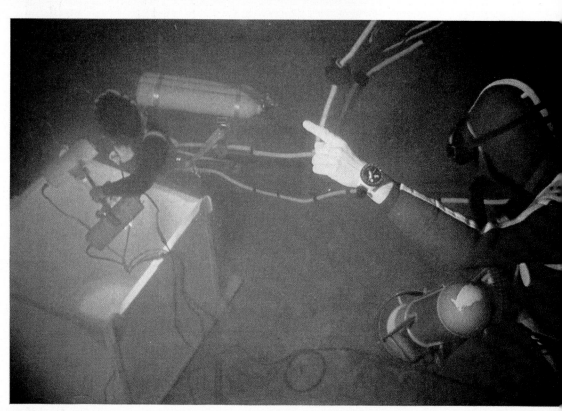

150 feet or more down cannot be efficiently maintained by surface-based divers, so that test drillers who hit oil in such depths customarily cap the well to await new methods of deepwater maintenance. We hoped to demonstrate that wells could produce profitably at more than twice the present depth.

If the oceanauts could man a wellhead at 370 feet, workers living in undersea stations could handle many other jobs, such as mining, submarine stock farming, and hydroarcheology. The marine sciences could be revolutionized by investigators residing in laboratories far below present-day diving access.

Wellhead Comes Down Like a Yo-yo

The lowering of the wellhead went poorly. The floating crane was rocked by eight-foot storm swells. As the wellhead sank into the oceanauts' lights, it bounced up and down like a five-ton Yo-yo; it trampled the bottom, exploded a pall of sediment, came plowing out, and jerked up out of sight in the dark.

The oceanauts felt fragile; they got back into the house. Falco, supervising the operation from the diving saucer, was equally cautious. If the berserk Christmas tree came

down on his submarine, the result would be similar to that of a one-pound hammer smiting a half-pound crab.

It took an hour to plant the monster and let go the hook. The oceanauts gave Falco a sign by thumb and forefinger. He returned it and floated through the black ceiling.

The oceanauts made their biggest impression on the peeping oil engineers by replacing the 400-pound McEvoy valve, the main component of the wellhead, while it was under pressure of 2,500 pounds per square inch. Because tools are lighter in water and the men didn't have to fight their own weight, they did the job in 45 minutes, quicker than the engineers had ever heard of its being done on land.

Storm sediments continued to hamper work below as we approached Day Fifteen, provisionally the final day of Conshelf Three. We had considered two weeks as a term sufficient to show results, but bad weather had robbed us of eight days' work. Photography was at a standstill, and the scientific experiments were not even begun. I felt justified in asking the oceanauts if they would stay on and complete as much of the plan as possible.

527

WATCH "THE WORLD OF JACQUES-YVES COUSTEAU" ON MOST OF THESE CBS TELEVISION STATIONS

(A few stations may schedule the program at a later date. Check your newspaper for day and time.)

ALABAMA
Birmingham WAPI-TV (13)
Dothan WTVY (4)
Huntsville WHNT-TV (19)
Mobile WKRG-TV (5)
Montgomery WCOV-TV (20)

ARIZONA
Phoenix KOOL-TV (10)
Tucson KOLD-TV (13)
Yuma KBLU-TV (13)

ARKANSAS
Fort Smith KFSA-TV (5)
Little Rock KTHV (11)

CALIFORNIA
Bakersfield KBAK-TV (29)
Chico KHSL-TV (12)
Eureka KIEM-TV (3)
Fresno KFRE-TV (30)
Los Angeles KNXT (2)
Sacramento KXTV (10)
Salinas-Monterey KSBW-TV (8)
San Diego KFMB-TV (8)
San Francisco KPIX (5)

COLORADO
Colorado Springs-Pueblo KKTV (11)
Denver KLZ-TV (7)
Grand Junction KREX-TV (5)

CONNECTICUT
Hartford WTIC-TV (3)

DELAWARE*

DIST. OF COLUMBIA
Washington WTOP-TV (9)

FLORIDA
Fort Myers WINK-TV (11)
Jacksonville WJXT (4)
Miami WTVJ (4)
Orlando WDBO-TV (6)
Tallahassee WCTV (6)
Tampa-St. Petersburg WTVT (13)

GEORGIA
Atlanta WAGA-TV (5)
Augusta WRDW-TV (12)
Columbus WRBL-TV (3)
Macon WMAZ-TV (13)
Savannah WTOC-TV (11)
Thomasville WCTV (6)

IDAHO
Boise KBOI-TV (2)
Idaho Falls KID-TV (3)
Lewiston KLEW-TV (3)
Twin Falls KMVT (11)

ILLINOIS
Champaign WCIA (3)
Chicago WBBM-TV (2)
Peoria WMBD-TV (31)
Quincy KHQA-TV (7)
Rockford WCEE-TV (23)
Rock Island WHBF-TV (4)

INDIANA
Evansville WEHT (50)
Fort Wayne WANE-TV (15)
Indianapolis WISH-TV (8)
Lafayette WFAM-TV (18)
South Bend WSBT-TV (22)

IOWA
Cedar Rapids-Waterloo WMT-TV (2)
Des Moines KRNT-TV (8)
Mason City KGLO-TV (3)
Ottumwa KTVO (3)
Sioux City KVTV (9)

KANSAS
Ensign KTVC (6)
Goodland KLOE-TV (10)
Hays KAYS-TV (7)
Hutchinson-Wichita KTVH (12)
Topeka WIBW-TV (13)

KENTUCKY
Lexington WLEX-TV (18)
Louisville WHAS-TV (11)

LOUISIANA
Baton Rouge WAFB-TV (9)
Lafayette KLFY-TV (10)
Monroe-West Monroe KNOE-TV (8)
New Orleans WWL-TV (4)
Shreveport KSLA-TV (12)

MAINE
Bangor WABI-TV (5)
Portland WGAN-TV (13)
Presque Isle WAGM-TV (8)

MARYLAND
Baltimore WMAR-TV (2)
Salisbury WBOC-TV (16)

MASSACHUSETTS
Boston WHDH-TV (5)

MICHIGAN
Cadillac-Traverse City WWTV (9)
Detroit WJBK-TV (2)
Kalamazoo WKZO-TV (3)
Lansing WJIM-TV (6)
Marquette WLUC-TV (6)
Saginaw-Bay City WKNX-TV (57)

MINNESOTA
Duluth KDAL-TV (3)
Mankato KEYC-TV (12)
Minneapolis-St. Paul WCCO-TV (4)

MISSISSIPPI
Columbus WCBI-TV (4)
Greenwood WABG-TV (6)
Jackson WJTV (12)
Meridian WTOK-TV (11)

MISSOURI
Cape Girardeau KFVS-TV (12)
Hannibal KHQA-TV (7)
Jefferson City KRCG (13)
Joplin KODE-TV (12)
Kansas City KCMO-TV (5)
Kirksville KTVO (3)
St. Joseph KFEQ-TV (2)
St. Louis KMOX-TV (4)
Springfield KTTS-TV (10)

MONTANA
Billings KOOK-TV (2)
Butte KXLF-TV (4)
Glendive KXGN-TV (5)
Great Falls KFBB-TV (5)
Helena KBLL-TV (12)
Missoula KGVO-TV (13)

NEBRASKA
Lincoln KOLN-TV (10)
Omaha WOW-TV (6)

NEVADA
Las Vegas KLAS-TV (8)
Reno KOLO-TV (8)

NEW HAMPSHIRE*

NEW JERSEY*

NEW MEXICO
Albuquerque KGGM-TV (13)
Carlsbad KAVE-TV (6)
Roswell KSWS-TV (8)

NEW YORK
Albany WTEN (10)
Binghamton WNBF-TV (12)
Buffalo WBEN-TV (4)
Carthage-Watertown WWNY-TV (7)
New York WCBS-TV (2)
Rochester WHEC-TV (10)
Syracuse WHEN-TV (5)

NORTH CAROLINA
Charlotte WBTV (3)
Durham-Raleigh WTVD (11)
Greensboro WFMY-TV (2)
Greenville WNCT-TV (9)

NORTH DAKOTA
Bismarck KXMB-TV (12)
Dickinson KDIX-TV (2)
Fargo-Valley City KXJB-TV (4)
Minot KXMC-TV (13)

OHIO
Cincinnati WCPO-TV (9)
Cleveland WJW-TV (8)
Columbus WBNS-TV (10)
Dayton WHIO-TV (7)
Steubenville WSTV-TV (9)
Toledo WTOL-TV (11)
Youngstown WKBN-TV (27)

OKLAHOMA
Oklahoma City KWTV (9)
Tulsa KOTV (6)

OREGON
Klamath Falls KOTI (2)
Medford KTVM (5)
Portland KOIN-TV (6)

PENNSYLVANIA
Altoona WFBG-TV (10)
Erie WSEE (35)
Harrisburg WHP-TV (21)
Johnstown WARD-TV (56)
Lancaster-Lebanon WLYH-TV (15)
Philadelphia WCAU-TV (10)
Pittsburgh KDKA-TV (2)
Scranton-Wilkes-Barre WDAU-TV (22)
York WSBA-TV (43)

RHODE ISLAND
Providence WPRO-TV (12)

SOUTH CAROLINA
Anderson WAIM-TV (40)
Charleston WCSC-TV (5)

SOUTH DAKOTA
Rapid City KOTA-TV (3)
Sioux Falls KELO-TV (11)

TENNESSEE
Chattanooga WDEF-TV (12)
Jackson WDXI-TV (7)
Johnson City-Bristol-Kingsport WJHL-TV (11)
Knoxville WBIR-TV (10)
Memphis WREC-TV (3)
Nashville WLAC-TV (5)

TEXAS
Amarillo KFDA-TV (10)
Austin KTBC-TV (7)
Beaumont KFDM-TV (6)
Bryan KBTX-TV (3)
Corpus Christi KZTV (10)
Dallas-Ft. Worth KRLD-TV (4)
El Paso KROD-TV (4)
Harlingen KGBT-TV (4)
Houston KHOU-TV (11)
Laredo KGNS-TV (8)
Lubbock KLBK-TV (13)
Lufkin KTRE-TV (9)
Odessa KOSA-TV (7)
San Angelo KCTV (8)
San Antonio KENS-TV (5)
Sweetwater-Abilene KPAR-TV (12)
Waco KWTX-TV (10)
Wichita Falls KAUZ-TV (6)

UTAH
Salt Lake City KSL-TV (5)

VERMONT
Burlington WCAX-TV (3)

VIRGINIA
Bristol WHL-TV (11)
Harrisonburg WSVA-TV (3)
Norfolk WTAR-TV (3)
Richmond WTVR (6)
Roanoke WDBJ-TV (7)

WASHINGTON
Bellingham KVOS-TV (12)
Pasco KEPR-TV (19)
Seattle KIRO-TV (7)
Spokane KXLY-TV (4)
Yakima KIMA-TV (29)

WEST VIRGINIA
Charleston WCHS-TV (8)
Clarksburg WBOY-TV (12)
Oak Hill WOAY-TV (4)
Wheeling WSTV-TV (9)

WISCONSIN
Green Bay WBAY-TV (2)
La Crosse WKBT (8)
Madison WISC-TV (3)
Milwaukee WISN-TV (12)
Superior KDAL-TV (3)
Wausau WSAU-TV (7)

WYOMING
Casper KTWO-TV (2)
Cheyenne KFBC-TV (5)
Riverton KWRB-TV (10)

*See neighboring states

Man's newest triumph: a workaday world 55 fathoms under the sea

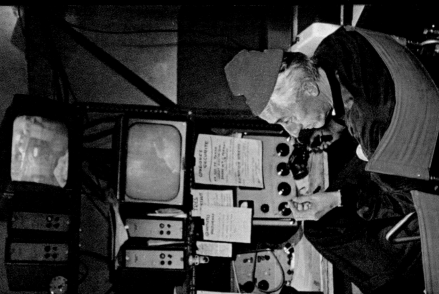

S UNK IN THE NUMBING COLD of perpetual gloom, you drift at the end of a slender dual hose circulating a lifegiving mixture of gases. A gleaming monster suddenly glides from the darkness—the fabulous diving saucer, coming to shepherd you and fellow oceanauts as you go about your daily work at the bottom of the sea. Later, a short swim brings you to a glowing "skylight," the door of a warm lodge where a dinner of pâté, veal chops, and peach melba awaits while a concerto sounds softly in the background.

This is the incredible "World of Jacques-Yves Cousteau" that you and your family will share for a thrilling hour on Thursday evening, April 28, when the National Geographic Society presents the fourth in its series on CBS TV (see station listings on back page). You will live with six oceanauts, among them Christian Bonnici, here working on an oil-well head.

Your home: Conshelf Three, 328 feet beneath the Mediterranean Sea. Keeping vigil with Captain Cousteau in his lighthouse command post (right), you will feel the triumph of conquering a new world. The color telecast, sponsored by Encyclopaedia Britannica, Inc., and Aetna Life and Casualty Insurance Companies, brings your Society's 1965-66 adventure series to a close.

The Electrowriter in the lighthouse dashed off a message in Rollet's handwriting: "To the Surface People: Have mercy on us, poor little oceanauts in the womb of the Immense Sea. Bring us back up . . . as late as possible."

Such was the spirit of their decision to go on. It was their choice alone. From the start, it was they who decided how they would work and how long. I kept watch on them, ready to bring them up if they showed signs of heavy strain. I went sleepless for days on end.

I began an intensive motion-picture campaign with Falco in the diving saucer. Each day we went down for five- or six-hour dives. I logged 40 hours below in the next week.

I continued to marvel at Falco's mastery of the diving saucer. He used it as a camera boom, practically framing my shots with his maneuvers. He shone our big light on Philippe's subjects. When the oceanauts went in for lunch, Falco simply parked the submarine under the house and turned everything off to save power for the afternoon's work. We lay on our backs and chatted in the dark.

To Falco the saucer was more than a photographic platform. Omer wrote in his diary: "I was laboring uphill with some heavy cables in my arms. Falco brought the saucer gently up behind and pushed me up the slope."

Sea Team Solves Its Own Problems

On the evening of Day Eighteen, the pump that brought back the exhaled breath from divers outside the sphere broke down. The depressor had given us trouble before. Now it simply exploded. It was pretty spectacular. Pieces of the machine rattled off the walls of the diving room.

It took two days to get a new depressor to the station, but the work outside did not stop completely. Since the wellhead sat 42 feet lower than the house, the oceanauts found their exhalations would travel up the black hose without mechanical inducement.

The Conshelf team, bottom and top, met and solved more unexpected engineering problems in three weeks than we had in all our undersea operations since 1950. To me the achievement was especially bright because

the team did the job without referring more than two or three decisions to me.

Despite all the safeguards we had devised, lives were at stake. Yet the men—aided by women, who stood long watches in the computer center—brought it off with smart and imaginative seamanship, or perhaps it should be called under-seamanship.

By Day Twenty-one, the sea-floor workers had been away from the known world for six extra days. Although they did not grumble, they could not conceal fatigue. It was telling particularly on Laban, the eldest and the one with the most responsibilities.

After Three Weeks – "Prepare to Surface"

The men of the sea bottom were willing to spend their last physical reserves to carry out the few remaining scientific experiments, which would take several days more. I decided to cancel them. "Let's start the surfacing procedure," I said to Alinat.

Every foreseeable aspect of the ascent was listed in detail. More depended on the oceanauts now than had on the descent. They completely controlled the return to the surface.

The next day would be the most dangerous of our continental-shelf campaign. The greatest risk—and an awful one—was a leak in the bottom hatch. If, on the trip up, helium escaped as outside pressures diminished, the pressure within the house would rapidly fall from 11 atmospheres to one, killing the oceanauts by massive decompression.

Day Twenty-two, the last day of Conshelf Three, opened bright and sweet. The sea was mirror-flat under lambent autumn sunshine. We needed every second of daylight. A night surfacing would be hazardous.

The arithmetic of surfacing began to click. The oceanauts were outside early, casting off cables, until they had only power and videophone left. Our research fleet rallied. In the museum, the data-processing machines stuttered out, engorged with their last ream of information on how oceanauts lived.

Around the ships the water was furrowed with the wakes of launches and inflatables. Walkie-talkies honked. I stood among the

Water can serving as cookie cutter, Rollet carefully collects cores of undisturbed sediment under the gaze of a sardinelike *mendoule.* Traces of radioactive fallout sifting down after nuclear-bomb tests may show up in such sea-floor samples. A ceaseless mild rain of debris builds sediment that roils like explosions when divers walk or drag equipment across the bottom.

TEAR OUT THE ATTACHED PAGE, fold, and keep as a reminder of a memorable evening to come, when you may enter, by way of television, the undersea "World of Jacques-Yves Cousteau." ▶

hundreds of onlookers on the lighthouse terrace, with a walkie-talkie turned low and a devout wish that nobody would pay any attention to me all day. That would mean all was going smoothly.

Ballast Drops but Station Stands Fast

The oceanauts returned from the final outside chores at 11 a.m. and closed the bottom hatch and turned the bolts. Through a porthole they looked at the outside depth gauge that would register their upward movement.

Everything stopped for two hours, while the oceanauts increased internal pressure to test the sphere for leaks. There were none.

Laban turned a crank to release the iron-pellet ballast; in the saucer, Falco saw an immense metallic hailstorm pounding the bottom and sending up mud clouds that hid the station. He hovered in mid-water, waiting to see the house come up. Nothing rose. The station held fast.

EKTACHROME BY PHILIPPE COUSTEAU © N.G.S.

Pressure-dimpled cans of juice and water fill the outside pantry bin. Sea salts penetrated a few tins of water, perhaps through tiny cracks in the soldered seams.

Inspecting intruders in its domain, an ocean sunfish glides by. The *Mola mola,* a young 2½-footer, may grow into a two-ton leviathan on its diet of jellyfish. Small sea animals swarmed unafraid about the fish men, but larger ones usually shied away.

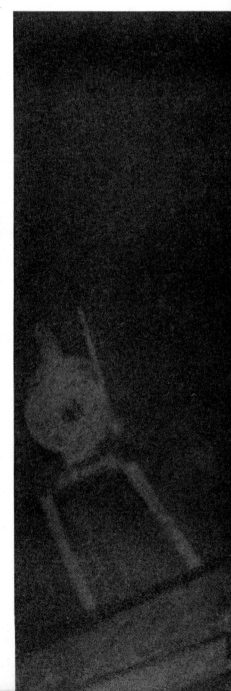

At the lighthouse I glanced at my watch: Less than two hours of daylight remained. I phoned Laban, suggesting that he blow a very small amount of compressed air into the water-ballast tanks, just enough to loosen the station. Too much buoyancy could send it rushing aloft to leap from the sea and wallow about, perhaps injuring those inside.

Laban squirted compressed air for two seconds. The oceanaut at the pressure gauge reported, "She's not moving."

I said to the station chief, "Give it another gentle injection, Dédé."

Laban needled two more seconds of compressed air. Still there was no result.

Conshelf Breaks Free at Last

Day Twenty-two was fading in a lyrical peace that contrasted grimly with the dilemma of the oceanauts, down in the icy dark.

Laban said, "Here goes a bit more," and twisted the aircock.

"Tiens!" exclaimed Coll. "We're shifting."

The deck trembled. The sea dwellers grinned at each other. Inches at a time, the station departed from its foundations. I heard Alinat cry, "She's coming!"

The oceanauts traveled back to their natural habitat much more quickly than they had gone to their adopted one. The trip took only three minutes. The water boiled, and the big checkered globe miraculously appeared on the surface. The red sun vanished over Nice.

Saucer Jets Hail Returning Oceanauts

The vessels gathered protectively around the steel globe. Divers rolled out of rubber boats to make lines fast. The diving saucer surfaced nearby, and Falco turned up his water jets like a New York fireboat hailing a new ocean liner.

In the dark the riggers, navigators, talkers, and divers went to work to undo what had been done the day before the oceanauts went down. Bernard Delemotte plunged under the house and disconnected the remaining power and TV cables from the lighthouse. In two hours he replaced them with lines to a generator and TV room aboard our research vessel, *Calypso*. On the screen we saw the oceanauts turning on the infrared heaters to prepare dinner. I said to Alinat, "These men are great." *Calypso* took up the tow in a mild sea.

At the time the station unstuck itself, the oceanauts had been working and living continuously on the bottom in pressures 11 times normal for 21 days, 17 hours, and 16 minutes. There was nothing in the computer-processed data, self-administered daily medical checkups, or biological samples they had sent to the surface to indicate that their submarine stay had harmed them in any way.

Calypso dragged the undersea house behind the Monaco harbor jetty whence it had started (pages 536-7). Clinging to the sphere were white sea anemones, which had taken up squatters' rights on the house. Inside, the oceanauts began their carefully computed period of decompression. Its duration: 84 hours.

High above us in the stony peaks, the first light touched a colossal Roman monument, the Trophée des Alpes, built in 6 B.C. to honor

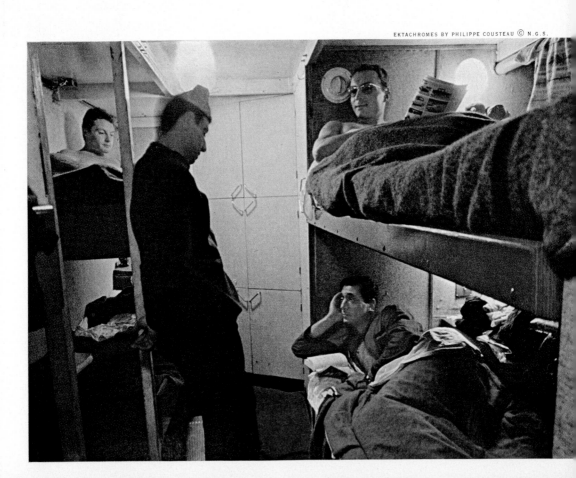

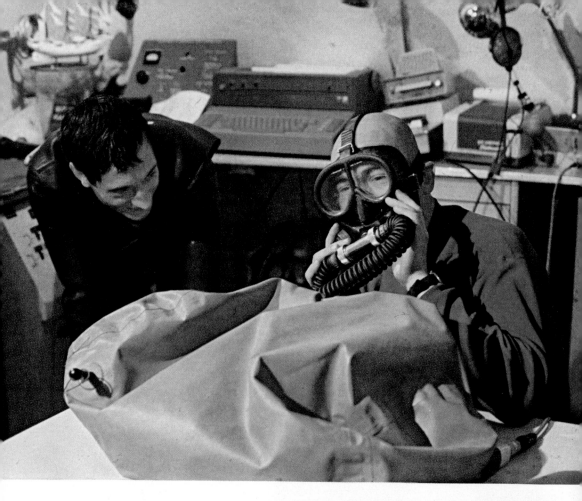

"**Conshelf calling Sealab.**" Two undersea settlements make a historic first contact as Laban talks by telephone to aquanauts of Sealab II, the United States Navy's undersea experiment conducted in 205-foot depths off La Jolla, California. With Coll eavesdropping, Laban speaks first in English, then shifts to French in talking to a bilingual scientist in Sealab 6,000 miles away. Giant neon lung feeds "neox"—neon and oxygen—to help rid Laban's voice of helium squeaks.

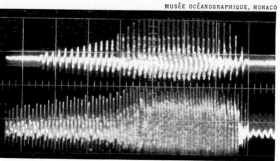

Squiggles of oscillograms contrast Laban's baritone on the surface, upper graph, with his rasping heliox falsetto on the sea floor. Oceanauts soon learned to avoid high-pitched sounds that garbled words. Voices raised in anger produced comical squeals—a deterrent to any argument. The croaks of two frogs sent down with the divers changed to canarylike chirps.

In their undersea Pullman, all six oceanauts could sleep at one time—though the watch-stander's bunk always remained empty. The exhausted men "slept as if dead," said Philippe Cousteau.

Caesar Augustus for his conquest of the Alpine tribes of Gaul. The oceanauts, too, had subdued a hostile territory. Theirs was larger than all Transalpine Gaul. They had helped to double the habitable and exploitable region of the world's continental shelf.

In the falling pressure, the men swallowed and blew their noses to clear their ears. Treble speech reverted to baritone. They did not recognize each other's voices in the masculine register. Somebody phoned the prisoners, "The sun is bright and clear." They groaned. They had not seen the sun for 27 days.

We asked the public what it wanted to know

Par ce système IBM M050 les océanautes sont en liaison directe avec le centre de calcul.

Ils adressent à l'ordinateur les masses des diverses valeurs, effectuées sur place.

Ils ont immédiatement connaissance du résultat des calculs...

about the oceanauts, and passed the questions in to them by teletypewriter.

An elderly woman asked, "Could you have tolerated a longer stay?" Four oceanauts said, "Yes, but not much longer," while two were ready to stay two weeks more. All six replied "No" to a small boy who asked if they'd had nightmares.

Watches Explode As Pressure Drops

A young lady wanted to know if they thought life downstairs would be more agreeable with feminine company. "No," said four oceanauts. One said women would be "agreeable but impossible," while another declared bravely, "One must try."

Many of the questioners asked what was the first thing the oceanauts wanted to do when they emerged. Two of the adventurers were going to see their parents first. One wanted to rest "far from everything;" another preferred "a walk in the country." Still another said he wished to "see other people and let them pamper me."

During decompression, Laban heard a small muffled explosion. In his sea chest, where it had lain unworn since Day Two, was his impressive new deep-sea wristwatch with a shattered crystal. The timepiece had withstood water and exceptional pressure, but had been infiltrated by helium. When the house pressure fell, the helium expanded and smashed its way out. As Laban looked at his broken timepiece, he heard his comrades' watches exploding one by one.

On the evening the oceanauts came out, crowds covered the mole and threatened to capsize our vessels at their berths. Movie lights bathed the sphere as Western Europe watched on television.

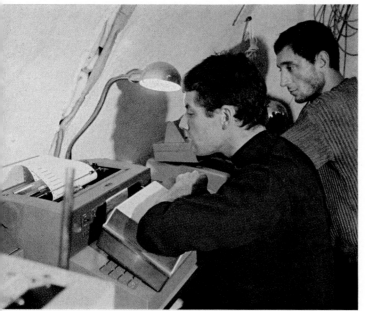

As numbers flash in a memory test sent from shore, Yves Omer tries to type them on a boxlike transmitter that feeds into a computer. Coll awaits his turn. In some instances the men did better below than ashore, perhaps because concentrating was easier in the sphere. A series of tests revealed no deterioration of the oceanauts' reflexes, coordination, or physical well-being. Except for weariness and paleness from lack of sun, they came up exactly as they went down.

"There no longer exists any physiological or psychological obstacle to the occupancy of the entire continental shelf," asserts Captain Cousteau.

EKTACHROMES BY PHILIPPE COUSTEAU; KODACHROME (OPPOSITE) BY BATES LITTLEHALES © N.G.S.

Rampart of clicking computers and communicators, arrayed in the main hall of the Oceanographic Museum at Monaco, serves as the expedition's intelligence center. Manned 24 hours a day, it processes torrents of data emanating from underwater men and machines. Guy Levi-Soussan transmits a memory test to Conshelf Three. TV monitors flash round-the-clock coverage from the sphere and wellhead. Thousands of visitors, watching on sets ringing the center, saw the most candid scenes: Once a naked oceanaut strolled unknowingly before a camera on his way to a shower. Monaco's "Savant Prince," Albert the First, stands watch on a marble flying bridge in the museum he founded 56 years ago.

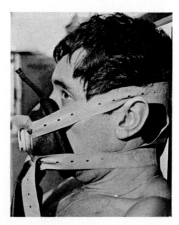

Up at last! Coll breathes deeply of oxygen during decompression.

Homeward come heroes as their sea house, towed by the research vessel *Calypso,* floats safe in Monaco harbor. Before they step ashore, the oceanauts must decompress for 3½ days inside the sphere.

Jubilant captain greets exultant divers. Total time in the sphere: 30 days, 10 hours, 52 minutes. Television audiences in 17 countries watched the moment over Eurovision.

From the top hatch, a red diver's cap and the blanched visage of André Laban appeared. He carried a full briefcase. Dédé had brought his homework back from the office. Grinning, blinking, and greeting friends, up came the other pale hostages to our dream. Six red caps went bobbing through the crowd (left).

A reporter asked Philippe, *"Etes-vous fatigué?"* The cameraman of Conshelf Three said: "Of course; I have never been so tired in my life. But we lived wonderful days. We have the rest of our lives to recover."

Conshelf Three was an epic of triumphant men and failing machines. In this day of automatamania, or worship of gadgets, the oceanauts served up a healthy reminder of how vastly superior to mechanisms old *Homo sapiens* remains.

Of course the equipment was first-class on land, but manufacturers have little experience with machines that must operate in exotic gases under heavy pressure. The oceanauts were forced to battle continually against the equipment in order to maintain their foothold on the bottom.

Vital Steps Toward Conquering the Sea

In addition to the oceanauts' fine accomplishments on the oil-well head, I think Conshelf Three contributed significant gains to the art of occupying the deep-sea bottom:

—We proved our high-pressure breathing system on its first application.

—By using incompressible vests, we showed that full suits of microbead material will lessen hardship for future oceanauts.

—By reducing the ties to the world above, we enabled the station to survive weather that would have forced earlier undersea installations to close down.

We have heeded our own discoveries and learned the lessons they present. The greatest of these is that if man is to make an undersea creature of himself, he must do it wholeheartedly and without a backward glance. As with a newborn infant, the umbilical cord must be severed.

We are now planning Conshelf Four. Our principal effort is to further reduce dependence on the surface. We are confident that within a few years we will entirely eliminate ties to the world above. Then, for the first time, oceanauts will have true freedom of the deep.　　　　THE END

537

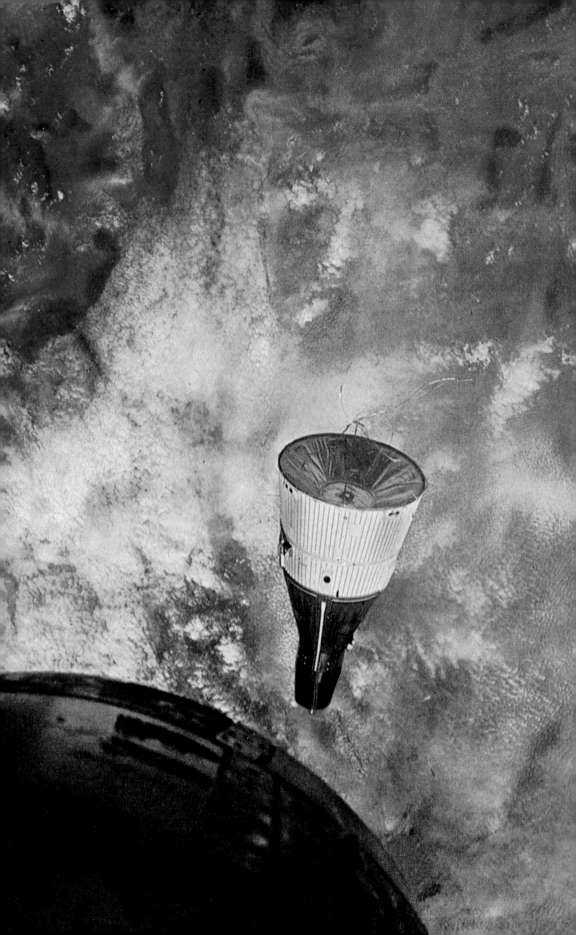

NASA EKTACHROMES BY THOMAS P. STAFFORD

Chase in space nears its triumphant end as Gemini 6 homes in on a moonlike Gemini 7 for the world's first spacecraft rendezvous. Distance between them: 275 feet.

Flying at five miles a second, the two-man American spaceships perform a stately dance (left). Gemini 6 looks straight down at its twin, 90 feet away, and beyond to the cloud-dappled Pacific Ocean, 185 miles below.

Space Rendezvous

MILESTONE ON THE WAY TO THE MOON

By KENNETH F. WEAVER
National Geographic Senior Staff

"IT WAS NIGHTTIME, just becoming light. We were face down, and coming out of the murky blackness below was this little pinpoint of light. The sun was just coming up and was not illuminating the ground yet, but on the adapter of Gemini 6 we could see sunlight glinting, and as it came closer and closer, just like it was on rails, it became a half-moon. At about half a mile we could see the thrusters firing, like water from a hose. And just in front of us it stopped. Fantastic!"

Astronaut James A. Lovell, Jr., thus recalls how he and Frank Borman, command pilot of Gemini 7, saw the historic rendezvous with spacecraft Gemini 6, piloted by Walter M. Schirra, Jr., and Thomas P. Stafford.

Fantastic it was, indeed. For on that December day last year, a day that will live in the annals of exploration of the universe, man cleared away one of the major obstacles on the hard road to the moon. He proved that he could find and reach his fellow man in the vastness of space.

When these American astronauts brought their spaceships

539

EKTACHROMES BY JAMES M. GODBOLD (BELOW), WILLIAM TAUB (LOWER), AND JAMES A. LOVELL, JR.

Rocketing off in pursuit of Gemini 7, G-6 trails a snowy wake as it streaks into space. Winds aloft twist the plume like a pretzel. Camera-bearing Air Force chase planes sweeping up beside the Titan rocket stripe the sky with smaller contrails.

Huge Kennedy Space Center, from 135 miles up, shows as a small bulge on Florida's Atlantic coast as G-7 Astronauts Frank Borman and James A. Lovell, Jr., soar over the peninsula. At this moment, down on Pad 19, technicians labor feverishly to ready G-6 for launch. Command pilot Walter M. Schirra, Jr. (below, foreground), and pilot Thomas P. Stafford check controls in the cabin. After two thwarted attempts, they roared heavenward on December 15, 1965, to rendezvous with G-7.

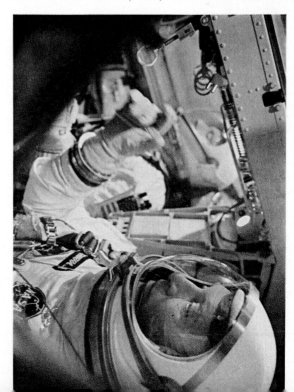

NASA EKTACHR

almost within touching distance 185 miles above the Pacific on December 15, 1965, they pioneered a technique that must be mastered before men can make a round-trip flight to the moon. After exploring its surface, they can return only by making successful rendezvous with their mother ship (pages 552-3).

For that reason the remaining Gemini flights, all scheduled for 1966, are designed primarily to practice rendezvous maneuvers. Indeed, by the time you read this article, Astronauts Neil A. Armstrong and David R. Scott may already have gone into orbit aboard

Gemini 8, seeking to hook up with an Agena spacecraft—an unmanned rocket specially fitted with a docking collar.

What do men say to each other on such an unprecedented occasion as the first meeting in space? When 200 feet still separated G-6 and G-7, Schirra greeted his fellow astronauts with a laconic, "Having fun?"

The words, garbled perhaps, were not heard on the ground, nor was G-7's response:

"Hello, there!"

And then, his eyes aching from the intense glare of the rising sun on the other spacecraft,

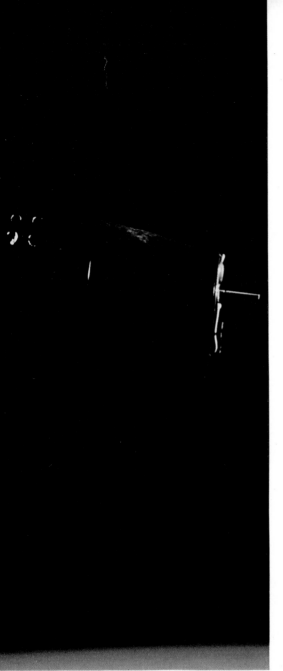

Splash of sunlight marks lines of strain in the bearded face of Navy Commander, now Captain, Lovell during G-7's 14-day, 220-orbit flight.

With the cool skill of a seasoned pilot, Navy Captain Schirra nudges within 14 feet of G-7. Later he closed the gap to a single foot. Smoke from jettisoned staging rockets thinly clouded the windows, but the crews could see each other.

Friendly taunt, carried to space by Schirra and his fellow Annapolis graduate, Air Force Major, now Lt. Col., Stafford, urges football victory over West Point, the alma mater of Air Force Lt. Col., now Colonel, Borman. White shield covers a radar unit used to track G-7.

Schirra said, "Hey, Frank, I see your hatch is on fire!"

A little later, Schirra told ground controllers in Hawaii:

"There seems to be a lot of traffic up here!"

To which Borman shot back, "Call a policeman!"

But the astronauts, for all their joshing, knew better than anyone else the meaning— and the difficulty—of their accomplishment. Their rendezvous came as the climax of an extraordinary chase through space—100,000 miles at speeds of more than 17,300 miles an hour before Gemini 6 closed in on its target (diagrams, pages 546-7). It took nearly six hours of complicated maneuvering, using radar, a global tracking network, and one of the world's largest assemblages of computers, as well as that more primitive instrument known to astronauts as the "Mark I Human Eyeball."

And yet, ironically, it all seemed so simple to the earth-bound audience when Schirra and Stafford eased their four-ton vehicle to

within a single foot of Gemini 7, to look through the windows and marvel at Jim Lovell's 11-day-old beard. Or when they slowly circled in a stately minuet, then settled down to fly nose to nose for hundreds of miles.

Schirra himself noted this irony while flying from Bermuda to Cape Kennedy the day after the Atlantic splashdown. Frowning as he read a sheaf of glowing press reports on the rendezvous, he remarked: "I'm real sorry

they made the rendezvous sound so easy. It may have looked easy, but it was only because we had practiced so much."

Tom Stafford agreed: "I figure we must have worked out at least 80 times in the simulators, an hour and a half each time."

Wally Schirra reacted also to suggestions that if two spacecraft come within three or four miles of each other—as the Russians' Vostok 3 and 4 did momentarily in 1962—then a true rendezvous has been accomplished.

"That's when the job really starts," said Schirra. "I don't think rendezvous is over until you are completely stopped, with no relative motion between the two vehicles, at a range of approximately 120 feet. From there on it's station keeping. That's when you can play the game of driving a car, or driving an airplane; it's about that simple."

Other astronauts agree. "It's easier to fly in

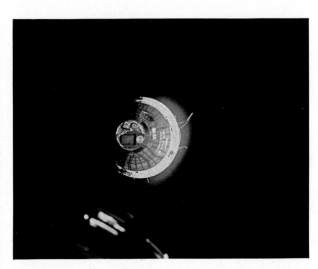

Spaceships part company (above) when Schirra fires his thrusters and moves away from a radiant G-7; both craft orbited the earth at 17,300 miles an hour.

Lovell, watching G-6 recede, photographs it from a quarter mile away (below). Nose of G-7 partially hides a horizon aglow with bands of color at sunset.

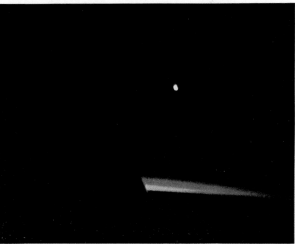

"Brightest thing I've ever seen in my life," Schirra described the sunlight blazing on G-7's white skirt (left). Nose to nose, the vehicles glide through the void in a game of near-tag, and later of celestial ring-around-a-rosy.

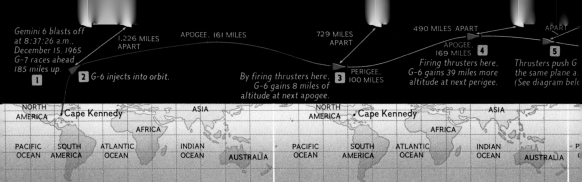

Gemini 6 blasts off at 8:37:26 a.m., December 15, 1965. G-7 races ahead 185 miles up.

1

2 G-6 injects into orbit.

1,226 MILES APART

APOGEE, 161 MILES

By firing thrusters here, G-6 gains 8 miles of altitude at next apogee.

729 MILES APART

3

PERIGEE, 100 MILES

490 MILES APART

APOGEE, 169 MILES **4**

Firing thrusters here, G-6 gains 39 miles more altitude at next perigee.

APART

5

Thrusters push G the same plane a. (See diagram belo

NORTH AMERICA — Cape Kennedy — ASIA

AFRICA

PACIFIC OCEAN — SOUTH AMERICA — ATLANTIC OCEAN — INDIAN OCEAN — AUSTRALIA

NORTH AMERICA — Cape Kennedy — ASIA

AFRICA

PACIFIC OCEAN — SOUTH AMERICA — ATLANTIC OCEAN — INDIAN OCEAN — AUSTRALIA — P O

How Gemini 6 caught its twin in a 6-hour, 100,000-mile chase

LIKE A RACE HORSE on the rail, with less ground to cover than an outside horse, G-6 circled the earth faster than higher-flying G-7. This helped G-6 catch up with G-7. But G-6 also had to climb into G-7's orbit (diagram above). The rules of motion in space helped G-6 rise: Each burn of its thrusters automatically raised its altitude. As G-6 moved farther from earth, Schirra needed less speed to offset the pull of gravity. Thus, G-6 went slower in the higher orbit. Schirra began the chase at 25,414 feet per second. Burns of his thrusters totaled 208.6 feet per second, but by raising his orbits, they slowed him finally to G-7's speed of 25,366 feet per second at rendezvous.

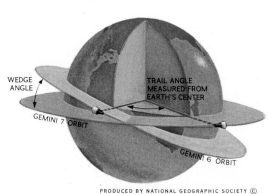

PRODUCED BY NATIONAL GEOGRAPHIC SOCIETY ©

Whirling in different planes, G-6 and 7 could not have rendezvoused without delicate maneuvers. G-6 went into orbit 1,200 miles behind G-7 (trail angle). To catch up, Schirra kept his craft in a lower and faster orbit. While still 439 miles behind, he jockeyed into G-7's plane by turning at a right angle to his line of flight and firing aft thrusters for 40 seconds. This erased the fraction-of-a-degree difference in their orbital planes (wedge angle). The execution of such intricate tactics marks the rendezvous as a masterful feat of flying. The angles in the diagram are exaggerated for clarity.

space than to pilot an aircraft, once you've mastered the controls," says Frank Borman. And Neil Armstrong adds: "Docking is like putting a car in the garage."

Gemini 6 and 7 did not touch, leaving still unanswered the question of whether a spark of static electricity will jump between two docking spacecraft. As a safeguard, the Agena's collar wears metal "whiskers," like a lightning rod, to bleed off any charge.

When Gemini 6 went into orbit, it trailed more than 1,200 miles behind Gemini 7. Its orbit was lower and was tilted slightly to the orbital plane of the other craft.

To correct these differences, Wally Schirra fired his thrusters in a series of skillfully controlled "burns," timing them according to instructions from the ground and computations made by Tom Stafford with the spacecraft's own computer. Stafford, incidentally, was so busy with his navigation duties that he was able to look out of the window no more than 15 minutes during the first six hours of flight.

Schirra, who had more opportunity to observe outside the spacecraft, said later of the cloud-banked earth: "If we four had come from another planet, I'm sure we would have said, 'That's not inhabitable. Let's leave!'"

In the wave of excitement over the successful rendezvous, it is easy to lose sight of the importance of the equally successful 14-day flight of Gemini 7. Dr. George E. Mueller, the National Aeronautics and Space Administration's Associate Administrator for Manned Space Flight, says:

"It's true that we could not go to the moon until we learned to rendezvous. The first astronauts who set foot on the moon will have to rendezvous with the mother ship orbiting 92 miles above them, or they will have no possible way to return to earth.

"But neither could we go to the moon until we learned whether man could function successfully in space for days at a time, and then

288 MILES APART

197 MILES APART   PERIGEE, 170 MILES   APART

APOGEE, 169.5 MILES

G-6 sights G-7 **8**
visually for
first time.

9

APOGEE, 171 MILES

10

G-6 establishes radar
contact with G-7; by a
tweak burn gains 1/2 mile
of altitude at next apogee.
GEE, 139 MILES

7 G-6 fires thrusters
again to gain 31 miles
of altitude at next perigee.

Thrusters begin transfer
of G-6 into G-7's orbit.

After three minor course
corrections, G-6 and G-7
rendezvous 120 feet apart.
Two hours later, they close
to within one foot.

Cape Kennedy   ASIA   NORTH AMERICA   Cape Kennedy   ASIA   NORTH AMERICA

AFRICA   AFRICA

SOUTH AMERICA   ATLANTIC OCEAN   INDIAN OCEAN   AUSTRALIA   PACIFIC OCEAN   SOUTH AMERICA   ATLANTIC OCEAN   INDIAN OCEAN   AUSTRALIA   PACIFIC OCEAN

PRODUCED BY
NATIONAL GEOGRAPHIC SOCIETY ©
GEOGRAPHIC ART DIVISION

adjust easily to gravity on earth after a long period of weightlessness."

The experience of the Gemini 7 pilots with weightlessness is reassuring. They did react to retrofire, the reverse blast of rockets that slows a spacecraft and starts its fiery plunge to earth. But they said they had no real problems after returning to the ground.

"After being desensitized to G's [weightless] for 14 days," reported Borman, "we felt we were going backward when the retrorockets fired—I think John Glenn said back to Hawaii—I felt we were going back to Japan. But when we got back on the carrier, if we had any deterioration at all, it was that our legs were heavy because they hadn't been used. We were able to run a mile the day we got back to the Cape. In my opinion, with proper crew-comfort provisions, people will have no difficulty going a month, two months, or as long as they want to in space."

Both men stressed the necessity of comfort, noting that they functioned much better when they took off their bulky pressure suits.

"One of our biggest problems," says Jim Lovell, "was the same thing that everybody faces here on earth—eating, sleeping, and housekeeping. We were worried that we'd sort of get pushed out of the spacecraft with all the debris that would accumulate. So we spent many hours prior to the flight finding little spots and crevices in the spacecraft

Tail feathers of tape, part of the insulating material used to minimize blast damage at separation, float behind G-7. They flapped on 7's roof during its third orbit, mystifying Lovell and Borman until G-6 reported sighting the cords.

NASA EKTACHROMES BY THOMAS P. STAFFORD

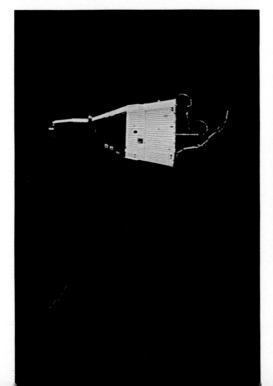

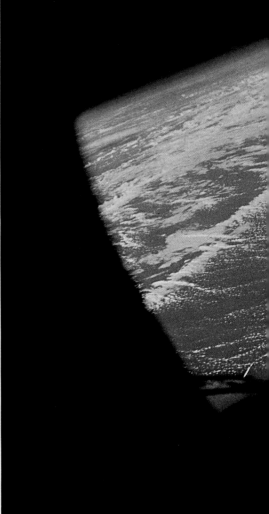

Eye test occupies Borman in this motion-picture sequence taken by cabinmate Lovell. He holds a biteboard that, clamped between his teeth, maintains the proper distance from his face to a binocular device used for testing ability to see detail. Borman has shed his space suit and wears only underwear, as did Lovell during much of the flight.

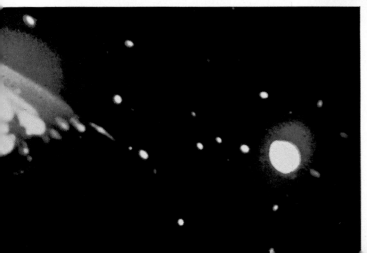

"You guys are really a shaggy-looking group with all those wires hanging out," G-6 radios to G-7 as both pass over the Pacific, 600 miles west of Chile. G-7 to G-6: "You have some too." Gold curtain guards the instrument package from solar radiation.

"Constellation Urion," Astronaut Schirra jokingly labeled this photograph at the postflight press conference. Droplets of urine, vented from G-7 at twilight and instantly frozen in space, follow as miniature satellites. They eventually sublimate and vanish, like dry ice.

where we could pack things. We would eat three meals a day, and Frank would very nicely pack the containers in a small bag, and at the end of the day he would throw it behind the seat. We managed to get nine days' debris behind those seats."

The spacecraft returned surprisingly clean.

"Other Gemini crews," says Lovell, "have reported that they became increasingly tired due to the fact that one person would be on watch and the other sleeping, and communication between the ground and the spacecraft would wake the sleeping person. So we decided to sleep simultaneously.

"We worked on a Houston day. Our watches were set on Houston time. We had a regular work day, had three meals a day, and then at night we went to bed. We put up light filters in the windows and didn't look out, and to us it was nighttime.

"We had absolutely no sensation of movement. Our world was inside the spacecraft. We even had some books along. Frank had one which was quite apropos: It was called *Roughing It,* by Mark Twain!"

These December flights climaxed a year in which five Gemini teams orbited the earth for a total of 650 hours, covering more than

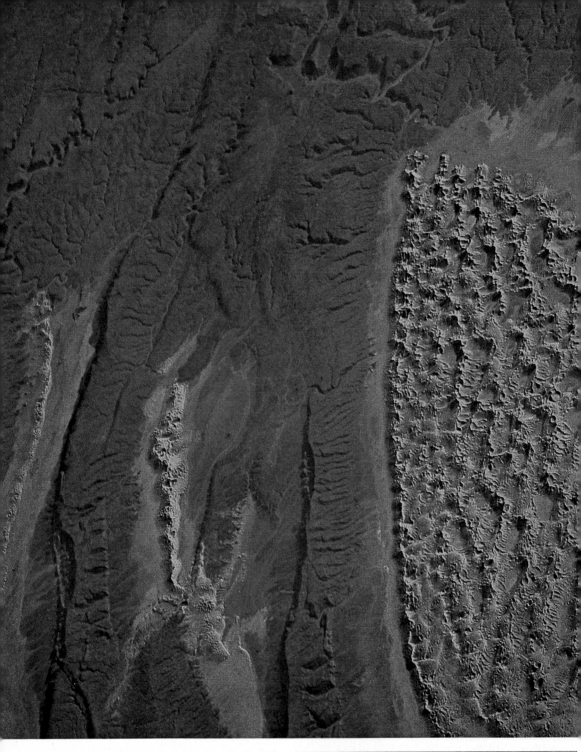

"**We spent many hours** just observing the beautiful tones and colors," Lovell said of North Africa. With hand-held Hasselblad camera, Borman captured the thousand-foot-high Tifernine sand dunes in Algeria from 150 miles up. His 250mm lens looked south as the setting sun burnished the tops of the dunes against a desert darkened by dusk. Filtering effect of the atmosphere tints the earth blue. As Heinz Haber wrote in the GEOGRAPHIC ten years ago—even before the first satellite—ours is "the most beautiful planet of the solar system. It is Earth, the blue planet, the home of man."

550

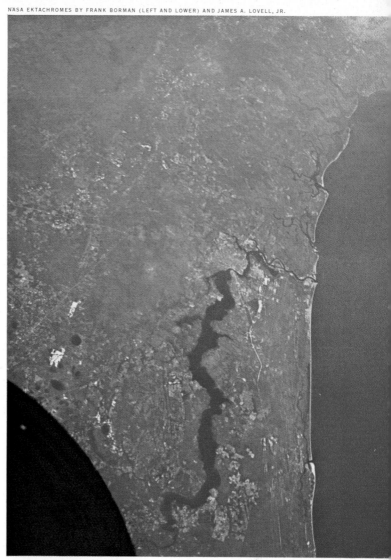

St. Johns River forms a broad path in the low-lying region of northern Florida before narrowing at Jacksonville. Southward, the inlet at St. Augustine appears as a tiny notch in the coast. Gemini pictures are the clearest yet made from space.

Island of Socotra, source of myrrh, frankincense, and dragon's blood—resin of the dragon tree—covers 1,400 square miles, about the size of Rhode Island. This view from G-7, 185 miles high, looks southwest. Islands at top center, The Brothers, lie between Socotra and the African coast. For this and most of their earth photographs, Borman and Lovell used an 80mm lens and a basic exposure of 1/250 at f11.

551

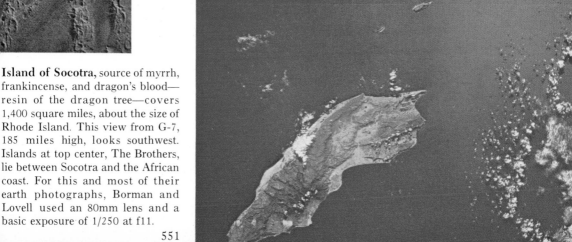

11,000,000 miles—nearly fifty times the distance from here to the moon.

What lies ahead now on the road to the moon? Dr. Mueller forecasts a wind-up of the Gemini program this year, with five two-man flights of from one to three days' length.

"On each flight," he says, "the astronauts will practice rendezvous and actual link-up with an Agena or a similar target. Then they may use the fuel supply of the Agena to propel both vehicles into new orbits and maneuvers. On each flight an astronaut may leave the Gemini vehicle to 'walk around the earth.' * And once the Gemini and Agena have docked as a unit, they may seek out and rendezvous with a second Agena to be left in orbit from a previous Gemini flight."

As Gemini comes to an end, the real moon

*"America's 6,000-Mile Walk in Space," in the September, 1965, GEOGRAPHIC, described this feat.

NASA EKTACHROME BY JAMES A. LOVELL, JR.

Beckoning destination of America's space program, the pearl-like moon rides high over the Pacific. NASA's Apollo astronauts hope to reach it by 1970.

Homeward bound from the moon, a LEM (lunar excursion module) fires its guidance rockets to dock with its orbiting mother ship. The Apollo pilot uses an overhead cross-hair sight to line up with the craft that will return the crew to earth. Artist Meltzer's look at the future incorporates the knowledge and advice of NASA experts, astronomers, and the Apollo contractors, Grumman Aircraft and North American Aviation. Dated June 24, 1969, 12 noon, Greenwich mean time, the painting shows the stars in their true positions for that date.

program, Apollo, gets under way. With the success of G-6 and 7, it is now conceivable that the first manned Apollo vehicle, boosted by the huge Saturn 1B rocket, will carry three astronauts into orbit before the end of 1966. To NASA officials, the goal of Americans on the moon by 1970 now seems within grasp.*

Far beyond Apollo, scientists visualize space crews rendezvousing above the earth to assemble orbiting laboratories, or eventually to put together space ports from which travelers will set out for Mars and even more distant points. And they regard as certain the day when these techniques will permit rescue of astronauts stranded in space and examination of potentially hostile satellites.

Rendezvous—our newest space achievement—makes all this possible. THE END

*See "Footprints on the Moon," by Hugh L. Dryden, NATIONAL GEOGRAPHIC, March, 1964.

WYOMING
High, Wide, and Windy

By DAVID S. BOYER
National Geographic Staff

FOR A MAN who narrowly escaped hanging ninety times a year, Mr. Clover Sturlin seemed remarkably cheerful. He was not the least bit bothered about the grisly fate that threatened him every summer evening in Jackson, Wyoming.

"It's a living," he said, stroking a desperado-type mustache.

A few minutes earlier, with hundreds of other visitors, I had seen "Clover the Killer" get his daily dose of frontier justice. Along about sundown we had heard a distant clatter of hoofs. Looking eastward, we saw a rider on a galloping black horse, pursued by a dozen others.

Near Jackson's main intersection, the posse caught Mr. Sturlin.

TRIGGERED BY EARTH'S INNER FIRES, *geysers steam above a wintry Yellowstone National Park. Old Faithful puffs a cloud that weather researchers have seeded with silver iodide. Gleaming ice crystals fall as man-made snow. Measuring the amounts caused by various chemicals, scientists hope to learn more about weather control.*

554   KODACHROME BY VINCENT J. SCHAEFER © N.G.S.

All four feet off the ground, a flying bronco tries to unseat a Wyoming cowhand at the Frontier Days rodeo in Cheyenne, bringing to life the symbol on the state's license plates. A high, often dry land straddling the Continental Divide, Wyoming pastures three times as many cattle—more than a million head—as it has people. In recent years, petroleum has displaced agriculture (livestock and farming) as the leading industry. Stark mountains, blue lakes, and sweeping plains draw millions of visitors each year; entertaining them ranks third among Wyoming's industries.

EKTACHROMES BY LOWELL J. GEORGIA (ABOVE) AND ROBERT W. FULLER © N.G.S.

Still mounted but with his hands tied behind him, he was led to the town square, where a noosed rope was thrown over an arch of elk antlers. But at the last moment, Mr. Sturlin was granted a chance to shoot it out with the sheriff. There was a popping of blanks, and both men fell "wounded." The tourists loved it.

"It's just like television!" I heard a small spectator exclaim.

As the make-believe ended, Mr. Sturlin made his exit draped across the saddle of his horse. For another 24 hours he would be back in real life—a peace-loving retired cowboy who has never committed any crime more heinous than overtime parking.

With this and other Old West touches, Jackson amuses visitors while housing them in neon-bright motels with swimming pools. Wooden sidewalks boom hollowly under the high-heeled boots of genuine cowpokes and Eastern dudes. In a cocktail lounge, customers marvel at a bar inlaid with 2,231 silver dollars. At the Pink Garter Theater, where college students perform in gaslight-era melodrama, the audience roundly hisses the villain.

Jackson, an authentic Western town despite its modern trappings, serves as a rousing introduction to Wyoming. And a hearty, outgoing expanse of America it is, this second highest state of the Union (after neighboring Colorado). A resort and ranching center close to the Idaho border, Jackson Hole is a fair sample: green valley rimmed by the majestic Teton and Gros Ventre Ranges . . . high country abounding with elk, antelope, and bighorn sheep . . . moose standing tall in swampy willow brakes . . . rushing streams and placid lakes alive with giant trout . . . and always an unbelievably blue sky over craggy peaks rising from an infinity of grassy rangeland.*

A vast upland more than a mile high, Wyoming owns half a dozen mountain ranges outright, and goes partners with neighbor states on a few more. It straddles the Continental Divide, sending its melting snows to both oceans (map, pages 578-9).

In Laramie, the Nation's highest university town, Wyomingites smile at lowland football teams. The visitors bring bottled oxygen to help them battle the husky Cowboys of Wyoming U. on their 7,200-foot-high field.

Yellowstone: First National Park

Besides being one of the highest states, Wyoming is one of the most spectacular. It is also one of the wildest, windiest, and coldest —and, in places, one of the drabbest, saddest, and loneliest. Only a salt-shakering of people live here, a mere 340,000 sprinkled across nearly 100,000 square miles—an area twelve times the size of Massachusetts. Twice as many people live in Boston alone. Of all the states, only Alaska has fewer.

At least two chunks of Wyoming—Yellowstone and Grand Teton National Parks—are household words.

Trapper John Colter discovered the scenic wonders of Yellowstone in 1807; it became the world's first national park, in 1872.†

The Tetons became a park in 1929, and the story of how Jackson Hole came to be added to this public preserve is best told by Horace M. Albright. Mr. Albright, now in retirement in Los Angeles, was Superintendent of Yellowstone back in the 1920's; later he served as Director of the National Park Service.

"In 1924," Mr. Albright told me recently, "Yellowstone had a very important visitor— Mr. John D. Rockefeller, Jr.—with his three older sons. I showed him around and urged him to visit the Jackson Hole country, but did

*Lynda Bird Johnson describes her visit here in "I See America First," GEOGRAPHIC, December, 1965.
†Conrad L. Wirth tells of the start of the Nation's Park System in "Heritage of Beauty and History," NATIONAL GEOGRAPHIC, May, 1958.

Oil-boom city, Casper presents a shining, prosperous face in this time exposure of Center Street. Automobile lights streak and squiggle; street lamps shine like stars. The town boasts 40 millionaires—one for every 1,100 people.

Just 35 miles north lies Teapot Dome, a rich oil field made notorious in the 1920's when the Secretary of the Interior illegally leased Government oil reserves to private companies. Supreme Court action returned them.

Town hat hung like a six-gun on his hip, an off-duty cowboy takes the measure of Cheyenne's 17th Street on a Saturday night.

not mention our hope of adding it to the park.

"Two years later the Rockefellers returned to Yellowstone. I took them to see the Tetons, and the mountains, lakes, and forests made a profound impression upon them. The spectacular beauty of this land, they thought, surpassed anything they had ever beheld.

"I called Mr. Rockefeller's attention to the growing disfigurement along the roadsides—hot-dog stands, dance halls, filling stations, ramshackle buildings, and the like. All I had in mind was showing him the Jackson Hole country and then telling him of our program for getting national-park status for the region.

"Mr. Rockefeller, however, at once saw the possibility of preserving for all time the scenery and the wildlife for the benefit and enjoyment of the public. He asked me to compile a map showing the private properties and to estimate the cost of acquiring them.

"It was an immensely complicated business, of course, and it took years. But the final re-sult was that Mr. Rockefeller purchased more than 33,000 acres of Jackson Hole, for about $1,500,000, and presented them to the people as part of Grand Teton National Park."

Today one of the donor's sons, Laurance S. Rockefeller, who visited Yellowstone with him that summer, continues this pursuit of conservation for public use as the President of Jackson Hole Preserve, Inc.

Visitors Find New Hotel a Boon

Rambling Jackson Lake Lodge (following pages) and the camping and recreational area at Colter Bay command breathtaking panoramas of the Tetons. Laurance Rockefeller, a Trustee of the National Geographic Society, told me one afternoon how the hotel and the campsite were born.

"On one of our trips to Jackson Hole, about 1951," he said, "my father heard that so many people were visiting the park they *(Continued on page 564)*

MONARCHS IN RAIMENT OF SNOW, *the Tetons dwarf Jackson Lake, its lodge and cottages. Immense picture windows of Jackson Lake Lodge frame fantastic views of the peaks. The buildings, accommodating 1,100 guests, lie low on the land—in harmony with the setting.*

560   KODACHROME BY WILLIAM ALBERT ALLARD © N.G.S

OPPOSITE PAGE FOLDS OUT

couldn't find accommodation. Many were sleeping in their cars. It was then that he thought of building a hotel so that others could enjoy the beauty of the Tetons, as we had on many trips over nearly thirty years.

"With park officials, we chose the site— Lunch Tree Hill, where we had often picnicked. The Park Service supplied land, utilities, landscaping. Jackson Hole Preserve, Inc., built the hotel. All profits go to conservation."

Like millions of others, I have marveled at the Tetons, framed in the big picture windows of Jackson Lake Lodge. I like the scene even better through the trees from Colter Bay. Here the Rockefellers made a home for those who take their parks a bit more basically.

Colter Bay: Haven for Kitless Campers

For the family that has never camped, that doesn't own a tent, a sleeping bag, or even a frying pan, Colter Bay has the answer—log-shelter campsites and camping gear for rent, by the night or by the week (page 590). Even an especially designed trailer camp is provided, where people who take their homes with them can tie on to electric power, sewer, and other connections, and find a cafeteria, laundry machines, showers, and grocery store within walking distance.

Fittingly, between them Yellowstone and Grand Teton National Parks attract more than two million visitors a year to Wyoming —seven times the state's own population. But countless others use Interstate Highway 80 across the southern part of the state as a sort of transcontinental racetrack, scarcely stopping for hamburgers or gasoline.

Wyomingites consider this dash across their land a sorrow. A few think it should be made a misdemeanor. After seeing the rest of Wyoming, I'm inclined to agree.

My travels took me to Cheyenne, the lively capital; to oil-rich Casper, the "other city," whose population almost equals Cheyenne's 52,000; and to dozens of towns. I remember most fondly the little places with the poetry of a rugged young country in their names.

The Indians named Ten Sleep, because they reckoned the site was ten days' travel from Fort Laramie or from the Yellowstone hunting grounds. Chugwater Creek is named for an Indian legend that a tribe once drove buffalo over a bluff to slaughter them, and the beasts landed with a chugging sound.

The most graceful name of all belongs to a pleasant town in the Bear Lodge Mountains of northeastern Wyoming, not far from Devils Tower National Monument (page 588). It is

Plume of vapor towers 150 feet (opposite) as Old Faithful erupts in Yellowstone. Though it performs every 67 minutes on the average, the geyser is hardly faithful enough to set a watch by; it has waited as long as 96 minutes and as little as 33. Ten to twelve thousand gallons shoot out during each four-minute burst.

Fighting fiery gas, a workman sprays water on a well near Cody. Reaching for oil, the drillers hit instead a pocket of natural gas; a spark in the drill rig ignited it. Twelve million cubic feet burned in four days and nights before firemen put it out.

Fifth among states in oil production, Wyoming harbors reserves estimated at a billion and a half barrels. Twenty-seven million acres, though leased, remain to be explored.

Gnarled fingers of lightning stab sand dunes at Rock Springs. Interstate 80 appears as a luminous band, painted by automobile headlights. "The thunder here is not like the tame thunder of the Atlantic coast," wrote 19th-century historian Francis Parkman of a summer storm. "Bursting with a terrific crash directly above our heads, it roared over the boundless waste . . . seeming to roll around the whole circle of the firmament with a peculiar and awful reverberation. The lightning flashed all night . . . revealing the vast expanse . . . and then leaving us shut in as if by a palpable wall of darkness."

EKTACHROME BY JACK E. RICHARD (UPPER) AND KODACHROME BY LOWELL J. GEORGIA © N.G.S.

Ball game, Indian style: Feathered braves and booted squaws, linked wrist to wrist by handkerchiefs, run after the ball during the All American Indian Days in Sheridan. Each summer 2,000 Indians from some 40 tribes across the continent gather here to stage the three-day festival, climaxed by a beauty contest to select Miss (Indian) America.

Oil-drum horse, towed by a vintage roadster, bucks through Cheyenne as members of "Forty-and-Eight," a veterans' organization formed after World War I, help celebrate Frontier Days. Loosely mounted tail wheel adds eccentric motion to the steed. A week-long carnival in rawhide, Frontier Days will erupt for the 70th consecutive year this July.

EKTACHROME (BELOW) BY LOWELL J. GEORGIA; KODACHROME BY DAVID S. BOYER © N.G.S.

moon Lake, treating us to glassy, inverted images of Cloud Peak and Bomber Mountain. Deep down in the cold, dark mirror flickered the stars, half a million diamonds set in the lake floor, washed and sparkling. The Wyoming heavens were winking upward.

Edward Schunk, a young rancher from Sheridan, reined in, tilted back his ten-gallon hat, and took a long look. So did the rest of us: Dr. William F. Schunk, who moved to Wyoming from North Dakota before his son Ed was born; businessman John Ferries and his son Greg, who had just moved to Wyoming weeks before; and I.

Will and Ed had ridden to this Cloud Peak Primitive Area dozens of times. For me, it was a first pack trip in the snow; for John and Greg, a first into high country at all. Now we sat still in our saddles, transfixed, near the top of a very high world.

Dr. Will rested a gloved hand on the rump of his patient old mountain horse, Socks, and waved out toward Mistymoon.

"You see," said Doc, "you've got to move off the highway and get up into the hills to see the real Wyoming!"

We pushed across a snowy pass above the Christmas-card lake. Before the moon set we had built a fire, broiled a steak, and unrolled sleeping bags in a white silence beside another lake, called Solitude.

Next to wife and kids, Will Schunk loves Solitude best. A physician in Sheridan, Doc has devoted half a lifetime to protecting wilderness areas. There are eight in Wyoming—some of the most extensive and spectacular reaches of unspoiled land in the Nation.

The Wilderness Society, of which Doc is a member, scotched plans to slash a road in to Solitude and lower its waters for irrigation. Now there was no road, and we were very much alone in these high mountains.

"Someone once called Wyoming 'the land of high altitudes and low multitudes,'" said Doc, as we crawled into our sleeping bags. "The only thing we're sure of today is the first part. High multitudes may be on their way."

I knew what he meant. Bumper-to-bumper traffic in Yellowstone-Teton suggests that tourists may become a stampede. The whole tempo of Wyoming life is accelerating.

A hundred years ago, Wyoming was a land of trails: the Oregon Trail (pages 572-3), the California Emigrant Trail, the Mormon Trail, and others—wagon ruts across the plains and through the Rockies, the highroads of the Old West. For the pioneers, this was a region of cruel mountains, battering rivers, and hostile

Sundance, so called for the festivals once common to all Plains Indian tribes.

I also saw places called Goose Egg and Greybull, Mule Creek Junction and Lightning Flat, Little America and Pitchfork, Lost Cabin and Recluse, Wolf and Moose. Others hint at Wyoming's frontier past: Crazy Woman Creek, Powder River, Whiskey Gap, Rattlesnake Range, Baby Wagon Creek, and Hell's Half Acre. Most amount to little more than a building or two at a wide place in the road; they serve as trade centers and post offices for cattle and sheep ranchers who live miles away on far-flung spreads.

Wyoming Hoards Scenic Treasures

My most indelible experience was an October pack trip into the Bighorn Mountains. For hours we rode through deep snow, with only the blowing of horses and creak of leather breaking the silence. Night overtook us, and moonlight through the evergreens cast picket-fence shadows across the trail.

Our horses whinnied up a sudden conversation, nickering back and forth. We straightened up in our saddles. There it was: Misty-

Man-made Grand Canyon:
To bare rich veins of uranium ore, miners gouged 30 million tons of barren rock from this pit near Jeffrey City.

The Dave Johnston Power Plant, largest in the Rocky Mountains, casts rapierlike reflections on the North Platte River near Glenrock. Fueled by coal, the plant serves as a nighttime landmark for airplane pilots a hundred miles away.

Begrimed taconite miner Jack Finley comes off duty at U. S. Steel's mine in Atlantic City, Wyoming.

KODACHROMES BY DAVID S. BOYER (ABOVE AND OPPOSITE) AND LOWELL J. GEORGIA © N.G.S.

Indians—obstacles and miseries overcome at oxen pace.

Early travelers left their names here on trailside rocks, their dead in shallow graves, and sagas of hardship in the history books. Some liked the looks of the land and stayed.

Wyoming Territory came into being in 1868 because of the Union Pacific Railroad. The U. P. had picked the flattest possible right of way through 440 miles of dreary sagebrush hills from what is now Nebraska to Utah. It spawned five brawling Wild West children along its way—Cheyenne, Laramie, Rawlins, Rock Springs, and Evanston. As five county seats, the towns governed great slices of wilderness country during territorial days. But by 1890, when Wyoming achieved statehood, the number of counties had grown to 12.

Ever since covered-wagon days, travelers have drifted by and dropped off. Most Wyomingites still seem to come from somewhere else. They find here an echo of early Western comradeship. Wyoming is where a stranger gets a cheery "Good morning!" even if it isn't. And where no man stays a stranger.

Partly for these reasons, Wyoming has been rediscovered. A new wave of pioneers is pressing in, many to develop the state's dormant natural resources. Having located untold mineral wealth in Wyoming, they see a snowballing economy, cities building, an era of manufacturing, people rolling in by millions.

"The good Lord," a newcomer said, "made a lot of Wyoming into desert. But He made up for it with what He left underground."

No Coal Worries for 300 Years

Somehow I had never thought of Wyoming as an important state in oil production. But it ranks fifth in the Nation. More than anything else it has coal, God's plenty of it. Its reserves could supply the entire United States for 300

IN THE GOLDEN DUST, *a vision of the past.*
Early-morning roundup brings in a string of
saddle horses at Eatons' Ranch near Sheridan.
But the Wild West has changed; these mounts
will carry vacationing dudes rather than cowboys.

KODACHROME BY DAVID S. BOYER © N.G.S.

Oregon or bust! Hundreds of prairie schooners buck "this cursed wilderness." In the picture by William H. Jackson, pioneers trudge across the Continental Divide at South Pass. Francis Parkman, who followed the Oregon Trail in 1846, reported "abundant and melancholy traces of their progress. . . . Sometimes we passed the grave of one who had sickened and died on the way. The earth was usually torn up, and covered thickly with wolf-tracks. . . . One morning, a piece of plank . . . attracted our notice, and riding up to it, we found the following words very roughly traced upon it, apparently with a red-hot piece of iron: *Mary Ellis, Died May 7th, 1845, Aged two months.* Such tokens were of common occurrence."

Ruts of prairie schooners, cut more than a century ago, still scar the limestone plain near Guernsey.

Arrowhead in a bison skull — a Plains Indian nearly hit the bull's-eye. The relic at Farson survives from an age when buffalo provided every need for the red man: food, clothing, shelter, beds, ropes, saddles, fuel, boats, and skins for trading.

years. Uranium ore, too, bulks large; the state bows only to New Mexico in annual production. Wyoming also mines most of the Nation's bentonite, a versatile clay used principally in steelmaking and to condition oil-well drilling muds; and virtually all its trona, a mineral used in manufacturing glass, soap, textile dyes, and paper.

Sheep and cattle outnumber people in Wyoming better than ten to one—except possibly during the tourist season, when a stampede of free-spending visitors makes cash registers jingle to the tune of ninety million dollars a year.

Nearly a billion dollars of new investment has been pumped into Wyoming industry in a decade. Many of the millions went into huge new plants to exploit low-grade iron ore, high-grade gypsum, and coal for electric power. Economists foresee an even faster growth in industry. And, of course, in people.

Not all Wyomingites view such a future with enthusiasm. One old-timer told me:

"Sure, new year-round industry would help us in the winter, when the tourists are gone and there's some unemployment. But how many people can come in and settle before our towns start growing into cities and the whole state starts to change? The way things are, we've got God's country pretty much to ourselves. And that's the way I like it."

Rangeland Bristles With Minutemen

Cheyenne, once a roistering railroad and cowboy town whose streets frequently resembled shooting galleries, now has a major industry a hundred million times more lethal than the wildest of the Wild West. The men with fingers on today's triggers are a new breed, absolutely sober and clean.

I met a pair of them deep underground. Air Force Maj. James M. Donohue and Capt. Gerald W. Buchman wore spotless white coveralls, punctuated by black pistols on their hips. They showed me the "triggers"—actually two keyholes, so far apart that no one man could reach both—which could send ten Minuteman missiles screaming over the roof of the world, carrying awesome nuclear power.

Around Cheyenne clusters the free world's greatest concentration of combat intercontinental ballistic missiles. Here, a rifleshot away from Wyoming's Capitol, lies Francis E. Warren Air Force Base, headquarters of one of the Nation's newest missile sites.

The 90th Strategic Missile Wing controls 200 of the Nation's more than 800 Minuteman missiles. The wing's installations lie scattered

Fishing in rock, Dr. Paul O. McGrew lands sunfish, herring, and *Notogoneus* (foreground) that swam 50 million years ago, when southwestern Wyoming was covered by a lake. The University of Wyoming professor studies fossils from the Green River shale near Kemmerer.

Like a bullet in a cocked pistol, a Minuteman missile stands as a deterrent against enemy attack. The solid-fuel rocket can deliver a nuclear warhead 6,300 miles from its silo in the prairie. Maintenance crew slides open the four-foot-thick protective lid.

across 8,300 square miles of rangeland extending into Colorado and Nebraska. Miles apart, the missiles present an almost inconceivably difficult target to any enemy, for they are buried in underground silos, invulnerable except to a direct hit.

Twice a week, for a 24-hour day, Major Donohue and Captain Buchman control ten missiles. These Minutemen could be fired in less than a minute after receiving a verified "fast-reaction" Presidential order.

We were deep down inside a "launch-control facility." This steel-and-concrete underground fortress has an electronic core, a two-man heart.

"If we ever do get the word, we'll *know* it has come from the President!" Jim Donohue assured me. "If people could only know how elaborate and absolutely foolproof the system is—the system to prevent the arrival of a false message—they would never worry. But, of course, the details are secret.

"Also, there isn't much we can say about how we rule out the possibility of an unauthorized firing, but there are many safeguards against its happening," Major Donohue continued. "In order to launch a Minuteman, for example, more than one crew must authenticate firing orders and throw switches before any missile can get off the ground."

These "hardened" underground missile sites bespeak U. S. policy of striking back, or waging war only in retaliation. The system is built to ride out an atomic attack; then, with men and missiles still intact, to destroy an enemy with a counterblow.

"Obviously," Jerry Buchman said, "an enemy will try to knock our missiles out, but we feel perfectly safe down here."

Jim Donohue had a parting word.

"We even feel safe about Cheyenne, where our wives and kids live," he said. "You see, we really believe that it is our being here, ready to retaliate, that protects them, and everybody else. It's more than just a clever slogan when we say 'Peace Is Our Profession.'"

Cheyenne Relives Its "Frontier Days"

It seemed a long jump backward into Wyoming's past, from a nuclear-missile silo to Cheyenne in the frenzy of Frontier Days. For a week in July the city bulged and throbbed with people (page 566).

A sort of Mardi Gras in rawhide, Frontier Days has been held annually since 1897. Crowds up to 45,000 watched each performance of this granddaddy of rodeos. Riders risked their necks in feats of calf roping,

bulldogging, broncobusting (page 556), and wild-horse racing. Afterward there was dancing in the streets and action in the bars.

"Hell on Wheels," they had once called Cheyenne, back in the late 1860's, the years of the town's tumultuous birth as a division point on the westward-pushing Union Pacific Railroad. The U. P.'s arrival set more than the stage for a state. It launched one of the most ripsnorting booms in American history. With the railroad builders came swarms of gamblers, land speculators, claim jumpers, and other bellicose types who looked for trouble and usually found it.

Now, the people who had crowded with me into Cheyenne were simply looking for fun—and finding it.

Northwest from Cheyenne, nearly the breadth of the state away, lies the little ranching center of Pinedale. There I looked further back into Wyoming's beginnings.

Mountain Men Ride Again

Wyoming, some say, got its first reputation because of a hat. In the early 19th century beaver hats were the rage in New York, London, Paris, and Vienna. And in Wyoming trappers and traders penetrated some of the West's best beaver country (and some of its worst Indian country) to furnish the pelts.

Autumnal gold floods a valley as hayfields yield their abundance beneath peaks already heavy with snow. Hay covers half of Wyoming's cropland; sugar beets, wheat, oats, barley, and corn grow on the remainder.

Indians, with beaver pelts to trade for guns and powder, knives and traps, blankets, tobacco, and liquor. While here, they tested their prowess against the white men in wrestling, horsemanship, and drinking.

"There are thousands of people watching here today," said Jim Harrower, Pinedale's mayor, "more than have come together for any event in Sublette County in 125 years. But there were more here for some of those original rendezvous. Of course, 95 percent of them were Indians then."

But things didn't look much different at this rendezvous. The cowboys, wives, and kids of Sublette County had ridden into Pinedale in "tribes," wearing Indian costume. With a few buckskinned cowboys and ranchers playing the roles of the mountain men, they brought Wyoming history alive.

They plan to immortalize it further. Late this spring they hope to break ground for a Museum of the Mountain Men.

Indians Lived Here in 11,000 B.C.

Leapfrog a few mountain ranges northward to the town of Cody, and you stand in a museum where the Old West already lives in elegance. Paintings and sculpture by cowboy artist Charles Russell and his contemporary, Frederic Remington, enhance a gallery of art and artifacts.

I talked with Western author Harold McCracken, Director of the Whitney Gallery of Western Art.

"It is the Wyoming cowboy who has captured the world's fancy, you know," said Dr. McCracken. "Our Crows, our Blackfeet, our Sioux, and our Shoshoni are the Indians that are best known across the world, as well."

Moreover, Dr. McCracken is making known to the world some of the Indians who inhabited Wyoming as early as 6000 B.C. He directs excavations, supported by the National Geographic Society, at Mummy Cave near Cody.

Across the state, at Hell Gap in eastern Wyoming, another expedition, sponsored by our Society and Harvard University's Peabody Museum of Archaeology and Ethnology, has discovered traces of the oldest houses yet known in the Americas. Circles of postholes mark the sites of two round huts built some 10,000 years ago. Prof. J. O. Brew, Peabody

Several of their annual rendezvous took place in the valley of the Green River.

Names of these mountain men became legends—Gen. William H. Ashley, Jim Bridger, Kit Carson, Thomas Fitzpatrick, Joe Meek, Robert Campbell, Andrew Drips, Lucien Fontenelle, Jedediah Smith, David E. Jackson, William Sublette, and many more.

Now, in Sublette County, just outside Pinedale, the mountain men ride again each July. It is the Green River Rendezvous—held where the stream flows down from the cloud-piercing Wind River Range—a wild, swirling re-enactment of the annual gathering.

To the original rendezvous flocked the

MONTANA
WYOMING
IDAHO
UTAH
COLORADO
110°
108°
44°
42°
Yellowstone
Emigrant
Absaroka Range
Gallatin
Madison Ra.
Miner
Corwin Springs
Electric Peak
Gardiner
Mammoth Hot Springs
Gallatin Ra.
Hebgen L.
Mt. Holmes
Mt. Washburn
Canyon Village
YELLOWSTONE
NATIONAL
PARK
West Yellowstone
Surprise Pool
Morning Glory Pool
Old Faithful
W. Thumb
Shoshone L.
Yellowstone L.
Heart L.
Lake
Fishing Bridge
Sylvan Pass
Lamar
Nye
Granite Peak
Silver Gate
Cooke City
Pilot Peak
SHOSHONE
Indian Peak
Dead Indian Peak
Trout Pk.
Mummy Cave
NATIONAL
TE Ranch
Bobcat Ranch
Valley
S. Fk. Shoshone
Needle Mt.
Two Ocean Pass
Younts Pk.
Francs Pk.
FOREST
Togwotee Pass
Continental Divide
Pacific Creek
Colter Bay
Jackson L.
Moran
Jackson Lake Lodge
GRAND TETON
TARGHEE
TETON
NAT. PARK
Grand Teton
Kelly
TETON NATIONAL
Moose
Jackson Hole
Jackson
Wilson
Gros Ventre
Gros Ventre Ra.
FOREST
Teton Pass
Marysville
Felt
Tetonia
Driggs
Victor
Snake River Ra.
TO IDAHO FALLS
Palisades Res.
Alpine
Snake
Hoback
Bondurant
Hoback Pk.
Etna
Star Valley
Thayne
Bedford
Turnerville
Salt River Range
Wyoming Range
Auburn
Grover
Afton
Fairview
Smoot
Merna
BRIDGER
Daniel
Fremont L.
Pinedale
SUBLETTE
NATIONAL
Boulder
Circle Ranch
Marbleton
Big Piney
Wyoming Peak
FOREST
La Barge Cr.
Geneva
Montpelier
Calpet
La Barge
Cokeville
Bear Lake
Smiths Fk.
Hams Fk.
Fontenelle Reservoir
LINCOLN
Sage
Frontier
Kemmerer
Diamondville
Opal
Elkol
OREGON TRAIL
Randolph
Woodruff
Bear
Evanston
Fort Bridger
Urie
Lyman
Carter
Muddy Cr.
UINTA
Altamont
Aspen
Piedmont
Mountainview
Robertson
Lonetree
Blacks Fork
McKinnon
Elizabeth Mt.
Manila
Dutch John
Uinta Mountains
Kings Pk.
Marsh Pk.
Mt. Lena
Weber
Uinta
Whiterocks
Tridell
Maeser
Vernal
Zenobia Peak
DINOSAUR NATIONAL MONUMENT
Greystone
Sunbeam
Maybell
Yampa
Lay
Craig
Hayden
Milner
Steamboat Springs
Elkhead Mts.
Hahns Peak
Baggs
Dixon
Savery
Slater
Little Snake
Shell Cr.
Pine Mt.
FLAMING GORGE NAT. RECREATION AREA PROPOSED
Flaming Gorge Reservoir
Green
Boyd
Edgar
Roberts
Fromberg
Bridger
Red Lodge
Washoe
Belfry
Bearcreek
Clarks Fk.
Pryor
BIGHORN CANYON RECREATION AREA
Yellowtail Reservoir
Warren
Frannie
Elk Basin
Clark
Deaver
Cowley
Garland
Powell
Ralston
Lovell
Kane
Byron
Heart Mt.
Shoshone
Himes
Cody
Buffalo Bill Res.
Emblem
Greybull
Shell
Burlington
BIG HORN
Otto
Basin
Tatman Mt.
Manderson
Hyattville
Greybull
Meeteetse
Pitchfork
Sunshine Res.
Fifteenmile Creek
Worland
Ten Sleep
Nowood Cr.
Gooseberry Cr.
Grass Creek
Winchester
Neiber
HOT SPRINGS
Hamilton Dome
Gebo
Kirby
Lucerne
WASHAKIE
No Water Cr.
Thermopolis
East Thermopolis
Owl Creek Mts.
Boysen
Boysen Res.
Duncan
Dubois
Union Pass
Wind River
Wind River Range
Downs Mt.
Gannett Pk.
BRIDGER
Fremont Pk.
NAT.
Crowheart
WIND RIVER INDIAN RES.
Bull L.
Pavillion
Kinnear
Ocean L.
Shoshoni
Bonneville
Lysite
Lost Cabin
Moneta
Poison Cr.
Armito
Hiland
Waltman
Hell's Half Acre
FREMONT
Fort Washakie
Riverton
Roberts Mt.
Wind River
St. Stephens
Arapahoe
Hudson
Lander
FOREST
SHOSHONE NAT. FOR.
Wind River Pk.
Atlantic Pk.
Granite Pk.
Atlantic City
South Pass City
South Pass
Sweetwater
Muskrat Creek
Gas Hills Uranium Mining Dist.
Ervay
Rattlesnake Range
Jeffrey City
Granite Range
Green Mountains
Alcova Res.
Independence Rock
Pathfinder Res.
Muddy Gap
Whiskey Gap
Bairoil
Lamont
Seminoe Dam
Seminoe Reservoir
Little Sandy Cr.
Big Sandy Reservoir
Pacific Cr.
Eden Valley Res.
Bear Cr.
Farson
Eden
Sandy Cr.
Bad Lands Hills
Lost Cr.
Hay Res.
Lost Creek Lake
Red Lake
Mahoney Lakes
Steamboat Mountain
Superior
South Superior
Thayer Jct.
Stansbury
Reliance
Point of Rocks
Westvaco
Granger
Verne
SWEETWATER
Bryan
Little America
Green River
Rock Springs
Aspen Mts.
Black Buttes
Bitter Creek
Table Rock
Tipton
Pine Butte
Wamsutter
Creston
Continental Divide
U.P. Mammoth Kill Site
Muddy Cr.
CARBON
Rawlins
Sinclair
Ft. Fred Steele
Walcott
Bridger Pass
Sierra Madre
Saratoga
MEDICINE
Encampment
Riverside
Bridger Pk.
NATIONAL
Garryowen
CUSTER BATTLEFIELD NATIONAL MONUMENT
St. Xavier
Lodge Grass
Rosebud Mts.
Wyola
Tongue River Reservoir
Parkman
Dayton
Ranchester
Acme
Sheridan
Bighorn Mountains
Sheep Mt.
BIGHORN
Hunt Mt.
NATIONAL
FOREST
Wolf
Big Horn
Banner
SHERIDAN
CLOUD PEAK PRIMITIVE AREA
Cloud Peak
L. Solitude
Mistymoon
Powder River Pass
Mayoworth
Bigtrails
Middle Fk.
Buffalo Cr.
Powder River
NATRONA
PRODUCED BY NATIONAL GEOGRAPHIC SOCIETY © CARTOGRAPHIC DIVISION

WYOMING

WITH ITS JAGGED PEAKS, green valleys, and sagebrush plains, Wyoming bears the indelible stamp of the Old West. Cowboys still ride the range, though they sometimes drive jeeps or helicopters. The population totals only half that of Boston, Massachusetts. Across the open rangeland lie scores of missile launching sites, their weapons in underground concrete silos. Minerals lead the economy; Wyoming ranks fifth in petroleum production, ninth in natural gas. Deposits of soft coal could supply the entire United States for centuries. The state's tallest mountain, Gannett Peak in the Wind River Range, rises to 13,785 feet. South of matchless Yellowstone, 13,766-foot Grand Teton mirrors itself in the cool blue lakes of Grand Teton National Park.

Equality State, so called because of its early adoption of woman suffrage. **AREA:** 97,914 sq. mi., ranks 9th. **POPULATION:** 340,000, ranks 49th. **ECONOMY:** minerals (oil, natural gas, iron, uranium), ranching (2d in U. S. in wool), farming, tourism. **CLIMATE:** Summer temperatures, though ranging above 100° F. in desert areas, are generally temperate. An average elevation of 6,700 feet results in prolonged winters. **MAJOR CITIES:** Cheyenne, pop. 52,000, capital (State Capitol shown below); Casper, 45,000; Laramie, 20,000. **ADMISSION:** 1890 as 44th state.

EKTACHROME BY LOWELL J. GEORGIA © N.G.S.

POSTER COURTESY BUFFALO BILL MUSEUM, CODY, WYOMING; KODACHRO
BY TED SPIEGEL (BELOW) AND DAVID S. BOYER © N.

Fighter for the vote, Esther Hobart Morris helped inspire the act that gave Wyoming its nickname: Equality State. The territorial government in 1869 became first in the world to grant women the vote. The statue, standing before the State Capitol in Cheyenne, contrasts with the drum majorette leading the University of Wyoming band at Laramie.

Annie Oakley, "Peerless Lady Wingshot," appeared with Buffalo Bill Cody's Wild West show. Her name became a synonym for free tickets, which usually bore perforations resembling the bullet holes she shot in playing cards during her act.

director, and field leaders Cynthia Irwin-Williams, Henry Irwin, and George Agogino have uncovered a continual sequence of cultures here from 11,000 B.C. to the present. They have also found some of the finest flint artifacts of North America.

Outside Cody's Whitney Gallery, with Winchester rifle raised high, a familiar figure rides a bronze horse—the man for whom the town was named, Col. William Frederick "Buffalo Bill" Cody, among the most colorful heroes the West has known.

Iowa-born Cody moved to Kansas with his parents and while still a boy became a Pony Express rider. Later, as a professional buffalo hunter, he supplied tons of meat to railroad construction crews.

He won his nickname fairly, no doubt, but one story still told pokes a little fun. A buffalo gored his horse and chased him across the prairie. A colleague, hearing of the incident, roared with laughter: "That's our Bill, our Buffalo Bill!"

By 1872 Cody had become a widely known figure, picturesque in fringed buckskin and with flowing yellow locks and whiskers. Encouraged by admirers, he organized a Wild West show. For years the troupe thrilled crowds all over the United States and Europe with its daredevil cowboys, howling redskins, clattering stagecoaches, and the astounding feats of Annie Oakley, "Little Sure-shot."

Cody also served as an Army scout, helping

BUFFALO BILL'S WILD WEST·

CONGRESS, ROUGH RIDERS OF THE WORLD.

A. Hoen & Co., Baltimore, U.S.A.

MISS ANNIE OAKLEY,
THE PEERLESS LADY WING-SHOT.

Gen. Philip H. Sheridan quell Indian uprisings. Soldiers with Colonel Cody told how he killed Cheyenne Chief Yellow Hand, taking his war bonnet and claiming "the first scalp for Custer."

Buffalo Bill became a rancher in his final years, though his main interest continued to be his Wild West show. At Cody, his Irma Hotel, named for his daughter, still does a brisk summer business, with guests rocking in a long row of chairs on the porch. He died in 1917 and was buried on Lookout Mountain, just west of Denver, Colorado.

Next door to Cody's TE Ranch was the Bobcat Ranch, today the prized possession of Wyoming's junior Senator and former Governor, Milward L. Simpson.

"Buffalo Bill used to be a great hit with us kids," Senator Simpson told me. "Sometimes we'd see him out in front of the Irma. I remember he'd have someone toss up a silver dollar, and he'd blast it out of the air with a .22 rifle. I used to have a dented souvenir dollar myself. It seems like only yesterday."

The past is never far away in Wyoming. At Senator Simpson's urging, I drove to Laramie to visit a stimulating scholar who has traced that past back as far as it can be read—Professor Samuel H. Knight, retired head of the University of Wyoming's Department of Geology and Mineralogy.

Oil Helps Build a University

"The rocks exposed in Wyoming cover much of the scope of geologic time," the professor told me. "The state is a tremendous workshop for us, with an amazing diversity of earth structures. Several other universities maintain summer geology camps in Wyoming; with our summer weather we hardly ever lose a day in the field."

Professor Knight, who still teaches part-time, pointed out the warm pink limestone of the university's handsome buildings. "Quarried near the campus," he said. And he told me of the curious relationship between these buildings and the geologists he has trained over the past fifty years.

Wyoming's Legislature, he explained, long ago earmarked part of the state's royalties from oil and gas wells to be used for construction at the university. Meanwhile, geology graduates, finding jobs with Wyoming oil companies, helped discover the oil that further financed their alma mater's growth.

Capital city of the state's leading industry is Casper (pages 558-9), where petroleum money has sprouted plush new homes, colorful office buildings, sophisticated shops, and an ultramodern bank with a domed roof that suggests an astronomical observatory. The city claims a millionaire for every 1,100 persons—some 40 of them. It also admits to a fairly frequent rangeland wind that howls into town and down Center Street.

Landmark Recalls a National Scandal

Twenty-six miles north of Casper stands Teapot Rock, an outcrop big enough to brew a nationwide tempest back in the 1920's. Teapot Dome, an oil structure underlying the land to the north, became a blot on President Warren G. Harding's Administration.

After almost a decade of investigations and trials, Albert B. Fall, Harding's Secretary of the Interior, went to prison. A Supreme Court decision took Teapot Dome out of private hands and restored it to Government control.

The area still contains vast oil reserves. In the adjacent Salt Creek oil field, the wells began producing in 1890, and in 1923

KODACHROME BY JAMES R. SIMON © N.G.S.

Early snowstorm surprises hare and people. The white-tailed jack, crouching in its Yellowstone igloo, will turn a camouflage white later in the season.

Campers, caught in the park's first storm of the season, huddle beneath a tarpaulin. Snow closes Yellowstone each year from November 1 to April 30, but during the summer months two million persons come to visit. Set aside for public enjoyment in 1872, Yellowstone became the first national park in the world and remains the largest in the United States, with 3,472 square miles.

poured forth a fantastic 97,000 barrels a day. Then the wells slowed. But today, thanks to water-injection techniques, they flow again at 34,000 barrels a day, with a quarter of a century at that rate still ahead of them.

I drove 26 miles east out of Casper one night to photograph a monument to Wyoming's second mineral industry—coal. On an improbable superhighway beyond Glenrock, crossing black and virtually uninhabited rangeland, I rounded a lonely hill and met it face to face.

The largest power plant in the Rocky Mountains advertises its own product, electricity. If you stumbled on Chicago's Wrigley Building spotlighted there you could not be more startled. The Dave Johnston Power Plant is a tower of light that airline pilots say they can see a hundred miles away (page 569).

Dave Johnston himself got out of the car with me, and we stood there on the old Oregon Trail, watching his plant burning Wyoming coal and churning out nearly half a million kilowatts of power.

"I came out here in the 1920's from Wisconsin," he said. "This is still young people's country today. The fishing hooked me on Wyoming 45 years ago. The fishing, the great outdoors, and the people still keep me here."

Dave had launched the Natrona Power Company, which later became Mountain States Power, at Casper. Now, Pacific Power & Light Company, Wyoming's biggest investor, had merged with Mountain States and built the Glenrock plant. They named it after Johnston—a well-merited tribute to a man who had pioneered in building an industry and a community.

Rusting Locomotives Stir Nostalgia

North of Glenrock is Gillette, another coal town, and between them lie vast coal beds nearly 100 miles long. Estimated to contain 47 billion tons, they could supply the Dave Johnston plant for 20,000 years.

The southwestern towns of Evanston, Green River, and Rock Springs have long looked sad to cross-country travelers racing the length of Wyoming (map, pages 578-9). Union Pacific steam locomotives stood rusting

on pedestals, sorry souvenirs of the demise of steam, reminders that this depressed area once supplied coal to the railroad.

But there has been a revival, in nearby Kemmerer.

"During the next five years," President Glenn E. Sorensen of the Kemmerer Coal Company told me, "we'll mine twice as much coal a year as we ever did for the U. P. By 1970, we'll mine two million tons a year. Utah Power & Light Company's new plant here will take more than half of it."

A few miles west of Green River—and a third of a mile beneath the Wyoming plains—several companies are tapping another vast mineral deposit, buried in the bed of an ancient lake. The miners are honeycombing a 15-foot-thick deposit of trona, the yellowish-white mineral that yields soda ash, a chemical widely used by United States industry.

The lake bed yields a million tons of trona annually, yet the deposit is so extensive that Wyoming can continue to mine it for a century or more.

Recent cutbacks in the Federal Government's requirements have dulled the luster of one of Wyoming's most glamorous minerals, uranium. But in Rawlins I met a

KODACHROME BY LOWELL J. GEORGIA © N.G.S.

millionaire miner who refuses to accept the idea of a depression in his business. He was among the first to dig the radioactive ore for atomic weapons during Wyoming's uranium boom, and expects he'll still be digging it when peaceful atomic power creates a second boom.

Robert W. Adams was not long out of a German prisoner-of-war camp when he came to Rawlins to open a restaurant and night club. Then came a uranium strike in the nearby Gas Hills. Mr. Adams mortgaged his holdings, borrowed from friends, and in 1955 set up the Lost Creek Oil and Uranium Company, with offices in Rawlins.

The company later changed its name to Western Nuclear, Inc., and for its 200 employees it built a town, Jeffrey City, in country where the deer and the antelope still play. (The old town here had been called Home on the Range.)

Until recently Western Nuclear had been mining by the open-pit method—digging ore close to the surface (page 568). Now it goes underground in search of higher grade ore. Twelve hundred tons of high-grade ore are already coming daily out of an 860-foot shaft on the company's Golden Goose reserves, 11 miles from Jeffrey City. In a state that has been selling nearly 30 million dollars' worth of uranium annually, the golden eggs are not yet all laid.

Sheep Ranchers Face Varied Woes

Rawlins is the seat of Carbon County, where more sheep are raised than anywhere else in the United States, except two counties in Texas. Carbon County woolgrowers, however, have Texas-size troubles.

I listened to a few over a predawn breakfast at a Rawlins restaurant. Curtis Rochelle, Bus Rendle, Charles Vivion, and Elmer Peterson are early risers and hardy hangers-on in a traditional Wyoming industry hard hit by sagging lamb prices, foreign wool competition, synthetic fibers, periodic drought, and troubles with fences. They have troubles, that is, with conservationists and hunters, who say fences—thousands of miles of them across leased Federal land—restrict the movement of deer and antelope.

"One reason we put our sheep behind fences," Curt Rochelle was saying, "is that we can't get enough good sheepherders any more.

"We'll have to come to some kind of compromise with the hunters, I guess," Curt continued. "The Wyoming Game Commission recommends a fence low enough for a deer to jump, and high enough for an antelope to crawl under. This may satisfy the conservationists too.

"As far as conservation is concerned, sheep *should* be fenced and not herded around. Herding ruins a lot of forage, and leaves sheep trails that encourage erosion.

"Sheep themselves are just like human beings," he

Sheep command the right of way as they move to winter range, stalling a motorist near Powell. Basque shepherds once herded vast flocks on open range; today more and more sheep grow up behind fences. Second only to Texas in wool production, Wyoming supports some two million sheep.

HELICOPTER HERDERS *drive elk toward corrals in the annual thinning
of the Northern Yellowstone Herd. The elk increased to about 7,000
during the calving season, more than the range could feed, and
were cut back to 5,000 last winter to prevent starvation. Park rangers
ship surplus animals as far away as Michigan and Texas.*

586   KODACHROME BY JACK E. RICHARD © NATIONAL GEOGRAPHIC SOCIETY

Gigantic stone stump, Devils Tower rises 1,280 feet above the Belle Fourche River in northeastern Wyoming. It took shape millions of years ago when molten rock, forced up from below, cooled near the surface. Water has since eroded away the softer stone around it.

Near-vertical columns of Devils Tower National Monument provide a challenging rock climb, as these members of the Iowa Mountaineers discover. Legend ascribes the cracks to the claws of bears; when the animals tried to catch Indian maidens, the girls jumped onto a low rock that saved them by soaring skyward.

went on. "They do better when they aren't pushed around. Some want to eat salt sage, and some want grass. Some want to go for water often, and some don't. Especially at lambing season, we're better off with fences. Ewes tend to lose their lambs in all the confusion of being herded."

Curt's final reason for defending fenced prairie was, to me, absolutely unassailable: He has 360 miles of fences flung across Wyoming—at $1,000 a mile.

"We used to raise sheep for money and cattle for respectability, behind the same fences," Charlie Vivion said. "Now you can't get either one out of either one."

"That's right," Bus Rendle said. "I'm operating with one man and myself, and I'm thinking of firing me."

Then Bus took off in his private plane to sell some sheep over on the Idaho border.

Back in the old days, raising sheep and cattle together would have been unthinkable. For years, Wyoming cattlemen, first on the scene, accused sheepmen of denuding the range and draining water holes with their hungry, thirsty flocks. There was a vicious war and much bloodletting.

"I remember talk about sheep wagons on fire in the hills when I was a kid," said cattleman Danny Budd. His great-grandfather, a cattle rancher, started the town named Big Piney in the 1880's.

Danny introduced me to Everett Curtis of Big Piney. Everett remembered back to the days before fences, almost to the era of bad blood among cattlemen, in the 1890's, when cowboys died in range wars because they'd put their brand on another man's calves.

Winter Begins at 40 Below

"My dad came to Wyoming in a wagon train bound for California," Everett told me. "He dropped out because he liked the looks of the land. I was the first white baby born in Big Piney. My folks laid me out on a table, and everybody filed by to get a good look."

We were riding out to a cattle branding on the Circle Ranch of James F. Michelson, a spread of about 60,000 acres. Everett punched cows here for 25 years, and now owns a small herd of Herefords himself.

"Big Piney's temperatures are always being talked about on the radio," I mentioned. "Is it pretty bad here in the winter?"

"You know," he said, "we never noticed it till the radio picked it up. We don't even get

into our long johns until it hits about 40 below. Of course, that happens pretty often."

All across Wyoming cattle country, I had vaguely wondered about the kindergartens of calves clustered in the sagebrush around a single cow.

"Cows are smarter animals than you'd think," Everett told me. "They'll leave one or two old cows to baby-sit all day with 20 calves, while the mothers go off to find grass and water and salt.

"I don't know how they decide who does the calf-sitting. But I do know that if you roped one of those ornery little critters and dropped him off from a truck miles away, he'd be back in the same patch of sagebrush with his baby-sitter almost before you could get back yourself."

False Teeth Save Pampered Cattle

I picked up another odd bit of range lore that afternoon.

"What did you say about false teeth?" I asked a rancher who was at the branding.

"That's right," he said. "Several years ago quite a few cattle wore 'em. Particularly registered purebreds. A few still do, especially in areas where there is a lot of grit."

Grazing animals, he explained, often pick up dirt, bits of stone, and other abrasive materials together with grass. With steers, there's no problem, since they go to market pretty young. But over the years the teeth of valuable breeding stock wear down. Some of the animals are worth thousands of dollars apiece. Unable to chew a full ration, they might eventually starve.

"In the old days, we just slaughtered stock that had reached that point," the rancher said. "Then a dentist came along and invented stainless-steel crowns that fit right over the lower incisors, adding years to their lives."

The original cattle of Wyoming were the buffalo. They fed and clothed the Indian for centuries, then became nearly extinct at the hands of the paleface. A few years ago a meat packer from San Francisco thought buffalo might be made to feed and clothe modern Americans, and started one of Wyoming's strangest enterprises.

It was in the town of Buffalo that I heard about the 66,000-acre B-Bar-B Buffalo Ranch of D. C. (Bud) Basolo, Jr. The route to the ranch goes east to Gillette, then south. I followed a four-lane highway for 70 miles without seeing a filling station. Livestock herds

In the lee of the Tetons, Colter Bay pioneers a partnership between the National Park Service and a nonprofit foundation, Jackson Hole Preserve, Inc. Hundreds of sportsmen from across the Nation launch boats from the Jackson Lake marina for fishing, boating, and skiing. Spray flies from the ski of Mrs. Peter Mead, daughter of Wyoming Governor Clifford P. Hansen.

Colter Bay's economical facilities range from campsites, trailer park, and tent village to actual homestead cabins, moved to this site and newly equipped with hot and cold running water. General store, restaurant, laundromat, and tackle shop serve campers. No one need bring even a sleeping bag; all gear may be rented on the spot.

use underpasses to avoid the infrequent but very fast traffic.

Basolo started with 125 bison bought from a ranch in Texas. Now he grazes thousands and ships the frozen meat all over the U. S.

"We herd these fellows with jeeps," he said. "They're pretty docile for the most part. You can walk among them or lead a horse. But don't *ride* a horse into a herd. Chances are you'd wind up gored or trampled or both. You'd almost think they have a lingering, hereditary memory of men on horseback hunting them down. Buffalo Bill Cody, you know, personally killed about 4,000 head when he was supplying meat to the railroads."

A chance discovery by Mr. Basolo's wife Georgia has opened up new possibilities for buffalo-ranching. Seated one night on an old buffalo robe, she ran a hand through the hair, admired its texture, and wondered aloud, "Why can't a buffalo hide be sheared and used as a fur?" Her husband echoed, "Why not?" and sent several sample hides to a furrier.

The result: Handsome, durable buffalo coats, jackets, hats, and after-ski boots, designed by Mrs. Basolo, have gone on the market. But the B-Bar-B turns out an even stranger by-product—bleached buffalo skulls.

"Interior decorators are snapping them up," said Mrs. Basolo.

Bighorn Mountains Challenge Motorists

In my rear-view mirror, the shaggy brown bison dwindled into the prairie landscape. My car was aimed at Wyoming's far west. Now, in late September, the standing-room-only signs were coming down in Yellowstone and Grand Teton National Parks.

The least traveled route over the Bighorn Mountains is U. S. Alternate 14. I took it.

Driving down the breathtaking switchbacks into the Bighorn Basin, you see vast reaches of flaming desert color, rivaling that of Arizona. Half a dozen mountain ranges march away like a deep stage with many banks of sets. The Absarokas—Yellowstone's eastern wall—pinprick a horizon 100 miles away through the clear Wyoming air—whenever you dare take your eyes off the next curve to look at them. At places on Alternate 14, it's better to park before viewing the scenery.

In the town of Lovell I stopped for coffee to settle my nerves. "There's no other road like it in the world," I was told. "Only a few tourists take Alternate 14. Some come down as if from seventh heaven. Others reach here petrified. Their fingers have been embedded in the steering wheel, their eyes locked on the middle of the road, and their foot mashed against the brake pedal for an hour."

I flexed my toes inside my right shoe and said nothing. Cal Taggart, who was talking, seemed a nonchalant sort of mayor to me.

Scenic Grandeur in Town's Back Yard

An hour later, in a high wind, Cal had me up in his private plane, showing me the town of Lovell, and a miniature edition of the Grand Canyon of the Colorado River—the magnificent Bighorn Canyon. Across the line in Montana, the Department of the Interior has built the Yellowtail Dam on the Bighorn River. Soon vacationers will enjoy boating and fishing and water-skiing on the upper end

of the reservoir, right in Lovell's back yard.

Also aboard the plane was Joe Rumburg of the National Park Service, Superintendent of the new Bighorn Canyon Recreation Area.

"Down in Utah there's practically a twin for this recreation area, Flaming Gorge, with water backed up the Green River into Wyoming, just like this," Joe told me. "In the first eight months of last year, more than half a million people came to use it.

"If we get a highway over the Bighorns that isn't quite so terrifying, we may get half a million here, too."

There had been two million tourists at Yellowstone during the season. When I pulled in at Old Faithful Inn, only a handful remained,

warming themselves before a fire crackling in one of the eight hearths beneath the lobby's 85-foot stone chimney.

I related a rumor I'd heard that they were going to demolish Old Faithful Inn, a vast, rambling masterpiece of weathered pine logs, and replace it with a modern building.

"Tear this old log cabin down? No! Why Yellowstone would never be the same." *

The reaction came from George D. Marler, veteran park geologist and geyser expert.

"I have heard, though," he said, "that

*For earlier GEOGRAPHIC accounts of the park, see: "Springtime Comes to Yellowstone National Park," by Paul A. Zahl, December, 1956; and "Fabulous Yellowstone," by Frederick G. Vosburgh, June, 1940.

EKTACHROME (ABOVE) BY JAMES W. ELDER; KODACHROME BY JAMES R. SIMON © N.G.S.

Leaping skier trails snow from a small cliff at the Jackson Hole Ski Area, newest of Wyoming's dozen developed slopes. Skiers can descend 4,135 feet—greatest drop in elevation of any ski resort in the country. Developers anticipate that within five years as many as 15,000 skiers a day will use the area's facilities. Already, slopes like Snow King (left) lure hundreds of winter visitors, turning Wyoming's tourist season into an all-year affair. This home of the schuss and sitzmark overlooks the town of Jackson.

they're thinking of moving other accommodations out of the park, or at least away from Old Faithful Inn. The pressure of visitors around here in the summer is terrific. It's like Times Square."

I mentioned that a nice lady in Sheridan had told me to be sure to watch Old Faithful erupt under the colored lights at night.

George smiled resignedly.

"There are no colored lights," he said. "Never have been. But lots of people seem to remember them. And you'd be surprised how many recall when we had Old Faithful on the other side of the highway. 'When did you move it?' they want to know."

I decided to play straight man for him once more.

"There's a bill before Congress to give the Secretary of the Interior authority to lease public domain for the development of geothermal energy. Have you heard any talk about tapping the Yellowstone geyser basins?"

"No, and I hope I don't," George Marler said. "I know they get commercial power from underground steam in Italy and New Zealand, and I think Iceland, too. And there's a geothermal power plant in California.

"They drilled some test holes here years ago, and I think they calculated that Yellowstone's underground heat could melt six tons of ice a second. But of course, if they tapped into our hot springs, even miles away from Old Faithful, for example, it might be the end. It could upset the thermal balance of all that interconnected underground plumbing."

Quake Changes Flow of Springs

The slightest alteration of temperature or pressure can suddenly change a spring's way of life. In August, 1959, a severe earthquake, centered at nearby Hebgen Lake in Montana, gave Yellowstone a memorable jolt.* The underground convulsions, Marler said, had altered many springs and geysers. Some beautiful geysers became dormant; others, previously insignificant, sprang to furious and photogenic activity.

"What we need," George said, "is not more power, but more respect for these wonders of nature. It's a crime what people will do to them. One morning we drew water out of Morning Glory Pool and made it erupt. It reswallowed most of what it had regurgitated. But around its chin we picked up 75 towels

*See "The Night the Mountains Moved," by Samuel W. Matthews, NATIONAL GEOGRAPHIC, March, 1960.

and bath mats, any number of sticks and marbles, two wristwatches, a wedding ring, and $115 in coins."

I drove southward through the rest of Yellowstone. It was quiet. The park bears, hold-up artists of the highways, weren't bothering the lonely likes of me. They would hibernate till spring, when bumper-to-bumper tourists would make the begging worthwhile again.

Wyoming's Future: Higher Multitudes

Grand Teton National Park, like Yellowstone, had survived another summer's tourist onslaught. Some Wyomingites regard this fact with wonder at the end of every season. How many more visitors, they ask, can these areas take before the parks come unraveled from the heavy wear?

Staring out at the splendid crags from Jackson Lake Lodge, I pondered what Laurance Rockefeller had told me in Washington, D. C.

"Open space isn't the problem," he said, "but how we use it. For example, about 95 percent of Yellowstone—one of our most heavily traveled parks—is still unused. Visitors concentrate at a few well-known landmarks in the remaining 5 percent.

"I think eventually we'll have to turn to a zoning concept—keeping the wilderness hearts of our parks intact, surrounding them with buffer zones of trails and footpaths, then, around that, developing areas for high-density recreational use. This seems a practical compromise between a sort of 'deep-freeze' philosophy and wide-open development of the parks."

Still in the shadow of the Tetons, I watched a onetime little cow town sigh and try to settle down for the winter. Jackson had been trying to act like Las Vegas all summer, providing food and games and souvenirs for an invasion two million strong. Now Jackson was tired.

But it wouldn't be allowed to sleep this winter. Developers were spending nearly thirty-five million dollars to turn a mountainside near Jackson into one of the highest, most dramatic ski resorts west of Switzerland. In five years, they told me, they'd have a dozen lifts and tramways, and 10 to 15 thousand skiers a day on their slopes.

More multitudes on their way. This time mostly by plane. From both coasts. In the wintertime.

Doc Schunk was right. Maybe only the high altitudes would last.

NATIONAL GEOGRAPHIC

E NATIONAL GEOGRAPHIC MAGAZINE VOL. 129, NO. 5 COPYRIGHT © 1966 BY NATIONAL GEOGRAPHIC SOCIETY, WASHINGTON, D.C. INTERNATIONAL COPYRIGHT SECURED

CALIFORNIA
The Golden Magnet

PART I: THE SOUTH

By WILLIAM GRAVES
National Geographic Senior Staff

Illustrations by National Geographic photographer THOMAS NEBBIA

WILL ROGERS, the much-beloved humorist, once attended a meeting of the "Old Settlers of California."

"No one," he wrote later, "was allowed to attend unless he had been in the State 2 and one-half years."

Will's settlers were fictitious, but he made his point: California is a land of many newcomers. A friend of mine in Los Angeles recently put it another way. "Californians," he said, "are people who were born somewhere else and then came to their senses."

Human Explosion Creates a Giant

Naturally, that's Los Angeles and you have to make allowances; Angelenos are impossible about their city. So, for that matter, are Californians about their state. They insist it's the only place to live. Of course, that's just talk, and no one else takes it seriously—except about 1,000 new residents every day.

California, in other words, is an irresistible magnet, luring 400,000 settlers across its borders each year. At the moment, some 19,000,000 people—roughly one out of every ten United States residents—make their home in the Golden State.

The trouble with statistics about California is that they rarely stay the same for long. During the three months that I recently spent exploring the state, for example, some 100,000 more people became Californians.

Practically the only thing constant in the third largest state is its vast area—158,693 square miles.

"Everything else," says a census taker wearily, "is in a perpetual state of explosion."

The explosion reaches far beyond population to an endless variety of items. Among other things that California has more of than any other state are national parks, national forests, and military bases. It also has more

LIKE A BOLT OF STARRY FABRIC *unrolled from mountains to sea, Los Angeles sprawls in grandeur, metropolis and lodestone of southern California. Second most populous urban area in the Nation, city and suburbs attract tens of thousands of new residents yearly. Hollywood Freeway, painted by automobile lights, forms one strand of a luminous 330-mile maze that throbs with Angelenos' four million vehicles. Hollywood Bowl audience applauds the Beatles*

teachers, students, automobiles, superhighways, and motorcycles—not to mention more major-league baseball teams (three) and more members of the National Geographic Society (630,000)—than any other state.*

What California produces is equally impressive. Golden State manufacturers in recent years have obtained almost a quarter of all prime contracts for military equipment; nearly half the money allocated for civilian space research and development is spent here. In addition, California provides a vast portion of the country's food and 80 percent of all the wine consumed in the United States.

Blessings Mixed With Problems

One thing, contrary to common belief, California does not do—produce more oranges than Florida. The Sunshine State still outharvests its rival by more than three to one.

Not all California's distinctions are enviable ones. Others include one of the largest prisons in the country (San Quentin, with 5,000 inmates), and the greatest number of traffic deaths among the states, 5,000 a year. Recently, too, California suffered one of the

598

Nation's grimmest riots—when, in a single violent week at Watts, in Los Angeles, more than 30 people lost their lives.

California's problems, like many of its blessings, stem mainly from sheer size. In terms of people, the burden falls far more heavily on southern California than on the northern half of the state.

Just where the boundary falls between southern and northern California is a matter of opinion; or rather, of 19,000,000 opinions —every Californian has his own. No one disputes the fact that San Francisco is the center of northern California, or that Los Angeles belongs with the south. Somewhere between —roughly around Fresno, in the San Joaquin

*The most recent NATIONAL GEOGRAPHIC articles on this diverse and colorful state include: "The Magic Worlds of Walt Disney," August, 1963, and "Los Angeles, City of the Angels," October, 1962, both by Robert de Roos; "California's Wonderful One," by Frank Cameron, November, 1959; "Giant Sequoias Draw Millions to California Parks," by John Michael Kauffmann, August, 1959; "Bristlecone Pine, Oldest Known Living Thing," by Edmund Schulman, March, 1958; "Huntington Library, California Treasure House," by David S. Boyer, February, 1958; "Californians Escape to the Desert," by Mason Sutherland, November, 1957; and "New Rush to Golden California," by George W. Long, June, 1954.

Valley—north and south merge in a geographical no man's land where personal preference or map-making convenience decides the division (see the new supplement map of **California**, which divides it about in half).

Los Angeles: Colossus of the South

There is no question whatever about the focal point of southern California. Los Angeles is less a city than a human galaxy, a vast cluster of 75 smaller cities fused together by endless suburbs and freeways. All lie within gigantic Los Angeles County—4,060 densely populated square miles, the second largest urban area in the country, after New York City. The City of Los Angeles alone, with 2,731,000 residents, ranks third in size in the Nation, behind New York and Chicago.

Los Angeles, like many giants, often suffers the taunts of a world built to a slightly smaller scale. Even Californians make fun of their colossus. "Los Angeles," runs the quip, "speaks unkindly of San Francisco, but San Francisco never mentions Los Angeles at all."

Angelenos are accustomed to being chided about their home: about its smog, its traffic, its endless size, and—most unjustly of all—its lack of culture. Not all Angelenos, especially adopted ones, take it kindly.

"Why do people criticize Los Angeles?" demands Romain Gary, the brilliant French novelist and a former

Guide to a dream factory, Miss Cherie Hamilton escorts Hollywood visitors around outdoor sets at Universal City Studios. When movie production permits, tourists may witness a mock war or watch lovers emoting before the cameras.

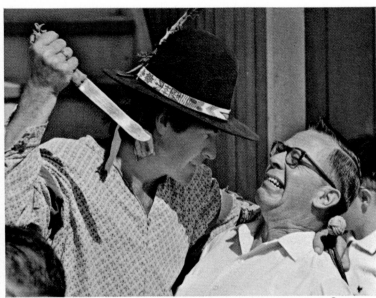

KODACHROME (LEFT) AND EKTACHROMES BY THOMAS NEBBIA © N.G.S.

"Paleface, you die!" The fierce Indian turns out to be quite gentle. Pilgrims to movie shrines join the action at Universal City's Studio Entertainment Center. Even the Creature From the Black Lagoon, from the movie of the same name, plays host behind a thin aquarium that gives the illusion of an underwater lair.

With the opening in 1913 of Hollywood's first film studio in a $25-a-month barn, the obscure hamlet began a climb to world fame. In the twenties, Mary Pickford ruled as "America's Sweetheart"; Charlie Chaplin mixed laughter with pathos. In the thirties, Clark Gable and Carole Lombard enchanted movie-goers. After losing its audience to television and foreign movies following World War II, Hollywood came back strong.

French consul general there. To Gary, Los Angeles has the beauty of endless vitality. "It is a city," he says, "bursting with life." Julie Andrews, another Angeleno by choice, puts it a slightly different way.

I called on Miss Andrews at her home in Coldwater Canyon, a wooded section above Beverly Hills. The slender young Englishwoman who has become Mary Poppins to a generation of Americans had earned an afternoon off from her new film, *Hawaii*.

"The beauty of Los Angeles," she said, "is what I would call 'pulse'—that wonderful steady beat of energy. You feel it in the early morning, when the sun is barely up, the air is cool and quiet, yet there is already a hint of excitement." She waved toward the vast reach of Los Angeles below us.

"Then you drive down into that busy life, and you can't help thinking—'It's going to be another wonderful day!'" She smiled. "What more can anyone ask of a city?"

What more indeed—though whatever one asks, Los Angeles is likely to have it. One morning along Sunset Strip, the famous entertainment section of Sunset Boulevard, I passed a sign that read "Budget Rent-A-Car System." Beside it stood two gleaming Rolls-Royce "Silver Clouds"—each worth about $18,000—for hire.

Fascinated, I stepped into the office and asked the clerk if anybody could rent one of his Rolls-Royces.

"Naturally, sir," he replied with dignity. And what would it cost?

"Actually, it's quite a bargain—seventy-five dollars the day, and a modest twenty-five cents the mile." He held up a warning finger.

"Of course, sir, you understand that at that rate, you must furnish the petrol yourself."

Night Reveals a Second City

That evening, having reluctantly passed up a bargain Rolls-Royce, I watched what seemed to be all of Los Angeles County's 4,000,000 vehicles in action. In a small plane I took a tour of the city at dusk, just as rush-hour traffic reached the flood stage.

Los Angeles during the day admittedly can be a monotonous sight from the air—a city packed in the dingy cotton batting of its own smog. Only the thousands of back-yard swimming pools glint upward through the haze like scattered bits of bright turquoise.

At night, however, the scene comes alive, pulsing like some vast bed of coals (pages 596-7). To the east, on the great rampart of the San Gabriel Mountains, the first flickerings of light begin. As though tumbling downhill, they collect in pockets and ravines, spilling out at last onto the glowing plain of the city itself. Through it all wind the great conveyer belts of the freeways, heavy with their diamond-and-ruby chips of light.

We flew over the immense darkened tureen of Pasadena's Rose Bowl and swung southeastward toward Anaheim. Suddenly beneath us rose the jagged claw of Disneyland's miniature Matterhorn, its bobsleds still busy in the glare of floodlights.

Other lights rimmed the waterfronts of Long Beach and Los Angeles, two of the country's busiest deep-sea ports. The ports seemed strangely still—their huge traffic, some 39,000,000 tons a year, consists mainly of

EKTACHROME (OPPOSITE) BY THOMAS NEBBIA AND DUOTONE BY OTTO ROTHSCHILD, PHOTOGRAPHY © N.G.S.

A dream came true for music-hungry Angelenos when their majestic new Pavilion opened its doors in December, 1964. The soaring glass-granite-and-marble Pavilion dominates a downtown Music Center that will eventually house theater, opera, and ballet companies and a chamber-music society. The grand foyer glitters with chandeliers.

Maestro Zubin Mehta, whose brilliant performances have won critics' acclaim, leads the Los Angeles Philharmonic. Mehta, 30, is the youngest permanent conductor of a major U. S. orchestra.

Heap of talent: Carol Channing collapses over David McCallum in feigned exhaustion during a show that brings on stage the Spirit of '76, cabaret girls, fur-hatted Russians, and a Bavarian band. The scene highlighted CBS's "An Evening With Carol Channing."

Arrival of television in the 1940's at first hurt the movie industry deeply, but as more and more studios began filming television shows, Hollywood gained new prominence in the world of entertainment. Today television brings the film capital more than $460,000,000 a year.

oil and oil products pumped to and from tankers.

Flying over what sprawling Los Angeles arbitrarily calls its downtown area, we passed clusters of state and federal buildings in the new Civic Center and came on a view dear to the hearts of all Angelenos—the great honeycomb of light marking the superb new Music Center, an architectural masterpiece coveted even by San Francisco (page 600).

San Francisco, in fact, has more than the Music Center to consider in its cultural race with Los Angeles. I talked about this one day with Richard F. Brown, until recently the director of another major landmark, the new Los Angeles County Museum of Art on Wilshire Boulevard.

The museum is a magnificent blending of practical design with the grace of a marble temple. I strolled through elegantly simple rooms of Cézannes, Botticellis, and Van Dycks to Mr. Brown's glass-walled office.

Dues-paying Patrons Stimulate Art

I remarked that the museum certainly should settle any doubts about Los Angeles' love for the arts. Mr. Brown shook his head.

"There shouldn't be any doubts at this late date. Los Angeles has valued great art for years and attracted it with any number of fine institutions—the Henry E. Huntington Library and Art Gallery over in San Marino, for one. And that's not just a native Angeleno boasting," he said with a smile. "I'm an immigrant from New York, myself.

"But the main thing about our new museum is that it's supported by more than just a handful of great fortunes. Today we have some 30,000 dues-paying members—school children, dentists, bus drivers, carpenters."

He gestured around him. "All Los Angeles helped to buy what you see here."

Los Angeles pays an increasingly stiff price for anything involving space. With the influx of tens of thousands of new Angelenos each year, suburbs and shopping centers have all but erased the city's once-vast fringe of citrus orchards.

"When I bought my first parcel of land here 40 years ago," a friend in the real estate business told me, "it was ten dollars down and ten dollars when they caught me. I should have bought the whole city."

The era of bargains has long since vanished. And owners of choice land in the downtown area usually prefer to lease their property rather than sell it, in the expectation of continued rise in values.

"I don't care if you have the Great Pyramid of Cheops on the acreage I want," another developer said. "I'll take the land and move the pyramid anywhere you say, free of charge."

Fortunately for the developers, pyramids are rare in Los Angeles, although I have seen an Amazon jungle and a Swiss Alpine village. Both were outdoor sets at Universal City, where Charlton Heston and I made our movie.

Mr. Heston of course did most of the work —I spent only a day as one of his extras. Quite frankly, I wouldn't go through it again for half the box office receipts.

I arranged the one-day job through Herb Steinberg, a friend at Universal, the huge movie and television studio just north of the Hollywood Bowl (pages 598-9).

"Don't look for glamor," Herb warned me ahead of time. "Making movies is 50 percent backbreaking work—and 50 percent waiting around to do it over again. Out of eight hours' shooting on a major film, we're lucky to get three minutes of final footage."

Herb's warning proved the understatement of the year: I did the same thing not twice, but 13 times. The casting office had signed me for *The War Lord,* an 11th-century adventure story starring Mr. Heston. With 20 other extras dressed as Norman cavalry and crossbowmen, I rushed into make-believe battle.

Rushing into battle with cavalry and crossbows can be almost as fatal as battle itself —especially when one happens to be nearsighted. The wardrobe department tactfully pointed out that my eyeglasses would hardly lend authenticity to an 11th-century epic. Off they came. After an hour of racing half-blind past the camera along with ten horses and my fellow bowmen, I had multiple shin scars from flying hoofs and a dozen bruises from flailing bows. The only reason I'm alive today is that Norman crossbowmen wore helmets.

Our director proved a hard man to satisfy. After half a dozen unsuccessful takes, he called a five-minute break. I noticed Mr. Heston in costume beside the camera, and I asked him a question that had bothered me all morning. No one had told me whose side I was on.

"You're on my side, one of the good people," Mr. Heston explained, smiling. "It's going to be a tough battle, but we win it."

The director called us back and ran the scene seven more times. Finally it began to rain and we stopped, so I never took part in the battle. I don't regret it. Considering the wounds I got just running onto the field, I'm sure they would have carried me off it.

Lobsters Play a Space Age Role

While Charlton Heston battles flesh-and-blood villains, other Angelenos wage war against an invisible foe. At North American Aviation, Inc., the enemy is the vast, hostile reach of space.

North American is deeply involved in Apollo, the United States' project to land two men on the moon some time before the year 1970.

I walked one morning through North American's huge plant in Downey with

EKTACHROME BY THOMAS NEBBIA © N.G.S.

Alley—oop! Traditional acrobat's signal echoes across Santa Monica's "Muscle Beach" as young athletes rise on the hands of a strong man. Tanned instructor directs the trick with open arms.

Threading the pilings, a surfer "shoots the pier" while riding the curl, or steepest part of the wave, at Hermosa Beach. Surfers may stand almost upright in a "trim" position, or they may "hot dog"—do acrobatics. Moving to the front and sticking his toes over the nose of the board, a surfer "hangs ten." If only one foot protrudes, he "hangs five." Surfing, native to Hawaii, now counts half a million followers in California alone.

George Hoover, a program manager in the Life Sciences Division. Among other problems, George's division studies the possible harmful effects of prolonged space travel on the human body.

We inspected a mock-up of the Apollo spacecraft, three separate giant vehicles: one to carry the astronauts on their round trip to the moon; another to furnish fuel and power; and a third, the spider-legged LEM, or lunar excursion module, for actual landing on the moon's surface.

I asked George why North American isn't building all three vehicles.

"We probably could," he said, "but Apollo is really too big, and too complicated, for any one company to handle. Altogether there are twenty *thousand* private firms working on the moon project, not to mention the Government side of things—our overall boss, for example, the National Aeronautics and Space Administration."

The monumental scope of Apollo becomes even clearer when one considers Douglas Aircraft Company, Inc., the contractor for the top stage of the huge Saturn V rocket. Even Douglas, with its vast experience and skill, has hired 5,000 smaller firms to help.

In the endless quest to make space travel safe for man, George Hoover has played some unusual roles. Once, he ran a study on weightlessness with the help of six live Maine lobsters.

"Our purchasing department thought I was crazy when I ordered them flown across the country," George said. "But New England lobsters are very special beasts—quite different from our Pacific spiny lobster. For one thing, they stick grains of sand in their heads to tell them which way is up."

I looked skeptical, and George explained that in its nearly weightless state in water, *Homarus americanus* has trouble keeping its bearings. To solve the problem, the lobster inserts a grain of sand in an opening near the base of each of its two feelers. Gravity exerts a faint but constant downward pull on the grain, giving the lobster what amounts to a built-in plumb line.

"When the lobsters got here," George explained, "we substituted iron filings for the grains of sand in their heads, and then tried to confuse them with magnets.

"We confused them, all right. When we put a magnet against the side of the tank, the lobsters mistook the side for the bottom—they crawled right up and tried to hang on.

"It was interesting work, and we might have learned a thing or two, but we called it off. Another company was studying the same thing with human subjects in a centrifuge."

"What happened to the lobsters?" I asked. George gave me a wink.

"We ran a final experiment with boiling water and some melted butter. Scientifically, it was a great success."

Dazzling Crop Creates a Traffic Hazard

From Space Age Los Angeles I turned to California's past, by driving along magnificent coastal Route 1, roughly following historic El Camino Real, or King's Highway.

El Camino dates back to the early days of Spanish settlement of California, when the great Franciscan from Majorca, Father Junípero Serra, helped to colonize the new land with his chain of missions. The missions, eventually 21 in all, still span California's coast, from San Diego north to Sonoma, with their graceful names, most of them commemorating saints—Juan Capistrano, Luís Obispo de Tolosa, Juan Bautista, Rafael Arcángel. . . .

Beyond Mission San Luís Rey de Francia at Oceanside, I came to what surely is one of the world's most charming traffic hazards—Mr. Edwin Frazee's seed and bulb flower farm.

High-tailing through the blue, a new DC-9 short-haul jet completes a test. Twenty-eight airlines have ordered the plane, built by Douglas Aircraft Company, Inc., on the same Long Beach assembly line that produces its big brother, the four-engine DC-8.

Aircraft manufacturers led California into the space business; last year, 45 percent of the four billion dollars in prime contracts signed by NASA went to the Golden State. From its workshops come the Apollo ships to carry men to the moon, the Mariners to peer at Mars and Venus, the Rangers that photographed the moon close up, and the Surveyors to search out later landing sites.

Villain-black biplane flies out of aviation's youth. It carried evil Jack Lemmon in a contest with virtuous Tony Curtis during Warner Brothers' movie *The Great Race*. The plane, with a four-cylinder Continental engine, copies an early Glenn Curtiss design.

At first sight of the farm, some 500 acres of seed-producing anemones, freesias, and ranunculuses, it is wise to stop the car. On the landward side of the road the eye is almost overwhelmed by an explosion of color—on the other side, far below, lies the Pacific.

At Mr. Frazee's invitation, I wandered knee-deep in a dazzling world of crimson, lavender, orange, and gold that seemed to stretch beyond the horizon (page 614).

As so often in rain-scarce southern California, the crop was heavily irrigated. Scores of rotating sprinklers like giant water pistols threw a perpetual mist over the fields. Now and then the mist trapped a rainbow, the only one I ever recall that seemed colorless.

Shark Appetites Defy Analysis

South of Oceanside I had a close-up view of another brilliant side of California—this one in La Jolla, or more exactly, 50 yards offshore from it. The small community in northern San Diego is famous not only for its quiet charm and its elegant cliffside houses, but also for one of the world's leading centers of underwater research, the famed Scripps Institution of Oceanography.

The institution—actually a branch of the colossal University of California—had just taken part in Sealab II, the U.S. Navy's project to maintain three teams of men 205 feet underwater for a minimum of two weeks. One person who has contributed heavily to the safety of such ventures is James Stewart, the institution's chief diving officer.

Jim has taught hundreds of Scripps graduate students and scientists to use scuba gear as a basic tool in undersea research. His pupils' first meeting with him is likely to be a sobering one, for Jim bears a terrible crescent-shaped scar above one elbow—the result of a brush with a shark off Wake Island in 1961.

"Lots of people have theories about sharks," Jim told me in his office, "and that's about all they are—theories. The only thing certain you can say for sharks is that there's nothing certain about them.

"Take the hammerheads we have here on the Pacific coast. A lot of swimmers will tell you that hammerhead sharks are just curious,

and that if you leave them alone, they'll wander off." He shook his head.

"That doesn't prove anything at all about hammerheads; it only proves that some lucky swimmers live to talk."

Another creature worth avoiding in California waters is the occasional large electric ray. Jim told me that a few weeks earlier, north of La Jolla, a diver had come up under a big ray, which promptly draped its "wings" down over his head and turned on the current.

"Luckily, the diver was wearing a rubber hood against the cold," Jim explained, "and that *may* have given him some protection. But he said later, when his companion helped him out of the water, that it was like putting his head in a giant lamp socket."

That afternoon Jim took me for a dive in

KODACHROME BY THOMAS NEBBIA © NATIONAL GEOGRAPHIC SOCIETY

CALIFORNIA

SUPERLATIVES seem almost commonplace in California: Most populous state (with 19,040,000); continent's lowest point (Death Valley, 282 feet below sea level) and highest waterfall (Yosemite, 2,425 feet); tallest of all living things (coast redwoods) and oldest known (bristlecone pines); first ranking in value of agricultural products, number of cars, and military installations; leadership in the space industry. Vulnerable to earthquake, fire, and flood, it also owns some of the world's most spectacular mountain and coastal scenery. Early explorers included Sir Francis Drake. Spanish friars seeking converts and forty-niners in search of gold helped bring civilization.

CALIFORNIA REPUBLIC

Golden State. **AREA:** 158,693 square miles; third largest state, after Alaska and Texas. **MAJOR CITIES:** Los Angeles (Nation's second most populous urban area, after New York, and third most populous incorporated city, after Chicago), San Francisco, San Diego, Sacramento (the capital). **CLIMATE:** Most of state enjoys Mediterranean-type climate, with temperature extremes in high mountains and southern desert. **ADMISSION:** 1850 as 31st state.

La Jolla Bay, and we spent a delightful half hour below. The water had an almost magic clarity, and we saw a steady but always changing procession of California marine life, including the spiny lobster.

There was a small moray as well, several varieties of crab, and endless species of small fish that hovered around us in schools like clouds of brilliant gnats. Happily, the hammerheads and electric rays were busy elsewhere that day.

Electricity Helps Protect Mothball Fleet

South of La Jolla, at the U. S. Naval Base on San Diego Bay, man has borrowed a trick from the electric ray. I learned the story while touring the Navy's mothball fleet with Comdr. Derwood Duncan.

San Diego has been a seafaring community since discovery of its great natural harbor—and thus of California—in 1542 by Juan Cabrillo, a Portuguese navigator in the employ of Spain. Curiously, California is believed to have earned its name before Juan Cabrillo ever set foot ashore. Around the year 1510, before the conquest of Mexico, a Spanish writer of romantic fiction described an island "on the right hand of the Indies... very near to the Terrestrial Paradise...."

Carried away by his vision, the author told of a race of beautiful women, "without any men among them." Their weapons, he said, were entirely of gold, "for in all the island, there is no other metal." The queen was called Calafia, and the writer named his mythical realm California.

Nearly a quarter of a century later, so the story runs, Spanish mariners cruising the waters northwest of Mexico sighted the coast of what they fancied to be the golden realm. Word of the discovery spread, and in 1542 when Juan Cabrillo sailed into what today is San Diego Bay, the name California sailed with him.

Cabrillo and his men found little if any gold and still less in the way of beautiful women. Centuries later, however, the Spanish writer proved a prophet: California became famous for both.

In early times San Diego exported what Californians called "leather dollars"—cured hides that were hauled from the great inland cattle ranches and tumbled down San Diego's cliffs to waiting longboats.

Today the leather dollars, together with choice California beef, go east by rail and truck, while San Diego handles more formidable traffic: Many U. S. warships bound for Viet Nam waters clear through San Diego (pages 624-5).

One morning I toured half a dozen installations, including the recruit training center, the Naval Air Station on North Island, an underwater demolition unit, and an antisubmarine warfare school, all part of the Navy establishment

Firework flowers bloom over Disneyland: Sleeping Beauty's castle glows like a mirage as crowds enjoy a summer evening. More than six-and-a-half million visitors—three-quarters of them adults—revel here at Anaheim every year, a record made possible by California's gentle climate. "Sunshine built California," Walt Disney told the author. "Just about everything else followed it here."

that spends more than a million dollars a day in San Diego. Finally we ended with the mothball fleet, scores of cocooned and silent ships at ghostly anchorage.

Walking beside the aircraft carrier *Philippine Sea* with Commander Duncan, the fleet's maintenance officer, I noticed a slender electrical cable running down into the water beside the hull. Commander Duncan explained that the cable helps to protect the hull against corrosion.

"Without protection," he said, waving toward the carrier, "a hull that size can lose hundreds of pounds of steel a year through corrosion. And the corrosion isn't always uniform—it attacks certain points in a hull and forms pits or craters that eventually could eat right through.

"Basically, corrosion is an electrical and chemical process. We've found we can slow it down, or even eliminate it, simply by running a current to the hull of the ship through the water from what we call anodes—bars of lead, graphite, platinum, or other metals that in a sense do the deteriorating in place of the

hull, only at a much slower rate." He smiled.

"That way, if the Navy ever needs these ships in a hurry, we can get them to sea ready for a fight without having to patch them up like old inner tubes."

Market Research Aids War on Smuggling

For all its role in national defense, San Diego still finds time to enjoy itself. The possibilities are broad, for the city has one of the world's finest zoos (page 623), some of the best fishing and surfing beach in California, and a brand-new waterfront recreation area, Mission Bay Park, that draws yachtsmen and vacationers from as far away as the Atlantic coast. In addition, of course, there is San Diego's colorful next-door neighbor, the Mexican border town of Tijuana.

Tijuana, with its bull ring, its *jai alai* matches, and its slightly faded air of endless fiesta, lures Californians across the border by the scores of thousands each weekend and returns them, as a rule, happier and slightly poorer. On weekdays the human tide reverses itself, as thousands of Mexicans cross the

KODACHROMES BY LAWRENCE SCHILLER © NATIONAL GEOGRAPHIC SOCIETY

Hardy campers line Pasadena streets on New Year's Eve. Their reward for the chilly, night-long vigil: a close-up view of the resplendent Tournament of Roses Parade. A million and a half spectators jammed the route to watch the procession last January 1; more than a hundred million saw it on television.

Blaze of blossoms on Burbank's float honors Walt Disney, 1966 grand marshal. Floral music staff and artist's palette resting on an open book represent "the three important elements in the Disney legend: story, music, and art." The float uses 5,000 orchids, 75,000 chrysanthemums, 1,000 roses, and 50 potted azaleas.

border northward to shop or, in some cases, to work in San Diego.

I stood by the human floodgate—the border station of San Ysidro—one weekday morning with a U. S. Customs Bureau inspector. San Ysidro is famous for its stories of smuggling, and I asked if there was any truth to them. The inspector nodded.

"We make more individual seizures of narcotics than any other United States point of entry," he said.

Marijuana and heroin, I learned, are the drugs most frequently smuggled, and the Customs Bureau has found them hidden in practically everything—salt shakers, ladies' compacts, hollowed-out vegetables, and once in a set of extremely false teeth.

"Don't get the idea that smuggling is particularly a Mexican affair," the inspector told me. "No country has a monopoly on it. Our troublemakers hail from every part of the world—and usually come to grief right here."

He sounded very sure of himself, considering that customs never sees the contraband that slips past it. The inspector smiled.

"We don't need to," he said. "We have agents all over southern California who know the going price for—let's say heroin—on the black market. If the price is high, that means the supply is low, and we're doing all right at San Ysidro. But if the price of heroin takes a dive"—the smile faded—"we spend a little more time with certain visitors."

Lawyer's Skill Overcomes Intolerance

For all the human traffic between California and Mexico—some 22,000,000 people a year pass through San Ysidro alone—influence on the Golden State from south of the border has long been declining. Mexico's brief rule over California ended more than a century ago. In 1848, after the war with Mexico, the territory was ceded to the United States by treaty.

"We gave California some of our music and architecture," Ramon Castro observed one night at dinner in San Diego. Ramon is a brilliant young lawyer whose Mexican parents immigrated to California from the State

Gardener's palette splashes color on fields of Edwin Frazee, Inc., at Oceanside. Yellow, orange, and red beds of ranunculuses contrast with more distant carpets of anemones. Frazee's 500 acres produce bulbs and cut flowers for shipment around the world.

KODACHROME BY THOMAS NEBBIA © N.G.S.

of Durango before he was born. "Luckily for all of us," he continued, "we gave you the taco and the enchilada, too.

"But those are minor contributions, and the trend is the other way. Many Mexican Americans in California today go what I call all-out 'native'—strictly U. S.

"It wasn't always that way," he added, frowning. "When I was a boy here in California, I hated the gringo with a passion. I remember excursions when we traveled in separate rail coaches—one for Mexican American kids, and the other for the 'real Americans.'

"But we've learned a lot on both sides since then. Today in San Diego I'm just another American who happens to speak a second language, Spanish."

As a successful lawyer, Ramon has helped to bring down the barriers of misunderstanding between Californians and their neighbors south of the border. Not long ago a San Diego court appointed him to defend a young man accused of murder.

"When I walked into his cell," Ramon explained, "the first thing he said was, 'I guess you ought to know I don't like Mexicans.'

"So I told him that was fine, that I didn't want his case anyway, but now that I had it, I was going to win it. We did win it, too; the jury acquitted him and he's free today.

"I receive news of him now and then, and he's changed his mind about Mexicans. That's one man whose kids will never ride in a separate coach."

East of San Diego, beyond the great rain barrier of California's coastal ranges, Mexico and the Golden State work side by side. The business is agriculture; the place, the Imperial Valley; and the result, $200,000,000 a year.

Imperial Valley, that vast larder for the Nation, is in part a happy accident of nature —silt piled as deep as 2,000 feet by former meanderings of the Colorado River. What transforms murderous desert into one of the world's richest farming areas is man's diversion of Colorado waters into the All American Canal.

Through a system of barriers upstream on

Devils Golf Course, a fossilized lake in Death Valley, holds the dry remains of a watery expanse 100 miles long and 600 feet deep. Wind and rain carved its salt into jagged pinnacles. Hottest place in the Nation, the valley once recorded 134° F. in the shade.

the Colorado—the great concrete scallop shells of Imperial, Parker, Davis, Hoover, and Glen Canyon Dams—the gravity-flow canal can deliver 15,000 cubic feet of water every second to Imperial Valley's nearly fifty assorted crops. As a result, farmers on both sides of the border take a dim view of that valley rarity—rain.

"That's the last thing we want," one Im-

perial grower told me. "Rain drowns the plants, washes away the soil, and makes a quagmire out of everything."

He waved a hand across the green velvet of a broccoli field.

"When my crops need water, I pick up the telephone and ask the water district to open its sluice gates and send me some. Within a day I get just what I asked for—almost down

to the drop." He spread his hands. "No rain-storm on earth can do that."

I mentioned the grower's remarks later to Father Jerry Sims, the Roman Catholic pastor of a church in El Centro, Imperial Valley's major city. Father Sims nodded.

"Rain is a touchy subject in the valley," he agreed. "It's a problem even in church. Now and then the bishop of our diocese over

Magic of water conjures a lush green golf course on Palm Springs' burning desert. A score of courses in the area attract many celebrities, including former President Dwight D. Eisenhower. Dry, warm winters, elegant shops, and luxurious accommodations make the city California's best-known desert resort. Almost every home has its pool; water flows from 400-foot-deep wells and from the nearby San Jacinto Mountains (left).

617

in San Diego issues a special prayer for rain, and that's fine for San Diego—they can use it.

"But I'll tell you this: It takes a brave priest to read that prayer in the valley."

Not every part of southern California has a Colorado River to tap, or even much hope of rain. North of Imperial Valley and its great drainage sump, the Salton Sea, lies a vast stretch of seared and empty land known to Californians simply as "The Desert."

Actually, the California desert has many parts, the two largest being the Colorado and the Mojave. Together the two giants cover some 20,000 square miles—an area four times the size of Connecticut.

Maps give the Mojave a deceptively gentle look, with their blue tracery of lakes and rivers. The map maker's blue is more phantom than real—the symbol of water long vanished. The lakes and riverbeds for the most part are dried-up fossils of the great sea that drowned southern California in prehistoric times (page 615).

For all the Mojave's barren hostility to man—a soldier on desert maneuvers once called it "the proving ground for Hell"—it is a land of haunting beauty.

Like bowling balls, cantaloupes tumble into a truck as college students help with the harvest near Huron. Fringed sombreros from south of the border became rare when the Government in 1965 halted seasonal migrations of *braceros* —field workers from Mexico. Local farm hands help fill the gap, but a shortage of labor still plagues some areas despite increasing use of machinery.

Driving north from Imperial Valley, I passed ranges of jumbled rock, scorched and blackened as though by a giant blowtorch. Yet among the rocks rose the slender shafts of yucca plants, lifting their clusters of silver blossoms like candelabra against the sky.

Altimeter Unwinds to Minus 80 Feet

Loneliness enfolds the Mojave like a cerement. Often the traveler's only companions are the dust devils—miniature whirlwinds that do their ghostly dance across endless miles of sand. Sound, too, comes rarely to the desert, except for the solitary wind. Now and then against the stillness, high out of sight, a jet aircraft rips a seam across the sky.

Curiously, the desert offers a hospitable side to the aircraft that invade its silence. So endlessly flat and hardened are the dry lake beds that they make perfect auxiliary landing strips. The most famous example is the vast expanse of Rogers Lake, at Edwards Air Force Base.

One morning at the base, the Air Force's great flight-test center in the western Mojave, I sat buckled in the rear seat of a T-38 jet trainer behind a test pilot, Capt. David Livingston.

Earlier I had toured the base and learned that in today's aviation test work, all is not supersonics and the Space Age. Close beside the X-15, the bulletlike rocket plane that has flown six times the speed of sound,* I saw half a dozen familiar propeller-driven aircraft. All

were vintage types that I had thought of as long since tested, yet all were obviously being readied for experimental flights by green-overalled ground crews.

"No Air Force plane ever really graduates from the test line," Dave Livingston told me. "For one thing, aircraft designers are always coming up with improvements to make their products do a better job—or even do a brand-new one.

"All the drawing boards in the world won't tell you for certain how some change may affect an airplane in flight. Our job is to find out for sure, not only with the supersonic

*Test pilot Joseph A. Walker described how it feels to fly the X-15 in the September, 1962, GEOGRAPHIC.

California gold: Sunkist oranges go into crates at Rancho Sespe, near Ventura. The Golden State provides 90 percent of the Nation's lemons, but Florida outproduces it in oranges by three to one. Groves of oranges, lemons, and grapefruit earn California $150,000,000 a year. Because of sky-rocketing land values, however, many groves have yielded to expanding cities and suburbs.

Carpet of cotton, woven with machine precision, covers a seemingly endless expanse of the San Joaquin Valley at Lemoore. Daredevil pilots leave contrails of pesticides over the

fields. Scientific fertilizing, irrigation, planting, and harvesting make this valley the

state's most important farm region and California the Nation's leading agricultural producer. High cost of labor and its short supply have spurred the development of complex
machinery to operate the huge factorylike farms.

621

types, but with what people nowadays consider the Model T's."

Our jet trainer was neither the Air Force's fastest plane nor in any sense a Model T. Dave lifted the slender nose and we streaked upward through the desert haze, leveling off in the crystal morning at 15,000 feet. The dry lake bed below us had dwindled sharply, its network of emergency strips like a scattering of arrows in the dust.

I had asked to fly over Mount Whitney in the Sierra Nevada, the United States' highest point—at 14,494 feet—until Alaska brought Mount McKinley (20,320 feet) into the Union. Afterward I hoped to see the Western Hemisphere's lowest point, near Badwater in Death Valley, at 282 feet below sea level.

Dave swung northward over the Tehachapi Mountains, long a traditional dividing line between southern and northern California. Today, with faster transportation and closer

dependence between the two halves, the boundary is less easily defined.

Beyond the Tehachapis we banked eastward, and suddenly the great upturned saw blade of the Sierra flashed beneath us. Even in early summer, the grooves of the blade— the high mountain passes—were clogged with snow. Here and there among the peaks, small frozen lakes glinted like tarnished coins.

Dave circled Mount Whitney and followed the Sierra northward, along the jagged ridgeline. Clouds drifted in on the Pacific's westerly winds, striking the massive mountain barrier and coiling upward in a violent froth. Winds tipped the froth over the ridge, so that it curled and tumbled down the eastern slopes and vanished over the desert; we seemed to be flying beside an enormous waterfall.

We followed the clouds in a shallow dive, and suddenly the great, vivid scar of Death Valley opened before us.

KODACHROMES (INCLUDING PAGES 624-5) © NATIONAL GEOGRAPHIC SOCIETY

Oasis of wonders: Balboa Park, San Diego's chief recreational and cultural center, borders the downtown business district. Its 1,158 acres contain wild and landscaped grounds, museums, a concert bowl and theater, golf courses, and a zoo where children may feed and pet some of the animals. Amid sun-drenched gardens, students (opposite) paint beneath the Spanish-colonial California Tower, designed by Bertram Grosvenor Goodhue for the 1915-16 Panama-California International Exposition.

Tall-masted pleasure yachts share San Diego Bay with steely men of war. California possesses few good harbors; boats jam every available space such as at man-made Shelter Island. Across the water, jets line the aprons of North Island's Naval Air Station. Home of the U.S. Navy's First Fleet, San Diego serves as headquarters for a huge defense complex that includes shipyards, depots, and training installations. Viet Nam-bound troops and supplies also stage through the port.

"We'll take a close look at it," David said over the intercom and went into another shallow dive. The air-speed indicator in front of me showed 400 knots as we leveled off some 200 feet above the valley floor.

I can't say that I saw Badwater as we streaked by, but Dave assured me it was there. I was more impressed by the fact that we were flying approximately 80 feet below sea level. Dave climbed and provided a final variation, rolling the T-38 slowly on its back. For a moment I hung suspended upside down in the harness—and Death Valley streamed by overhead.

It took only minutes, right side up, to cover the 165 miles between Death Valley and the town of Mojave near Edwards—a brutal

week-and-a-half trek for the 20-mule teams that hauled borax from the valley in the 19th and early 20th centuries.

Today a different sort of mule helps California harvest her underground riches. The mules—Californians sometimes call them "donkeys" or even "grasshoppers"—are mechanical pumps that operate the state's 41,000 oil wells, endlessly nodding and drawing wealth from the land (pages 636-7).

California's mechanical donkeys graze in unlikely places: on downtown streets in Los Angeles; in a Beverly Hills high school yard; in vineyards and cotton fields; even miles at sea, atop offshore wells.

I walked one day through a herd of the donkeys near Bakersfield, at the southern tip

Careening on two wheels, a sand sailor races across the dry bed of El Mirage Lake. His single-sail land boat can scoot 2½ times the speed of the wind, sometimes attaining 60 to 70 miles an hour on the hard flats.

At the feet of mighty giants, tiny humans stand in awe. Sequoia National Park in the Sierra Nevada, established through Government and private efforts, including grants from your Society, preserves forest patriarchs in their primeval splendor. Some of these *Sequoia gigantea* near Crescent Meadow first took root 3,500 years ago. Although scarred by countless forest fires, the trees' thick bark helps insulate the heartwood against flames.

bing donkeys. Like many a stranger to the petroleum industry, I had thought of oil wells in terms of gushers that had to be restrained rather than encouraged to flow. Ray nodded agreement.

"You're partly right," he said. "When a well first comes in, underground water or natural gas usually lifts the oil up, and you may have to slow it down. But after a while the pressure drops off, and then these"—he waved at the pumps—"take over.

"Finally," he added, "the pressure gets so low that even the pumps aren't enough."

I asked if that meant the end of the well, and Ray shook his head emphatically.

"Not necessarily. The cost of discovering a field can be enormous, and the ratio of producing wells pretty low. When the pressure is really gone, you recharge the well by forcing water, gas, or nowadays even steam, back into the ground to start things moving.

"It's just like shaking a soda pop bottle to make it fizz a little more. Only this is pretty valuable fizz."

Sea Water Supports Sinking Land

Shaking the pop bottle too long and hard can lead to trouble, as Californians have learned to their dismay. In some areas of the state, so much oil has been pumped out of the ground that the land above it has actually begun to settle. In coastal regions engineers have hit on an ingenious solution—stabilize the land by pumping tons of sea water underground to replace the depleted oil.

East of Fresno, along the shoulder of the mighty Sierra, lies one of southern California's greatest treasures. Sequoia and Kings Canyon National Parks, although technically separate domains, join to form a 1,314-square-

of the San Joaquin Valley. The San Joaquin and its northern counterpart, the Sacramento Valley, join in a great 500-mile-long trough, called the Central Valley, running between California's Coast Ranges and the Sierra.

The San Joaquin and Sacramento are two huge greenhouses, between them producing an infinite variety of crops. Bakersfield and surrounding Kern County, while blessed with rich farmland, are equally blessed in what lies beneath. In a state whose oil production is exceeded only by that of Texas and Louisiana, Kern County contributes nearly a third of all California output, with 98,000,000 barrels a year.

Ray Arnett, a geologist with Richfield Oil Corporation, led me on review past the bob-

mile federal preserve. The reason for the preserve—its spectacular mountains and gorges aside—is *Sequoia gigantea,* the big tree (preceding pages).

Many National Geographic Society members are familiar with their Society's role in preserving the world's finest stands of giant sequoias. Susan Baisden, for one, knows all about it.

I met Susan, who is ten years old, at Lost Grove, one of the roadside stops in Sequoia park, where her family had come for the weekend from their home in Bakersfield. She and I fell to discussing the great fire scars

that etch the sequoia trunks as far up as the eye can reach, recording countless assaults by flames.

One of the park naturalists had told me that a healthy redwood may even withstand a "crown fire"—a forest fire that races through the tops of the tall trees. The bark of *gigantea,* like that of its cousin, *Sequoia sempervirens* —the coast redwood of northern California— has an almost asbestoslike quality. Although it can be burned, a mature redwood, because of its thick, fire-resistant bark, rarely dies as a result of a single fire.

That fact, I said, may help to account for

the sequoias' fantastic age, estimated as high as 3,500 years. Susan nodded unhappily.

"Yes, but it's sad that they aren't the oldest living thing any more," she said. "I suppose you've read about those bristlecone pine trees in the GEOGRAPHIC—the ones in the White Mountains, beyond the Sierra. We read about them in school."

I said I knew of them. One of the incredibly gnarled bristlecones has an estimated age of more than 4,600 years. And one tree across the line in Nevada has lived 4,900 years.

Susan considered matters soberly for a moment, and then brightened.

"A plane in every garage" could be the motto of Sierra Sky Park, near Fresno. The "town square" is a 3,200-foot-long grass airstrip, making this a suburb with a real difference. Planes taxi on streets that bear signs reading "Watch for Aircraft on the Roadway." Children skateboard along the driveway of their futuristic home. Their father, a lumber company owner, uses his plane for business and family recreation.

631

"After all," she said, "it isn't so bad, really —most bristlecones are Californians, too."

For every national park and monument within its borders, California has dozens of state parks and monuments all its own. For sheer contrast with Sequoia's untouched splendor, nothing quite matches San Simeon (page 639).

Empty Bottles Return to Wine Cellar

Even the term "castle" seems scarcely adequate for the lavish former home of the late William Randolph Hearst, on the Pacific coast north of Morro Bay. Castles, as a rule, follow a single architectural style; San Simeon exuberantly follows half a dozen.

The vast mansion, with its soaring bell towers, formal gardens, and statuary, exhibits such styles as Florentine, Moorish, Roman, Greek, and Peruvian, with a dash now and then of ancient Egypt. Yet somehow the castle at San Simeon, far from being an eyesore, has unmistakable grace. It also has a very curious wine cellar.

I learned about the cellar from Barbara Sewell, an attractive member of the state historical monument's staff. She had shown me the lavish Neptune Pool, done in marble with a Roman temple on the side. Mrs. Sewell remarked that the State of California, now the mansion's proprietor, allows guides and maintenance staff to use the pool after hours.

But the state, unhappily, refuses to heat the pool, as Mr. Hearst did for his guests.

Indoors, we came to the enormous Refectory, the main dining hall of the mansion. At one side of the room on a long buffet stood a magnificent silver wine bowl, more accurately called a wine cistern. Mrs. Sewell explained that San Simeon in its day had been famous for its wine cellar, part of which still remains.

Recalling the pool privileges, I asked if she were personally acquainted with the wine cellar. She shook her head.

"I made several recommendations about that," she said smiling, "but the State of California didn't agree."

Actually, I learned later, California doesn't own San Simeon's wine—it still belongs to Mr. Hearst's family. But to maintain the cellar's original appearance, California and the Hearsts have made an ingenious agreement.

The Hearsts, who no longer live in the main mansion, now and then remove a few cases of wine for their own use. Once the bottles are empty, the Hearsts return them to San Simeon's cellar to help preserve its authentic historical atmosphere.

South of San Simeon, just off California's coastal Route 1, something happens to the salt sea air. It is suddenly drowned in a fragrant wave of chocolate, followed by others of nutmeg and cinnamon. The reason is Solvang, a town of some 1,500 that would seem to have no business being in California at all.

Solvang, with its immaculate, half-timbered houses and its Hans Christian Andersen bakeries and candy shops, properly belongs on the other side of the Atlantic, in Denmark—the birthplace of about half the town's residents. Happily for California, Solvang's Danish-Americans are quite content where they are.

EKTACHROMES © N.G.S.

Rainbow robes of Japanese O Bon dancers paint swirls on Fresno's city mall—and fill a child's eyes with wonder. Traffic once clogged this business district where today flowers, fountains, and a sculptured clock tower adorn an open promenade. City planners hope to convert an entire 85-acre business "superblock" to pedestrian use, erecting a convention center and other public buildings. Japanese-Americans honor their dead during the O Bon Festival; they constitute only a small proportion of Fresno's population, but represent the active and prosperous Nisei community of the entire state.

Solvang began more than half a century ago as a small colony of Danish-Americans from the Midwest. Over the years other Danes followed, both from the homeland and from many parts of the United States. With them they brought the magic of Danish cookery, craftsmanship, and a genius for farming.

Solvang's sidewalks are perpetually awash with non-Scandinavians—visitors drawn by the town's endless store of fresh-baked pastry, delicate cheese, and hand-blocked linen.

But the charm of Solvang and its surroundings, to me, stretches beyond the gift shops and the bakeries. North of the town in a quiet valley stands a red frame building as surprising in California as is a Danish village.

In a state whose exploding numbers demand education on a massive scale, the two-room school seems hopelessly out of place. Yet the small public school of Ballard goes unconcernedly ahead training some two dozen pupils every year, just as it has since 1882.

Gopher Umpires a Sand-lot Game

I sat one morning on the schoolhouse steps with Joan Brace, Ballard's principal and one of its two teachers until she left recently to be married. We talked of California's educational system, for all its massive size one of the best in the country. I asked how Ballard

"Queen of the Missions," Santa Barbara relives its colonial glory during the Old Spanish Days Fiesta. Padre Choristers open the August festival on the steps of the old church. Beguiling dancer twirls to the music of guitars and castanets. Established in 1786, the mission forged a link in the chain of 21 outposts—from San Diego to present-day Sonoma—that helped Spain colonize California's coast.

fitted into a network noted for such giants as the University of California, Stanford University, and Los Angeles' University of Southern California.

"Perfectly," Joan answered. "Ballard graduates have gone on to take higher degrees in those places, and a good many others. It's true that the big elementary schools outdo Ballard in the extras—music, mechanical training, and that sort of thing. But basically we all follow the same pattern." She waved around her.

"What Ballard has that the others don't is something that's precious in California because it's vanishing—space, and the wonder of natural things. Look there, for example." She pointed toward the schoolyard, at a small form investigating what appeared to be a sandwich crust.

"That gopher is a school pet, and every one of my 28 pupils knows him on personal terms. What's more, he knows them. I've seen him at baseball games, standing attentively right next to third base. If you didn't know better, you'd say he was an umpire. I'm convinced *he* thinks he is." She smiled as I stood up to go.

"You won't find that in San Francisco or Los Angeles."

Ballard, at least, has a schoolhouse with

children; lonely San Nicolas has hardly any life at all. I learned of San Nicolas during a visit to Santa Barbara, once the site of a Spanish *presidio,* or colonial garrison, as well as a Franciscan mission.

Lonely Vigil Proves Futile

Santa Barbara has an air of untroubled charm that disguises two historic ordeals—a disastrous earthquake in 1925 and a forest fire that engulfed the city's outskirts less than two years ago.

It was at Mission Santa Barbara, called "Queen of the Missions" (preceding page),

that I learned of Juana Maria. Juana Maria's story goes back to the year 1835 and to remote San Nicolas, a speck of land lying some 50 miles southwest of Los Angeles in the Pacific Ocean.

During the fading years of Mexican rule over California, authorities decided to evacuate the small band of Indians living on San Nicolas. As a boatload of islanders set out for the waiting ship, one mother, Juana Maria, discovered that her child was missing. She was returned to the island, but while she searched, a fair wind sprang up and the ship set sail for the mainland. For 18 solitary years

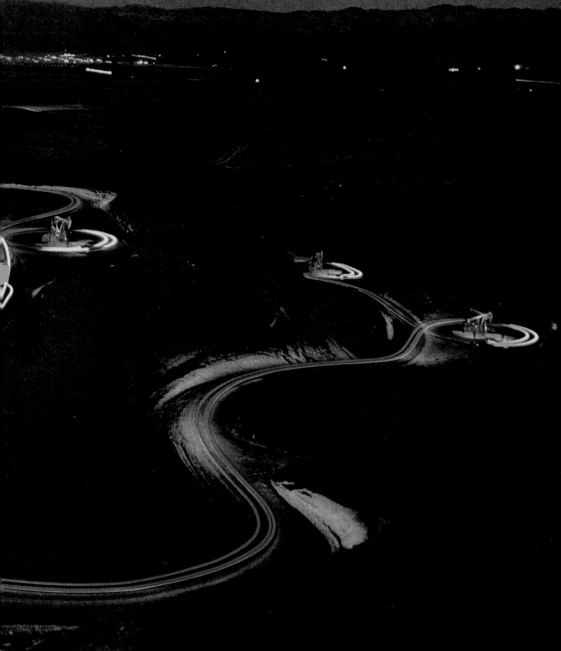

Juana Maria lived marooned on San Nicolas, until rescuers sent by the Franciscans at Mission Santa Barbara found her and returned her to the mainland. There she died a few weeks later and was buried by the Franciscans in their quiet cemetery.

No trace of the child has ever been discovered on the island.

Fascinated by the story, I determined to visit San Nicolas. The island today provides a link in the Pacific Missile Range, a 3,000-mile-long test corridor from the Navy's missile test complex at Point Mugu all the way to tiny Johnston Island west of Hawaii.

Whorls of light outline oil wells at Coalinga. With his camera set on a hilltop and the shutter open, NATIONAL GEOGRAPHIC photographer Thomas Nebbia drove through the maze of roads serving five wells and stopped at each pump to set off a flash. In the process, he captured his own silhouette at least once—in the circle at far left.

California wells produce nearly 11 percent of the Nation's petroleum, surpassed only by Texas and Louisiana. Yet, because of the state's huge number of motor vehicles —11,000,000 registered in 1965—it must import motor fuel.

The Navy kindly flew me to San Nicolas from range headquarters at Point Mugu. The flight took us south, past the magnificent Channel Islands National Monument to the west of Santa Catalina, Los Angeles' offshore vacation center. Finally the ten-mile-long outline of San Nicolas appeared below us through the haze.

San Nicolas is hardly a reassuring sight to passengers in an aircraft about to land. As we circled low for a final approach, I noticed a grim line of wreckage beside the runway. There were battered sections of fuselage, a crumpled tail fin or two, and the charred remains of half a dozen wings. The pilot ignored them and banked evenly into the wind, touching down and rolling to a stop beside the control shack.

Only then did I learn that San Nicolas' junkyard is a source of pride rather than shame to the Navy.

"They're target drones, brought down in practice shoots and then fished out of the water," said Comdr. Harold R. Megrew, the island's officer in charge. "Beautiful sight, aren't they?" I admitted they were breathtaking.

Commander Megrew took me for a brief tour of the island in an open jeep, and I learned why Californians speak of the "San Nicolas tilt." A constant half gale tore at our clothes and raised miniature dust devils beside the road. Old-timers who used San Nicolas as an occasional station for hunting sea otters insisted that to walk anywhere on the island, they had to maintain a constant 45-degree tilt to windward.

I found San Nicolas a bleak and forbidding spot, wind-scourged and treeless. Only the grim silhouettes of the Navy's great radar tracking antennas relieved the low line of dark hills.

My thoughts turned to Juana Maria and her years of lonely exile, gazing endlessly out on an empty sea. San Nicolas had begrudged her even the comfort of wild companions: The island proper has few natural inhabitants save for lizards and the elusive Channel Islands foxes.

Yet Juana Maria had not watched alone. To seaward of the coves where she had gathered abalone and small mussels, rise dark spires of rock—lookouts to this day for other sentinels of the lonely ocean, the cormorant and the sea lion.

Where South Ends and North Begins

Flying back toward the mainland at dusk, we passed Los Angeles' great plain of light and turned northwestward to follow the coast. Gradually the city dropped behind like some enormous incandescent cloud, drifting across the dark reach of space. At last I turned away and picked up the lights of Point Mugu before us. From there the coast lay north and west, outlined by other lights of small towns like a row of beacons set awry.

Beyond them lay another California.

                                        *   *   *

La Cuesta Encantada—The Enchanted Hill—William Randolph Hearst's San Simeon estate, houses a fabulous collection of paintings, sculptures, and antiques. The palatial home towers like a Spanish cathedral over surrounding guest cottages and landscaped grounds. A colonnade flanks the outdoor pool. Donated to California by the Hearst Corporation, the property has become a state historical monument.

Newspaper editor William Randolph Hearst, Jr., rides on the family's 75,000-acre ranch surrounding the San Simeon estate.

KODACHROMES BY THOMAS NEBBIA © N.G.S.

ABOVE THE DOORWAY of a state building in Sacramento, California's capital, runs a legend carved in marble:

BRING ME MEN TO MATCH MY MOUNTAINS

Providence, it seems, having created California on a vast scale, generously answered the request. From its earliest beginnings, California history has rung with great names in discovery and achievement—Cabrillo, Serra, Drake, Frémont, Vallejo, Stanford.

Yet for all its dramatic past, California remains a land of endless challenge. In a recent speech near San Francisco, President Lyndon B. Johnson declared: "Those who believe the frontiers of America are closed should be out here today . . . the era of the pioneers is not over —only the area of pioneering has changed."

One of California's greatest challenges lies in binding two divergent parts into a single, smoothly working state. What distinguishes northern California above all from its southern counterpart is the ratio of men to mountains—of men to the land.

"Southern California has the people," runs a saying. "Northern California has everything they need." The saying exaggerates; yet the fact remains that two out of three Californians make their home in what is regarded as the southern part of the state, while many of the resources—timber, undeveloped land, and water—lie largely in the northern half. The result is a state divided in character, yet unified by the needs of its vast population.

Open Spaces Hold Key to Future

Northern California's wealth lies not only in its resources but in the sheer majesty of the land itself—in the great coastal ramparts that buttress the land against the sea, in the timeless grandeur of the redwood groves, in rolling grasslands and grim volcanic peaks—and in

the glitter of a stately city at night high above San Francisco Bay.

I began my tour at Big Sur, still in the southern half of the state but scenically the beginning of nature's north. Big Sur has become famous both for its dramatic confrontation with the sea and for the artists and writers who are drawn to its natural beauty (pages 650-53). I saw it first on a day when fog wrapped the great headlands in gauze, smoothing the rough contours of the coast.

At least one of Big Sur's residents, the noted architect Nathaniel Owings, believes such uncluttered beauty holds the key to California's future. "Our problem is people," he told me when I called on him. "Not just thousands or even millions of people, but *tens* of millions. California's population is expected to triple by the end of the century, and our cars even now are increasing at something like a thousand a day."

CHROMES BY JONATHAN S. BLAIR (BELOW) AND TED MAHIEU © N.G.S.

CALIFORNIA
PART II

Nature's North

By WILLIAM GRAVES

*Photographs by JAMES P. BLAIR
and JONATHAN S. BLAIR*

Beloved city by the bay, San Francisco dons her nighttime glitter beneath a tawny sunset sky. Double decks of the majestic Bay Bridge carry spangled streams of auto lights. The vibrant city of St. Francis blends gold-rush gusto and Nob Hill sophistication, whistle of ships and clank of cable cars (above). Queen of northern California, she reigns over a domain of farmland and forest, pleasant towns and rugged mountains—and water to nourish the state's parched south.

"Someone has said jokingly that eventually California will be entirely paved—with the possible exception of Lake Tahoe. It might almost come to that, unless we treat the land with respect. Today, instead, we treat it with contempt, sprawling all over it with suburbs.

"We have a lesson to learn from some other Americans," Mr. Owings added, "the Pueblo Indians, who were here on the continent centuries before us. They needed land for agriculture and beauty just as we do, and what did they do about it? By building early versions of high-rise apartments, they concentrated their living areas.

"That way they saved the open spaces for all the people—not to mention future generations. We would do well to consider history."

California Adds 31st Star to Flag

Californians are seldom more than a step or two from the past. Just north of Big Sur lies a city steeped in tradition, the old Spanish garrison town of Monterey.

Curiously, for all Monterey's fame as a colonial stronghold—first Spanish, later Mexican—it speaks to Californians of independence. There, on July 7, 1846, the United States flag was first raised as a permanent symbol in California, signifying a free territory. Four years later a slightly different flag followed, with a 31st star—California's.

Monterey is something more than a historic landmark, as both golfers and gourmets can testify. On Monterey Peninsula lie five famous golf courses, among them the spectacular Pebble Beach Course, beside the equally spectacular Seventeen Mile Drive. Almost within iron shot, along Monterey's waterfront, runs a street known as Cannery Row.

Cannery Row has changed surprisingly little in appearance since 1945, when John Steinbeck's novel by that name captured the bizarre life of Monterey's sardine packers. The great canning factories still line the Row in drab ranks, but the sounds and smells that once engulfed them are only memories. In

Market Street pierces downtown San Francisco like an arrow, its flaming tip the Ferry Building tower. The financial district —Wall Street of the West—stretches to the left. Wells Fargo's bank-in-the-round sits like a top hat beneath Crown Zellerbach's skyscraper; the Shell Oil Building lifts an amber crest beyond.

Early-bird brokers open the Pacific Stock Exchange at 7 a.m. to synchronize workdays with their New York counterparts.

Dungeness crabs delight a small diner at San Francisco's Fisherman's Wharf. Each day before dawn, sturdy mariners stream out into the Pacific to net flounder, shrimp, salmon, and crabs for the wharf's renowned restaurants.

Dazzle of Chinatown bursts upon sightseers in a motorized ricksha. Grant Avenue's pagoda rooftops mark the home of 25,000 American Chinese—largest Chinese settlement outside the Orient.

EKTACHROME (BELOW) AND KODACHROME BY NATIONAL GEOGRAPHIC PHOTOGRAPHER THOMAS NEBBIA © N.G.S.

1946, the sardines that formerly blackened Monterey Bay began to depart, as did eventually the jobless cannery workers.

Today new businesses restore life to the Row. In the shadow of the silent factories stand several elegant restaurants, an antique shop or two, and a mecca for alpinists—the Himalayan Pak Company, a well-known mountaineering supply firm.

Where once only Spanish commands rang through Monterey's historic presidio, or military headquarters, the sounds today are of Swahili, Turkish, Greek, and Mandarin Chinese. The reason is something called the Defense Language Institute (West Coast Branch), a school administered by the United States Army for military personnel assigned to special jobs overseas.

Sea Lions Provoke Linguistic Feud

One morning I toured the institute with Capt. Dolores Hubik, an attractive staff officer. We visited half a dozen classes out of the more than 250 that offer 25 different languages to some two thousand students.

No one took notice as we passed through the rooms on what seemed a tour of the Tower of Babel. Military rank had little place in the classroom: Officers and enlisted men treated one another on equal terms as fellow students. Later I asked Captain Hubik what sort of assignments the graduates drew.

"According to the Russians and the Communist Chinese," she answered, "we're running an espionage school. Of course we get students from all branches of the military, but," she said, "I've yet to see a cloak or a dagger here.

"The fact is," she added seriously, "that the services today in every line of work need fluent language specialists, from military attachés to combat interpreters."

She pointed to one student with his leg in a cast, whom I had taken to be a casualty of California's ski slopes.

"He got that in parachute training at the Army's Special Forces school in Fort Bragg, North Carolina. You can't jump from a plane with a broken ankle, but you can study a language while it heals. After graduation, he'll go back to jumping."

The institute's curriculum is a reasonable gauge of world tensions and United States commitments. Three years ago the average class in Vietnamese numbered roughly 50 students; today it is closer to 300. Russian

and Chinese—both Cantonese and Mandarin —account for other large classes.

Courses are so concentrated that the students become deeply absorbed in their adopted languages, but the institute fortunately has its occasional lighter side.

"We had a second lieutenant here not long ago," Captain Hubik said, "who was studying for an assignment in Thailand. He took to going down on his day off to watch the sea lions in Monterey Harbor. I asked him one day why he spent so much time there, and he told me he had a theory the sea lions were speaking Thai. Apparently, he had quite an argument about it with a friend—the friend claimed they were speaking Serbo-Croatian."

With apologies to the second lieutenant and his friend, sea lions have a language all their own. I went to see them one day in a dramatic setting, Point Lobos Reserve State Park, south of Carmel-by-the-Sea. The park takes its name from a spectacular arm of land called by the early Spaniards after their term for sea lions: Punta de los Lobos Marinos—Point of the Sea Wolves.

The Spaniards, it seems, were as prone to illusion as the young lieutenant—sea lions are a far cry from wolves. To be fair to the Spaniards, one has to admit they are just as far a cry from lions.

I watched a herd of the ponderous creatures shuffling and hitching their way over the offshore rocks. Once they took to the water, clumsiness vanished; they were all grace and effortless speed.

In and out of water, the herd kept up a running commentary, a series of honks and blasts that echoed among the coves and windbowed cypresses. The sound reminded me of neither man nor beast; the nearest thing to it is an antique-car rally.

Fortune-seekers Build a State

If Monterey represents the birthplace of California statehood, the Mother Lode might be called the cradle. The wild and beautiful mountain region lying roughly between Sacramento and the high Sierra gave the state its first true magnet—gold.

For more than three centuries the vision of quick wealth had beckoned conquistadors and other adventurers to California's shores. Actually, James Marshall's discovery at Sutter's mill in 1848 was only one of several clues to treasure beneath the soil. Six years earlier, a small strike had been made in what is now

Reaching for the Golden Gate, Carinita-class sailboats race seaward beneath bald headlands of Marin Peninsula. Awesome currents surge through this majestic passage between the Pacific Ocean and San Francisco Bay; each tide rams an estimated one-sixth

of all the bay's waters in or out. A waterman's paradise, the bay wears a white-flecked pattern of sailing canvas the year round. Golden Gate Bridge, its roadway 246 feet above the water, points traffic northward from San Francisco toward the Redwood Empire.

the Los Angeles area. The find, however, attracted little notice.

Marshall's discovery not only attracted notice; it touched off a world-wide epidemic of "Sutter's fever" and laid the foundations of modern California. During the first frenzied three years of the gold rush, the forty-niners rocketed California's population from 15,000 to close to 100,000. They also gave California a new name—Golden State.

Today the hills of the Mother Lode are virtually silent. The gold—California's harvest ultimately reached more than 2⅓ billion dollars—is not, as many believe, exhausted. Many veins still exist, but the price paid for the metal, legally fixed at $35 a fine ounce, has closed all but a handful of small mines.

Driving through the Mother Lode, I found the names of its former mining towns poignant reminders of an era both sordid and heroic. There were courage, greed, hope, and a touch of loneliness in such names as Challenge, Rescue, Smartsville, Rough and Ready, Enterprise, and Tragedy Springs. There was humor, too, in such misnomers as Drytown—the settlement, in its heyday, had 26 saloons.

Other memorials in the Mother Lode tell more personal stories, ones of nostalgia or of longing for a distant land. In a cemetery at Jamestown I came across an inscription to one Victor Belli.

A Frenchman, Belli apparently had contracted Sutter's fever and sought a cure for it thousands of miles from home. In tribute to

KODACHROMES BY THOMAS NEBBIA © NATIONAL GEOGRAPHIC SOCIETY

his attachment to France, friends had inscribed the stone in his native language:

Ici repose
VICTOR BELLI
Né à Paris, France
Décédé à Peoria Flat
Le 12 Février, 1877

To at least one town in the Mother Lode, tradition means something more than gold. When spring creeps north along the Sierras, the talk in Angels Camp turns to frogs.

The reason is Mark Twain's riotous story, "The Celebrated Jumping Frog of Calaveras County." For more than a century, readers of all ages have delighted in the tale of Jim Smiley, the gold-rush gambler who bet a

California sherry in a glass-ended cask casts a roseate halo over tour guide Sally Paolini at Almaden Vineyards, Los Gatos.

Burden borne high, seminarian Michael C. Carey hurries a pan of grapes between a vineyard's stripped rows. His white Sémillons will ferment into golden sauterne at the Novitiate of Los Gatos; thus lives the tradition of California's mission fathers, who introduced viticulture two centuries ago. Today vines by the hundreds of thousands drape hillside and valley from Shasta to San Diego, producing 80 percent of all wine drunk in the United States.

MOUNTAINS BOUND FROM MISTY SEA *as dusk etches the rock ribs of Big Sur—a storied stretch of sculptured coastline. Taillights trace a car's progress on State Highway 1, notched into the soaring slopes.*

KODACHROME BY NATIONAL GEOGRAPHIC PHOTOGRAPHER JAMES P. BLAIR © N.G.S.

stranger $40 that his pet frog, Dan'l Webster, could outjump all comers.

While Smiley obligingly went in search of a frog for the stranger to match against Dan'l, the stranger prudently fed the champion a dose of quail shot, successfully ensuring his own victory.

Every spring since 1928, Angels Camp in Calaveras County has marked the tale with a county fair and a Jumping Frog Jubilee. Frog fanciers from all over the United States, and even from foreign countries, enter their favorites in the jumping tournament.

The visitor who wishes to compete but who has no frog is invited to catch one in a pool stocked for the occasion. Officials guarantee that none of their frogs has been fed a diet of quail shot.

Unfortunately, the guarantee says nothing about other handicaps. My borrowed frog, whom I hopefully christened "Paul Bunyan," thoroughly disgraced us both. In the three consecutive hops allowed by jubilee rules, he covered an embarrassing 4 feet, 7½ inches.

Later, after a frog by the less glorious name of "Hops" had swept the field with a creditable 14 feet, 8 inches, I asked a veteran frog-handler what Paul Bunyan's trouble was. He took a long look at Paul and another one at me.

"Mister," he said pityingly, "the first thing you do is get a new name for that frog. If it was me, I'd pick 'Paulette' or maybe 'Gertrude.' She's expecting, and she's carrying half a pound of eggs."

Some 40 miles to the southeast of Angels Camp lies a treasure far more dazzling and durable than gold. Yosemite National Park, another of California's great magnets, attracts more than 1,600,000 visitors each year.

Actually, Yosemite is not one magnet but hundreds of them, ranging from

On a lonely strand, a curl of kelp garnishes froth-laced Point Sur beach. Other Big Sur beaches—isolated in high-walled coves—reward beachcombers with jade, agate, jasper, iridescent bits of abalone shell, and moonstone smoothed by sand and tide. Residents value a greater treasure: privacy in a wild symphony of sea, mountain, and sky. The seafront country was the *sur,* or "south," to the Spanish settlers of old Monterey.

the massive granite bulk of Half Dome to the lacy miracle of Bridalveil Fall (pages 662-3). Most of the park's famous features lie along seven-mile-long Yosemite Valley, although the entire preserve roughly equals Rhode Island in area—1,200 square miles.

To Californians and their countrymen, the Yosemite region has long stood for breathtaking beauty. To a handful of scientists, it has recently become a possible laboratory for studying characteristics of the moon's surface.

Volcano Offers Clue to Moon

I learned of the development from Dr. Joel S. Watkins, a member of the U. S. Geological Survey's Astrogeology Branch, with headquarters in Flagstaff, Arizona. Recently the survey has conducted studies of the lunar surface for the National Aeronautics and Space Administration, through telescopes and by examining close-up photographs taken by the Ranger lunar probes. One of the objects of the study is to determine the type of terrain the Apollo spacecraft may encounter when Americans first land on the moon.

"Last summer," Dr. Watkins told me, "we had an exciting discovery in the Mono Craters area just east of Yosemite. A geologist there found permafrost —perpetually frozen ground that usually occurs in higher latitudes than ours. But the elevation of Mono Craters— some 8,500 feet—makes for low temperatures."

I failed to see a connection with the moon. Dr. Watkins explained.

"It's a question of the type of ground," he said. "The Mono Craters area, being volcanic, contains lava and pumice. Some scientists believe that parts of the lunar surface likewise are covered with

EKTACHROMES BY JAMES P. BLAIR © NATIONAL GEOGRAPHIC SOCIETY

At home in "Wild Bird," an A-frame retreat perched high on a cliff, 600 feet above the surf (top and page 651), Mr. and Mrs. Nathaniel Owings battle to keep Big Sur unspoiled. A world-famous architect, Mr. Owings heads a Presidential commission charged with face-lifting Pennsylvania Avenue in Washington, D. C. Wood sculptor Harry Dick Ross and his wife Eve, a painter, dwell among other artists of Big Sur's Partington Ridge.

"Butterfly trees" glitter at Pacific Grove on the Monterey Peninsula. Here monarch butterflies by the millions—fluttering in from as far as Canada—brighten winter every year. Citizens greet them with a parade, and a city ordinance protects the migrants from molesters. (See "Mystery of the Monarch Butterfly," by Paul A. Zahl, NATIONAL GEOGRAPHIC, April, 1963.)

Powder-fine white sand, rimmed by cypress and pine, invites loungers at Carmel-by-the-Sea's crescent beach. But a sign warns, "Surf Unsafe. Riptides and Undertow."

Nonconformists, Carmelites ban television antennas, house numbers, mail delivery, and billboards. The community's 4,580 residents take pride in their artists, writers, restaurants, and dollhouse architecture.

KODACHROMES BY JAMES P. BLAIR (LEFT) AND THOMAS NEBBIA © N.G.S.

lava and pumice. The Russians' recent Luna 9 photographs, in fact, lend weight to that theory.

"Now, suppose there is water, too, below the lunar surface. Because of the intense cold a few centimeters down, the water would almost certainly be permanently frozen. Then what do you have? Something like permafrost in volcanic material.

"In any event, Mono Craters' rocks may be close relatives to lunar rocks. If our Apollo astronauts find permanent ice under the lunar surface, the similarity between Mono Craters and the moon could be even greater."

The Golden Gate: Heaven's Portal

While some men lay plans to invade the celestial world, others claim to have lived there for years. Nothing can shake San Franciscans' belief that heaven is located on San Francisco Bay (pages 640, 646-7). To them, it is more than mere chance that the entrance is called Golden Gate.

San Franciscans, admittedly, have a point: There is something almost celestial about their city. Seen from Marin County across the bay at evening, its hills lie embroidered with light, as if—in the words of one San Franciscan—"God dropped all His leftover stars on them."

San Francisco is hardly less spectacular by day. On early mornings when fog sifts low through the Golden Gate, filling the bay with a ghostly high tide, the city soars

into the sunlight above like some Atlantis returned from the sea.

San Francisco, however, is more than mere scenery; to begin with, it is home for some three quarters of a million people and the focus of a metropolitan area population numbering roughly three million more. The result is northern California's unofficial capital, one of the world's most beautiful cities.*

San Francisco is also the Nation's third busiest port (if one includes all waterfront cities in the bay region) after New York and New Orleans; a world center of finance and of scientific research; a lodestone for both

*See "Boom on San Francisco Bay," by Franc Shor, NATIONAL GEOGRAPHIC, August, 1956.

Oriental and Western arts. Not every distinction, though, is a source of pride: For all the beauty and charm of its surroundings, San Francisco has a higher rate of suicide than any other city in the country.

City Cherishes Antique Trams

One way to risk death, or at least severe injury, in San Francisco is to criticize the cable cars (page 641). San Franciscans are fiercely protective about their antique mode of transport, so much so that the owner, the San Francisco Municipal Railway, trembles at the thought of any change.

"I remember the time we put windshield wipers on the cars," Charles Smallwood told

me one day in the repair shop at Washington and Mason Streets. Mr. Smallwood, a large and kindly man, oversees all maintenance of the city's 39 venerable machines.

"People raised no end of fuss," he said. "One old gentleman even told me that if cable cars had needed windshield wipers, the good Lord would have built them that way."

San Franciscans are like that, slow to change where tradition and sentiment are involved. It is no accident that the city's best-loved hotels—for example, the stately Fairmont or the Huntington on Nob Hill—carefully preserve an air of bygone elegance while sparing no modern convenience.

Elsewhere San Franciscans welcome change, yet always with a protective eye on the past. The city already is hard at work on a Bay Area Rapid Transit system—BART—to link the downtown with such bay cities as Oakland, where a great Californian, Chief Justice of the United States Earl Warren, started his law career. Other plans are less easily accepted—for example, an unobtrusive second deck on the cherished Golden Gate Bridge was approved only after years of civic controversy.

San Franciscans maintain the same watchful eye on the heart of their city. Along Market Street, the traditional main artery, blocks of disheveled buildings have given way to sleek new skyscrapers (pages 642-3). Not far away, yet immune to the wrecking hammer, stands the beloved San Francisco Opera House—a monument to yesterday's elegance.

Elegance occasionally can be overdone, as with some of San Francisco's famous restaurants. The emphasis in a few seems heavier on interior decor than on the interior of the customers themselves. Other restaurants face the opposite problem of emphasizing perfectly good food amid distractions to the guests. Those on Fisherman's Wharf are in constant competition with some 200 crab and fishing boats moored beneath their windows.

At least one type of restaurant in San Francisco solves the problem of atmosphere by ignoring it. To residents of Chinatown, the sole business of restaurants is food. Atmosphere belongs outside, on Grant Avenue.

Grant Avenue, with its pagoda-type street-lamps, its neon aurora, and its garish rows of Chinese variety shops, runs like a strip of tinsel through the heart of Chinatown, luring visitors and San Franciscans alike in seemingly inexhaustible numbers (page 644).

Behind the avenue, in narrow streets of quiet row houses and apartment buildings, lives a sober community of some 25,000 American Chinese, the largest Chinese settlement outside Asia. Approximately 17,000 other American Chinese are scattered elsewhere throughout San Francisco.

KODACHROME BY JAMES P. BLAIR © N.G.S.

With banshee howl, natural steam escapes the earth near Geyserville. Workmen protect ears from the din with muffs as they repair pipes carrying scalding vapor from The Geysers—a teakettle area of fumaroles and hot springs. The ready-made steam spins generators of Pacific Gas and Electric Company. Bores 700 to 5,000 feet deep tap ground water set boiling by heat from magma, or molten matter in earth's fiery interior.

Nation's highest dam, rising in the Feather River canyon 70 miles north of Sacramento, promises a solution to California's water problem. To be completed by 1968, Oroville Dam will impound enough water to supply every household in the state for a year. Key unit of California's farsighted State Water Project, it will supply cities as distant as San Diego through a system of rivers, aqueducts, and tunnels. Oroville's 1¼-mile-long earthen embankment will climb 770 feet above the canyon floor, to the level of the highest roadway at right. Dark streak marks a slab of impervious clay, heart of the massive dirt dam.

Fearsome looking but tranquilized by drugs, a chinook salmon rides an elevator of water-filled compartments from "dope pound" to tank truck for a lift past the Oroville Dam site. A hatchery below the dam will replace spawning streams disturbed by the project.

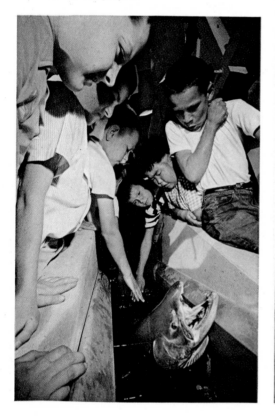

Chinatown today is neither the tinseled world of Grant Avenue nor the murky realm of the tong war and the opium den favored by fiction writers.

"Outsiders think of our tongs in terms of Murder, Incorporated," says Alan S. Wong, an energetic young worker in Chinatown's antipoverty program. "Of course it's true that at one time the tongs weren't above settling their differences with the hatchet and the cleaver, but then"—he grins—"I don't recall

that the old forty-niners took many of their arguments to court, either."

The tongs of San Francisco once wielded enormous power in their roles as business cartels, courts of justice, and crime syndicates, all in one. Today, like many another traditional feature of Chinatown, they have lost a great deal of their influence. The last killing attributed to a difference between tongs occurred forty years ago.

The associations now more closely suggest

combinations of business groups and fraternal orders. I asked Alan Wong how the change in traditional patterns influenced Chinatown's younger generation.

Words of Wisdom From an Oven

" 'Influence' is hardly the word," he replied. "Our children are changing the patterns themselves, just as your own children are.

"Naturally, our kids are in love with everything modern—cars, television, the way-out dances—though to them it's all strictly 'American.' You see, they think they're rebelling against outdated Chinese culture, when all they're really doing is what kids everywhere do—rebelling against their own parents."

At least one American influence in Chinatown is hardly modern; it's a book of Benjamin Franklin's sayings. The owner, an American Chinese named Ernest Louie, quotes it to millions of Orientals and Westerners alike.

Ernie Louie has an influential job: He

composes the messages that go into Chinese fortune cookies. With his brother Ed, he owns a successful firm known as the Lotus Fortune Cookie Company.

Passing their plant on Chinatown's Pacific Avenue one day, I dropped in and made Ernie's acquaintance. He showed me the ingenious machines like small carousels that pour and bake the cookies—more than 30,000 a day—in endless succession. Women tending the machines deftly scoop each finished cookie from its small oven, inserting a fortune and bending the still pliable pastry into final shape before it cools.

Ernie, I discovered, is not one for cute phrases or frivolity when it comes to fortune cookies. "People need a little philosophy, something meaningful at the end of a meal," he said. "Jokes are bad for the digestion."

I asked where he got his inspiration—the Lotus Company prints more than 4,000 different fortunes—and he waved toward a shelf of heavy books.

"I'm fond of the regulars, Confucius and Lin Yutang," he said, "and now and then I lean heavily on Plato. But my favorite is this one." He held up an incredibly battered book. "You can't beat *Franklin's Wit and Wisdom.*"

Fortune cookies, it seems, can be just as appealing to Chinese as they can to Westerners.

Ardent conservationist, Governor Edmund G. ("Pat") Brown pledges his administration will never sacrifice the state's prized groves of coast redwoods to freeways.

Crackling skies match the brilliance of a floodlighted capitol dome at Sacramento. A booming gold-rush town when it became the state capital in 1854, Sacramento served as western terminus for the Pony Express and the first transcontinental railroad. Today's city of 266,000 people prospers as a food-processing, trade, and transportation center.

"Even I can't resist them," Ernie confided sheepishly. "When I see one in a restaurant, I've got to know what's inside—even if I wrote it myself. But what kind of a fool would I look like, opening a fortune cookie, when everybody knows the business I'm in?"

I asked how he solved the problem, and Ernie blushed.

"I usually go with friends," he said. "They open my cookie for me, and then pass the fortune under the table."

Fortune and its companion, disaster, are old acquaintances of the city beside San Francisco Bay. Many San Franciscans remember, and all are aware of, the horror that overtook their city one morning 60 years ago. At 5:13 a.m. on April 18, 1906, the great San Andreas Fault, running roughly north and south beneath San Francisco Bay, split for a distance of some 270 miles, loosing a series of jackhammer blows at San Francisco and neighboring towns.

Shock and Fire Level a City

The blows themselves lasted less than a minute, but as with many major shocks in populated areas, fire took up where the heaving earth left off. The price to San Franciscans after days of anguish was some 700 lives lost and roughly half their city demolished.

EKTACHROME (OPPOSITE) BY JAMES P. BLAIR; KODACHROME BY TOM MYERS © N.G.S.

Gouged by glaciers, breathtaking Yosemite Valley dazzles 1,600,000 visitors a year to California's top scenic attraction—Rhode Island-size Yosemite National Park. El Capi-

tan's granite prow soars vertically at left, Bridalveil Fall plunges below Cathedral Rocks, and distant Half Dome hulks nearly two-thirds of a mile above the valley floor.

San Francisco, of course, eventually was rebuilt, together with a safeguard that remains to this day. What had cost the city cruelly in its struggle with fire was lack of water—the first shock had severed most of the mains.

Today San Francisco firemen run little risk of facing a holocaust with limp and useless hoses. At 152 points around the city, on the crests of hills and at major intersections, lie great subterranean cisterns, independent of the city's water system—precious weapons against earthquake and its aftermath.

Actually, the cisterns are nothing new to San Francisco: Smaller versions existed even before the great fire. Several were located in the notorious Barbary Coast area, near Pacific Avenue and Kearny Street, where they helped to save the Coast in 1906; it suffered scarcely a casualty or a burned-out saloon. Today enlarged cisterns safeguard the Coast's would-be successor, the dazzling but somewhat tamer North Beach entertainment district.

EKTACHROME (BELOW) AND KODACHROMES
BY JAMES P. BLAIR © N.G.S.

California's Average: Tremor a Day

Californians are constantly reminded of the terrible spasms that can seize their land. Every year some 350 tremors—an average of roughly one a day—are recorded in the northern and central parts of the state.

"Of course, those are just the ones we can locate accurately," explains Dr. Bruce Bolt, Director of the University of California's Seismographic Station at Berkeley. "Many tremors are too remote or too slight to allow our seismographs a proper fix. Of the total number of shocks, between 30 and 60 are strong enough and close enough to people in California to be felt by them. Fortunately, none so far has equaled the 1906 shock for strength and damage combined. But all of them remind us that California is a land in perpetual motion."

Dr. Bolt's town recently has earned a name for quite another type of upheaval. More than one political or academic battle has raged through the headquarters of California's vast state university.

The Berkeley campus of the University of California has about 27,000 students—a figure matched and even exceeded by several other universities in the country. Yet all together UC comprises nine separate campuses throughout the state, with 80,000 students and a faculty of 6,000.

Perhaps Berkeley's greatest fame rests on the genius of such men as Ernest O. Lawrence, the inventor of the cyclotron and founder of the great Lawrence Radiation Laboratory that stretches across the hillside behind the Berkeley campus.

Other northern California universities, notably Leland Stanford at Palo Alto, have contributed enormously to the state's role in research and academic achievement. Yet, as a Berkeley senior remarked to me, "We have more Nobel Prize winners per square inch than any other place on earth."

Weird wool-knit masks, copied from those worn by Peruvian Indians, warm cheeks and noses of youngsters skiing at Squaw Valley. Spill-conscious, one youth plays it safe with a hard hat.

Streaming a rooster tail of fresh powder snow, a skier races lengthening shadows beneath a chair lift to Siberia, the highest ridge above Squaw Valley. The Sierra Nevada resort near Lake Tahoe, scene of the 1960 Winter Olympics and now a state park, lures skiers with slopes carpeted white into early summer.

One of the first states to protect its natural wonders from encroaching civilization, California maintains a system of 183 state parks and 8 state forests.

I talked one day with another senior, 21-year-old JoAnne Schwartz, who came to California from New Jersey. JoAnne went through two major crises that have recently shaken Berkeley—the so-called Free Speech Movement and the furor over United States policy in Viet Nam. I asked how it was that the scholarly world of Berkeley could erupt so suddenly into chaos. Her answer shed light not merely on Berkeley but on much of California as well.

"The Viet Nam demonstration is a poor example," she began, "because it wasn't really Berkeley. Only a few hundred students were involved out of thousands—most of the demonstrators didn't even come from here.

"But the Free Speech Movement is something else; in the end, nearly all of us got in-

volved. I won't argue the pros and cons of it, because that's been done to death. But you asked me how it could happen." She paused.

"I guess I would answer: 'Because it's California—and California hasn't settled down yet.' In a way, I hope it never will, because I suspect it would lose something vital.

"People are new and rootless here," she said. "California attracts that kind because, in a sense, it's still a frontier. Not in the old way, of course, but in other respects: in the experimental architecture, for example, or in new sports and fashions—even in those way-out religions Los Angeles is so fond of.

"But you see, that's part of the way Californians are: Always trying for something different, always in search of the new—and not always thinking whether it's good or bad.

KODACHROME BY B. ANTHONY STEWART © N.G.S.; LOOMIS MUSEUM ASSOCIATION (RIGHT)

"Sometimes we come up with nothing more than a new style of bathing suit, sometimes with a campus revolt." She waved toward the laboratories behind us on the hill. "And now and then we produce an Ernest Lawrence. California pioneers come in all sizes."

Wedge of Earth Blocks Feather River

In their long and dramatic history, California pioneers have worked a succession of miracles on their land. The most massive to date is Oroville Dam, the great earthen wedge now being built across the Feather River in the Sacramento Valley (pages 658-9).

The key to California's ambitious State Water Project, Oroville Dam in 1970 will begin delivering millions of gallons to parched areas as far south as San Diego, more than 500 miles away. It may also spell the end of an age in hydraulic engineering—the age of the great concrete storage dam.

"We get visitors almost every week from the so-called underdeveloped countries," says an Oroville engineer proudly. "They can't all afford to throw great concrete slabs across their rivers, but they've sure got the manpower and materials to copy Oroville.

"What's more," he adds, "they'll have just as good a dam as the old concrete ones. Thanks to Oroville's inner core of impervious clay, we expect to measure our leakage almost with a medicine dropper."

Southwest of Oroville, across the Sacramento Valley in the heart of the Coast Ranges, another pioneer project takes shape. Amidst an infernal realm of steam clouds and sulphur

667

fumes, drilling crews at The Geysers puncture the earth to harness natural steam wells to waiting dynamos (pages 656-7).

Not all California miracles, however, are the work of giant machines—the dragline, the steam shovel, the bulldozer. At the foot of the Sacramento Valley, where the San Joaquin and Sacramento Rivers meet, lies a monument to the wheelbarrow and the spade.

The delta, or slough country, as northern Californians call it, represents a contradiction in the Golden State: Where men historically have struggled and even killed to preserve water, pioneers in the slough country strove to banish it. Their enemies were the Sacramento and the San Joaquin, which sought to drown rich farmland in periodic floods.

Beginning with mere farm tools in the days of the gold rush, settlers in the delta walled themselves off from the rivers. Gradually their earthen dikes encircled vast areas of marshland—and the island farms of the delta were born. The waterways, or "sloos," meandering among the islands, became the delta people's country roads. One day I traveled part of the 1,300-mile labyrinth by power boat with Wallace McCormack, a native of the quiet delta town of Rio Vista.

Only in recent years, Mr. McCormack explained, have roads and bridges begun to supplement the sloughs.

"When I was a boy here and someone got sick," he said, "you often went for the doctor in a rowboat. It meant two round trips of several miles each, and of course you didn't ask a doctor to help row. By the time you were all through and got back home, you almost needed the doctor yourself."

Like residents of another water-beleaguered land, the Netherlands, delta people cherish tales of heroism and quick action among their kind. Perhaps the most famous concerns Jesse Thomas, a farmer who was inspecting a levee on horseback. Suddenly he came on a dangerous break; even as he watched, surging water widened the gap to nearly a yard.

"It was a hard decision," Wallace McCor-mack explained, "but Jesse knew he could never seal the break alone. He rode his horse directly into the gap and then killed it where it stood with a blow of his hatchet. Leaping free, he scooped up dirt by hand and kept throwing it into the break. Soon others came to lend a hand, and the levee was saved."

I asked whose levee it had been, and Wallace McCormack shook his head.

"Nobody's in particular. And everybody's."

Sacramento: Seaport 91 Miles Inland

Today a new kind of flood occasionally tops the levees, although the delta people scarcely notice it. It lasts only a moment and is caused by the wake of some ocean-going ship on its way up to Sacramento.

Californians are still slightly astonished that their capital has become a deep-sea port. Dredging of the Sacramento River and construction of a new terminal, at a total cost of $55,000,000, now bring heavy freighters 91 miles inland from the Golden Gate.

At least one resident of Sacramento sees nothing surprising in such developments. California's Governor Edmund G. Brown (page 660)—known everywhere as "Pat"—already has his mind on the year 2000.

"Managing California," he told me in his office, "is a little like tuning a car going 65 miles an hour. It isn't just a problem of taking care of the engine." He grinned. "It's the running alongside while you do it."

Governor Brown does better than keep up with his state. Many of California's vast new projects for highways, water development, education, and other needs took shape in his office at the capitol. One development that did not, and that may bring change to California, is the United States Supreme Court's ruling on reapportionment.

Under the ruling, California must revise its state senatorial districts by population rather than on county lines. The prospect disturbs northern Californians, who fear domination by the more numerous southerners. I asked Governor Brown what he thought.

Vermilion shaft of light, bouncing from mirror to mirror, illuminates a new kind of three-dimensional photograph, a hologram. In ordinary white light, it would appear to be merely a piece of gray glass. But in the pure red light of a laser at Stanford University's Systems Techniques Laboratory, the hologram takes on color and lifelike depth.

In this triple exposure, the immensely powerful red pencil of light has overexposed the film, creating a yellow line. A piece of ground glass, moved along the beam almost to the picture frame, makes the light visible, and a lens flares the beam to illuminate all of the hologram. Now experimental, holography holds potential for 3-D television. This test hologram shows a stack of coins, keys on a ring, and a laboratory signboard. Engineer David Jackson adjusts one of the mirrors that show how laser light can be bounced around corners to the point of use.

Students take a break between classes at the University of California's Berkeley campus. The Associated Students pennant hangs above Sproul Hall Plaza, named for famed President Robert G. Sproul. Here a coed may study in the sun (above) or a campus politico may take to the soapbox. Oldest of nine UC campuses, Berkeley enrolls a third of the system's 80,000 students. An annual budget exceeding half a billion dollars spurs growth of the "multiversity"; all California high-school graduates who meet admission standards may attend tuition-free.

Hanging like chandeliers, closed-circuit TV screens bring the blackboard to students in the 550-seat Physical Sciences Lecture Hall. Remote-controlled camera, monitored in foreground, trains on Professor of Physics Harvey White as he lectures on kinematics, the dynamics of motion. Dr. White's stage, of his own design, rotates so that aides behind it can set up experiments to be swung into view for the next class.

With nine Nobel Prize winners, the Berkeley faculty has achieved such breakthroughs as isolating viruses and building the Nation's first atom smasher.

"To begin with," he answered, "we're all Californians together—we need one another too much to become divided. But beyond that, our northern part of the state is on the verge of enormous expansion itself. If Californians are going to triple by the end of the century, where will a lot of them go? I'll tell you one place, and that's in our far north. Go take a look, and you'll discover why."

Water Jug Triggers a Holocaust

I followed the Governor's advice, and ended up in a dilemma: where to settle if I ever become a Californian.

There is the Sacramento Valley, broad and rich in the sun, its silos standing like great stacks of silver coins on the green baize of endless level fields.

There are the smaller valleys, Sonoma and Napa, famous for the gift of fine California wines and steeped in the saga of a state's

struggle for birth. Here in the closing days of Mexican rule, Gen. Mariano Vallejo governed California, and here in 1846 Californians called for independence with that stirring symbol, the flag of the Bear Republic.

North of the Sacramento Valley the land sheers upward in the giant thrust of two volcanic peaks, Lassen and Mount Shasta (pages 667 and 678-9). Barely half a century ago, long-silent Lassen thundered to life, immolating thousands of acres of grassland and turning stately forests of pine and Douglas fir into enormous open-hearth furnaces.

Fire still presents California with a dreadful balance sheet, claiming an average of 300,000 acres a year and sparing little, often taking human life. Not every fire, it seems, is the result of a lightning bolt or of a carelessly dropped match.

"I've known a fire to start from a jug of cold water left in the shade by a logging crew,"

671

EKTACHROMES BY JA

one forester told me. "Gradually, the sun worked around to where it hit the jug, and then fire had everything it needed—bright sunlight, a makeshift magnifying glass, and made-to-order tinder."

Other forest fires have spread in macabre ways. A friend of mine tells of seeing a wall of flame checked by a logging road. Suddenly a rabbit, its fur ablaze, streaked across the road and doomed the forest on the other side.

Rustlers' Tools Invite Suspicion

Northeast of Lassen Peak I came to the rolling grasslands of cattle country around Alturas. California's beef cattle are valued at nearly $450,000,000, and the beef industry follows such modern techniques as diet feeding and inoculation against epidemic disease.

Charlie Demick remembers the days when the only doctoring of cattle had to do with their brands—and could get a man in serious trouble. I talked in Alturas with Charlie, a retired cattleman of 91, about early ranching in California. Gradually the subject turned to branding and to the ingenious ways rustlers had of doctoring brands.

"They used what we called a 'running iron,'" Charlie explained, "really no more than a long bar bent at one end to make a sort of 'L.' Actually, people used running irons

now and then to burn legitimate brands, but a rustler could take one and doctor the brand on a calf so that even the owner couldn't tell his property.

"I remember one job they did on the old ZX brand that belonged to an outfit just across the line in Oregon. They turned the letters into the prettiest six-pointed star you ever saw in your life. Look here."

He borrowed my pencil, and with a slow but deliberate hand, traced two designs in my notebook. On the left he drew the original brand and on the right the doctored version, with the forgery shown in dotted lines.

$$ZX \quad \text{\ensuremath{\mathbb{Z}}X}$$

I asked if there was any truth to the old legend that a rustler's court often consisted of the nearest tree. Charlie shook his head.

"Not for cattle rustling," he said, "though it was a serious business. The branch of a tree was for stealing horses, because a horse was your life—taking it amounted to murder.

"Still, if a stranger rode in one side of town with a running iron on his saddle, people took what you might call a special interest till he rode out the other side."

Autumn was slipping south across the Oregon border as I came to Tule Lake. The sky above the great national wildlife refuge at

672

"Suicide row" greets chinook salmon entering Smith River. Treacherous tidal currents drown some ten sportsmen a year—thus the name for their anchored formation. When an angler hooks a fish, he slips anchor and drifts to avoid snarling. Most salmon escape the gantlet.

Twenty-pound armful makes Lewis Haller beam. He dangled anchovy bait to hook his prize, average in size for a chinook. Sportsmen take a third as many as commercial fisheries.

Still fighting, a chinook rises in the net of a Yurok Indian guide at the mouth of the Klamath River, a major highway of spawning salmon.

673

times showed only dimly through the migrating birds, as if through some vast, threadbare canopy. Across the surface of the darkened lake, Canada and snow geese mingled with avocet, grebe, mallard, and redhead—major species among more than two hundred that use the stopover on their long winter retreat down the Pacific flyway.

Beyond the mountains west of Tule Lake I reached Crescent City, California's northernmost coastal town. Crescent City is famous among Californians for an event that had its origin 1,600 miles from the Golden State. The terrible earthquake that battered Alaska in March of 1964 set up a seismic sea wave that some six hours later wiped out almost the entire Crescent City waterfront.*

One crab- and salmon-boat owner, whose moored vessel survived the disaster, recalled the night Crescent City heard that the wave was coming. "Right then," he told me, "I would have sold you that boat for a dollar and given you 75 cents change. Then the next morning I looked out and there she was by the pier, worth all of $20,000 again."

Of some 100 boats in the harbor that night, nearly a third were sunk or badly damaged.

South of Crescent City for nearly 350 miles runs a strip of unimaginably beautiful land. Northern California's frontier with the sea is a miracle of sloping, grassy headlands, majestic stands of redwood and fir, and dark

*Author Graves reported on the Alaskan disaster in "Earthquake!" NATIONAL GEOGRAPHIC, July, 1964.

World's tallest living thing, a coast redwood towers 367.8 feet above fireside campers. Dr. Paul A. Zahl, Senior Natural Scientist of the National Geographic Society, discovered the spire in a glen of giants cupped by this question-mark curve of Redwood Creek in Humboldt County. Here also stand the third and sixth tallest trees.

Seedling about a year old (right) pokes from a stony bed in an area lumbered and reseeded by Arcata Redwood Company, owner of the giants. In another 600 years the baby *Sequoia sempervirens* could measure 12 feet thick and 350 feet high. Arcata now preserves the Redwood Creek grove. Bills before Congress seek to protect it in a national park.

Wall of redwood soars out of sight in dust kicked up by a highballing truck. From this stack, called a "cold deck," trucks relay the logs to feed band saws of the world's largest redwood mill, Pacific Lumber Company's plant at Scotia.

Decay-resistant and richly hued, redwood makes durable outdoor furniture and siding as well as striking interior paneling. A single giant such as the one at left, measuring 10 feet across its base with 170 feet of usable trunk, yields enough lumber to build and furnish three large homes.

Screaming teeth of a chain saw sink into a coast redwood near Scotia. Steep slope forces the logger to make his cut high on the downhill side. Fellow worker (below) clears a cavernous notch that aims the brittle behemoth's fall toward a cushion of earth loosened by bulldozing.

battlements of rock fringed with offshore spires—a land alternately drenched in mist and golden sunshine.

The names of some of the counties bordering the coast are almost poetry in themselves—Sonoma, Marin, Del Norte, Mendocino.

Often the northern coast is a bright and tranquil realm, garlanded with flights of gulls on a steady northwest breeze. Occasionally, however, storm winds come up out of the southwest, building great waves before them. Then there is thunder all along the coast, and the offshore spires are besieged by spray.

Other sections of the California coast have the booming surf and tall headlands, yet none has the majesty of the coast redwoods. The immense stands and groves of *Sequoia sempervirens* extend in a scattered chain beside the Pacific from the Muir Woods National Monument area, near lonely Point Reyes, to just beyond the Oregon line.

Cathedral of Timeless Giants

From Crescent City south, I followed the coastal route that runs like a great nave between cathedral ranks of dark spires.

Some of the most famous redwood groves take the names of those who fought relentlessly to preserve them—Rockefeller Forest in Humboldt Redwoods State Park, Williams

677

EKTACHROME (BELOW) AND KODACHROMES BY JAMES P. BLAIR © N.G.S.

"Old White Lady," as pilots in northern California fondly call snow-maned Mount Shasta, looms 14,162 feet. Airmen respect her as a navigation reference point, yet keep their distance, since downdrafts created by her bulk can send small aircraft plummeting earthward. Four California summits rear higher than Shasta, but none more spectacularly. No nearby mountain competes with her stately eminence amid virgin wilderness. Seventy miles away in Oregon, the snowy heights of 9,495-foot Mount McLoughlin peek above the horizon.

Grove, Stephens, and Jedediah Smith. North beyond Eureka stands the tallest known living thing, a 367.8-foot-high redwood discovered in 1963 by Dr. Paul A. Zahl of the National Geographic Society (pages 674-5).*

Recently, through their dues, members of the Society financed another farsighted project—a detailed survey of the great coast redwoods belt, conducted by the National Park Service, which pointed out the need for saving one of the last stands of virgin redwoods.

*See "World's Tallest Tree Discovered," by Melville Bell Grosvenor, and "Finding the Mount Everest of All Living Things," by Paul A. Zahl, July, 1964, GEOGRAPHIC.

Today such a park, the vision of all conservation-minded Americans, stands close to reality: President Lyndon B. Johnson, in a recent message to the Congress, has asked for its early establishment.

Reminders of Nature's Powers

In safeguarding a great and irreplaceable treasure, Americans give fresh meaning to the words of Secretary of the Interior Stewart L. Udall: "In an era when man's role in altering the face of the earth is conspicuous, we need reminders of nature's own forces, events, and ultimate powers."

On my way back to San Francisco I stopped once more in Sonoma Valley, gentle in the autumn sun. The first chill had touched the leaves of the vines, barren now of grapes after the harvest. The valley lay awash in a tide of yellow tinged with scarlet and green.

To the north, winter had brushed Mount Shasta's flanks with new snow and paved the edges of Tule Lake with ice. As I turned at last toward San Francisco and the end of my trip, I suddenly found I had company. High overhead I caught the faint chatter of Canada geese, moving south across the golden land.   THE END   679

California: First State Map in New United States Atlas Series

SIR FRANCIS DRAKE strode ashore in 1579 near what is now San Francisco and left a name for map makers to ponder: Nova Albion, or New England. But, through the centuries, settlers flocking to this rich and beautiful land have preferred another name—one bestowed by Spaniards who fancied they had found the golden realm of a mythical queen, Calafia.

California becomes the first state to be mapped in the new National Geographic United States Atlas Series. The map is distributed to the Society's more than five million members with this issue of their magazine.*

California's 840-mile north-south span required a double map, just as the Nation's most populous state called for a two-part article to do it justice. (See "California, the Golden Magnet," by William Graves, in this issue.)

The two-sided Atlas Map outlines all 58 counties, with a color code of red and yellow tracing the state's highways and freeways. Distinctive symbols denote state parks, ski resorts, redwood groves, even notable individual trees. Insets enlarge metropolitan areas—San Francisco, the bay region, Los Angeles, and San Diego—as well as Yosemite Valley, part of Sequoia National Park, and the northern redwood forests.

On the northern California side of the 20-by-15¼-inch sheet are names to send the imagination soaring: Donner Pass, Golden Gate—and Drakes Bay, where the English sea dog may have anchored his booty-laden *Golden Hind.*

Drake saw here a "goodly country," with "some special likelihood of gold or silver." He must have had a nose for treasure. A mere 125 miles inland, while building a sawmill on the American River for Capt. John A. Sutter, James Marshall found gold in January, 1848.

Run a finger down State Route 49, and you trace the Mother Lode that by 1850 had lured 80,000 newcomers to California. To get to the promised land, easterners sailed 100 days or more around the Horn to San Francisco. Or they dragged covered wagons over the Sierra Nevada through passes such as the infamous Donner —now crossed by new Interstate 80—where 34 pioneers had perished in the deep snows of 1846-47.

Today, ocean ships can steam inland past San Francisco, via new deep-water channels, into the fertile valley heartland of a state that grows more than one-third of the Nation's fruit and vegetables. Freighters berth at Stockton, California's largest inland port, or at the capital, Sacramento, 91 miles from the Golden Gate.

From San Francisco to the Oregon border, U. S. 101 ribbons past towering forests. An inset, the Northern Redwood Corridor, pinpoints the world's tallest known tree (page 674).

At the three forks of the Feather River, 70 miles north of Sacramento, the map locates Oroville Dam, which will be the Nation's highest—770 feet—when completed in 1968. A man-made river now under construction, the 444-mile California Aqueduct, will funnel the water downstate to Los Angeles and San Diego reservoirs.

Highest Peak Loses a Foot

Half the southern California side of the map is sprinkled with the names of a thirsty land: Mojave Desert, Death Valley, Devils Playground, Sand Hills. Temperatures soar above 130° F. in Death Valley, where land sinks 282 feet below sea level, lowest on the continent.

A solid blue oval to the south marks the Salton Sea, an accident turned into a recreation area. Its waters first flowed from a break in a Colorado River levee 60 years ago. Salt leached from the soil and inadequate outlets to the sea have made the waters as briny as the ocean. But they provide a bone-dry country with water sports—boating, fishing, and water-skiing.

California's highest point, Mount Whitney, stands not as high as once believed: Official survey figures have shaved a foot off the peak, now listed on the map at 14,494 feet.

Offshore lie "certaine Ilands" where Sir Francis Drake found "plentifull and great store of Seales and birds." Sea lions and birds still frequent the Farallon Islands, lonely bits of land that the frontier never reached.   THE END

*Extra copies of the map may be obtained for 50 cents each, postpaid, by writing to Dept. 305, National Geographic Society, Washington, D. C. 20036. Other state maps will be issued periodically as supplements to NATIONAL GEOGRAPHIC; members meanwhile will continue to receive World Atlas Maps until that series is completed.

Snaking subdivision entwines a mountainside south of San Francisco, shrouded by haze in the distance. Rapidly spreading cities alter the face of the Golden State.

TROPICAL RAIN lashed at the thatched roof of my hut. I sat alone at the preserving table skinning a batch of arrow-poison frogs—*kokoá,* the local Indians call them—to prepare an extract of deadly venom.

No sixth sense gave me warning that within half an hour pain would rack me and I would be fighting for my life against the effects of the powerful poison in the skins.

Through the doorway I could see the swollen San Juan River rushing past the mud-and-palm-frond village of Playa de Oro, my base for biological collecting in the Chocó jungle of Colombia (map, page 688).

Rain is the normal weather in the Chocó, one of the wettest spots on earth. Nearly twenty-five *feet* of rain drench this Pacific coastal region each year.

Kokoá Venom, an Aid to Medicine?

The hothouse climate nurtures small creatures of the forest floor, among them the black, yellow-striped frog *Phyllobates latinasus* (opposite and page 685). The jewel-like kokoá fits into a teaspoon, yet its skin exudes a venom more potent than any other known. For centuries the local Cholo Indians have smeared kokoá poison on their blowgun darts.

Similar primitive arrow and dart poisons —curare from South America and strophanthin from Africa, for example—provide drugs useful in surgery and in the treatment of heart ailments. Might kokoá venom also be of medical value? The National Institutes of Health in Bethesda, Maryland, wanted very much to know.

I picked up another moist, limp frog and opened the skinning scissors. Accidentally—incredibly—I jabbed the point of one blade into my finger! I put the finger to my mouth and sucked the blood. A strong metallic taste —then my throat began to close.

Panic sent sweat coursing down my face. *There is no antidote,* I thought. Gasping for air, I lay down on a cot, repeating to myself, "You can breathe. You can breathe." Spasms shook me for an hour. Each time my throat constricted, I forced down another swallow of the only fluid immediately at hand—canned tomato juice.

Turning my head, I saw half a dozen wet figures gathered outside the front doorway. Holding captured frogs in twists of green leaves, my hunters were waiting for me to count the day's take and pay them.

How close I came to death remains a guess.

The spasms gradually subsided. Luckily it had been raw, not concentrated venom, and I had quickly sucked it from the wound. I was not going to die.

Within two hours I was on my feet again, buying arrow-poison frogs and popping them into cages.

Indians Revealed Kokoás' Secret

As a professional collector of rare animals for scientific study, I have specialized in capturing the lesser creatures of jungle and highland: birds, monkeys, snakes, rodents, and—most memorable —the poison frogs of the Colombian swamps.

Although known to naturalists since the mid-19th century, the kokoá attracted little interest until 1961, when I learned from the Cholo Indians of the frog poison's remarkable potency. During an expedition to collect giant earthworms, my Indian hunters bagged 50 of the tiny frogs. I shipped them by air to NIAMD—the National Institute of Arthritis and Metabolic Diseases— which is part of the National Institutes of Health. These were the first live

On mist-soaked Andean ridges or in tropical forests, Indian friends help the author stalk rare species for science. Chief quarry was this tiny jungle frog, the *kokoá*, which exudes the deadliest venom known. On cloud-wreathed heights (left), she sought giant earthworms (pages 692-3).

Capturing Strange Creatures in Colombia

By MARTE LATHAM

Photographs by TOR EIGELAND

SLIGHTLY LARGER THAN LIFE-SIZE

He's got one! An Indian lad, ankle-deep in a Colombian swamp, captures a black-and-gold kokoá frog for the author. Centuries ago his Cholo tribe learned to smear blowgun darts with the frog's toxic skin secretion, which can induce paralysis, convulsions, and death in minutes. Weighing only a gram, the 1¼-inch-long kokoá yields enough poison for 50 darts.

Today, researchers study the venom, hoping to uncover medical uses. Curare—another Indian arrow poison—proved valuable as a muscle relaxant, especially in surgery.

SLIGHTLY LARGER THAN LIFE-SIZE

Deadly denizens of Colombia's wild Chocó region, these jewel-like frogs produce poison: the kokoá, *Phyllobates latinasus* (top), and the less toxic "painted" frogs, subspecies of *Dendrobates tinctorius*. Biochemists at the National Institutes of Health, Bethesda, Maryland, isolated the kokoá venom and named it batrachotoxin.

KODACHROMES (BELOW AND TOP) AND EKTACHROMES © N.G.S.

1 1/2 TIMES LIFE-SIZE

specimens of kokoá sent beyond Colombia's borders for study.

"Of the 50 frogs you sent," Dr. Bernhard Witkop later told me, "only seven reached us alive. Of these, six died overnight and the last was moribund. Enzyme action destroys the toxic principle immediately upon death."

From that fiftieth frog, scientists extracted enough venom to want to study it further. On a subsequent expedition I sent back raw venom from 2,400 kokoá. Yet even this number yielded only 30 milligrams of the crystalline pure venom—a smidgen, but enough to kill three million mice.

Now, in the summer of 1964, I was once more in the Chocó—this time accompanied by my 14-year-old son Billy, on vacation from school, and by photographer Tor Eigeland. I had orders for more kokoá frogs, and for giant earthworms from the Andean highlands.

We traveled to our wilderness base camp at a progressively slower pace: jet to Bogotá, four-engine plane to Medellín, two-engine plane over green rain forest and muddy rivers to Condoto, then launch up the swift San Juan River to Playa de Oro.

Jungle Villagers Descend From Slaves

Young friends from my previous visits ran down the steep riverbank to greet the boat and unload our bags and boxes of gear. Playa de Oro had not changed. It was still a village of desperately poor Negroes, descendants of slaves brought to Colombia by the Spanish centuries ago. They eke out a living by tending small banana plots and working tiny gold and platinum mines with simple tools.

Adobe huts, once whitewashed, line the single muddy street; a statue of the Virgin in blue and white stands squarely in the middle of the road. Automobiles have yet to reach Playa de Oro.

Our hut was waiting for us. We swept the floor, strung the last hammock, and collapsed in sleep.

Next day we posted signs stating that we would buy giant cockroaches, monkeys, kinkajous, anteaters—and, of course, poison frogs. In no time Billy had acquired a night

monkey and a blue-headed parrot. He named them Abercrombie and Fitch.

The forest Indians usually drift into Playa de Oro toward the end of the week. The Cholos have always been my best frog catchers, and I wanted to enlist them again.

It was Sunday morning when I finally heard Billy shout, "Here come the Indians!"

I looked out and was delighted to see Químico, who had taught me to find the kokoá, with his family and several friends. Like some of the other local Cholos, they were *civilizados* now, wearing shorts, hats, and shirts.

Hunters Imitate Quarry's Call

But their world was still the jungle world, and when I said to Químico, "Will you come with us to hunt kokoá?" I knew what the answer would be, even before the long, meditative pause, the quizzical glances exchanged, and the final abrupt nod of the proud head.

The next day we headed into the rain forest, over big round hills, toward the mountains. Químico and his family led the way, followed by camera-laden Tor, Billy, and myself.

Hidden in the jungle, the tiny frog is hard to see, even though nature gives him poster-bright stripes, as if to warn other animals that a kokoá dinner is a dangerous venture.

How do the Indians locate the frogs? From the trail we watched Químico at work in the black swamp. He crouched—then his hand went to his face, and with a finger vibrating his taut cheek, he whistled in imitation of the peeping of the frog (page 688). *"Chee-chee-chee-chee-chee,"* stop, then repeat. He squatted quietly for a minute, then took up the chirping call again.

"Chee-chee-chee-chee-chee," answered the kokoá. But where? My civilized ear could not pinpoint its location.

Químico did not hesitate. He hopped like his quarry, landing on all fours a yard away; his hand was a blur. He tore a leaf from a plant and swirled it into a funnel. He plugged one end with a dab of mud, dropped the frog in, and tied the top with a vine.

The hunt was on. The Indians listened intently, judging distance. Too far for a clean

Spellbound Cholo mother and sons watch the author, whom they call the "frog lady," dump their catches into a wooden cage. Indians carry kokoá in swirled leaves, since prolonged contact with the creatures can cause irritation such as that roughening Mrs. Latham's hands. These tribespeople along the San Juan River cling to the dress and the ways of jungle living. But even children puff cigarettes bought at the Playa de Oro store with frog-hunt earnings.

EKTACHROME (ABOVE) AND KODACHROME © N.G.S.

"Chee-chee-chee-chee-chee," Químico imitates the kokoá's voice, drumming his cheek while whistling. The Cholo hunter finds frogs by listening for their answering cries.

Safely past rapids that nearly swept them from their balsa-log raft, Mrs. Latham and her Indian guides journey a swift highway, the San Juan River. They look behind to see how a trailing raft fares in the turbulence.

The San Juan curls through the Chocó, a savage region of jungled hills walled off by the Andes from the rest of Colombia. Indians roam the lush forest, while descendants of African slaves, brought by the Spanish to mine gold, populate the scattered communities. Nearly 300 inches of rain annually drench the Chocó, one of South America's— and the world's—wettest places.

catch? They crept forward, stopped, then chirped. The tiny kokoá answered, and the hunters pounced. Soon I had 25 frogs.

We had witnessed a scene as old as the Cholo culture. Once the Indians hunted kokoá in preparation for the warpath. Now they use poisoned darts only to hunt game.

I explained to Billy and Tor how they prepare the darts, as Químico had once shown it to me. The frog exudes the poison when under the stress of heat, cold, or pain. Each kokoá is impaled alive on a stick and held over an open fire. As venom seeps from the skin, the hunter rolls the dart point over the frog's back. Spiral grooves in the tip pick up the poisonous secretion. One kokoá can poison as many as fifty blowgun darts. Dried venom has remained lethal for 15 years.

At my preserving table I extracted the venom from the morning's catch. Killing the kokoá with ether, I removed the skins with scissors and forceps. (It was a careless moment some days later, when I neglected to use the forceps, that cost me those agonizing hours and that very bad scare.) Cut into pieces, the skins were soaked in alcohol, and later the solution was poured into bottles.

This was the extract from which scientists at NIAMD—Dr. Witkop, Dr. Fritz Märki, and later Dr. John W. Daly—prepared the crystalline venom found to be about ten times as powerful as that of the Japanese globefish, or puffer, the deadliest previously known.

"There is always hope," Dr. Witkop had told me, "of developing helpful drugs from a substance with such strong action as kokoá venom. Maybe in low concentration it will have beneficial action on the heart. Related venoms are used as heart stimulants.

"Who can tell? It is truly a remarkable substance and deserves careful attention."

Day after day the Indians came into Playa de Oro carrying captured kokoá frogs in leaf cages. They brought other creatures, too: less toxic but more glamorous "painted frogs" (page 685), small mammals, and birds. Occasionally we accompanied our helpers into the jungle, where we found that even Cholo children were amazingly skillful—and enthusiastic—frog hunters (page 684).

Once we ventured by dugout canoes to the upper Tadosito River in search of frogs, returning overland to Playa de Oro. Immense hardwood trees arched the crystal-clear Tadosito. Giant white anthuriums, red-and-yellow lesser bird-of-paradise flowers, long-stemmed water lilies, and lavender orchids adorned the banks. Scattered palm-frond huts with banana plots edged the river.

"God and a Japanese gardener must have joined forces here," said awestruck Tor.

Bird-eating Toad Remains a Rumor

From the settlement of Tadosito (five thatched huts, a school, and a mission building) we plunged into the great swamp at the headwaters of the river, led by a young local Cholo chief and a group of his people. It was tropical fairyland and green hell—a wild tangle of palms and hardwoods, vines and thornbushes—through which we sometimes had to hack our way with machetes.

We skirted a waterfall of breathtaking beauty, then heard a parrot's scream followed by the coo of a dove. Almost at the same moment, from the distance, came the throbbing beat of a tom-tom.

"I expect to see Tarzan swinging down from a tree any minute," Billy remarked.

One of the creatures we sought was a giant toad rumored to eat birds as big as chickens —an animal supposedly deadly just to touch. This *sapo de loma*—toad of the hills—had been on my investigation list for years.

"Do you know where we will find the toad that eats birds?" I asked the young chief.

He shook his head, no.

"Kokoá?"

EKTACHROME © N.G.S.

Probing secrets of the lethal frog toxin, Drs. Bernhard Witkop (in glasses), John W. Daly, and Henry Fales use a mass spectrometer at the National Institutes of Health. The machine reveals the chemical nature and molecular structure of the venom.

Make-believe matadors flap their *ruanas*—Colombian ponchos—to corner a dog-size rat. The Andean rodent, or pacarana, bit one captor but quickly submitted to kind treatment from Mrs. Latham (right). Billy, her 14-year-old son (above, left), named his unusual pet "Rodie."

Excited by a sudden lurch on its first jeep ride, Rodie leaped from Billy's arms onto the driver, sending the vehicle plunging down a steep embankment. Extricating themselves from jumbled camping gear, giant worm specimens, and cages of screaming monkeys and coatimundis, the occupants recaptured Rodie with the help of fascinated bystanders (left). For the rest of the trip the huge rat rode in a box.

Extremely rare in captivity, pacaranas, also called Branick's rats, may measure a yard from nose to tail tip.

The Indian swept his arms in an arc to indicate "many, many."

As he led us overland back toward the San Juan River, we kept a sharp lookout for a toad the size of a hat. But if the bird-hungry beast exists in that region, it eluded us.

Deep in the forest, we at last heard kokoá peeping. In a few hours, the Indians had captured as many as we could use.

These frogs were of a different coloration from those near Playa de Oro. Instead of a yellow double stripe down the back, here the markings were bright orange.

Giant rhinoceros beetles climbed over rotted logs, and golden-winged locusts sang. Finally we came to scattered houses set in small banana plots.

When, after ten hours on the trail, we stumbled into the gorge of the San Juan, my knees were shaking and my face dripped with sweat. Our legs were scratched, our clothes muddy, and we were dumb with fatigue. Playa de Oro across the San Juan had never looked so good.

Before long, I had prepared venom extract from 150 arrow-poison frogs. In cages I kept two dozen live specimens, both painted frogs

EKTACHROME BY TOR EIGELAND © NATIONAL GEOGRAPHIC SOCIETY

and kokoá. Billy by now had a fine start on the animal collection he would take back as a science project to his school in Florida. We left the Chocó jungle feeling satisfied.

On the Trail of an Andean Giant

A week later, after a brief rest in Medellín, we were in pursuit of even stranger quarry, in a dramatically different setting.

Pre-Columbian artists, I once was told, modeled giant earthworms on pottery. But until I tracked the elusive creatures down in 1956, I could find only scattered reports and a single photograph to verify their existence. In that year, mountain people high in the Andes of southwestern Colombia found five worms, each 30 inches long, while searching on my behalf. Later I journeyed to their lofty region myself and dug up giant worms by the score.

Tor, Billy, and I now flew to the mountain-girt colonial city of Popayán, where my old friend Alfonso Valencia met us with his jeep (map, page 688).

Hour after hour we climbed long switch-backs into the blue-velvet Colombian Andes, until at last we reached our base, the *finca,* or farm, of Luzselva, at 7,800 feet elevation. The adobe house perches on a narrow plateau between two brawling streams.

In the cold morning we took to the saddle. I huddled deep in my *ruana*—a woolen poncho—against the Andean chill. As we rode up into the heights, I called out at every house we passed, *"Venga, lombrices!"* My entreaty, "Come, worms!" was a familiar call from my previous trips here, as was the response, *"Cuanto vale?*—How much?"

Where the trail climbed out of a gorge, a group of Indian men, women, and children—short, stocky, hardy people—waited for us.

Maria, Feliz, and their children welcomed me with shouts and embraces; over the years they had been the best of the worm diggers. Today they had with them another man and three of his children.

"Lombrices! This way," they shouted, and gestured up the slope.

We soon reached the place the Indians had selected for digging, and I fell to with my machete. Fifty strokes, perhaps, and little Maria pounced on a monster.

"Look, a big one!" The girl's face spread in a delighted grin.

Just another earthworm? Not exactly. This one measured an inch shy of five feet long and

Monster worms the size of rattlesnakes tunnel Andean highlands at 13,000- to 14,000-foot elevations. Mrs. Latham heard that pre-Columbian Indians depicted the giant earthworms on pottery, but many people thought them legendary until she discovered specimens near Popayán a decade ago.

Champion digger of the hunt, an Andean girl holds her prize catch, an earthworm just under five feet long. Billy Latham admires the wiggler from a distance.

more than two inches in diameter. Deepest blue and green flashed from the moist skin. It was, I suppose, a repulsive creature, its gross accordioned sections rippling back and forth, and the snout probing blindly for the soil. But to me it was a beautiful sight, a living creature whose very being until recently had been in question.

The worms live in a quite restricted band of elevation from 13,000 to 14,000 feet, above the hardwood forests and in the high-altitude grasslands, the Andean *páramos*. Colonies of them burrow just below the surface on the crests of ridges and mounds, and in the banks along the trails.

Once you have located a worm's burrow, the trick is to excavate the tunnel and its inhabitant. The quarry will always dig inward and down when pursued, and you must uncover at least half of it. These are strong animals: The harder you pull, the tighter they grip the soil. Often they break in two.

At times we could simply pick the worms off the open ground in the early morning. Torrential rains sometimes helped us by forcing our quarry out of their flooded burrows.

When we ran out of worms at one site, we sought them elsewhere. Day after day our horses zigzagged through the forests and upward to the treeless 14,000-foot páramo. Indians whom I knew would pop out of their houses along the road, offering me worms in old cooking pots, burlap bags, tin cans.

Indians Find Dog-size Rodents

The whole area is a paradise for the hunter of strange creatures. Overhead wheeled an Isidor's crested eagle, chestnut with black breast stripes. Once the Indians brought us a pair of pacaranas—rare rodents that sometimes grow as big as a good-size dog. Here, too, I found the scarlet cock-of-the-rock, one of the most colorful of birds.

From previous efforts, I knew there was little point in trying to ship my giant worms

KODACHROME BY TOR EIGELAND © NATIONAL GEOGRAPHIC SOCIETY

home alive. Out of hundreds I have sent, only one ever survived for as long as four months. And when one of these creatures dies, within hours nothing remains but a streak of slime.

This time I would preserve my catch and ship it to a biological supply house which furnishes specimens to many American universities for dissection and study.

Preserving demands patience, rubber gloves —and protective eyeglasses. The worms, even after being anesthetized and killed, often spurt back the formalin injected into each segment. Finally I packed the worms in formalin-soaked moss and wrapped them in plastic.

Adding Up the Catch

By departure date we had preserved 250 worms to distribute in Colombia and the United States. At Medellín we picked up the preserved frogs and venom extract which we had carried out of the jungles of the Chocó.

I sent a new supply of kokoá venom extract to NIAMD, and two dozen frogs (painted and kokoá) to the Philadelphia Zoo. I also assembled a collection of Chocó snakes and lizards and "pickled" Andean worms that would find their way to universities, zoos, and other places of study.

Billy's animal collection included three coatimundis, two night monkeys, a parrot, and a silky anteater, as well as Rodie, his pet pacarana (page 690).

It had been a memorable trip; Billy and I had shared many adventures and made many new friends. It had also been most rewarding professionally; I had obtained specimens of all the odd creatures I had hoped to find. As we turned for home, I could not help but wonder what medical marvels scientists might discover in them.   THE END

Mighty monuments to Ramesses II endured for 3,200 years beside the Nile at Abu Simbel. But as waters rose behind the new Aswân High Dam, only a mammoth international campaign—spearheaded by the United Nations and United States—could enable Egypt to save the shrines. In a remarkable series of paintings and photographs, NATIONAL GEOGRAPHIC shows how skilled ancients carved the cliffside temples and how, with equal skill, modern engineers lifted them above the river's reach.

Saving the Ancient Temples at Abu Simbel

Article and photographs by
GEORG GERSTER, Ph.D.

Paintings by ROBERT W. NICHOLSON
National Geographic staff artist

THE DERRICK WHIRRED. Slowly the god-king Ramesses' face separated from his ears—a sight I shall never forget.

It had been a long, busy night. The first cut in the statue had been made at dusk. Then, with the great head bathed by floodlights, two workmen inched a ten-foot handsaw down through the rock, cutting between the god-king's cheeks and ears.

A near-full moon shone on two other colossal heads of Ramesses gazing enigmatically over the silver-plated Nile. Their turn would come later.

At midnight the crew had changed. Twice I had slipped down from the camp above the temple site. The second time, at three in the morning, lacking transport, I had walked for an hour through the haunted desert to get there. I had to make sure the event would occur on schedule.

Dawn brought a selected few to the site. The sun had barely risen when the derrick operator received the long-awaited signal. The face took to the air (above and pages

730-31). For a moment I had the wry thought that ancient Egypt's great king was being ruthlessly defaced by modern barbarians. As the face hung on the hoisting rope, it revolved. In seconds it took on all the fleeting expressions—from somber to benign—that the sun, in daily passage across the sky, normally bestowed on its immovable features only by slow degrees. Then it was gently bedded onto a specially constructed trailer for removal to a storage area.

Lifting Ramesses' 19-ton face was only one, though the most spectacular, step in a salvage job without precedent.

The two temples of Abu Simbel on the Nile, 180 miles upstream from Aswân, are the most prominent of a priceless heritage of monuments threatened by man-made Lake Nasser

---

About the paintings: How did Ramesses II's magnificent shrine look when it basked in the Egyptian sunshine of three millenniums ago? NATIONAL GEOGRAPHIC staff artist Robert W. Nicholson went to Egypt to find out. He consulted eminent scholars on three continents, notably Dr. Henry G. Fischer of the Metropolitan Museum of Art in New York City and Louis A. Christophe, Egyptologist at Cairo and Abu Simbel for the United Nations Educational, Scientific and Cultural Organization. For accuracy of detail he ranged from Abu Simbel and Nefertari's tomb at Luxor to the Louvre and the British Museum.

A graduate in architecture of Clemson University in South Carolina, Mr. Nicholson drew plans and built models as preparation for his brushwork. "I know more about Abu Simbel now than I do about my own house," he comments. The artist has undertaken similar re-creations for other GEOGRAPHIC articles: "Exploring the Drowned City of Port Royal" (February, 1960) and "Conquest of the Holy City" (December, 1963).

730-31). 696

behind the fast-rising Aswân High Dam (map, page 698).* Hewn out of a rock bluff 3,200 years ago, they pay perpetual homage to Ramesses II, god-king of Egypt, and his favorite consort, Queen Nefertari.

Four seated colossi of Ramesses, each 67 feet high and weighing 1,200 tons, guard the entrance to the Great Temple. The upper body of one of these has broken off and lies at the statue's feet. Before the neighboring Small Temple, six giant statues of Queen Nefertari and Ramesses stand sentinel side by side.

In the campaign to salvage the treasures of flood-threatened Nubia, the lands south of Aswân, Abu Simbel's two rock-hewn shrines have been of primary concern. Nevertheless, work got off to a late start. Now engineers from many nations race the rising Nile to cut both temples into manageable blocks and move them to safety, above the future maximum reservoir level. Just to reach the innermost rooms of the shrines, the engineers had to excavate nearly 190 feet down through the cliff above the temples (page 721).

Re-erection at the new site, 212 feet above the old and 690 feet back from the shore, started last January, and the cutting and dismantling continue. The temples must be removed by August 15, when Nile waters are expected to wash over the cofferdam, a temporary structure erected to keep Ramesses' and the engineers' feet dry (pages 724-5).

The day Ramesses lost his face, October 10, 1965, was the most exciting one for me. But for the engineers the crucial day had come

---

*Recent GEOGRAPHIC accounts of Abu Simbel appeared in *"Yankee* Cruises the Storied Nile," by Irving and Electa Johnson, May, 1965, and "Threatened Treasures of the Nile," by Georg Gerster, October, 1963.

Sailing the sacred Nile, Ramesses' royal scribes, architects, and overseers set out for Abu Simbel, proposed as the site of Pharaoh's temple. Linen sails hang limp on the windless river as oarsmen drive the vessels ahead. Finally the flotilla arrives at the imposing cliffs. Here, the learned men agree, is the perfect place to build a monument worthy of a king claiming kinship with the gods.

On their return, the overseer of works presents to the ruler diagrams for a rock-hewn temple. A scribe holds plans for a smaller temple to honor the Pharaoh's favorite queen, Nefertari.

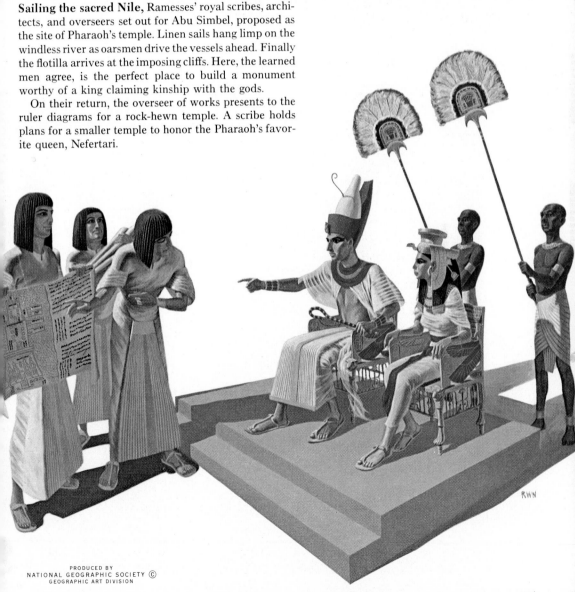

Pharaoh's engineers, putting their knowledge of astronomy to work, line up the axis of the Great Temple. They orient it so that twice yearly the sun will shine into the innermost chamber and bless the statues of the ruler and of Amun, god of Thebes. Egyptologist Louis Christophe believes that this may have been planned to occur first on the day of Ramesses' 30-year jubilee—about October 20 in the year 1274 B.C. (or, by another reckoning, in 1260).

Thirty-two centuries later the rising sun still streamed into the Sanctuary twice each year and bathed the seated figures (page 708).

Ramesses' domain spanned more than a thousand miles from Syria to the Sudan. Today the waters of Lake Nasser gradually submerge most of his Nubian realm. The new reservoir for irrigation and power will ultimately stretch 310 miles and average six miles wide.

four and a half months earlier—when the first block had been cut and was ready for lifting.

The scene is vivid in memory. I held my breath like everyone else, as the deafening noise of the heavy construction equipment suddenly ceased. It was a moment of heart-stopping silence—for everyone from the project manager to the humblest workman.

Karl-Fredrik Wård of Sweden, representing the consulting engineers, stretched prone on the bluff below the crest of the temple cliff. Project manager Carl Theodor Mäckel of Germany, as befits a general during battle, took a position right at the edge of the excavation pit. Pino Lucano of Italy, chief of the section directly responsible for dismantling, moved busily on the rock crest. Egyptian resident archeologist Dr. Anwar Shoukry stood on a vantage point nearby.

It was late forenoon and the weatherman would have said the temperature was 100° F. in the shade—but there was no shade. Still, neither heat nor dust had kept the sidewalk superintendents from strolling over from the

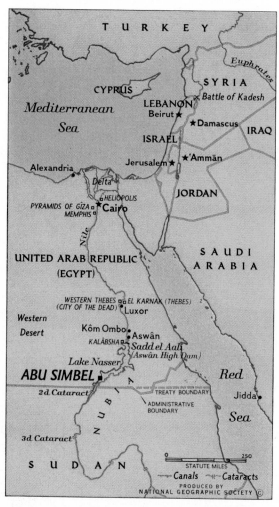

698

base camp. One was Stefan Lindström, aged 12, who stood next to his Swedish engineer father and trained his binoculars with tense anticipation on the north end of the cliff. There a narrow cut, barely visible to the naked eye, traversed the rock.

One of Wård's assistants had motioned aside the bulldozers that ripped gashes in the rock of the excavation pit. Seconds earlier the Egyptian workmen had silenced their pneumatic hammers. Now the only sound was the rumbling of the winch. Suddenly the fine line of the cut widened to a gaping fissure—as if the mountain were yawning silently. A large block separated. Gingerly, inch by inch, the derrick's tackle swung over. For endless minutes the load hovered motionless against the majestic Nile and Nubia's drowning palms.

"Go, baby, go," a spectator behind me said.

The "baby" was heavy. It weighed 11 tons. And it had a name: GA1A01. This designation stood for Great Temple, Treatment A, Zone 1, Row A, Block 1. The zone, row, and block symbols indicated the piece's position at the topmost section above the façade. Treatment A designated the area framing the sculptured façade. The cliff behind the Treatment A slabs had already been excavated. Now the Treatment A area projected like a vertical fin above the floor of the pit.

"Baby" also got its cradle: a sand-cushioned trailer. The tractor moved it to storage at a snail's pace to avoid vibration. There the slab would wait a year and a half until reassembly in the great jigsaw puzzle, since the first pieces removed must be the last pieces in.

Pharaonic Puzzle: Cut, Float, Lift?

This initial step in precision removal, on May 21, 1965, marked the end of five years of agonizing uncertainty. Since the first call from the United Nations Educational, Scientific and Cultural Organization (UNESCO) to save the Nile's flood-threatened treasures of antiquity, Abu Simbel's two massive shrines had been alternately rescued on paper and given up as doomed.

(Continued on page 706)

"**His Majesty** commanded the making of a mansion in Nubia by cutting in the mountain. Never was the like done before except by the son of Amun." So reads an inscription at Abu Simbel. These paintings illustrate how the army of artisans built the temples.

Guided by the painted red line established by the rising sun's rays (preceding page), quarrymen first hacked off the rough sandstone and smoothed the surface. Draftsmen, projecting the red line onto the rock face, drew lines to help proportion the figures. Masons chipped away the background, and monolithic blocks emerged. Stairsteps representing feet, lap, and crown developed into stylized forms resembling robots. From these, master sculptors softened harsh lines into muscular legs, chests, and arms. Others delicately molded curved lips more than three feet wide with dimples at the corners.

Clambering over scaffolding, painters apply red ocher to the monarch's body. The god Re-Harakhti, who seems to stride out of the wall above the entrance, wears the same hue. A solar disk crowns the falcon-headed deity. Beneath his right hand, sculptors carved the jackal-headed staff, User; beneath his left (obscured by overseers), the figure of Maat, goddess of truth. The triumvirate represents User-maat-re, Ramesses' coronation name. The Pharaoh in bas-relief on either side therefore presents offerings not only to the god, but to himself.

Through the ages, sand and weather wore away the figures' vivid coloring, but archeologists have found that Egypt's ancient monument builders followed standardized color schemes in painting their statues.

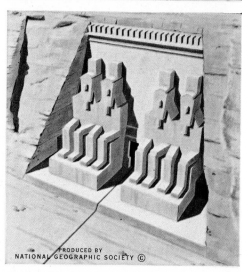

700

A living god walks the earth of Nubia as Ramesses dedicates his own monument. To the blare of trumpets, jangle of sistra, and beat of drums, the king and his queen Nefertari lead a procession from the monument in celebration of his 30-year jubilee. Ramesses II wears the blue crown associated with the New Kingdom; he carries the crook and staff, royal symbols. Nefertari holds sistra, musical instruments sacred to the goddess Hathor. Her headdress of horns, disk, and feathers also honors the female deity.

Temple priests shoulder the golden solar bark containing images of gods who preside over the Sanctuary. Linen draperies hide the hallowed figures from the common people. Priests and priestesses stream from the entrance.

What a glorious day! To reconstruct the event, all record of which is lost in antiquity, artist Nicholson followed a bas-relief in the Great Temple showing the king and queen on a ceremonial occasion. The painter faithfully copied many details, including the queen's musical instruments, leopard skins worn by the priests, ceremonial fans, and the sacred bark adorned with falcons on bow and stern.

A Nubian boy in the line of warriors peers at the god-king with mouth agape. One soldier looks sidewise in disapproval at the unmilitary intrusion into the martial rank.

THIS PAGE FOLDS OUT

Engineers from many countries pitted their imaginations against this unparalleled challenge. The leading contenders were a French and an Italian scheme. The French plan called for a rock-and-sand-filled dam to protect the two temples. To guard the monuments against seepage would have required an elaborate pumping installation, which would have been too costly.

The Italian plan suggested freeing the temples from the rock and using jacks to raise each in a single huge mass, one weighing 291,500 tons, the other 60,500 tons.

One-piece Move Hits Cost Snag

Several other ingenious solutions were proposed. A French engineer wanted to float the shrines up to high ground on two huge rafts. He didn't propose to wait for the new lake's rise; he envisioned a mammoth concrete bathtub for each temple. Nile water would be pumped into the tubs to lift the rafts to safety.

An American construction expert proposed building barges of concrete under and around each of the two temples and allowing the rising water level of the reservoir to float them up.

A Polish engineer suggested leaving the temples under water, protected by reinforced concrete domes. Another Polish engineer would have surrounded the Great Temple with a circular reinforced concrete wall and placed the Small Temple in a smaller concrete cylinder with a glass roof.

A British film producer proposed a curved membrane to separate the muddy waters of the reservoir outside from clear, filtered water inside; the wall need not be thick, since pressure on both sides would be equal. Visitors, standing in underwater observation galleries, would then be able to admire Ramesses in a kind of aquarium within the membrane.

Inside at last! For centuries drifts of sand concealed the Great Temple. Then in 1813 Swiss traveler John Lewis Burckhardt stumbled upon "what is yet visible of four immense colossal statues." Four years later Giovanni Battista Belzoni, a bearded six-foot-six Italian who sometimes wore Arab dress, penetrated the sand barrier at the entrance. Torches illumined "one of the most magnificent of temples, enriched with beautiful intaglios, painting, colossal figures."

Sunlight "falls like fire from heaven upon the altar at the feet of the Gods," wrote Amelia Edwards, pictured above, who visited Abu Simbel in the 1870's. "It is fine to see the sunrise on the front of the Great Temple; but something still finer takes place on certain mornings of the year, in the very heart of the mountain. As the sun comes up above the ... hill-tops, one long, level beam strikes through the doorway, pierces the inner darkness like an arrow, penetrates to the sanctuary. ...

"No one who has watched for the coming of that shaft of sunlight can doubt that it was a calculated effect, and that the excavation was directed at one especial angle in order to produce it."

When Ramesses' Great Temple has been reassembled beyond the river's grasp, the sun will once again shine full on the figures of the god Amun and the god-king himself each mid-February and mid-October, as it first did some 3,200 years ago.

UNESCO and the United Arab Republic once favored the Italian scheme to move each temple in one piece. But early in 1963, it became clear that the final word would come from the fund raisers, not from the engineers. UNESCO's members shrank from astronomical estimates that ranged as high as $90,000,000.

Egypt and UNESCO then decided upon a plan for dissecting the temples in as large segments as possible. This plan offered a fighting chance to win over the rising waters despite the late start. It also offered the lowest cost—$36,000,000. The Swedish consulting engineering firm of Vattenbyggnadsbyrån (VBB) drew up contract specifications. Bids were requested and received.

Egypt allocated almost one-third of the required funds. The United States, using its local currency holdings from sale of surplus agricultural commodities, pledged another third in the fall of 1963. This was decisive, making possible the signing of a contract with an international group of bidders on November 16, 1963. Other UNESCO nations partly underwrote the last third of the funds, with the remainder to be raised by private donations, about half, it is hoped, from the U. S.

The group, Joint Venture Abu Simbel, managed by the West German firm of Hochtief of Essen, includes Atlas of Cairo, Grands Travaux de Marseille of Paris, Impregilo of Milan, and two Stockholm firms, Skånska and Sentab. This group executes the VBB project under VBB and Egyptian supervision.

In addition, committees made up of internationally known engineers, archeologists, and architects act as advisers to the Egyptian authorities. The United States is represented on these advisory bodies.

Wise Crocodile Flees Bedlam

The project has been termed a "minimum program." I have heard archeologists call it a "solution of despair," and even engineers regret abandonment of the more daring proposals. Professor Walter Jurecka, Joint Venture's chief adviser and at one time acting project manager, told me: "Each and every one of us will loyally do his best for the project. But there is such a thing as keeping faith with the spirit of engineering, and I must say only the raising of the temples in one piece would have done justice to the broad vision of their builder."

My earliest recollection of Abu Simbel, as I saw it only ten years ago, approaches the idyllic: flowering acacias, a spit of golden sand flowing down from desert to river, and the giant statues of the regal deity gazing serenely across the Nile. On that occasion I shared the sandbank only with a crocodile.

A dozen visits later, in May, 1965, the salvage work had changed everything—even the crocodile had moved out. Capt. Abdel Rahman Serafi, chief pilot of the air shuttle that had brought once-remote Abu Simbel within an hour of Aswân, flew me over the sand bar from which the reptile had judiciously fled the bedlam of the relocation work.

Bustling Town Springs Up in Desert

The acacias had been chopped down, and Ramesses had been blinded under 5,000 truckloads of sand. Engineers had buried the statues of both temple façades to their crowns to protect them from falling stones during removal of the overburden of rock (pages 714-15 and 718). The cofferdam had been completed: 504,400 cubic yards of rock and sand rising 80 feet above the riverbed.

Two harbors had been roughed out for barges and supply boats. Gravel and sand pits pocked the area. There was an airstrip a mile away, although vehicles could get to it only by using four-wheel drive—but, still, a regular airfield. I was not sure I liked all this.

"What a change!" I said a little disconsolately to the receptionist in the contractor's office on the desert plateau above the temples.

"Yes, what a change," the girl echoed cheerily. "Plenty of life now!"

The new bustle struck me with special intensity, contrasting as it did with the dying land around us. Nubia had always been mostly empty space, and the Nubians had ever felt themselves to be denizens of the horizon. But after the modern Nubians were relocated to save them from the rising flood, the area lost its last trace of life. Not a soul, not a sail. Mournful palm trees foundered in the water (pages 726-7). Houses crumbled, avidly swallowed by the mounting river. Abandoned villages on the rocky heights awaited their coup de grace. A calculated agony.

But now, how right the girl was! Abu Simbel pulsed with more life today than at any time since its construction.

On the day the first block of Treatment A swung out, nearly 3,000 persons lived around Abu Simbel. Settlements for engineers, workmen, and clerical employees, including 50

ETCHING BY A.

European and Egyptian families with 46 children, had been conjured out of the desert sands (pages 738-9). Front yards revealed the first timid signs of greenery. Eight miles of roads laced the area, but only the road between the operation site and the main storage yard enjoyed a hard macadam surface; it was more important to ensure a smooth ride for Abu Simbel stone than for Abu Simbel people. The community had a hospital, police station, two stores, and a bakery; a water-purification plant would soon be in operation.

The camp map even showed a Honeymoon Road—and with good reason, for several engineers had brought brides with them. But the school everyone had hoped for did not exist, frustrated by the polyglot make-up of

the population. Languages spoken in Abu Simbel, besides Arabic, include English, German, Italian, Swedish, French, and Danish.

The community's international flavor reaches beyond language. At my first lunch in the mess hall, I learned where all the principal dams had been built in recent years in Africa, Asia, and South America.

Most of Abu Simbel's new residents never saw the acacias bloom before the temples. For them the record began in the autumn of 1964. I made a moonlight Nile cruise with Werner Emse, a German engineer who lived on Honeymoon Road. He was showing his young wife the sights of Abu Simbel's past, known to her only from his letters.

"Here," he pointed out, "is the former

gravel pit. . . . Here the road used to run. . . ." And, pointing to some rickety houseboats aground on the bank of the Nile, "Here we were quartered in the beginning."

Older Shrines Fixed Temple Sites

Werner's intensely personal view of Abu Simbel's past set me wondering about my own limited concept of its history. I had never reflected much on its beginnings as long as Abu Simbel was untouched. Now that men and machines had invaded the place, writing finis to the temples' three millenniums of history at the old site, I was intrigued by questions of how, when, and why.

Ancient Egypt's whole civilization, fortunately, is so well documented that we need

Glacier of sand spreads from plateau to river in an etching from an 1817 drawing by Belzoni. He distorted dimensions of the cliff and placed the Great Temple too high on its face. But he can be forgiven the overabundance of sand; it must have seemed monumental to the first man to begin removing it. "The sand ran down in a slope from one side to the other," reported Belzoni, "and to attempt to make an aperture straight through it to the door would have been like making a hole in the water."

In 1819, an expedition cleared enough sand to reveal that the statues were sitting. Diversion walls built in 1892, not seen in this turn-of-the-century photograph, kept the desert's invasion to a minimum. Sand no longer threatened the Great Temple after reinforcement of diversion walls in 1910.

not speculate entirely about the how. As for the when and why, the years during which Abu Simbel's reconstruction dossier wandered about among committees yielded much new information through an intimate study of the temples at their site. First and foremost, French Egyptologist Louis A. Christophe, UNESCO's man in Egypt for the Nubian archeological campaign, deepened our knowledge of Abu Simbel's creation.

From inscriptions at the scene Christophe concludes that the sites of the two temples were already holy ground, occupied by shrines to local divinities—the god Horus of Meha and the goddess Hathor of Ibshek. Though Ramesses appropriated the sites, he paid due homage to both by having images of them placed in his new and much larger temples.

(Continued on page 717)

Gilded by sunlight, finely shaped figures of Ramesses II greet the visitor entering the Great Temple. Each holds the crook and flail, symbols common to Pharaoh and the god Osiris, king of the dead. Such statues usually flank the Great Hall, or open court, of surface temples. The four 30-foot-high figures on the north (photograph) wear the double crown of Upper and Lower Egypt; those on the south (not visible) wear only the crown of Upper Egypt.

Belzoni erred again in depicting the Great Hall; he drew double crowns on all figures (below). "The heat was so great in the interior of the temple," the Italian recalled, "that it scarcely permitted us to take any drawings, as the perspiration from our hands soon rendered the paper quite wet."

ETCHING BY A. AGLIO, AFTER A DRAWING BY GIOVANNI BATTISTA BELZONI

ABU SIMBEL, 1964: *Salvage begins as sand pours from an overhead conduit. Bulldozers pile high the yellow mounds to protect the façade from falling stone during removal of the rock above and behind it.*

714

Man and machine carve away a cliff. When plans to move the temples intact proved too expensive, Egypt and UNESCO adopted a plan to cut the monuments into movable blocks and reassemble them on the plateau above.

For bulk excavation over the temple chambers, steel rippers gouged out rock (left). When one layer of rock resisted the ripper's bite, engineers nervously resorted to dynamite. The carefully calculated blasts caused no damage to the temples.

Chain saw (right) cuts a slab immediately over the chambers. An Egyptian (above) slices sandstone with a Swedish handsaw. Workmen cut seams less than a quarter of an inch wide in the façade and interior walls.

Throughout Ramesses' reign, which began in 1304 B.C. (or, by another reckoning, in 1290 B.C.), fact and fiction tended to merge. He dreamed of restoring the Egyptian realm as far as the Euphrates, but failed. After years of striving against his Asiatic foes, the Hittites, he had to settle for little better than the status quo. Nevertheless, when he died after 67 years of rule, he had already gone down in history as a great conqueror.

A forest of obelisks and colossi from the Delta to Nubia, more gigantic than any constructed before, proclaimed his renown. In all antiquity, he was probably the most prolific builder of monuments to his own glory.

Great Temple Oriented to the Sun

The ceremonies attending the founding of an Egyptian temple centered on the placing of the four corners of the ground plan, using measuring tape and boundary stakes. This ancient and sacred ritual was no doubt enacted at Abu Simbel, even though for a rock-hewn temple it could have only symbolic meaning. Possibly animals were sacrificed to propitiate the mountain before wounding it with mallet and chisel.

We can be sure that high court officials did not shrink from the tedious journey to

KODACHROME BY WERNER EMSE © N.G.S.

Nubia, on the fringe of the civilized world. But history fails to tell us when—or even if—Ramesses himself visited Abu Simbel. Our artist has assumed his presence with his queen, Nefertari; a bas-relief inside the Great Temple shows the royal couple taking part in a similar ceremony (pages 703-5).

The chief palace architect directed the construction. Surveyors laid out the axis of the Great Temple from a point on the eastern horizon. Christophe suggests that Ramesses' orders were that the rising sun's rays must strike 180 feet back into the Sanctuary on the day of his 30-year jubilee, around October 20 in 1274 B.C.—or possibly 1260 B.C.

Stonecutters chiseled the façade into the mountainside, imitating the pylons of a temple in the open. Draftsmen painted guide lines on the smoothed façade to facilitate their drawing of the colossi's contours. With eyes fixed on plans sent from the court, the sculptors began the seated figures of the king with mallet and bronze chisel. At his colossal feet, they sculptured the standing figures of his family. Finally, painters swarmed over the images with fiber brushes (pages 700-702).

Specialists from the City of the Dead at Thebes drilled tunnels into the rock, at first advancing in narrow parallel galleries. Later they broke loose the rock masses that separated the tunnels. Workmen used tools of bronze and hard wood in the soft stone. They hollowed out the temple in the cliff as if it were built in the open, leaving pillars in place as ceiling supports.

How they solved the problem of lighting deep inside the mountain remains a mystery. Smudgy torches or burning wicks would have choked the workers. Did they use smudgeless alcohol-burning lanterns? But we have no evidence that distillation was a known art in ancient Egypt. Perhaps bronze mirrors reflected sunlight into the interior.

In the Great Hall of Ramesses' temple, sculptors transformed the pillars into statues holding the crook and flail, symbols common to both Ramesses and the god Osiris. In the adjoining hall they merely gave the pillars four smooth sides. In the inner sanctum they carved out of the rock four seated figures, representing Ramesses and the great gods Ptah, Amun, and Re-Harakhti. Draftsmen traced sketches on the smoothed walls, and sculptors, following these outlines, chiseled bas-reliefs. Then painters brushed on brilliant color.

Clerks in white-linen garments moved

Enemy turns friend: Desert sands that once hid the wonders of the Great Temple now provide a cushion for the immense but fragile figures to protect them from falling debris during removal of the cliff top. Workmen on scaffolding covered inscriptions and stone baboons above the images with planks.

Reinforcing Ramesses' nose, Abd Es Samya of Egypt's Antiquities Department squirts polyvinyl acetate into a nostril. Where the soft sandstone threatened to crumble, this resin compound strengthened the rock surface.

"Because of the bad quality of the stone," said project manager Carl Theodor Mäckel, "Abu Simbel would have been lost long ago had it not been for the area's exceptionally dry climate."

among the artisans, checked the work against the plans, and drew up progress reports that went by express downriver. Barges brought in supplies. Dulled or broken chisels had to be recast and resharpened; club-shaped mallets needed replacement. Court executives constantly dropped in for the grand tour. Special vessels manned by high-speed rowers brought the latest instructions from the royal court. As far as we can learn, work on the Great Temple and Small Temple went on simultaneously.

Ramesses' Favorite God: Ramesses

What, I wonder, went through the minds of the artists who decorated the north wall of the Great Hall with a heroic representation of the Battle of Kadesh? They had orders to make this encounter of Ramesses with the Hittites an overwhelming victory. But the artists must have known the truth: This "victory" had been merely a successful retreat. Ramesses avoided disaster only by personal valor, inspiring his troops to fight bravely. And I would dearly like to know what these artists thought of the king's increasing self-deification.

The Great Temple actually glorifies Ramesses himself; all other deities are only invited guests. A rebus over the entrance spells out the name of the host: User-maat-re. This is the king's coronation name, his throne name. He is a deity by virtue of his office and sits in the innermost hall, a god among gods.

Christophe concludes that the king had the temple built for the feast of his *sed,* the jubilee marking 30 years of his reign and a milestone in his life. The sed was probably a symbolic survival of a prehistoric ritual: the slaying of the ruler while still in the prime of life. At the sed the Pharaoh, with great pomp, became, as it were, his own successor. The renewal

Taking apart a mountain, workmen lay bare the Great Temple. Stonecutters moved not only the temple face but also the rock that framed it, so that the reassembled monument will appear in as natural a setting as possible.

Cutaway drawing reveals that Ramesses' architects designed his subterranean temple with a floor plan similar to that of one built in the open. Traditional entrance leads into the Great Hall (pages 706-7 and 712-13). Beyond lie Hypostyle Hall, Transverse Chamber, and Sanctuary.

A red trace on the ground shows the direction of the rising sun's beams when they penetrate twice each year into the Sanctuary and light the statues of Ramesses and Amun. Side rooms probably held ceremonial utensils or gifts to the gods.

of his rule was likened in the religious texts to the restoration of Egypt to order after a time of chaos, and also to the recapture of a fortress usurped by an enemy. On the day of Ramesses' sed, the rays of the rising sun would penetrate along the carefully aligned axis into the bowels of the mountain to flash across the statue of the king; thus the sun god himself would vouchsafe to Pharaoh the renewal of his earthly realm.

A few years later, perhaps for a celebration in the 34th year of his reign, Ramesses took the final step. As the hieroglyphs reveal, he assumed his place among the gods not only under his ceremonial

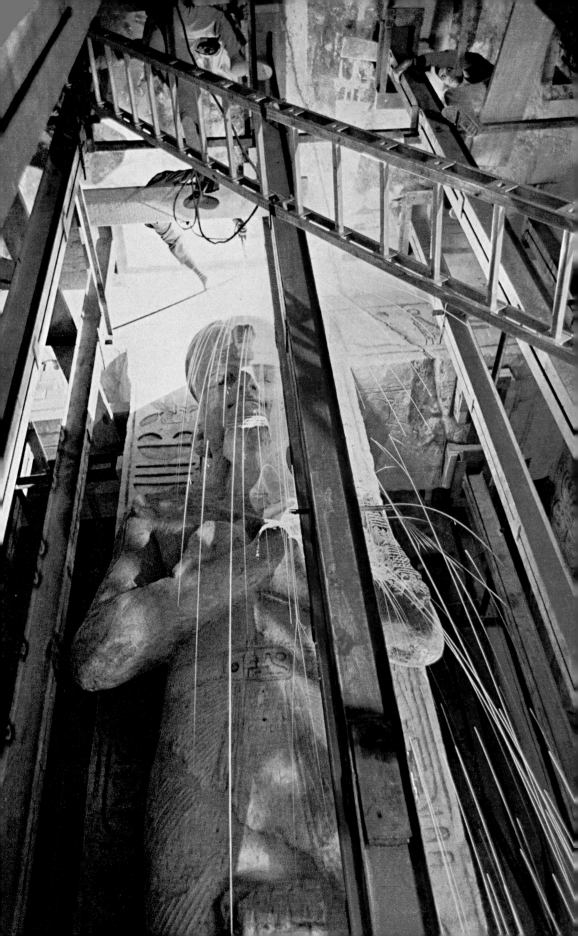

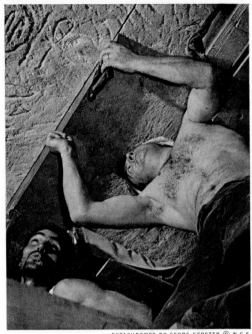

Shower of sparks cascades past an impassive Ramesses as a welder applies his torch to steel girders within the Great Hall. Because of changing stresses in the rock after removal of the cliff top, the ceilings and walls might have collapsed without these supports. The 156 tons of scaffolding will be re-erected at the new location before the chambers take shape once again.

With the skill of surgeons, bearded Egyptian Abbas Ali Ali Omar and Italian Giovanni Greco saw into the ceiling of the Great Temple. Slender steel pins driven through the slit enable chain-saw operators, slicing down from above, to locate the cut and meet it.

EKTACHROMES BY GEORG GERSTER © N.G.S.

name but also as Ramesses, his name at birth. The man as well as the king was now a god.

A sculpture in the Great Temple strikingly documents the king's audacity. This relief originally showed Ramesses standing before the seated god Amun and goddess Mut, offering them Nubian captives. Then, obviously on orders from the palace, artists recut the relief to seat the deified Ramesses between the two deities. To make room for this divine latecomer, the artists moved Mut to the right and made her smaller. A touch-up with plaster and paint, abetted by the chamber's gloom, concealed Ramesses' earlier status as a mere mortal.

Royal Shrine Rises in Hinterland

Why did Ramesses choose Abu Simbel as the place to create the most spectacular of his works?

The answer must lie in the nature of Abu Simbel's setting, at once a stimulus and a challenge to Egyptian artists. Since the beginning of their civilization, Egyptians had responded to the inherent possibilities of the materials at hand. The greatness of Abu Simbel springs from the combination of superb architecture with a dynamic setting, and the completed monument is truly worthy of the grandeur of a god-king.

But Ramesses built half a dozen other temples in Nubia, four of them partly rock-hewn, and made numerous additions to existing shrines in Egypt. He also deified himself in

other temples. Does it seem illogical from a religious or political point of view that he should make the overwhelming display of his power and majesty in such an isolated part of his realm?

To us it would appear that these colossi were raised by a megalomaniac to impress his subjects and the mammoth shrines to accommodate vast hordes of worshipers, but this is not true. To the Egyptian mind the colossi were living things, a mystical extension and enlargement of Pharaoh's being. They needed no worshipers to give them meaning.

Temples to the Egyptians were simply redoubts of the gods, represented by their living statues, standing guard between chaos and an ordered world. That is why at Abu Simbel small statues of the gods were borne out of the Sanctuary on a ceremonial bark to greet the sun. Abu Simbel was no subterranean cathedral with a congregation, but more like a military installation, a secret command post obsessed with problems of security and clearance of its selected personnel, the priests.

Inscription's Position Gives Clue to Date

The two temples, many years in building, were completed before Ramesses' 34th year of reign. Christophe deduces this from the fact that a happy communique announcing the reception of the daughter of Hittite King Khattusilis into the royal harem in that year had to be placed outside rather than within the Great Temple. No space remained for the

inscription inside, for the walls were covered with painted reliefs.

"But bad news had also reached Abu Simbel," Louis Christophe told me. "Ramesses' first chief consort, Iset-nefert, presumably died shortly before or after construction got under way. Bent-Anta, Ramesses' and Iset-nefert's first-born daughter, is portrayed in the Great Temple's Great Hall, sometimes as a princess, sometimes as the queen of her father-husband. As long as Iset-nefert was alive, Ramesses would hardly have elevated her daughter to a position equaling that of Nefertari, his other famous royal spouse."

The Small Temple is believed to have been completed ahead of the Great Temple, and was decorated in Nefertari's honor. It pays homage to the queen and the goddess Hathor, and in contrast to the solemnity of the larger shrine, it displays a boudoirlike intimacy and charm. Here, as in the Great Temple, Nefertari's lovely face and figure appear repeatedly, usually near her royal spouse, as in our painting (pages 703-5).

Buried Temple Sleeps Away the Ages

While Ramesses yet lived, Christophe believes, the upper portion of the second colossus from the south side fell to the sands, where it lay through the centuries. Pharaoh's experts had underestimated the fissures and stresses in the rock. A second seated figure and the temple interior required extensive repairs.

For a while after Ramesses' death, the priests continued to maintain the temples. But by 1000 B.C. Lower Nubia had begun to fade from the pages of history, and the sands of the Western Desert started to invade the Great Temple.

In the sixth century B.C., Greek and Phoenician mercenaries marching against Nubia climbed the heaped-up sand to carve their names on the seated colossi. Two of the

Before salvagers began their task, statues fronting the temples gazed on a serene riverscape (top). As work began, a wall of steel pilings—core for a shielding cofferdam—fenced the monuments from the Nile (center). Men labored night and day in 1964 to complete the dam to its 80-foot height when the annual Nile flood rose higher than expected. Corrugated metal conduits formed tunnels into both temples, providing access through the rising sand cover. With protective measures completed by 1965, Abu Simbel wore a new face (bottom).

KODACHROME (ABOVE) AND EKTACHROME BY GEORG GERSTER © N.G.S.

Drowned forest of date palms spikes the waters of growing Lake Nasser. Soon the trees will vanish forever. Passing boatmen pick a few clusters of the last harvest. A deserted Nubian village, two miles downstream from Abu Simbel, awaits inundation. The United Arab Republic has resettled more than 60,000 Nubians of the area in new villages in the Kôm Ombo region, north of Aswân.

727

EKTACHROME BY GEORG GERSTER (BELOW); KODAC

"Ramesses II made . . . a mansion and great and mighty monuments for the great royal wife Nefertari," reads an inscription on the Small Temple. Two statues of Ramesses and one of Nefertari stand on each side of the doorway (see cutaway drawing). Laborers remove the shielding of sand from the 33-foot-high figures. In the Tranverse Chamber, artisans carved one of the most beautiful reliefs (lower photograph), in which the goddesses Hathor and Isis crown Nefertari.

"On every pillar . . . we find the names of Rameses and Nefertari 'coupled and inseparable,' " wrote Amelia Edwards. "We see that the Queen was fair . . . the King was in his prime. We divine the rest; and the poetry of the place at all events is ours. Even in these barren solitudes there is wafted to us a breath from the shores of old romance."

soldiers, not content with a simple "Kilroy was here," scratched across Ramesses' shin this military communique:

"King Psammetichus having come to Elephantine, those who were with Psammetichus, son of Theocles, beyond Kerkis as far as the river permitted, have written this: Potasimto led the foreigners and Amasis the Egyptians. We have written this, Arkhon, son of Amoibikhos, and Pelekos, son of Oudamos."

These two soldiers bequeathed us one of the older texts in Greek, and never has science defended more staunchly the mischievous habit of decorating other people's shins and walls with signatures.

"Colossal Statues" Astound a Daring Traveler

The Hellenistic period listed among the Seven Wonders of the World Egypt's Pyramids and the Pharos, or lighthouse, of Alexandria. Not a word about Abu Simbel. Its Great Temple slumbered on in a cocoon of sand, not to be rediscovered until 1813.

John Lewis Burckhardt, traveling as a Moslem, was one of the first in modern times to follow the Nile almost to the Third Cataract, about 210 miles upriver from Ramesses' temple (map, page 698). On his return downriver he looked for the "temple of Ebsambal," of which he had "heard many magnificent descriptions."

This was the Small Temple, which had not been buried and served villagers in Burckhardt's time as a refuge from marauding Bedouin. As Burckhardt was leaving the site of the Small Temple, he suddenly espied "what is yet visible of four immense colossal statues." He saw little—only the double crown, head, and part of the torso of the most southerly statue and the "bonnets" of the two northerly ones projecting from the sand.

I had always found it hard to visualize the circumstances of this

First face lifting: Pharaoh's head glows under floodlights as work continues into the night. Guido Roncaglia severs block 120, as marked on the blueprint (below), with a six-foot saw. Sponge rubber protects the forehead. In clear morning light, a staff member with arms outstretched (opposite), guides the 19-ton face to a sand-filled trailer bound for storage.

Curved lines of the blueprint, like a contour map, show the shape and dimensions of the rock as taken from stereoscopic photographs.

EKTACHROME (ABOVE) AND KODACHROME BY GEORG GERSTER © N.G.S.

discovery. No longer—for I myself have now seen the Great Temple purposely engulfed in a protective mass of sand.

Burckhardt surmised that sand hid the entrance to a temple hewn from the rock, but he could not even tell whether the colossi were seated or standing.

Giovanni Battista Belzoni journeyed to Abu Simbel in 1817 and gained entrance to the Great Temple. The British consul general in Egypt had turned to this adventurous Italian to collect antiquities for the British Museum.

After weeks of digging, the six-and-a-half-foot Belzoni and his helpers pushed aside enough sand to slide into the cavernous hall (pages 706-7). He and his companions marveled at the work of Ramesses' artists, unseen since ancient times. They attempted to make drawings, but it was so hot inside that perspiration ruined their sketchbooks.

The southernmost colossus was dug out in 1819 and the general sand level reduced, revealing the four seated statues of the façade. This revelation set off a rush of tourists, just as did news of Abu Simbel's imminent flooding 150 years later.

Excavation Betrays a Slayer

The creation of Abu Simbel in the 13th century B.C. was a story of struggle and triumph, of pride, and perhaps of strife and murder. And so has been the story of its rediscovery.

Belzoni's success for the British roiled French competitors. As the Italian left Abu Simbel after one visit, a Turkish soldier on a dromedary overtook him to deliver two threatening letters written in Arabic and signed, Belzoni reported, with fictitious names. Later a French agent warned him that if he continued his activities in Nubia, his throat might be slit. At one heated confrontation, Latin tempers rose over French and English claims; a pistol was fired, luckily missing Belzoni.

Murder was actually committed in the modern-day relocation of the temples. After a planned blasting in a quarry was abruptly postponed in October, 1964, a Swedish engineer noticed an arm projecting from the rubble. An Egyptian had killed a fellow workman, counting on the explosion to make the murder look like an accident. Before the

murderer was caught, a hundred workers from his village quit their Abu Simbel jobs, fearing the vengeance of the slain man's kin.

In the evening, when men relax, many stories make the rounds: stories of horror, of poisonous scorpions, or of the scourge of Abu Simbel—the horned viper. Or the talk may be of the visitors who take sand as a souvenir, some of them almost piously.

Today the sand is blanketed by flourlike white dust from the sawing and excavating. Phase No. 1 of the salvage operation was aimed at protection. Engineers, after building the cofferdam and shielding temple façades with sand, shored up the interiors with prestressed scaffolding (page 722). Test borings in the sandstone and measurements of its strength and stresses had revealed that the ceiling not only rested on the rock pillars but also was kept in place by lateral thrusts. The scaffolding would prevent ceiling slabs from falling when, during removal of the mountain above the temples, changes in stress occurred within the rock.

The rising waters of the Nile posed the chief problem of protection. The cofferdam helps to keep the construction site dry. A drainage system collects unavoidable seepage. Tunnels intercept any water filtering through the cliff's sandstone from the river. Deep wells help lower the water table around the site to prevent its rising higher than 40 inches below the sill of the Small Temple. Beyond that level, water

drawn up into the stone by capillary action would wet the monuments. Pumps supporting this complex drainage system can siphon off as much as 200 gallons a second.

The cost of the cofferdam and drainage system is about a sixth of the estimated salvage cost—a $6,000,000 price tag for delay. If the work had started two years earlier, this costly rear-guard action against the Nile would have been unnecessary.

Phase No. 2 comprised removal of the cliff and excavation behind the façade to reach

Bare bones of the Great Temple lie exposed after the cutters take off the cliff top (page 720). Slab by slab, the roof and walls move by trailer from their age-old home to storage areas. Dismantling continues simultaneously on rooms and the façade.

For the first time, daylight streams into the innermost rooms from above (right). Ceiling gone, decorated walls await removal. The thin cable of this wire saw, running over grooved wheels, makes a fine cut.

the temple ceilings. The engineers planned to do this without blasting, to avoid risk to the temples. But they struck a massive layer of iron-rich sandstone that fouled the teeth of the ground-ripping equipment. Dynamiting was the only way out. The echoes of the explosions resounded in UNESCO's Paris headquarters, but the vibrations, as measured in the temple, were smaller than those caused by the bulldozers.

Pino Lucano, chief of the section superintending excavation and dismantling, told me that bulk excavation around the Great Temple involved 142,000 cubic yards of rock.

Another 29,200 cubic yards had to be painstakingly excavated by hand, using pneumatic hammers only. This careful excavation included removal of the sandstone to within less than a yard behind the façade, above the ceiling, and along the side walls.

Relics Excite Dreams of Treasure

Pino showed me what looked like pieces of petrified palm tree found embedded in the sandstone. Paleontologists are still analyzing these, but if they are true fossils, they must have been washed in at least a million years ago as the sandstone formed.

Finding these relics spurred the instincts of treasure hunters. One of the Nubians on the site, a dark, fine-featured workman, confessed to me, "Never would I take a job at the High Dam; but Abu Simbel, that's something else again."

No one could fool him; he knew exactly why men and machines were driving into the cliff. He intended to be there when the gold hoard was brought to light. He had to shout his confession above the noise of the pneumatic hammers; obviously, he would have preferred to whisper it.

Even Pino Lucano's fellow countrymen, the *marmisti,* stonecutters from northern Italy's marble quarries, cling to dreams of finding treasure—"a mummy, a scarab, anything," as one said to me almost pleadingly.

The engineers, however, are too busy to give the possibility of treasure much thought. Diether Fuchs, superintendent of the civil engineering works, reviewing Phases 1 and 2 with me, said: "I do not think that management at any other construction site has ever had to coordinate so many operations. On some days we have several hundred operations going at the same time. And everything, of course, is complicated by the multiplicity

73

Lesson in Egyptology: Resident archeologist Dr. Anwar Shoukry explains to Stefan Lindström, a Swedish engineer's son, an inscription in the cliff near the Great Temple. The stela, showing Ramesses' viceroy Setau, proclaims the sovereign's might in the 38th year of his reign.

"Watchers for the dawn," sacred baboons squat in a storage area, awaiting return to a high perch above the entrance of the reconstructed temple.

Gauze bandages cover the feet of painted figures on pillars from the Great Temple. Wrapping prevents brittle edges from crumbling away.

of languages. Then, what trouble to procure spare parts! It takes at least three months to get them from Europe. No matter how large a stock we have on hand, the part you want is always missing. Just go over to the workshops and ask them what working at Abu Simbel means: Improvise, improvise!"

Boy Becomes Expert on Abu Simbel

I asked in many places how it felt to be at Abu Simbel, and I received many answers. The most enthusiastic was, "The time of my life!" This came from 12-year-old Stefan Lindström (preceding page).

Although I often trudged the site with the engineers, I soon found that there was no better guide than Stefan. Before he came to Abu Simbel, he had watched his father build a port in Liberia. This new faster-paced project enchanted him. Any free time he had—when his mother, who was his teacher, let him

escape from his studies—he roamed among men and machines.

He knew the intricacies of each piece of machinery, and all the men knew young Lindström and his field glasses. He had a grasp of details. For instance, he could differentiate scrupulously between a D-8 bulldozer and a D-9. He could also expertly distinguish between Hathor and Isis in the Small Temple's bas-reliefs. He knew when the iceman was due, and he was an authority on the quality of the fish peddled at noon among the Egyptian workmen.

He and I watched as the workmen blasted to level a storage lot and then set up the gantry crane. We stood in the excavation pit above the temples, amid the rumbling of bulldozers with steel rippers that looked like the stingers of giant angry scorpions as they struck into the rock (page 716).

Through a steel conduit piercing the sand

Rebuilding begins: In January, 1966, laborers ease the first stone of the Great Temple into place at the new site high above the rising Nile. Special mortar will attach the block to the foundation. Resin paint, shining at the base, prevents water in the mortar from discoloring the sandstone. So carefully were measurements computed that blocks fit into place with a precision of 1/25 of an inch or less—like parts of a three-dimensional jigsaw puzzle.

King-size manicure: Dismantling continues down to the finger tips as workmen slice Ramesses' extremities into neat blocks. Crane cables will attach to the steel lifting bars. Engineers expect to complete the dismantling and reconstruction of both temples late this year—two years earlier than predicted. Completion of the setting will require another year and a half.

EKTACHROME (OPPOSITE) AND KODACHROME BY GEORG GERSTER © N.G.S.

before the façade, we ventured into the Great Temple. We could hardly move between the uprights and struts of the scaffolding. Above us, through layers of stone, the pneumatic hammers throbbed like a summer rain on a tin roof. To protect himself against the infernal dust, Stefan donned a mask.

"Now I look like a pig. Or like a spaceman," he commented happily.

Phase No. 3, dismantling and removing of the temples, was in full swing. Outside earlier, Stefan and I had seen the derrick lift the first block of the Treatment A series. Inside now, we watched skilled marmisti wield their saws, some tailor-made for this unique job.

These men had spent their working lives in cutting and moving stone. "We know rocks like hearts," one of them quipped. "We know when they break."

Soon their chain saws had bitten four feet deep into the rock on the bias, where ceiling and walls met. These cuts would prevent splintering of the temple ceiling when the mountain readjusted itself after removal of the rock overburden.

Other marmisti, working in two-man teams, cut vertical four-inch-deep grooves into the painted ceiling at regular intervals. To manipulate their saws, they crouched on a scaffold beneath the ceiling in a painfully cramped posture (page 723). I thought of the tortures suffered by Michelangelo while painting the ceiling of the Sistine Chapel.

The men, however, showed little concern for their physical discomfort. They were interested only in the width of their cuts. If they made a finer cut—by a hairline or perhaps a full millimeter (.039 of an inch)—than the maximum six-millimeter width stipulated in the contract, they felt well rewarded.

Diether Fuchs joined Stefan and me, and he explained: "The joints in all painted or

sculptured surfaces must be as thin as is humanly possible. This is true for the façades as well as the interiors of the temples. With saws we cut only an inch or so deep into the sculptured side of the slabs, then drill holes through which we drive steel pins. When by careful excavation we have approached from the outside to within 80 centimeters—31 inches—of ceiling or walls, we begin to cut from that side. Using power saws, we make a much wider cut but work faster. The steel pins tell us where to run the cuts from the outside so that they coincide with the thin cuts made from inside."

At the time of our conversation, Diether did not know yet how they would work a slab loose when the cuts approached each other. "One possibility," he told me, "is to use wedges" —the method finally adopted.

Many people believe the ancient Egyptians split granite with moistened wooden wedges. I recalled this to Diether. Half seriously, he answered: "If you want to stay around, you better banish the word 'water' in connection with the temples, even in your dreams."

The temples are sandstone, and archeologists fear not only the damage but also the discoloration that water can cause. That is why special care must be exercised in any use of reinforcing cement.

When the two temples of Abu Simbel are completely dismantled, they will form a jigsaw puzzle of 950 pieces. Of

CONTRACTOR'S COLONY

MESS HALL

MAIN STORAGE AREA

EKTACHROME (BELOW) BY JOHN M. KESHISHIAN, M.D.; KODACHROMES BY GEORG GERSTER © N.G.S.

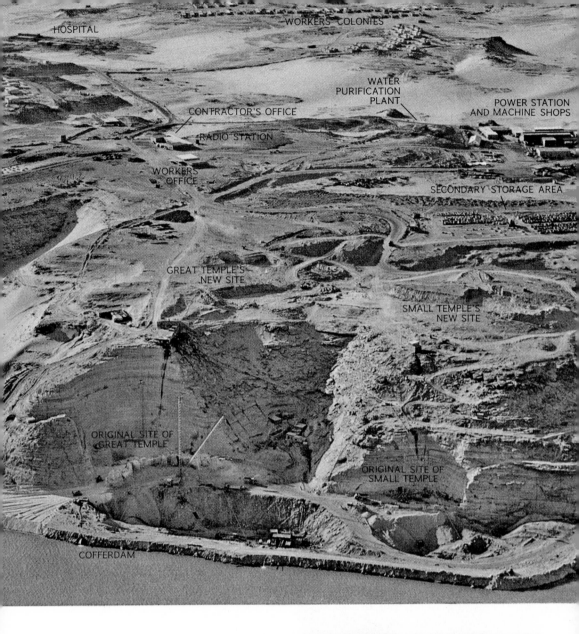

HOSPITAL

WORKERS COLONIES

WATER
PURIFICATION
PLANT

CONTRACTOR'S OFFICE

POWER STATION
AND MACHINE SHOPS

RADIO STATION

WORKERS
OFFICE

SECONDARY STORAGE AREA

GREAT TEMPLE'S
NEW SITE

SMALL TEMPLE'S
NEW SITE

ORIGINAL SITE OF
GREAT TEMPLE

ORIGINAL SITE OF
SMALL TEMPLE

COFFERDAM

New town blooms on the desert waste. Homes for engineers and workmen dot the plateau. The complex at left will become a tourist facility upon completion of the project. Resembling a race track, the main storage area stretches the length of a small promontory. A gantry crane, moving along the track, deposits each block in its preassigned place. Later, the crane will pick each one out again when its turn comes in the reassembly. Three faces of the colossi (opposite) rest in the area's soft sand.

German engineer Wolfgang Heyder concentrates on the problems of reconstruction. Working with a gypsum model of the Great Temple and a simulated derrick, he seeks the best places to set up cranes so that they can reach all parts of the monument in reassembling the blocks 212 feet above their original location.

KODACHROME BY JOHN M. KESHISHIAN, M.D. © N.G.S.

GEOGRAPHIC ART DIVISION © NATIONAL GEOGRAPHIC SOCIETY

Reassembled for new dawns, the Great and Small Temples of Abu Simbel rest high and dry in this artist's reconstruction, which also shows the old site, now ghostly beneath the waters. On certain mornings of the year the sun will again strike the statue of Ramesses seated in the Sanctuary of the Great Temple. The fallen head of one colossus lies in its age-old tumbled position.

Speedy hydrofoils like the *Hatshepsut* will carry wondering visitors to see the reassembled temples.

FINAL RESTORATION OF ABU SIMBEL MAY DEPEND ON YOUR HELP

UNLESS an additional $7,000,000 is raised, work on Abu Simbel may stop short of complete restoration. Present funds do not cover all costs of the reassembly, which includes reconstruction of the adjacent cliffs to complete the setting. If you wish to help with this historic project, send tax-deductible gifts to the American Committee to Preserve Abu Simbel, Box 3456, Grand Central Station, New York City, New York 10022.

these, 750 make up the Great Temple. Maximum weight for ceiling or wall slabs is 20 tons; for façade slabs, 30 tons. By hollowing out some blocks from behind, a maximum surface can be obtained within weight limits.

Derricks hoist the slabs, and low-bed trailers move them to the main storage yard. There the gantry crane picks them up and carries each to its preassigned position. While in storage, interior slabs are covered with straw mats; the water archeologists fear can also come from the heavens, even in parched Abu Simbel. In 1962 a cloudburst struck the surrounding villages and melted down many mud-brick houses. Just last September a severe rainstorm lashed the site, raising Nile waves that nibbled at the cofferdam.

Each slab gets the red-carpet treatment. Cracks and fissures riddle Abu Simbel's ailing rock, and its grains of quartz are only feebly cemented together. Before the slightest cut is made in any decorated surface, workers apply a coating of synthetic resin, except on the saw line, to guard against crumbling (page 719). Deeply injected resin must not spread near a future line of cut since it would stop the saw blades. Once a block is cut, it may need further strengthening.

Rods Anchored in Stone Aid Lift

Surveyors measure each slab and compute its center of gravity in order to place drilled holes for the lifting bars. Engineers fix the bars with epoxy resin. When the resin hardens, the engineers screw these anchoring bars to a yoke attached to the derrick hook. At first they lift the block only a finger's breadth, so that the load indicator in the derrick hook can register the weight. Then hydraulic pressure is put on the slab to create a 10- to 20-percent overload; if the slab shows signs of cracking, it will be strengthened or subdivided.

When Joint Venture Abu Simbel signed its contract, none of the participating firms knew exactly how to make the quarter-inch cuts they had agreed to make or how to hold together the weak sandstone (sometimes more sand than stone) without arousing the archeologists' ire. Though Hochtief had successfully removed and relocated the Temple of Kalâbsha, near the Aswân High Dam, the project had yielded little pertinent experience, since Kalâbsha was built of blocks in the open, not hewn from rock.

VBB had supervised the removal of three small rock temples in Nubia. But these were mere finger exercises, for no block exceeded seven tons.

While engineers feverishly built the coffer-dam, others conducted tests with all kinds of saws—wire saws, chain saws, disk saws, specially hardened handsaws. Chemists ran hundreds of tests to determine the proper synthetic resins and their admixtures.

VBB's towering Karl-Fredrik Wård told me, "Most outsiders, and even many insiders, overlook the key technological principle of our salvage scheme. In a negative sense, it means doing entirely without hydraulic jacks, ropes, slings, cables, and similar hoisting equipment; in a positive sense, it means the use of lifting bars.

"With the bars' help we can handle big slabs and still keep the cutting lines to a minimum width. We do not have to make room in the cut for a bulky sling. And also we do not need to move the block first to get a sling around it. That's why lifting bars are the safest solution; they minimize risk of damage."

Even so, because of the poor quality of the sandstone, some breakage must be anticipated. Early in the work a stela broke. Carl Theodor Mäckel, the project manager, explained: "That accident brought the problem of risk up for discussion. Everyone concerned should know this is an experiment. We take every possible precaution, within the time available. We could perform the dismantling work virtually free of risk, but to do this we would need two or three years. That would mean we might as well pack up right now. By August 15, 1966, we must clear the site."

Impossible to Set Insurance Value

Although Egypt obtained nominal insurance against monument damage, the coverage by no means reflected esthetic value. For what is the value of Ramesses' legs? How much is his nose worth in dollars and cents? The archeologists despaired of setting price tags on this priceless legacy of history.

Pharaoh's move is one of the most daring in history. Certainly it is the most costly. It will take at least five years from signing of contract to completion of landscaping.

In the final phase the temples are being re-erected with utmost precision over the same scaffolding system that shored up their interiors during removal. The blocks from the ceilings, walls, and façades are anchored to a structure of reinforced concrete. The rock framing the façades, consisting of 970 Treatment A blocks and some 5,500 blocks even farther out (called Treatment B), will also be returned to place. Artificial hills heaped atop the monuments will restore the original aspect of the whole (preceding pages). Concrete domes above the temples will relieve them from all pressure of this overburden.

Survey work (300,000 theodolite readings for the two temples) guarantees the repositioning of the slabs down to a millimeter of accuracy. The precision of the watchmaker applied to colossi!

Will Pharaoh Ever Be the Same?

One day soon, perhaps by the end of 1966, Pharaoh will again smile serenely on a considerably wider Nile. And on certain days of the year the rays of the rising sun will once more penetrate past the colossal guardians into the Sanctuary.

Will these "million-year temples," as a contemporary inscription describes them, look the same after reassembly? At times when the reservoir is at its maximum of 597 feet above sea level, they will appear unchanged. They will be less so when the Aswân reservoir is at low ebb. Then visitors will have to climb about 120 feet to the sill of the temples.

The temptation will be strong to restore the fallen second colossus to its original splendor. Around 1910 an engineer commissioned by the Egyptian Antiquities Department deemed the project unfeasible. Today its feasibility is no problem, but many would question its desirability.

What about the wounds inflicted on Pharaoh by the move? I took the question to resident archeologist Shoukry, who also is retired director-general of Egypt's Antiquities Department (page 735).

In giving his answer, he posed a question: "Pharaoh's injuries will be healed. The joints will be treated with a filler up to a few millimeters of the surface. It would be easy to go further—not only to heal these wounds but to conceal them. But would this be honest toward our forebears, ourselves, and those who come after us?"

SIX-MONTH INDEX

As one of the privileges of membership in the National Geographic Society, members who bind their GEOGRAPHICS as works of reference will receive upon request an index for each six-month volume. The index to Volume 128 (July-December, 1965) is now available.

VOL. 129, NO. 6

NATIONAL GEOGRAPHIC

JUNE, 1966

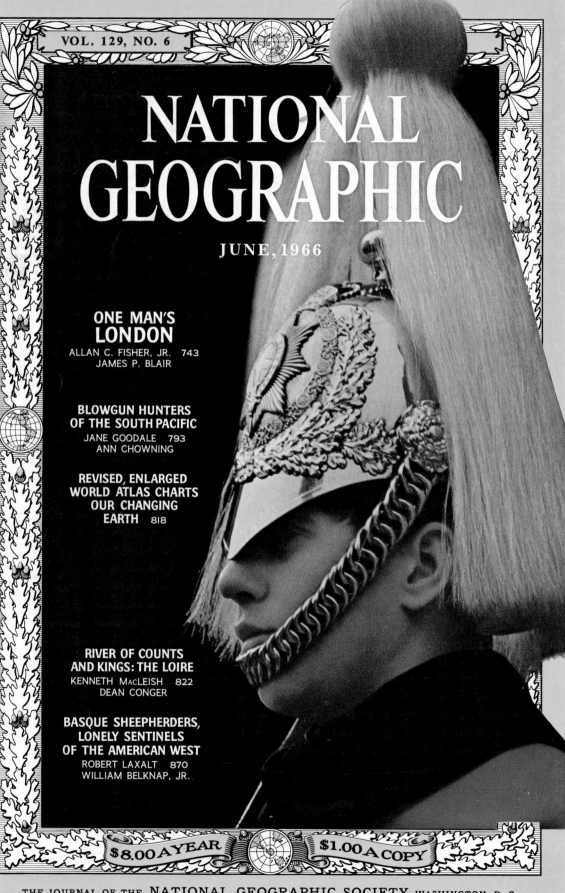

$8.00 A YEAR $1.00 A COPY

THE JOURNAL OF THE NATIONAL GEOGRAPHIC SOCIETY WASHINGTON, D. C.

COVER: Resplendent Life Guard in London symbolizes Britain's heritage and love of pageantry (page 743).

This is Caprice Custom Coupe with roof styling unlike any other car's, with side view mirror and seven other standard safety items.

The Chevrolet "convertible" that doesn't convert

Clever. The vinyl roof covering available for your Caprice Custom Coupe creates the impression it's a convertible. But Caprice is really a luxurious hardtop with all the advantages of Chevrolet hardtop design. Inside, Caprice allows only luxury, like foam-cushioned seats, thick carpeting and paneling to highlight doors. Padded dash and seat belts, front and rear, for added safety. Want to top the Caprice? That's easy. Just tell us whether you want the black or beige vinyl roof cover.

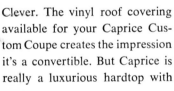 *Caprice* UNIQUE THE CHEVROLET WAY

Chevrolet Division

Shown: Model 100, under $150, including flash.   POLAROID®

You can get color prints like this in 60 seconds with a Polaroid Color Pack Camera. Is there any other way to take pictures?

Prices start at under $60.

Arizona arch salutes a noted geologist

TALL AS A 15-STORY BUILDING, Wrather Arch in northern Arizona dwarfs two visitors. The great sandstone buttress was first spotted by a local pilot, Royce Knight, as he flew over a remote gorge west of Glen Canyon. Reaching the arch by helicopter in 1963, Knight and GEOGRAPHIC staff man Walter M. Edwards calculated its height as 165 feet.

This year the Government named the natural wonder for the late Dr. William E. Wrather, who, as Director of the U. S. Geological Survey from 1943 to 1956, vastly expanded the uses of aerial photomapping. Dr. Wrather was a National Geographic Society Trustee for 12 years and a valued member of its Committee for Research and Exploration.

NATIONAL GEOGRAPHIC SOCIETY MEMBERSHIP

Mail to: The Secretary, National Geographic Society
Washington, D. C.   20036

$6⁵⁰ CALENDAR YEAR 1966 MEMBERSHIP DUES INCLUDE SUBSCRIPTION TO THE NATIONAL GEOGRAPHIC.

Annual dues in the United States and throughout the world are $6.50. To compensate for international postage differentials, remit in U.S. funds or equivalent, $7.00 for Canadian membership; $8.00 for all other countries. 80% of dues is designated for subscription to the magazine.
Life membership for the U.S., its outlying areas, and Canada is $150, elsewhere, $200. Remittances should be sent direct to the National Geographic Society in U.S. funds or equivalent.   6-66

I NOMINATE for Society membership the person named at left. (Use separate sheet for additional nominations.)

(GIFT MEMBERSHIP) I nominate and enclose $_____ for dues of the person named at left. Send gift card signed:

. . . .

I DESIRE INFORMATION concerning membership and the NATIONAL GEOGRAPHIC. (Fill in at left.)

NEW
MEMBER_____
PRINT NAME OF AN INDIVIDUAL ONLY (MR., MRS., MISS)

STREET_____

CITY, STATE, ZIP CODE

MY
NAME_____
PLEASE PRINT (MR., MRS., MISS)

STREET_____

CITY, STATE, ZIP CODE

Fly the quick & quiet jets:
Douglas DC-8 or DC-9

The famed Douglas DC-8 has flown faster, higher, and farther than any other commercial jet.

Ask for them by name. Request a quick and quiet Douglas DC-8 or DC-9 next time you fly.

When you board the DC-8, you'll enter a world of big jet travel like no other. You'll experience the ultimate in smooth, fast, reliable flight. Did you know the DC-8 was the first jetliner to be designed with fan jet engines as original equipment? And that the DC-8 has flown faster, higher, and farther than any other commercial jet?

Take the new DC-9 to places jets could never go before. Take it on hops as short as 100 miles. Every fleeting minute of the trip will be smoother and quieter and more comfortable than you ever imagined.

Look for a quick, quiet Douglas jet on the following 49 airlines:

Aeronaves de Mexico • Air Afrique • Air Canada • Airlift International • Air New Zealand • Alitalia • Allegheny • Ansett-ANA • Bonanza • Canadian Pacific • Capitol • Caribair • Continental • Delta • Eastern • Garuda Indonesian • Hawaiian • Iberia • Japan • KLM • Korean • Middle East • National • North Central • Northeast • Northwest Orient • Overseas National • Ozark • Pacific Southwest • Pan American • Panagra • Philippine • SAS • Saudi Arabian • Seaboard World • Slick • Southern • Südflug • Swissair • TWA • Trans-Australia • Trans Caribbean • Trans International • Trans-Texas • UTA • United • Varig • Viasa • West Coast.

The Douglas Royal Family of Jets

Sylvania's color tube brightened the whole TV picture. How did it make GT&E look sharp?

It all began in laser research. That's when GT&E scientists found that a rare-earth element —Europium—could be made to produce an unusually brilliant red hue. GT&E's Sylvania subsidiary took over from there. The result: the *color bright 85*™ picture tube.

Sylvania's unique process for applying phosphors to the face of each tube produced the sharpest, most colorful picture in television.

You might say we made everyone take a new look at color TV.

Innovation in communications comes from GT&E. Expect it anytime from any member of the family: General Telephone Operating Companies · General Telephone Directory Company · Automatic Electric · Lenkurt Electric · Sylvania Electric Products · General Telephone & Electronics Laboratories · General Telephone & Electronics International. We're 116,000 strong and dedicated to Total Communications.

Who says gasoline credit cards have to stop with gasoline?

We don't even call ours a credit card. It's the Gulf Travel Card. Because you can use it for almost all of your travel expenses.

You can charge delicious, well-prepared meals at all Holiday Inns of America. And when you and your family are ready to call it a night, your Gulf Travel Card will cover rooms at every one of more than 600 Holiday Inns.

The card also handles all Gulf services and products available at dealers' everywhere in the country ... including NO-NOX® premium gasoline and Gulfpride® Single-G Motor Oil.

So next trip don't pack a lot of cash. Pack a Gulf Travel Card. Pick up an application where your driving takes a turn for the best at the Sign of the Orange Disc.

GULF OIL CORPORATION

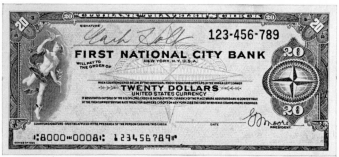

Other travelers checks are every bit as good as <u>First National City Bank's</u>

...until you lose them!

You can cash First National City travelers checks all over the U.S. and abroad—even here in faraway Lima, Peru. But their *big* advantage is a faster refund system.

Other leading travelers checks, like First National City travelers checks, can be cashed all over the world. But if you think all travelers checks are alike, you may be in for a rude shock if you *lose* your checks.

With other leading travelers checks, elaborate and time-consuming inquiries often have to be made. It may be days—even weeks—before you get your money back. Who wants to wait?

But, if you lose First National City travelers checks, you don't have to worry. There are more than 20,000 places around the world authorized to give you a *fast refund—right on the spot!*

First National City travelers checks come from the *leader* in world-wide banking, and have been in use over 60 years. They are known and accepted in more than a *million* shops, hotels, restaurants, air terminals, etc., the world over.

Next time you travel, *insist* on First National City travelers checks.

They cost just one cent per dollar.

First National City Bank Travelers Checks
Sold by banks <u>everywhere</u>

The Redcoats are coming! Again? Again.

Reach for your camera and shoot! This is pure colour, pageantry, the kind of thing you can't see at home. (This is Changing the Guard on Ottawa's Parliament Hill, by the Regiment of Canadian Guards.) We're willing to bet you thought this sort of thing only went on at London's Buckingham Palace.

Well, it goes on just north of the border, too...every single summer day. And you don't need a visa or passport to see it! Clip this coupon for free maps and booklets about our exciting (red-coated and otherwise) events in Canada this summer.

Canada!

600 miles takes one hour up here,

or all day down here.

An hour's rest in a Boeing jet can take you as far as a long day's drive in your car.

Compared to driving, you gain a *day* for every hour you fly aboard a Boeing jet. Boeing jets give you extra time to spend *there*. They bring every part of America, and all the world, within easy reach.

And if you've never flown before, you'll enjoy an exhilarating new experience.

You'll discover why even veteran air travelers find Boeing jet flight the most enjoyable part of their trips.

Boeing jets have carried more than 120 million passengers. They serve 301 cities in 121 countries, and average a takeoff or landing every 13 seconds, around the clock. Boeing jets have set more speed and distance records than all other jetliners combined.

Next trip, fly Boeing.

Now flying Boeing jets: *Air Congo, Air France, Air-India, Air Madagascar, All Nippon, American, Ansett-ANA, Avianca, BOAC, BWIA, Braniff, Continental, Eastern, El Al, Ethiopian, Flying Tiger, Indian, Iran Air, Irish, JAL, Japan Domestic, Lufthansa, MEA, National, Northeast, Northwest, Olympic, PIA, PSA, Pacific Northern, Pan American, Qantas, Sabena, Saudi Arabian, South African, TAA, TAP, TWA, United, Varig, Wardair Canada, Western, World.* In service later: *Aerolineas Argentinas, Air Asia, Alaska, American Flyers, Braathens, Caledonian, Frontier, Mexicana, Northern Consolidated, Pacific, Piedmont, Southern Air Transport, Wien Air Alaska.*

BOEING JETS
World's first family of jets: 707 · 720 · 727 · 737

They're cleaning our windshields on the 34th floor

Some of today's new skyscrapers have much in common with our Mustangs and Mercurys. The glass for both was made by Ford.

Ford has the largest single flat-glass facility in the world. Our total yearly production is equal to a sheet of glass of almost one-quarter of a *billion* square feet. Glass used for skyscraper walls, insulating windows, mirrors, shower doors. Even glass for bullet-resistant windows in armored cars.

Today, we go wherever new ideas take us.

Our Philco subsidiary designed NASA's Gemini Mission Control Center. A new electronic teaching aid, "Savvy," is helping children think logically. Our idea of two front axles for pick-up trucks means a smoother ride.

A company of bold new ideas in many varied fields—that's what the familiar blue Ford oval stands for today.

"What's that make us, Frank, windshield wipers?"

The only guidebook to America that snitches on motels, hotels, resorts and restaurants.

good ★

very good ★★

excellent ★★★

outstanding ★★★★

one of the best in country ★★★★★

✔ unusually good value

We run an honest guidebook. There are no advertisements in it.

Nobody can buy his way in.

The only way a place can get into the Mobil Travel Guide is if we go out and inspect it and rate it.

And nobody knows when one of our Inspectors is going to show up.

When he gets in a motel or hotel room, he checks it out like nobody else would.

He bounces on the bed, runs the hot water, flushes the toilet.

He turns on the TV, the air conditioner, the heat, everything he can get his hands on.

Then he turns everything off.

He lies down on the bed. And he keeps very quiet.

He listens. For noises from other rooms, dripping faucets, anything that could disturb a guest's peace and quiet.

And when he finishes his inspection, he judges the place as honestly as he can. Fairly, but strictly.

The same goes for the way he inspects restaurants.

He notices everything. Cleanliness. The grades of meat and butter used. Whether fish and vegetables are stored separately. How food is prepared. All the things that make the difference between a good kitchen and a poor one.

When he finishes his inspection, he puts it all down in a detailed report to our central office. His findings are compared with previous inspections and comments from Mobil Travel Guide users (we get about 7,500 every year). And after all these factors are carefully gone over, we give a place a final rating.

We're the only guidebook to America that does it this way. With on-the-spot inspections of over 21,000 motels, hotels, resorts and restaurants. (And reinspections of every one, every year. In case a place lets things slip. Or improves.)

And the ratings aren't all you get in the Mobil Travel Guide.

You get an interstate highway map, a mileage map (that gives you distances between places), and city street maps.

You get a lot of useful tips on traveling.

And you get Guest Certificates that save you money on local attractions and things you would probably see and do anyway. (Most people find that the Mobil Travel Guide more than pays for itself this way.)

The Mobil Travel Guide covers the entire U.S. (except Alaska and Hawaii) in 7 regional editions, at $1.95* each. There are about 500 pages in each edition.

The easiest way to get one is at any Mobil Station.

Or you can mail this coupon.

Every year, more and more people travel with the Mobil Travel Guide.

In fact, last year more people bought it than any other U.S. guide.

We checked up on that, too.

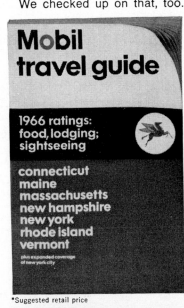

Mobil travel guide

1966 ratings: food, lodging; sightseeing

connecticut
maine
massachusetts
new hampshire
new york
rhode island
vermont

plus expanded coverage of new york city

*Suggested retail price

GENERAL ELECTRIC HAS IT!

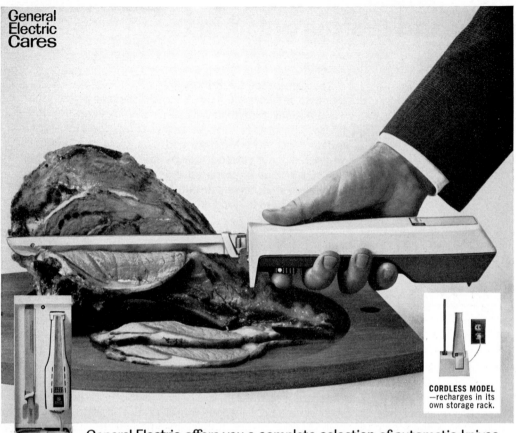

General
Electric
Cares

CORDLESS MODEL
—recharges in its
own storage rack.

CORD MODELS—
like this, with
rack for wall or
drawer storage.

General Electric offers you a complete selection of automatic knives, in a full price range. Quality knives. With features like hollow-ground stainless steel blades and tungsten carbide edges which stay sharp. Cord or cordless, they're the best – they're by General Electric!

General Electric Company, Housewares Division, Bridgeport, Conn. 06602

TOASTS—AND BAKES! General Electric's Toast-R-Oven* toasts both sides at once. Top-browns... bakes potatoes, frozen foods, and pies... reheats foods, too!

*TM General Electric Company

WHAT A CLEANER! The General Electric Portable Cleaner is less than 12 in. long, yet powerful enough to clean everywhere — home, car, workshop. All attachments.

ALL STAINLESS STEEL...completely automatic! Dial mild, medium or strong; light signals when ready... coffee stays hot, reheats without reperking. 2-9 cup capacity.

Progress Is Our Most Important Product

GENERAL Ⓖⓔ **ELECTRIC**

Hospitals were once looked upon as places for patients whose chances of recovery had all but slipped away.

Now, people go to hospitals to live.

Today, hospitals have become centers of hope where professional skills, medicines, diagnostic aids and equipment are concentrated to increase and hasten chances of recovery.

Thanks to doctors and hospital staffs, more and more patients walk out of hospitals now, relieved of ailments that were once almost always fatal.

Physicians and hospital staffs place increasing reliance on new and better medicines—including many developed by Parke-Davis—to help people live longer and more healthful lives.

PARKE-DAVIS
BETTER MEDICINES FOR A BETTER WORLD

1866 1966
100th
ANNIVERSARY

 **Hawaii will go a long way to please you. And so will we.**

With cuisine by the incomparable *Maxim's of Paris*.

With a fine film, on most flights from California.

In fact, with the same luxurious international-style service that pampers passengers on their way to 128 cities in 88 lands on 6 continents.

So when would you like to leave for Hawaii? We have more flights from the West Coast than anybody else. Choose from three classes from Los Angeles or San Francisco. First Class President Special, Rainbow Economy, or Thrift. (No Thrift if you're leaving from Seattle/Tacoma or Portland.)

Ready to go? Leave the details to a Pan Am Travel Agent or call your closest Pan Am Office.

All the way to Hawaii with us, you'll have the good feeling that comes from flying the very best there is.

That's a pleasant thought, too.

World's most experienced airline
First on the Pacific   First on the Atlantic
First in Latin America First 'Round the World

A great new camera takes the guesswork out of fine photography

New Honeywell Pentax Spotmatic camera measures light precisely for perfectly exposed pictures.

The magnificent new Honeywell Pentax Spotmatic is simplicity itself to operate, yet it will never fail to delight you with what it (and you) can do. Because it has a wealth of professional know-how *built in*, the Spotmatic lets you step up to the world of fine photography without forcing you to acquire and master a roomful of equipment.

The secret is a remarkable through-the-lens exposure metering system that is both automatic and uncannily precise. It assures you that you will never again lose a once-in-a-lifetime picture because of poor exposure. It gives you absolute control over the most difficult lighting situations. And it saves you time and film because you can forget about those extra shots "just to make sure." With the superb new

Spotmatic camera, you *are* sure. **Here's how it works.** The Spotmatic's metering system reads the light coming through the taking aperture of the lens—*the same light the film sees.* Its highly sensitive cadmium sulfide sensors can't be fooled by light that does not reach the film. An ordinary exposure meter *will* read such extraneous light, and the result will be an approximate—and often disappointing—exposure. Expert photographers know how to compensate for difficult situations, but now, the amazing Spotmatic does the work for you, giving you professional quality exposures time after time.

Fast, foolproof operation. You simply set the Spotmatic for the film you're using (color slide, color print, or black and white) and

choose a shutter speed—1/125 or 1/250 for most average pictures. Then, you compose, focus, and flip the meter switch "on." Turning the diaphragm ring will center an easy-to-see needle in the eye-level viewfinder window. When it's centered, you shoot—confident that you've made a perfectly exposed picture. It's that easy! And, you've composed, focused, adjusted lens opening and shot *without removing the Spotmatic from your eye.*

Lightweight, compact, and magnificently built to deliver a lifetime of pleasure, the Spotmatic has everything you want in a fine 35mm camera, yet it sells for just $289.50. See it soon at your Honeywell Pentax Dealer's, or mail the coupon for illustrated literature. Other Pentax models start at $149.50.

Honeywell takes the guesswork out of fine photography.

Your State Farm agent can give you the same good deal on nine room ranch insurance

as he does on nine passenger station-wagon insurance.

If you're like most homeowners, you already know that a homeowners policy gives you all the protection you'll probably ever need for your home and belongings (Even coverage in case of lawsuits.) You may already have such a policy.

What you may not realize is that rates for homeowners policies vary considerably from company to company. So that, whether you own your home or rent, it will pay you to check with State Farm, the number one company in the sale of homeowners policies.

You'll find the name of your nearby State Farm agent in the Yellow Pages. (He's the same friendly professional who probably saves you money on car insurance.)

State Farm Fire and Casualty Company. Home Office: Bloomington, Ill.

In Texas, savings on State Farm Homeowners Policies have been returned as dividends. In Mississippi, we offer a Comprehensive Dwelling Policy similar to our Homeowners Policy.

100,000 lakes: choose yours

Manitoba has over 100,000 lakes and countless beaches to welcome the summer visitor. Here in Canada's great outdoor playground, you can enjoy all the pleasures of summer — soft, warm sands, sparkling blue waters, skimming along on water skis, power boating or sailing. Bring your picnic basket. Or barbecue. Some of the more popular beaches are just a stone's throw from Winnipeg, the lively provincial capital. At the larger resort areas, the beaches are lifeguard supervised. Experience that good-to-be-alive feeling in Manitoba's exhilarating climate. For full vacation particulars, just send the coupon.

TOURIST DEVELOPMENT BRANCH
6432 Legislative Building,
Winnipeg, Manitoba, Canada

Please send free literature to:

NAME_____

ADDRESS_____

CITY_____

STATE_____ ZIP CODE_____

MANITOBA

CANADA'S VACATION HEARTLAND

The Thunderbird Touch:
A Stereo-Tape System...Highway Pilot Control...
Overhead Safety Control Panel

Thunderbird Town Hardtop

This is Thunderbird 1966!

A new Stereo-Tape System is but one of many exclusive options. It surrounds you with music from four high-fidelity stereo speakers.

Highway Pilot Control is another. Mounted at your fingertips, within the spokes of the steering wheel, Highway Pilot lets you set, retard, and resume your cruising speed at the touch of a button.

And the Overhead Safety Control Panel, standard on Town Landau and Town Hardtop models, has lights to remind you if fuel is low, a door ajar, or to fasten seatbelts—and an Emergency Flasher that sets four exterior lights blinking. Thunderbird 1966 will touch your driving with total luxury. Drive one today.

Thunderbird

UNIQUE IN ALL THE WORLD

NATIONAL GEOGRAPHIC

THE NATIONAL GEOGRAPHIC MAGAZINE VOL. 129, NO. 6 COPYRIGHT © 1966 BY NATIONAL GEOGRAPHIC SOCIETY, WASHINGTON, D. C. INTERNATIONAL COPYRIGHT SECURED

One Man's London

By ALLAN C. FISHER, JR.
Senior Assistant Editor

Illustrations by National Geographic photographer JAMES P. BLAIR

MY WIFE MARY is not a jealous woman, but we did go through a period when she spoke darkly of "that rival of mine." At such times I would be packing a bag, intent on putting home and children behind me. Invariably, with candor if not tact, I would analyze for Mary her rival's appeal: good looks, irresistible charm, maturity, character, individuality.

Oh, but I was enamored! I still am. But my wife has been tolerant and understanding. She knows how it is with a traveling man. Sometimes he loses his heart to a certain place, one that lures him back again and again. And for some years now I have been totally, irrevocably, and unabashedly in love with London.

Let me concede at once that other cities outscore London in certain winsome municipal qualities. Paris is more beautiful, Rome friendlier, Rio de Janeiro more colorful, New York more exciting. No matter. In the aggregate, stolid old London tops them all. Great Britain's capital and premier city is one of those magical places that somehow manage to be greater than the sum of their parts.

743

Symbols of tradition in a changing city, mounted Life Guards brighten a foggy March morning.

GATEWAY TO LONDON TOWN, *Tower Bridge spans the glassy Thames. Domed St. Paul's Cathedral shares the skyline with the 582-foot Post Office Tower, Britain's tallest building, which beams telephone and television signals from its waist. The two structures, one old and beloved, the other new and boldly modern, symbolize the dual personality of the capital.*

744   KODACHROME © N.G.S.

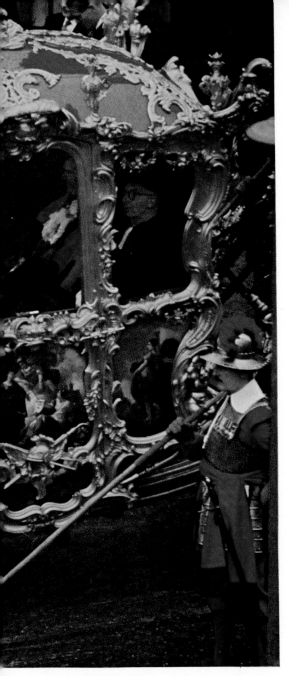

Annual "Show" of the red-robed Lord Mayor of London follows his election. His domain, the famous square-mile City in the heart of London, has been ruled by a mayor since 1192. Each year it pays the Crown a rent of six horseshoes, 61 horseshoe nails, a hatchet, and a pruning tool called a bill-hook. Pikemen of the Honourable Artillery Company, chartered by Henry VIII in 1537, flank the resplendent 4¾-ton coach.

Reflections of Remembrance Sunday: Backs turned to the ceremony and mirrors held high, girls catch a glimpse of their Queen as she lays a wreath on the Cenotaph, the monument honoring Britain's war dead.

Not that London's sum, in terms of sheer physical size and complexity, ever fails to impress. Greater London covers about 720 square miles. Here live more than eight million people, a population exceeded by only two other cities, Tokyo and New York.

This year London will play host to nearly two-and-a-half million foreign visitors, including 700,000 Americans. England's old colossus astride the Thames will house them in some 600 hotels. It will offer them an astonishing number of civic amenities: 124 museums and galleries, 39 legitimate theaters, 12 symphony orchestras. Some 200 principal banks will happily divest the visitors of their dollars and other foreign exchange.

Yet, despite its jumbo statistics and sprawling dimensions, London remains a city of distinct neighborhoods and of many secluded residential pockets—the narrow, hidden street, the little court, the old square. For a great city its character is surprisingly intimate.

Blue Plaques Blaze a Literary Trail

I had long wanted my wife to know her old rival. So recently we bade our maturing children a firm goodbye and, free as mud larks, flew to London for a prolonged stay. We rented a flat in Mayfair and began a memorable tasting of my favorite city: its landmarks, institutions, neighborhoods, pubs, museums, galleries (pictorial map, pages 750-52).

After a time Mary said: "This city is too big. Too crowded. And the climate—an absolute horror most of the time! But I'm almost as smitten with the place as you are."

My feeling for London is a compound of many things. Like most visitors I enjoy pilgrimages to Westminster Abbey and St. Paul's Cathedral, pre-eminent monuments to a great faith and a great people. I often go to the Mother of Parliaments, surely a shrine for every free man. Moreover, I dote on the archaic pageantry associated with Britain's monarchy and other old institutions, such as the office of the Lord Mayor of London. In these things I am typical. But much of my appetite for London is individual and personal.

I am an inveterate plaque spotter. The municipal government identifies many historic and literary landmarks with blue plaques, and I am seldom happier in London than when strolling the streets with one wary eye on the traffic and the other alert for telltale flashes of blue on the walls of buildings. Often I have experienced moving moments by chancing upon a site associated with one of my literary heroes: the home of William Blake

Winged archer known to Londoners as Eros, Greek god of love, actually represents the Angel of Christian Charity. The figure surveys bustling Piccadilly Circus from a bronze fountain memorializing the seventh Earl of Shaftesbury.

Broad Shaftesbury Avenue with its many theaters is but one of half a dozen streets radiating from the circus. The capital today enjoys a theater boom; nearly any night Londoners can take their pick of some three dozen plays, from the classics to exciting works by new dramatists.

"How do I get to Buckingham Palace?" A bobby provides the answer. His nickname honors Sir Robert Peel, founder of the Metropolitan Police Force. On the theory that force begets force, bobbies do not carry revolvers except on rare occasions.

on South Molton Street, the house in Kensington where Thackeray wrote *Vanity Fair,* the building on Doughty Street where Dickens penned *Oliver Twist.* Dickens House is now a museum, as are former homes of Carlyle, Keats, and Samuel Johnson.*

If one cares to embark upon a literary binge in London, it is quite easy to do so in a literal as well as a figurative sense. The city offers first-class pubs dedicated to the memories of such celebrated patrons as Pepys, Dr. Johnson, Boswell, Dickens, and Tennyson.

Green Islands: the "Lungs of London"

I am also a fancier of London parks. It seems I never can get enough of these magnificent open spaces, aptly called "the lungs of London." Sometimes on good days (in London any day when it doesn't rain is a good day) I pick a park at random, then wander through it as aimlessly as the addlepated pelicans that stroll beside the lake in St. James's Park. If the summer sun is out, thousands of Londoners lounge on the greensward, their pale faces turned, like Thomas Moore's sunflower, toward their god in the sky. Sometimes I join them, and I try not to watch the entwined young lovers, probably the boldest on public display in Europe.

Londoners owe some of their best parkland to the penchant of their monarchs for hunting. Royal decrees set aside preserves that ultimately became public parks, green islands in an ocean of stone and brick, among them Hyde, St. James's, Green, and Regent's. They give the central part of the city sweep and spaciousness and a bit of a countrified look.

Actually the Crown still retains title to the 5,684 acres in London's Royal Parks, but the public enjoys this land as freely as it does the 7,300 acres in the splendid park system administered by the Greater London Council (GLC), or the innumerable squares and commons, usually of two acres or less, maintained and manicured by the 32 boroughs.

In my career as a parkophile, I think I have visited most of the GLC's green islands. My particular delight is the Old English Garden at Golders Hill, where color riots in a setting as formal and stylized as a minuet. The last time I was there, superintendent Herbert Pocock discussed with me what to plant after taking up his tulips.

"The superintendent plants what he likes," said Mr. Pocock, "but if he is a good man, he gets ideas from the public. Someone may say to him, 'I notice you have no marigolds of a tangerine variety,' so maybe he puts some in. We try to make these parks what the people who use them want."

Some of the best-beloved "lungs" are the smallest: 6-acre Normand Park, built on a bombed site, and 7½-acre Hammersmith Park, with its little man-made waterfall. Both parks adjoin housing developments; mothers and children crowd the park pathways, seeking nature's solace and benison.

"The Englishman now, he loves his garden, he does indeed," says Mr. Pocock. "And if he can't have one, he likes to be near a garden."

Or even near a window box, Mr. Pocock
(Continued on page 757)

*See "Landmarks of Literary England," by Leo A. Borah, NATIONAL GEOGRAPHIC, September, 1955.

LONDON COLOSSUS ASTRIDE THE THAME

LONDON ADDRESS BOOK: NUMBERED
RED SQUARES SHOW FIFTY PLAQUE-
MARKED SITES WHERE FAMOUS
PEOPLE LIVED AND WORKED

1. SIR EDWIN ARNOLD, POET (5A)
2. SIR HERBERT ASQUITH, STATESMAN (2D)
3. JOHN LOGIE BAIRD, TELEVISION PIONEER (2E)
4. MICHAEL WILLIAM BALFE, MUSICIAN (2C)
5. SIR JAMES BARRIE, DRAMATIST, ROBERT
   ADAM, ARCHITECT, JOHN GALSWORTHY,
   AUTHOR, AND THOMAS HOOD, POET (3E)
6. WILLIAM BLAKE, POET (2D)
7. GEORGE BORROW, AUTHOR (4B)
8. JAMES BOSWELL, AUTHOR (2D)
9. ELIZABETH BARRETT BROWNING, POET (2D)
10. EDMUND BURKE, STATESMAN (3E)
11. FANNY BURNEY, AUTHOR (3D)
12. THOMAS CARLYLE, ESSAYIST (5C)
13. GILBERT KEITH CHESTERTON, POET (4A)

14. CLIVE OF INDIA, SOLDIER (3D)
15. WILLIAM WILKIE COLLINS, AUTHOR (2C)
16. CHARLES DICKENS, AUTHOR (2F)
17. BENJAMIN DISRAELI, STATESMAN (2F)
18. JOHN DRYDEN, POET (3E)
19. WILLIAM ETTY, ARTIST (3E)
20. MICHAEL FARADAY, SCIENTIST (2D)
21. FORMER PRIME MINISTERS RESIDENCE (3E)
    GLADSTONE, PITT, AND STANLEY
22. BENJAMIN FRANKLIN, STATESMAN (3E)
23. THOMAS GAINSBOROUGH, ARTIST (3E)
24. SIR WILLIAM S. GILBERT, LIBRETTIST (4B)
25. GEORGE F. HANDEL, COMPOSER (3D)
26. HEINRICH HEINE, POET (3E)
27. HENRY JAMES, AUTHOR (4B)
28. SAMUEL JOHNSON, LEXICOGRAPHER (2F)
29. RUDYARD KIPLING, AUTHOR (3E)
30. JENNY LIND, SINGER (5B)
31. GUGLIELMO MARCONI, INVENTOR (2A)
32. JOHN STUART MILL, PHILOSOPHER (4B)

33. GEORGE MOORE, AUTHOR (4D)
34. WOLFGANG AMADEUS MOZART, COMPOSER
35. NAPOLEON III, EMPEROR OF FRANCE (3E)
36. ADMIRAL LORD NELSON (3D)
37. SIR ISAAC NEWTON, PHILOSOPHER (3E)
38. SIR HUBERT PARRY, MUSICIAN (4B)
39. SAMUEL PEPYS, DIARIST (3E)
40. SIR JOSHUA REYNOLDS, ARTIST (3E)
41. DANTE GABRIEL ROSSETTI, POET, AND
    ALGERNON CHARLES SWINBURNE, POET (5C)
42. JOHN RUSKIN, MAN OF LETTERS (1E)
43. CAPTAIN ROBERT F. SCOTT, EXPLORER (5C)
44. THOMAS HARDY, AUTHOR, AND
    GEORGE BERNARD SHAW, AUTHOR (3F)
45. RICHARD B. SHERIDAN, DRAMATIST (3D)
46. WILLIAM M. THACKERAY, AUTHOR (4B)
47. ANTHONY TROLLOPE, AUTHOR (2C)
48. SIR ROBERT WALPOLE, STATESMAN (3D)
49. JOHN WESLEY, EVANGELIST (2G)
50. JAMES A. McNEILL WHISTLER, ARTIST (5C)

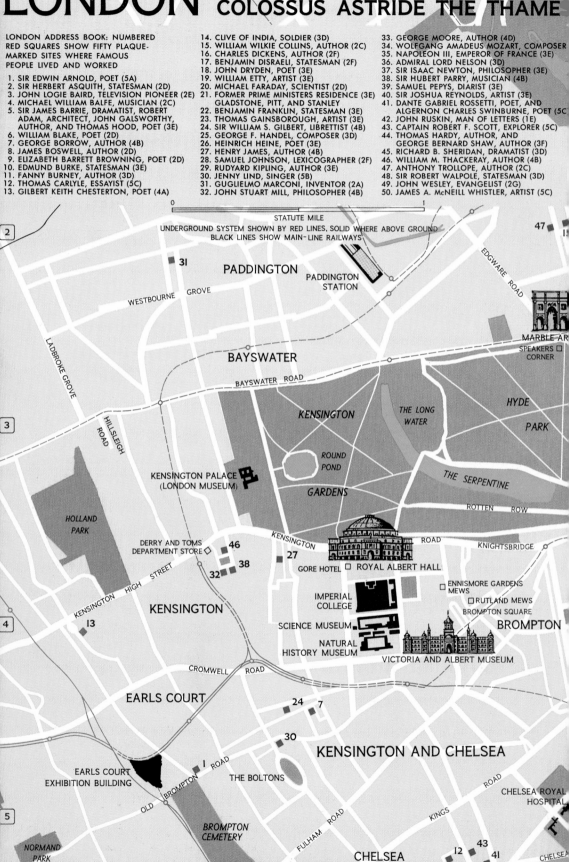

STATUTE MILE

UNDERGROUND SYSTEM SHOWN BY RED LINES, SOLID WHERE ABOVE GROUND
BLACK LINES SHOW MAIN-LINE RAILWAYS

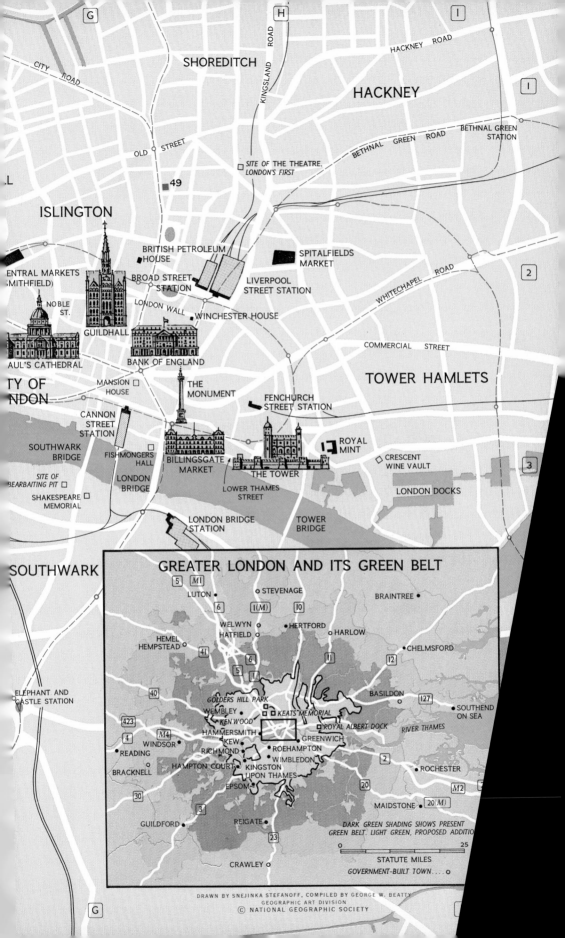

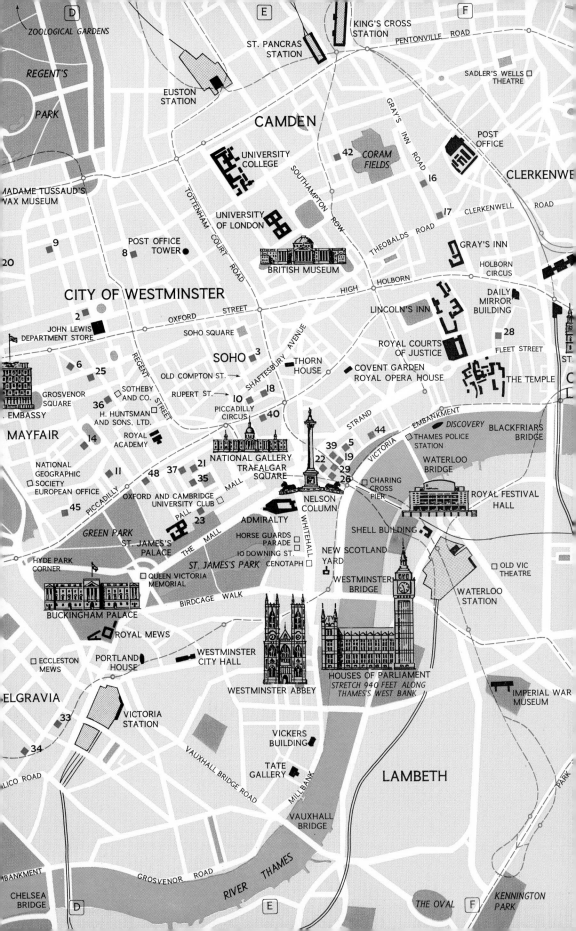

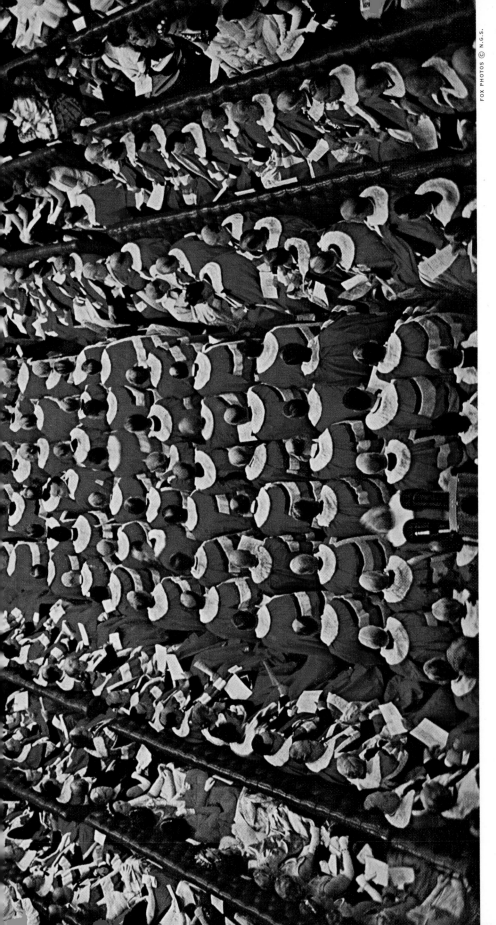

With full panoply of state, Queen Elizabeth II opens Parliament from her gilded throne in the House of Lords. She wears her Imperial State Crown and ermine-and-velvet Parliamentary Robe with 18-foot train. Bewigged High Court Judges and peers in scarlet robes fill the well of the Chamber. Members of the House of Commons (out of picture in foreground) stand behind them. Ambassadors, clergymen, peeresses, and guests occupy side benches and galleries. In Britain's constitutional monarchy, Parliament wields the power, but only the sovereign can convene a session of the legislature.

EKTACHROMES BY JAMES P. BLAIR © N.G.S.

Traditional cry, "Wench!" brings a hasty refill by a waitress when a cup runs dry at the Elizabethan Room in the Gore Hotel. Diners crowd around a community table laden with courses of roast suckling pig, peacock pie, boar's head, and syllabub—a dessert of cream, spices, and wine. "M'lords and ladies, prithee silence," requests a serving maid each time the strolling minstrel sings a ballad. Decor and menu recall the days of Shakespeare, Marlowe, and "Good Queen Bess."

"London is a man's town." Poet Henry Van Dyke's words ring true in the Oxford and Cambridge University Club. Women may hold associate membership but cannot enter the main building. In the South Library only whispers and rustled pages disturb the silence.

Wine like molten gold: Peter Thompson checks the quality of sherry in the Crescent Vault, an underground storeroom that the Port of London Authority maintains for wine merchants.

might have said. London abounds in colorful window boxes, and I like that. You may find them on the grimy brick façade of a docker's home or the imposing front of a rich and powerful bank in the financial sector. Tulips, daffodils, and narcissi, favorites in spring, yield to geraniums, petunias, and hydrangeas.

One day, not recognizing some flowers, I struck up a conversation with a window-box gardener in Mayfair. It turned out that the flowers were primula and salvia, and the gardener was worried about them.

"Raw weather. Beastly, really. Don't know as they can stand it," he said, and a farmer threatened with loss of his principal money crop could not have been more concerned.

It often seems that some kind of flower show is being held each day in London during the summer. These shows range from an improbable but charming one put on by the porters and fishmongers of Billingsgate, the historic fish market, to the very elaborate and impressive Chelsea Flower Show, attended on opening day by everyone who is someone —or who would like to become someone.

London's most unusual gardens, 100 feet above congested Kensington High Street, cover 1¼ acres atop Derry & Toms Depart-

ment Store. Americans seeking the gardens invariably tell cab drivers, "Take me to Tom and Jerry's." But they end up in the right place, delightedly exploring the Spanish, Tudor, or Woodland Garden. In the latter, which has a stream, I parted some bushes one day and found myself in a startled confrontation with a harlequin duck that had spiraled down to the rooftop for rest and refreshment. He paddled off, squawking raucous criticism.

Seeking the Rainbow's End in Chelsea

For a man who prefers the more sedentary pleasures, I display a remarkable avidity for walking when in London. There is much to delight the eye on side streets. Sometimes I wander through the byways of Chelsea, the city's arty area, feeling, as I pass between tiny row houses painted in vivid hues, as though I'm nearing the end of the rainbow. At other times I explore old neighborhoods that retain their fenced and tidily kept private squares, such as Brompton Square.

It's ultrafashionable in today's London to live in a mews, or area of horse stables. Of course the horses have long since moved out, and the coach rooms and lofts have been thoroughly—and expensively—renovated. 757

National Geographic, June, 1966

London abounds in these mews, tucked away behind the Victorian edifices they once served. Some have been refurbished to the point of poshness, such as Rutland Mews and Ennismore Gardens Mews, both near the Imperial College of Science and Technology, and Eccleston Mews in Belgravia.

I have a British acquaintance who, after years of country living in Surrey, paid a stiff price for a home in Kensington's Ennismore Mews. He had dreaded the lack of neighborly spirit, the unfriendly aloofness, of city living.

"My first Sunday in the mews," he told me later, "blast me if all of my neighbors didn't drag chairs and tables out on the cobblestones and sit around sipping apéritifs. Just like Paris, y'know. Later we played darts against a team from another mews. 'Straordinary!"

The Royal Mews is one of the few in London that still have four-footed residents. You can visit these stables behind Buckingham Palace and see the Coronation Coach, a masterpiece of the carriage-maker's dying art. Royal coachmen will explain things to you—and I wish you luck. The coachmen are Irish; I couldn't understand half of what they said.

Horses Enjoyed the Pause That Refreshes

Nearly all London's horses are gone, but I am charmed by the fact that a number of their drinking troughs remain. You find them occasionally along main thoroughfares. Most of these hardy survivors, shaped like fountains, remain impressively handsome, like an elaborately tiled one on Pimlico Road that I particularly admire. Many offer drinking facilities for humans as well as horses, and a number bear engraving dedicating them to the memory of some horse-loving person.

Water flows in a few of these troughs, but most survive as nostalgic Victoriana, more flavor for an already flavorful city.

No one ever tasted London with more appreciation than Samuel Johnson, who declared, "When a man is tired of London, he is tired of life." Johnson reveled in the vitality of the city; he was not one to confine his forays to fashionable areas, nor should you.

The irrepressible Cockney, his heritage rich on his tongue, can still be found in the East End, though the distinctive manner of speech is no longer commonplace. Take the tube to Bethnal Green Station, then stroll down Bethnal Green Road, where the produce stalls seem little changed from the street marts of the Cockney costers at the turn of the century. Bins overflow with vegetables brought during the predawn hours from Spitalfields Market, hardly a mile away. Women block the sidewalks as they gossip in pairs, while little children tug at their skirts.

Stepping on rhubarb stalks, breathing air that seems gray and clotted, you mingle with descendants of the original Cockney costers. You smell the fish and meats laid out for the flies and the sun and the housewives. "S. R. Kelly Live Eel and Meat Pies"—the sign catches your eye as you continue down this tawdry yet vital street. Listening to the talk and laughter, you begin to understand the inimitable Cockney spirit celebrated in such memorable shows as *Oliver!, Fings Ain't Wot They Used T' Be,* and *My Fair Lady.*

"Cockney is still alive, but dying," a young woman shopper tells you while the coster wraps her fish. "Take me; I don't speak at

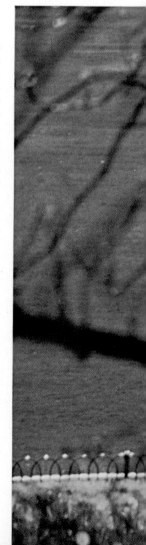

"Sweet lovers love the spring," wrote William Shakespeare. Taking advantage of a warm March day, a couple lolls on the grass in Hyde Park. Once the hunting field of monarchs, the park has been the personal playground of Londoners since King Charles I opened it to the public about 1637.

Hyde Park adjoins Kensington Gardens to form a square mile of green acres that gives city-dwellers one of their many bits of breathing room. Bird watchers peer up at trees; anglers fish in The Serpentine; riders canter on the sandy track; and anyone looking for an argument hastens to Speakers Corner at the northeast end of the park. There, orators sound off on politics, religion, or any subject that suits their fancy. The audience talks back, and both parties delight in the repartee.

work—or to you—the way I do at home. But we Cockneys are great talkers. We say what we mean and mean what we say, always in negatives, like 'You don't 'arf look a treat,' which means you look great. Or at the market, when my mother is looking over some nice meat pies, she'd say 'not 'arf nice.'

"We still have our children 'done,' meaning baptized. It's a big social occasion. Time for a chitchat. Cockneys all come from big families, and they have big families of their own. Sons and daughters will live with mum forever, so generations of large families grow up together. If someone dies, you have to put on a good funeral with lots of flowers, because the neighbors judge everything. Weddings have to be big too, and on Saturday, the established day. Oh, I'm proud I'm a Cockney."

Across town, in but not *of* the fashionable West End, lies another colorful enclave, Soho.

It is primarily a place for buying things, not a place of residence, and to most people it is a place to buy entertainment. Soho abounds in strip-tease clubs, nightclubs, coffeehouses, pubs, motion-picture theaters, betting shops. It also contains some of the finest restaurants in London. And it continues to be an area of small businesses: printers, shoe menders, sign painters, tailors, palmists.

Soho is London's Bohemian quarter, with a reputation for general naughtiness that has survived the city's war on prostitution.

The languages one hears on the streets suggest a new Babel: African dialects, French, Italian, American hipster slang. But the Soho habitués with the most bizarre appearance are some of London's own: the Mods, those young men with the tight, foppish clothes and the long, girlish hair.

"Soho used to be a wild place when the

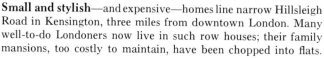
Small and stylish—and expensive—homes line narrow Hillsleigh Road in Kensington, three miles from downtown London. Many well-to-do Londoners now live in such row houses; their family mansions, too costly to maintain, have been chopped into flats.

760

Homes for thousands, high-rise apartments of Alton East and Alton West lift above the village of Roehampton and its spired church. Six miles from the heart of London, the development houses low-income families. One-story bungalows scattered through the parklike grounds provide accommodations for the elderly.

Town planning session brings prospect of relief for the crowded capital. The Borough Council of Thetford, 72 miles north of London, considers a redevelopment plan described by an architect of the Greater London Council. The GLC and towns outside London cooperate in building housing and industrial complexes to attract families and businesses from the city.

girls were on the street," says Niall, the door-man at a strip club on Old Compton Street. "A lot gayer. It's just a place to work now."

"Nothing to do of an evening here," says Joe the Flower Boy, who pushes a cart on Rupert Street. "It's no Chicago, is it? It's the name that draws people here, just the name."

And while one talks the traffic rumbles endlessly through the streets: Rolls-Royces, bikes, scooters, junk heaps driven by bearded beatniks, the black motorcycles and discreet unmarked Zodiacs of the police, the taxis and chauffeur-driven Rovers of the tourists.

Nearly everyone criticizes London's size and congestion—and has done so for the past 400 years. In 1580 Queen Elizabeth I, aghast that the old warren harbored 140,000 people, forbade construction of additional houses in the walled city or within three miles of its gates. No one took the order very seriously, but King James I later enforced it; he also ordered all noblemen who did not have busi-ness in the city to remain at their country homes unless Parliament was in session.

The king, and succeeding generations of wishful-thinking town planners, might as well have tried to restrain the tide on the Thames. London continued to grow outward from its ancient Roman center, expanding with the vigor of a mold in an ideal laboratory culture. Today, after engulfing many former subur-ban communities, the metropolis covers 620 square miles, if you count only the area ad-ministered by the Greater London Council, the 32 boroughs, and the City. More realis-tically, the metropolis can be said to encom-pass an additional 100 square miles of almost continuous development.

This growth has brought London to the boundaries of the Green Belt, a preserve, mostly of natural field and heath, held as soul-satisfying elbow room for confined urbanites. Totaling 840 square miles, the preserve now encircles the city like a constrictive girdle.

The pinch has been felt. Now, as never before, London is practicing girth control.

Heirloom hat of hard leather, passed from father to son, protects a porter carrying fish in Billingsgate's 1,000-year-old market.

Bearing ceremonial sculls, Thames watermen march around the tables when the Fishmongers' Company gathers in its grand hall for the annual presentation of Doggett's Coat and Badge. The guild, one of London's oldest, no longer insists that members be fish merchants, but it still samples seafood in Billingsgate to ensure no bad fish is sold.

Awarding of coat and badge dates from 1715, when actor Thomas Doggett offered a prize to the winner of a rowing race from London to Chelsea bridges.

All agree that the city must not "burst the Green Belt."

London, like some other cosmopolitan capitals, notably Budapest and Madrid, does not want to grow either in area or population. Although the London skyline boasts some impressive new skyscrapers, laws now severely restrict industrial and office construction anywhere in the city.

Other laws encourage—indeed, prod—companies and individuals to seek their fortunes outside Greater London. To accommodate this "overspill," as the planners call London's displaced persons, the national government built eight new towns around London, all at a minimum distance of 30 miles from the mother city. Twenty-five existing towns, 30 to 100 miles from the metropolis, signed agreements with the Greater London Council to absorb additional people and businesses and were designated "expanding towns."

London Grows at Expense of Other Areas

More than concern for the Green Belt dictated these bold control measures. The capital has long dominated all southeast England and, as a natural magnet, attracts people from all over Great Britain. For booming London this means greater congestion, and for the rest of the country a loss of economic opportunities. Britain, a small nation, no longer can tolerate this growing imbalance.

At last count, the GLC's Industrial Centre had moved 214 firms out of London and was negotiating moves with an additional 155.

"As you can imagine, in an old city there are a lot of industries that are badly located," said John Hartley, of the Centre. "They become nonconforming industries, in our jargon. We go to these firms and preach the gospel of moving out of London. We can only use persuasion to get them out, but if they will listen, we can give

762

Amid a galaxy of artificial stars, the City of Birmingham Symphony Orchestra plays for an audience seated across the water at London's Kenwood Lakeside. The orchestra shell needs no amplification system; the water acts as a sounding board.

He leaped to freedom: Russian dancer Rudolf Nureyev asked asylum in the West in 1961. One of the world's most acclaimed artists, he lives today in London and appears regularly as a guest with the Royal Ballet. Here he soars above the stage of the Royal Opera House, Covent Garden.

1086, at the time of the compilation of the Domesday Book. For centuries the town enjoyed modest growth. But Thetford declined after the dissolution of the monasteries by Henry VIII. A few years ago its population had dwindled to precisely what it had been nearly 900 years earlier, a scant 4,000 people.

That proved enough to stir the town fathers. With more unanimity than they had known in a long time, they came to the GLC and asked that their aged community be reborn with displaced Londoners.

Boom Hits Thomas Paine's Home Town

Thetford is the birthplace of Thomas Paine, the firebrand pamphleteer of the American and French Revolutions, and the little garden in front of the municipal building displays a controversial American-donated statue of Tom. Dramatically, he brandishes in one upraised hand a quill, but in the opinion of many, including me, he succeeds only in looking like a pub patron playing at darts. With the exception of the statue, Thetford is an attractive old town whose picturesqueness has been unimpaired by the addition of a handsome ultramodern industrial park and housing development on the town's outskirts.

More than 40 firms and some 1,000 families have moved from London to Thetford, and the population is now a bustling 9,500. It will grow to a planned 22,000 by 1972.

So far, more than 225,000 people have quit London for the new and expanding towns. Many moved because they could obtain housing, much of it new construction sponsored by the central government, the GLC, or the local communities. Although half a million new homes have been built in London during the past 10 years, a severe housing shortage still exists. Borough-council waiting lists for municipal housing contain 150,000 names. The problem is compounded by a tide of immigrants, including many Negroes from the

them quite a bit of help. We can buy their premises, help toward the cost of removal of their plant, equipment, and personnel to a new site, and even compensate in part for dislocation to their business during the move."

Nor is that all the help offered. Plans vary among the towns receiving these emigrants, but any industry willing to quit London can move into quarters specially provided for it— and in some cases built to its specifications.

Actually Mr. Hartley and his men needn't rely entirely on persuasion or offers of help. Nonconforming industries cannot get planning permission to expand or remodel their premises. The message is clear: Get out if you want to grow.

The little town of Thetford, 72 miles from London in Norfolk, is a good example of an expanding community ready to absorb Mr. Hartley's "customers." As the ancient capital of East Anglia, and a monastery town, it could boast a proud total of 4,000 souls back in

West Indies, flooding into already jammed neighborhoods.

Mrs. Evelyn Denington, the able and attractive chairman of the GLC's Housing Committee, described the relocation program to me as "a great success story, a wonderful story, a story of great human happiness. People who have lived under conditions of overcrowding and substandard housing that are difficult for you to imagine, now have their little gardens and are able to bring up their children in good surroundings. And the old towns around London that have received them have been revivified with a youthful infusion."

It is difficult to imagine a more paradoxical situation for a city than that confronting London, which finds itself not only driving ratepayers (taxpayers) from the fold, but subsidizing their resettlement elsewhere. Yet the various relocation programs have eased the city's problems. London's population has not grown in recent years; indeed, it has fallen slightly.

City Engulfed by Rush-hour Traffic

However, no lessening of congestion in the city's notorious traffic is evident, either to the naked eye or to the keepers of statistics. Each day, by various conveyances, nearly 16 million journeys are made within, into, or out of London, including 1¼ million to the central area, with its citadels of finance and government. At Hyde Park Corner, the busiest intersection, more than 145,000 vehicles stream by in a twelve-hour period.

At the risk of being thought a dangerous eccentric, I confess that at times I deliberately immerse myself in London's rush-hour traffic. It's stimulating, and the opportunity for studying the natives is unsurpassed. Londoners have a tendency to group themselves together in neighborhoods according to professions, and I have ridden into the central area by rail from Surrey with stockbrokers and bankers, from Richmond and Kingston with

How does a Londoner dress? Socialite, rebel, schoolboy, or executive—each has his uniform.

Coveted invitation to the Steward's Enclosure at the Henley Royal Regatta calls for fashionable attire—blazer, boater, and the inevitable umbrella.

Modern minstrel in Trafalgar Square prefers chin whiskers and locks as long as those of his young companion in blue jeans.

Cricketers at Harrow strap on leg pads; waiting batsman wears protective gloves.

Impeccable and resolute, a gentleman in morning dress with tightly-furled umbrella leads a bus-stop queue.

EKTACHROME (BELOW) AND KODACHROME BY JAMES P. BLAIR © N.G.S.

journalists, and from Tower Hamlets and Newham with workingmen. Aside from the occasional stockbroker who absentmindedly wields his rolled umbrella like a rapier, the British commuter seems notable for his patience and good manners.

In return, his city gives him a notably efficient transportation system. London's Underground, the world's first, operates seven lines with 215 miles of track. Each year this subway records 675 million fares. Topside, 8,000 buses and motor coaches and 7,000 taxicabs ply the city's 7,000 miles of streets. Numerous routes of British Railways converge on the city's center.

Gladstone is credited with advising some visitors: "The way to see London is from the top of a bus—the top of a bus, gentlemen." Many still favor this method, among them Sir William Fiske, leader of the majority party in the Greater London Council, who told me that, when in London on a Saturday, he likes to ride about on one of the famous double-decker buses. I do too. It's like being in a traveling red grandstand.

As for the London taxicab, I maintain it is the most sensible vehicle ever designed. Someone who never heard of Detroit gave the cab large doors, a flat floor, and a spacious interior with seats that, though comfortable, discourage slouching. Miraculously, you can enter and leave without feeling you are climbing in and out of a well. It has enough headroom for a man to wear a formal hat (I wore a topper once, so I speak with authority), and it will turn on a sixpence.

"Morale Poster" Scores With a Laugh

If I have a criticism, it is that the interior glass panels make conversation with the driver difficult. Yet I persist. Talking to cabbies is one of my major London enthusiasms. They know such wonderful stories about Americans.

"Had a nice old lady in my cab who kept talking 'bout morale posters," a cabbie told me recently. "She says, 'The war's been over for years. Why do you still have those signs to help your morale?'

"I asks her, 'What signs? Show me one, lady.' And right soon, guvnor, she did. Like that one."

The cabbie gestured toward a rooftop sign. I read the familiar words and dissolved into quaking laughter. "Take Courage," said the sign. It advertised a British beer.

"Americans wot comes over here, they wants the old stuff. That's wot interests

FLOODLIT TRAFALGAR SQUARE, *hub of London, swarms with Britons on election night. In the darkness high above, the cocked-hatted, empty-sleeved figure of Admiral Lord Nelson watches the unfolding destiny of his nation. Nelson lost an arm and an eye in naval engagements; he died in action at the Battle of Trafalgar, off the coast of Spain, where he defeated the French and Spanish fleets in 1805. His victory, a masterpiece of seamanship, ended forever Napoleon's hopes of invading England. And his words then, "England expects that every man will do his duty," still inspire his countrymen.*

them," a cabbie once said to me. Obviously he had a profound insight into the American character. And, although it was not planned for the convenience of Americans, some of London's most historic places—the Tower, remnants of the Roman Wall, Guildhall, St. Paul's, Parliament, Westminster Abbey—lie within easy cab distance, or even walking distance, of one another in the venerable City of London or the City of Westminster.

"City" Survives From Roman Times

In pursuit of an earlier article, I got to know the City of London well.* It is so small, only one square mile, that a visitor can get on quite intimate terms with it. A Britisher will refer to it simply as the City, with a capital "C," and everyone knows he means the oldest part of London, extending back to Roman and medieval times, once a walled city and still a political entity maintaining its old boundaries. Here the Lord Mayor of London presides with medieval pomp and ceremony (pages 746-7).

One might well wonder why there should

be two cities-within-a-city: the Square Mile, as it is often called, and adjoining Westminster, which together comprise the very heart of London. But, as A. G. Dawtry, Westminster's Town Clerk, once explained to me, "The title of city in England is now simply an honor bestowed by the sovereign, rather like a knighthood to an individual." In olden times only a community that boasted a cathedral could be called a city, and both the Square Mile and Westminster qualified in that respect.

Both survived last year's shake-up of London's municipal government, the result of an act of Parliament that reduced nearly 90 separate authorities to 34—the Greater London Council, 32 borough councils, and the City. In writing innumerable compromises into the act, Parliament may have assured municipal solicitors a generation of employment sorting out overlapping responsibilities and functions between the GLC and the boroughs. "I only hope our British genius for

*See "The City—London's Storied Square Mile," by Allan C. Fisher, Jr., NATIONAL GEOGRAPHIC, June, 1961.

muddling through will prevail," an official confided to me.

It surprised no one when Westminster emerged from the shakeup as a powerful new borough after absorbing two old neighboring boroughs. Westminster had long been the home of Parliament. It had long been rich—and, with its revised boundaries, became even richer, with a rateable (taxable) value of more than £100,000,000 ($280,000,000), twice as much as any other British municipality.

The little City, too, had long been rich and prestigious. But, unlike Westminster, it was, and is, controversial. Businessmen, organized into anachronistic trade guilds inherited from the Middle Ages, run the financial sector as they would a gentlemen's club. They run it efficiently and honestly through the Lord Mayor and a

Big Ben's famous voice bongs the hour from its tower above Westminster Bridge. The Union Jack flying from Victoria Tower proclaims Parliament in session. New skyscrapers dominated by 28-story Portland House (right, background) rise behind Westminster landmarks.

Four-thousand-year-old Egyptian statuette captivates a schoolgirl in the British Museum. Its treasures—among them the Rosetta Stone, the Elgin marbles, and a First Folio edition of Shakespeare's plays—prompted the oft-quoted remark: "Lucky are those who are unmarried, independent, and living near the British Museum."

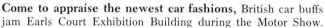

Come to appraise the newest car fashions, British car buffs jam Earls Court Exhibition Building during the Motor Show.

Brighton or bust! In his 1903 Renault Landaulette, Capt. P. Watters-Westbrook leads veteran cars out of Hyde Park in the 56-mile Commemoration Run from London to the popular seaside resort. Only cars built prior to 1905 may enter. The annual event celebrates an 1896 law that raised the speed limit from 4 to 14 miles an hour, eliminating the old regulation that a man with a red flag had to walk before every moving motor vehicle.

Silver Britannia, representing Great Britain and her dominions, identifies the Rolls-Royce of Queen Elizabeth the Queen Mother.

EKTACHROMES BY JAMES P. BLAIR © N.G.S.

council composed mostly of guildsmen, but they cheerfully admit their stewardship has little in common with modern democratic procedures.

When Parliament debated London's governmental reorganization, the City had its partisans and its vehement critics. Generally speaking, Conservatives pointed with pride and Labourites viewed with alarm. After the dust had settled, there stood the City, completely unscathed. Despite predictions, it had not been classified as a borough. It simply remained itself.

A friend of mine who is a pillar of the City Establishment and an unregenerate old Tory summed up the situation nicely: "The City is an anachronism, but there is not much advantage in eliminating it. The opposition to it is primarily doctrinaire pressure and not real conviction."

I was delighted one day when the mail produced an invitation for Mary and me to attend a formal reception and dinner at the Guildhall, given by Sir James Miller, then the Right Honourable the Lord Mayor of London, in

honor of delegates to a meeting of the Southeast Asia Treaty Organization. I knew SEATO would rate a showy performance by the City, and I suspected that my wife, as the evening progressed, would feel rather like Alice, as things got "curiouser and curiouser."

Pikemen Stand Guard Over Tradition

And so it proved. Mary was startled to find the magnificent old Guildhall, parts of which date from the 15th century, ablaze with pikemen in scarlet uniforms and helmets and breastplates of burnished metal. They stood about at strategic spots, looking determinedly picturesque. Sir James and some of his entourage added to the antique decor by wearing knee breeches and buckled shoes. The Toastmaster, his portentous voice fairly dripping with the upperclass inflections so prized by the British ear, announced the important guests, who then strode across a stage to receive a greeting from Sir James and his lady.

As I recall, only persons holding blue tickets were shepherded toward Sir James. Our ticket was a sort of undistinguished puce, but it entitled us to watch this show and, later, to enjoy an excellent buffet beside the scarred pillars of the Guildhall's old crypt. My wife was entranced. "I wonder what these people do in real life," she said.

To an American, one of the City's dress-up shows inevitably seems unreal, but the costumed participants never exhibit the slightest hint of self-consciousness. City fathers never forget that they are heirs of Great Britain's oldest traditions and custodians of ground hallowed by history.* Almost every time a foundation is dug in the City, workmen unearth objects dating back nearly 2,000 years to Roman Londinium. London Museum maintains a large collection of these Roman

*See "The British Way," by Sir Evelyn Wrench, NATIONAL GEOGRAPHIC, April, 1949.

Teetering between East and West, a youngster walks the Zero Meridian at the Royal Observatory in Greenwich. From this line geographers measure the longitude of every point on earth.

In ordered ranks, freighters line the quays of the Royal Albert and King George V docks, 42 miles from the sea. Across the Thames, ropes of light entwine the slopes of Woolwich.

Shipping helped create the sprawling city and still sustains it. Port of London Authority maintains five giant dock systems that can accommodate more than a hundred ocean-going vessels at a time. Together with prosaic necessities, cranes unload carpets from Iran, ivory from Africa, bananas from Jamaica, and spices from India and the South Seas.

artifacts: pottery, tile, coins, tools, knives. Remains of the old Roman Wall itself are still visible at a number of points, notably in the Tower of London and in the Noble Street-Cripplegate area.

If you like walking, I can recommend the City on a Sunday; then the buildings stand deserted, and empty streets return the sound of solitary footfalls. Begin at the Tower, that grim old pile of long and bloody fame (pages 782-3). It will be thronged, but you will leave crowds behind as you walk down Lower Thames Street past old Billingsgate Market, a site where fish have been sold for a thousand years. Nearby stands the Monument, a fluted Doric column 202 feet high, designed by Sir Christopher Wren to commemorate the Great Fire of 1666, which reputedly started exactly 202 feet away, in Pudding Lane. The Monument's spiral staircase will make you feel like a fly crawling up a corkscrew, but, if you can manage the 311 steps, one of London's finest views will reward you at the top.

After catching your breath, strike out for St. Paul's Cathedral, whose massive dome will never be long out of sight as you stroll the historic streets (page 745). Once you have attained the cathedral, do some more climbing, if your feet permit and the weather is clear, and experience the magnificent view 77

Easy canter of a carrousel horse soothes a stoic matron on the merry-go-round, one of many amusements for those who gather at Epsom for the famed Derby. Race fans often camp out all night for a spot on the rails of the mile-and-a-half course.

EKTACHROMES © N.G.S.

Proper British reserve tempers emotions as a fashion-plate crowd watches the 1965 Derby Stakes from the Members' Stand at Epsom. Sea Bird II, a French horse, won this 186th running of the classic.

Parliament has been known to adjourn for the race, and the Queen and other members of the royal family often attend. The Derby (pronounced "darby") appeals equally to the thousands watching from the open Downs, who pay no admission. Germany's Otto von Bismarck once remarked to Prime Minister Benjamin Disraeli: "You will never have a revolution in England as long as you keep up your racing."

Amateur jockeys take their horses over the brush in a cross-country race in northeast London. They wear the silks of hunt members who own the jumpers. Perennially green turf is a gift of England's wet climate.

777

from the Stone Gallery encircling the foot of the outer dome.

In any bird's-eye vista of London, one immediately perceives the life-giving role of the Thames, a pulsing artery that loops through the very heart of the metropolis. Hulking ocean-going freighters ply the river as far upstream as London Bridge; downstream several watery mazes, man-made lakes containing the docks of the Port of London Authority, branch off from the main stream. For miles along the river, giant cranes tower above the wharves like monstrous praying mantises.

Together these various port facilities handle 58,000 ships and more than 61 million tons of goods a year (pages 774-5).

Many people think Old Father Thames a surpassingly ugly river. But to me it has the beauty of utility and vitality. Unlike the serene Seine of Paris, where riverbank wharves and factories are not permitted, the Thames throughout its London reaches continues its age-old role of working river. Some 5,500 barges serve the Port of London, and I have seen days when it seemed that all these barges, shepherded by chuffing tugs, were on the move at the same time.

Scotland Yard Guards River Commerce

The men who perhaps know the Thames best, since daily they play a vital role in the life of the river, are the personnel of Scotland Yard's Thames Division. This division, formed in 1798, is the oldest branch of the Metropolitan Police. It evolved from a watchdog force of tough rivermen organized by the West India Company of Merchantmen to protect cargoes against looting and pilfering.

In those days nearly a third of all port workers handling cargoes were known to be thieves or receivers of stolen property, and they made off with about half of all cargoes entering the port of London. But vigilant river police eventually broke up the gangs.

Today the Thames Division patrols 54 miles of the river, using 34 launches operating from six riverside stations. One lowering morning, when the sky was as gray as the surface of the Thames, I went on a prowl cruise with a sergeant and two constables from the Waterloo Pier. The sergeant, a loquacious and knowing veteran of 18 years on the force, huddled beside me in the stern and gave a wind-whipped commentary as we headed downstream.

"When you think that there is about a million pounds' worth of goods in transit on the river at all times and that only about five thousand pounds' worth is lost in a year's time, we don't do too bad a job," the sergeant said. "We get to know all the regular tug skippers and all the watermen who man the small boats that go back and forth among the bigger ones. A new boat, a new man, stands out a mile to us. And chummy, if the

Yoicks and away to a perfect fit! Astride a wooden horse, assaying his proud carriage in double mirrors, a gentleman of the hunt gets fitted for a morning coat at H. Huntsman and Sons, Ltd. The firm on Savile Row, celebrated street of custom tailors, outfits followers of the hounds with everything from handsewn buckskin breeches to silk cravats. It even maintains a button bank; members of more than a hundred hunt clubs can replace lost buttons merely by writing Huntsman's.

EKTACHROME BY ADAM WOOLFITT © NATIONAL GEOGRAPHIC SOCIETY

bloke tries to steal, believe me, he doesn't get away with it."

We were cruising one of the most storied areas of the Thames. Off to our right, on the south bank, I glimpsed the site of the infamous bearbaiting pit where bloody spectacles had been held in competition with the plays of Will Shakespeare, performed nearby.* I tried to draw out the sergeant on the river history of that earlier, romantic period. But the sergeant, intent on the present, would have none of that. He was very good at his job.

"See that?" asked the sergeant, pointing to a canvas-covered, nondescript barge tied up at a wharf. "It contains parts for Ford motorcars. Many's the bloke what would like to have those parts. But we know which barges have the valuable cargoes. The owners tell us. Storing cargo in barges is good, cheap storage, provided the stuff isn't perishable."

Moments later the sergeant pointed to another canvas-covered barge. "Brandy," he said. "Forty thousand pounds' worth. But nobody's going to pinch a drop of the stuff."

I believed him. Scotland Yard, whether cruising the Thames or patrolling the 780 square miles of the London Metropolitan Police District, is notoriously efficient.

Old Sailing Barges Work the Thames

Class consciousness still being quite marked in Britain, it is supposed to be foolhardy for a man in a white collar and business suit to prowl about London's dockland and try to initiate conversations. The dockers don't like it. But I have done so on occasion. I learned long ago that an American accent wins an acceptance from British workingmen that they would never give one of their countrymen who obviously did not work with his hands. "It's a ruddy Yank!" a docker will exclaim, and from then on conversation is easy.

It was on just such an expedition, deep into the Royal Albert Dock, that I met J. H. Norman, master of a battered and delightfully obsolete old tub, the *Ethel,* one of the sailing barges still plying the Thames. These squat vessels, operating between English Channel ports and London, still run under sail when they can, though all have been converted to auxiliary power. The 70-ton *Ethel,* a venerable 68 years old, is one of less than a dozen such vessels still sailing.

Norman wore the typical garb of a London waterman: threadbare dark jacket and trousers, scarf, battered old cap. He rolled a cigarette and talked while we waited for a lock to clear so that *Ethel,* loaded with soybeans, could enter the river.

"I am on ter sixty-five now and fer fifty year, ever since I left school, I been on these boats. I c'yam to London on a sighling

*See "The Britain That Shakespeare Knew," by Louis B. Wright, NATIONAL GEOGRAPHIC, May, 1964.

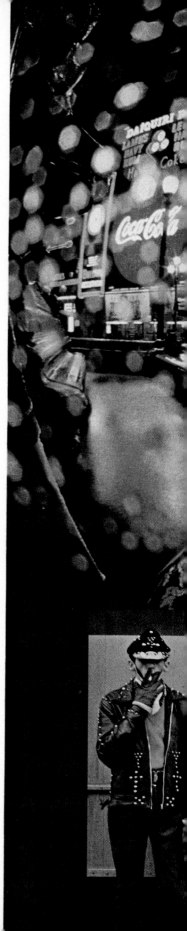

Sequins of light—raindrops on the camera lens—spangle Piccadilly Circus. When the blazing signs flashed on again after World War II's blackout, thousands of light-hungry Londoners blocked traffic to see the spectacle.

Studded leather jackets and rakish caps worn low across the eyes identify Rockers, members of a teen-age motorcycle set. Their garb sometimes includes German military insignia, like the Iron Cross on the boy at extreme right. Rockers frequently clash with rival Mods, who specialize in high-fashion dress. The result: a "punch-up."

EKTACHROME (INSET) AND KODACHROME BY JAMES P. BLAIR © N.G.S.

Teller of horror tales, a Yeoman Warder in the Tower of London spellbinds visitors with accounts of how Queens Anne Boleyn and Catherine Howard lost their heads in the fortress.

EKTACHROMES AND KODACHROME (RIGHT) © N.G.S.

"How big was the dragon?" Fascinated children, awed by the trappings of a knight, bombard armor-and-weapons expert R. E. Oakshot with questions. The White Tower houses suits of armor for men, horses, and even children.

Dark secrets of terror lurk among the stones of the Tower of London beside Tower Bridge. Since William the Conqueror built the square White Tower nearly 900 years ago, the fortress has served often as a prison. Here young Edward V and his brother Richard met mysterious deaths. Imprisoned, Sir Walter Raleigh and the future Queen Elizabeth I paced its rooms. The Tower once housed the Royal Mint and today, as always, guards the Crown Jewels.

barge 1913 or 1914, and I been sighling 'em back here ever since. No, I don't mind using 'er engine. Unless you have a fair wind of it, she won't do much alone, but when we put that sighl up, I tell you wot she puts you in mind of—a Chinese junk, that's wot she does. With sighl and 'er motor together she does eight knots. A right proper good old girl."

The lock cleared and Norman eased *Ethel* out into the stream under power. At that moment I made a resolution I hope someday to keep: To find J. H. Norman again and go sailing with him down the route of the sea dogs, the storied Thames, and beat up the Channel under *Ethel*'s patched old canvas.

Some of the most fascinating Thames-side activity takes place deep underground. There, in dimly lit caverns, the Port of London Authority stores some 83,000 casks containing wine and spirits. There are six of these huge man-made caves, but my favorite is the Crescent Wine Vault, built more than a century and a half ago by prisoners taken during the Napoleonic Wars. Being French, the prisoners thought the construction of a home for wine an excellent idea and fell to with a right good will. The result is one of the most picturesque scenes imaginable: Huge casks rest in files, seemingly endless, that stretch away beneath brick arches bearded and festooned with fungus and eerily illuminated by gas lamps flickering to an occasional spectral breath.

All casks in the Crescent Vault are held in bond for wine merchants, who permit the

For pleasure and profit, art plays an important role in London life. At the Tate Gallery a young family ponders modern sculpture.

Seated on his shooting stick, a visitor views paintings at a preview of the Royal Academy's Summer Show. The 1965 exhibition featured more than 1,600 works by contemporary artists and sculptors.

Tense hush settles over Sotheby & Co. as Rembrandt's "Portrait of a Man" goes up for auction. Peter Wilson, chairman of the firm, acknowledges a bid. Within two minutes, he sold the painting to Acquavella Galleries, Inc., of New York City for $392,000.

EKTACHROMES © N.G.S.

contents to age months or years before bottling.

"The fungus feeds on the wine," explained a guide. "The wine breathes, meaning it evaporates through the wood of the cask. So the vapor gets on the ceiling, and the fungus grows there. It's quite natural."

Quiet, Please — Wine Resting

Where newly formed, the fungus looked like Spanish moss; where old, it had solidified and had taken on the dank, dark look of congealed blood.

"What a marvelous place for a motion-picture dueling scene," I suggested. *"En garde,* Monte Cristo!"

"Oh, we couldn't have cinema people down here," said my guide. "No actors dashing about. It would disturb the wine's rest."

I have an uneasy feeling that the Crescent Wine Vault's days are numbered. Storing wine in casks is giving way to bulk storage, as exemplified by another PLA riverside installation, a warehouse containing huge glass-lined tanks. Ships fitted as wine tankers berth alongside the warehouse and disgorge their contents at the rate of 14,500 gallons an hour. When a merchant wants some wine, a tanker truck delivers it. The operation is similar to the way fuel oil and gasoline are handled.

Another guide showed me about this formidable enterprise. He said the plant could store 620,000 gallons of wine, and a similar installation being built nearby would add 346,000 gallons to the bulk-storage capacity. We examined a maze of pipe lines running from the dock to the tanks, which prompted my escort to say thoughtfully, "Some day we are going to pump some claret or burgundy into some sauterne. That's never happened yet, but it's the kind of nightmare I live with."

I confess thought of this possibility cheered me considerably. Not that I have anything against the chap who showed me through the plant; it's just that I hate to see the death of the old, careful, colorful ways for handling wine. That evening, unnerved by the wine industry's wave of the future, I indulged myself in a very fine burgundy that had never tried to breathe in a glass-lined tank. And I toasted the old Crescent Vault.

Port of London Authority facilities are not open to casual visitors, but you can get an excellent look at a vibrant part of dockland by taking an excursion boat from Westminster Pier or Charing Cross Pier downstream to Greenwich, home of the Royal Naval College and site of the Greenwich Zero Meridian (page 774). Doughty little sightseeing craft also push upstream to the Royal Botanic Gardens at Kew and to Hampton Court Palace, given by the luckless Cardinal Wolsey to his mercurial sovereign Henry VIII.

View From the Bridge Improves With Age

London's most celebrated river view can best be seen not from the deck of a boat but from Westminster Bridge. "Earth has not anything to show more fair," wrote Wordsworth in describing the city from a vantage point on the bridge. The structure Wordsworth stood upon has long since been replaced, and certainly the London skyline is vastly different. But the view now may well be more fair; when Wordsworth penned his poem, the turreted, richly Gothic Palace of Westminster (Houses of Parliament), stretching 940 feet along the riverside, had not been built. Begun in 1840 and completed in 1860, the Palace replaced the centuries-old Parliamentary home, St. Stephen's Chapel, destroyed by fire in 1834.

Fortunately, fate dealt more kindly with nearby Westminster Hall, begun by William Rufus in 1097, and with Westminster Abbey, the British shrine-of-shrines started by Edward the Confessor before the Norman Conquest. The saintly Confessor, with scores of the nation's most famous sons, lies buried in the Abbey, Great Britain's house of history.

Palace, Hall, and Abbey—they stand together, a trinity rich in meaning to people far beyond the isles of Albion (pages 770-71).

Without exception all Americans who come to England seek tickets admitting them to the visitors' galleries of the House of Commons— or so it seems to the United States Embassy in London, which gets a prescribed ration of tickets to distribute to Americans.

I will never forget the reaction when I asked an embassy official for tickets not only to Parliament *but also* to Trooping the Colour, an annual military spectacle in honor of the Queen's Birthday and in which the Queen herself participates (pages 790-91). Apparently I had parlayed two of the most impossible requests that one can make of a harried State Department employee. Well, I won't do it again; I just hate to see a grown man cry.

If you want to watch the Mother of Parliaments in session, write to the embassy months in advance of your visit. Better yet, try my tactic: Get a British friend to obtain tickets from a Member of Parliament. Otherwise you may have to queue up for hours awaiting admission to the Public Gallery.

Even if the day's business in the House of Commons is prosaic and the debate lethargic (as it always seems to be when I attend), that wonderful little unvarying show, the Speaker's procession, makes it all worthwhile. It takes place in the Central Lobby, where visitors with tickets have gathered before the House goes into session. A voice calls out, "Mr. Speaker!" Another orders, "Hats off, strangers!" Then quick-marching in perfect cadence, six men in black go by—the Senior Doorkeeper; the Serjeant-at-arms, carrying the mace; the Speaker, wearing wig and silk knee breeches with buckled shoes; his Train-bearer, holding up his robe; his Chaplain; and his Secretary. Within moments these unsmiling men, looking neither to the right nor left, have walked through the Central Lobby and into the House Chamber, leaving one with the feeling that he has seen ghosts from centuries past.

Yanks Invade a Select Affair

My wife and I were privileged to attend a memorable and altogether different show in the House of Commons: the annual dinner of the Parliamentary Press Gallery, a traditional affair given by the newspapermen who cover Parliament and often attended by the Prime Minister himself. I suspect a few eyebrows were raised when Tom Lindsay, chairman of the Gallery, invited my wife and me, for we were the only Americans present at this very clubby gathering. With the delicious feeling of being spies, we took indelible mental note of everything, from the fit of Prime Minister Harold Wilson's dinner jacket (a bit snug) to

Acrobatic elephants, begging for handouts, balance on the edge of a moat at the Zoological Gardens in Regent's Park. This spring the zoo's giant panda, Chi-Chi, went to Russia to mate with An-An, a male in the Moscow Zoo; no others exist outside China and North Korea.

Children of all ages with a yen for the sea gather at Round Pond in Kensington Gardens. A trim yacht, launched with a pole, embarks on a voyage across the seven-acre lake. Rules forbid powered models; their racket would frighten birds that enjoy sanctuary here.

7

EKTACHROMES BY ADAM WOOLFITT (ABOVE) AND JAMES P. BLAIR © N.G.S.

an amusing display of partisan political hauteur that occurred during a predinner gathering off the banquet hall.

My wife happened to be chatting with a Welsh lady of emphatic Tory sympathies when Prime Minister Wilson entered the room. With formal politeness, everyone turned toward him—everyone, that is, but the Welsh lady, who kept her back to the Prime Minister, her shoulders eloquent with disdain. "My dear, don't cut him so noticeably," whispered her husband, with ill-concealed delight. The lady smiled angelically and continued her explanation of Welsh place names. If Mr. Wilson noticed, he gave no sign.

Witty Give-and-take Spices Dinner

Such manifestations of extreme political feeling are not uncommon in Great Britain. The British, more than most Americans, take their politics with deadly seriousness, particularly in recent years. But no partisanship intruded during the remainder of an evening featuring after-dinner speeches, all off the record, of an urbanity, subtle wit, and felicity of expression that I have seldom heard equaled during similar gatherings in the United States.

Of course, one official of the British Government remains above politics and is rarely subjected to any serious criticism: the Queen.

"If we didn't have a monarch, we would have to hire one for you Yanks," a British friend once said to me.

He was right. I can't imagine London without its omnipresent reminders of royalty: cavalrymen in scarlet clattering through the streets for the changing of the guard ... the iron immobility of sentries in the guard boxes at Buckingham Palace ... a stirring "God Save the Queen" at football match, concert, formal banquet ... even the

"This happy breed," Shakespeare called his fellow Englishmen. And indeed the faces of Londoners reflect stability, confidence, and independence.

In Hyde Park a member of the St. John Ambulance Brigade enjoys afternoon tea.

Cheerful dustman wears an ever-bright rose on his jacket. The plastic bloom will not wilt, even when a "heat wave" sends the temperature soaring to the 70's.

Oak leaves sprout from the bemedaled tunic of a World War I veteran at the Chelsea Royal Hospital. He wears them in honor of Charles II, founder of the hospital, who escaped capture at the Battle of Worcester in 1651 by hiding in an oak tree.

Blush of youth paints the cheeks of a girl watching a tennis match at Wimbledon.

KODACHROMES © N.G.S.

familiar royal face on the pounds you spend.

Most Americans think of the British monarchy as a colorful, pleasant, but almost entirely ceremonial appendage of the government. It is considerably more. I was reminded of that fact recently when a British friend pointed out to me a messenger from Buckingham Palace getting out of a royal carriage in Whitehall.

"Returning government dispatches," my friend said. "The Queen sees them all, y'know. Secret. Most secret. The lot."

I confessed I hadn't realized it, and he decided my education should be furthered in this most British of subjects. Soon I found myself in a series of discreet meetings with certain discreet and well-informed people— indeed, people so discreet that I can't mention their names.

Queen Active in Affairs of State

"Oh, yes, the Queen sees all secret papers," one gentleman assured me. "She must be kept informed; it is her right. She may also be consulted by her Prime Minister, and she can warn him or encourage him.

"A monarch who has been on the throne for a number of years is the best-informed person in the realm on affairs of state. You see, under our system, an incoming Prime Minister does not have access to the confidential papers of his predecessor, but the sovereign sees everything. A wise and capable sovereign will use this knowledge effectively."

The Queen, I knew, appointed the Prime Minister, and I suggested to another informant that her choice must be automatic.

"On the contrary, sometimes it's frightfully complicated," this man said. "It's clear enough if the party in power has elected a leader; he becomes Prime Minister. But until recently the Conservatives didn't hold such an election. The Queen was put into a most difficult position some years ago when she had to choose between Harold Macmillan and 'Rab' Butler. Similarly, the leadership of the party was equally uncertain when Macmillan's retirement became imminent due to illness. The Queen could have been put in a devilishly awkward spot. However, Conservative opinion was canvassed by Macmillan, who advised the Queen that the choice was Lord Home."

I learned that there are only oblique references in statute law to the powers of the monarch. Those powers that remain are almost entirely the result of evolution. Yet

"Trooping the Colour," proud men and parading horses of the Queen's Household Brigade stride to martial music in honor of the monarch's "official" birthday each June. Her actual birth date: April 21. Seven regiments comprise Her Majesty's personal troops.

Iron discipline never fails an Irish guardsman; even when he faints in the ranks, he falls at attention. His comrades move not a muscle.

The Queen is never officially late for the trooping ceremony. Should she not appear by 11 a.m., an officer stops the hands of the tower clock and starts them again on her arrival.

EKTACHROMES BY JAMES P. BLAIR © NATIONAL GEOGRAPHIC SOCIETY

even today any number of things and any number of appointments simply cannot legally take place without the Queen's signature.

"You say she has to sign, and of course she must in this age," my informant continued. "But there is nothing in law that says she must, and it is still conceivable that she may not. We regard this as a safeguard to freedom. Confronted by madness or treason in a Prime Minister, the sovereign, by not signing, can force a general election."

An early dusk had crept into the quiet office where we talked, and when I reluctantly took leave, my host walked with me to the street door, where we stood for a time looking at a rain-swept London.

"There is nothing quite like her in your country," said my host very quietly. "Here our sovereign—particularly in times of national emotion, such as war—is the living symbol of all the patriotism and feeling that we have for our homeland. She is the very embodiment of our national existence in a way no politician can be. In your country I think only your flag quite assumes that national identity and elicits that response."

I agreed and went out into the night, feeling that somehow I had drawn closer to

London and understood it better as a result of the series of meetings.

A few days later my wife and I left London for home. As usual, it was raining, and as a cabbie drove us to the airport, I kept my head close to the rain-flecked window, bidding a last goodbye to the bobbies with their tall helmets, the scurrying figures at intersections, the flower dealer huddling by his stand, the glistening plane trees. In my heart I embraced old London—and never mind its climate or what Henry James called its "horrible numerosity of society."

It was then I recalled something Sir William Fiske, the Greater London Council Leader, had told me. "I know there are many people who can't stand London," he had said, "but there are also a great many who simply cannot stand to be anywhere but in or near its center. You often hear the phrase 'not half way.' It's an expression used to describe the reluctance to live anywhere else but in the heart of London."

Recalling this incident to my wife, I said, "I'm tempted to say 'not half way,' and go back."

Mary sighed. "That rival of mine! What can a poor girl do?" THE END

Blowgun Hunters of the South Pacific

By JANE C. GOODALE, Ph.D.

Photographs by ANN CHOWNING, Ph.D.

"FOR A FEW GLORIOUS DAYS I've been deluged with fresh meat. Boiled bat on Sunday, baked snake on Tuesday, roast eel on Monday and Wednesday. Back to canned meat tonight ... but it's been a pleasant interlude."

I read these lines, in a letter from my colleague Ann Chowning, just as I was about to open a tin of corned beef for dinner. The words filled me with envy. Never mind the boiled bat or roast eel. I've tried them, and they aren't too bad. But there's nothing better, Ann tells me, than six or seven inches of prime young python cooked to a turn in a wrapping of bark or leaves. It tastes rather like lizard, which in turn tastes rather like chicken.

No Snake for Dinner, Says Author's Cook

But snake was taboo among the New Britain aborigines with whom I lived for 13 months. My cook flatly refused to serve python, and I never did get to try it. Ann's hosts, in a village 10 miles away, had their own lengthy list of taboos, but snake was an approved food there.

One might ask: Why did we give up the security and luxuries of New York and Philadelphia, taking leave of our comfortable teaching jobs, to live among such primitive people in one of the most remote and least explored regions of the world?

Ann and I are anthropologists. We study and teach what we learn about man—his habits, environment, folkways, group relationships, history, religion.

Subjects of our study were two groups of people,

Brawny arm flexes for a spear throw; mighty puff rockets a 3-foot dart skyward through a 15-foot blowgun. For 13 months anthropologists Jane Goodale and Ann Chowning lived among primitive hunters in New Britain and studied their ways. Until recent years these people strangled widows and engaged in murderous warfare. Some now wear religious medals—gifts of missionaries— but taboos and magic still guide their every act.

the Kaulong and the Sengseng, living in the Passismanua area of southwest New Britain (map, page 799). These people and their close neighbors practice a skill not found elsewhere among Melanesians—they hunt with blowguns. They also bind their infants' skulls to elongate them into a shape regarded as fashionable (pages 806-7).

Island Made Headlines in World War II

Despite these differences, the Kaulong and Sengseng speak languages related to those of other Melanesians. We had to learn their tongues, for only a handful of Kaulong and Sengseng had acquired a knowledge of pidgin English, the "trade language" spoken throughout New Britain and elsewhere in the Trust Territory of New Guinea.*

Few Americans had even heard of New Britain until World War II, when the Japanese fortified Rabaul and slowed the Allies' island-hopping campaign. Fighting also flared around New Britain's western end and in adjoining waters. In the Battle of the Bismarck Sea, in March, 1943, Allied air and naval units destroyed a huge enemy convoy. Since 1947, the island has been part of a United Nations trust territory administered by Australia.

*John Scofield wrote of New Guinea and its peoples in the May, 1962, NATIONAL GEOGRAPHIC.

Bandaging cuts, treating burns, and dispensing aspirin, Dr. Chowning aids the villagers of Dulago. She left teaching duties at Barnard College, New York City, to accompany the author to New Britain. Dr. Goodale, on leave from Bryn Mawr College in Pennsylvania, lived in Umbi, half a day's walk from Dulago.

Resting after a day's hike to Lapalam, the author and her porters wait for a dinner of taro to cook on the fire in foreground. In this land of heavy rains, officials encourage construction of plank houses raised on stilts.

Fortunately, the forest-dwelling Kaulong and Sengseng lived some 250 miles from Rabaul and safely inland from the other battles. They had first come to our attention through films and published reports of the late E. Thomas Gilliard, ornithologist of the American Museum of Natural History. In late 1958 and early 1959 Dr. Gilliard and his wife spent several months exploring the area, collecting rare birds and small mammals.*

Kandrian was the jumping-off place for our 30-mile trek into the interior. The route was known to us, for we had spent six weeks there in 1962. Now, in July of 1963, we were back for more than a year of research, with a grant from the National Science Foundation and additional support from the National Geographic Society for the first extensive studies of these people ever made.

At Kandrian we recruited 35 bearers to carry our supplies—which included enough canned food to last for a month. As we passed villages, the pack-train personnel kept changing. Some bearers dropped out and collected their wages of a shilling (11 cents) an hour; others took their places.

* Dr. Gilliard, leader of two trail-blazing American Museum—National Geographic Society expeditions to study New Guinea's birds of paradise and Stone Age men, described "New Britain's Land of Fire" in the NATIONAL GEOGRAPHIC of February, 1961.

79

Forest-walled village of Umbi stirs with unaccustomed
bustle as "residents" prepare for the annual inspection and
census by Australian patrol officers. Its 78 inhabitants
actually prefer to live in bush huts near their gardens,
some as far as a three-hour walk from Umbi. "Every
Monday they come in to straighten up a bit," says
Dr. Goodale. "Then, in the week before the officials'
visit, they scurry about patching and rebuilding."

Many of the porters fanned out along the route, traveling at their own pace, some ahead of us, some behind. Since they were out of our sight most of the time, we feared part of our property might vanish forever. But when the reckoning came at the end of the march, only an umbrella had been misplaced.

A cast had just been removed from Ann's knee—dislocated during our stay in Rabaul—so the trek took us four days instead of the usual three. Our policeman-escort, genially accepting our snail's pace, expressed high regard for the stamina of American women.

Ann and I parted at Pomalal and went on to the villages of Dulago and Umbi, our respective bases, ten miles apart. In Dulago live the Sengseng; in Umbi live the Kaulong. For each of us there was a little house, built by the villagers since our 1962 visit.

To say the people "live" in these villages is to use the word loosely. They prefer to spend most of their time in the surrounding forest, where they can be close to the gardens and game that provide their food. Here they sleep in small huts and tend plots of taro, manioc, tobacco, sugar cane, and other crops.

Only on special occasions, such as the weekly cleanup days, the day of the annual census, or other rare visits from government officers, do all the people gather in the villages, which they built on official orders (pages 796-7). Each family has a house of hand-hewn planks; a large "men's house" shelters the community's bachelors.

A recent census credited Umbi, largest village in the region, with 78 occupants in a dozen homes. Dulago, one of the smallest communities, had 40 people living in seven or eight houses.

Wealth Reckoned in Gold-lipped Shells

Most Kaulong and Sengseng readily accept Australian or other currency as pay, but they attach far greater value to gold-lipped pearl shells for barter among themselves. If a man owns many shells, he is wealthy.

The large shells, handsome, almost circular, with gleaming inner surfaces, come mainly from the island of Manus, northwest of New Britain. To the Kaulong and Sengseng, shells range in value from five shillings to three Australian pounds, depending on size and quality.

Once a year labor contractors recruit small numbers of Kaulong and Sengseng to work at the Australian naval station on Manus. These highly prized jobs offer the opportunity to dive for, or buy cheaply, many pearl shells.

Other shells reach the interior via native

Preening forest maiden stares into a trade-goods mirror backed with a photograph of an actress. She combs stylish blackening into her mushroom hairdo. Tattoos beautify her cheeks.

Volcanic New Britain, 300 miles long, leaped into the headlines during World War II. Japanese troops converted Rabaul into a powerful base that blocked the Allied advance for two years. Today the island, a part of the Australian-administered U. N. Trust Territory of New Guinea, still harbors in its interior a people barely brushed by civilization. Enlarged map shows trails followed by Drs. Goodale and Chowning as they studied New Britain's Kaulong and Sengseng peoples.

KODACHROME BY ANN CHOWNING © N.G.S.

79

trade routes along the New Britain coast. Some find their way into trade stores in Rabaul. Here the bush people can exchange their wages, earned by working on coconut and cacao plantations nearby, for the one medium of exchange that has supreme value in their homeland.

Ownership of shells, and their use in complex financial transactions, offers the traditional road to personal prestige in the forest culture. Unmarried young men are considered too immature to be trusted with complete control of their own fortunes; they must give their shells over to the care of married relatives.

Sun Seldom Penetrates Forest

Ann and I wrote to each other frequently, the letters traveling through the forest by runner. Once a month one of us would go to the other's village; this plan involved four-to-six-hour hikes over sharp, ankle-twisting limestone ridges and down into valleys to cross a bog or a swift stream (page 813).

Tramping through the gloomy forest between Umbi and Dulago or on the trail to the coast, we seldom saw sky or sunlight. They were shut out by frequent rain clouds and by towering trees, some with vast exposed root structures.

We had to cross flood-swollen streams, where strong currents threatened to carry us away. In this area the annual rainfall totals about 250 inches, much of it coming in sudden, savage cloudbursts. Such storms quickly turned the Apaun and other rivers, with their myriad smaller tributaries, into raging brown torrents. Some streams we crossed on logs or crude shaky bridges; others we forded, at times clinging to a vine in depths that occasionally were over our heads (page 814).

Once during our stay, Ann and I met at Pomalal and walked to Kandrian to replenish our supplies and enjoy a taste of civilization. We timed our vacation for New Year's Day, so we could celebrate it with our friends at the government post and watch an exhibition of tribal dancing.

Aside from this brief trip, we remained in our isolated villages for more than a year and rarely saw another outsider.

For the most part we slept in the almost uninhabited villages and made daily trips to the forest to visit the people. Once I was forced to abandon my house and take refuge in the forest with the natives,

Lizard-skin drumheads boom the cadence for prancing tribesmen in a massive New Year's Day sing-sing—pidgin English for song-and-dance fest. Many participants traveled for days to reach the celebration in coastal Kandrian. These dancers, neighbors of the Kaulong and Sengseng, live near the sea and have access to Western goods. They daubed cardboard headdresses with paint and topped them with parrot plumes. Medical gauze binds ankles, knees, and wrists. Clusters of dyed fibers dangle beneath leafy bustles.

While attaching heads to their slim wooden drums, the Sengseng observe a taboo of strict silence to ensure that the tree-sap glue will hold.

KODACHROMES BY ANN CHOWNING (LEFT) AND JANE GOODALE © N.G.S.

Writing six-foot python struggles to burst a bond securing it to a stake. To prove his courage, Litem—son of Umbi's *luluai,* or headman—grasps the pole. People of Umbi fear these reptiles and place a taboo on eating them. Dr. Goodale sent this one to Dr. Chowning in Dulago, where no taboo bars snake dinners.

Parrot, frog, and bat—delicacies in the islanders' diet. A young Kaulong man captured the parrot in his garden after the bird gorged so greedily on taro that it could hardly fly. "Very tough, with a gamey flavor," recalls the author.

Children comb stream banks for frogs. "Tender and sweet," reports Dr. Goodale. Another tasty morsel: grubs.

Boy bites a fruit bat which has been wrapped in green bark and steamed in a fire. Largest of these night fliers have three-foot wing spans. Often felled on the roost by blowguns, bats proved the most frequent source of fresh meat for the anthropologists. Their verdict: "Very pungent."

KODACHROMES BY JANE GOODALE (UPPER LEFT) AND ANN CHOWNING © N.G.S.

who had fled their garden huts to hide from an epidemic which they envisioned as an evil spirit stalking victims in the bush (pages 812-13). Since we were a part of their world, we governed ourselves by their code.

Despite a sprinkling of religious medals acquired from missionaries, our friends had not been noticeably influenced by the teachings of Christianity. Almost every activity was controlled by taboos, fears, and beliefs in magic spells.

The Kaulong and Sengseng taught us their languages and modes of behavior in the same way they taught their own children. There was this difference: We had but 13 months to absorb what a youngster learns over years.

"Don't tickle that dog, or you will die!" I was admonished as I played with a puppy.

"The baby will die!" I was told by a horrified mother after I complimented her on the fine new tooth of her infant.

"Don't disturb the ashes of the fire!" Fire, a most sacred entity, was offended, and I would be burned.

From Dulago Ann reported a list of Sengseng taboos: "If you throw pumpkin peelings where pigs can eat them, the pigs will die."

"If, as an adolescent boy, you scuffle with

EKTACHROME BY JANE GOODALE © N.G.S.

Make-believe pig bites the dust as boys with willowy spears skewer a rolling disk of banana stalk. When they grow older, the youths will participate in real wild-pig hunts —favorite pastime of their elders. But until they reach their late teens, children of the forest have little responsibility; the younger ones while away daylight hours wrestling, playing hide-and-seek, and tobogganing down hills on sheets of bark.

girls, the blackening will fall off your teeth, and you'll be left with ugly white incisors."

"If you poke a stick down a rathole, the earth will open and swallow you."

Among Melanesians, only the Kaulong, Sengseng, and neighbor tribes of southwest New Britain use blowguns for hunting. With these they kill fruit bats as well as parrots, other birds, and small tree-dwelling animals. For larger game, such as wild pigs, they use spears and native dogs. With elaborate spring traps, they catch wallabies and cassowaries.

I enjoyed watching the hunters at work with their remarkable blowguns, fashioned of bamboo lengths tied and glued to form tubes 12 to 20 feet long. With these weapons the tribesmen launched slender shafts of palm-wood, as long as three feet, feathered at one end, sharpened at the other (page 793).

Favorite victims were the fruit bats, or flying foxes. These nightmarish creatures, when airborne, soared on a three-foot spread of wings. Mostly they were killed as they roosted during the day, forming dense black clusters in the trees.

Little marksmanship was required. Poking his blowgun close to the quarry, the hunter filled his lungs with air and expelled it with a mighty puff. Often the bat was impaled before the dart was fully out of the tube.

During our journeys among the forests and hills, we uncovered evidence that an earlier people once used tools far simpler than blow-guns. These were hundreds of flints, chipped into shapes resembling knives and scrapers (page 815).

Were these the relics of our friends' ancestors? Or were they left by a different people? We have turned many of the flints over to Australian archeologists for study, and Ann and I hope to undertake further investigations ourselves before too long.

In my village, Umbi, Monday was always a day when anything might happen. This was

KODACHROMES BY ANN CHOWNING © N.G.S.

Oblivious to stinging smoke, mother and daughter tempt a toddler with bits of starchy taro root, staple food of the area. Underbrush smolders in the garden patch that the family helped slash and burn in the forest.

In a still-burning field, women prepare to plant taro tops salvaged from harvested plots. Each family maintains two taro gardens simultaneously—one in harvest and a new one to replace it. Harvested plots lie fallow for at least five years to avoid depleting the soil. For bountiful yields, growers invoke the aid of Wolio, the taro spirit, with incantations.

the day when the people, by order of the Australian Government, were supposed to work on community projects, such as cleaning up the village and clearing forest trails.

Monday became something more to the villagers: a day to go visiting, to talk, to trade, to collect debts, to settle arguments and to start new ones.

While the adults talked, quarreled, and often had a fist fight, the children played games. A favorite was "killing wild pigs," in which the youngsters threw sharpened sticks at rolling disks of banana stalk (page 803).

Bamli's Visit Causes an Uproar

On one memorable Monday I was chatting with a group of villagers in the shade under my stilted house when a stranger approached on the path from the forest. He bore all the signs of a "finish-time," one who has completed a work contract on one of the coastal plantations near Rabaul. He wore a bright-

red cotton skirt fastened with a shining new leather belt. On his broad feet were rubber sandals. In one hand he carried a padlocked wooden chest, in the other a bulging sack.

Without a word the stranger calmly climbed the ladder into my house. Ningbi, my No. 2 houseboy and cook, followed him.

"That's Bamli," Ningbi said in passing.

I listened as Ningbi and Debli, the No. 1 houseboy, conducted Bamli on a tour of the house. First he inspected the living room, then the houseboys' bedroom, the kitchen, the storeroom, and finally my private quarters, a bedroom and washroom.

Then there was silence. Mystified, I made inquiries. Bamli, I was told, belonged to the village of Iombon, had been away two years, and was just passing through on his way home. Bamli did not come down to join us, nor did any villager move to join him. I became aware of something unusual in the people's behavior toward this man.

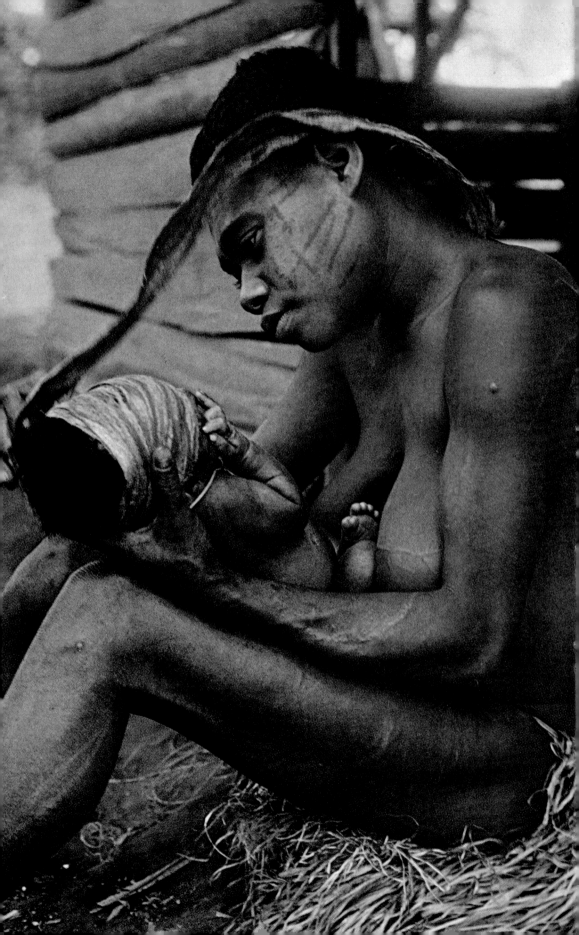

"Come down here and join us," I suggested.

"I'm afraid," he replied.

"Why?"

Bamli just smiled and shrugged. He sat on the bed for four more hours, saying nothing.

House Invaded by Knife-wielding Women

Late in the afternoon, Ningbi suddenly asked me if Bamli could hide in the storeroom. Just as I was about to say no, we were invaded. Up the ladder swarmed a dozen women, all brandishing long bush knives. Ningbi, Debli, and two other young men repelled the main assault at the door, disarming the women. But one agile girl clambered over the five-foot wall and gained entrance through

I thought it an odd request at such a time, but I quickly counted out 20 shillings and handed them to him. The fighting stopped as abruptly as it had begun.

Bamli distributed coins to the women. Then he reached into his sack and handed out tobacco, combs, razors, mirrors, and bits of cloth. The women gathered up their loot and their knives and departed, quietly and happily.

Just as I opened my mouth to ask for an explanation, the whole performance was repeated. A second wave of eight belligerent women swarmed over the wall and through the door. Again Bamli was pummeled, again he handed out money and trade goods.

This time, however, there was no general

To shape her baby's head into a fashionable elongated form, a mother binds the infant's skull with bark cloth. For several months following the child's birth, she will carefully loosen and rewrap the cloth daily to take up slack.

Two-week-old namesake of the author nurses at right. Rattan twine secures the head binding on "Goodao," the closest her mother could come to pronouncing Goodale. Dirt cakes the baby's face.

the gap between the wall and the leaf roof.

She leaped to the floor in the houseboys' room and advanced with upraised knife upon the cornered Bamli. He stood quietly, remarkably so, attempting no defense.

A couple of youths abandoned their stand at the door; one of them wrenched the knife from the girl's grasp and tossed it over a low partition into the storeroom. But the attack went on; the women pummeled poor Bamli with their fists. By this time the house was shaking dangerously on its five-foot stilts; pots and pans rattled; cans toppled from a shelf; female shrieks and hoarse male bellows added to the din as the battle raged.

Somehow Bamli extricated himself, thrust a pound note at me, and asked if I could change it into shillings.

retreat. The house was filled with laughing, chattering women, men, and children. Bamli laughed and talked as gaily as anybody.

Later, as my boys cooked supper, I got the answer to my question.

"All the women fought this man because he made them cry," Ningbi said. "Now this man has paid all the women, it is straight."

Payment Made for Needless Grief

While Bamli was away at work, it seemed, his people heard he had been accidentally killed. There was a great outpouring of grief, especially by female relatives. Then Bamli appeared. What I had witnessed was the normal Kaulong reaction to anyone who causes fright or undue sorrow among his kinfolk.

Bamli had been beaten the day before as he

Affection engulfs Dr. Goodale during a happy reunion with children of Umbi after several days' separation. One girl balances a palm-frond basket on her head.

Wild-eyed pig rides a rail to doom; its slaughter will climax a night of singing and dancing. To gain prestige and wealth, tribesmen raise enormous porkers to kill in honor of dead relatives, then sell the meat to guests at the ceremony.

Owners often knock out the upper canines of young boars so that the lower ones will grow into huge, curving tusks. Warriors decorate the tusks with strands of tiny shells to make highly prized ornaments, which they clench in their teeth during warlike dances (below, left).

KODACHROME (RIGHT) BY JANE GOODALE;
EKTACHROME (BELOW) AND KODACHROME BY ANN CHOWNING © N.G.S

passed through Arihi. Doubtless he would receive even worse punishment when he reached his home village of Iombon. He raised no objection to this, or to the drastic inroads upon his wealth. If a man turned up alive after being reported dead, such a homecoming ordeal was correct, proper, and just what he expected, however extraordinary it might seem to an outsider.

Dulago's Pigs Eat Ballpoint Pens

Meanwhile, Ann Chowning was having her adventures among the Sengseng at Dulago.

"Life here has unexpected hazards," she reported in a letter brought by a runner. "So far pigs have eaten two of my precious ballpoint pens and the ground wire of my radio. Their passion for plastic and rubber seems just a little strange.

"The people here," she continued, "are so avaricious that food, for example, is fully as expensive as in New York, but at least they are refreshingly frank about it. Just after I shelled out a large sum to the men who carried my month's supplies from Kandrian and those who built my house, one of them announced: 'I think we'll all cry when you leave. We make so much money out of you.'

"'You'll cry just because of the money?' I asked, hoping for a show of sentiment.

"'Yes,' they said, 'we love money,' with never a hint that they loved me for myself alone."

The *luluai,* or headman, of Dulago proposed to Ann that his people build an airstrip so that they would not have to work so hard carrying our cargo from Kandrian.

"I'm not sure why he doesn't think it would be equally hard work to build an airstrip," Ann wrote. "I suspect the whole thing is tied

in with a 'cargo cult' that seems to be flourishing on the coast. The luluai was asking me about it just before he mentioned the airstrip.

"Leaders of these cults teach that dead ancestors will return, by ship or plane, bringing all the white man's goods, of which the white man has wrongfully deprived the natives."

When I asked the Kaulong about the cargo cult, they laughed.

"Some Sengseng talk foolish," said one. "Our ancestors, they have died. Once a man has died, he is nothing but bones. They cannot come back among us."

Children Smoke Big Green Cigars

Both Kaulong and Sengseng grow tobacco, and they start smoking it, and also chewing betel nut, a mild stimulant, in early childhood.

"I still find the sight of a very small child smoking a large green cigar rather startling," Ann wrote.

Our friends preferred trade tobacco to their own product, and rolled it in newspaper. When my supply of newspaper ran out, I

persuaded the Kaulong to use magazine pages. Ann did likewise at Dulago, but, she reported, her people complained that coated paper gave them headaches.

Magazine illustrations were an endless source of wonder to the natives. Ann described the reaction:

"I have an extremely tough time explaining the pictures. Their favorite, so far, has been a photograph of the moon, and this they rather surprisingly accepted without question. They are most disturbed by blowups, especially of faces, most of them being convinced that evil giants are represented. But at least they're gradually learning to tell the men from the women by clues like hair length and lipstick."

Ann also reported on a forest romance:

"A young man and an adolescent girl turned up here on their way home from a dance in another village, and one of the men here, who is some sort of uncle to the girl, suddenly decided to marry her off to the young man. He was willing, but she was shy, and fled to the bush. The prospective groom took another

Spears plunge into sacrificial pigs, signaling the end of a nightlong sing-sing at Dulago. Prancing, drumming, singing at the top of their lungs, dancers had worked themselves to fever pitch, menacing each other with words and spears.

"Ann and I held our breaths as Kaulong faced Sengseng and the air grew thick with tension," reports the author. In earlier years such confrontations often led to bloody fighting. Spearman at left wears a rain hat, probably acquired when he labored on a coastal plantation.

Pugnacious dancer shouts defiance from behind his patterned wooden shield. Crushed limestone creates a white mask above his bone-pierced nose, and a pig-tusk ornament curls below his ear. Girdle of *tambu,* or sea shells, encircles his waist.

path, announcing that he'd really rather wait till they got home (her father is chief of his village).

"So suddenly a bunch of us were deep in the bush, separate ones pursuing the boy and the girl, and all the women of this village giggling madly about it. I was with the group following the girl. When we caught up with her, one old man tried to persuade her to accept a large pearl shell, as a sign that she was willing to marry the boy, while she, apparently in agonies of embarrassment, stood protesting and chopping down small trees with the knife she was carrying. She eventually fled without giving in."

In another letter, Ann commented on her neighbors' reaction to musical programs picked up from Radio Rabaul on her battery-powered set. She wrote:

"The people here (who sing beautifully) have a low opinion of the cowboy songs that make up the bulk of the program. They say the singers sound as if they have colds and as if they're drowning (although the latter may be the fault of my radio)."

(Continued on page 816)

811

Aerial roots of a giant banyan provide a shadowy shelter for three Umbi children. Such retreats often provide sanctuary from a monstrous spirit—the people's concept of an epidemic. When a "sick" stalks villages, young and old flee to the forest and hide. In past days of constant warfare, people camped close to these labyrinthine *Ficus* trees and scurried into them at the first hint of attack.

Preferring wet feet to a fall, Dr. Goodale wades a stream. Ihimei tries the rickety log bridge ahead of her husband Ningbi, the author's cook. She carries Dr. Goodale's bucket and pan on her head and clutches personal belongings in a basket.

EKTACHROMES BY ANN CHOWNING (ABOVE) AND JANE GOODALE © N.G.S.

Water sprite in a leaf skirt playfully whips a vine stretched across a river as a handhold for travelers in time of flood. Peroxide has transformed her hair into a fiery pompadour. Forest folk seldom

bathe for cleanliness, but the younger ones often splash for sport during hot weather.

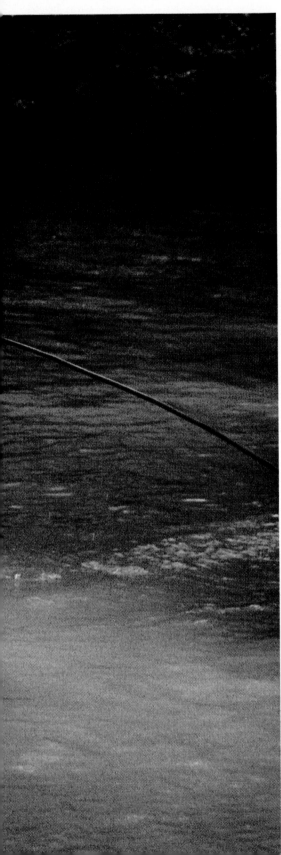

Woodsmen split a trunk into boards with wedges and a steel axhead. They will build houses with solid plank walls, as recommended by Australian administrators.

Cutting and scraping tools chipped from chert, a type of flint, are among three hundred found by the author and Dr. Chowning. Their origin—who made them, who used them, and how long ago—remains a mystery. The anthropologists shared their finds with the Australian National University at Canberra, whose archeologists are studying the discovery sites.

ONE-THIRD ACTUAL SIZE

Looking over the files of our letters, I find that Ann and I devoted much space to discussions of food. We were grateful when the people killed a pig and sold or gave us a chunk.

"I was brought a leg of half-baked pork yesterday," Ann wrote, "and happily devoured large bloody chunks of it on the spot. I decided years ago that I'd rather have pork when the chance arose than worry about its condition, and it's so much better baked than safely boiled that I continue to work on the probably

two wives (polygamy is permitted but not widely practiced), and they alternately fought and threatened suicide. Finally Kasli took the extreme step of divorcing one of them, by paying shells to her family and telling her to go. Because his remaining wife was lazy, his pigs ran wild. These and other pigs broke into his gardens and destroyed his taro.

Kasli had other troubles. No one would listen to him when he tried to enforce a new government order. His one area of success

erroneous theory that there is no trichinosis in these parts. Reminds me of the definition of anthropologists: 'Otherwise intelligent and educated people who do not accept the germ theory of disease.' But I'm happier if I don't watch my cook wash the dishes."

Feuding Wives Add to a Man's Woes

I found myself becoming more and more absorbed by my neighbors—their personalities, their problems. For example, there were Kahamei and Kasli, the government-appointed headmen of Umbi, who respectively bore the titles of luluai and *tul-tul*.

Like most of the men, Kahamei was small but heavily muscled. His skin was covered with ringworm blemishes, undesirable in a woman but the mark of an important man. He had many pigs, much taro, and a goodly stock of gold-lipped pearl shells; this wealth made him a power throughout the region.

Kasli, the No. 2 man, was quite different. He was a younger man, with little wealth but big ambitions and many problems. He had

was in hunting wild pigs. Since little went right for him when he stayed home, he often took off with his dogs to the peace and solitude of the forest, returning in glory with a feast for the village.

Then there were the teen-age girls—Ihimei, Tihimei, Wadelmei, and others. They worked hard tending the gardens and looking out for the younger children, but most of their off hours they devoted to courting my two bachelor houseboys, Ningbi and Debli.

One evening I was quietly reading, when my boys dashed into the house, breathless.

"The girls are fighting us!" they gasped, and I could see great welts swelling across their arms and backs. They hid behind my mosquito net just as Ihimei and Tihimei charged through the door, brandishing long whips made from supple sticks. I, too, cowered in a corner as the girls struck viciously at the men.

"Why don't you fight back?" I yelled.

"We can't," the men said. "This is our way."

The fight finally ended when the boys gave the girls some tobacco, but broke out anew whenever the girls reappeared on the scene.

For one couple, however, the battles ended. To this day I wonder why the marriage of Ningbi and Ihimei surprised me so. Perhaps it was because I knew my other houseboy was very fond of Ihimei and in fact allowed himself to be beaten by her far more than Ningbi had. Perhaps it was because no one had told me yet how marriages happen here.

It was after dinner one night when Kasli, Ihimei, and two of her cousins entered my

a new name. She decided to call him Lucas.

The period following the marriage was one marked by the tremendous difference between the married and the unmarried. Taboos forced the couple to change much of their vocabulary, making it difficult for them to talk and for me to understand. They could not eat many foods. Until they had given pearl shells to their numerous in-laws, they could not dine with them or even speak to them.

But the biggest change was that Ihimei was

house and began talking earnestly to Ningbi.

"You must marry," said Kasli.

"I can't," said Ningbi. "I'm too young."

"Ihimei says she likes you. Her parents say you must marry her."

"I won't. I'll run away and go to work."

Debli, busy in the kitchen, broke in angrily. "Ihimei is too young to marry. Her parents have said she is too expensive, and Ningbi has no shells."

Ihimei said nothing, as was proper, keeping her face turned to the wall as her cousins argued her case. After more than two hours of persuasion and rejection, everyone left.

The next morning I was greeted by a young neighbor: "Good morning, Jane. Ningbi and Ihimei are married."

"What happened?"

"Oh, Kasli put the two of them in the same house and kept them there all night so that they couldn't run away, so they are now considered to be properly married."

Because of a taboo, Ihimei could no longer call her husband Ningbi, and had to select

Gliding home with a load of sago-palm thatch, Nakanai tribesmen pole their slender outrigger off the north shore of New Britain. Jane Goodale and Ann Chowning concluded their expedition with a visit to this coast, where Ann had spent many months in 1954.

transformed from a giggling adolescent to a sedate, hard-working, charming young wife.

The unexpected marriage proved a highlight of my stay among the Kaulong, for it illustrated one of their fundamental attitudes and set me to speculating about their future.

The Kaulong regard premarital relations as a major offense, and it is not unusual for a man to marry as late as 30 years of age. (Some men are so marriage-shy that the approach of an eligible girl will send them away into the forest at a run.)

Denied many advantages of a modern world in their remote fastness, the Kaulong will, in all likelihood, also be spared one of its thorniest problems—the population explosion —for a long time to come. **THE END** 817

PUT THE WORLD ON YOUR BOOKSHELF—
138,000 place names at your fingertips and a
treasury of knowledge at the turn of each page—with
the enlarged, completely revised **National Geographic
Atlas of the World.** Among the expanded volume's many new pages,
large-scale maps portray the Low Countries, Denmark, and the smaller
states of Europe; physical maps show the wrinkled face of earth at a
glance—its mountains and plains, the depths of its seas. Decorative end papers
explain the science of map making, pinpoint earth's place in space, and sketch
the achievements of history's greatest astronomers, geographers, and cartographers.
Standard edition appears above, de luxe edition on the following page.

818

Revised, Enlarged World Atlas Charts Our Changing Earth

By WELLMAN CHAMBERLIN, Chief Cartographer, National Geographic Society

"WHAT DOES a cartographer do *between* maps?" a friend recently asked me. I could not answer. For in my 31 years with the National Geographic Society, the ever-changing world has never allowed me a lull.

Just three years ago the Society published its monumental **National Geographic Atlas of the World**. Members and professional cartographers hailed it with gratifying enthusiasm: "Exciting to the eye and intellect...." "None more convenient, current, or complete."

We had estimated the long-term demand—generously, we thought—and printed 140,000 copies. But now, sooner than anticipated, the entire stock has been sold out. And orders continue to pour in.

The easy answer would have been simply to reprint the Atlas. But we cartographers, painstakingly cataloguing events on this restless earth, concluded that changes in the world in only three years were so great that the Atlas should be brought right up to date.

Our course was clear, if costly: Nothing less than a completely revised, enlarged second edition would do. I now take considerable pride in announcing its publication.

Computer Sorts Index Automatically

Unseen behind its exhaustive, 161-page index lies a major breakthrough in atlas production. Our Space Age tool: an RCA 301 computer.

Under the direction of Associate Secretary Herman J. A. C. Arens, our staff explored ways to speed the tedious task of preparing the index for publication—a task that had required ten man-*years* for the first edition,

819

29 new pages
of maps and
information

EKTACHROMES BY PATRICK THURSTON © N.G.S.

Once Dutch, now German, children of Elten changed nationality without leaving home. In 1963 West Germany and the Netherlands realigned a frontier; at the stroke of a pen, some 7,700 people in areas under Dutch rule since 1949 became German citizens. Elten's name remained unchanged, but road signs switched from Dutch (upper) to German.

820

containing 11,000 fewer entries. This time the computer recorded and "memorized" on magnetic tape each of 138,000 index entries, more than can be found in any other American world atlas.

From this information storehouse the computer in a matter of hours automatically sorted and selected data, and then rolled out 30 *miles* of coded paper tape. Converted for use in the Society's Linofilm phototypesetting machines, the tape ran off the entire 161-page index—already alphabetized and set in columns!

Among new entries appear the infant island of Surtsey, spawned in volcanic eruption off Iceland in November, 1963, and new cities such as Reston, Virginia, designed for 75,000 inhabitants. And 10 new countries take their places among the family of nations (flags at right).

In Africa, Tanganyika and Zanzibar merged into Tanzania (pronounced "Tan-zan-EE-uh"); Nyasaland took the title of an ancient Bantu empire, Malawi; Northern Rhodesia adapted the name of its mighty river, the Zambezi, and became Zambia; Southern Rhodesia became simply Rhodesia. Other new countries with more familiar names: The Gambia, Kenya, Malaysia, Malta, the Maldive Islands, and Singapore.

Special Maps Reveal Earth's Wrinkles

To wrap up the world in one small package is like trying to pour an ocean into a bucket. But that is the task of the atlas maker.

Within this **Atlas of the World** you can find earth's extremes, from its longest river—the Nile—and largest sea—the South China Sea—to its tallest structure, a 2,063-foot television tower in Blanchard, North Dakota. You can see earth's interior from crust to core, and trace a newly mapped crack in the crust that zigzags entirely around the globe. You learn that the world's population now stands at 3.3 billion, an explosive gain of 10 percent over the 3 billion of just three years ago.

New physical maps of North America, South America, Europe, Asia, Africa, and Australia present each continent as nature forged it. Mountains appear in sharp relief; color tones accurately depict lowland contours and water depths.

Three added maps—England and Wales, Scotland, and Ireland—bring the British Isles into closer focus. Denmark now appears on a map of its own. So do Europe's smallest states: Liechtenstein, Andorra, San Marino, Vatican City, Monaco, and Malta.

A new double-page map separates the India-Pakistan subcontinent from the rest of Southwest Asia and spotlights disputed Kashmir. Two special maps, bearing capsule historical notes, revive the rich pasts of the Holy Land and the Nile Valley. A double-page plate, revised to include latest findings, shows Antarctica in unprecedented detail. Here scientists from 12 countries work together, under a 30-year treaty suspending all territorial claims, to unlock earth's last land-based frontiers.

Throughout the Atlas, inset maps of major cities locate points of interest for the traveler. Touring tips describe scenic and historic Europe. Half again as many places appear in the valuable climate table, which details the world's weather around the calendar.

Atlas was the giant of Greek mythology who supported the universe on his shoulders. Since 1595, with a work of the great Flemish cartographer Gerard Mercator, the name has been given to a bound collection of maps—such as the revised **Atlas of the World** that the National Geographic Society now proudly presents.   THE END

New banners unfurl as infant nations emerge. Since our first World Atlas edition in 1963, 10 countries—with a combined population of 42,900,000 and area of 1,145,000 square miles—have come into being.

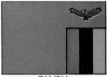

MALTA

ZAMBIA

MALAYSIA

MALAWI

THE GAMBIA

KENYA

TANZANIA

RHODESIA

SINGAPORE

MALDIVE ISLANDS

We flew southwest

from Paris in the cool summer morning, low, under puffball clouds. Pale wheat rippled on the Normandy plain like water in a wind. The paired spires of Chartres Cathedral notched the level skyline to my right. My son signaled that our course was good. We droned on in companionable silence.

A light plane is no place for conversation, but there is no better one for thinking beyond the barriers that beset a man on the ground. The sense of a region can be savored. And its past, considered in the lucid context of the land, becomes a reality, lying just over the horizon of time as a familiar region may lie out of sight over the curve of the earth.

One hour out. Trees ahead, and a break in the plateau. Glints of water, then a broad sweep of silver. We swung out over the stream above Blois and followed it westward. This was our destination: the Loire, the "River of France," which here flowed through its heartland, the famed Val de Loire. This was the chateau country, the country of kings.

Water made the Val de Loire, carving it out of the ungenerous soil of a broad plateau and paving it with rich loam. Wind made it too—the mild, moist breath of the sea, floating up the valley. Counts and kings made it, building forts to defend its natural barriers.

It was the epitome of France—was, because the royal influence that graced it with particular magnificence ended in the 16th century with the return of the court to Paris and its outskirts. But the castles are there, statements in stone of five centuries of brilliant, brawling human adventure. And the sea breeze still blows, and the river flows.

The Loire flowed now 600 feet below our wings, brown as cider in its sculptured sand bed. We passed quickly over pale castles half hidden among trees. Then we turned south toward the loveliest of the Loire's palaces, the Chateau of Chenonceaux. We found it astride its gentle stream, the Cher, framed in glowing gardens. I dropped my left wing and held the tip on the rooftop (pages 824-5). Magically, Chenonceaux pirouetted below us, revealing all its elegant aspects to our seemingly stationary seat in the sky.

For awhile we circled the great relic of the regal years, the age of personal wealth and power, of vanity and daring, of excitement

River of Counts and Kings

The Loire

CROWN AND SALAMANDER OF FRANÇOIS I, ADAPTED BY JANET FITCH SEWALL

about beauty. Then, as fuel gauges signaled the end of our stay, I banked north toward Paris. The "Garden of France," as Rabelais called it, lay behind us.

I would come back to explore the Val and its castles by land. But in what sense? Perhaps the river's own, starting where it starts in the Cévennes mountains and following its 625-mile course (map, page 832, and foldout, pages 826-8). For a stream is special among all the features of the earth: It has the three dimensions of length and breadth and depth like the rest. But it also goes somewhere; it has motion and direction. Thus it has a fourth dimension: the dimension of time.

A journey from source to sea through the four dimensions of the Loire would reveal the heart of France, the river's own biography from birth to majestic maturity, the monuments of men marking the successive stages of the human comedy played upon its banks.

THE OLD MAN with mournful mustache shuffled through the stable, brushing aside fat hens. He picked up a bucket and held it under a jet of clear water that curved from a spout in the wall into a watering trough. It took 12 seconds for the Loire to fill the pail. For this, said Monsieur Moulin, was indeed the Loire.

I watched a party of French visitors drink from the icy spring and touch the water with almost ritual awe (page 830). "But look! One can catch the Loire in one's two hands!"

The Moulin farm stands by a towering plug of lava called Gerbier de Jonc—"sheaf of rushes"—which its steep shape suggests. This monument to the Loire's birth juts out of the rolling meadows of a verdant highland forged in the fires of ancient volcanoes.

In the hollow below, from which the new-born Loire goes out to water towns and cities across the nation, a calm-faced peasant set down his scythe as I approached, following the rivulet. I greeted him in more or less Parisian French, picked up during childhood and more recent years in the capital. He answered in the unfamiliar but understandable accent of the southern mountain people.

"You've been to see the source? Well, that's what my neighbors up there call their spring. But there's another farm beyond those pines, and it has a spring too. Better look at it." His broad blade sliced through the sweet flower-spangled grass and he nodded farewell.

At the second farm a lean young man led me to a plank-covered spring in a pasture.

"*Le voici*—this is it," he announced firmly. "Just over the rise, all water flows to the Rhône and the Mediterranean. But this water goes north, all the way to the Atlantic."

He showed me where the overflow vanished into a brushy swale with a splash and a whisper. An old man approached, slow and straight-backed, holding his wooden rake like a banner.

"I am the owner of this place. I give you authority," he gestured grandly, "to study my farm as you please. I'm over 80, though you might not think so to see me raking hay, and all my life the Loire has flowed out of my pasture. It always has and it always will."

He paused, then added diffidently, "I hope you will send me a copy of your article. Don't worry, I can pay; and no one is more interested in me than I." He trudged away, rake erect.

Leaving the battle of the sources to its protagonists, I drove off down the course of the stream, following it as best I could. On the high mowings black-clad men and women pitched hay into cow-drawn carts and hauled it away to crooked, tightly clustered houses of dark stone where beasts and men would winter under the same red-tiled roofs. Here the new stream, a lusty infant, cut through overlying earth to rush noisily away over the bedrock of a harsh chasm untamed by time.

On a broad boulder I found four campers listlessly dangling lures in an eddy.

"Any fish?"

"Ha! There exist fish. One sees fish. But! But! One does not *catch* fish. We are here since a week, and soon we shall starve."

A few miles downstream at Arlempdes, the roughness of the river is matched by the gaunt bastions of a crumbling medieval chateau-fort (pages 832-3). Arlempdes is a relic, but a relic of a young culture, crude and vital, not

(Continued inside foldout, page 830)

By
KENNETH MacLEISH
Assistant Editor

PHOTOGRAPHS BY
DEAN CONGER
National Geographic Staff

823

LIKE A BRIDGE TO THE PAST, *the elegant castle of Chenonceaux spans the River Cher in the chateau-studded Val de Loire. Author Kenneth MacLeish dips a wing in a pilot's salute above the estate's exquisite formal gardens.*

GULF OF ST. MALO

N

MAYENNE

SARTHE

B R I T T A N Y

ANGERS

ANGERS

LE THOUREIL

LES PONTS-DE-C

A

N

J

O

U

BAC
DOUÉ

L O I R E

NANTES

SAUMUR

ST. NAZAIRE

BAY OF BISCAY

Janet

CHURCH OF ST. LIPHARD *at Meung*

JOAN OF ARC

SULLY

CHURCH OF JOAN OF ARC

ORLÉANS •

GIEN •

MEUNG •

BEAUGENCY •

SULLY •

BRIARE •

BLOIS

COSSON

CHAMBORD

CHAMBORD •

SANCERRE •

BLOIS •

B L O I S

CHEVERNY •

AMBOISE

LES MONTILS •

CHAUMONT •

CHEVERNY

CATHEDRAL OF ST. GATIEN *at Tours*

AMBOISE •

CHAUMONT

CHER

VOUVRAY •

CHENONCEAUX •

VALENÇAY •

T O U R A I N E

TOURS •

LANGEAIS •

VILLANDRY •

AZAY-LE-RIDEAU •

LOCHES •

CHENONCEAUX

VILLAINES •

INDRE

NGEAIS

RIGNY-USSÉ •

VOINE •

CHINON •

MUR

VIENNE

AZAY-LE-RIDEAU

CHINON

KODACHROME (ABOVE) BY KENNETH MACLEISH;
EKTACHROMES BY DEAN CONGER © N.G.S.

yet softened by sophistication. The stronghold, as raw as the rock on which it stands, tops a cliff above the valley.

Young country, young culture. The great buildings of the headwaters are old in years but young in architectural evolution. Along the lavish lower Loire, evolved elegance is of a later date. And so the theme develops: As the river flows onward, scenery and civilization mature together.

In the village below the ruin I found a cheerful crone, and asked her if she knew anything of its history. She shook her head. "No one lives there to tell. But it's very old. It's been there all my life, and *I'm* very old."

I climbed up to sit among the moss-bound stones that once were walls. Swallows darted around a topless turret. Far below, the river sighed down the valley. A fisherman stood motionless in midstream. The golden evening hummed with summer sound.

To some local lordling of the upper Loire, watching from his battlements in the days before France was France and this region of Velay was part of it, the scene would have been much as I saw it now. But how had he lived, that other watcher, centuries dead?

He lived in primitive austerity. A single big room in a square wood or stone keep was kitchen, bedroom, and living room all in one. A hearth, where meat turned on spits, warmed as best it could the chill hall. Daylight entered only through archers' slits. Torches flickered on walls where weapons hung.

The Loire leaps to life as a clear, cold spring beside a rocky volcanic peak in southeast France. A farmer at the foot of Gerbier de Jonc pipes the water into his barn, where thirsty tourists can say they caught France's longest river in a bottle (far right).

Or have they? In a nearby pasture an inquisitive boy pushes aside the rough-hewn planks sheltering a second spring, also claimed by its owner to be the mother of the Loire. A tactful government refuses to choose between them.

Winner by a whisker: In holiday mood, boys race their pet goats through the village of Les Estables. In the high, open country of the Loire's headwaters, winter-wise farmers conserve heat by sheltering flocks and families under the same roof.

829

GIEN

Val de Loire
Garden of France

NEVERS

0   10
STATUTE
MILES

Prince and peasant,
milkmaid and fal-
coner, countess and
cavalier: Royal
France lives on in
this map embellished
with figures taken from
tapestries of that era.
Artist Janet Fitch Sewall
re-created the life of
court and countryside
after a pilgrimage
to the chateaus.

BOURBON-LANCY

ALLIER

MARCIGNY

BURGUNDY

PINAY

FOREZ

LOIRE

ALLIER

VELAY

POLIGNAC
LE PUY

CÉVENNES

LES ESTABLES

GOUDET   GERBIER DE JONC
                5,089 FEET
ARLEMPDES

He lived in boredom. In this prisonlike protection, safety became stifling. He left when he could, to run down a stag or attack a neighbor or join a crusade. He was illiterate, or close to it, and in any case, books were rare and costly. He learned what little he knew of the literature of his day from the poems and songs of itinerant minstrels.

For later chieftains, home was no longer a single hall but perhaps three or four rooms. The bedroom was private and the kitchen separate. There would be a bath—a diminutive stone swimming pool filled with lukewarm water. Windows let in the sun to shine on painted walls and carpeted floors.

In this quiet ruin, haunted by its lusty past, history came alive. Feudal phantoms stood almost at the edge of sight. Lutes and flutes sounded just out of earshot. Below, the Loire lay in shadow. The fisherman had gone.

I went, too, and came quickly to the village of Goudet, where Robert Louis Stevenson arrived on just such a day 80-odd years ago and called the stream coursing through it "an amiable stripling of a river, which it seems absurd to call the Loire."

By nightfall I had reached Le Puy, the market center of Velay. I left my car in a quiet square. I found it next morning buried in a frantic melee of carts, quacks, curses, bleats, bellows, and the full-throated soprano protest of pigs being hoisted by an ear and a tail. I had got myself a ticket and an audience.

"You should not have parked in a market place on market day," a member of the audience announced in carrying tones.

"I didn't know it would be market day."

"Saturday is always market day!"

"Not in my village. Ours is Wednesday."

"Tiens!" shouted my interrogator.

A policeman removed the ticket, two pushcarts, and a sow, and I drove off in a blue haze of friendly obscenity.

FROM MARKET to cathedral seemed a proper progression. The original cathedral at Le Puy is of the 11th century, of the style called Romanesque—heavy, thick-walled, Roman-arched—to which belong the earliest churches in France (pages 836-7). This one is special. A place of pilgrimages and reputed miracles, it was born of a fourth-century legend:

A woman dying of fever was told by the Virgin to go to a certain pagan table stone on a remote hill and lie down on it. This she did, and arose cured. Around the stone a stag traced with hoofprints in the snow the outline of a chapel. The structure built to this supernatural plan has vanished, but the present cathedral stands in its stead, sheltering the "fever stone."

Downstream to the north, in sight of the crag which towers over the cathedral, the impregnable eyrie of the Counts of Polignac loomed on its sheer-sided table rock. I approached it across mist-dimmed meadows where the predatory feudal lords swooped down to take their toll from passing pilgrims.

The path to the summit is steep and narrow. I climbed it in the moist heat of noon. The place seemed deserted. Glancing upward at the forbidding portal, slotted for the delivery of boiling oil and arrows upon intruders, I did not see the dim figure propped in a corner.

"Go away," she suggested cordially. "Allez-vous-en; I am going home for lunch."

"But this is perfect," I blandished hopefully. "I had particularly wanted to explore the ruins alone. Surely you, a curator, will understand the problems of a writer. . . ."

"Lunchtime is lunchtime," she stated with flawless logic. Then, leavening triumph with mercy, "However, one can wait half an hour when one's family has served the Polignacs for three centuries. Forty centimes, please."

THE GRASSY cliff-rimmed plateau, where peasants from the village camped in days of danger, was punctuated now with ruins and wild roses. Crumbling walls and corpse-shaped graves carved in bedrock lay shrouded in fragrant briars. Only the tall feudal keep retained its old, bold appearance; but its floors had fallen away, leaving fireplaces arrayed in emptiness. Of the raiders' lair there remained only silent stones and memories.

In the village cafe lunch was over. The proprietress brought me two slabs of fresh bread, a mound of butter, a crock of pâté, pickles, a pitcher of red wine, her apologies, and a bill for three francs—60 cents.

Driving north along the Loire, I felt the country changing. Hilltops lowered. Poplars appeared, their leaves shivering like silver sequins in the hot breeze. Small wheat fields replaced the upland mowings, and the farmers no longer wore the black of highland people. The villages, too, had changed; houses here were plastered, and deployed along streets.

The river ran through small steep gorges, widening between them into quiet runs. In one such I stopped to swim, lying in the caressing current and listening to the clink of pebbles stirred by the stream's soft surge down toward the region called Forez.

The eerie Forez plain, sour, soggy, peppered with ponds, is a country of legends— 831 apocryphal tales of romance and horror, told, perhaps, to brighten its drab reality. Precious pens of the 17th century peopled the place with imaginary figures—courtly shepherds, delicate shepherdesses and, no doubt, gallant sheep. Other tales, more appropriate to this dim marshland, told of monstrous beasts which ate Forezians in epic numbers.

This was not castle country. The Loire, not yet broad enough to serve as a barrier or as a mirror for magnificence, cut through the valley in gentle, slow-running curves.

At Pinay, where Louis XIV had built a flood-control dam to tame the stream's excesses, it swept again through gorges, swirling and foaming in its last struggle with stone before breaking free to meander seaward in a sandy bed of its own making. Then it left Forez and, deflected northwest by the Mountains of Morvan, skirted the edge of Burgundy.

In this region of fertile fields and noble vineyards a new architectural form began to appear: the stone fantasy of the Gothic, an elaborate expression of 13th- and 14th-century

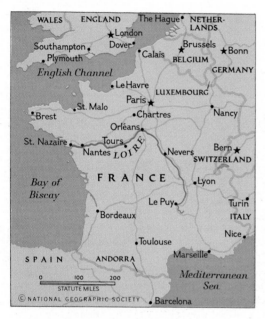

Flowing through the heart of France, the Loire swells from brook to stream to majestic river as it courses north to Orléans, thence westward to the Atlantic.

The verdant Val de Loire is rich in remembrance of the past. Feudal lords fought one another and even the king for the right to rule it in the Middle Ages. During the Renaissance sumptuous castles rose beside the river. Nobles and royalty alike spent carefree summers, entertaining lavishly and hunting in the forests, before the wars of religion ravaged the region.

Gallic charm still pervades the valley. Today's visitors, touring its show places, step back into a magnificent past.

Singing waters of the young river, tumbling over rocks and boulders, beckon a fisherman. The ruins of Arlempdes, a massive feudal fortress, loom on the clifftop.

civilization. The style could better be called pointed, based as it is on high-peaked arches and combinations of arches which suggest the interlacing branches of tall trees.

Gothic churches boasted another impressive novelty, the flying buttress. This ingenious support carried the weight of the vault so that the walls could be cut away and replaced with glowing expanses of stained glass. Churches and houses alike were decorated with intricate carvings.

Examples were not hard to find: a beauti-

fully beamed mill at Marcigny; a clock tower astraddle a street in Bourbon-Lancy near a happily cockeyed timbered house.

Near this pleasant town, now a spa for arthritics who come to soak in hot springs where Caesar may have sweated, I found two urchins fishing in a setting as pastoral as a Watteau painting. Did I say fishing? They wore gaudy cowboy hats, jiggled in time to American rock 'n' roll blasting from a portable radio, puffed on lumpy hand-rolled cigarettes, and tossed down their soda pop as if

Dining out in Le Puy, a top-knotted gourmet savors the delights of cafe cuisine.

Sunny Saturday: Market day brings farmers into Le Puy from the country to sell their fresh fruits and vegetables. Discerning housewives, a few with children in tow, watch closely as vendors weigh purchases on old-fashioned balance scales.

Le Puy, in the Auvergne dialect, means "the peak." Citizens of this ancient center of lace-making live in centuries-old houses built along hills so steep that some streets serve merely as stairways.

it were corn likker. They were also experts on all that concerned the river.

"Plenty of fish," yelled the smaller boy, handily outsounding his raucous radio. *"Regardez!"* He held up a netful of wriggling, glittering minnows. "We catch them with tiny hooks and eat them whole. But one must know where to find them. Swimming? Of course. Enjoy yourself."

I stripped and approached the shore a few yards away. "Not there!" shrilled my mentor. "One must know where to swim, too. The current would take you to the bend, where the quicksand would swallow you. Now, if you will do just as I say...."

I emerged some minutes later cooled, unscathed, and living proof that the youngster knew his river.

In the evening, after a supper served by a muscular lady whose face presented the color and expression of an apricot ("the meal pleased you," she stated, omitting the question mark), I found a clean, quiet room above a honeysuckle hedge. Next morning I took the river road to Nevers.

There is much to see in this land of transition from the simplicity of the upper river to the Renaissance opulence of the Val de Loire. Nevers, a supply center since Roman times, is a good place to see it.

For France, the Renaissance was not so much a rebirth of culture, as the name implies, but a great outpouring of new ideas in the arts and sciences, most of them coming at first from Italy. The Duke of Nevers was a Gonzaga from Mantua, and he brought to his French domain both crafts and craftsmen of his native land. The city's 400-year-old ceramics industry is his legacy (page 853).

In the showroom of his establishment, M.

Montagnon walked carefully among his fragile faïences, selecting and showing them with sure hands.

"There were a dozen *faïenceries* in the old days, and hundreds of artisans. Now there are three shops, of which only ours is original. You must understand that we make faïence *of* Nevers, not simply faïence *at* Nevers. It is hand-glazed, hand-painted, and always hand-formed. Most pieces are one-of-a-kind."

HALF AN HOUR'S run down the left bank brought me to a hilltop huddle of red roofs dominating the valley. This was Sancerre, center of a little land of flocks and vineyards, a village famed for its wine, its goat cheese, and the horror of its history. A Huguenot town, it was besieged and starved by royal troops during the 16th-century wars of religion, until its natives turned for food to rats, dogs, and weeds, and, even in a few frightful instances, to the flesh of the dead.

Nothing remains of the home of the Protestant Counts of Sancerre except a round tower from whose height the Loire—and a barge canal which parallels it here—can be followed into the far distance. Some twenty miles downstream at Briare this canal takes an unusual turn: It crosses the river. Borne across the Loire by a 2,000-foot aqueduct, which connects it with another canal on the far side, this lofty waterway permits boats to cross the stream without touching it. And just beyond this singular crossing lies Gien.

It is at Gien that the special conditions of wind and water which define the Val de Loire first coincide. The mildness of the still-distant sea begins to be felt. The widening waters begin to deposit strips of rich soil. Here, too,

835

RINSED BY RAIN, *blessed by a rainbow, Le Puy clusters around table-topped Corneille Rock and its imposing centerpiece, a statue of Notre Dame de France. Cast from Russian cannon captured in the Crimean War, the iron figure surveys a sea of red-tiled roofs and the rugged countryside of the upper Loire. During the Middle Ages, pilgrims flocked to the massive Cathedral of Notre Dame to pray before a statue of the "Black Virgin." French Revolutionaries burned it, but a replacement still attracts worshipers.*

836

the downstream traveler finds his first royal castle, though not a very elaborate one, and built by a king's daughter rather than a king. And now the hills are left behind, the sky is big, and the river reflects its light.

I watched Gien across the water, arrayed along the river with the chateau resting on a rise above its roofs—a sensible, solemn, semi-feudal mansion. Toward twilight, clouds coursed the sky like homing herds. Children who had been aiding the river in its timeless task of moving sand from one place to another picked up their pails and went home. So did I, to my hotel, where there was bird-shot in the pheasant to prove its authenticity.

Anne de Beaujeu's castle at Gien (below) presents no decorations and no expensive accoutrements of war. The long struggle with England was over when she built it, late in the 15th century, and Anne was not one to waste money on useless elaborations. She was a practical woman of simple tastes. It was perhaps in recognition of these qualities that her parsimonious and misogynic father, Louis XI, said of her, "She is the least foolish woman in France; for of wise ones, I know none."

The Chateau of Gien now houses a handsome museum of shooting and falconry and the dreary precincts of the recently vacated Palace of Justice and local jail. When I entered the building, its rooms rang with the age-old call of the hunting horn; no spectral sounds but those of the curator, M. Henri de Linares, practicing in his quarters (opposite).

Soon he joined me, a gentleman as courtly as any of his predecessors in these antique halls. He spoke fondly and knowledgeably of his superb weapons, pointing out a crossbow, beautifully decorated with staghorn, an ivory-encrusted arquebus, an antique air rifle, then sent me with a guide to the unseen subterranean spaces below the castle halls.

There, in musty darkness, our flashlights revealed the studded doors and bolts of ancient oubliettes, and the sad stigmata of imprisonment: stenciled numbers and regimented grease stains of the abandoned modern lockup.

In a beautifully vaulted room of great age,

Music of the hunting horn echoes through the Great Hall of the Chateau of Gien. Now a museum, the castle houses a collection of weapons, tapestries, paintings, and engravings depicting the history of the chase. Curator Henri de Linares, at left, himself a hunter, wears the habit of a *veneur*—one who rides to hounds after stag and boar.

Warm sands of Gien lure sunbathers and swimmers, but a barricade warns against a treacherous stretch of the Loire. Beyond the river rises the severe castle built in 1484 by Anne de Beaujeu, eldest daughter of Louis XI. The 15th-century bell tower at left is all that survives from the original church of Joan of Arc, a gift to the town by Princess Anne.

KODACHROMES © N.G.S.

strange iron hooks were set in the wall "to hang meat, perhaps," suggested my guide with a macabre smile, and added, "Over there are bits of evidence from recent trials. See, a boot with a bullet hole, poachers' snares, broken bottles...."

I emerged in time into sweet air and sunlight and followed the left-bank road to Gien's exact antithesis, the Chateau of Sully. A white-walled fighting fortress, Sully was born of battle. Massive, moated, turreted, it is a lovely monument to feudalism. I stood for a while among its sighing cypresses and saw in its blind windows the shadows of its medieval masters.

SULLY was a military outpost of Orléans, the walled sanctuary of the eastern Val. Today a clean, prosperous town, bombed out and rebuilt, richer in the remembrance of things past than in its physical legacy, Orléans was once the key city of central France. The English recognized it as such and laid siege to it in one of the crucial engagements of the bitter Hundred Years' War. It was here that the illiterate farm girl Joan of Arc won the day for her faltering ruler Charles VII; her heroism led eventually to her trial and death.

The strange alliance of Joan and Charles began in March, 1429, at the fortress of Chinon, where the weak-willed successor resided while England threatened his throne. The simple girl, driven by voices and visions, came before Charles as he hid among his courtiers. Strong, dark-skinned, unabashed, she singled him out at once and begged him in God's name to assume his crown and drive the English from the land.

Charles believed in her, it seems, because only in doing so could he believe in himself. He gave her a small army. She entered Orléans, exhorting its exhausted citizens to rally to her banner and counterattack. On May 8 the city was freed.

MODERN MAIDS OF ORLÉANS *stroll the Place du Martroi, where a bronze Joàn of Arc commemorates the young farm girl who vanquished English invaders five centuries ago. The grateful city still celebrates its deliverance every May.*

Joan, accused by her enemies of sorcery and heresy, was later sold to the English and burned alive after a long, false trial during which the triumphant Charles, aptly nicknamed "the Well Served," did nothing to save her. She was not yet 20 years old.

Below Orléans' urban sprawl lies the village of Meung, and in Meung there are many millers. Here, in earlier days, the harvests of the northern plateau were milled by the force of brooks rolling down to the river where the Loire's merchant navy, plying between Orléans and the sea, carried the flour away.

Over the whirr and clatter of his machinery, a dusty young man with the build of an acrobat and the speech of a collegian commented on milling at Meung.

"The locale was perfect," he shouted. "Supply, power, transportation, all at our doorstep. We still have the supply. Loire shipping died a hundred years ago with the silting up of the river, so we use the railroads. The brooks have dwindled, so we use electricity. And people still eat bread. Ours is an old trade, a good trade."

Nearby, on the river flats, a blue-smocked farmer was engaged in a profitable new project. He climbed off his tractor-sprayer to tell me about it.

"See all these apple trees, trained on wires to spread out like fans? You've seen such trees espaliered against the walls of our old buildings, to beautify them. Here the practice is practical: The two-dimensional trees take sun and spray well, and the harvest is easy. The oldest are only ten years old, yet observe how they produce.

"Once this was all vegetable country. We made big crops and little money, and we worked too hard. Now the work goes quickly, and the prices are good." He mounted his rig and trundled away in a cloud of insecticide.

A SHORT drive brought me to Beaugency, stretched beside the stream in enchanted sleep, dreaming of other days. A single square tower rises near the river, remnant of a feudal fortification. Elsewhere venerable houses, set along winding ways, comfortably encompass fragments of still older structures.

The town's bridge is one of the finest on the Loire, and naturally there is a story about it: The devil built it in a single night to trap the soul of the first person to cross it. But the wise citizens sensed his purpose and prudently sent

Aflame with light, the Chateau of Blois brings the past hauntingly alive in the spectacle of *Son et Lumière*—a pageant combining music, dialogue, and ingenious lighting.

A succession of owners turned the castle into an architectural catalogue of styles from Romanesque to neoclassical. In this wing, the spectacular creation of François I, a winding staircase open to the air spirals from ground to roof. Some experts believe Leonardo da Vinci influenced its design during the years he spent in the Val de Loire as a guest of François.

"Most joyous utterance of the French Renaissance," writer Henry James called this white limestone masterpiece.

Secret cabinets that may have held the poisons of Catherine de Médicis fascinate young visitors to Blois. Scene of dark intrigue, the chateau witnessed the murder of King Henri III's political adversary, the Duke of Guise, at the ruler's command.

Pride of Sancerre — creamy goat cheese and deliciously light white wine. Straw embedded in each biscuit-shaped cheese guarantees the buyer that a farmwoman made it in her home.

Vouvray's grape harvest brings pickers to the region north of Tours whose fruity white wine evokes accolades from connoisseurs the world over. Harvesters with buckets on backs gather Chenin grapes and gently tamp them in wooden vats.

Sunshine in a bottle, sparkling Vouvray bubbles like champagne and resembles it in taste. Most Vouvray wines are still, but the addition to this variety of a little sugar before corking causes a second fermentation and a head of foam.

KODACHROMES BY DEAN CONGER AND HÉLÈNE JEANBRAU (OPPOSITE) © N.G.S.

a cat instead of a man. One cat's soul was all "the Other One" got for his trouble.

The trickle in the mountain meadow and the spout in the stable seemed far away. Here the Loire flowed forcefully, a quarter of a mile wide. Already it was well into the legendary Val de Loire, the region of royal residence, whose full flowering would appear just ahead at Blois, and beyond.

At first glance the famous Chateau of Blois seems unremarkable. It is not nearly so large as the imagination would make it. It has no unity. Its wings are of different ages, different styles, and different materials, seeming to ignore each other's existence.

Yet in its detail and in its separate parts the Chateau of Blois is beautiful and impressive, even though it is richer in its past than in its present. And it is the perfect place to encounter the shades of the Val's great men and to begin an exploration of their special and individual creations.

I entered Blois as part of a large, noisy, and cosmopolitan tour group. It included a dozen different nationalities plus perhaps a hundred happy, supercharged little Italian schoolgirls who, with their high speed and low center of gravity, outmaneuvered everyone in the doorways and stairways.

We ambled dutifully from wing to wing, from epoch to epoch: through the great hall of the 13th-century Counts of Blois; the red brick Gothic gallery of the poet Charles of Orléans, who, in his 71st year, fathered Louis XII; the late Gothic additions of Louis XII; the white limestone Renaissance elegance

of François I's 16th-century wing; and finally the dreary 17th-century classical wing of Gaston d'Orléans. We saw within the confines of this court the full succession of styles, from medieval onward.

When the tourists had gone, I presented to the chief guard an assortment of credentials and received from him, literally, the keys to the castle. I climbed François' marvelous octagonal stairway and wandered alone through the empty rooms, larger now in their natural state of silence.

My footsteps echoed as if others followed. The painted eyes of portraits watched. Locks squeaked and hinges creaked. Here, in Catherine de Médicis' "office," four panels out of 237 open at the touch of hidden levers to reveal secret compartments legend fills with poisons (page 842). Here were rooms where the Duke of Guise, rabid anti-Protestant and

Enchanting island of stone, forested with towers, chimneys, and dormers, Chambord became a passion of its builder, François I. Though "too poor" to pay the ransom of his sons held captive in Spain, he raided church treasuries to keep 1,800 workmen busy raising this largest of the Val de Loire's chateaus.

Succeeding kings of France, great huntsmen all, chased deer and boar in the surrounding Forest of Boulogne. Their ladies watched tournaments and festivals from the rooftop terrace. "A court without ladies," François once remarked, "is a springtime without roses." With the storms of the Revolution, Chambord fell into disrepair until the French Government restored it in the 1930's.

As if expecting the courtiers to reappear, artisans of today keep carvings and embellishments in immaculate condition.

political rival of Catherine's son, Henri III, was assassinated as the King hid listening in his study and two priests in his private chapel prayed for the success of the scheme.

But it is at night that the Chateau of Blois becomes truly believable. In the spectacle of *Son et Lumière*—sound and light—music matched to its several styles adds a new dimension. Light, played like an instrument, directs the eye to this façade or that, blazing and fading; to a single window glowing, to a gallery alive with the shadows of unseen dancers (page 843).

A voice speaks from the castle: "The spirits love the night. Darkness erases form and time." It is true. The spirits live as voices speak for them. Kings and queens converse in tones of men and women. And this, their home, isolated by night and accented by light, lives too as never under the sun.

Having seen the spectacle of sound and light at Blois, the wise traveler will hurry on before his soaring imagination is shot down by the town's brisk contemporary bustle.

Across the river, bright among dark woods, I could see Chambord, the most fanciful and complicated castle in France. Only François I, that brash, swashbuckling egotist and paragon of the French Renaissance, could have ordered so wildly spectacular a dwelling. I approached it down a perfectly straight road more than a mile long, at the end of which its forest of lantern towers, chimneys, pinnacles, and turrets loomed in frozen fantasy (preceding pages).

An American airman standing near me stared thoughtfully for a few moments, then shook his head. "Wow!" he said. It was as valid a critique as any.

Chambord is the biggest of the hundred-odd chateaus of the Loire, and had the least reason for being. It has been called "passionately personal" and "a true domicile of abso-

lute monarchy." François loved it and emptied the national treasury to build it. Then he used it as a hunting lodge.

It took a man of vivid personality to live happily at Chambord. François' son Henri II managed a few visits, but no other king came to live in that limestone extravaganza. It was given by the crown to a series of deserving friends and relations, who no doubt lived out their privileged stay in overawed boredom.

FRANCOIS' funhouse is the first of an alliterative trio of chateaus which adorn the region of Blois: Chambord, Cheverny, Chaumont—names that sound like a song. The three could hardly differ more.

Cheverny, a 17th-century classical mansion, is a lordly dwelling rather than a royal residence. Strangely, this blandest of chateaus is the product of a misalliance and a murder. The Count of Cheverny, finding his wife in another man's arms, killed her lover on the spot and offered her a choice between

KODACHROMES BY DEAN CONGER AND HÉLÈNE JEANBRAU (BELOW) © N.G.S.

Room fit for a king: Persian silk graces bed and canopy in the King's Chamber in Cheverny. Tapestries portray scenes from the Odyssey; paintings adorn ceiling and mantel. In royal times, every chateau reserved its most handsome room for a visit from the monarch.

Sunshine streaming through its windows pierces the rich brown gloom of the Guardroom (upper right). The 15th-century tournament armor conjures up the days of chivalry.

"A light, sweet mansion . . . looking over a wide green lawn and groups of trees," Henry James wrote of Cheverny more than half a century ago, and so it appears even today.

Cheverny, unlike most Loire chateaus, is used by descendants of its builders. When the tide of tourists ebbs each fall, its owner, the Marquis de Vibraye, returns for the hunting season.

849

Mirror-calm waters of the Loire part for the Ile d'Or as they glide slowly past the town of Amboise and its chateau. During the Renaissance, Charles VIII imported Italian sculptors and decorators to

embellish his favorite castle, but in 1560 a massacre of Huguenots stained its glory. Abandoned by royalty, the buildings decayed; the few still standing represent only a dim shadow of past magnificence.

poison and the sword. She chose the former.

For his breach of good taste, the count was confined for some years to his lands on the Loire. There, having nothing else to do, he married his bailiff's daughter. Later he wearied of her and went off to serve his king. To divert herself, his bride began to build the present chateau. In time her husband returned, fell in love with her creation—and perhaps herself—and devoted his fortune to completing it.

The particular glory of Cheverny is its sumptuous interior (pages 848-9). One of the few castles still occupied by descendants of its builders, it has been kept as it was 300 years ago. It is alive with color and the warmth that can come only from human residence.

In the old days the poor land around Chambord and Cheverny remained in its natural state and served its natural purpose, which was to supply game. Chateau country was hunting country. Now small farmers work the meager soil, making modest crops in patchwork fields between hedgerows. The villages are peaceful and unpretentious. They suggest the indolence of the Val people, which is epitomized in a famous parable:

"Are you hungry?"

"Yes!"

"Then fetch your bowl and get some soup."

"I'm not hungry any more."

In one such hamlet, called Les Montils, I heard the unhurried ring of a blacksmith's hammer and stopped to watch him in the darkness of his shop. He beckoned lazily.

"*Entrez donc*—come in. Forgive me if I continue to hammer. I am making a horseshoe, and the horse is on his way. A writer, eh? Then you're interested in the artistic side of life. The old skills, like mine. I am not just a shoer of horses. Here! A 17th-century piece, a wrought-iron wall bracket. Made it myself. Ah, the devil, here comes the horse."

In the empty street he and the man who came with the horse exchanged gossip as they lifted and trimmed the great, docile hoofs.

THE SOUTHERN plateau skirts the river in this section, raising its limy cliffs a hundred feet or so above the Loire. Chaumont, the third of Blois' great outlying chateaus, stands on the height of the land, commanding the river (page 854). Its entrance is a drawbridge set between towers. Unlike florid Chambord and genteel Cheverny, designed for gracious living, Chaumont is a strong point.

No king dwelt at Chaumont, but it has close royal connections. Upon the death of Henri II, his widow, Catherine de Médicis, acquired the place as an instrument of vengeance. During the king's lifetime, Catherine, an

Wands of willow flick back and forth in the deft hands of Nestor Metezeau and his son Claude, as they weave wicker chairs and screens in their cave workshop at Villaines-les-Rochers.

The Metezeaus pick the slender branches on the banks of the Indre River in January, then let them stand in water until May before stripping off the bark. Stored dry until needed, the willow must soak for 24 hours to become pliable enough for weaving.

"My great-grandfather was a wicker worker," says young Claude, "and maybe even his father before him." Some families in Villaines trace furniture-making forebears to the 1600's. In 1849 the village priest organized the artisans into a cooperative that still functions.

Wielding an oarlike spoon in a giant pot, chef Jean Gaudin stirs a fish sauce at the canning plant of Amieux Frères in Nantes. Needing no recipe, he relies on memory to add just the right amount of each ingredient as he blends crab meat, tomatoes, flour, butter, white wine, and Armagnac. Fresh vegetables grown in the Loire Valley ride a cart to the processing tables.

EKTACHROMES © N.G.S.

Blue flowers bloom beneath the brush of an artist at the Montagnon pottery shop in Nevers. Hand-glazed, always hand-formed, most pieces are unique. An Italian from Mantua, who became Duke of Nevers in 1565, introduced the making of faïence to the townspeople.

853

Grace of Chenonceaux and strength of Chaumont mirror the spirit of different ages. Chenonceaux' Renaissance façade sweeps across the placid Cher River, inviting guests to pursue a life of peaceful pleasure. Only 12 miles away, Chaumont's feudal towers (below), built for war, command a hill above the Loire.

Rivals for a king's heart changed the history of two chateaus. Diane de Poitiers (left) received Chenonceaux as a gift from King Henri II. She lavished attention on the castle, building a piered bridge to the right bank, and laying out the huge formal garden. When the thrust of a tournament lance killed Henri, his embittered Queen, Catherine de Médicis (right), seized Chenonceaux and forced the grim fortress of Chaumont (opposite, lower) upon her rival. Catherine added a two-story gallery over the bridge; from it guests viewed mock naval battles fought for their amusement on the Cher.

Italian commoner with a quick mind and a sour face had been powerless against her husband's mistress, Diane de Poitiers. Henri had given Diane the castle of Chenonceaux, perhaps the finest in the Val. Now Catherine forced Diane to exchange Chenonceaux for Chaumont. The triumphant queen mother went to live in her rival's lovely castle and Diane, banished from her cherished home, dimmed slowly and died.

There were dull explosions downstream. From Chaumont's terrace I could see smoke trails rising into the belly of a swollen thunderhead a few miles to the west. Again the mortarlike thumping sounded and more trails streaked up into the roiling mass, purple-green as an old bruise. I turned to the guardian watching beside me. "What . . . ?"

"Rockets. The farmers' cooperative has them all over the Val to protect the wheat and the vines from storms. When a big cloud comes, they shoot it right in the bottom with their rockets. Don't think they're not expensive, those rockets; they contain rain-making explosives. But if they make the cloud release

855

its rain before it can become hail, the crops are saved. Look! Here it comes now! Run for it!"

The stagnant air moved restlessly. Then thunder crashed and the cloudburst smothered the land. I followed the left-bank road along the rain-blurred river toward my next goal, Amboise. But soon the downpour forced me off the road into a pleasant interlude.

Across the narrow pavement were several caves cut straight back into the cliff, some

Huddled beneath the battlements, houses of Langeais crowd the castle built to block threatened incursions by the Bretons in the 1460's. But the marriage of Anne of Brittany to King Charles VIII in the chateau's chapel erased the danger.

The somber gray building with its heavy overhanging cornice and slate-roofed towers belies an opulent interior. Jacques Siegfried, an Alsatian, bought the castle in 1885 and spent the rest of his life collecting furnishings to give life to the rooms. His daughter, Mlle. Agnès Siegfried (above), still lives in the chateau. Each summer morning she arranges fresh flowers for visitors.

fronted with proper doors and windows, some opening into velvet blackness. A gnome with spectacles peered from one of the latter and hollered, "Come in and have some wine!"

I ducked out of the rain into a fragrant grotto with an alcove at the back containing a wine press. On one side was a large sooty fireplace and on the other a spavined table bearing wine bottles.

"My vineyards are right overhead," said the small troglodyte. "That's why this cave belongs to me."

He set out glasses, fastidiously dipping each one into a bucket of river water and polishing it with his shirttail. "Here, try the white." He filled two glasses, toasted me with a wink, and drained his.

"Terrible, isn't it," he apologized cheerfully. "Here, try the rosé. It's good. Expensive, though. I have to ask two francs [40 cents] a bottle for it. Try the red. Try them all. But if you're going to buy any, buy the rosé. *Santé!*"

I went away refreshed and entered Touraine under a clean sky scoured by the retreating storm.

TOURAINE is the heart of the Val, just as the Val is the heart of the Loire (and, some say, of France itself). Henry James wrote of it, "In that soft, clear, merry light ... everything shows, everything speaks."

In such a light I first saw the gray bulk of Amboise, a chateau that is more a place than a building (pages 850-51). It is a fortified vantage point. For several centuries Amboise was the stage for the brutal and brilliant accomplishments of a succession of rulers, commencing with counts and concluding with kings. It was a home for every crowned head who ruled France from the Loire.

In succession came Charles VII, to make the place a royal redoubt; Louis XI, to improve it and keep his wife in it; Charles VIII, to import artisans from Italy and make the castle a center of the Renaissance; Louis XII, to start new living quarters; and François I, to finish them.

François also brought men of arts and letters from beyond his borders, among them Leonardo da Vinci. It is certain that the aging genius, showman that he was, produced brilliant settings and all sorts of illusions for his patrons' parties. Leonardo lent himself more willingly to such transitory achievements than he did to the tiresome task of completing paintings for posterity.

Fairy-tale castle, Ussé inspired author Charles Perrault, who gave the modern world
Cinderella, Bluebeard, and other classics, to retell the ancient legend of Sleeping

Beauty. The chateau, rising from the Forest of Chinon, provides the ideal setting for a
fantasy about an imprisoned princess, magic spells, romance, and happiness ever after.

Glowing above dark waters of the River Indre, Azay-le-Rideau reflects the tranquil era of the early 1500's, when nobles and financiers raised luxurious mansions in the Val de Loire. Its banker-builder, Gilles Berthelot, spared no expense; indeed, he plundered the royal treasury to assure its grandeur. Fine furnishings and art objects fill the chateau, now a national museum.

was once the beating heart of the French monarchy.

Still, the easy, lazy life of the valley survives with all the timelessness of the river itself. Below the melancholy castle there is a green island. And on this summer day it was decorated with the blue and orange tents of campers idling inexpensively between the cool arms of the Loire.

I LEFT THE big river now and headed for its pastoral tributary, the Cher, and the building whose beauty had inspired my pilgrimage. Unlike Amboise, Chenonceaux charms the senses. It is a *château de plaisance,* a pleasure palace. Here no fortification intrudes on elegance (pages 854-5).

Henri II was the last monarch to see Amboise at its height. Following his death, his Queen, Catherine, was left as regent for their son, the boy King François II. Troubled times were at hand. The magnificence of Amboise was suddenly fouled by an orgy of slaughter. In 1560, at the outbreak of the wars of religion, hundreds of Protestant activists were butchered there under the eyes of the court. The gay terraces were stained with blood and the place stank of corpses.

Never again did a King of France live at Amboise. Sickly young François II died, with the massacre fresh in his mind, and his two brothers, who succeeded him, ruled from Blois. Then the court left the Val forever for Paris and its environs.

The glittering castle became a prison, then a private residence, rotting with the passing years. Today the ruins have been cleared away, and what remains has been restored. But there is little left to proclaim that this

Chenonceaux' builder was Thomas Bohier, commoner and financier, who got the land by systematically exploiting the ill fortunes of its original and noble owners. He left the building in his wife's charge and went off in the fiscal service of his king. After Bohier's death in the 1520's, an examination of his books showed him to be deeply in debt to the royal treasury. François I received the castle as restitution.

Chenonceaux has a feminine feel to it, with its delicate decor, its mirroring water, its original and discreet arrangement of rooms around a central hall, its revolutionary straight stairway, better suited to spectacular entrances than the standard spiral. And indeed it has always been ruled by women. Diane de Poitiers beautified the building before Catherine took it from her, and Catherine improved upon her predecessor's plans. Other great ladies kept the creation of the renowned rivals in

Cloud-scraping citadel, the Chateau of Saumur sits above the Loire and the town it once defended. Built in the 14th century, the bastion became a Protestant stronghold during the wars of religion in the 1500's. Its collection of antiquities includes ceramics and Limoges enamels and a "Museum of the Horse." In World War II, the castle suffered heavy bomb damage.

perfect repair and magnificently furnished.

I came out onto the drawbridge of Chenonceaux dazzled as much by its treasures as by the slanting sun that gilded its pale stone. For here was an expression of special accomplishment through special privilege beyond the reach of modern monarchs. Such was the spirit of France's absolute monarchy. It destroyed itself, but in its time it created beauty.

Such also was the spirit of Touraine and, according to great writers of the past, of Tours, its capital, toward which I now traveled. Balzac, proud son of that city, wrote:

"Tours has always had its feet in the Loire, like a pretty girl who bathes herself and plays with the water ... for this town is more smiling, merry, loving, fresh, flowery, and fragrant than all the other towns of the world. . . ."

BALZAC might not recognize his city. Heavily damaged in recent wars, the old artistic and intellectual community has become a market town, a railhead, a tourist center. Yet it is still very much the provincial capital, with a rich tradition and, as always, its feet in the Loire.

But Tours' pace has changed with its appearance. A secretary at city hall said, "Today Tours is like any other place. Everyone gets up early; everyone eats at 12:30, an uncivilized hour; everyone hurries and makes money. You won't find the old ways of Touraine here. Look for them in the villages."

I went looking in Vouvray, a commune famed for its wine, and sought out the dean of Vouvray wine growers, Jules de la Leu. The old man led me into his dining room and ordered up a sparkling white wine from his stock.

"This is a true house of Touraine," he told me. "The front is built up, the rear is dug in. The kitchen goes right into the living rock. There are caves under us and over us. I was born in one of them. Seven generations of de la Leus have lived in this very house. We've always made wine."

He glanced at me. "How do you like it?"

He acknowledged my praise with a nod.

"That, you see, is Vouvray. And what is Vouvray? A wine made of grapes grown on the Vouvray slopes—the slopes, mind you—not the valley below or the plateau above. Our region is small and very sharply defined.

"Buyers tell me that there is not enough Vouvray, that more of the local wines should carry the name. I say nonsense. Only Vouvray is Vouvray, just as only I am Jules de la Leu."

Spirited horses and spirited men of the Armored Corps and Cavalry School at Saumur carry on a proud tradition of horsemanship, even though graduates spend more time in tanks than in saddles. The school's crack riding team, the Cadre Noir, wears uniforms of Empire days as it wheels its steeds in intricate mounted drills.

Mechanized mounts pass in review during the July Carrousel, an annual show in which Saumur cadets display their skill with horses, tanks, motorcycles, jeeps, and helicopters.

Saumur's heritage of gallantry includes a battle at the town itself. In the summer of 1940, the students and their officers, greatly outnumbered, held a crossing of the Loire against a German division for three days. Hundreds of cadets died in the fight.

Restored by my brief sojourn in the present, I plunged again into the past at a place which four centuries of writers have acclaimed the jewel of Touraine. Azay-le-Rideau is no clifftopping keep but a sumptuous little palace of the valley, seated squarely in the quiet water of the Indre (page 860).

The original castle, a military emplacement controlling the tributary stream, was burned five centuries ago, when Charles VII passed that way and was insulted by the garrison. Later the present chateau rose out of the Indre, just as Chenonceaux, at the same time, was rising out of the Cher.

The resemblance did not end there: Both were the creations of financiers. Gilles Berthelot, Azay's owner, considered himself in direct competition with Bohier of Chenonceaux. Berthelot's wife, like Bohier's, directed the construction. Both gentlemen dipped too frequently into the royal till. François I got both castles in payment of their debts.

No one lives at Azay now, or has for half a century. But its rooms are museums of Renaissance art and artifacts and warm with reflected life. So kind and timeless is this fine place that it seemed no more than natural that a group of noisy youngsters were playing in its halls, to run off laughing at the guardian's approach; or that a dozing fisherman drifted a lazy line in the shadow of its walls.

IN THE castle-crowded country of central Touraine, no traveler can plot a simple course along the Loire without missing the finest creations of the Garden of France. It is best to roam the tributary valleys of the Cher, the Indre, and the Vienne, following one's fancy and varying one's esthetic fare. But with Azay-le-Rideau, I had ended my wandering south of the river. It was time to regain the main stream at Tours and follow it on its westward way.

Below Tours, in the western part of Touraine, two chateaus guard the riverside routes of the right and left banks. Both were built in the uneasy days of Louis XI, when the form of France was not yet fixed. The first, Langeais, was raised at the king's orders on the right bank to block the path of any invaders from Brittany, which was not yet part of his domain. He could have saved himself the trouble. His son's marriage to Anne of Brittany established peace, and eventually union, between her duchy and France.

Today the frowning feudal building looks almost exactly as it did in the 15th century, largely because its subsequent owners were never sufficiently sure of their royalty-derived tenure or sufficiently fond of the stern old pile to change it. Its formidable towers rise straight from cheerful village streets, pleasantly pretending to threaten the cars creeping past under its weathered flanks (page 856).

Langeais' left-bank neighbor, Ussé, is situated delectably between the edge of the Forest

KODACHROMES BY NATIONAL GEOGRAPHIC PHOTOGRAPHER DEAN CONGER © N.G.S.

of Chinon and the leafy water garden formed where the Indre and Loire lie briefly side by side before joining. It appears as a tangle of white towers among trees (pages 858-9). It, too, has serious defenses designed for the brutality of siege and countersiege. But while Langeais is a manor that remained a fortress, Ussé is a fortress that became a manor. Its owners did not owe their tenancy to royal whim and so, secure in their residence, they beautified the place devotedly, adding to the Gothic design the graces of the Renaissance. Its present aristocratic owner, the Count de Blacas, continues the tradition.

FOR A TRAVELER faced with innumerable marvels, occasional and violent contrast is almost essential. A staggering one exists between Azay-le-Rideau and the huge silver ball of France's first atomic power plant. The Chinon plant consists of three units—the newest ranks as the world's largest power-producing reactor—together capable of more than 700,000 kilowatts.

French tourists filled the little glassed-in pavilion where models and diagrams illustrated the workings of the station. A crisp electronic voice explained it. The visitors stared at the ball in admiration and listened solemnly.

"*Magnifique!*" exclaimed an old man. "I don't understand it, but how big and round it is!"

"One must admit that it shines brightly in the sun," conceded a young man,

KODACHROMES BY DEAN CONGER (ABOVE) AND HÉLÈNE JEANBRAU © N.G.S.

Gladioli flood a field near Angers, in a region where the deep, sandy soil sustains more than 200 nurseries. The Ernest Turc Company, which grows these blooms, also raises dahlias and begonias. On the horizon a *château d'eau,* or "water castle," stores water for irrigation.

Grim towers of Angers dwarf tame fallow deer grazing in the castle's long-dry moat. Shrubs sprout from windows and narrow slits that once rained death on attackers. King Louis IX built the fortress. Henri III ordered it demolished. Delaying tactics employed by the governor of the city saved all but the upper parts of the 17 prodigious stone towers.

At home underground, the family of Jean-Baptiste Marion sits down to lunch. They live near Le Thoureil in a cavern, one of hundreds in the region. Most consist of two or three rooms; some boast electricity and running water. Their coolness makes them popular summer retreats for city folk.

Many of the caves date from Roman times, when invading legions of Julius Caesar attempted to smoke out Gauls hiding in the rocky lairs.

Mysterious grotto, part of a labyrinth carved out of limestone 30 feet below the village of Doué-la-Fontaine, once sheltered worshipers. Its pointed arches resemble those of Gothic churches built in the 13th to 15th centuries. A deep-dug well suggests that the grotto provided refuge during the Hundred Years' War and the later wars of religion.

EKTACHROME BY DEAN CONGER © N.G.S.

less easily impressed. A small girl asked if the sphere was full of electricity, and the blasé young man, charmed by the thought, intoned: "One has only to open the spigot at the bottom, *et voilà!* Out pours electricity."

THE LEFT-BANK ROAD, leading out of Touraine and into Anjou, crowds the Loire's shore as it moves among its antiquities to Saumur. The old capital of eastern Anjou is an airy town of white houses, scarred by innumerable bullets and topped by a handsome shell of a chateau. As at Tours, the town has lost its archaic aura.

But one great tradition survives from Saumur's gallant past: horsemanship claimed to rival any in the world. The famed 1763 cav-

alry school of Saumur, now largely concerned with tanks, continues to produce superb riders. The equestrian tradition goes back to the days when the chateau on the heights was the scene of jousts and tourneys (pages 861-3).

"We stress riding, even though our young officers will command armored vehicles," a Saumur instructor told me. "An officer should learn to dominate another living creature before he is called upon to dominate men."

As we walked among the drab buildings, students hurried past, saluting. Horses' hoofs thumped in the training ring. Engines whined and iron treads clanked near the tank sheds.

"It is a school like another," the instructor said with a shrug. "To the eye, I mean. Not to the spirit."

The martial sounds of Saumur brought to mind a campaign that rocked this region in relatively recent times. North of the Loire, Lt. Gen. George Patton began his daring dash across France in the summer of 1944. For the protection of his long southern flank, Patton relied solely on the river and the reconnaissance planes and fighter-bombers of the XIX Tactical Air Command, under Brig. Gen. O. P. Weyland. When asked if this did not worry him, Patton gave a characteristic answer: "Let the enemy worry about *his* flanks."

The surroundings of Saumur boast sights that span civilization. If the steel steeds of the cavalry school are ultramodern, the weird dolmen of Bagneux is older than history. I found it behind a small cafe, a few miles and

a few millenniums away from busy downtown Saumur.

It is a long, gloomy hut of stone slabs set on edge and roofed with others, most of them 15 feet on a side and about two feet thick. The weight of these pieces is immense. They are not of local rock. How were they brought here? How put in place? Archeologists may guess, but an old man of the neighborhood felt he knew.

"The Gauls were not afraid of work. They went to a lot of trouble to build this thing, and they could do so because they were immensely strong. And big, like Americans," he added. "You might not believe me, but I've often seen Americans eight feet tall. Such were the Gauls."

I did not spoil his tall tale by admitting my own American nationality, but set my five-foot, eleven-inch self once more on a downstream course.

BELOW SAUMUR I crossed to the right bank and the beginning of a new kind of country. Here the plateau was set far back from the river, which passed through thousands of acres of fine alluvial fields protected by dikes. The forests were gone. Houses were no longer of close-fitted limestone blocks but dark-walled, rough-surfaced, built of thin courses of slate and schist. This was the "Black Anjou." Ahead was Angers, the last city of the Val de Loire and the site of its last kingly castle (page 864).

The colossus of Angers did not begin as a royal edifice. It was for two centuries the lair of those perpetual predators, the Foulques, Counts of Anjou. From its somber walls Nerra, fiercest of Foulques, galloped throughout the Val to become part of each town's most violent history.

At Tours, he waged war against the archbishop. At Saumur he set fire to the monastery, then, as the building burned, sought to divert divine wrath by making pious promises. He earned disfavor by having a courtier murdered under his king's very eyes.

From here, too, he set out on pilgrimages to the Holy Land to atone for his crimes, returning, refreshed, to commit still greater ones.

French kings took the fort and rebuilt it in its present 17-towered form. So it stands today, shorn of its uppermost battlements, encircled by the honking traffic of a metropolis. There is no echo of human occupancy.

Henry James defined the fortress well: "You cannot do more than look at it, and one good look does your business. It has no beauty, no grace, no detail, nothing that charms or detains you; it is simply very old and very big—so big and so old that this simple impression is enough, and it takes its place in your recollections as a perfect specimen of a superannuated stronghold."

I found the "one good look" richly rewarding, then left to regain the Loire at Les Ponts-de-Cé, where seven bridges cross its seven branches.

Here, says Michelin's excellent guide to the chateau country, a 16th-century captain named Strozzi committed the unforgivable discourtesy of drowning 800 camp followers; these undisciplined women slowed his march, so the rough captain had them thrown into the Loire.

The road west from Angers leads out of the Val, which ends before Nantes, a city that properly belongs to Brittany. The Val's last lands bridge the gap between antiquity and modernity. They complete a sequence begun in the rude ruins of Velay, where the Loire and its civilization were young. Here the river, like the imposing manors along its shore, is big and serene. It is an old, sophisticated stream flowing seaward in casual curves.

AS I DROVE westward, the Loire lands changed; villages were denatured by modern incongruities. The first ships loomed over the fields near Nantes. A refinery sprawled on the right bank, bigger than any palace. Then St. Nazaire, all new, all clean, smelling of salt wind. Beside the Loire, no river now but a wave-streaked estuary, the gray mass of a former Nazi submarine base squatted, forced by function into the massive mold of all fortified keeps.

From the top of an abandoned lighthouse I watched the Loire lose in its last few miles the character of a regal waterway and begin its maritime metamorphosis. Ferries crossed its widening mouth. Fishing boats huddled in a protected basin where terns wheeled. A freighter flying the American flag stood outbound for home. The Loire vanished quietly and completely into the all-engulfing sea.

THE END

River's end: At St. Nazaire the Loire merges with the Atlantic. Submarine pens built by the Nazis still flank the channel, despite relentless Allied air attacks aimed at destroying them. Now, with peace, only sea birds soar above the stout fishing smacks that moor along the quays.

Lonely Sentinels of the American West

Basque Sheepherders

By ROBERT LAXALT

Photographs by WILLIAM BELKNAP, JR.

T HE OLD SHEEP CAMP lay in a sheltered hollow. In this high place, the only thing above us was the shoulder of the Sierra Nevada, looming so near that its tattered fringe of wind-blasted trees stood out in clear relief against the skyline.

My father spoke from where he knelt by the open campfire. He said in Basque that he could remember the day when these mountains were filled with sheep: *"Oroitzen naiz mendi horiek ardiez betezielarik."*

"Bai," I said in assent, knowing what he really meant. In those days, we had had our own sheep in these mountains, too. And here at his old campsite, he was recalling that time.

Sun-bronzed shepherd Fermin Alzugaray, like thousands of Basques, came from the Pyrenees to herd flocks in the western United States. Orphaned lamb rides a gunny sack until the herder finds it a foster mother (pages 876-7).

KODACHROME © N.G.S.

The Author: A second-generation Basque, Robert Laxalt, right, watches sheepshearing with his father Dominique. As youths, Robert and his brothers—one of them now Lieutenant Governor of Nevada—herded sheep for their father. Director of the University of Nevada Press, author Laxalt recounted the visit of Dominique to his French birthplace in *Sweet Promised Land* (Harper & Row, New York, 1957).

Though retired, the elder Laxalt still enjoys camp life. Below, he helps funnel sheep into shearing pens.

Late spring had come, and the earth was still moist from the winter's snow. The wild canaries and jays had returned to the mountains, and the first flowers were raising their faces to the uncertain warmth of the sun. I found it hard to conceive that the bright glitter of Reno, Nevada, lay less than thirty miles away to the north.

I raised up on an elbow to watch my father by the fire. He stooped over the blackened rocks in a pose as old as my memory.

From where I lay on the rough canvas camp bed, I could see the outline of his lean frame and a bronzed face creased with the fine lines that a lifetime of wind and sun had etched there. But now, his wild shock of hair was white.

My father is a Basque, his homeland the Pyrenees mountainland shared by France and Spain (map, next page).* He came to America sixty years ago, at the age of 16, to herd sheep in the lonely mountains and deserts of the Far West. The chronicle of his life is that of thousands of other Basque sheepherders who, for more than a century, have been coming to America to make their lives in that same harsh setting.

Their role in our history has gone nearly unrecorded. Yet, without their incredible capacity to endure hardship and solitude, the great era of western sheep raising would not have been what it was.

Descendants of an ancient race whose origins and language still remain a mystery, the Basque sheepherders of America were urged here by the same restless spirit that lured their forebears around the world as sailors with Magellan and to South America as soldiers with the conquistadors.

Basque sheepherders still come to the West, though the total number of herders in the United States is declining. The old method of raising sheep on the open range is giving way to the trend toward small farm flocks.

This trend and the diminishing of the western range in the face of population needs have spelled the decline of the range-sheep industry. In Nevada, for example, there are some thirty range-sheep outfits operating today. There were twice that number in the years immediately preceding World War II. In another generation, the lone sheepherder and his wandering band may well become a thing of the past.

Campsite Conjures Up Childhood Summers

My father read my thoughts when he recalled the mountains filled with sheep. I well remembered. And though it ended for us when my father sold his sheep, it is still a way of life in Basque sheep camps throughout the West.

I looked about me at our camp nestled once more under tall pines that rose like feathered shafts into the arch of blue sky. I saw the worn leather pack bags our burros had carried, the weathered tent in which we had huddled through so many storms, the scarred carbine hanging by its strap from a tree.

And, in the twinkling of an eye, I was carried back to the time when my father had sheep on this same mountain. In the summers, he would take my brothers and me to the

*See "Life in the Land of the Basques," by John E. H. Nolan, NATIONAL GEOGRAPHIC, February, 1954.

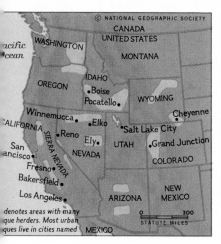

Two homelands of the Basque sheepherders lie 5,500 miles apart. In the mid-1800's the first Basques came to America from the rugged Pyrenees border region of France and Spain. Today they and their descendants in the western United States number an estimated 60,000.

Spring reunion: In late May or early June, herders of the Allied Land and Livestock Company bring their sheep to the shearing sheds at Scraper Springs, Nevada. Camping in wagons and tents on the slopes, they share their experiences and adventures of the past year. Few speak English; they converse in Basque, a tongue unrelated to any other European language.

Golden loaves of herders' bread rise high in Dutch ovens; one wears the lid's cross imprint on its crusty top. Basques once scratched every loaf with the sign of the cross before cutting it. Santiago Camino works as camp tender and cook for Allied.

range to help him with the band. The camp had been a bustle of activity then.

In the early dawn, when the first gray light was pushing back the night sky, we had tumbled out of our canvas beds laid on mattresses of pine boughs. We dashed our faces with spring water cold as ice. Breakfast was steaming coffee, sweetened with canned milk and filled with crusts of sourdough bread. Then off to start the sheep.

By the time we arrived at the meadow where the band had bedded down, the leaders would be up and waiting. Then would come a multitude of sounds to break the silence of the mountains—the bells of the leaders, the bleating of ewes, the plaintive calls of lambs searching for their mothers, the barking of sheep dogs urging on the stragglers, and our own shrill whistling.

When the sheep had been set on the day's course, they would fall quiet as suddenly as if on a single command. As they moved through the forest, grazing on wild grass and flowers rich with milky fluid, the only sound to mark their presence in the mountains was the faint tinkling of bells.

At midday they stopped to rest in a familiar aspen grove. We would hike back to the camp, following deer trails through rocks and manzanita. Then came the main meal of our day—an omelet filled with bacon and potatoes, washed down with jets of strong wine from the goatskin *bota* (page 885).

Stock Trucks Come for the Lambs

And so it went through the long sun-drenched days of summer. When September came, and with it the first hint of autumn frost, we trailed the several bands of sheep down to the shipping corrals near the highway. There the big stock trucks were waiting, and the grown lambs would be separated and shipped away to market, while the rest of the sheep went back to the range. This was the

Newborn lamb curled beneath its mother still wears patches of the bright yellow that naturally stains its coat at birth. In the sagebrush beyond, a herder checks the condition of another ewe and her minutes-old lamb.

Camouflage coat saves a life. Finding a dead lamb, a herder removes it from the mother and quickly skins it. Then he fits the pelt like a dog sweater onto an orphaned lamb (right) and nestles the foundling at the side of the ewe that has lost her offspring (left). She usually accepts the substitute as her own because it carries the smell of her dead baby.

EKTACHROME (BELOW) AND KODACHROMES © N.G.S.

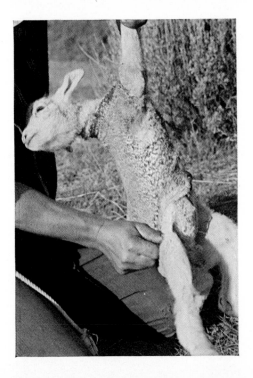

time, too, when we would have to lay off one of the herders and say goodbye to him until the next year.

I remembered so well the Basque herders who had worked for us through the years.

There was young Ascona, with his long wedge-shaped face and merry eyes, who sang melancholy Basque songs to us around the campfire at night. There was tragic old Joanes, who longed to go home to the Basque country, but who lost all his savings twice.

The first time came when the bank failed. After that, he saved his money in a suitcase, but it was stolen from him in San Francisco. By that time he was too old to begin saving again, and, heartbroken, he had to give up his dream.

Herders' Lot: Loneliness and Hardship

There had been my uncle, whom we called "Oita." My father told us he was the best herder who ever lived. He could bring back the fattest lambs from the summer range and lose less than a handful of sheep to coyotes, mountain lions, and poisonous plants. He had herded past his time, but he refused to quit. One day, in sight of this very camp, he fell from a stroke, and my brother Paul carried him in his arms all the long way down to the main camp near the highway, where the truck was waiting. He never really recovered, and the last time we saw him in the hospital, he had forgotten all his English and could speak only Basque.

Then I remembered Peyo of the wizened face, who lost his mind in the hills. Though Peyo could never afterward herd sheep, my father often hired him to help in the busy lambing and shearing times.

I asked my father how Peyo lost his mind.

"From the loneliness and the suffering," he said. "It happened mostly in the deserts. If a man was unlucky enough to be sent there when he first came, it was a terrible shock.

"I remember how it was for me. I wasn't much more than 16 years old, you know. And they sent me into the deserts with a dog and 3,000 sheep.

"I can remember waking up in the morning, and, as far as I could see in any direction, there were only sagebrush and rocks and runted little junipers. Though the Basques are used to being alone, these deserts were something else. In the first months, how many times I cried in my camp bed at night —remembering my home, remembering the beautiful green Basque country.

"In the summer, the desert burned your

SNOW POWDERS RIMROCK *of a Nevada canyon as a herder heads his band southward toward winter ranges, with their milder climate and better grazing grounds. Ahead lie days of travel across raw hills and frost-rimed meadows. During the journey, the shepherd on horseback must stay ever alert for the bleating of strays and for hungry mountain lions and coyotes.*

878   KODACHROME © NATIONAL GEOGRAPHIC SOCIETY

asylum, but we arranged to send him home. Do you know? As soon as he got to the Basque country, his mind cleared up and he never had trouble again. It shows you what home-sickness can do."

A few weeks after our visit to the old sheep camp, I made a trip with my father to see the shearing of the sheep at the Allied Land and Livestock Company camp in northern Nevada. Allied is one of the last major range outfits operating in the West. On the way, we stopped overnight at Winnemucca, for more than fifty years a sheep and cow capital.

Memories Haunt Nevada Range Town

The Winnemucca Hotel is a Basque hotel. There is a saloon with an ornate bar and oil-cloth-covered card tables where the herders play at *mus,* an old Basque game that is much like poker, a dining room with long tables where everyone eats family style, and rooms upstairs for the sheepherders who come to town.

As we walked in, I noticed that my father's attention was caught by a picture of a mule team on the wall. Before I could ask him about it, a man with chiseled Basque features detached himself from a group and approached us.

"Euskalduna zera zu?" he said, asking my father if he was Basque.

"Bai. Ni eskualduna naiz." My father nodded in acknowledgment.

The other's name was Joe de Arrieta, a second-generation Basque like myself, whose father had been a sheepherder, too. I knew better than to ask him how he knew us as Basque —there is a saying that the Basques can recognize one another anywhere in the world.

Over bittersweet *picon* drinks, De Arrieta said to my father, "I've never seen you before. Have you ever been in Winnemucca?"

"Not since 1915," my father answered. "I used to know the town well. When we were running sheep in the northern deserts, I would come in once a month on the railroad to buy provisions and grain for the mules and horses. *Kazu!* I would fill a carload with all the supplies."

De Arrieta nodded. "But not any more," he said. "When I was a boy, I worked in the hardware store. Then, sheep outfits would buy wholesale lots of tents and ammunition, and Dutch ovens by the dozen. Now maybe one Dutch oven a year is sold."

"I thought so," said my father. "I don't see as many Basques around. In the old days, you know, this was a good town for the

EKTACHROME BY DAN McCOY © N.G.S.

Newcomer to America, Isidoro Aquirre from the Spanish Pyrenees arrives at New York's International Airport. Like the 300 to 400 Basque herders who come to this country annually, he holds a contract for three years' work on western ranges.

lungs, and every day you had a scare with rattlesnakes and scorpions. In the winter, the blizzards tore at you and soaked you so that you were wet and freezing day and night.

"Those first few months, you thought you would go insane. Then, suddenly, your mind turned the corner and you were used to it, and you didn't care if you ever saw people again."

Because the Basques do not like to discuss it, I said hesitantly, "But there were some like Peyo who didn't turn the corner."

"Of course there were some," my father answered. "I remember one in particular, because what happened to him was so strange. We called him Garazi, which was the name of the valley he came from. When he lost his mind, he thought he was in the Basque country. Every day, he would tell us something that had happened in his village that morning.

"The doctors wanted to put him in an

Basques. What times I had here! But I guess most of the Basques who were my friends are gone now." He began mentioning names, and at almost every one of them, De Arrieta would nod his head that he had died.

"And him, too," said my father, pointing to the mule skinner in the picture on the wall. "Do you know? The last time I was here, I came on that mule team, leading one of my horses behind. I had lost my best saddle horse in the deserts. He cost me $150, and that was about as much as you could pay for a good horse then. The rustlers had taken him. So I set out to follow. But I got lost, and I almost starved. Then I ran into that mule team, and it was a pleasure to sit down on the wagon after so many days in the saddle."

"Did you ever get your horse back?" asked De Arrieta.

"Oh, yes," said my father casually. "There was a Basque in town who had been herding sheep near the rustlers' hideout. He showed me the way. We went out at night, and I got my horse back without any trouble. We laughed all the way home, thinking how surprised those rustlers would be when they woke up the next day."

After dinner, I took De Arrieta aside and thanked him for his kindness.

"For me, it's a pleasure," he said. "I love to talk to the old Basques. There are so few left. We owe them so much for what they went through in those hills to give us, their children, our start in this country. If we turn out half the men they were, it will be enough."

Gentle Valley Stirs a Basque's Vision

Next day, we turned off the main highway near Winnemucca and moved along a good dirt road through Independence Valley, which pierces the gray sagebrush desert like a green broadsword. It was in this same valley that the saga of Basque sheepherders in America really began.

A young Basque adventurer named Pedro Altube sailed to California in 1850 in the gold rush. His experiences there are somewhat obscured, but unlike so many others, he made enough to buy a sizable herd of cattle. He trailed the herd over the Sierra and across the deserts of Nevada until he chanced on Independence Valley. He was so struck by its beauty and the opportunity it offered that here, in 1873, he founded the historic Spanish Ranch.

In the years that followed, he brought scores of relatives and friends to America to help him with his growing empire. In time,

Constant companion, the sheep dog shares his master's work by day and sleeps at his side under the stars or outside his wagon. He works to hand or whistle signals, but a well-trained dog can keep the band together and round up strays without supervision.

they launched out on their own with cattle or sheep, spreading from California to Colorado and from Arizona to Washington. For this, Altube was to earn the name *"Euskaldunen aita Ameriketan Mendietan—*Father of the Basques in the Far West."

Though no accurate count has been made, an estimated 60,000 Basques live in the western United States today. This number includes both the Basques who emigrated to America and their descendants.

As they became successful, the Basque pioneers sent for their sweethearts, who had stayed behind in the Basque country. Many also sent for brothers and sisters, nephews and nieces. The men worked with the livestock and the women with the myriad chores of housekeeping and cooking, gardening, and conserving that a ranch demands. And so started the Basque colonies of the West, and the generation of American-born Basques that was to follow.

As for Basques who did not become sheep owners or foremen, but remained herders all their lives, very few married. It was one thing to be an owner who could make a ranch his home base, another to be a herder whose only home was a lonely sheep camp.

Many of the older Basques are still in the sheep business—either as owners or as herders—but their children have gone mostly into city occupations or professions.

Fortunes Fall With Sheep Prices

"The big movement of the Basques came after the century had turned," my father said. "Thousands like myself came between then and the 1930's. We all came the same way, without much more than the clothes on our backs. But we were young and strong, and willing to work and suffer for a chance in life we couldn't have had in the old country.

"Though we talked about going home—and some did go—underneath, most of us realized the opportunity was here. It was a raw new land, and we were helping to build it. There wasn't anything a man couldn't do in this western country with work and luck.

"We all started the same way, taking our wages in sheep instead of cash. We would run our sheep with the owner's, until we were big enough to break away on our own."

As he talked, I recalled the famous Nevada sheep names that had begun this way—names like Garat, Itcaina, Elia, Jaureguey, Etchart, Saval, and the massive Smoke Creek outfit of the Poco, Duc, and Iriart brothers, who at one time ranged 40,000 head of sheep. Of Pete Elia, I could remember sheepmen saying he wasn't quite sure just how much land he owned, but that it was somewhere over a million acres.

This had been the big time of sheep in the West—when the Basques who had come as sheepherders twenty years before suddenly found themselves rich men. They kept town houses, dressed in the best suits money could buy, and drove expensive cars. I could remember the legend that if it weren't for the Basques, the Cadillac agency in Reno would have gone broke.

Then, without warning, came the livestock crash of the 1920's. The market dropped out from under the stockmen, and sheep were worth next to nothing. In an instant, most of the Basques lost everything for which they had endured so many hardships—their sheep, ranches, land, and all the elaborate dressings of town houses, cars, and jewels. It happened to my father, too.

But it was not in their nature to give up in despair. They had begun with nothing, and the memory of it was not that far away. Without shame, they went back to the mountains and deserts, roaming from one outfit to another, taking whatever work there was.

Many of the hardy Basque women followed their husbands through this wandering time, working as ranch cooks. Others stayed behind in the towns, finding jobs in the Basque hotels and restaurants until they could be together again with their husbands. And

though many of the Basque men never regained their former heights, they saw the day when they had their own outfits again.

Shearing Time Takes Over Camp

We had left the lush greenery of Independence Valley. Now we struck out with our pickup truck deep into the back country, jolting through narrow ravines and under long bluffs of sheer rimrock that towered like fortresses over the desert hills.

The Allied sheep camp lay in a shallow ravine, and the sight of it was like that of every sheep camp in the West—a forlorn speck of life in an immensity of loneliness (pages 874-5). There were the weathered corrals enclosing little postage stamps of earth beaten bare by countless hoofs, a cluster of crude sheds sided with brown boards, the trailerlike camp wagons where the Basque herders slept and ate their meals, dusty pickup trucks with stock racks and loops of baling wire, and the tiny pond of spring water that is life itself in the thirsty desert.

The familiar sounds of the sheep camp at shearing time awoke a nostalgia in me for the years our family had been in sheep—the bleating of ewes being crowded into the shearing pens, the barking of dogs and the shrill shouts of the herders working in the corrals, the whine of clippers wielded by the shearing crew, and the terrified cries of lambs separated from their mothers.

Sheep foreman Tony Mendiguia paused in his corral work to welcome us. Born in the Basque country, Tony became foreman after

Lunch-hour music maker, Santiago Mendieta entertains rangemen with Basque melodies on his accordion.

Leaping lambs dash through a chute at Columbia Basin, Nevada. A buyer operates the gate and diverts those ready for market into the shipping corral. Lambs that need further fattening—called feeders—go to another corral. White-faced ewes, the best wool producers, return to the range for breeding.

EKTACHROMES (BELOW) AND KODACHROME © N.G.S.

eight years as a sheepherder and camp tender. His good-natured features, covered with a thick film of gray dust, crinkled into a smile as he told us he had just lost an argument with the boss of the shearing crew.

"I wanted them to shear 200 more head a day," he said. "Yesterday, I won the argument. Today, I lost. Tomorrow, I hope to win again." He glanced at my father. "But that must be an old story to you."

My father nodded. "It doesn't look like anything's changed." He asked Tony how many sheep Allied Land and Livestock was ranging.

"About 14,000 head in Nevada, and 3,000 more in Oregon," Tony explained. "We'll run 5,000 head through the shearing at this camp alone. I have the bands spotted in the hills around us, waiting for their turn in the shearing pens." He made a sweeping gesture with his hand. "Did you see them on the way in?"

"I saw their dust," said my father. "They seemed like small bands."

"Well, we keep each band down to 1,000 or 1,200 head, with two men to each band," said Tony. He grinned apologetically. "From what I understand, it's not like the old days of big bands with one herder alone."

Shortage Eased by McCarran Act

My father shrugged. "But it makes sense, if you've got enough herders. They can choose the best feed that way, and the sheep aren't moving like crazy all day long to get enough to eat. It's a protection for the herders, too, in case one of them gets sick or hurt."

Tony nodded. "We've got enough herders." He explained that now they come mostly from the Spanish provinces of the Basque country under a special provision in the United States immigration law. The late U. S. Senator Pat McCarran of Nevada in 1952 put a specific

clause for sheepherders into the law to save the western range-sheep industry, floundering after World War II. Under the McCarran Act, as now amended, nearly 1,200 Basques throughout the West are here today in temporary employment.

Tony took a stub of pencil out of the pocket of his worn Levis and made figures on the board fence. "It works like this," he said. "The typical herder is under a three-year contract to the Western Range Association, a group of the largest outfits. The sheep outfit that needs him agrees to pay part of his plane fare to America, and the herder works out the remainder. After three years, he goes back to the old country for a visit, and then he can apply to come back to America for another three years."

Exuberant Basque Festival each summer attracts sheepherders and other Basques from all over the West to the northeastern Nevada town of Elko. Reno lawyer Peter Echeverria, last year's master of ceremonies, squirts wine from a goatskin *bota* without spilling a drop—a feat worthy of his heritage. Dancers dressed in traditional old-country costumes introduce spectators to the spirited but exhausting *jota*. Brawny Benito Goitiandia wins one of the many strength contests by hoisting a 304-pound steel "stone" to his shoulder nine times in three minutes.

I asked if a herder could save enough money to make six years in the hills worth it.

"It's not like the days when the Basques could make big fortunes," Tony answered. "But it's pretty good money even now. The herder makes at least $230 a month, and also his board and room."

Repeating an old sheepman's joke, my father said, "Well, it's a pretty big room."

Tony rubbed his stubble of beard. "Yes, about a hundred miles across, I'd figure."

"Well," said my father, "it's a chance these young Basques never would have had unless they came to America to herd sheep. With the money they save, they can go back to the Basque country, buy a little farm, marry, and start their own families."

Tony grinned. "You can be sure they save their money, too. Take young Santiago, the sheep-camp cook, for example [page 874]. He hasn't been to town in months."

In the lonely life of a sheepherder on the open range, it is only at shearing and shipping times that the scattered bands of sheep come together. And so, supper that night in the narrow confines of the cookwagon was a rare reunion. The herders had bedded their sheep in the surrounding hills, taken time to shave and put on clean denims, and come down to the main camp for the evening meal.

In honor of the occasion, Santiago the cook had fixed a special meal of potato salad filled with boiled eggs, a dish of macaroni and tomato sauce, a stew of mutton and onions, and applesauce dessert.

For the sheepherders, it gave a welcome respite from usual fare. By the time the sheep have stopped grazing at the end of a long day, the herder usually is too tired to cook anything but an omelet or warmed-over beans before crawling into his bedroll.

Their faces glowed ruddy in the light from the single lantern. They sat as Basques will sit, with elbows planted firmly on the table, talking and gesturing as they ate. There was

serious talk, and they would lean forward intently with furrowed brows. There was happy talk, too, and features would be transfigured in rare laughter. There were bursts of song, and the men would suddenly become melancholy, remembering homes and families and sweethearts thousands of miles away.

Festival Brightens the Lonely Year

Talk turned to the Basque Festival that would be held in August in the nearby town of Elko. An annual affair, it draws Basques from nearly every state in the Far West.

Basque dancers would wind through the streets in a vivid blur of berets and crimson sashes, white rope sandals, and gay green skirts. There would be singing of old country songs in Elko's many Basque bars, storytelling, and much debate about Luis Basterrechea's chances in the weight-lifting contests against the champion, Benito Goitiandia of Idaho (page 885), and whether an unknown woodchopper might emerge to challenge "Little Perrico," who could cut his way through logs like a machine saw.

Above all, the festival would bring a reunion for the old Basques, with their narrow Stetsons and sun-creased faces. For the shy young sheepherders, the festival would be their only touch with civilization in a year.

Santiago wondered how many Basques would come to Elko for the festival this time. I told him. "Lou Uriarte and Ray Goicoa say they expect 2,000 or more. At least 1,000 pretty Basque girls," I added with a grin.

Santiago whistled and looked imploringly at Tony, the sheep boss. *"Debria*—the devil!" said Tony, "you can go. You've been in the hills too long. But for the rest of you, I can't say yet. We will have to arrange who can go and who stays with the sheep." He ignored the chorus of moans by upending the wine pouch and taking a drink.

After dinner came the storytelling, and the bota made its rounds. Emilio, barely past 20 and enamoured of western horses, wanted to hear of the range wars between sheepmen and cattlemen. My father told him that most

Trailing through autumn snow, sheep search the ground for edible shrubs. Herdsman rides in the middle of the flock, where he can see both pacesetters and stragglers. After months of lonely life on the range, he yearns for the sound of other human voices and the comforts of civilization.

of the trouble had really been in Wyoming and Montana, where lone sheepherders were murdered by bands of masked riders, their valuable dogs burned alive, and the sheep dynamited or stampeded over cliffs.

My father remembered well one incident in Nevada. A cow outfit had brought in a professional badman to harass the sheepherders.

"One time, the badman sneaked into a sheep camp when the herder was gone and put cyanide into the bread," my father related. "When the herder cut the new loaf—he scratched the sign of the cross on it, as we all did —he gave the first piece to his dog. So he saved his own life."

Emilio was indignant. "Didn't the Basques do anything about it?"

My father raised his hand. "The time came when the badman went too far. He roped a herder and dragged him to death over the desert. It was an awful thing to see how he must have suffered. So the Basques got their rifles and went after the badman. He died with a dozen holes in him, and that ended all the trouble in a hurry."

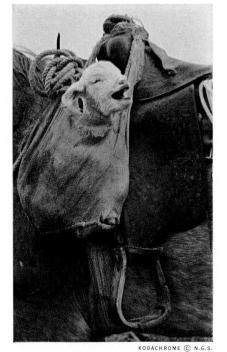

KODACHROME © N.G.S.

Forlorn foundling rescued by a compassionate Basque bleats plaintively as the herder searches for a new mother.

Fermin, a stolid young Basque who was going home in a few months, wanted a snowstorm story to take with him. My father obliged, and told him how a herder far out in the deserts had suddenly gone snow blind.

"He was in a bad situation, you can imagine. He couldn't see to find his way back to the camp. And he knew that if he started wandering, he would get lost and freeze or starve before the camp tender found him.

"Then he heard the sheep, and got the idea that saved his life. He stumbled and crawled in the direction of the sounds. When he was in the middle of the sheep, he caught hold of one by the wool. He held on to that wool for a whole day and a night until the camp tender found the band, and him with it."

Santiago Mendieta, a trapper for Allied (page 883), had come into the wagon to listen. Santy is notorious for his wry humor.

He added a story of his own for Fermin.

"It happened one winter," Santy began, "when the snows had bogged down thousands of sheep and cattle in the deserts. The Air Force was carrying hay to them in their Flying Boxcars. Anyway, this one plane passed over a band of sheep and saw the herder waving. So it dropped bales of hay.

"One bale killed the herder's burro, and another leveled his tent. The funny thing about it was that the herder was only waving to signal that he was fine. But he sure wasn't fine after that."

Before dawn on the day we were to say good-bye, I climbed high up on the hillside to watch the sheep camp come to life. By the time I reached the bottom of the rimrock, the eastern horizon was edged with silver. Range upon range of mountains stretched out on all sides, lying one past the other as far as the eye could see.

In the crystal morning air, the waking sounds of the sheep camp carried up to me clearly. I heard the clink of a washpan, the scuff of a boot on bare ground. I smelled the woodsmoke rising from the slender chimney of the cookwagon.

The distant barking of a dog reached me, and when I turned, I saw a band of sheep streaming slowly out of a ravine. The first sunshine was glowing on their backs. Behind them, wooden staff in hand, moved the solitary figure of a Basque sheepherder.

This was the life our fathers had led, and this was the land they had known when it was new and untouched. And it was a passing thing. The day of the Basque sheepherder was almost done. It had come without fanfare, and it would die as quietly.

It was for our generation to know city occupations and professions. But we had been witness to the kind of men our fathers were. We had tasted the life they had led, the vastness of the land they had walked, the loneliness they had known. We, the sons of Basque sheepherders in America, would remember.

When a Buick owner makes the first (the very first) team, he buys an Electra 225.

No doubt you assume that any Buick owner has made the first team. You're right.

But there are teams and there are teams. Some are just a little bit "firster" than others.

Similarly, there are Buicks and there are Buicks. All have that certain Buick quality; the Electra 225 just has "Buickness" on a slightly grander scale.

All Buicks are tuned cars. The four basic components of a car — ride, performance, handling and styling — are all tuned. All together. (That's what sets a Buick apart from the throng on the throughway.)

But the Electra 225 is tuned to provide not just luxury and comfort, but the ultimate in those noble qualities. (Life may not actually be a bed of roses, but our plan is to have you think it is while you're in the car.) We start with a majestic 401-cu. in. V-8. And a

Super Turbine transmission. Then we go on from there. So do you. (We also put in all the standard Buick safety items. We mention this, not because we expect to surprise you, but because it gives us a chance to recommend using those front and rear seat belts regularly.)

Then, there is the Electra Fiscal Policy. All Buicks are built to give you the most car for your money. With the Electra 225, though, a little more money — and thus more car — is involved. We keep that clearly in mind. And build the car to last. (Not as much money is involved as most Electra 225 admirers imagine, but let that be our secret. Yours and ours.)

Now then. If you aren't yet on the first team of your choice, get an Electra 225 and see how it feels, in advance. Remember, it's not whether you win or lose, but how you get to the game.

1966 Buick. The tuned car.

BUICK MOTOR DIVISION

One reason lasers are working to keep down phone costs is that Western Electric is part of the Bell System.

It's all because Western Electric is concerned about your telephone rates.

Our contribution to keeping them low is keeping down the price of the equipment we make for the Bell telephone companies. And we do *that* by continually searching for better, more efficient ways of doing things.

That's why we've become the first company to apply the laser for mass production purposes.

We use the laser to burn holes in diamonds. We use diamonds as dies in making fine wire. These diamonds are only tiny chips, but drilling holes in them by conventional methods took several days. The laser can do it in about two minutes.

It does it with a beam of light 100 million times brighter than a spot of equal size on the sun. Controlling this beam so that it would make a hole half the size of a human hair exactly where we wanted it took a lot of work. Particularly since an operator cannot directly watch the beam in action. (We solved that problem with closed circuit television.)

This use of the laser will help us save thousands of dollars this year, and more in the future, on wire and cable. But the laser holds the promise of significant savings in many other areas, too. And our engineers are hard at work converting that promise to reality.

Because keeping phone costs low is as important to Western Electric as it is to your Bell telephone company. We're on the same team. We have been since 1882, working together with the same purpose: to keep bringing you the world's finest communications at low cost.

Western Electric
MANUFACTURING & SUPPLY UNIT OF THE BELL SYSTEM

how do you say "pride" in Japanese?

Or Hawaiian? Or Chinese? It's the same in any of the languages spoken in the eleven ports across the Pacific that Continental Airlines serves. Language is no barrier when it comes to expressing pride, because pride is said with actions ... not with words. Continental Airlines people express their great measure of pride by being more helpful ... doing things more willingly. And Continental passengers, in whatever part of the world they may be, feel comfortable, at ease, almost at home because of it. The reason Continental's people have so much pride in themselves and in their airline is understandable.

You see, as major airlines go, Continental is not a great big, impersonal one. So Continental's people can and do maintain their individuality ... their interest and involvement in how their airline is run. It's not so much what they do as how they do it. You feel it all around you all the time, and it feels good. Unless you're a member of the military you can't take Continental across the Pacific ... yet. But you can take Continental across America. We serve 22 cities between Los Angeles – Chicago and Los Angeles – Houston. Travel with us, and feel the difference pride makes. Your travel agent or Continental will arrange it ... please call.

CONTINENTAL The Proud Bird with the Golden Tail

All it has in common with other luxury cars is luxury.
Otherwise it wouldn't be a Pontiac.

We won't belabor Bonneville's luxury. It's been public legend and an industry blueprint for years. You open the door and sink up to your knees in it. But we would like to remind you that Bonneville is also a Pontiac. Taut Wide-Track suspension and a tiger under the hood are standard equipment. (Along with front and rear seat belts—be sure to use them.) What it all adds up to is the one luxury car you don't feel out of place in if you're not wearing somber gray. So don't think of Bonneville as just a luxury car. Think of it as a luxury car for people who refuse to take their luxury standing still. People like yourself, for instance.

WIDE-TRACK PONTIAC/'66 GM

Pontiac Motor Division

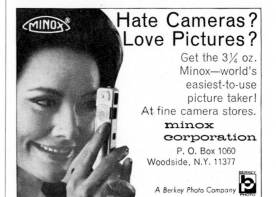

méXico is an outdoor museum, a history book, three civilizations to the south. There's more to do in Mexico.

Only in Mexico can a day's travel take you from primitive pyramids to a way of life reminiscent of the grandeur of medieval Spain and architecture as progressive as tomorrow. Just an easy drive from modern metropolitan Mexico City, you can explore the ancient temples of Teotihuacan, stroll along streets lined with tile-roofed cottages in Taxco, admire the colonial splendor of Guanajuato. You can enjoy this unique blend of past and present nowhere else in the world. Only in Mexico.

This professional camera has some amateur features.
Like price.
And automation.

"The Lens Alone is Worth the Price"

It looks and performs like the luxury, professional camera it is. But you don't have to be a 'pro' to own it. Or use it. The fast, sharp Hexanon f1.8 lens is cross-coupled to a super sensitive CdS electric eye. They work together to give you perfect pictures, automatically, under most any lighting conditions. The bright range/viewfinder window shows you exactly what the camera sees. No more, no less. You say, "smile", and Konica Auto-S2 does everything else. Under $110 *(plus case)* and as any pro will tell you, *"the lens alone is worth the price"*. See your dealer or write for free brochure: Konica Camera Corporation, P.O. Box 1070, Woodside, N. Y. 11377. A BERKEY PHOTO COMPANY

Konica Auto-S2

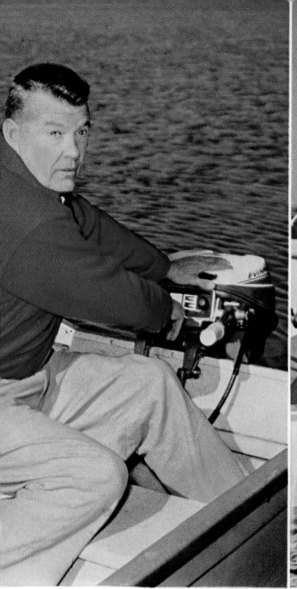

don't start that Evinrude Sportwin!...it's already running

They warned us it would happen — when we asked our engineers to make the new SPORTWIN smoother and quieter.

We told them to go ahead anyway. Fact is — there wasn't much else we could think of to do to improve the SPORTWIN for 1966.

No point in making it lower. You can fish right over the top now — just as though the motor wasn't there.

We couldn't make it any lighter and still keep it rugged.

We couldn't make it go any faster without ruining its sunny disposition. Some people swear it goes fast enough now to ski with.

There wasn't much we could add. It already has full gearshift and all deluxe features — including sixteen tilt positions — eight of them just for running in weeds and shallow water.

Oh, yes — we did add a new trolling adjustment that lets you pre-set trolling speed and then return to it — automatically.

Mostly, for 1966 we made the SPORTWIN quieter. But unless we can add a warning light to let people know when it's running — we've gone about as far as we can go in that direction.

Come to think of it — this could be a pretty good year to buy yours.

See your Evinrude dealer, listed in the Yellow Pages. Catalog free. Write Evinrude Motors, 4381 N. 27th St., Milwaukee, Wis. 53216.

EVINRUDE
first in outboards
DIVISION OF OUTBOARD MARINE CORP.

We'll give  your holiday a foreign flavor all the way (just north of the border)! Rail way with us through the Canadian Rockies o enjoy spectacular scenery in spectacular omfort. Then play mile-high at Banff prings Hotel, North America's fabulous ountain resort:entertainment nightly, utdoor activities, service in European style.

the scenic Banff-Lake Louise route through the Canadian Rockies rd "The Canadian." You'll see 2,881 miles of spectacular scenery from omfort of a scenic-dome streamliner as you travel between Montreal, nto, and Vancouver. You'll enjoy gourmet dining, tasty budget meals, ks. All accommodations, from coach to first class, are reserved.

Relax mile-high in the Canadian Rockies at Banff Springs Hotel. This internationally famous resort offers golf, tennis, swimming, fishing, boating, riding, climbing, dancing—you name it. And there's nearby Lake Louise, Victoria Glacier, and Emerald Lake to visit. With its continental cuisine and gracious service, Banff Springs is an unforgettable holiday. May 25-Sept. 14.

Holiday all the way in Canada with

Canadian Pacific

TRAINS • TRUCKS • SHIPS • PLANES • HOTELS • TELECOMMUNICATIONS • WORLD'S MOST COMPLETE TRANSPORTATION SYSTEM

You get twice the "grip" on rain-slick roads with 4-wheel drive

'Jeep' Wagoneer.

When the road turns slick and "skiddy", shift smoothly at any speed from 2-wheel to 4-wheel drive. That extra traction lets you hug slippery curves and hills with greater safety. And off where there are no roads, a 4-wheel drive 'Jeep' Wagoneer can churn through mud, plow through snow, go places other wagons can't. New power, too: 250 hp V-8 or Hi-Torque

*TRADEMARK GENERAL MOTORS CORPORATION

6 cylinder engines. Options? You name it: Turbo Hydra-Matic* automatic transmission; power steering, power brakes...the smoothness, comfort and response you'd expect in any fine wagon. Plus "picture window" visibility. Big cargo area. Your family will be safer, go more places, have more fun in a 'Jeep' Wagoneer with 4-wheel drive. **KAISER Jeep CORPORATION**

TOLEDO 1, OHIO

You've got to drive it to believe it. See your 'Jeep' dealer. Check the Yellow Pages.

Having trouble with weight control?

The Special K Breakfast can help you reach and hold the line

This is the famous low-calorie breakfast that helps you <u>reach and hold the line</u>—so over-weight never becomes a problem. It has everything. Good protein nourishment. Crisp, delicious taste, day after day. When you eat sensibly like this in the morning, it's easier to eat sensibly at noon and night. You look better. Feel better. Don't put it off. Let Kellogg's Special K Breakfast help you reach and hold the line.

The Special K Breakfast
Only 240 Calories

4 ounces orange or tomato juice —or half a medium-size grapefruit

1 ounce (1½ cups) Special K with 1 teaspoon sugar

4 ounces skim milk

Black coffee or tea

(99% fat-free)
(Only 0.62 grams of fat)

The Nutrition Story of Kellogg's Special K

One serving of Special K (1½ cups with ½ cup skim milk) supplies 14% of the recommended daily protein allowance for an adult man, and approximately these percentages of his minimum daily requirements as established by the Food & Drug Administration:

Thiamine (B$_1$)	44%
Riboflavin (B$_2$)	60%
Niacin	51%
Vitamin C	38%
Calcium	22%
Phosphorus	22%
Iron	36%

Kellogg's

SPECIAL K